The History of Islam
in Africa

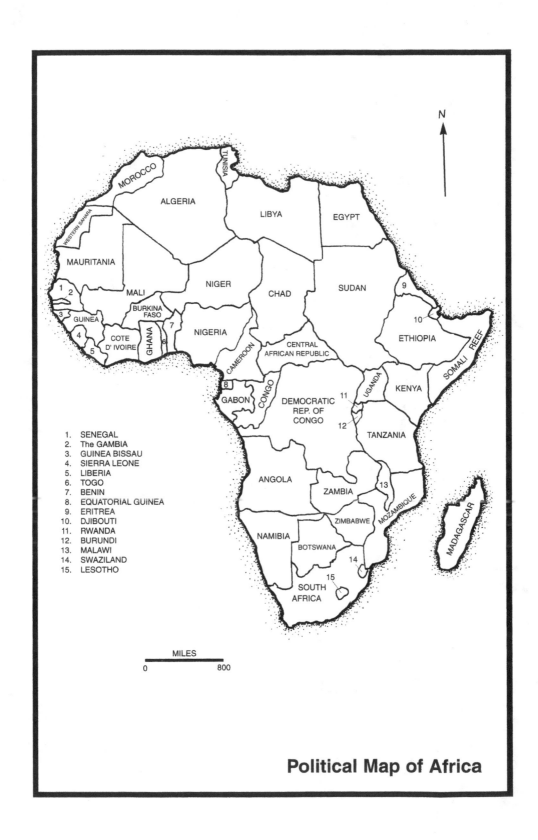

1. SENEGAL
2. The GAMBIA
3. GUINEA BISSAU
4. SIERRA LEONE
5. LIBERIA
6. TOGO
7. BENIN
8. EQUATORIAL GUINEA
9. ERITREA
10. DJIBOUTI
11. RWANDA
12. BURUNDI
13. MALAWI
14. SWAZILAND
15. LESOTHO

MILES
0   800

Political Map of Africa

The History of Islam in Africa

edited by Nehemia Levtzion & Randall L. Pouwels

Ohio University Press
Athens

James Currey
Oxford

David Philip
Cape Town

First published 2000 in the United States of America by
Ohio University Press, Athens, Ohio 45701

Published 2000 in the United Kingdom by
James Currey Ltd, 73 Bodey Road, Oxford OX2 OBS

Published 2000 in Southern Africa by
David Philip Publishers (Pty) Ltd,
208 Werdmuller Centre, Newry Street, Claremont 7708, South Africa

Ohio University Press books are printed on acid-free paper ⊗ ™

20 19 18 17 16 15 14 13 12   9 8 7 6

Jacket/cover photographs:

Front: Mosque at San, Mali.
Photograph by Eliot Elisofon, 1971
EEPA EECL 16303
Eliot Elisofon Photographic Archives
National Museum of African Art
Smithsonian Institution

Back: Worshippers attending prayers at Mosque, Sokoto, Nigeria.
Photograph by Eliot Elisofon, 1959
EEPA EECL 6353
Eliot Elisofon Photographic Archives
National Museum of African Art
Smithsonian Institution

Library of Congress Cataloging-in-Publication Data

The History of Islam in Africa / edited by Nehemia Levtzion and Randall L. Pouwels.
   p. cm.
 Includes bibliographical references and index.
 ISBN 0-8214-1296-5 (cloth: alk. paper). - ISBN 0-8214-1297-3 (paper:alk. paper)
1. Islam-Africa-History. I. Levtzion, Nehemia. II. Pouwels, Randall Lee, 1944-
BP64.A.1H62 1999
297'·096–dc21

                                  99-27729
                                  CIP

A CIP record of this book is available from the British Library
ISBN 0-85255-782-5 (James Currey cloth)
ISBN 0-85255-781-7 (James Currey paper)
ISBN 0-86486-454-X (David Philip paper)

Contents

Maps

Preface

This volume is intended to pioneer an approach to the history of Islam in Africa on a continent-wide scale. The editors are gratified that the balance has been redressed between East and West Africa. Although the study of Islam in West Africa is by far more advanced than the study of Islam in East Africa, the two regional sections of this volume, Part II on West Africa and Part III on Eastern and Southern Africa, have been given roughly equal weight. The editors do not know any other work on Islam in Africa in which Islam in East Africa achieves such prominence in a continental context.

We have been particularly concerned with the dynamics of religious interaction between the "essentials" of Islam—those elements that fostered unity and continuity within a discernible community of discourse—and the particular historical, cultural, and environmental factors that produced diversity and local forms of Islam. Our aim was to provide comprehensive studies of the experience of Muslim communities all over Africa.

In Africa, diversity has produced rich traditions of widely varied religious meanings, beliefs, and practices. Islam energized, enlivened, and animated life in African communities, and at the same time Islam has been molded by its African settings. As a result of the interaction between Muslim and African civilizations, the advance of Islam has profoundly influenced religious beliefs and practices of African societies, while local traditions have "Africanized" Islam. The ways Islam has thrived in the rich panoply of continent-wide historical circumstances have fostered discord at least as often as these ways of Islam have helped realize unity and agreement.

The main challenge for all of us who participated in this project has been to limn specific ways in which Islam and Muslims have played creative roles in the story of Africa's development. Muslims were important in the process of state-building, in the creation of commercial networks that brought together large parts of the continent. Muslims introduced literacy that, in addition to its religious significance, also made Muslims scribes to African rulers in charge of state records, as well as exchanges of inter-state diplomacy, inside Africa and beyond.

Preface

The twenty-four chapters of this volume have been written with the personal authority of the best scholarship in the history of Islam in Africa. Some of our authors began writing on Islam in the 1960s, when African history in general, and the history of Islam in Africa in particular, were first recognized as academic disciplines in their own right. Other authors joined the ranks in the seventies and eighties, and the youngest authors bring the fresh fruits of scholarship derived from their recent dissertations.

The volume greatly benefited from a conference sponsored by the Van Leer Jerusalem Institute. We met after the first drafts of most of the chapters had been circulated among all participants. The dynamics of the conference enabled interaction at two complementary levels: among authors who wrote on adjacent regions or on consecutive periods, as well as among authors who wrote regional chapters and those who wrote the general thematic chapters.

Following an introduction by the editors, who chart the principal themes of the volume, there are two very special chapters brought together as Part I, "Gateways to Africa." Those gateways are Egypt and the Maghrib from the north and the Indian Ocean from the east. Hence, the history of Islam in the continent of Africa is further expanded by presenting it in the wider context of the rest of the Muslim world. The next fourteen chapters (Parts II and III) are regional and chronological in scope, while the last nine chapters (Part IV) are summary and integrative. The authors of the chapters in Part IV, "General Themes," have been encouraged to draw on the regional and chronological chapters in order to enrich and to enliven their comparative studies.

The editors wish to express their deep gratitude to the contributors to this volume, who in addition to their excellence in scholarship have also proved their comradeship and devotion to the idea of producing this comprehensive volume.

We extend our thanks to the Van Leer Jerusalem Institute for generously hosting the conference in June 1997.

Finally, our thanks go to Gillian Berchowitz, senior editor at the Ohio University Press; to the copyeditor, Dennis Marshall; the typesetter, Karol Halbirt; the cartographer, Chris Akers; and all those at the Press who contributed to the production of this unique volume.

The History of Islam in Africa

Patterns of Islamization and Varieties of Religious Experience among Muslims of Africa

Nehemia Levtzion and Randall L. Pouwels

slam reached Africa through two gateways, from the east and the north. From both directions the carriers of Islam navigated across vast empty spaces, the waters of the Indian Ocean, and the desert sands of the Sahara. Both ocean and desert, which so often are considered barriers, could be crossed with appropriate means of transportation and navigational skills, and they were, in fact, excellent transmitters of religious and cultural influences. Densely populated lands, on the other hand, functioned as filters, their numerous layers slowing down the infiltration of religious and cultural influences.

From Egypt, Islamic influence extended in three directions, through the Red Sea to the eastern coastal areas, up the Nile valley to the Sudan, and across the western desert to the Maghrib. In the eleventh century, Arab nomads drove southward from Egypt to the Sudan and westward across North Africa. These nomads contributed to the Islamization and Arabization of the Sudan and North Africa. At the same time, Muslim seamen from Egypt and Arabia established commercial centers along the Red Sea and Africa's east coast.

By the twelfth century, the last indigenous Christians disappeared from North Africa, and by the fifteenth century the Christian Coptic population of Egypt itself was reduced to a minority of some 15 percent. The Christian Nubians, who resisted Muslim expansion for almost six centuries, steadily lost ground between the twelfth and the fourteenth centuries (chapter 5). It was only in the Horn of Africa that the power struggle between Islam and Christianity remained undecided. Ethiopia endured as a Christian state even after the number of Muslims had grown considerably; Muslims could not own land and were excluded from higher government offices.

On the East African coast, Islam faced the challenge of Christianity between the sixteenth and the eighteenth centuries. Religion was important in the struggle of Arab and Swahili Muslims. The struggle concluded with the withdrawal of the Portuguese from the coast north of Mozambique after 1698. However, Muslims lost to the Christians the control of the maritime trade in the Indian Ocean. Muslims had dominated this trade for more than seven centuries, though they had faced competition from Asian Hindus and Buddhists. The Saharan trade, on the other hand, remained completely at the hands of Muslims. Europeans interfered in the Saharan trade only indirectly after the fifteenth century, when they began diverting some of the gold to the coast.

Because Islam spread to West Africa from North Africa, Muslims there followed the Maliki school of law dominant in North Africa. On the other hand, in East Africa, where Islam came from the Arabian peninsula, Muslims followed the Shafi'i school of law that prevailed in Arabia. Both regions, however, were exposed to the influence of the Ibadiyya sect. Ibadi merchants opened up trade across the Sahara, and were among the first Muslims who reached western Sudan—as early as the eighth and ninth centuries. But whatever converts they had made were reconverted to Maliki Islam by the eleventh century. The Ibadiyya had been established in Eastern Arabia during the first centuries of Islam and became dominant in Zanzibar after the Omani conquest of this island in the eighteenth century. The Ibadis of Zanzibar maintained their distinct Arab identity, and did not engage in missionary work among Africans.

The Progress of Islam in North and West Africa

Soon after they had defeated the Byzantine imperial forces in the middle of the seventh century, the Arabs gained control over coastal North Africa. But for some time, the Arabs failed to impose their authority over the Berber tribes of the interior. Successive revolts of the Berbers, that forced the Arabs to withdraw, were referred to as *ridda,* the same term used when Arab tribes deserted the young Muslim community after the death of the Prophet. In both cases, political submission and conversion to Islam were considered one and the same act. Similarly, when the Arabs consolidated their rule over the Berbers the text reads "after the *islam* of the Berbers had been made good" *(ba'da ma hasuna islam al-barbar);* the word *islam* here carried the two meanings of submission and conversion.

The next phase of the Berbers' resistance to Arab rule occurred within Islam, through adherence to heterodox sects, first the Ibadiyya and then the Isma'iliyya. The Almoravids finally secured the victory of Sunni-Maliki Islam in the eleventh century. Under their Almohad successors, Islam in the Maghrib became imbued with the mysticism of the sufis, who became the principal agents of Islamization in North Africa after the twelfth century (chapter 1).

Berber-speaking nomads reached the southern Sahara and touched the Sahel in pre-Islamic times. They were well positioned to mediate Islamic influences between the Maghrib and the Western Sudan (known to the Arabs as "Bilad al-Sudan"). As the Berber nomads occupied both shores of the Sahara, the dividing line between "white" and "black" Africa, to use French colonial terms, was where the desert meets the Sahel, and where Berber-speaking nomads interacted with the Sudanic sedentaries. Along this line they cooperated in creating the termini of the Saharan trade. Today, this dividing line cuts across the modern African states of the Sahel—namely, Senegal, Mali, Niger, Chad, and the Sudan. In all these states, except the Sudan, political power is with the black people of the south; it is also only in the Sudan that the dividing line is not only an ethnic but also a religious frontier.

As early as the eleventh century, Manding-speaking traders, ancestors of the Juula, traveled between the termini of the Saharan routes and the sources of the gold. They created a "commercial diaspora," based on a shared religion as well as a collective language. A common legal system—the law of Islam *(shari'a)*—even if not strictly observed, contributed to mutual trust among merchants in the long-distance trade. Conversion to Islam became necessary for those who wished to join commercial networks. Though merchants opened routes and exposed isolated societies to external influences, they did not themselves engage in the propagation of Islam.

Conversion to Islam was the work of men of religion who communicated primarily with local rulers. The latter often became the first recipients of Islamic influence, an indication to the importance that states had in the process of Islamization. Thus, for some time Muslims lived under the hospitality of infidel kings, who generally were praised by Muslims for their benevolence toward the believers. This was the situation in eleventh-century Ghana as in nineteenth-century Asante. The process of Islamization advanced when Muslim clerics helped African kings to overcome severe droughts, as in the case of eleventh-century Malal, or to secure victory, as in fourteenth-century Kano and in sixteenth-century Gonja (chapter 3). But, because only the king and his immediate entourage came under the influence of Islam, the ruling aristocracy adopted a middle position between Islam and the traditional religion, patronizing both Muslim divines and traditional priests. It was through the chiefly courts that Islamic elements filtered the culture of the common people. The symbiotic relations of Islam with the traditional religion has been illustrated in a novel by Ahmadou Kourouma, who remarked that everyone publicly proclaimed himself a devout Muslim, but privately feared the "fetish" (chapter 23). Muslim clerics who rendered religious services to Islamized chiefs became integrated into the sociopolitical system of the state by playing roles similar to those of traditional priests. Like traditional priests, Muslim clerics were politically neutral and could therefore act as peacemakers. Mosques, like shrines, were considered sanctuaries.

Allah bestowed beneficent power *(baraka)* on those closest to him. The latter, clerics and saints, transmitted his blessings to devotees and to communities. During long years of training, they acquired specialized and hidden knowledge. The ability to know which chapter or verse or the combination of passages to be used and at what time and for what purpose required esoteric knowledge (chapter 21). The

Wolof *marabout* (cleric) in Birago Diop's novel *Les Contes d'Amadou Koumba* combined the spiritual power he brought from Mecca with the ancestral source of power. The power of the word is inseparable from the status of the agents—both poets and saints—who articulate it (chapter 23).

In the great kingdoms of the Sahel, with international trade, Muslim centers of learning, and close connections with the Muslim world, the kings developed greater commitment to Islam. But even these kings, like Mansa Musa of Mali and Askiya Muhammad of Songhay, were unable to relieve the monarchy of its pre-Islamic heritage. Ibn Battuta attested this during his visit to the court of Mali in the middle of the fourteenth-century, and a scholar from Timbuktu witnessed pre-Islamic customs when he visited the court of Askiya Dawud in the middle of the sixteenth century (chapter 3).

Scholars like those of Timbuktu lived as an autonomous community under the leadership of the *qadi* (the Muslim judge). Such a community was that of Diaba, "the scholars' town," where the king of Mali did not enter. Anyone who entered this town was safe from the king's oppression and his outrage, and it was called "the town of Allah." Jealous of their autonomy, proud of their erudition, and committed to follow the law of Islam strictly, the scholars of Timbuktu were not politically neutral, unlike clerics who lived close to chiefly courts. As a result, there were tensions between the scholars of Timbuktu and the political authorities. These scholars were the avowed enemies of Sonni Ali in the middle of the fifteenth century, and they led the resistance to the Moroccan conquest a century and a half later. There were even tensions between the pious Askiya Muhammad and Askiya Dawud and the contemporary qadis.

Chiefs used to send their sons to study with Muslim clerics as part of their princely education. Such offspring were not meant to become Muslims, but some converted and became scholars. A qadi of Jenne in the second half of the sixteenth century was "from among the sons of the chiefs of Kala. He withdrew from authority and became a scholar." Bakary, the son of Biton Kulibali, ruler of the young eighteenth-century Bambara state, became a Muslim; he was deposed and killed because he failed to maintain the delicate balance between Islam and tradition. In fifteenth-century Kano, the king's son Umar became a sincere Muslim; when he succeeded his father, the contradiction between being a Muslim and a warrior chief became apparent to him, and he resigned the kingship. He repented during the rest of his life for the wrongs he had done as a king (chapter 3).

Though they entertained Muslim clerics in their courts, prayed, and exhibited some external signs of Islamic influence, the chiefs were not considered Muslims because, as warriors, they drank alcohol and shed blood. Among the Wolof, tension developed when the rulers rejected the call of the clerics to repent (to the military and the political elite, repentance, or true conversion to Islam, implied abandoning their way of life and joining the clerical community). In the Saharan society, too, tension between clerics and the warriors was an important feature. Toward the end of the seventeenth century, Nasir al-Din, a member of a clerical group in the southwestern part of Mauritania, rebelled against the Banu Hassan warriors, and for a few years the Hassan were on the defensive: Wolof and Fulbe-speaking Muslims joined the jihad of Nasir al-Din and succeeded in overthrowing the ruling dynasties of the states of Cayor, Walo, Jolof, and Futa Toro. Within a few years, however, a coalition of the warriors, the traditional political elite, from the Sahara and the Senegal valley, with some support from French trading interests, defeated the clerics and regained power. The final victory of the warriors consolidated the division of Saharan society into two main estates—warriors and clerical clans. The Hassan exercised political and military domination; the *zawaya (marabouts)* controlled religious instruction, adjudication, and most of the economic activities in commerce and agriculture (chapter 6).

Around Lake Chad, the trade of Kanem to North Africa was mainly in slaves. As a result, Islam did not spread to the lands south of Lake Chad, which remained hunting grounds for slaves. When its power grew, Kanem expanded northward to the Sahara and as far as Fezzan. In Kanem, and in its successor state Bornu, Islam was not restricted to the court but reached out the whole population. In the sixteenth and seventeenth centuries, Birnin Gazargamo, the capital of Bornu, was an important center for Islamic learning. Quranic manuscripts from Bornu dating from as early as the seventeenth century had interlinear translations and glosses in the local language. Bornu attracted many students from neighboring regions, and Bornu scholars officiated as teachers and imams in Hausaland, Yorubaland, Borgu, and further west (chapter 19). By the end of the eighteenth century, Islam was deeply rooted in the everyday life of the ordinary man in Bornu. But even there, pre-Islamic elements persisted, which the Fulbe of Sokoto used as a pretext for the jihad against Bornu.

The spread of Islam among the Yoruba began in the nineteenth century and advanced as a result of the fall of the northern Yoruba to the Fulbe jihad. Except in the emirate of Ilorin, which was part of the Sokoto caliphate, Islam took root among the Yoruba as a religious practice, but it did not become associated with a state tradition. The progress of Islam did not obliterate traditional patterns of authority.

Farther to the east, on the Nile, Christian Nubians had arrested the advance of Islam for six centuries. From about 1500 onward, three major states in the grasslands south of Nubia had developed with a veneer of Islam. In these kingdoms—Funj, Dar Fur, and Wadai—Islam was corporate and communal. All obedient subjects were considered Muslims, whatever their way of life, while disobedience implied rejection of the corporate Islam of the community, and therefore apostasy (chapter 5).

All over Africa, holy men were able to convert charisma, spiritual or "symbolic capital," to economic power. Where central political authorities were weak, or completely absent, holy men could also build up political power.

Conversion in the Horn and South of the Equator

Muslims settled on the Ethiopian coast of the Red Sea as early as the eighth century. By the ninth century, there were Muslim communities along the trade routes to the interior. The town of Harar developed as the most important center for trade and Islamic learning. These communities grew to become Muslim principalities that challenged the hegemony of the Christian Ethiopian State.

The most important outcome of the jihad of Ahmad Gran in the first half of the sixteenth century was the weakening of both the Christian state and the Muslim principalities. The fertile highlands became subject to mass migrations of the pastoral Oromo. By the eighteenth century, the chiefly families of the Oromo embraced Islam. Muslim religious leaders gained prominence in the Oromo principalities of Ethiopia. Scholars received grants of land to sustain themselves, but they also criticized local rulers and ordinary believers, threatening to avoid performing the proper funeral prayers to those they considered lax in observing Islam. Sufi shaykhs established centers for higher learning, spiritual training, and devotional practice and made written contributions to Islamic scholarship. By the middle of the nineteenth-century, Islam also took root among the Oromo commoners. They fasted, turned to Islamic rather than to customary law in matters of marriage and inheritance, paid the *zakat* (the obligatory "tithe"), circumcised their sons at an earlier age than before, and went on pilgrimage to Mecca. In the nineteenth century, Muslim traders opened up new regions in the southwestern parts of present-day Ethiopia to procure slaves. Between 1800 and 1830, new Oromo states emerged at the termini of the trade routes from the coast. Sufi teachers who accompanied the slave merchants converted their rulers (chapter 11).

While Islam was present on the east coast as early as 780, it became the religion of the majority of the Swahili-speaking peoples between 1200 and 1500. At that time the Swahili also developed a distinct culture. This Swahili Islamic civilization became quintessentially urban. Stone houses, often two-storied, walled off prosperous Swahili families from commoners and encouraged a lifestyle imbued with a special urban elegance (chapter 12).

Compared with West Africa, where connections with the heartland of Islam in the Arabian peninsula were only through the *hajj* (pilgrimage), East Africa, closer geographically, has been in direct and continuous communication with the Arabian peninsula. In the past two centuries at least, boys have been sent to study in Hadhramaut and in Mecca and Medina. Direct cultural influences have been detected in music, and in fact whole Arabic instrumental ensembles and their repertories have been adopted. West African societies, by contrast, have not exhibited such clear Arab musical influences (chapter 24).

Until the nineteenth century, Islam in East Africa remained confined to the coast, unlike in West Africa, where Islam spread far into the interior. What follows is an attempt to explain the different patterns of the spread of Islam in East and West Africa. Merchants and other settlers on the east coast were part of the Indian Ocean trading diaspora. Their commercial connections were with lands around the Indian Ocean, rather than with the African interior, and to the extent that African goods reached the coast before the nineteenth century, usually they were carried by traders from the interior (e.g., the Shona, and later the Makua and the Yao). The spread of Islam conveniently took place within a wider context—one of cultural influences and migrations. In West Africa these movements were in the same direction, from north to south, as that taken by Islam. In East Africa, on the other hand, migrations and the movement of goods, from the interior to the coast, were contrary to the direction Islam would have taken, that is to say, from east to west.

In the nineteenth century a new class of merchants and landowners with wealth from plantations and trade contributed to religious revival on the East African coast. This new bourgeoisie was responsible for a dramatic increase in the number of mosques and schools, which further augmented the opportunities of employment for men of religion. The more important 'ulama' (scholars) spent time in Arabia, mainly in Mecca and Medina. Along with the increasing depth of scholarship, literacy became more popular and widespread, due to the growing importance of sufi brotherhoods in the nineteenth century (chapters 2 and 12).

The Omani sultans encouraged migration from Hadhramaut to the East African coast. But the new arrivals were not assimilated in the Swahili society. For them, the term *Swahili* implied lower status and even contempt. Those who claimed Arabian origins maintained close ties with their homeland and cultivated what may be described as normative Islam, thus widening the gap with the ordinary Swahili. Mutual estrangement between Swahili and Arabs explains why the former cared nothing for Islamic revivalism or Pan-Islam, which bore an Arab stamp (chapter 2).

The slow process of Islamization in East Africa beyond the narrow coastal strip started only in the nineteenth century, when people of the immediate hinterland began frequenting Mombasa with products of the interior. The process was accelerated in the third quarter of the nineteenth century, when Muslims from the coast settled in farms in the interior, and Africans who had converted in the coastal towns returned to their original rural homes. Islam thus penetrated deeper into the interior of East Africa only when Muslim merchants from the coast ventured inland in search of ivory and slaves. Not many Africans accepted Islam along the trade routes and in the settlements of the Arabs and Swahilis. Those who converted were mostly members of the immediate entourage of the Arab and Swahili merchants: spouses and their relatives, porters and other employees of the merchants (chapter 13).

The Yao are the most Islamized people in the interior of Mozambique and southern Tanzania. Though they had traded with the coast since the seventeenth century, they were converted only in the nineteenth century with the coming of Muslim traders and scribes to the interior. Matrilineal social principles among the Yao and the Makua created tensions with Islam's patrilineal order. A Makua shaykh who had succeeded his matrilineal uncle as *mwene* (chief elder) of his lineage was obliged to abandon his position in the Qadiriyya *tariqa* (sufi brotherhood) but remained a practicing Muslim (chapter 14).

Buganda is the only centralized state in East Africa that might have experienced patterns of Islamization similar to those of kingdoms in West Africa. Kabaka Mutesa came under the influence of Muslim merchants, built mosques, and obliged his chiefs to pray. Muslims held important positions as heads of provinces and as commanders of the royal guard. The influence of Islam in Buganda was arrested, particularly after the British conquest, because of fierce competition with the Protestant and Roman Catholic missionaries (chapter 13). Nevertheless, Bugandan Muslims migrated throughout the region of the Great Lakes and became important agents of conversion well outside their homeland.

Islam reached South Africa with free and slave migration from Malaya and the islands of the Indian Ocean. The process of conversion during the last decades of formal slavery (1798–1838) might have constituted South Africa's golden age of Islam. In 1838, manumission among Muslims was faster than among Christians, and became a powerful inducement to embrace Islam. Slaves appear to have enjoyed being of a religion opposed to that of their owners (chapter 15).

State-driven Reforms (c. 1500)

Pre-Islamic elements persisted because Islam became integrated into the religious, social, and cultural life of African societies without a break with the past. A reform was needed to make such a break and to bring about more literate forms of Islam.

Chiefs and kings who undertook the *hajj* became acquainted with different ways of practicing Islam and were also exposed to the teachings of some of the greatest scholars of the day. The Almoravid movement originated in the encounter of a Sanhaja chief from the Southwestern Sahara with Abu 'Imran al-Fasi in Qayrawan. Mansa Musa strengthened Islamic institutions in Mali after making the pilgrimage to Mecca and a visit to Cairo. Askiya Muhammad was invested with the title of caliph in Cairo, and exchanges with scholars of Cairo added depth to the intellectual life in sixteenth-century Timbuktu.

About 1500, there were attempts at reform in three contemporary states: in Songhay under Askiya Muhammad, who sought the advice of the 'ulama'; in Kano at the time of King Rumfa, who ordered the felling of a sacred tree, under which the original mosque had been built; and in Bornu, where the contemporary reformer king was Ali Ghaji. Both Songhay and Kano were visited by the militant North African scholar al-Maghili, who called for the purgation from Islam of all its accretions. Al-Maghili urged the anathemization *(takfir)* of those who had accepted the accommodation of Islam with traditional beliefs and customs. His zealous teachings were mitigated by the advice of the more moderate and pragmatic Jalal al-Din al-Suyuti, one of the greatest scholars of Egypt at that time. These reforms, however, were initiated by the rulers themselves, and were by far less radical than the Islamic revolutions of the eighteenth and nineteenth centuries, when ruling dynasties were overthrown and 'ulama' assumed power (chapter 6).

It is significant that about this same time, in the first half of the sixteenth century, Islam in the Horn of Africa became more militant. The power struggle between the Christian state of Ethiopia and the Muslim principalities reached its highest point in the jihad of Imam Ahmad Gran (chapter 11).

Brotherhoods

In the Maghrib, the land of sufism par excellence, there had been no structured hierarchical brotherhoods, only independent *zawaya,* seats of marabouts. They all followed the Shadhili sufi tradition, which at that time lacked any meaningful organization. Only after the late seventeenth century did new brotherhoods evolve on a wider geographical and societal scale out of the local zawaya.

In the sixteenth century, the leading scholars of Timbuktu were sufis, but like contemporary Egyptian sufis, they were not affiliated to any sufi brotherhood *(tariqa).* Likewise, in Bornu, communities *(mallamati)* were also without tariqa affiliation. In the Sudan, the old brotherhoods of the Qadiriyya and the Shadhiliyya had been assimilated into localized holy clans. The relationship between the shaykh and his followers was direct, face-to-face and personal, without any further organizational elaboration.

There is evidence that the Qadiriyya was present in Harar as early as 1500, but oral hagiographic traditions do not associate pre-eighteenth-century holy men in the Horn with a particular brotherhood, as they do in regard to holy men who lived after 1800. Rather, holy men are remembered as the founding fathers of various Somali clans. In southern Somalia and East Africa, the affiliation of sufi communities with a particular tariqa was weak. It was only in the nineteenth century that named tariqas became important in Somalia. After the early 1800s, religious settlements from various clans lived together as *ikhwan* (brothers), jointly engaged in agriculture, livestock husbandry, and religious study and worship (chapters 11 and 20). Along the east coast, the saint-centered 'Alawiyya brotherhood probably arrived in Pate as early as the sixteenth century, with the immigration of large numbers of Hadramis from the holy city of Inat and its vicinity. From Pate and the Lamu archipelago, the 'Alawi *sharifs* (those who claim descent from the Prophet) and shaykhs and their adherents spread southward along the coast, exerting a tremendous degree of religious prestige and charisma (chapter 12).

During the eighteenth century, there was a meaningful shift in sufi brotherhoods away from the old patterns of decentralized and diffusive affiliations toward larger-scale and more coherent forms of organization. In the process of restructuring, the role of the shaykh was expanded and brotherhoods became centralized, disciplined organizations that included networks of deputies *(khalifas).* It is clear from the evidence that the hierarchical, centralized organization of the tariqa was a novelty. Organizational aspects of the brotherhoods, rather than the content of their teaching, rendered them potential political actors (chapters 3 and 20).

The Qadiriyya brotherhood had first been introduced into the Sahara probably at the end of the fifteenth century. But the Qadiriyya had been loosely organized and rather ineffective until its resurgence, in the second half of the eighteenth century, under the leadership of Sidi al-Mukhtar al-Kunti. He skillfully used his religious prestige to acquire wealth and political influence as individuals and communal factions sought his patronage. He reinforced the dependency of these

9

clients by fostering the spiritual chains of the Qadiriyya. Sidi al-Mukhtar's emissaries spread the new branch, known as Qadiriyya-Mukhtariyya in the Sahara, the Sahel, and as far as Futa Jalon (chapters 3 and 20).

In the Sudan, the opening up of commercial connections with the Mediterranean and the Red Sea toward the end of the seventeenth century encouraged the development of towns and the rise of an indigenous, urban-based middle class. The new class needed the stabilizing influence of the *shari'a*. A rise of literacy in Arabic, public prayers, and conformist dress gave this urban society an entirely new cultural and ethnic identity as Arabs. Observance of the rules of Islam became the criterion to evaluate one's status as a Muslim (chapter 5).

The two trends of Islam—the popular Islam of the holy men and the more conformist Islam of the urban population—were brought together by reformed brotherhoods that developed in the Sudan since the last quarter of the eighteenth century. The new sufi brotherhoods—the Sammaniyya, Khatmiyya, and Rashidiyya—incorporated local holy families into large-scale organizations. In the Sudan, local scholars and saints were drawn into new and wider networks, which were also interethnic and interregional (chapters 20 and 5).

Popularly-based brotherhoods reached the East African coast much later; only near the end of the nineteenth century did the Qadiriyya and the Shadhiliyya become active. The Qadiriyya attracted some new converts, but its greatest impact seems to have been to encourage African Muslims to live their faith more enthusiastically and with greater conviction (chapters 12 and 13).

Jihad Legitimation

Sidi al-Mukhtar did not advocate militant jihad. His son opposed the jihad of Shaykh Ahmad of Massina and his grandson that of al-Hajj 'Umar. But Sidi al-Mukhtar, the nonmilitant sufi, supported the jihad of 'Uthman dan Fodio in what is now northern Nigeria. The mystical encounters of 'Uthman dan Fodio with 'Abd al-Qadir al-Jilani, founder of the Qadiriyya, helped legitimize the jihad in Hausaland.

The dramatic point of no return in the development of Islamic militancy was when radical reformers introduced the concept of takfir, which implied that those who had previously been considered Muslims were declared infidels. In arguing against the jihad, al-Kanemi insisted that the general consensus *(ijma)* is against anathematizing Muslims; people might be sinners, but they had not rejected Islam. 'Uthman dan Fodio justified the jihad against the Hausa because of deeds that for centuries had been accepted as a legitimate accommodation of Islam with traditional religions.

An anti-jihad ideology is attributed to al-Hajj Salim Suwari, the architect of the ways of life of the Juula and the Jakhanke, who lived probably in the late fifteenth century. He taught that some people may remain in a state of ignorance longer than others and that true conversion will occur only in God's time; hence, actively to proselytize is to interfere with God's will, and jihad is unacceptable as a method of conversion. Muslims may accept the authority of non-Muslim rulers, and even support them through the provision of religious services, so far as they are able to observe Islam strictly. The wars of Samori Touré in the last decades of the nineteenth century were perceived as a threat to the Juula way of life. As the Juula refused to collaborate with Samori, he sacked their towns of Buna and Kong and executed the imam of Buna and forty of the senior ʿulama' of Kong (chapter 4).

In the seventeenth and eighteenth centuries, Islam spread from towns to the countryside. Whereas trade served as the economic basis for urban scholarship, rural Islamic scholarship depended on slave farming and on the work of students *(talamidh)*. Among the clerical lineages of the Sahara, scholars and students moved together in nomadic and seminomadic groups. In Bornu, radical scholars withdrew from the centers of political power to establish autonomous religious communities. These autonomous enclaves of rural scholarship, known as *mallamati*, maintained only minimal communications with the wider society. In the Nilotic Sudan, rural centers of learning that combined legal teaching with sufism developed after the sixteenth century. In the more fertile regions of southern Somalia, scholarly groups established themselves between powerful and rival tribes (chapters 19 and 20).

Itinerant Muslim preachers moved among the rural Muslim communities. ʿUthman dan Fodio himself addressed the peasants and articulated their grievances, criticizing rulers who killed people, violated their honor, and devoured their wealth. His son Muhammad Bello evoked the wrath of Allah over "the *amir* who draws his sustenance from the people but does not bother to treat them justly."

It is significant that all leaders of the jihad movements in West Africa came from the countryside and not from commercial or capital towns. The challenge to the marginal role of Islam in African societies did not come from ʿulama' who were spokesmen for the traders, nor from clerics who rendered religious services in the chiefly courts; it came mostly from the autonomous rural and pastoral enclaves.

In the period 1880–1918, three forms of Islamic militancy became interconnected in the Horn. One was against adherents of indigenous religions and lax Muslims; a second opposed the Christian Ethiopian state; and a third resisted European colonialism. In Somalia, Sayyid Muhammad Abdallah Hassan began a jihad in 1898 to purify the country from the Ethiopian and European "unbelievers." The sayyid belonged to the Salihiyya brotherhood, an offshoot of a tariqa founded by a disciple of Ahmad ibn Idris. He confronted the Qadiriyya, which collaborated with Europeans (chapter 11).

In South Africa, a movement of Islamic revivalism was ushered with the arrival in 1862 of a Kurdish scholar, Shaykh Abu Bakr Effendi. He sought to integrate the Cape Muslims into the wider Muslim world and to impose Islamic orthodoxy. To the extent that he succeeded, the price was a slowdown of conversion to Islam compared with an earlier period, when Cape imams converted all and sundry (chapter 15).

Islamic Vernacular Literatures

The expansion of Islam to the countryside widened the popular basis for religious teaching and preaching. Knowledge of Islam was disseminated to the illiterate peasants and herdsmen in the vernacular languages. Parallel to the transformation of Islam as a popular religion and as a political force, Muslim reformers developed a pious literature. Poems, easily committed to memory, became a major vehicle for teaching and preaching. Vernacular poems were disseminated in handwritten copies among Muslim literati, who recited them in public.

Some of the oldest known written texts in Fulfulde, dating from the second half of the eighteenth century, were poems written by reformers who sought to reach people of all walks of life. The reformers produced a huge mass of devotional, didactic, and legal literature in Arabic and in local languages. Under the rule of the Almamis of Futa Jalon, a large corpus of religious and didactic poetry in Fulfulde was created. When 'Uthman dan Fodio saw that his community was ready for the jihad, he began inciting them to arms, setting this to Arabic verse *(qasida ajamiyya qadiriyya)*. This mystical verse had a hypnotic effect upon devotees on the eve of the jihad.

With the development of the preaching activities of the leaders of the future jihad movements, local languages were increasingly used for religious and didactic purposes, if necessary with translators. Poetry in Fulfulde and Hausa became a major tool for the propagation of Islamic morals and doctrines. It was under the impact of the jihad that Hausa written literature was created, especially in the field of religious and moral poetry (chapter 19).

On the East African coast, before the seventeenth century Arabic seems to have been confined to first-generation immigrants and to those few who obtained religious education abroad. Swahili was the language of daily discourse, Arabic remaining confined to religion and to correspondence. There was relatively little interaction between the two languages until the seventeenth century, and no extensive borrowing of Arabic words by Swahili. Only after the middle of the seventeenth century were Arabic loanwords absorbed in Swahili. As Hadhrami scholars became assimilated into the local coastal society, they began to write in Swahili. The earliest surviving manuscripts of written literature in Swahili date from the seventeenth century, though the beginnings probably go back further in time. Many of the texts were translations of Arabic religious and didactic poems, but a new genre of epic poems *(tendi)* was created in the early eighteenth century, with themes drawn from the life of Muhammad and other prophets. The genre itself marks a new stage in the adaptation of Islamic lore to the interests of a broader local public (chapters 12 and 19).

The Post-Jihad States

The Fulbe and Somali who provided the main fighting forces to the holy wars were able to participate fully in the consummation of the military and political victory by abandoning pastoralism and settling down. The process of sedentarization often was made possible only with the help of slave farming, which freed the pastoralists from their political, religious, and educational pursuits (chapters 6 and 11).

In Futa Toro, the Almamy Abdul Qadir Kan established mosques, schools, and qadi courts in the villages. He came into conflict with the powerful regional lords, members of Fulbe families who were closer to the older traditions of pastoralism and did not share his commitment to Islam. His death in 1807 marked the end of a strong central government in Futa Toro. But the people of the Futa preserved a strong sense of Islamic identity and commitment to holy war, which was later exploited by al-Hajj 'Umar.

In post-jihad Sokoto, mosques and schools multiplied in urban as in rural areas. Sufi practices of the Qadiriyya were encouraged to support the process of Islamization. The emirs named qadis to administer Islamic law, but they maintained a large judicial role for themselves. Aspects of the Islamic law were discussed in relation to situations and events that were familiar to their audience (chapters 6 and 17).

Seku Ahmadu established in Massina the most centralized post-jihad regime. He regimented the lives of people in the towns and in the countryside. He settled pastoralists in designated areas. The Kunta scholars of the southern Sahara considered his severe interpretations of Islamic practice to be wrong, the product of a very limited Islamic education.

Hence, a formal judicial system was established throughout Africa only in the post-jihad states, where qadis were appointed to administer the law of Islam. Earlier, the administration of the shari'a was informal, as people typically approached the imam, a Quranic teacher, or any person with a pious reputation to solve legal questions. Local 'ulama' served in advisory capacities to local rulers, who themselves adjudicated (chapter 17).

Because of the constraints of war, al-Hajj 'Umar was unable to consolidate an Islamic state. He did not establish judicial courts, schools, mosques, and other institutions of an Islamic state that might have brought the Bambara and other conquered peoples into a more orderly practice of Islam (chapter 6).

Leaders of jihad movements, like al-Hajj 'Umar and Samori, who were still at their expansionist stage, came into confrontation with the expanding colonial powers; they were defeated. The Sokoto caliphate, on the other hand, survived into the colonial period because it had been consolidated early in the nineteenth century and accepted British rule after a token resistance.

Islam under Colonial Rule

Only a minority of Muslim leaders resisted colonialism or tried to avoid conquest by making the *hijra* (migrating beyond the reach of colonial authorities). The majority, however, chose accommodation and collaboration. Public opinion in West Africa was not critical of the elites that collaborated with the colonial powers. Indeed, religious leaders sometimes replaced the defeated aristocracies as intermediaries with the colonial authorities, as was the case among the Wolof. Juula traders, whose trade benefited from the consolidation of colonial rule, adopted the same attitude to the new rulers as they had toward the previous non-Muslim rulers (chapter 8). Likewise, the 'ulama' of the East African protectorates were co-opted into the regime's service as salaried qadis and other "native" officials (chapter 13).

The expansion of Islam accelerated during the colonial period. The opening of routes and railways facilitated the installation of Muslim colonies in southern regions. In Northern Nigeria, the British helped the expansion of Islam by extending the rule of Muslim emirs to neighboring "pagan" areas.

In East Africa, under British and German rule, Muslim trading stations developed into administrative centers, where most of the government officials were Muslim. People from the countryside migrated to those growing urban centers, like Tabora, where they came under Muslim influence. In Malawi, freedom and security of movement to Muslim traders and clerics facilitated the expansion of Islam, as did the fact that most of the British colonial troops were Muslims (chapters 13 and 14).

Farther into the interior of East Africa, in the eastern provinces of the Congo and in Burundi and Rwanda, Swahili-speaking Muslims were recruited by the Germans to serve as interpreters and soldiers. Their quarters became the nuclei of urban centers, where rural people migrated and settled. A process of mutual acculturation took place, as the indigenous people converted to Islam while the foreign Muslims adopted the local language (chapter 13).

The French colonial administration seems to have cultivated an Islamic policy that changed over time. At first they encouraged Islam, which they perceived as an advanced stage in the evolutionary process from "animism" to Western civilization. But when they felt threatened by Islam, the French invented the concept of Islam Noir, to distinguish African Islam from Arab Islam. In the 1920s, the French constructed an imagined struggle between Islam and "animism." In the 1950s, they supported traditional Muslim leaders against attacks by the reformers, who sought to "Arabize" African Islam (chapter 8).

During their brief conquest of Ethiopia, in order to undermine the foundations of the Christian state, the Italians pursued a pro-Islamic policy. They granted Muslims full freedom of religion, encouraged mosque building, appointed qadis, and introduced Arabic in all Muslim schools. They facilitated the pilgrimage, and allowed the propagation of Islam (chapter 11).

Brotherhoods changed roles in their relation to the colonial authorities; whereas in Algeria the Qadiriyya resisted the French and the Tijaniyya collaborated with them, in West Africa the Tijaniyya led resistance to the French. With the consolidation of colonial rule, most leaders of the brotherhoods, including the Tijaniyya, collaborated with the authorities. The French administration supported those movements, which already had become accommodated to colonial rule, and repressed those who challenged these movements. This was the case of the Hammaliyya, which challenged the main stream of the Tijaniyya (chapter 8).

Following the defeat of the Mahdiyya in the Sudan, the British became allied with Sayyid Ali al-Mirghani, the Mahdi's rival. Cooperation with the Khatmiyya gave a certain aura of Islamic legitimacy to British rule. The British policy that aimed to suppress the Mahdiyya changed when the Mahdi's son, Sayyid Abd al-Rahman al-Mahdi, set out to reconstruct the Ansar as a successor to the Mahdiyya, within the tradition of popular Islam and in reconciliation with the British authorities. The two largest Muslim associations—the Ansar and the Khatmiyya—were accepted as representing the voices of Sudanese society. Leaders of holy families also became involved in nationalist movements and politics during the Condominium (chapter 7).

During the colonial period, the existence of an alternative Muslim educational system insulated the Muslim community from the modernizing tendencies associated with Western education. Where Muslims lived close to Christians, as in Lagos, Freetown, Mombasa, Capetown, and Durban, they organized earlier and more aggressively to create a modern school system that would combine Islamic and Western education. This was the case of the Young Ansar-Ud-Deen Society, founded in 1923, that established and ran Western schools among Yoruba Muslims (chapter 19).

During the colonial period, women took an active part in movements of popular learning and piety. Women, some of them Western-educated, devoted time to prayers, learned the Koran, preached to other women, and performed voluntary services. Female participation in the Arabic schools is very high, often reaching more than half of the student population. Many women went to Mecca off-season. Hence, the 'umra, which unlike the hajj may be performed at any time of the year, became known as the "women's pilgrimage" (chapter 9).

Efforts to give women a greater role in religious life were opposed by the reformers. Women responded to the challenge of the fundamentalists by embracing distinctive Muslim dress, including the veil, but at the same time they became more active politically and formed their own organizations. Under the Islamist regime in the Sudan, fewer women enrolled to certain types of medical and technical training. Women became excluded from high-ranking and better-salaried positions (chapter 18).

Modern Reformism

After independence, the traditional religious elites lost their hold on education—on the one hand to those educated in the French schools, and on the other to a new Muslim elite educated in Arab countries. Many of the new generation of young Muslim intellectuals combined Western education with studies in Islamic institutions in Arab countries. After the 1980s, this young Muslim elite asserted themselves as a distinct cultural and political group, set aside from the older generation of Muslim scholars and leaders (chapter 19).

The introduction of new types of Arab schools, which had started in the 1930s and 1940s, gained in momentum in the 1960s. From the 1970s onward, a dense network of Arabic schools emerged in many Muslim regions. In the 1960s, Egypt supported Islamic educational projects. In the 1970s, the oil-producing nations of Libya and Saudi Arabia competed in giving out grants to create cultural and educational institutions (chapter 19).

The call for reform came in the 1950s from graduates of Al-Azhar university-mosque in Cairo. The reformers sought to purify the practice of Islam by eradicating saint worship associated with maraboutism. They prayed with their hands crossed and were recognized by their beards and by the *chemises arabes,* which they put on instead of the more common *boubou.* They sought to isolate themselves from the rest of the community and had their own mosques. Violent and bloody confrontations with the sufi brotherhoods took place, particularly in Bamako (chapter 9). The reformers rejected accommodation with pre-Islamic relics of the past. In the 1950s in Guinea, Muslim zealots managed to get the "fetishes" burned. The mysteries of the Koma secret society were exposed to the eyes of women and the non-initiated. Since then, Koma rites have been discontinued in the village concerned, now completely Muslim. Muslim zealots also destroyed the wooden sculptures and drums of the Baga of the Guinea coast (chapter 24).

The reform movement in the French-speaking countries of Mali, Guinea, and Côte d'Ivoire, as in Nigeria, appealed to the rich merchants. Piety enhanced the prestige of merchants and raised their credit among fellow merchants. Performing the pilgrimage was highly regarded as an act of piety. Rich merchants in Maradi, Niger, are known as Alhazai—that is, those who performed the pilgrimage. In order to further advance their economic and political interests, wealthy merchants who had already been to Mecca became engaged in acts of charity *(sadaqa),* building mosques and financing other religious activities, and thereby benefited the reform movement. Middle-class businessmen and civil servants were also involved (chapter 9).

In Nigeria, Abubakar Gummi, the grand qadi of the north, was the most outspoken critic of sufi Islam. He advocated an Islamic reform that was modernizing and fundamentalist at the same time. His young followers were organized in the Yan Izala and in the Muslim Students Society. Police were called to discipline preachers who used abusive language to stir the rabble. One such preacher, Muhammad Marwa, known as Maitatsine, built a formidable following in the late 1970s. In December 1980, a disastrous conflict developed: federal troops were called in and some four thousand people were killed. Since the early 1980s, the Islamic zeal has caused periodic clashes between Muslims and Christians in both urban and rural areas (chapters 10 and 17).

After Gummi's death in 1992, his successor as the leader of Islamic fundamentalism Shaykh Ibrahim al-Zakzady used inflammatory rhetoric, appealing to the same population as Maitatsine did in 1980—namely, young Muslim mendicants from the countryside. He was arrested in September 1996, but his followers continued to clash with the security forces in Kaduna and Kano in 1996 and 1997, with fatal casualties (chapter 10).

A literary expression of the crisis created by modern reformism is Ibrahim Tahir's *The Last Imam* (1984). A brilliant and unbending imam strove to bring a pure form of Islam into the lives of the people of Bauchi. He also opposed his father, his predecessor as imam, who was willing to accommodate with traditional customs and the political authorities (chapter 23).

In the 1950s, there were violent clashes between adherents of the Qadiriyya and the Tijaniyya, who represented conflicting political interests and orientations. But under the attacks of the Yan Izala and other "fundamentalists," the rival sufi brotherhoods—Qadiriyya and Tijaniyya—became reconciled in the 1970s (chapter 10).

Since the late 1980s, individuals and groups have adopted a lifestyle of greater personal piety and have adhered more strictly to the tenets of Islam. In French-speaking countries the common enemy of Islam was secularism. The rival reformers and marabouts became reconciled, and mutual respect has replaced inflammatory statements (chapter 9).

Politics

At the end of the colonial period, Muslims participated in social and economic activities and benefited from the politics of cultural nationalism and the growth of the informal economy. But with independence, Islam became politically marginal. Only in Senegal did Muslims play a significant role, because Senghor's political interests converged with those of the brotherhoods. In Côte d'Ivoire, Houphouet developed strong personal relationships with the traditional Muslim leaders. But Islam remained the religion of the savannah peoples and Muslims felt themselves to be second-class citizens. After Houphouet's death in 1993, legislation that defined most Muslims as foreigners determined the succession dispute between Bedie the Roman Catholic and Ouattara the Muslim. The former was the winner, and Muslim Juula were purged from the army and from the civil service (chapter 9).

In Mali, soon after independence, Modibo Keita attacked Muslim reformist organizations and placed their schools under state control. In Guinea, Sékou Touré's policies found expression in an official document, issued in 1959, that called on the populace to fight marabouts and other forms of mystification and exploitation. After 1970, however, Touré changed strategy and used Islam to legitimize his regime. His speeches became loaded with Islamic themes. Both Wahabi and sufi groups alike enjoyed his support (chapter 9).

In northern Nigeria until 1966, the political competition was between two Muslim political parties. Seeking to preserve the integrity of the northern emirates, the ruling NPC advocated gradual modernization through education and economic development. The opposition NEPU, under Aminu Kano, claimed that true progress for the north would never occur under the hegemony of emirs (chapter 10).

In Nigerian politics at the federal level, religion created the most serious cleavage. During the preparation for the return to civilian rule and in drafting the constitution of the second republic, between 1976 and 1978, there was a dispute over a federal shari'a court of appeal. For the Christians, this move was perceived as a threat, signaling the Islamization of the Federal Republic. Muslims, on the other hand, considered opposition to a federal shari'a court as sheer anti-Islamic prejudice. Yoruba Muslims played an important role in achieving reconciliation, and the proposal to create a shari'a court of appeal was withdrawn (chapter 10).

Muslims in East and Central Africa, though minorities, and making up a smaller proportion of the population than those of West African states, are nevertheless important in politics. In 1992 the Kenya government suppressed attempts to create a Muslim party, described as the party of the "Arabs." In Uganda, Muslims' political influence is more than might be expected, given their numerical strength (10 to 15 percent of the population). In the 1970s and 1980s, hundreds of Ugandan Muslims studied at the University of Medina. On their return, they led an activist Salafi movement that, by the mid-1980s, became alienated from the old, traditional 'ulama' and worshipped in separate mosques (chapter 16).

In Tanzania, the nationalist party of TANU was most successful in the Muslim areas, and Muslim traders were active in TANU. But Nyerere insisted that Tanzania's politics know no religion: no party based on religious affiliation was permitted. Nyerere was succeeded as president by Mwinyi, a Muslim from Zanzibar. He was urged by Muslim groups to increase the number of Muslims in government positions and in higher institutions of learning. In Zanzibar, young people increasingly seek to identify the island with Islam (chapter 16).

Farther south where Muslims are even fewer in numbers, Islam is still important. In Malawi a Muslim president was elected in 1994. In Mozambique, the Portuguese were greatly troubled by the political implications of the allegiance of Muslims to the sultan of Zanzibar. In their war against FRELIMO, the Portuguese colonial authorities sought to win conservative Muslim leaders of the brotherhoods. After independence, the Muslim leadership was discredited and the new government banned some Muslim organizations. Within the Muslim community, sufi leaders and the majority of the Muslims in the northern part of Mozambique were in conflict with the more radical Muslim reformers based in the south (chapter 14).

In South Africa, the apartheid state (1948–1994) created a fertile climate for the radicalization of Islam. In 1994, the new governing party, the ANC, appointed a Muslim as minister of justice in the government of unity. After 1994, there was a resurgence of "Malay" identity, as trade and cultural links with Malaysia increased (chapter 15).

Part 1

Gateways
to Africa

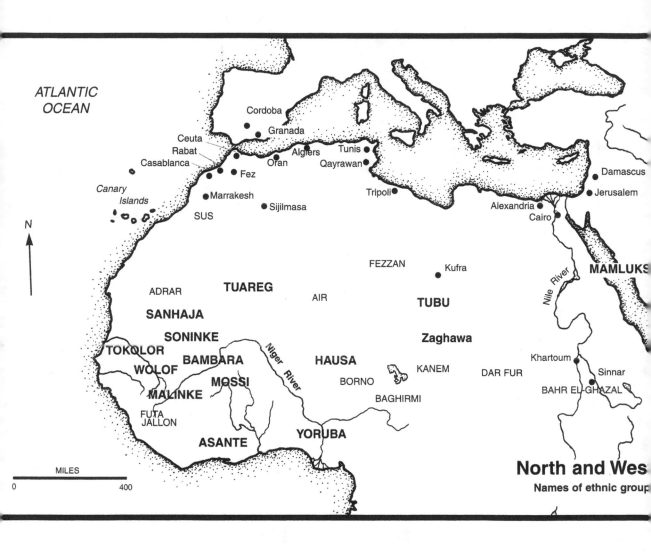

ATLANTIC
OCEAN

N

Canary
Islands

• Cordoba
• Granada
Ceuta
Rabat
Casablanca
• Fez
Oran
Algiers
Tunis
Qayrawan
Tripoli
Damascus
Jerusalem
Alexandria
Cairo

Marrakesh
• Sijilmasa

SUS

MILES

0   400

FEZZAN
Kufra

Nile River

MAMLUKS

ADRAR
TUAREG
AIR
TUBU

SANHAJA
SONINKE
Zaghawa
TOKOLOR
BAMBARA
Niger River
HAUSA
KANEM
Khartoum
WOLOF
BORNO
DAR FUR
Sinnar
MOSSI
BAHR EL-GHAZAL
MALINKE
BAGHIRMI
FUTA
JALLON
ASANTE
YORUBA

North and Wes
Names of ethnic group

CHAPTER I

Egypt and North Africa

Peter von Sivers

In May 1989, an eighteen-year-old woolcarder set fire to the Husayn Mosque in Cairo. The incident was written up in an Islamic newspaper by a journalist who deplored the act. The article began by asking why this young man would travel from his northern suburb all the way downtown to pray in a mausoleum-mosque—a place where, because of his stance on saint veneration, he believed prayer would be invalid; could he not instead have gone to any of the many mosques of Cairo that did not have tombs? In the remainder of the article, the journalist presents authoritative opinions by establishment figures on the specific requirements of order and decorum during mausoleum visits and on ordinary Muslims wrongly taking the law into their own hands. The article concluded that the woolcarder's act was indefensible.[1]

This incident illustrates a typically modern conflict in northern Africa. A Muslim accepting the teaching of absolute separation between God and his creation literally takes drastic action to end the deeply rooted popular tradition of saint veneration in Egypt. And a believer in the traditionally broad Sunni orthodoxy defends saint veneration, provided it occurs in an orderly fashion according to accepted custom *(adab)*. The conflict is not without precedent in earlier centuries, but it is only today that the two positions are seen as irreconcilable.

This chapter deals with, first, the formation (700–1250 C.E.) and dominance (1250–1800 C.E.) of a broad Sunni orthodoxy as the religion of the majority of the inhabitants of northern Africa; and second, modern efforts at political centralization and a narrowing of orthodox Sunnism, both of which have contributed to the rise of contemporary Islamism (1800 to the present).

The Formation and Dominance of Sunni Orthodoxy (700–1800)

The promotion of a specific religion as orthodoxy by an empire is a relatively late phenomenon in world history. The first to be so promoted was Zoroastrianism, adopted by the Persian Sasanids (224–651 C.E.) as their state religion. Islam, supported by the Arab caliphal dynasties of the Umayyads and ʿAbbasids as the religion of their far-flung empire after their rise in the seventh century C.E., was the most recent. In all cases—be it Zoroastrianism, Buddhism, Confucianism, Christianity, or Islam—the endorsed religion was attributed to a founding figure who preceded the empire. These religions went through more or less extended formative phases in the empires before they crystallized into dominant orthodoxies and a variety of heterodoxies that either died out or became marginal.[2]

Christianity, the state religion of the Roman-Byzantine Empire from the fourth century C.E., was in the last stage of its doctrinal evolution toward imperial orthodoxy when the Arabs occupied Byzantine Syria and Egypt in 634–55. It appears that it was the still unsettled question of a Christian orthodoxy for the Byzantine Empire that inspired the rulers of the new Arab empire to search for their own, independent, religion. Caliph ʿAbd al-Malik (685–705) was the first to leave us an idea of the beginnings of this new religion in the inscriptions of the Dome of the Rock in Jerusalem (691). He called this new religion "Islam" and proclaimed its superiority over Christianity.[3]

During the early seventh century, Byzantium had been racked by the controversy between the patriarchs of Constantinople and Alexandria over the orthodox interpretation of Christology. Constantinople advanced the doctrine of Christ's mysteriously double nature, divine as well as human (the Nicene Creed). Alexandria insisted on the more rational doctrine of God's single, divine nature descending into the human form of Jesus (Coptic monophysitism). While the emperors vainly sought to impose a compromise formula, the caliphs took advantage of their disarray. "Do not speak of three (gods)," warns one of the inscriptions on the Dome of the Rock, disposing of Christology altogether.[4] Islam was presented as the new, superior religion, built on a clear, rational separation between a single, non-Trinitarian God and the world.

Proclaiming a new religion was one thing; turning it into an orthodoxy was another. Inevitably Islam underwent the same process of rancorous divisions as did Christianity before orthodoxy eventually emerged. The rancor began over the nature of the caliphate and its ability to define doctrine. The caliphs interpreted themselves as representatives (caliphs) of God, and said that their decisions, therefore, were divine writ. On the other hand, it was claimed that because the divine word was laid down (probably by the 700s) in scripture, in the Quran, no one was privileged over anyone else to make law; the interpretation of scripture was held, in this view, to be a collective right.

At first the caliphs continued to issue laws and formulate dogma as they saw fit, but in the ninth century the tide turned. Pious critics, claiming to speak for all Muslims, increasingly gained the initiative. What had hitherto been caliphal law now was turned into the alleged precedents *(hadiths)* established by the prophet Muhammad. Ad hoc dogmas promulgated by the caliphs were replaced by a progressively systematic theology formulated by the critics. By the mid-thirteenth century, the separation between religion and state was complete: the critics, now officially recognized as the autonomous body of "religious scholars" *('ulama)*, controlled dogma and law; the rulers had been demoted to the position of executive organs of religion.[5]

While the 'ulama' were busy establishing the basics of scriptural orthodoxy, a parallel development was occurring on the level of religious practice. Early evidence comes from what began as a military institution during the period of the Arab conquests—the sentry post *(ribat)*. Such posts—towers, forts, castles—existed by the score in northern Africa, along the Mediterranean coast, and in Anatolia, for protection against Byzantine counterattacks. In the ninth century, many of these posts lost their military purpose and evolved into autonomous religious foundations *(waqfs)*, in conjunction with agricultural enterprises, mosques, and meeting rooms, and supported by alms and gifts. In the ribats, committed Muslims met for Quran recitation and ascetic practices, imitating the prophet Muhammad's life. (The Quran and the biography of the Prophet became available as scriptures probably in the early 700s and 800s, respectively.) Many were mystics *(sufis)* and wrote manuals on how to acquire divine knowledge *(ma'rifa)*, or were revered as "friends of God" *(walis)*—that is, saintly figures whose prayers and rituals for rain, healing, or exorcism were reported as effective and who attracted pilgrims and religious fairs to their ribat.[6]

As orthodoxy was being hammered out during these early centuries, dissenters essentially had two choices. Either they rejected the authority of caliphs and scholars altogether, a position taken by the so-called Kharijis ("Seceders"), and made the fulfillment of all laws and duties incumbent on Muslims as individuals. Or they deplored the caliphal retreat from law and dogma as a betrayal and labored for the reestablishment of the true caliphate, or "imamate" [(true) leadership], whose holder was held to be divinely empowered. The latter position was taken by the Shi'is ("partisans" of 'Ali, who is traditionally listed as the fourth caliph). At the center of the Islamic Empire, adherents of both positions were ruthlessly persecuted and they therefore generally mounted their oppositional movements on the periphery.

North Africa, or the Maghrib (the "West"—that is, Tunisia, Algeria, and Morocco) was one such peripheral refuge for dissenters. It was a sparsely inhabited imperial province of limited agricultural resources located on the coastal plains along the Mediterranean and the Atlantic, the adjacent mountains (the Kabylia in eastern Algeria, the Atlas in northern Morocco), and the oasis clusters of the northern Sahara. The steppes of the vast interior high plateau supported only pastoralists. The sedentary, mostly Christian population of indigenous Berbers in Byzantine Tunisia and Morocco (Tangier and Ceuta) had officially surrendered to the Arabs by 711 after half a century of intermittent fighting. The mountain villagers, high-plateau pastoralists, and desert nomads, fiercely devoted to their independence, either avoided the new Arab conquerors or fought them, stirred into action by Khariji refugees from the Arab heartlands.

In the middle of the eighth century, the Khariji refugees and local Berber converts founded a number of small mountain and oasis states that quickly supplemented their limited agricultural resources with camel-borne trans-Saharan trade. Baghdad, the capital of the ʿAbbasid Empire, was in the process of developing into a cosmopolitan cultural and economic center with intensive trade interests in East Africa, India, China, Scandinavia, and the western Mediterranean. Cordoba, the capital of the Spanish Umayyads, was an almost equally impressive rival. The trade in both empires was based on a bimetallic monetary system of gold and silver coins. Most of the gold was obtained from Nubia, on the upper Nile to the south of Egypt, and West Africa, in the region of the upper Niger and Senegal Rivers. Nubia and West Africa were outside the Islamic empire. The merchants were Egyptian Copts and North African Kharijis who traded cloth and copperware for gold, ivory, and slaves. The Kharijis maintained permanent residences as well as mosques in the northern market towns of the Sudanic kingdoms and thus were the first carriers of Islam into West Africa.

As opponents of any strong central political authority, the Kharijis were content with small realms, far removed from the caliphs and religious scholars in Baghdad. By contrast, the Shiʿis favored a return to the original concept of the caliph as the sole representative of God—a concept that was being transformed in emerging Sunni orthodoxy into the caliph-ʿulamaʾ coregency. When their emissaries preached the message of the *mahdi* to establish a realm of justice, peace, and unity on earth, they clearly had the replacement of the ʿAbbasid caliphate and its clerical scholars in mind.[7]

But even the Shiʿis had to start their proselytizing far away, in the mountains of Lesser Kabylia in eastern Algeria. There, at the end of the ninth century, a missionary from Iraq converted the Kutama Berber villagers to the cause of the Ismaʿiliyya, a Shiʿi branch devoted to immediate revolutionary action. The missionary Abu ʿAbdallah was part of a worldwide network of missionaries (*daʿi*, plural *duʿat*). They carried a religious message in the name of the descendants of Ismaʿil, the eldest son of Jaʿfar the sixth *imam* of the Shiʿa. Ismaʿil died before his father and his supporters, the more militant among the Shiʿis, rallied around his son Muhammad, and split from the main stream of the Shiʿa.[8]

In the early 900s, the Kutama Berbers conquered Tunisia from a local dynasty of ʿAbbasid governors. The original missionary relinquished leadership to ʿUbayd Allah the Mahdi, who had lived in an Ismaʿili center in Syria before he was forced by ʿAbbasid persecution to flee to the Maghrib. Once in power, the first Fatimid caliph began to implement his idea of the utopian realm of justice on earth (909–34). He and his descendants interpreted this to mean no less than the vanquishing of the ʿAbbasid Empire—a feat they in fact almost accomplished. In 969, they conquered Egypt, Syria, and western Arabia; and in 1058/59, a Fatimid general briefly held power in Baghdad. Impressive as these conquests were, however, reality soon fell short of utopia: the justice of the Fatimids was no more equitable than that of the ʿAbbasids. They collected the same heavy taxes from the peasants and confiscated the properties of merchants and officials with the same arbitrariness. Furthermore, in spite of major propaganda and conversion efforts, they never succeeded in supplanting the nascent, but tenacious, Sunni orthodoxy in their empire. When the Fatimids eventually collapsed in 1171, their version of Islam disappeared rapidly from the central Islamic lands.[9]

Not surprisingly, while Fatimid imperialism was still dangerous it instilled militancy into the rising Sunni orthodoxy. From the mid-eleventh century onward, newly converted ethnic groups—Turks from Central Asia and Berbers from northern Africa—made themselves the champions of nascent Sunnism against the Shiʿis, the Christian Crusaders in Palestine, and the Christian *reconquistadores* in Spain.

☾ ☾ ☾

The rural Berbers in northern Africa had barely been touched by Islam prior to the eleventh century. However, camel-breeding nomads such as the Sanhaja Berbers in the western Sahara had been involved in the trans-Saharan trade ever since the Kharijis pioneered this trade. The Saharan merchant city of Awdaghost, which had Muslim residences and mosques, was initially in the Berbers' pastural territory, but around the turn of the tenth to the eleventh century it recognized the authority of the king of Ghana, a non-Muslim.

In 1035–36, a Sanhaja chief from near Awdaghost went on his pilgrimage to Mecca. On his return journey, seeking an Islamic instructor for his tribe, he met a Sunni scholar in Qayrawan, Tunisia. He recommended to him another scholar, the head of a school in southern Morocco, a sunni stronghold in the midst of a country infested with heresies. One of his disciples, Abdallah Ibn Yasin (d. 1059), accompanied the Sanhaja chief to the Sahara.

Ibn Yasin succeeded in harnessing the Sanhaja into a disciplined movement, the *murabitun,* known in Europe as Almoravids. They were committed to strictly observe the letter of the law, according to the Maliki *madhhab.* At its height, the Almoravid empire (1042–1148) encompassed Mauritania, Morocco, western Algeria, and the southern half of Spain. However, both Almoravid military power and religious orthodoxy were on shaky foundations: The original tribal troops were not easily transformed into a professional army, since most troops preferred settlement over continued service, and their nontribal replacements, recruited in the conquered territories or from abroad, failed to coalesce into effective units. As for Almoravid orthodoxy, "guardsman" Islam proved too narrow in comparison with theological developments in Islamic civilization generally. In the twelfth century, eminent scholars (e.g., Abu Hamid al-Ghazali; d. 1111) were proposing the limited use of philosophy, mainly for the interpretation of dogma, so as to combat more easily the counterorthodoxy of Shi'ism; they wanted to explain with the help of rational arguments the superiority of Sunni Islam. The Almoravid scholars, unfamiliar with philosophy, lacked theological sophistication and therefore found it difficult to defend their narrow Sunnism.[10]

On both military and religious grounds, the Almoravids were thus unable to consolidate their empire. Their regime was challenged at the beginning of the twelfth century by the Almohads. The founder of the Almohad movement, Abu 'Abdallah Muhammad Ibn Tumart (d. 1130), a Masmuda Berber from the Anti-Atlas mountains in southern Morocco, staunchly supported Ghazali's theological position within rising Sunnism. Ibn Tumart's central doctrine was that of the unity of God as distinct from the multiplicity of the things making up the world. Since all-encompassing divine oneness is rationally incomprehensible Ibn Tumart proposed to interpret it with the help of the theological tool of analogy *(ta'wil)*. The followers of this theological interpretation, called *al-muwahhidun* ("Unitarians"), or Almohads, built an empire that at its height was even more impressive than that of the Almoravids, comprising all of the Maghrib as well as Islamic Spain (1148–1269).[11] Like its predecessor, the Almohad empire disintegrated during the transition from fielding conquering armies to garrisoning troops, although its religious legacy—a broad Sunni orthodoxy—proved to be a lasting accomplishment. The empire was succeeded by a set of regional successor states in the Maghrib and Spain.

By this time (mid-thirteenth century), Sunni orthodoxy had reached its mature phase: law and theology had been fully formulated and the mystics and saints who had hitherto practiced Islam in the ribats began to move into lodges (*zawiyas;* lit. "retreats") in the countryside. Scriptural Islam was taught and studied in urban colleges, such as the Qarawiyyin in Fez and the Zaytuna in Tunis. Mystical and popular Islam began to include the population outside the cities and away from the coast. The zawiyas in the countryside, with their saint's mausoleums, guardian families, and religious rituals were supported by alms from the surrounding peasants or nomads and provided basic education in reading and writing to promising young men. The rituals were named after their patron saints and often became the distinctive practices of entire brotherhoods of lodges, called *tariqas*, with branches throughout the Islamic world.

The earliest saint whose full biography and writings we possess was Abu Madyan Shu'ayb Ibn al-Husayn (1126–90), a Spaniard who became the patron saint of Tlemcen in western Algeria. One of his disciples was Abu al-Hasan al-Shadhili (d. 1256), a Moroccan whose Shadhiliyya tariqa became one of the most influential and widespread brotherhoods in the Islamic world (today it has its own website).[12] Thus it is only from the thirteenth century and the establishment of Sunni orthodoxy onward that we can speak of the full Islamization of the Maghrib.

In Egypt, the final establishment of Sunni orthodoxy occurred when the Kurdish-descended Saladin (Salah al-Din; ruled 1171–93), with his Turkish cavalry troops, destroyed the Fatimid empire in 1171. Saladin was a champion of the Turkish-endorsed version of broad Sunni orthodoxy that Ghazali had formulated half a century earlier. Two types of new urban institutions were devoted to the promulgation of this orthodoxy, the college *(madrasa)* for the teaching of scripturalism and the seminary *(khanqa)* for the teaching of mysticism. Both were religious foundations similar to the ribats mentioned above, financially independent from the government and maintained by rents collected from urban real estate or villages. Both madrasas and khanqas maintained salaried professors and instructors and provided lodging and scholarships for their students. As in the Maghrib, the ribats gave way to zawiyas that dotted city neighborhoods and the countryside. Here the general population received oral instruction in the basics of Islam and congregated for the practice of local religious customs.[13]

Saladin's descendants, the Ayyubids (1193–1250), and the Turkish Mamluks (1250–1517) further broadened orthodoxy by endowing sufi seminaries and encouraging the teaching of the Shafi'i law for the people of lower Egypt, the Maliki law for the people of upper Egypt and Alexandria, and the Hanafi law for Syrian residents and for the Turkish-speaking elite.[14] The same broad orthodoxy was maintained by the Turkish Ottomans who conquered Egypt in 1517 and established tributary regimes in Algeria (1518), Libya (1551), and Tunisia (1574). In fact, under the Ottomans the previously distinct career paths of 'ulama' and sufi shaykhs in Cairo and Alexandria merged, and only brotherhoods and lodges with distinctly local practices and customs remained separate. During the Ottoman period (1517–1798), religious scholars at the prominent Azhar University could be enrolled in as many as two dozen sufi circles, and many sufi shaykhs were distinguished teachers of law.[15]

Only a small handful of 'ulama'/sufi shaykhs expressed discomfort with local saint cults or brotherhood practices that they considered to be beyond the pale of orthodoxy. On a theological level, they criticized the concepts of sainthood and miraculous powers as "associationism" *(shirk),* "unbelief" *(kufr),* and blameworthy "innovation" *(bid'a),* since God alone was all-powerful. On a moral level, they criticized the pilgrimages, processions, fairs, music, dances, self-mortifications, and exorcisms connected with a number of popular tombs and brotherhoods as unruly, disorderly, and against prevailing custom. However, combating heterodox minority movements of the Khariji and Fatimid variety was one thing; taking on heterodox popular religious customs supported by perhaps as many as 90 percent of the Egyptian population was quite another. Hence the absence of any resonance among the population at large.

Only one case is known where criticism provoked a commotion, and that was short-lived. This case involved a Turkish preacher, Ibrahim Gülsheni, who in 1711 incited his listeners to go out from his mosque and combat blameworthy innovations in the Turkish and Arab shrines. A crowd surged forth to the Zuwayla Gate (which was believed to be the seat of the unseen master of all saints) and attacked the dervishes (popular sufis) holding ad hoc sessions on the streets around the gate. The chief jurisconsults *(muftis)* issued legal opinions *(fatwas)* in which they affirmed the reality of miracles and refused to transform saintly retreats into law colleges. The chief judge *(qadi al-askar)* refused to debate the preacher and on the second day the government put down the riot. The Turkish preacher was exiled and his mosque closed down. A poet who witnessed the events cleverly turned the preacher's own moral argument against him: "He exceeded the proper bounds, he exaggerated, he incited the army against us!"[16]

In Algeria, Libya, and Tunisia, the Ottomans pursued the same broad policy of Sunni orthodoxy. Since they were not numerous enough to impose a firm regime on the tribal populations of the interior, they tacitly allowed many zawiya shaykhs to assume rudimentary political functions, such as arbitration in tribal disputes, collection of taxes, and even maintenance of auxiliary cavalry troops. Morocco remained outside the Ottoman Empire, mainly thanks to the rise of the Sa'dids, a southern Moroccan family of zawiya shaykhs claiming descent from the Prophet.

The Sa'dids (1510–1613) were self-declared champions of the liberation of the country from the Portuguese, who had held all major ports for varying time periods (1415–1578). Unwilling to exchange one set of invaders for another, the Sa'dids vigorously repelled the Ottomans. In 1591 the Sa'di Sultan al-Mansur sent a Moroccan expedition force across the Sahara. With the superiority of firearms the Moroccans defeated the Songhay kingdom, and took possession of Timbuktu. The Pashalik of Timbuktu was ruled directly from Morocco during a short period (1591–1618), and then became autonomous until the second half of the eighteenth century.[17] After a period of disunity in the country, another Prophet-descended zawiya family, the 'Alawids from central Morocco, established a more modest regime (1668 to the present).[18]

Political Recentralization and Religious Reform (1800 to the present)

By the 1700s, Europe had completely supplanted the Middle East and northern Africa as the main commercial hub of the world. Not surprisingly, after the Middle East had been relegated to secondary status, the ensuing financial crisis crippled the central institutions in the existing empires. Northern Africa was no exception. The Ottomans were barely able to hang on to control in Egypt, and they lost Algeria, Tunisia, and Libya to autonomous rulers or even dynasties whose own power, in turn, was largely limited to the coasts. In Morocco, the 'Alawids effectively controlled only about one-third of the country, largely on the central plain around Rabat. After the shock of Napoleon's invasion of Egypt in 1798, northern African rulers bestirred themselves and introduced reforms designed to recentralize their states' institutions.

Muhammad 'Ali (ruled 1805–48), the Ottoman governor in Egypt, set the pace for this recentralization. In the religious domain, in 1812 he issued a decree that installed the sufi shaykh Muhammad al-Bakri (d. 1880) as the head of all brotherhoods, lodges, and saints' mausoleums. Although al-Bakri's family had held the position since the seventeenth century—in part by virtue of their claim to be descendants of Abu Bakr, traditionally the first caliph—their role had been without executive power. The Bakris led the annual celebrations of the Prophet's birthday *(mawlid);* for the rest, religious institutions administered themselves as they saw fit. Now the position was given teeth: all shaykhs had to receive official appointments from al-Bakri before acceding to their positions as heads of their brotherhoods, lodges, or saints' mausoleums. Muhammad 'Ali's primary intention was to put some structure and organization into the diffuse amalgamation of theologically and financially autonomous religious organizations. But he also aimed at curtailing the reach of Azhar University, the country's flagship institution, whose professors in his view were double-dipping in a large number of religious brotherhoods. Finally, through this act of "divide and rule," Muhammad 'Ali sought to minimize resistance against his subsequent land- and tax-reform decrees of 1812–14, which affected the landholdings of all religious institutions.[19]

Although intended to increase the supervisory control of the state, Muhammad 'Ali's decree changed very little in the intricate web of religious institutions. Furthermore, since his successors' energy slackened in the recentralization drive, the government's declared assumption of power over the religious appointments remained theoretical. Much more drastic was the centralization process in Algeria, where it was carried out by the French through their policy of colonial centralization. An initial French expedition in 1830 resulted in the removal of the autonomous Turkish regime on the coast, and further efforts in 1841–47 brought about the destruction of a state under the zawiya of 'Abd al-Qadir (d. 1883) in the interior;[20] but this system broke down when the zawiya embarked on his own centralization drive. Once fully in control, however, the French systematically destroyed the autonomy of the brotherhoods, sometimes with the help of military repression and land confiscation.

The most spectacular destruction of a brotherhood occurred in 1871, when France had been defeated in its war against Prussia. At this moment, when the colonial regime appeared to be vulnerable, a tribal leader, Muhammad al-Muqrani, and a Rahmaniyya shaykh, Haddad, concluded an alliance and led a powerful uprising that engulfed most of eastern Algeria. At first the rebels achieved surprising successes against the depleted French troops, but after the death of Muqrani in one of the battlefield encounters, the uprising lost its momentum, and a year later it was completely crushed. The consequences were devastating: some eight hundred thousand Algerians (one-quarter of the population) were condemned to fines of 35 million francs and the loss of 450,000 hectares of agricultural land (equivalent to 70 percent of their properties). Thereafter, the autonomy of the population in the interior of the country, including the lodges and brotherhoods, was essentially broken.[21]

As recentralization took hold in Egypt and Algeria, lodge and brotherhood leaders who were determined to maintain the autonomy of their institutions had little choice but to establish themselves in regions traditionally outside the reach of northern African states, such as southern Libya, Mauritania, and Africa south of the Sahara.

Libya was a special case: the Ottomans, in pursuit of their own centralization program, deposed the provincial dynasty of governors in 1835 and reestablished direct rule. But after crushing a few rebellions in the north they dug in on the coast around Tripoli, Benghazi, and Derna and left the interior of the country (except for the Fezzan oasis) largely to its own devices. Thus, for the two hundred thousand or so inhabitants of the remote eastern province of Cyrenaica (Barqa), little was altered from the preceding century. In 1841, shaykh Muhammad Ibn ʿAli al-Sanusi (d. 1859) arrived there with his followers to found a brotherhood eventually known as the Sanusiyya.

Al-Sanusi was an Algerian from Mostaghanem who had spent nearly two decades in Mecca as a student of one of the most prominent scholarly sufis of the time, the Moroccan Ahmad Ibn Idris (d. 1838). Other students of Ibn Idris would become the founders of brotherhoods in Sudan, Somalia, and Eritrea; thus, Ibn Idris's mystical treatises became influential not only in Libya, Chad, and Niger, but also in eastern Africa. The Ottomans in Cyrenaica abandoned their initial suspicions after they had assured themselves of the immense learning of al-Sanusi; it was more advantageous for them to deal with one man seeking to maintain order than with hundreds of tribes playing hide-and-seek and disrupting the security of the country. The Sanusi family dutifully asked the Ottoman authorities for building permits and religious foundation status for its lodges dotting the oases of the Libyan Sahara. After their expansion to the Sahel, the Sanusis obtained similar permits from West African rulers. By 1900, there were close to 150 lodges.[22]

The southward movement of another of the Algerian brotherhoods, the Tijaniyya, followed a different trajectory. The brotherhood was founded by Ahmad al-Tijani (d. 1815) in the western Algerian Sahara at the end of the eighteenth century. The Tijanis had successfully defied the Turks on the coast and—advancing an unusual bid for preeminence—they claimed to have superseded all previous brotherhoods. But after a failed bid for a Saharan state, they submitted to the French and one descendant even married a Frenchwoman. They established lodges in all the Maghribi countries and, via the affiliation of Mauritanian pilgrims returning from Mecca in 1789, extended their influence to the far southwest of the Maghrib.[23]

Mauritanian society had undergone a drastic restructuring in the centuries after producing the Almoravids. Bedouin tribes had arrived from Arabia, Arabizing most of the Maghribian Berber nomads, except for the Tuareg, as they swept through North Africa. When they established themselves in Mauritania, a complex system of tribal dependencies emerged. On the one hand were the unarmed *zawaya* tribes claiming saintly status and supporting a high level of legal education and practice; on the other hand were the secular warrior tribes. The latter depended on the zawayas for the conclusion of truces and occasional periods of peace, but they also collected tribute from them, both in oases and when the zawayas were traveling as merchants. Both the zawayas and the warriors controlled the tributary farmers and pastoralists who made up the bulk of the population. Prior to the end of the eighteenth century, most zawayas were affiliated with the Qadiriyya, the oldest brotherhood in the Islamic world. The Tijanis, in spite of their efforts, managed to enroll only one, hitherto mostly unaffiliated, zawaya tribe in Mauritania. As proud believers in Tijani supremacy, they had no other choice but to carry their beliefs further south of the Sahara. There the Tijanis became spectacularly successful through the jihad-leader Hajj ʿUmar (d. 1864).[24]

❨ ❨ ❨

To return to the situation in Egypt: al-Bakri worked diligently during his long and respected tenure to bring administrative order into the diffuse world of brotherhoods, lodges, and saintly mausoleums. What initially had been a purely administrative mandate of centralization gradually shifted into a government-led redefinition of what constituted Sunni orthodoxy. The traditional division between state and religion, in force since the thirteenth century, was attenuated. Few Egyptians seemed to mind, except perhaps those whom al-Bakri administered. In fact, a few Egyptian administrators and Western-educated professionals expressed embarrassment about "crude" popular religious practices that they viewed as incompatible with (Western) "civilized" life. Thus, during the turbulent years after 1876 when a heavily indebted Egypt lost its sovereignty to a French-British financial commission, a number of Azhar shaykhs, Western-educated journalists, and European consuls supported a drastic religious-reform decree devised by the new khedive of Egypt, Tawfiq (ruled 1879–92), and promulgated in 1881.[25]

According to this decree, the following rituals were to be removed from all religious meetings and parades: the use of swords, needles, and other instruments for self-mortification; the eating of live coals, serpents, and glass; chanting the liturgy; hyperventilating while chanting the name of God; the alternate bowing of adepts facing each other in rows; jumping up and down from one foot to the other; beating drums and other musical instruments; carrying anything but banners; and riding on horseback over a carpet of prostrate adepts. The list amounted to a virtual outlawing of any ecstatic state, and hence of mysticism itself if a brotherhood's practices were deemed unbecoming to a modern, progressive, civilized nation.[26]

As it turned out, the 1881 decree moved no further than the paper it was written on—as with its predecessor of 1812. Muhammad al-Bakri had died just prior to the promulgation of the decree and he was succeeded by his thirty-year-old son Muhammad Tawfiq al-Bakri (d. 1911), who lacked both the erudition and experience of his father. The government was in no position to enforce the decree, and even the British, who took over in 1882, were unwilling to assemble the totalitarian state that would have been necessary to suppress popular culture. The decree was reissued in 1905, but its only effect was a discreet disappearance of some brotherhoods from the streets into private homes.[27]

It appears that the prominent religious reformers of the late-nineteenth century, Jamal al-Din al-Afghani (d. 1897) and Muhammad ʿAbduh (d. 1905), had no influence on the 1881 decree, although they greeted it warmly, of course, and in their subsequent writings advocated similar reforms. Thus the important movement of the Salafiyya (from *salaf*, "ancestors") that they inspired and that advocated a return to the allegedly pristine, rational, and progressive religion of the ancestors surrounding the prophet Muhammad was a consequence, rather than the fountainhead of the narrow orthodoxy that came to dominate the twentieth century. The line from the broad traditional to the narrow modern Sunnism of northern Africa clearly passed through the modern, centralizing state of Muhammad 'Ali.[28]

Paradoxically, both 'Abduh and many Salafis of the subsequent generation of religious reformers were well trained in sufi practices. They therefore did not categorically condemn mysticism as unbelief, but they made clear that it was quite unnecessary for the faith of the reformed Muslim, just as were the detailed legal compendia from the time of broad orthodoxy (1250–1800). All a Muslim needed was the Quran, the Prophet's biography, and the precedents Muhammad set for living an Islamic life (called hadiths)—all as formulated by Islamic scholars in the period between the late-eighth and eleventh centuries.

In the 1930s, Egypt experienced its first stage of industrialization, with a beginning rural-urban migration, rising birth rate, and expanded literacy. But it also felt the effects of the worldwide economic crisis following the U.S. stock market crash of 1929. Islamic fundamentalism or "Islamism"—that is, the narrowed Sunni orthodoxy of the Salafiyya that was disseminated in the form of popular tracts—became an attractive alternative to the secular, formal democracy of the wealthy Egyptian landowners who were in control of Egyptian politics. Although there was still opposition to the alleged unbelief of mystics, Islamists were more concerned with condemning secular democracy and praising strict religious rule under a caliphate they wanted to see reestablished. (The Turks had abolished the caliphate in 1924 when they created the Republic of Turkey on the ruins of the Ottoman Empire.) By far the largest Islamist movement was, and is, that of the Muslim Brothers (Ikhwan al-Muslimun), founded in 1928 by Hasan al-Banna (d. 1949), a modern-trained school teacher. The movement expanded rapidly in the late 1930s and in the 1940s to several hundred thousand members. In the Maghrib, still under complete French colonial control, the tumultuous 1930s were experienced in more muted form, but even there, small Islamic associations devoted to adult education and social activities left their mark.[29]

After World War II, these fundamentalists were overshadowed by nationalist parties fighting for independence in northern Africa. These parties recruited their militants from the nontraditional urban professional, student, and worker milieus. The members were usually at least nominal Muslims who, once in power after independence, focused on the pursuit of large, state-led industrialization programs and expanded education. The educational curricula included a strong dose of what one perhaps can call a secularized version of Islamism. In this version, it was not the allegedly original Islam of Muhammad, his companions, and the early caliphs that was emphasized, but the alleged Arabism of these figures. Arabism was assumed to have been corrupted in the later centuries, particularly during the period from 1500 to 1800, when the Ottoman Turks were said to have oppressed the Arab nation. Given the appropriate circumstances, however, it was easy for students to shift from Arabism to Islamism.

These circumstances arrived in the 1960s. Once again, urbanization, birth rates, and literacy rose, this time explosively. In contrast to the 1930s, the urban masses were much larger, crowded more densely together in dysfunctional cities, and 50 percent of them were youths under twenty-one years of age. Not surprisingly, Islamism experienced a rebirth, beginning in the late 1960s and expanding rapidly in the 1970s. Tracts were again written and distributed in large numbers. Nationalism and socialism were condemned as godless Western ideologies—alien to northern Africa—that had corrupted the Muslims. Mysticism was denigrated as a relic of the past. When the governments hastened to de-emphasize their nationalist roots and socialist programs and expressed their support for a "moderate," broadly defined Sunni orthodoxy, small militant minorities went over to terrorism. In the eyes of these terrorists, the secular, Westernized government elites were composed of "hypocrites" *(munafiqun)* and unbelievers whom good Muslims had a holy duty to destroy.

The Tunisian and Moroccan governments succeeded in suppressing their small terrorist movements after brief episodes in the 1980s. In Egypt, too, terrorist organizations, operating since the early 1970s, were largely mastered by the late 1990s. Only Algeria was racked by a protracted stalemate between the government and Islamists. There have been more than seventy thousand victims of violence in Algeria since 1992, when the government canceled an electoral victory of the Islamists. The chances for an Islamic solution, however, seem to be dim since the Algerian government so far has been able to hang on to large revenues from exports of gas and oil. Behind the scenes, the military and its pervasive secret service have regained the initiative and since spring 1999 terrorism has declined sharply.[30]

The ultimate problem for Islamists is that in spite of the huge demographic burgeoning in all northern African countries, they have failed so far to attract more than, at most, 20 percent of the populations. Particularly in Egypt, the broad orthodoxy of mysticism and popular Islam discussed above is alive and well. Today's Egyptian governments have retreated from Muhammad 'Ali's all-too-close control of religion in the name of administrative centralization. Short of becoming totalitarian, no government would be able to gain control over popular religion and destroy allegedly unorthodox practices. Consequently, the decrees of 1812 and 1905 were abrogated, and a much broader and more tolerant new decree concerning the organization and practice of religion was issued in 1976. Defenders of the traditional, broad orthodoxy feel far less intimidated now to engage in public debates, as the reaction to the mosque incident cited at the beginning of the chapter demonstrates. Perhaps traditional broad orthodoxy will weather the current Islamist assault.[31]

Notes

1. Story taken from Johansen 1996.

2. For a comparative discussion of empires devoted to the promotion of monotheism, see Fowden 1993.

3. During the last three decades, a number of scholars have begun to distinguish between the historical and the theological origins of Islam. The sources on the Arab occupation of Syria and Iraq in the seventh century C.E. say very little about the religion of the occupants. By contrast, the Islamic sources of the eighth and following centuries present a detailed picture of the seventh-century origins, but with the theological intent of demonstrating the development of a fully developed religion of Islam in the Arab desert, prior to its imperial expansion by the Arabs beginning with Syria and Iraq. See Wansbrough 1978; Crone and Cook 1977.

4. On the siginificance of the Dome of the Rock for the formation of Islamic religion, see Rippin 1990.

5. On the history of the caliph-'ulama' dispute and its role in the formation of orthodoxy, see Crone and Hinds 1986.

6. A detailed discussion of the evolution of ribat is found in Halm 1991, chapter entitled "Ribat and Gihad."

7. The leading specialist on the Kharijis is Lewicki. See especially Lewicki 1960, 1962, 1971, and 1976. A more recent study is Schwartz 1983.

8. On the early Ismailiyya, see Daftary 1990.

9. The two leading historians on the Fatimids are Halm (1991) and Madelung (1961).

10. Norris 1971; Levtzion 1979.

11. The best study in English of the Almohads is Le Tourneau 1969.

12. Mackeen 1971; Ibn al-Sabbagh 1993.

13. Fernandes 1988.

14. Ibid., 33–110.

15. Winter 1992.

16. Ibid., 158–60.

17. Cook 1994.

18. el-Mansour 1990.

19. de Jong 1978, 7–95.

20. Danziger 1977.

21. von Sivers 1994, 555; the best survey of modern Algerian history is Ruedy 1992.

22. Vikør 1995.

23. Abun-Nasr 1965.

24. Scholarship on Mauretania is woefully underdeveloped. An exception is Oßwald 1986.

25. de Jong 1978, 96–97.

26. Ibid., 97–121.

27. Ibid., 124–68.

28. Ibid., 97 n. 8. See also Keddie 1972; Kerr 1966.

29. Mitchell 1969; Merad 1967.

30. Kepel 1985; Burgat and Dowell 1993.

31. Johansen 1996.

Bibliography

Abun-Nasr, Jamil M. 1965. *The Tijaniyya: A Sufi Order in the Modern World,* Middle Eastern Monographs 7. London: Oxford University Press.

Burgat, François, and William Dowell. 1993. *The Islamic Movement in North Africa.* Austin: University of Texas.

Cook, Weston F. Jr. 1994. *The Hundred Years War for Morocco: Gunpowder and Military Revolution in the Early Modern Muslim World.* Boulder, Colo.: Westview.

Crone, Patricia, and Michael Cook. 1977. *Hagarism: The Making of the Islamic World.* Cambridge: Cambridge University Press.

Crone, Patricia, and Martin Hinds. 1986. *God's Caliph: Religious Authority in the First Centuries of Islam.* Cambridge: Cambridge University Press.

Daftary, Farhad. 1990. *The Isma'ilis: Their History and Doctrines.* Cambridge: Cambridge University Press.

Danziger, Raphael. 1977. *Abd al-Qadir and the Algerians: Resistance to the French and Internal Consolidation.* New York: Homes & Meier.

Farhat, Halima. 1993. *Le Maghreb aux XXIe et XIIIe siècles du foi.* Casablanca: Walada.

Fernandes, Leonor. 1988. *The Evolution of a Sufi Institution in Mamluk Egypt: The Khanqah.* Islamkundliche Untersuchungen 134. Berlin: Klaus Schwarz.

Fowden, Garth. 1993. *Empire to Commonwealth: Consequences of Monotheism in Late Antiquity.* Princeton: Princeton University Press.

Halm, Heinz. 1991. *Das Reich des Mahdi: Der Aufstieg der Fatimiden.* Munich: Beck (in English as *The Empire of the Mahdi: The Rise of the Fatimids.* Trans. Michael Bonner. Leiden: Brill, 1996).

Ibn al-Sabbagh, Muhhamad. 1993. *The Mystical Writings of al-Shadhili: Including His Life, Prayers, Letters, and Followers.* Trans. Elmer H. Douglas. Albany: State University of New York Press.

Johansen, Julian. 1996. *Sufism and Islamic Reform in Egypt: The Battle for Islamic Tradition.* Oxford: Clarendon.

de Jong, Fred. 1978. *Turuq and Turuq-Linked Institutions in Nineteenth-Century Egypt: A Historical Study in Organizational Dimensions of Islamic Mysticism.* Leiden: Brill.

Keddie, Nikki. 1972. *Sayyid Jamal ad-Din "al-Afghani": A Political Biography.* Berkeley: University of California Press.

Kepel, Gilles. 1985. *Muslim Extremism in Egypt: The Prophet and Pharaoh.* Berkeley: University of California Press.

Kerr, Malcom. 1966. *Islamic Reform: The Polititcal and Legal Theories of Muhammad Abduh and Rashid Rida.* Berkeley: University of California Press.

Le Tourneau, Roger. 1969. *The Almohad Movement in North Africa in the Twelfth and Thirteenth Centuries.* Princeton, N.J.: Princeton University Press.

Levtzion, Nehemia. 1979. "Abd Allah b. Yasin and the Almoravids." In *Studies in West African Islamic History,* ed. John Ralph Willis, vol. 1, *The Cultivators of Islam.* London: Cass.

Lewicki, Tadeusz. 1960. "Quelques extraits inédits relatifs aux voyages des commerçants et des missionnaires ibadites nord-africains aux pays du Soudan occidental et central au Moyen Age," *Folia Orientalia* 2:1–17.

———. 1962. "L'Etat nord-africain de Tahert et ses relations avec le Soudan occidental à la fin du 8e et au 9e siècles," *Cahiers d'Etudes Africaines* 8:513–35.

———. 1971. "The Ibadites in Arabia and Africa," *Journal of World History* 13:51–130.

———. 1976. *Etudes maghrébines et soudanaises.* Warsaw: Editions scientifiques de Pologne.

Mackeen, A. M. 1971a. "The Early History of Sufism prior to al-Shadhili," *Journal of the American Oriental Society* 91:398–408.

———. 1971b. "The Rise of Shadhili (656–1256)," *Journal of the American Oriental Society* 91: 427–86.

Madelung, Wilferd. 1961. "Das Imamat in der frühen ismailitischen Lehre," *Der Islam* 37:43–135.

el-Mansour, Mohamed. 1990. *Morocco and the Reign of Mulay Sulayman.* Wisbech, U.K.: Middle East and North African Studies Press.

Merad, Ali. 1967. *Le reformisme musulman en Algérie de 1925 à 1940.* Recherches méditerranéennes 7. Paris: Mouton.

Mitchell, Richard P. 1969. *The Society of the Muslim Brothers.* London: Oxford University Press.

Norris, H. T. 1971. "New Evidence on the Life of Abdullah b. Yasin and the Origins of the Almoravid Movement," *Journal of African History,* 12:255–68.

Oßwald, Rainer. 1986. *Die Handelsstädte der Westsahara: Die Entwicklung der arabisch-maurischen Kultur von Shinqit, Wadan, Tishit, und Walata.* Marburger Studien zur Afrika- und Asienkunde, Serie A: Afrika, vol. 39. Berlin: Dietrich Reimer.

Rippin, Andrew. 1990. *Muslims: Their Religious Beliefs and Practices,* vol. 1, *The Formative Period.* London: Routledge.

Ruedy, John D. 1992. *Modern Algeria: The Origins and Development of a Nation.* Bloomington: Indiana University Press.

Schwartz, Werner. 1983. *Die Anfänge der Ibaditen in Nordafrika, Die Beiträge einer islamischen Minderheit zur Ausbreitung des Islams.* Wiesbaden: Harrassowitz.

Vikør, Knut. 1995. *Sufi and Scholar on the Desert Edge: Muhammad b. Ali al-Sanusi and His Brotherhood.* Evanston, Ill.: Northwestern University Press.

von Sivers, Peter. 1994. "Nordafrika in der Neuzeit," in Ulrich Haarmann, ed., *Geschichte der arabischen Welt,* 3rd ed. Munich: Beck.

Wansbrough, John. 1978. *The Sectarian Milieu: Content and Composition of Islamic Salvation History.* Oxford: Oxford University Press.

Winter, Michael. 1992. *Egyptian Society under Ottoman Rule (1517–1798).* London: Routledge.

CHAPTER 2

The Indian Ocean and the Red Sea

M. N. Pearson

This chapter describes the role of the Indian Ocean, and more specifically the western corridor or sector of this ocean, the Arabian Sea, in the spread and continuance of Islam in eastern Africa. It will begin by sketching some salient characteristics of this vast entity, looking first at "deep structure" matters like winds and currents and topography.[1] The account moves on to consider connections across these waters, looking at matters like trade and the dissemination of crops and disease. It then focuses on the circulation, via the ocean, of religion, with particular reference to the role of seaborne Muslim religious specialists and ideas. However, in what follows I will aim only to write about external matters in the wider Muslim world that affected Islam in eastern Africa. What happened when these influences arrived in our area is the concern of several other chapters in part 3 of this book.

At first glance, it may seem that one would expect few connections across and around the Indian Ocean before our modern era. We are often told that the world today is far more integrated than ever before—that we live in a global village. Yet there was, as we will see, copious interaction over long distances across the Indian Ocean for at least the last two millennia. A matter that may seem to hinder communication is the sheer extent of the Indian Ocean. This is an ocean that stretches from 28 degrees north latitude in the far north at the head of the Red Sea to around 26 degrees south latitude in the far south of Mozambique. Indonesia is in longitude 95 to 140 east, as compared with about longitude 38 east for Mozambique. By comparison, the continental United States occupies only from 50 to 30 degrees north latitude, and from longitude 125 to 75 east. The coast with which this chapter is most concerned, that is the west coast from the head of the Red Sea to southern Mozambique, stretches for more than five thousand miles. A direct passage from east Africa to Indonesia is more than four thousand miles. Again by comparison, the United States at its greatest extent is fewer than three thousand miles from east coast to west coast. Consequently, travel times in this ocean area were very large: often some months to go from one major entrepôt to another. Yet people were able to overcome these difficulties, helped in part by particular deep-structural factors.

The pattern of winds in the Arabian Sea is familiar enough. Many authorities stress the divide of the coast at Cape Delgado. As a rule of thumb, down to Cape Delgado is the region of one monsoon, from Arabia and India; south of there is the region of two. The northeast monsoon starts in November, and one can leave the Arabian coast at this time and reach at least Mogadishu. However, the eastern Arabian sea has violent tropical storms in October and November, so for a voyage from India to the coast it was best to leave in December. By March, the northeast monsoon was beginning to break up in the south, and by April the prevailing wind was from the southwest. This was the season for sailing from the coast to the north and east. At its height, in June and July, the weather was too stormy, so departures were normally either as this monsoon, the southwest monsoon, built up in May, or at its tail end in August.[2] Ocean currents also affected travel by sea.

The third geographical matter that affects the influence of the ocean on travel and the land is coastal topography. Broadly speaking, no matter how favorable the winds and currents may be, no one is going to want to travel to an uninhabited desert shore. Equally unattractive would be an unproductive coastal fringe cut off from a productive interior by impenetrable mountains. But in fact, most of the shores of the Arabian Sea are not quite as inhospitable as these examples. In India, a fertile coastal fringe, especially in the south, the area of Kerala, is backed by the high mountain range called the western Ghats, but these are nowhere completely impenetrable. So also on the Swahili coast, where again behind a productive coastal zone is the *nyika,* a mostly barren area difficult, but not impossible, to travel through on the way to more fertile land farther inland. On the northern shores of the Arabian Sea, the coastal fringe is mostly much less productive, and leads to inland areas that often are hostile deserts. This may help to explain a long history of out-migration from such areas as the Hadhramaut and Oman.

Who are some of the people who traveled around and across the Indian Ocean? We will deal in detail with people transporting religious ideas later. For now, we can note merchant groups from very diverse areas indeed. Armenians traveled from their homeland in Iran all over the littoral of the ocean, and far inland. Everywhere they traveled they found hospitality from fellow Armenians. Jews were to be found all around the shores of the ocean, and especially on the west coast of India. Muslim merchants traveled and traded far and wide. From bases in Egypt or southern Arabia, their reach extended all around the shores of the ocean, and as far as China: indeed, Patricia Risso considers that their fortunes in faraway China influenced importantly their activities in the ocean.[3] Hindu merchants were to be found in little colonies or merely as sojourners in every major port city all around the ocean's shores, including the so-called exclusive Muslim heartland of the Red Sea. More recently, various other communities have traveled and settled very extensively. The Goan Christian population are to be found in other Portuguese colonies, especially

Mozambique, and more recently in the Gulf oil states. Nor did people travel only for trade or to find employment. About fifteen hundred years ago, a vast, and as yet poorly understood, movement of people from what is now known as Indonesia resulted in the population of the huge island of Madagascar. This influence is plain to see today in many areas of life. Many questions remain unanswered: Was this a more or less individual, or even accidental, enterprise, or was there some directing hand? Was any contact maintained with their homeland far to the east?

Other people who traveled and sometimes settled are legion. One example, giving a glimpse of very diverse connections indeed, is the actual people on the ships. Merchants, or their agents, traveled far and wide in search of profit. The famous Asian peddlers, an important part of Asian sea trade for centuries, were pure itinerants, who often had no home at all. Skilled navigators seem to have been a group of their own, their skills being recognized internationally. The pilot who fatefully guided Vasco da Gama from Malindi to Calicut in 1498 is one example; da Gama was so impressed with him that he took him back to Portugal, where he was quizzed on his knowledge by, among others, Italian merchants.[4]

The most discussed, and the most notorious, of all human movements was trade in humans themselves. This topic is hardly germane to a discussion of the Indian Ocean and Islam in eastern Africa; just because many of the traders were Muslim, and some slaves were sold into Muslim areas, does not mean this was an "Islamic" trade. Similarly, as western Europe industrialized, the slave mode of production became outmoded and inefficient. This did not happen in the Indian Ocean world, and hence, for Arab traders and producers, the trade continued; this however was not a function of their being Muslim but of their not yet having made the transition to capitalism. There was an extensive trade to ʿAbbasid Iraq from eastern Africa, primarily from the northern areas of Ethiopia and Somalia, from at least the eighth century. Severe oppression and backbreaking work in the marshlands of southern Iraq led to numerous revolts, the largest being the Zanj revolt of 868–83. This revolt may well have contributed to the weakening of the ʿAbbasid empire, while in turn this weakening led to economic decline in the Middle East and hence a smaller demand for slaves. Later we find African slaves serving on board ships, and as military elites, in India; indeed, even some Indian Muslim rulers were technically slaves. From the late eighteenth century, this trade expanded enormously, with slaves from eastern Africa being destined for date plantations in Oman, plantation agriculture on the Swahili coast and in Zanzibar, and European plantations on the French islands, especially Madagascar, and in the Americas, notably in Brazil.[5]

Early contacts around and across the ocean were primarily for trade. We know, for example, of a quite extensive trade between Mesopotamia and the Indus Valley civilization some five thousand years ago. Romans traded with India, and from this same time of about two thousand years ago, Indians, and possibly Arabs, were active on the east coast of Africa. By the early modern period, trade had increased, and linked together very far-flung areas.

The general point here is that eastern Africa was solidly geared into the Indian

Ocean world long before the rise of Islam. Arabs certainly had come down from the Red Sea and so along the coast; in the seventh century, these traders converted to Islam, and kept on trading. Indians had been in the area for centuries before Islam. Pre-Islamic Sassanian pottery testifies to ties with the Gulf before Islam, while Chinese porcelain fragments again point to very early contacts. It is not, then, a matter of newly converted Muslims "opening up" the Swahili coast. Trade patterns continued, relatively unchanged at first.

This was a very long-distance trade, and one where a vast variety of products were traded—both humble items like cloths and food and luxuries like gold and ivory. High-cost luxuries made up a considerable, and glamorous, part of the trade. Some came from outside the ocean, such as silks and porcelains from China. Others originated in the ocean area. Spices—mace, nutmeg, cloves, cinnamon, and pepper—came mostly from Indonesia, with some pepper from India and cinnamon from Sri Lanka, and were universally valued to flavor food. Spices thus flowed all around the ocean, and far beyond. China was a huge market for pepper, as was Europe.

Precious metals also were in demand everywhere, at first for hoarding and ornamentation, but increasingly to be used for money. The Indian Ocean area produced little here. The exception was gold from the Zimbabwe plateau, which reached a peak of production before 1500. Soon after this, precious metals flowed in from the Americas in a complicated pattern. Some came across the Pacific to Spanish Manila, and then on to China. From about 1550 to 1700, Japan produced much gold and silver, most of which ended up in China. The bulk of the supply for our area came across the Atlantic from South America to Spain. From there some came via the Cape of Good Hope to the Indian Ocean in Portuguese ships, and later with the Dutch, but much more flowed through the Mediterranean and to the ocean via the Red Sea and the Gulf. Other luxury products were legion: for example, ivory from eastern Africa was much in demand as being far superior to Indian and Southeast Asian equivalents. This product was to be found all along the shores of the ocean, and indeed far away in China.

Probably the greatest bulk of trade items were cotton cloths from India. Some of these were very fine things indeed, with gold and silver woven into the diaphanous material, but much of it was cheap stuff for poor people's everyday wear. Huge amounts of such cloths were exported from the three main Indian production zones of Gujarat, Coromandel, and Bengal. It was only in the nineteenth century, when English machine-production undercut Indian handicrafts, that India ceased to be the region that clothed virtually the whole littoral and far inland in the Indian Ocean. Today this trade has again reverted to the control of countries around the ocean: India again, and also many countries in Southeast Asia, not to mention vast production in China. *Kanga,* long strips of colorfully dyed cloth very widely worn on the coast, provide a specific modern example. In the nineteenth century, these were imported from England. Later in the century, India was allowed to develop a modern textile industry, and kanga came from there. Now some are made locally, some in India, and some in China.

Most cloths must be considered to be necessities, not luxuries. Another necessity is food, and basic foodstuffs like rice and wheat were carried very long distances in the early modern Indian Ocean. Several of the great port cities—Melaka in the sixteenth century, Zanzibar in the nineteenth—imported most of their food. Another item was lumber. Mangrove poles from the Swahili coast, and teak from India, were valued for house building and ship construction.

Products were not only traded across the ocean; sometimes they were transplanted to grow in new places. One famous modern example is cloves, which in the nineteenth century were taken from their major production area in the Malukus in eastern Indonesia and grown, very successfully, in Zanzibar. They thus moved from the far east of the ocean to the far west. As one would expect in an oceanic zone so open to exchange and contact, many other plants have moved, and indeed they have become so indigenized that today we think of them as native. Hot chili peppers, for example, are often thought of as typifying Indian curries, yet they were introduced only in the sixteenth century, from the Americas by the Portuguese.

Some products and styles that today are spread all around the ocean originated in the distant past in one particular area. The best example is bananas, which came from Indonesia with the migrants to Madagascar, and subsequently were much modified and improved in Africa. The areca nut, a mild stimulant that originated in Southeast Asia, again is ubiquitous around the ocean. Ibn Battuta was offered some in Mogadishu as a gesture of respect for his learning. Newitt and Middleton provide quite long lists of products, techniques, and crops imported into, and indigenized in, East Africa: cotton, rice, bananas, coconuts, mangoes, outrigger canoes, looms, square houses, and the use of coral cement in construction.[6] Many other products apart from chili peppers were introduced to the Indian Ocean from America by the Portuguese: pineapples, maize, cassava, cashew trees, cucumbers, avocados, guava, and tobacco.

Another importation from American to the Indian Ocean was apparently a much more virulent version of syphilis. It is believed that someone on Columbus's second voyage was responsible for bringing the infection into Europe, where it spread with remarkable rapidity to Asia. There is a case reported from Canton as early as 1502, and in 1505 the Italian Varthema in Calicut claimed that the ruler had "the French disease ['Frangi'] and had it in the throat."[7]

David Arnold has written more generally about the Indian Ocean as a "disease zone." Bubonic plague, for example, may well have spread to Europe not only by land but also by sea via the Indian Ocean, and of course this fearsome disease was to be found also around the shores of the Indian Ocean. Cholera and smallpox also spread out from India all over the ocean. In the early eighteenth century, leprosy spread in South Africa. Its origins may well lie on the other extreme of the ocean, with the Malay servants and slaves recently introduced to this Dutch colony. A century later, as communications became more frequent and intense, a series of cholera epidemics spread out from India all over the ocean. In 1821, cholera reached Java, where it killed 125,000 people, and at the other end of the ocean, in eastern Africa, there was a particularly serious outbreak in 1865. The *hajj* was a great transmitter of this disease, and mortality at Mecca itself was often fearsome. In 1865, fifteen thousand out of a total of ninety thousand pilgrims died. In the 1880s, rinderpest was introduced into Ethiopia, probably again from India, and in the next decade spread, with devastating effects, down the east coast of Africa.[8]

A recent trend in history writing has been the effort of "world historians" to transcend state boundaries. The Indian Ocean is a particularly suitable area for this sort of analysis, for states, and more generally politics, played little role for most of its history. It is in fact precisely five hundred years since politics was introduced into the ocean. Before the arrival of the Portuguese, there is very little evidence of landed states attempting to extend their power to control over the ocean. By and large, the seas were, in contemporary Western juridical terms, mare liberum, where all might travel freely.[9] To be sure, the controllers of port cities levied taxes on those who called to trade, but on the other hand they made no attempt to force seafarers to call at their ports. And even if they had wanted to do this, two major limitations would have rendered their efforts nugatory. First, none of them had armadas effective enough to roam over the vast ocean and force people to call at a particular port. Second, in areas such as the eastern African coast and the western Indian coast, these port cities competed with each other. Sea traders were looking for entrepôts where the products they wanted were available; they also expected taxes to be reasonable, and they wanted no arbitrary confiscation of their goods or other abuses. If they were ill-treated in one port city, they had the option to turn to another; hence, the ocean's long list of port cities that rose and declined.

This is not the place to describe in detail the impact of western European powers on the Indian Ocean. Suffice it here to note that it was them, and the Portuguese first of all, who introduced politics and naval power into the ocean. The Portuguese tried to monopolize trade in some products, and direct and tax other trade. From the seventeenth century, they were imitated by the Dutch and the British, and later by the Omanis, and indeed the British in the nineteenth century were able to monopolize and limit to themselves the use of force in the ocean. As we will see, this had little effect on the subject of this chapter—the role of the Indian Ocean in the spread and changing nature of Islam in east Africa. The point for now is merely that naval power and "politics" played a small role in integrating the ocean—really none before the arrival of Europeans, and even then, very little.

We can now turn to cultural connections and so lead into our main concern; that is, Islam in the ocean and its shores. The aspect of culture that most concerns us is religion, more specifically Islam, but it is best to look more generally at cultural connections first. The key concept here is littoral society. The subject is far from fully studied yet, but the general notion is that there is a certain commonalty about all societies located on the shores of the Indian Ocean. We may note here that the very term *Swahili* means "shore folk," those who live on the edge of the ocean. It is argued that such societies, whether they be in eastern Africa or western or eastern India, around the shores of the Gulf and the Red Sea, on the southern Arabian shore, or in insular Southeast Asia, share certain characteristics. Heesterman stresses that it is transitional, permeable: "The littoral forms a frontier zone that is not there to separate or enclose, but which rather finds its meaning in its permeability."[10] In an earlier discussion, I sketched the case for identifying such a society, which has certain links and a commonalty to do with society, religion, and economy.[11]

East African specialists have contributed to this discussion. Chittick argued that the monsoons made the Indian Ocean a united entity. "This has resulted in its constituting what is arguably the largest cultural continuum in the world during the first millennium and a half C.E. In the western part of the basin, at least, the coasts had a greater community of culture with each other and with the islands than they had with the land masses of which they form the littorals."[12] Or, as Pouwels has it, by 1500 Swahili culture was "a child of its human and physical environment, being neither wholly African nor 'Arab,' but distinctly 'coastal,' the whole being greater than the sum of its parts."[13] A useful new concept here, which seems to get the essential relationships of coastal people very well, is resac. This refers to "the three-fold violent movement of the waves, turning back on themselves as they crash against the shore, [which] seeks to elucidate the way in which [like] the to-and-fro movements of the Indian Ocean, coastal and inland influences keep coming back at each other in wave-like fashion."[14]

The precise elements of commonalty of littoral society have not yet been adequately worked out. We could look at food, obviously largely derived from the sea. Houses may well be different from those inland, as they often use materials, especially coral, available on the shore. The whole rhythm of life is geared to the monsoons. Ship architecture historically may have been similar, characterized by the use of lateen sails. Certainly, littoral society was much more cosmopolitan than that of inland groups, for at the great ports, traders and travelers from all over the ocean, and far beyond, were to be found. There seem also to have been certain languages that achieved wide currency, such as Arabic in the earlier centuries. Jan Knappert finds that there are some five thousand words of Arabic influence in Malay, and more than that in Swahili, and about 80 percent of these are the same (that is, in Malay and Swahili) so that we have a "corpus of traveling Arabic words."[15] Freeman-Grenville tried to find links and commonalties between Swahili and the language of the Sidis of Sind.[16] Later, a sort of nautical Portuguese, and today variants of English, have achieved a similar, quasi-universal status.

Folk religion on the littoral similarly is to be distinguished from inland manifestations. On the coast, religion had to do with customs to ensure safe voyages, or a favorable monsoon. Particular gods were propitiated for these purposes. Specifically maritime ceremonies marked the beginning and end of voyages. Thus, folk religions on the littoral were functionally quite different from those found inland, precisely because the concerns of coastal people were usually quite different from those of peasants and pastoralists inland. It was the increasingly cosmopolitan aspect of the Swahili coast that contributed to its conversion to Islam.

James de Vere Allen, in one of his provocative but frustratingly erratic overviews, claimed that among the elements that contributed to an Indian Ocean world was indeed the Muslim religion. This means that he excludes from this world Sri Lanka, Burma, and Thailand, as they were not Muslim, but he includes South India, since this region, while not Muslim, is too important to be left out of the Indian Ocean world.[17] Despite these inconsistencies, Allen's central point is valid: Islam indeed provided a crucial link around most parts of the Indian Ocean, while on the other hand, any consideration of Islam in eastern Africa must include a maritime dimension, one focused on the Arabian Sea and the Red Sea. I will now turn to this central task.

The central thesis is that the Indian Ocean tied in eastern Africa to a vast, diverse, and cosmopolitan Muslim world. We have shown how the Indian Ocean has always been a place of movement, circulation, contacts, and travel over great distances. It could be that Islam fits well into this sort of environment. The Quran itself has positive things to say about travel by sea: "It is He who subjected to you the sea that you may eat of it fresh fish, and bring forth out of it ornaments for you to wear; and thou mayest see the ships cleaving through it; and that you may seek of His bounty, and so haply you will be thankful."[18] Islam has spread over very great distances. The travels of the famous scholar-traveler Ibn Battuta illustrate this very well, for in the fourteenth century he traveled about seventy-two thousand miles in nearly thirty years, and all the time virtually was in a Muslim world, from West Africa to China. It could be that Islam is more peripatetic than the other great world religions. Famous scholars and saints attracted, and continue to attract, the faithful from very wide areas.

In particular, Islam involves travel and movement because of the central role of the hajj, where historically hundreds of thousands, and today millions, gather together in one place at one time for one purpose. No other world religion has anything exactly similar. The role of Mecca and the hajj has been much studied. It is here that Muslims for the last thirteen hundred years and more have been brought face-to-face with the numbers and diversity of their fellow Muslims. The hajj then is a remarkably efficient method of integrating the worldwide community.[19]

A few more or less random case studies will demonstrate these far-flung ties of Islam over the Indian Ocean, before we turn to a more chronological description of the various Muslim influences coming into the eastern coast of Africa. Here are a few from Southeast Asia. A. H. Johns has investigated the career of Abd al-Rauf of Singkel, and this gives us a clear picture of the many ties and networks and connections established in seventeenth-century Islam, as well as of the centrality of the holy places in this process. Abd al-Rauf was born in North Sumatra around 1615. In about 1640, he moved to the Hijaz and Yemen to study. In Medina, his main teacher was the Kurdish-born Ibrahim al-Kurani. Abd al-Rauf spent a total of nineteen years in Mecca and gained very considerable prestige. In particular, he taught hundreds, even thousands, of Indonesians there, and initiated many of them into the order of which he was a distinguished member, the Shattariyya. He returned to Sumatra, to Aceh, in 1661, and was a revered teacher there for nearly thirty years. He kept in touch with Ibrahim in Medina and taught what he had learned from him to the many Indonesian, especially Javanese, pilgrims who stopped for a time in Aceh on the way to the Red Sea.[20]

Another Asian example stresses the role of Medina; it, too, shows the extreme cosmopolitanism of Islam, in this case in the eighteenth century. Muhammad Hayya, the teacher of Ibn 'Abd al-Wahhab, founder of the Wahhabiyya movement, studied in Medina with scholars from India, Persia, Algiers, and Morocco. His students came from Turkey, India, Yemen, Jerusalem, Baghdad, Damascus, and other Muslim cities. As Voll notes, "The Medinese scholarly community in general was able to contact people from throughout the world of Islam because of the Pilgrimage."[21]

Now two examples from India. Hajji Ibrahim Muhaddis Qadiri was born near Allahabad in northern India. He did the hajj and then studied in Cairo, Mecca, and Syria. He was away twenty-four years, but then returned to India, settled in Agra, and was a prestigious teacher until his death in 1593.[22] The international character of Islam at this time, and the pattern of a career for a Muslim religious specialist, is well illustrated in the history of a founder of the Suhrawardiyya sufi order in India. Shaykh Bahaud-Din Zakariyya was born late in the twelfth century, near Multan. He memorized the Quran, and undertook further study in Khorasan for seven years. Then he traveled to Bukhara, did a hajj, and subsequently studied hadith for five years in Medina. Later he traveled and studied and taught in Jerusalem and Baghdad, the latter place being where he joined his order.[23]

The career of Sayyid Fadl, a Hadhrami sayyid very influential in the Mappilah community of Malabar in the nineteenth century, provides yet another example. Early in his career, he spent four years visiting Mecca and the Hijaz. It may have been during this time that he became an authority in Shafi'i law and a member of the 'Alawi *tariqa,* a sufi brotherhood. Later, his political activities in Kerala annoyed the British rulers, who after some time, in 1852, made him emigrate to Arabia. Subsequently he spent time in Istanbul and became one of the most important theoreticians of the Pan-Islamic movement, along with Jamal al-Din al-Afghani. When he was resident in Mecca, he influenced the some two thousand *hajjis* from Kerala who each year made the pilgrimage.[24]

Finally we turn to eastern Africa for a sketch of the career and travels of Sayyid Ahmad bin Sumeyt. His father Abubakar was a Hadhrami sharif, born in Shiban, who was a trader and scholar and was made *qadi* (judge) of Zanzibar in the time of Majid (1856–70). Ahmad, too, grew up to be a trader and scholar. He interrupted his trading to study religion in Grand Comoro under the supervision of two scholars, one of them his father, who had retired there. Then Ahmad studied under an Iraqi scholar in Zanzibar, where he was made qadi in the 1880s. Even so, he later visited the

Hadhramaut three times to study yet more under famous scholars and get their *ijaza*—that is, a certification, license, or permit. While away between 1883 and 1886, he spent time in Istanbul and studied with Sayyid Fadhi Basha bin Alwi bin Sahi, a famous Hadhrami scholar, and through his influence received an Ottoman order from Sultan Abdul Hamid. In 1887, he studied in Al-Azhar and Mecca, and in 1888 returned to Zanzibar. From then until his death in 1925, he was famed as a scholar and teacher; students came from all over the coast. Indeed, he had an international reputation, for he was asked by the mufti of Mecca himself to settle a quarrel between two Zanzibari 'ulama' (religious specialists). Even prestigious scholars in Egypt sometimes sought his opinion, such was his reputation.[25]

We now turn to a more chronological analysis of Islamic influences flowing into eastern Africa. These began even during the time of the Prophet, for there were Africans in Mecca at the time of the Prophet, and some became his Companions, such as Bilal, the freed Ethiopian slave. Close ties with Ethiopia, just across the Red Sea, are also demonstrated by the way before the *hijra*, Muhammad's migration from Mecca to Medina, some members of the new faith fled there. Islam spread across the Red Sea to the Dahlak Islands very early on, maybe by 700. Another important beachhead was Zayla, in the Gulf of Aden, from whence Islam was disseminated to southern Ethiopia. Moving farther south, Islam also spread to the Horn very early on. Even the interior was converted in perhaps the twelfth century C.E., or even earlier. Shaykh Barkhandle, whose religious name was Shakh Yusuf al-Kawneyn, is given much credit for this. His tomb is in the north of Somalia.[26]

As we would expect, Islam first spread into Somalia from the coast. By the tenth century at least, there were Arab merchants from Aden, Yemen, and the Hadhramaut in Mogadishu, Brava, and Marka, but while the local Somali population converted, it was not "Arabized," there being no large-scale Arab settlement in the area; rather, there evolved a mixture of local and Arab influences. Later there also was extensive contact with the Gulf.

What we have just noted about a mixture of Arab and Somali elements applies even more strongly farther south, in the Swahili coast proper. It used to be claimed that Arab colonies were established, and that these colonies owed nothing to the interior; they looked out, to the Indian Ocean and the Red Sea, never inland to the interior. Today we know that this is far from the case. The earliest mosques so far excavated, possibly dating from the eighth century, were for the use of visiting Arab merchants, or merchants who even had already settled. Wholesale conversions of the existing Swahili indigenes came later, in the twelfth century and a few decades on either side of this. In this context, an observation by two outstanding younger African scholars, F. T. Masao and H. W. Mutoro, is apposite: "The role of outsiders in the early history of the East African coast cannot be denied, but it is one thing to be part of a process of change and completely another to claim responsibility for the process."[27]

Muslims from the heartland of Islam, Hadhramaut especially, moved south for various reasons. Often they were traders, for the strong nexus between trade and the spread of Islam has been much noted all over the Indian Ocean world. Some moved

The Indian Ocean and the Red Sea

as a result of push factors; in other words, they exchanged a life of poverty in the inhospitable regions of southern Arabia for the more benign region of eastern Africa. It used to be claimed that many of these migrant Hadramis established or took over city-states on the coast. In seeing how this can square with the current rejection of any notion of Arab colonization, it is important to note two things. First, while many were no doubt from the Hadhramaut or Oman originally, they rapidly became merged into the Swahili world; that is to say, through acculturation and intermarriage they became another element, albeit a politically important one, in the Swahili world. Second, historically, and especially during the Omani period, a claim to an ancestry deriving from the heartland of Islam was a matter of prestige, and clearly many genealogies were manufactured, or at least embossed, in order to support such claims. A detailed analysis of this matter may be found in chapters 12 and 14 of this book.

To continue on the topic of Arab colonization, it used to be thought that some of the early settlers and rulers were Shirazis, from the eastern shores of the Gulf. This also is now generally discounted. We noted some settlement from the Gulf on the Benadir coast of Somalia, and it seems that some people claiming Shirazi ancestry moved on south from there. Indeed, it could be that the (perhaps mythical) place of origin of the Swahili people, called Shungwaya, probably located somewhere around the Tana River area in the north of modern Kenya, may be linked to the Shirazi origins myth. Anyway, whether these purported Shirazis came from there or somewhat further north, they certainly succeeded in establishing ruling dynasties in several of the major port cities, whose rulers then proudly proclaimed their Shirazi ancestry. These rulers shared a common myth of origin, and had lineage ties with each other. But the claim of a direct link with Shiraz, or the Gulf in general, can be discounted. There was, however, extensive trade with that region during the period that the 'Abbasid caliphate, centered in Baghdad, was at its height, from the ninth to the thirteenth centuries. This was also a time of very extensive trade with China. Baghdad was very thoroughly sacked by the Mongols in 1258 and the focus of trade on the eastern African coast then shifted to southern Arabia, and especially the Red Sea and Hadhramaut area.[28]

What we see here are very extensive connections across the Indian Ocean, with rulers claiming origins in very distant, but still maritime, locations. These rulers, regardless of origins, interacted closely with religious specialists, and indeed in terms of Islam in Africa it is these people who are most important for our purposes. We can, then, now turn to the role of Hadhrami religious specialists on the coast.

We must first note that while contact between these two areas is most important for our purposes, in fact this was all part of a much wider flow, by which Muslims from the heartland, in this case southern Arabia, spread far and wide across the Indian Ocean. It seems that push factors at several times led to an outflow of men from the Hadhramaut, and indeed also from Oman to the east and Yemen to the west. Thus they moved to India after about 1200, and even today the "Arab" community in Gujarat preserves stories of their Hadhrami origins. They also, unlike other Muslims of northern India, belong to the Shafi'i *madhhab*. In Hyderabad in the Deccan, Hadhramis arrived in the eighteenth century to serve as soldiers for the Nizam, the ruler of this state. They also retain their Shafi'i allegiance despite being surrounded by Hanafi Muslims.

The flow to eastern Africa began after about 1250, and to Malaysia, Indonesia, and then the Philippines after about 1300. Thus were created vast, far-flung lineages, merchants and scholars mixed together, who had connections for both piety and pelf all over the ocean. Stephen Dale's exemplary work on the Mapillas of Malabar provides further detail. He notes that in this area, today called Kerala, Islam is of the Shafi'i madhhab, as compared with the Hanafi school of the Turkic-Persian rulers of the great inland empires. Scholars came to Kerala from Yemen, Oman, Bahrain, and Baghdad. From Kerala, Islam flowed on, to Southeast Asia, especially to the north Sumatran state of Aceh in the sixteenth century, and even to the Philippines. Indeed, in their wars against the Portuguese in the sixteenth and early seventeenth centuries, the Acehnese were helped by Muslims from southern Arabia and by Mapillas from Kerala. Further to demonstrate wide ties, some military support was supplied by the Ottoman Turks, whose sultan the Acehnese recognized as caliph.[29] Given this, there is a question about whether the Shafi'i madhhab is peculiarly suited to maritime locations. Certainly it is the dominant school in eastern Africa, the Comoro and Maldive Islands, the west coast of India, and Indonesia. The Shafi'i madhhab expanded to all those lands that surround the Indian Ocean, from the port towns of southern Arabia and the Gulf, through the work of itinerant merchants, scholars as well as migrants. They crossed the ocean or made their way from one port to the other.

While contact, and migration, was more or less continuous between other Muslim areas around the Arabian Sea and the African coast, a particular area, the Hadhramaut, and two particular times, the thirteenth to the fifteenth centuries and the later nineteenth century, are when there seems to have been most extensive contact between the coast and southern Arabia. If we think of the whole Indian Ocean, or even just the Arabian Sea, as a cultural corridor, then we have what may be called a subcorridor linking these two areas, that is coastal towns in the Hadhramaut such as al-Shihr and al-Mukalla, and also inland towns, connected to the Swahili coast.

In the fourteenth century, the Swahili city-states were at their most flourishing, and contact with the Hadhramaut was at its height. Large numbers of prestigious Muslims came to the area. These migrants brought with them the Shafi'i madhhab and, if they were sharifs or sayyids, very considerable *baraka,* or prestige, based on their claim to be direct descendants of the Prophet.

In the north, in Ethiopia and Somalia, these contacts seem to have been close throughout, given their location, so that there were continuing and extensive contacts with Hadhrami, Yemeni, and Hijazi migrants. But this northern area is also subject to other influences from the north, so that while the Shafi'i madhhab predominates on the Swahili coast, on the west bank of the Red Sea and further inland, the situation is more diverse, no doubt a result of location, and also of the continuing Coptic Christian presence in the area. In Ethiopia and the Horn, we find the

Shafi'i school, which clearly demonstrates influences from Arabia, but also the Maliki, from the Sudan, and the Hanafi, which comes in with the Ottomans.

On the Swahili coast, as we would expect, contact was especially close in the north, in the Lamu archipelago. A Portuguese observer noted of Pate, about 1570, that it "has considerable trade with Mecca and other parts. The town is very large and has many buildings. It was here that a Moorish caciz, the greatest in the entire coast, resided."[30] Late in the sixteenth century, a new group of Arab settlers, called Hatimi, arrived in Pate from Brava, a little way to the north, but who claimed to have originated in far-distant Andalusia.

This first wave of Hadhrami influence was succeeded by a more negative presence from across the sea—that is, the Portuguese, who came up from the Cape of Good Hope after 1498. Certainly they aimed to combat Islam wherever they found it, and here again we can see very wide connections indeed. The visceral hatred of the Portuguese for Muslims derived from their own experience in conquering their homeland from Muslims. Even after this, the Portuguese experience in fighting Muslims in Morocco all through the fifteenth century continued their tradition of a curious mixture of hatred and fear toward Muslims. The impact of the Portuguese on the coast is traced in chapter 12.

If it can be said that the Portuguese presence had mixed effects on Islam in the region, what can we say of the next major political change—that is, the Omani hegemony of the nineteenth century? The connection between Oman and the Swahili coast provides yet another example of close ties and connections all across the Arabian Sea, albeit a political rather than a religious one.

The major port of Oman, Muscat, had been ruled by the Portuguese until 1650, when they were expelled by the Ya'rubi dynasty. Soon after, Muslims in Mombasa, at this time ruled by the Portuguese, wrote to the Omanis asking for help to expel the foreign rulers. Oman responded and sacked Mombasa in 1661, raided Mozambique in 1670, and in 1689 destroyed the Portuguese settlement at Pate. In 1698, they captured Mombasa. In the second half of the seventeenth century, there was extensive Omani naval activity in the Hadhramaut area, near the Bab al-Mandab, and at Mocha and al-Shihr.

Early in the eighteenth century, Omani interest in and activity on the coast declined due to instability at home, but around the middle of the century, a new and much more mercantile dynasty, the Busaidi, gained control and increasingly focused on eastern Africa, especially as their activities in India were curtailed by the beginning of the establishment of British rule there. Zanzibar became the center of Omani power in East Africa, and in 1840 replaced Muscat as the capital of the Omani empire. Contact, both in terms of movements of people and trade, continued to be intense throughout the century, with especially large numbers of slaves being taken off to work on the date plantations of Oman.

On the face of it, one could predict quite major changes in religion on the coast. The Omani rulers, after all, belonged to the Ibadi group within Islam, and thus apparently had quite different religious practice than did the Swahili, with their adherence to the Shafiʽi madhhab. Further, the Omanis established a powerful state in Zanzibar, one that had profound political and economic effects on the coast. For the first time, and the last, most people whom we call Swahili were being ruled under one authority and by fellow Muslims. Yet in fact the Omani state neither achieved, nor wanted to achieve, deep penetration into the lives of its more or less nominal subjects on the coast. Ibadi Islam is one of the more moderate tendencies among the Khawarij schism within Islam. In theory, the leader of the Ibadis was to be the one with military and religious knowledge, rather than the more usual emphasis on tribe or family or race. This was greatly diluted under the Busaidi dynasty, who indeed even took the title of sultan. But even at its purest, Ibadi Islam differs from Sunni or Shiʽa mostly in terms of "theology," not in, say, ritual, taxation, marriage, or inheritance.[31] Hence, as other chapters show, the Omani impact on Islam in eastern Africa was again a mixed one, and appears to have been no more major, whether for better or worse, than was the Portuguese.

Wider connections were also in evidence in more social matters, and again we see the importance of the Hadhrami connection, which had a recrudescence under the Omanis in the nineteenth century. Family registers were kept to maintain linkages and the legitimacy of descent claims, especially for the dominant lineages, that is shurafa', or sharifs. Hadhrami sharifs keep family registers, the central one being in the place of origin of the lineage in the Hadhramaut. Lineage members, wherever they are, must report births and deaths to this center—that is, to the munsib, the lineage head. Thus the sharif of the Jamal-al-Layl sharif lineage keeps a genealogy of the eastern African branch in Mombasa. He keeps it up-to-date by corresponding with other lineage members on the coast, the Comoros, and Madagascar, and periodically he also sends it to the head of the Jamal-al-Layl in the Hadhramaut.[32]

Just as these scholars and merchants, and their lineages, were cosmopolitan in the extreme, so also were the sufi tariqas, arguably the most vibrant and important part of Islam in the nineteenth century, if only because it impacted much more on common Swahili than did the learned work of the scholars. Different brotherhoods were dominant at different times and places. In the north, Ethiopia, the Horn, and Somalia, the Qadiri order had long been important. During the nineteenth century, it was challenged by the reformist Idrisi strand from the north. Later in the nineteenth century, a new brotherhood founded in Mecca found its way over the Red Sea. This was the Salihiyya brotherhood, named after its leading shaykh, Muhammad ibn Salih al-Rashidi, who died around 1919. He was from the Sudan, but settled in Mecca and acted in a way typical of sufi orders in that he initiated men into his order as khalifas (deputies) who then went home to spread his doctrine. Sayyid Muhammad, as one would expect, had spent five or six years in Mecca, Medina, and Yemen studying, undertaking the hajj, and getting initiated into the order.

The most influential brotherhood on the coast was the ʽAlawi order, a very austere one, with its main shrine at Inat. Late in the nineteenth century, a branch of the main ʽAlawi order, the Shadhiliyya, won much support on the coast, even as far south as Mozambique. The founder of this branch, Shaykh Marʽuf, was from the

Comoro Islands; a sharif, he did the hajj. Here we see another example of widespread connections: one of the areas where he was most influential was southern Somalia. Shaykh Ma'ruf died in 1905 and his tomb in the Comoros is a place of pilgrimage for all the Shadhilis of eastern Africa.

The Qadiri brotherhood, followers of Abdul Qadir Gilani, were at least as far-flung across the ocean as were the 'Alawi. The legends of the founder have been translated into Swahili as well as Malay and Javanese. During the colonial period, the Qadiri network reached from Mecca and southern Arabia along the Somali coast past Brava, Kisimaiu, and Lamu to Mombasa, and then via Voi, Nairobi, and Kampala into the Belgian Congo. Other lines went to German East Africa, others west through the Sudan to Nigeria and Mali. Their teachings spread from the Hadhramaut ports to Indonesia. Not surprisingly, then, some textbooks found in the Belgian Congo were identical to those in use in Indonesia. This was a very rich and important network.

Several other interlocking strands from outside the area have been important during the last two centuries. Among them are the reformist Wahhabi movement, Pan-Islam, the Islamic reform movement associated with Muhammad Abduh, the influence of colonialism, and the impact of the so-called Islamic revival of recent times. As to the first, the Salihiyya order in the north was a strictly observant movement not unlike the reformist Wahhabi tendency that had arisen in Arabia late in the eighteenth century. It is interesting, however, that Wahhabism, while influential in inland Arabia, and to an extent in Ethiopia, and a source of continuing problems for the rulers of Oman, never gained much support in the Hadhramaut, and hence had little impact on the Swahili coast.

Pan-Islam, promoted by Abdul Hamid II, the Ottoman sultan, after 1880, had a wide impact on the Muslim world and frequently was tied in with anticolonial movements. Notions of Islamic unity and the centrality of the caliph in Istanbul were widely dispersed in our area. These ideas were given greater currency by the rulers of Zanzibar, as Pouwels notes in chapter 12.

This was a reciprocal matter, for some scholars from eastern Africa spent time in, and were influential in, Istanbul itself. So, for example, an important Zanzibar scholar, Ibn Sumayt, spent a year in Istanbul and studied with his fellow Hadhrami scholar Fadl b. Alawi, who was one of the theoreticians of the Pan-Islam movement. Yet when World War I broke out, the flimsiness of the ties to Turkey were revealed, as indeed they were also in India and in the Hijaz. In the former, the khalifat movement met with little success, while in the latter the sharifian dynasty in Mecca and Medina opted for the Arab Revolt and the Allies rather than the Ottomans and their German allies.

The broad impulse to moderate Islamic reform, associated with Muhammad Abduh in Cairo and his successors, met some response on the coast. However, this may have been tempered by the orthodoxy of the Shafi'i school and the Qadiri brotherhood, so that many Swahili desiring to study in the heartland went not to Cairo and al Azhar but to the traditional *ribat* (sufi lodge) at Tarim. Nevertheless, there was some influence, such as *Al-Islah* ("Reform"), a Mombasa paper established in 1932 that spread Islamic antiimperialist and nationalistic messages from Cairo.

Colonial rule from the late nineteenth century interacted with these various tendencies and influences from outside. A new wave of very confrontational proselytizers—in this case, Christian missionaries—were tolerated, sometimes supported, by the European colonial states. Their activities did much to produce a reaction that favored Islam as the more indigenous, and locally older established, religion. Colonial rule also involved speedier communications, and the widespread dissemination of ideas via the printing press. Knappert notes that textbooks for prayer sessions printed in Egypt, Bombay, Singapore, and Penang have been found in Jakarta, Mombasa, and Dar es Salaam. Texts for Shafii law were published in Swahili, Malay, Javanese, and Amharic.[33]

The end of colonialism, and the Islamic revival, have produced new trends in the Islam of eastern Africa, some positive and some negative. In Kenya, and to an extent Tanzania, the Swahili are now marginalized, considered to be collaborators with the slave-trading Omanis and then with the Western colonial rulers. In the face of this, some lineages "are now picking up on their Yamani or Umani patrilines where they can and going to Jeddah, Mecca, Muscat, Dubai and Abu Dhabi."[34] Others, no doubt the less prestigious, with no kin ties to the outside, have turned to Islam as a positive force and reaffirmation of a Swahili identity. Some have even converted to Shii Islam, this being considered to be more militant. Here for perhaps the first time in history we may see an influence from Iran, especially Iran since the revolution of 1979. In Zanzibar, the anti-Arab revolution of 1964 led to a period of downplaying of any foreign influences, but more recently, in 1985, an Omani consulate was set up, significantly not in the capital of Tanzania, Dar es Salaam, but in Zanzibar. Around the same time, discontent with what was perceived to be an anti-Islamic mainland regime led the island to join the Organization of Islamic Countries. Following a great outcry from mainland Christian politicians, this decision was reversed in 1993.

I want finally to locate all this material in a wider historiographical context. During the colonial period, Western authors presented Africa as a tabula rasa, on which European influence had a positive effect. Two tendencies have responded to these slights, but there is a tension between them. On the one hand, is a commendable effort to see Africa in its own terms—in fact, to indigenize African history. On the other hand, historians influenced by once-fashionable political-economy notions have written of African history as a long story of dispossession, and of deleterious foreign impacts.

Where, then, in a wider historiographical context, can we locate our data on religious flows and influences? We are not here dealing with the matter of the "quality" of the Islam of eastern Africa; other chapters deal with that in detail. All that need be said is that coastal Islam is a significant regional variant within the broad rubric of "Islam." The key point is reciprocity. It is not just a matter of Arabs and other foreigners impacting on the Swahili; nor is it merely the Swahili Africanizing the Arabs. Rather, it is a matter of to and fro, with input from both. Nor is this an unusual finding, for the same could be said about most other Islamic areas in the world, where local cultures have influenced profoundly what happens, and produced many regional variants—all of them, however, Islamic.

My concern is with external influences. Was eastern Africa merely a passive recipient of religious norms and practices from overseas, especially from Arabia? More than twenty years ago, the above-cited Allen noted with some despair that the received wisdom, which he hoped was not true, was that everything came from Asia, nothing from Africa.[35] We need to consider the extent to which the Islam of eastern Africa has merely drawn on, and modified, trends from the wider Islamic world around the Indian Ocean, as opposed to what it has contributed to the wider Islamic world.

The balance is heavily weighted toward the former. This is not to belittle Islam on the coast, for to an extent this applies to all Muslim areas around the ocean. Yet it seems to apply especially strongly to this area. This chapter has constantly stressed the centrality of the heartland. Local boys are sent off to study in Mecca, or Medina, or in the case of eastern Africa more likely in Tarim, and then come back with the prestige of an ijaza from these centers. Thousands, today even hundreds of thousands, of people from around the ocean go on hajj each year. This chapter has constantly noted the prestige, the baraka, of people who can trace their lineages back to the Prophet, or to some other acclaimed lineage from the Hadhramaut. Similarly, *madrasas* (Islamic schools) were set up in most of the major towns of the coast, but their founders, their inspiration, and their most prestigious teachers all came from outside.

In this regard, an Indian comparison may reinforce the point. The great madrasa of Deoband, in northern India, is generally considered to be second only to al Azhar in prestige for a traditional Sunni education. During its first one hundred (Islamic) years, it produced more than 7,000 graduates. Of these, 431 worked outside the subcontinent, with the greatest number in Afghanistan, Russia, Burma, China, Malaysia, and South Africa. There were even two who worked in Saudi Arabia and Kuwait, and one in Yemen.[36] Eastern Africa can boast no such prestigious college. To be sure, Muslims from outside eastern Africa attend some of the major festivals, but significantly these are considered to be in a way poor people's substitutes for the hajj itself.

In short, just as Swahili ships seldom left the coast, and very few Swahili traveled from the coast, so also we can say that norms and ideas came to the coast, but few went out. Possible exceptions are the occasional prestigious scholar from the coast who found a wider, Islam-wide audience (though most of these would claim to be Hadhrami, Meccan, or whatever by origin), the Mawlidi festival at Lamu, and the Ukitani Institute in Zanzibar, which have over the last century attracted people from many parts of Africa; these seem to be unique, and so atypical, examples. There never was, nor is, on the coast an Islamic center that attracts people from the wider Muslim world; obviously there is no Mecca or Medina, but also no shrine of a great sufi *pir,* no pilgrimage to the tomb of an imam, no influential variant, such as Shïi Islam in Iran since 1500, no educational institution such as Deoband or al Azhar, all of which cater to a worldwide Muslim constituency. The evidence, then—so far admittedly inconclusive—seems to be that, while the Indian Ocean network has operated to spread, and then influence, Islam on the coast, there has been little flow in the other direction, from the coast to the wider Muslim world.

Notes

1. For general accounts of the Indian Ocean, see Das Gupta and Pearson 1987, Arasaratnam 1994, Chandra 1987, McPherson 1993, Mathew 1990, 1995. For Southeast Asia, see Reid 1988–93. For a "popular" overview, see Hall 1996.

2. For details and references, see Pearson 1998, 51–54.

3. Risso 1995.

4. Subrahmanyam 1997, 121–28.

5. For a recent discussion and extensive references, see Alpers 1997.

6. Newitt 1994, 127; Middleton 1992, 202 fn. 8.

7. Varthema 1928, 63; Carmichael 1991.

8. Arnold 1991. On rinderpest, see Dahl 1979.

9. Subrahmanyam 1997, 109–12.

10. Heesterman 1980.

11. Pearson 1985.

12. Chittick 1980, 13.

13. Pouwels 1987, 31.

14. Caplan 1996. She is referring to the contribution of Jean-Claude Penrad in the book under review.

15. Knappert 1985, 125.

16. Freeman-Grenville 1988.

17. Allen 1980.

18. Arberry 1955, sura 16: verse 14; see also 2:164; 30:46.

19. Pearson 1994; Peters 1994; for the flavor of the hajj, by a participant, see Wolfe 1993, 1997.

20. Johns 1978, 471–72; Johns 1964, 8–11. The discussion here draws on Pearson 1990.

21. Voll 1975, 32–39.

22. For many other examples, see Rizvi 1978–83, 2:146–47, 294, 167, passim.

23. Rizvi 1978–83, 1:190.

24. Dale 1980, 6–7, 116–18, 128, 134–35, 167.

25. Salim 1973, 141–43; Pouwels 1987, 152–58.

26. Galaal 1980, 24.

27. Masao and Mutoro 1988, 586.

28. On the Shirazi matter, see Middleton 1992, 186–87; Spear and Nurse 1984, 74–79; Allen 1982.

29. Martin 1975. On Gujarat, see Misra 1964, esp. 78; for Malabar, Dale 1980, 26, 56–60.

30. Fr. Monclaro's account printed in Silva Rego, 1962–89, 8:355. A *caciz* is a Muslim religious specialist. For details, see Pearson 1994, 71–72.

31. See Risso 1986, 5, 22–33, for a concise introduction to the doctrine.

32. Shepherd 1984, 152–77; see esp. 157, 159.
33. Knappert 1985, 129.
34. Shepherd 1984, 172.
35. Allen 1980, 149.
36. Metcalf 1982, 110–11.

Bibliography

Abungu, George H. Okello. 1994. "Islam on the Kenyan Coast: An Overview of Kenyan Coastal Sacred Sites." In *Sacred Sites, Sacred Places,* ed. David Carmichael et al., 152–62. London: Routledge.

Adas, Michael, ed. 1993. *Islamic and European Expansion: The Forging of a Global Order.* Philadelphia: Temple University Press.

Allen, J. de Vere. 1980. "A Proposal for Indian Ocean Studies." In *Historical Relations across the Indian Ocean,* ed. C. Menaud, 137–51. Paris: UNESCO.

———. 1982. "The 'Shirazi' Problem in East African Coastal History." In *From Zinj to Zanzibar: Studies in History, Trade, and Society on the Eastern Coast of Africa (in Honour of James Kirkman),* ed. J. de Vere Allen and T. Wilson, 9–27. Wiesbaden: Steiner.

Alpers, Edward. 1997. "The African Diaspora in the Northwestern Indian Ocean: Reconsideration of an Old Problem, New Directions for Research." Paper presented at the conference on the Northwest Indian Ocean as Cultural Corridor, Stockholm, Jan. 1997.

Arasaratnam, Sinnappah. 1994. *Maritime India in the Seventeenth Century.* Delhi: Oxford University Press.

Arberry, A. J. 1955. *The Koran Interpreted,* ed. C. Mehaud. New York: Macmillan.

Arnold, David. 1991. "The Indian Ocean as a Disease Zone (1500–1950)," *South Asia* 14:1–21.

Bang, Anne. 1997. "The Hadramis of East Africa (ca. 1860–1910): A Diaspora Community in Context." Paper presented at the conference on the Northwest Indian Ocean as Cultural Corridor, Stockholm, Jan. 1997.

Barbosa, Duarte. 1918–21. *Livro.* 2 vols. Ed. M. L. Dames. London: Hakluyt.

Bouchon, Geneviève. 1973. "Les musulmans du Kerala à l'époque de la découverte portugaise," *Mare Luso-Indicum,* vol. 2, 3–59.

Braudel, Fernand. 1972. *The Mediterranean and the Mediterranean World in the Age of Philip II.* London: Collins.

———. 1981–84. *Civilization and Capitalism, Fifteenth to Eighteenth Centuries.* 3 vols. London: Collins.

Caplan, Patricia. 1996. Review of *Continuity and Autonomy in Swahili Communities,* ed. David Parkin (London: School of Oriental and African Studies, 1994) in *Journal of the Royal Anthropological Institute* 2:764.

Carmichael, Ann G. 1991. "Syphilis and the Columbian Exchange: Was the New Disease Really New?" In *The Great Maritime Discoveries and World Health,* ed. Mario Gomes Marques and John Cule, 187–200. Lisbon: Escola Nacional de Saude Pública.

Chandra, Satish, ed. 1987. *The Indian Ocean: Explorations in History, Commerce, and Politics.* New Delhi: Sage.

Chaudhuri, K. N. 1985. *Trade and Civilisation in the Indian Ocean: An Economic History from the Rise of Islam to 1750.* Cambridge: Cambridge University Press.

Chaudhuri, K. N. 1990. *Asia before Europe: Economy and Civilisation of the Indian Ocean from the Rise of Islam to 1750.* Cambridge: Cambridge University Press.

Chittick, H. Neville. 1980. "East Africa and the Orient: Ports and Trade before the Arrival of the Portuguese." In *Historical Relations across the Indian Ocean*, 13–22. Paris: UNESCO.

Dahl, Gudrun 1979. *Suffering Grass: Subsistence and Society of Waso Borana.* Stockholm: University of Stockholm Studies in Social Anthropology.

Dale, Stephen F. 1980. *Islamic Society on the South Asian Frontier: The Mappilas of Malabar (1498–1922).* Oxford: Oxford University Press.

Das Gupta, Ashin. 1979. *Indian Merchants and the Decline of Surat, c. 1700–1750.* Wiesbaden: Steiner.

———, and M. N. Pearson, eds. 1987. *India and the Indian Ocean (1500–1800).* Calcutta: Oxford University Press.

Dunn, Ross E. 1986. *The Adventures of Ibn Battuta, a Muslim Traveler of the Fourteenth Century.* London: Croom Helm.

Esmail, Aziz. 1975. "Towards a History of Islam in East Africa," *Kenya Historical Review* 3:147–58.

Freeman-Grenville, G. S. P. 1988. "The Sidi and Swahili." In *The Swahili Coast, Second to Nineteenth Centuries: Islam, Christianity, and Commerce in Eastern Africa.* London: Variorum.

Galaal, Musa H. I. 1980. "Historical Relations between the Horn of Africa and the Persian Gulf and the Indian Ocean Islands through Islam." In *Historical Relations across the Indian Ocean,* ed. C. Mehaud, 23–30. Paris: UNESCO.

Godinho, Vitorino Magalhães. 1981–83. *Os descobrimentos e a economia mundial.* 2nd. ed., 4 vols. Lisbon: Editorial Presença.

Goitein, S. D. 1954. "From the Mediterranean to India: Documents on the Trade to India, South Arabia, and East Africa, from the eleventh and twelfth centuries," *Speculum* 29:181–97.

Gonçalves, Fr. Sebastian. 1957–62. *Primeira Parte da História dos Religiosas da Compánhia de Jesus.* Ed. José Wicki. 3 vols. Coìmbra: Atlântida.

Hall, Richard. 1996. *Empires of the Monsoon: A History of the Indian Ocean and Its Invaders.* London: Harper Collins.

Heesterman, J. C. 1980. "Littoral et Intérieur de l'Inde," *Itinerario,* no. 1:87–92.

Horton, M. C. 1986. "Asiatic Colonisation of the East African Coastline: The Manda Evidence," *Journal of the Royal Asiatic Society:* 201–13.

Hourani, George. 1995. *Arab Seafaring in the Indian Ocean in Ancient and Early Medieval Times.* Rev. and exp. ed. Princeton: Princeton University Press.

Ibn Battuta. 1962. *The Travels of Ibn Battuta.* vol. 2. Trans. H. A. R. Gibb. Cambridge, U.K.: Hakluyt.

Johns, A. H. 1964. *The Gift Addressed to the Spirit of the Prophet*. Canberra: Australian National University Centre of Oriental Studies.

———. 1978. "Friends in Grace: Ibrahim al-Kurani and 'Abd al-Rauf al-Singkeli." In *Spectrum: Essays Presented to Sutan Takdir Alisjahbana on his Seventieth Birthday*, ed. S. Udin. Jakarta: Dian Rakyat.

Kelly, J. B. 1972. "A Prevalence of Furies: Tribes, Politics, and Religion in Oman and Trucial Oman." In *The Arabian Peninsula: Society and Politics*, ed. Derek Hopwood. London: Allen & Unwin.

Khoury, Ibrahim. 1983. *As-Sufaliyya, "The Poem of Sofala," by Ahmed ibn Magid, Translated and Explained*. Coimbra: Centro de Estudos da Cartográfia Antiga, Seção de Coìmbra, Série Separatas 148, Junta de Investigações Científicas do Ultramar.

Kirkman, James S. 1970. "The Coast of Kenya as a Factor in the Trade and Culture of the Indian Ocean." In *Sociétés et compagnies de Commerce en Orient et dans l'Océan Indien*, ed. M. Mollat. Paris: SEVPEN.

Knappert, Jan. 1985. "East Africa and the Indian Ocean." In Stone 1985.

Le Guennec-Coppens, Françoise, and Pat Caplan, eds. 1991. *Les Swahili entre Afrique et Arabie*. Nairobi: CREDU/Karthala.

Levtzion, Nehemia, ed. 1979. *Conversion to Islam*. New York: Holmes & Meier.

Martin, B. G. 1975. "Arab Migration to East Africa in Medieval Times," *International Journal of African Historical Studies* 7:367–90.

———. 1976. *Muslim Brotherhoods in Nineteenth-Century Africa*. Cambridge: Cambridge University Press.

Masao, F. T., and H. W. Mutoro. 1988. "The East African Coast and the Comoro Islands." In *General History of Africa*, ed. M. El Fasi, vol. 3. Paris: UNESCO, 586–615.

Mathew, K. S., ed. 1990. *Studies in Maritime History*. Pondicherry: Pondicherry University.

———. 1995. *Mariners, Merchants, and Oceans: Studies in Maritime History*. New Delhi: Manohar.

Mazrui, Alamin M., and I. N. Shariff. 1994. *The Swahili: Idiom and Identity of an African People*. Trenton, N.J.: Africa World History.

Mazrui, Ali A. 1985. "Towards Abolishing the Red Sea and Re-Africanizing the Arabian Peninsula." In Stone 1984.

McPherson, Kenneth. 1993. *The Indian Ocean: A History of People and the Sea*. Delhi: Oxford University Press.

Menaud, C., ed. 1980. *Historical Relations across the Indian Ocean*. Paris: UNESCO.

Metcalf, Barbara Daly. 1982. *Islamic Revival in British India: Deoband (1860–1900)*. Princeton: Princeton University Press.

Middleton, John. 1992. *The World of the Swahili, an African Mercantile Civilisation*. New Haven: Yale University Press.

Misra, S. C. 1964. *Muslim Communities in Gujarat*. London: Asia Publishing.

Newitt, M. D. D. 1994. *History of Mozambique*. London: Hurst.

Pearson, M. N. 1985. "Littoral Society: The Case for the Coast," *Great Circle* 7:1–8.

———. 1990. "Conversions in Southeast Asia: Evidence from the Portuguese Records," *Portuguese Studies* 6:53–70.

———. 1994. *Pious Passengers: The Hajj in Earlier Times.* Delhi: Sterling/Hurst.

———. 1998. *Port Cities and Intruders: The Swahili Coast, India, and Portugal in the Early Modern Era.* Baltimore: Johns Hopkins University Press.

Peters, F. E. 1994. *The Hajj: The Muslim Pilgrimage to Mecca and the Holy Places.* Princeton: Princeton University Press.

Pouwels, Randall L. 1987. *Horn and Crescent: Cultural Change and Traditional Islam on the East African Coast (800–1900).* Cambridge: Cambridge University Press.

Purchas, Samuel. 1905. *Hakluytus Posthumus or Purchas His Pilgrimes.* 20 vols. Glasgow: Hakluyt.

Reid, Anthony. 1988–93. *Southeast Asia in the Age of Commerce.* 2 vols. New Haven: Yale University Press.

Risso, Patricia. 1986. *Oman and Muscat: An Early Modern History.* New York: St. Martin's.

———. 1995. *Merchants and Faith: Muslim Commerce and Culture in the Indian Ocean.* Boulder, Colo.: Westview.

Rizvi, S. A. A. 1973–83. *A History of Sufism in India.* 2 vols. New Delhi: Manoharlal.

Russell-Wood, A. J. R. 1992. *A World on the Move: The Portuguese in Africa, Asia, and America (1415–1808).* New York: St. Martin's.

Salim, A. I. 1973. *The Swahili-speaking Peoples of Kenya's Coast (1895–1965).* Nairobi: East African Publishing.

———. 1992. "East Africa: the Coast." In *General History of Africa*, ed. B. A. Ogot, vol. 5. Paris: UNESCO, 750–775.

Schimmel, Annemarie. 1980. *Islam in the Indian Subcontinent.* Leiden: Brill.

Serjeant, R. B. 1963. *The Portuguese off the South Arabian Coast.* London: Oxford University Press.

Shepherd, Gill. 1985. "Trading Lineages in Historical Perspective." In Stone 1984.

Silva Rego, António da, ed. 1962–89. *Documentos sobre os Portugueses em Mozambique e na Africa Central (1497–1840).* 9 vols. Lisbon: National Archives of Rhodesia and Nyasaland, Centro de Estudos Historicos Ultramarinos.

Spear, T. T., and D. Nurse. 1984. *The Swahili: Reconstructing the History and Language of an African Society (A.D. 500–1500).* Philadelphia: University of Pennsylvania Press.

Stone, J. C., ed. 1985. *Africa and the Sea: Colloquium at the University of Aberdeen* (March 1984), proceedings. Aberdeen: Aberdeen University African Studies Group.

Subrahmanyam, Sanjay. 1997. *The Career and Legend of Vasco da Gama.* New York: Cambridge University Press.

Tibbetts, G. R. 1971. *Arab Navigation in the Indian Ocean before the Coming of the Portuguese.* London: Royal Asiatic Society.

Tolmacheva, Marina. 1993. *The Pate Chronicle.* East Lansing: Michigan State University Press.

Trimingham, J. Spencer. 1964. *Islam in East Africa.* London: Oxford University Press.

Van Leur, J. C. 1955. *Indonesian Trade and Society.* The Hague: Hoeve.

Varthema, Ludovico di. 1928. *The Itinerary of Ludovico di Varthema of Bologna from 1502 to 1508.* Ed. R. C. Temple. London: Argonaut.

Voll, John. 1975. "Muhammad Hayya al-Sindi and Muhammad ibn 'Abd al-Wahhab: An Analysis of an Intellectual Group in Eighteenth-Century Madina," *Bulletin of the School of Oriental and African Studies* 37:32–39.

————. 1994. "Islam as a Special World-System," *Journal of World History* 5:213–26.

Wilding, Richard. 1987. *The Shorefolk: Aspects of the Early Development of Swahili Communities.* Mombasa: Fort Jesus Occasional Papers no. 2. Mimeo.

Wilkinson, J. C. 1981. "Oman and East Africa: New Light on Early Kilwan History from the Omani Sources," *International Journal of African Historical Studies* 14:272–305.

Wink, Andre. 1990. *Al-Hind: the Making of the Indo-Islamic World.* Delhi: Oxford University Press.

Wolf, Eric R. 1982. *Europe and the People without History.* Berkeley: University of California Press.

Wolfe, Michael. 1993. *The Hadj: An American's Pilgrimage to Mecca.* New York: Grove.

————. 1997. *One Thousand Roads to Mecca: Ten Centuries of Travelers' Writing about the Muslim Pilgrimage.* New York: Grove.

Wright, H. T. 1993. "Trade and Politics on the Eastern Littoral of Africa (A.D. 800–1300)." In *The Archeology of Africa: Food, Metals, and Towns,* ed. Thurstan Shaw et al., 658–72. London: Routledge.

Zain al-Din. 1899. *História dos Portugueses no Malavar por Zinadim.* Trans. David Lopes. Lisbon: Imprensa Nacional.

Part II

West Africa and the Sudan

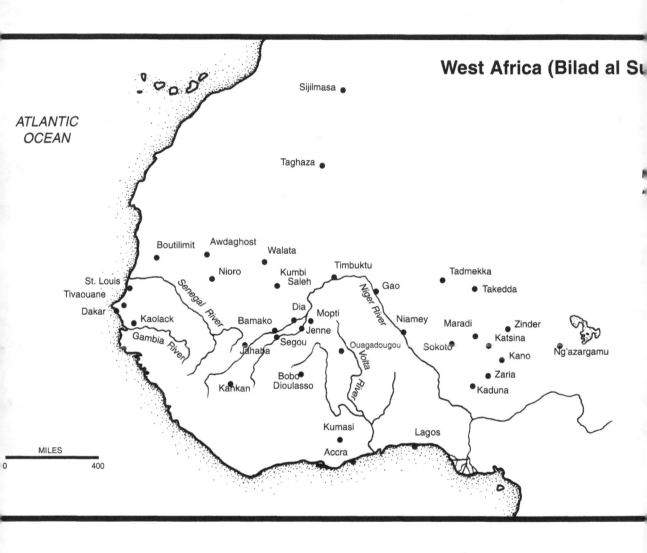

West Africa (Bilad al Su...

ATLANTIC OCEAN

MILES
0   400

Sijilmasa

Taghaza

Boutilimit   Awdaghost   Walata
Nioro   Kumbi   Timbuktu   Tadmekka
             Saleh   Gao   Takedda
St. Louis
Tivaouane   Dia
Dakar   Bamako   Mopti   Niamey
      Kaolack   Jenne   Maradi   Zinder
             Jahaba Segou   Katsina
Gambia River   Ouagadougou   Sokoto   Kano   Ng'azargamu
             Bobo   Zaria
             Dioulasso   Kaduna
      Kankan

Senegal River
Niger River
Volta River

Kumasi
Accra   Lagos

CHAPTER 3

Islam in the Bilaᴅ al-Suᴅan to 1800

Nehemia Levtzion

The earliest Arab expeditions in North Africa in the seventh and eighth centuries penetrated into the Sahara in two directions, the one from Tripoli toward Fezzan and the other from the Sus in southern Morocco. The Arab expeditions must have made their way on beaten routes along which trade had been moving for some time. Trade across the Sahara was carried by nomad Berbers, who occupied both ends of the Sahara. By the tenth century, Muslim traders from North Africa had their base in the commercial centers of Awdaghust and Tadmekka in the southern Sahara. From these towns, they traded with the capitals of the Sudanic kingdoms of Ghana and Gao.

It appears that the North African traders preferred to have their southern entrepôt in the domains of the Berbers, which they considered as being within *Dar al-Islam*. These traders might have observed the injunction by Ibn Abi Zayd (d. 996), the authoritative jurist of Qayrawan: "Trade to the territory of the enemy and to the Land of the Sudan is reprehensible."[1] In the following centuries, with the progress of Islam, the boundary between the Berber domains of the Sahara and *Bilad al-Sudan* (the Land of the Black People) became blurred, and the southern termini of the Saharan trade—Walata and later Timbuktu—had a Muslim population of Berbers and Sudanese.

In the eleventh century, the two capital cities of Ghana and Gao were composed in part of a Muslim town, which was separated from the royal town. Both parties seem to have been rather cautious to expose themselves to the full impact and consequences of unrestricted commercial and social relations between the Muslims and those local people who adhered to their ancestral traditions. This residential separation allowed each group to maintain and practice religious rites that may have been offensive to the other group.

Writing in 1068, the Andalusian geographer al-Bakri was able to gather precious information about Islam in three contemporary African kingdoms—Gao,

Takrur, and Ghana. The king of Gao was Muslim and the royal emblems Islamic, but "the common people worshipped idols as did the [other] Sudanese." Also, pre-Islamic customs persisted. The only-partial acceptance of Islam in Gao is contrasted with the zealous adherence to Islam of the king of Takrur on the Lower Senegal, who compelled his subjects to observe the Islamic law, and carried jihad against his infidel neighbors.[2] The Islamic militancy of Takrur was exceptional, whereas Gao represented symbiotic relations between Islam and the traditional religion that were typical of Islam in West Africa.

In Ghana, the Muslims lived under the auspices of a non-Muslim king who invited Muslim traders to the capital and employed literate Muslims in his court. According to the geographer al-Zuhri, writing in 1137, the people of Ghana converted in 1076.[3] This must have happened under the influence of the Almoravids, a militant Islamic movement in the southwestern Sahara. In 1154, according to al-Idrisi, Ghana was a Muslim state and was still among the most powerful in the Western Sudan.[4] But by the middle of the thirteenth century, the power of Ghana had declined and the political center of gravity shifted southward, where Mali, on the upper reaches of the Niger, emerged as the dominant power. Al-Bakri's distinction between Muslims and "followers of the king's religion" *(ahl din al-malik)*, and not between Muslims and local people, suggests that not all the Muslims in Ghana were foreigners. Al-Bakri referred to the Banu Naghmarata, "merchants who export gold to other countries." These were traders who were part of a commercial network that extended from the towns of the Sahel to the sources of the gold in the south. They opened routes among friendly non-Muslim people. When the traders "enter their country the inhabitants treat them with respect and step out of their way."[5]

☾ ☾ ☾

Muslims established new trading centers, which by the end of the fifteenth century reached the fringes of the forest. They created a "commercial diaspora," with a common religion, a lingua franca, and a common legal system, the Shari'a, a personal, extraterritorial divinely ordained law, that added to the mutual trust among merchants. Conversion to Islam became necessary for those who wished to join the commercial network. The first stage in the spread of Islam in West Africa was therefore the dispersion of Muslims. The next phase began when Muslim clerics began to communicate with the host kings. Another text of al-Bakri presents an account of such an encounter that brought about the Islamization of a West African king:

> The king of Malal is known as al-Musulmani. He is thus called because his country became afflicted with drought one year following another; the inhabitants prayed for rain, sacrificing cattle till they had exterminated almost all of them, but the drought and the misery only increased. The king had as his guest a Muslim who used to read the Quran and was acquainted with the Sunna. To this man the king complained of the calamities that assailed

him and his people. The man said: "O king, if you believed in God (who is exalted) and testified that He is One, and testified as to the prophetic mission of Muhammad (God bless him and give him peace), and if you accepted all the religious laws of Islam, I would pray for your deliverance from your plight and that God's mercy would envelop all the people of your country, and that your enemies and adversaries would envy you on that account." Thus he continued to press the king until the latter accepted Islam and became a sincere Muslim. The man made him recite from the Quran some easy passages and taught him religious obligations and practices which no one may be excused from knowing. Then the Muslim made him wait till the eve of the following Friday, when he ordered him to purify himself by a complete ablution, and clothed him in a cotton garment which he had. The two of them came out toward a mound of earth, and there the Muslim stood praying while the king, standing at his right side, imitated him. Thus they prayed for a part of the night, the Muslim reciting invocations and the king saying "Amen." The dawn had just started to break when God caused abundant rain to descend upon them. So the king ordered the idols to be broken and expelled the sorcerers from his country. He and his descendants after him as well as his nobles were sincerely attached to Islam, while the common people of his kingdom remained polytheists. Since then their rulers have been given the title of al-Musulmani.[6]

The Muslim divine succeeded in winning over the king by demonstrating the omnipotence of the great Allah. Praying to Allah saved the kingdom in a situation where all sacrifices performed by the local priests had failed.

Al-Bakri's account, like other traditions, emphasizes the role of the rulers as early recipients of Islamic influence, and therefore also the importance of kingdoms in the process of Islamization. Indeed, Islam did not penetrate into segmentary societies even when and where Muslim traders and clerics were present. Kings sought supernatural aid from external religious experts, because in the process of state-building they experienced situations of uncertainties and strain, like competition over the chieftaincy, fear of plots, wars with other states, and the responsibility for the welfare of the whole community. By contrast, the common people, even when integrated into the new states, did not undergo radical social and economic changes that called for a readjustment of religious life. Their way of life remained harmonized with the rhythm of the traditional religion: its fertility rites, ancestor worship, and the supplication of the deities.

This argument may be related to Robin Horton's theory of conversion, according to which the peasant who lives in his own community is likely to be taken up by the cult of the lesser spirits, whereas his ritual approach to the Supreme Being is intermittent and of marginal importance. On the other hand, kings and other office-holders, by being directly involved in long-distance trade or by interaction with merchants and interstate diplomacy, were opened to the wider world, beyond their own microcosms. They were cultivating and simultaneously performing the cults of communal and dynastic guardian spirits and the cult of the Supreme Being. For the latter, they drew selectively from Islam. Thus, the religious life of the rulers was the product of the adaptation of a unified cosmology and ritual organization, and imams that directed the rituals for the chiefs were part of the court, like the priests of the other cults.[7] In al-Bakri's account, the Muslim cleric taught the king of Mali only those religious obligations and practices that no one may be excused from knowing. Hence, the king was instructed only with the rudiments of Islam and was not heavily burdened from the beginning with the obligations of prescriptive Islam.

In Malal and, as noted above, Gao, only the king, his family, and entourage accepted Islam, whereas the commoners remained loyal to their ancestral religions. Situated between the majority of their pagan subjects and an influential Muslim minority, kings adopted a middle position between Islam and the traditional religion. They behaved as Muslims in some situations but followed traditional customs on other occasions. They patronized Muslim religious experts but referred also to traditional priests and shrines. From this middle position, dynasties and individual kings, in given historical circumstances, could develop greater commitment to Islam or fall back upon ancestral religion. This may be demonstrated by following the development of Islam in Mali from the eleventh to the fourteenth centuries.

☾ ☾ ☾

Malinke chiefs had come under Islamic influence before the time of Sunjata, founder of the empire of Mali.[8] Sunjata, a great hunter and magician, fought against Sumanguru, the king of Soso, another powerful magician. Though a nominal Muslim, he turned to the traditional religion for support, to the particularistic spirit of the nation, rather than to the universalistic appeal of Islam. Two centuries later, Sonni Ali, who made the small kingdom of Songhay into a large empire, behaved in a similar way. Kings like Sunjata and Sonni ʿAli, founders of empires, are the heroes of the national traditions, whereas the exploits of their Muslim successors—Mansa Musa of Mali and Askiya Muhammad of Songhay—were recorded by the Arabic sources.

From its center on the upper Niger, Mali expanded into the Sahel. Muslim towns became part of the empire, and Muslim traders traveled over the routes that traversed the empire. Through the control of the Saharan trade and when they performed the pilgrimage to Mecca, the kings of Mali came closer to the wider Muslim world. As the small Malinke kingdom turned into a vast, multiethnic empire, with influential Muslim elements inside and extensive Islamic relations with the outside, its kings moved along an imagined continuum, from attachment to the traditional heritage toward greater commitment to Islam. Mansa Musa (1312–37) was "a pious and righteous man, and made his empire part of the land of Islam." He built Friday mosques with minarets and instituted the public prayer. He attracted Maliki scholars and was devoted to Islamic studies.[9]

In 1352–53, during the reign of Mansa Musa's brother Mansa Sulayman, the Moroccan traveler Ibn Battuta visited the king's court and described the celebration of the two great Islamic festivals. The presence of the king made the public prayer an official occasion to which non-Muslims were drawn; in return, the prestige of the new religion was mobilized to exhort loyalty to the ruler. The alliance between kingship and Islam made the latter into an imperial cult. As the Islamic festivals became national feasts, they also accommodated traditional ceremonies. On the two festivals following the afternoon prayer, the sultan sat on the dais, surrounded by army officers, the *qadi* (the Muslim judge), and the preacher. Dugha the linguist, accompanied by slave girls, played an instrument made of reed with gourds underneath, and recited songs of praise to the king. He was followed by the bards *(dyali)*, dressed as birds in red-beaked masks of feathers. They recited the history of the kingdom and called for the sultan to be remembered by posterity for his good deeds.[10]

Ibn Battuta regarded this "ridiculous reciting of the poets" among "the vile practices" of the people of Mali. He criticized other practices, too, such as the custom of sprinkling dust and ashes on the head as a sign of respect before the king.[11] In eleventh-century Ghana, under a non-Muslim king, only those who followed the king's religion kneeled down and sprinkled themselves with dust; the Muslims were exempted from this practice and greeted the king by clapping hands.[12] In the Islamized empire of Mali, all subjects, Muslims and non-Muslims, had to follow the custom.[13] In other words, under non-Muslim rulers, Muslims were not obliged to perform some traditional ceremonial acts, but under Islamized kings, who themselves combined Islamic and traditional elements, pre-Islamic customs had to be accommodated. But Ibn Battuta was also impressed by the way Malian Muslims observed the public prayer on Friday, dressed in white clothes. He also commended their concern for the study of the Quran.[14]

Mansa Musa visited Cairo on his way to Mecca in 1324, where he was described by an Egyptian official as a pious man, who "strictly observed the prayer, the recitation of the Koran, and the mention of Allah's name." But, the same informant added that beautiful daughters of his subjects were brought to Mansa Musa's bed without marriage, as if these freewomen were slave concubines. When Mansa Musa was told that this was not permitted to Muslims, he asked: "'Not even to kings?' 'Not even to kings,' was my reply, 'ask the learned scholars.' 'By Allah,' he said, 'I did not know that. Now I will renounce it completely.'"[15] Shortcomings in the application of the Muslim law were most apparent in marriage customs and sexual behavior.

In the fifteenth century, Mali lost its control over Timbuktu, Jenne, and the other centers of the Sahel, thereby being cut off from direct contact with the trans-Saharan routes and the wider Muslim world. The capital declined and was deserted by the foreign Muslim community. As more ethnic groups escaped the domination of Mali, the kingdom gradually contracted back to its Malinke nucleus and the traditional particularistic spirit of the Malinke nation triumphed over the universal, supratribal appeal of Islam. Muslim divines remained attached to the courts of the successor states of Mali and continued to render religious service to those minor kings, but the latter lost the Islamic zeal and appearance of the fourteenth-century kings of Mali. The Malinke chiefs returned to the middle position between Islam and the traditional religion, with a greater inclination toward the latter. Muslims in the capital of the empire and provincial centers of government rendered religious service to Islamized kings and became integrated into the social and political system of the state. They were pious and observant believers themselves, but had to tolerate the more diluted forms of Islam as practiced by their kings, and even to take part in ceremonies in which pre-Islamic rites were performed. The situation of these Muslims was different from that of Muslims in commercial towns, which were often autonomous. The king of Mali did not enter Diaba, a town of the *fuqaha'* (jurists), where the qadi was the sole authority. Anyone who entered this town was safe from the king's oppression and his outrage, and it was called "the town of Allah."[16]

☾ ☾ ☾

Merchants were the carriers of Islam rather than agents of Islamization. Merchants opened routes and exposed isolated societies to external influences, but they were not themselves engaged in the propagation of Islam, which was the work of religious divines. The latter joined the commercial caravans and it was through them that Islam actually left traces along the trade routes. Clerics often abandoned the caravan when a local chief requested their religious services. Clerics followed the merchants to the commercial towns, where they served the Muslim community as imams and teachers. The clerics became integrated into African societies by playing religious, social, and political roles similar to those of traditional priests. Like traditional priests, Muslim clerics were peacemakers, who pleaded for the wrongdoers, and mosques, like the traditional shrines, were considered sanctuaries. Clerics were expected not to interfere in the political competition within African societies, and immunity of life and property was extended to Muslims only as long as they posed no threat to the existing sociopolitical order. Muslims had limited political objectives; they sought to win the favor of the rulers toward the Muslims. A non-Muslim ruler, the eleventh-century king of Ghana, was highly praised "on account of his love of justice and friendship for Muslims."[17]

Songhay and Timbuktu

In the middle of the fourteenth century when Ibn Battuta visited Timbuktu, it was still a small town inhabited mainly by the Massufa Berbers.[18] There was, however, a community of foreign Muslims in Timbuktu, because Ibn Battuta noted the tombs of two foreigners, the Egyptian Saraj al-Din ibn al-Kuwayk and the Andalusian Abu Ishaq al-Sahili. The former, a merchant from Alexandria, died in Timbuktu in January 1334,[19] on his way to Mali to claim a debt of loan from Mansa Musa. In Timbuktu, he was a guest of Abu Ishaq al-Sahili, a poet and architect from

Andalusia, who had accompanied Mansa Musa back from the pilgrimage. Abu Ishaq built a magnificent palace for Mansa Musa in the capital and then settled in Timbuktu, where he died in October 1346.[20] He must be credited also with the building of the great Friday mosque of Timbuktu, which according to Leo Africanus was built by an Andalusian architect.[21] The two chronicles of Timbuktu confirm that this mosque was built by the order of Mansa Musa.[22] But, during Ibn Battuta's visit, Walata was still more important than Timbuktu, and the descendants of Abu Ishaq al-Sahili preferred to live there and not in Timbuktu.[23]

Mansa Musa encouraged intellectual life in Timbuktu, and sent Malian scholars to study in Fez.[24] By the first half of the fifteenth century, the level of scholarship in Timbuktu was such that Sidi Abd al-Rahman al-Tamimi, who came from the Hijaz, realized that the scholars of Timbuktu surpassed him in the knowledge of Islamic jurisprudence *(fiqh)*. Sidi Abd al-Rahman himself therefore traveled to Fez to study fiqh before he settled in Timbuktu.[25] He became integrated into the scholarly community of Timbuktu, and his descendant Habib served as qadi of Timbuktu from 1468 to 1498.[26]

The senior scholar in Timbuktu under the rule of Mali was Mobido Muhammad, a native of Kabora, which had been mentioned together with Zagha (Dia) by Ibn Battuta, as two old Muslim towns on the Niger. Kabora was perhaps the most important center of Islamic learning on the Middle Niger, where famous scholars *('ulama')* who later held positions in Jenne and Timbuktu studied until the sixteenth century. Around the tomb of Mobido Muhammad al-Kabori in Timbuktu "were buried some thirty men of Kabora, all scholars and men of piety." Two prominent white scholars of Timbuktu, 'Umar ibn Muhammad Aqit and Sidi Yahya, also studied with Modibo Muhammad al-Kabori.[27] Under the rule of Mali, the imams of the Friday mosque were Sudanese. After the Tuareg conquest of Timbuktu in 1433, scholars from the oases of the northern Sahara replaced Sudanese scholars as imams of the Friday mosque. It was about the same time that the Sankore scholars, members of three Sanhaja families, who had migrated from Walata, became prominent in Timbuktu.[28]

Even a source as hostile to Sonni Ali as *Ta'rikh al-Sudan* admits that, notwithstanding Sonni Ali's persecution of the scholars of Timbuktu, "he acknowledged their eminence, saying: 'without the *'ulama'* the world would be no good.' He did favors to other *'ulama'*, and respected them."[29] The *'ulama'* favored by Sonni Ali were the descendants of scholars who had come from the northern Sahara and beyond, who unlike the Sanhaja of the southern Sahara, had no relations with the Tuareg, Sonni 'Ali's enemies. Except for his violent encounter with the Sankore scholars, Sonni 'Ali was a typical Islamized king of the western Sudan. Sonni 'Ali combined elements of Islam with beliefs and practices of the Songhay traditional religion, and was greatly respected as the magician-king. He observed the fast of Ramadan and gave abundant gifts to mosques, but he also worshipped idols, sacrificed animals to trees and stones, and sought the advice and help of traditional diviners and sorcerers.

He pronounced the *shahada* (the Islamic confession of faith), without understanding its meaning. He prayed but was careless in observing the correct time of the prayers.

Sonni 'Ali therefore was not different from most West African kings, who maintained a middle position between Islam and the traditional religion, but he encountered different historical circumstances. His successful military exploits brought him to rule over regions that had been under stronger Islamic influence. It was the political confrontation with the representatives of Islam, and not the deficiency in the practice of Islam, that brought about *takfir*, the declaration of Sonni 'Ali as an infidel. Since the early days of Islam, it was the consensus *(ijma')* of the scholars of Islam to avoid such declarations, so that those who proclaimed themselves Muslims by making the profession of the faith could not be anathematized. It was on the basis of this consensus that West African kings were not challenged as infidels. The legal and doctrinal justification to the declaration against Sonni 'Ali, against the general consensus, was provided by Muhammad b. 'Abd al-Karim al-Maghili.

☾   ☾   ☾

Shortly after Sonni 'Ali's mysterious death, his son was overthrown by Askiya Muhammad, a senior commander in Sonni 'Ali's army. He entered into an alliance with the 'ulama' of Timbuktu and with chiefs and governors of the more Islamized western provinces. A new balance was achieved between those provinces west of the Niger bend and Songhay proper, down the river, which remained strongly traditional and had hardly been affected by Islam. Askiya Muhammad made Islam one of the central pillars of the state and cultivated close relations with the scholars of Timbuktu. Shortly after his accession, he went to Mecca on pilgrimage. On the way he visited Egypt, where he met Jalal al-Din al-Suyuti. Al-Suyuti introduced Askiya Muhammad to the 'Abbasid caliph in Egypt. The caliph invested Askiya Muhammad with the title of caliph. In Egypt, Askiya Muhammad "learned from him [al-Suyuti] what is lawful and what is forbidden, . . . and benefitted from his advice and admonitions."[30]

Our sources suggest that Askiya Muhammad sought the advice of al-Suyuti and al-Maghili in matters of state. But these remained theoretical exhortations, because from what we know about Songhay under Askiya Muhammad and his successor, little was done in practice to reform the empire in line with Islamic political theory. The scholars of Timbuktu were less demanding, and were satisfied with their privileged position. They praised the askiya for his love of scholars and for his humility before the scholars and his generosity to them. The court ceremonies and the protocol were adjusted to accommodate Muslim scholars. Sharifs were permitted to sit with the askiya on his dais, and only they and other scholars could eat with the askiya.

In 1498, Askiya Muhammad appointed Mahmud ibn 'Umar Aqit as qadi. Mahmud ibn 'Umar was succeeded by his three sons, who held office until the end of the sixteenth century. The transfer of the office of qadi to the Aqit family marked the growing influence of the Sankore Sanhaja scholars, led by members of the Aqit family. The qadi Mahmud b. 'Umar asserted his independence in Timbuktu to the extent that he sent away Askiya Muhammad's messengers and prevented them from carrying out the askiya's orders.[31] The qadi Muhmad b. 'Umar behaved as mentor of Askiya Muhammad who requested the qadi to save him the fire of hell, by guiding him in the right way.[32] There were also tensions in the next generation, between Askiya Dawud, son of Askiya Muhammad, and the qadi al-'Aqib, son of the qadi Mahmud. Once, following an exchange of unworthy words, the qadi refused to see the askiya, who was made to wait before the qadi's home for a long time before being given permission to enter. The askiya humiliated himself before the qadi until the latter was reconciled. The character of the qadi al-'Aqib and his attitude toward the askiya and his officials were described by his nephew Ahmad Baba: "He was of stout heart, bold in the mighty affairs that others shrink from, courageous in dealing with the sultan and those under him. He had many confrontations with them and they would be submissive and obedient to him in every matter. If he saw anything he disapproved of, he would suspend his activities as qadi and hold himself aloof. Then they would conciliate him until he returned."[33]

There were other 'ulama' who fitted better to the traditional role of Muslim divines in a Sudanic state, as intimate advisers, whose relations with the rulers were devoid of the tensions between the askiyas and the qadis. These clerics prayed for the ruler and recruited supernatural powers to protect him and his kingdom.[34] These clerics received grants of land and charters of privilege. Such documents were known as *hurma* in Songhay, *mahram* in Bornu, both meaning "sanctity," "immunity," or "inviolability."

Askiya Muhammad was deposed by his son Musa in 1528. During the civil war that followed between Askiya Musa and his brothers, the qadi Mahmud b. 'Umar sought to bring about a reconciliation, but Askiya Musa refused. A provincial governor who had taken arms against Askiya Musa sought sanctuary in the house of the qadi of Timbuktu. Askiya Musa ordered to seize him at the qadi's house.[35] Askiya Musa's defiance of the qadi's intercession was a departure from the accepted norms of political conduct, a sign of unmitigated rule of violence, seemingly unconcerned even for its own legitimacy. The period of illegitimate despotism came to an end with the accession of Askiya Isma'il in 1537. He set free his father Askiya Muhammad, who in return ceremonially invested Askiya Isma'il with the insignia he had received in Cairo from the 'Abbasid caliph: green gown, green cape, white turban, and an Arabian sword.

Askiya Dawud, the last ruler in the line of Askiya Muhammad's sons, ruled for thirty-three years (1549–82). As a prince, he received a good Islamic education, and even as king he continued to study with a *shaykh,* who came to the palace every morning. He exceeded his father in his generosity to Muslim scholars. He gave his daughters in marriage to scholars and merchants.[36] Whenever Askiya Dawud passed near Timbuktu, the merchants of Timbuktu came out to greet him in his camp outside the city. But the askiya went in person to visit the qadi at his home, and then proceeded to pray at the great mosque.[37]

When one of the scholars of Timbuktu visited Askiya Dawud in his palace, he was shocked by the persistence of pre-Islamic practices at the court. "I was amazed," the scholar said, "when I came in, and I thought you were mad, despicable and a fool, when I saw the people carry dust on their heads." The askiya laughed and replied, "No, I was not mad myself, and I am reasonable, but I am the head of sinful and haughty madmen and I therefor made myself mad to frighten them so that they would not act unjustly toward the Muslims."[38] Even a devoted Muslim like Askiya Dawud was unable to relieve the monarchy of its pre-Islamic heritage.

☾ ☾ ☾

After Askiya Dawud's death in 1582, scholars and merchants of Timbuktu became involved in succession disputes among the Songhay princes. When one of these princes gave up his right to the throne and wished to retire to Timbuktu to become a student of the Islamic sciences, his wish was rejected and he was detained because the commanders of the army thought that if the prince resided in Timbuktu, officials and princes on visits to Timbuktu would be suspected of intriguing with him. In 1588, when the governor of Timbuktu and the Tuareg chief supported a rebellious prince, the merchants of Timbuktu also supported the rebel; they donated gold to the prince, and the imams prayed for him. Following the defeat of the prince by the reigning askiya, the political supporters—namely, the governor of Timbuktu and the Tuareg chief—were executed; the scholars and merchants, however, were pardoned, because they were not considered a political threat. Referring to a certain merchant, the askiya said: "He is a poor trader of no importance and not to be worried about."[39]

In the middle of the sixteenth century there were 150 or 180 Quranic schools in Timbuktu.[40] They formed the broad basis for the higher levels of learning in all the branches of the Islamic sciences. Students studied a subject with the scholar best known for his authority in that field. By the end of the century, scholarship in Timbuktu was highly regarded, and during Ahmad Baba's exile in Marrakesh (1594–1607), leading scholars of the Maghrib, including the qadis of Fez and Meknes and the *mufti* of Marrakesh, came to hear his lessons.

At that time, intellectual life in Timbuktu was influenced by Egyptian scholars, with whom scholars from Timbuktu studied when they visited Cairo on their way to Mecca. It is significant that almost all these Egyptian scholars were Shafi'is, with whom the Maliki scholars of Timbuktu must have studied subjects like *hadith* (Hadith), *tafsir* (Quran exegesis), and mysticism, rather than jurisprudence, which one learned with scholars of one's own school of law. Al-Suyuti boasted that scores of his books had been taken to the land of Takrur, as Egyptians called Bilad al-Sudan at that time.[41] Thus the scholars of Timbuktu had wider exposure than the parochial Maliki scholars of Morocco. Indeed, Ahmad Baba complained that Moroccan scholars were concerned only with the study of Maliki handbooks such as the *Risala* of Ibn Abi Zayd and the *Mukhtasar* of Khalil.[42]

On two issues that were central to West African Muslims—namely, the use of amulets and coexistence with non-Muslims—the scholars of Timbuktu accepted the advice of the more sophisticated Egyptian al-Suyuti than the admonitions of the zealous Maghribi reformer Muhammad b. 'Abd al-Karim al-Maghili. Whereas al-Suyuti saw no harm in the manufacture of amulets, provided there was nothing reprehensible in them, al-Maghili was against any trade in amulets. Al-Suyuti gave license to some forms of association with non-Muslims, whereas al-Maghili insisted that between Muslims and infidels there was only jihad.[43]

Sufism was brought to Timbuktu from the Maghrib and the northern Sahara in the fifteenth century. In the sixteenth century, the leading scholars of Timbuktu, on their way to Mecca, sought the blessing and guidance of Muhammad al-Bakri (d. 1545), the Egyptian poet and mystic. It is significant that, like al-Bakri and other Egyptian sufis of the sixteenth century, those of Timbuktu were also not affiliated to any sufi brotherhood *(tariqa)*.[44]

It seems that much of the wealth of the scholars of Timbuktu came from gifts by the askiyas and by the city's merchants. Donations by the askiya were in gold or in the form of grants of land with slaves to cultivate them.[45] Members of scholars' families were sometimes important merchants.[46] An individual might spend the first part of his life as a merchant before retiring to scholarship.[47] Scholars of Timbuktu referred to as saints and ascetics were known to have been quite wealthy.[48] Commerce seems to have been problematic to mystics. Sidi Yahya al-Tadilsi, the patron-saint of Timbuktu, not wanting to depend on donations, became engaged in commerce; gradually, he was deprived of his nightly visionary encounters with the Prophet. "Look," says the author of *Ta'rikh al-Sudan*, "to the misfortune caused by business, even though the blessed *shaykh* had been extremely heedful of what is forbidden in transactions."[49]

Timbuktu was a city of commerce and scholarship. The scholars of Timbuktu were spokesmen of the trading community of the city, which benefited commercially from being part of the Songhay empire. Even legal opinions were influenced by commercial interests; there was, for instance, Ahmad Baba's ruling on the lawfulness of tobacco because Timbuktu was an important center for the tobacco trade.

The Seventeenth and Eighteenth Centuries

Following the Moroccan conquest in 1591, the people of Timbuktu, under the leadership of the qadi, first adopted a policy of passive submission and noncooperation with the conquering army. The 'ulama' and the merchants were called on to provide slaves for the construction of the fort *(qasaba)*. The *shurafa* (believed to be descendents of the prophet Muhammad) led popular discontent and two of them were publicly executed. Timbuktu, after having been autonomous, became the seat of a military government. The presence of the occupying force disturbed life in a city of commerce and scholarship and led to unrest and disobedience of the civilian population, led by merchants and fuqaha'. The pasha and his troops resorted to harsh disciplinary measures, when all conventions were broken. People deposited

73

their valuables in the houses of the fuqaha', which in the past had been considered immune and sanctuary, but the pasha ordered the arrest of the leading fuqaha and let his soldiers pillage their houses and to take away what had been deposited there. Seventy prominent fuqaha' were deported in chains to Marrakesh, among them the qadi 'Umar and Ahmad Baba. The fuqaha' were under arrest in Marrakesh for two years, and the qadi 'Umar died in prison. Even after their release in May 1596, the fuqaha' were not allowed to return to Timbuktu. Only Ahmad Baba returned, after almost twenty years in exile.

After the exile of the fuqaha', according to the author of *Ta'rikh al-Sudan,* Timbuktu "became a body without a soul."[50] The line of qadis from the Aqit family that had held office for about a century was replaced by qadis from other families, but they did not enjoy the authority and prestige of their sixteenth-century predecessors.

During the seventeenth century, the elite of Timbuktu was made up of the *arma,* the descendants of the Moroccan conquerors, who held military and political power. The elite of the civilian population were the merchants and the 'ulama'. Under the rule of Songhay, the 'ulama' had served as spokesmen for the merchants and other sectors of the civil population; they acted as intermediaries with the political authorities. But under the rule of the arma, the political influence of the merchants increased, because the merchants contributed to defray the cost of military operations to secure the Niger waterway and other routes to Timbuktu. The merchants no longer needed the 'ulama' as intermediaries.

By the end of the seventeenth century, the impoverished mercantile community of Timbuktu was no longer able to support a large, specialized, scholarly community. Scholars left Timbuktu and the city went into a period of intellectual decline. Lesser scholars, known as *alfas,* earned their living as traders and artisans, mainly weavers and tailors.

The suffering of the people of Timbuktu increased as the struggle for power among the Moroccan military commanders intensified. The supply of food from the inner delta was cut off as the routes were intercepted by Fulbe and Tuareg. By the middle of the eighteenth century, the pashalik of Timbuktu was in total eclipse. About 1770, the Tuareg took possession of Gao, and in 1787 they entered Timbuktu and abolished the office of the pasha. Not only was military and political ascendancy taken over by the nomads of the southern Sahara; spiritual leadership, too, passed to the clerics of the southern Sahara. The harshness of the nomads was mitigated by the clerics, whose religious prestige also carried political influence, reaching its peak with the revivalist movement led by Sidi al-Mukhtar al-Kunti (1729–1811).

☾ ☾ ☾

Linked by the Niger waterway to Timbuktu, Jenne developed as a distribution center for trade to the south. Merchants from the Sahara and North Africa extended their business from Timbuktu to Jenne. Their agents were Juula, who carried the trade to the sources of gold and kola in the Akan forest (chapter 4).

In Jenne, deep in the world of the Mandingue, Islam gained ground slowly. Pre-Islamic customs persisted there until the end of the fifteenth century, when a pious Juula came to Jenne from the south and destroyed the house of the idols that the people continued to worship.[51] Clerics and scholars in Jenne—all Soninke and Mandingue—were highly respected by the rulers of Jenne, who sought their blessings.[52]

Between Jenne and Timbuktu, the Fulbe pastoralists of Massina, though they remained attached to magical-religious rites and observances to secure the prosperity of their cattle, became exposed to Islamic influences. Clans of Muslim clerics rendered religious services to the Fulbe chiefs, who gradually adopted Muslim names and began to practice some Islamic rites. There had been no signs to suggest that under the leadership of these Fulbe clerics a theocratic state would be established through jihad in Massina.

The Bambara state of Segu was established in the first half of the eighteenth century by Biton Kulibali, who forced greater centralization to overcome older egalitarian patterns of Bambara communal life. He was supported by Muslim merchants and clerics, but was careful to maintain the balance between traditional and Islamic elements.

It was customary for chiefs to send their sons to study with a Muslim cleric as part of their princely education. Though they were not meant to become Muslims, some of them did, and even turned scholars. A qadi of Jenne in the second half of the sixteenth century was "from among the sons of the chiefs of Kala. He withdrew from authority and became a scholar."[53] In this way, Bakary, the son of Biton Kulibali, became a Muslim. When he succeeded his father (c. 1755), the prospects of a growing Islamic influence at the court was unacceptable to the *ton-dyon,* the core of Biton's supporters, and Bakary was deposed and killed.

Ngolo Diara, a former slave of Biton Kulibali, seized power and established a new dynasty in Segu. Ngolo had spent some years in Jenne with an important Muslim cleric and was influenced by Islam, but he was also steeped in the Bambara traditions. He had been appointed by Biton Kulibali to the office of the "guardian of the four cults of Segu," one of the principal posts of the Segu state, and Ngolo retained this position after Biton's death. It was in the central shrine that he gathered the warriors in his move to seize power.[54] Ngolo skillfully maintained the balance between traditionalism and Islam. Muslim clerics extended their religious services at his court and the Muslim trading communities enjoyed the protection of the Bambara state. Though Ngolo followed Islamic customs, he also remained the great priest of the protecting idols.[55]

As subjects of the Islamized empires of Mali and Songhay, the Bambara had hardly been influenced by Islam, and might have even exhibited a tendency to resist Islam. But when Bambara clans became themselves involved in the process of state-building, their chiefs became exposed to Islamic influence. As ruling dynasties, the

Kulibali and the Diara became culturally differentiated from the peasants, though they shared with them most practices and beliefs. Through chiefly courts, where Islamic rituals were held, Islamic elements penetrated also the culture of the common Bambara, including the celebration of Islamic festivals as national feasts.[56] The Bambara worship Ngalla (Allah), but because they have a sense of impurity, they call on the help of Muslim clerics to approach him.[57]

Mungo Park, who visited Segu in 1796 during the reign of Mansong Ngolo's, was impressed by the influence of Muslims at the court of Segu. Mansong, he said, "would willingly have admitted me into his presence at Sego; but was apprehensive he might not be able to protect me against the blind and inveterate malice of the Moorish inhabitants."[58] In the rival Bambara state of Kaarta, Mungo Park observed that "the disciples of Mahomet composed nearly one half of the army," and therefore "the mosques were very crowded" when the whole army gathered into the capital. Mungo Park, however, recognized the persistence of pre-Islamic beliefs and practices, saying: "Those Negroes, together with the ceremonial part of the Mahomedan religion, retain all their ancient superstitions and even drink strong liquors."[59]

(((

The Maraka were Soninke that came to live among the Malinke and the Bambara, whose language they adopted. Bambara or Bobo that converted to Islam became identified as Maraka.[60] Whereas, during the age of the great empires, Islam had been mainly an urban phenomenon, restricted to merchants and scholars, in the seventeenth and eighteenth centuries Muslims made inroads into the countryside and won adherents among peasants and fishermen, who until then had hardly been influenced by Islam.

In the midst of the general sense of insecurity, caused by the violence generated by the demand for slaves, Muslims traveled as traders or pilgrims, and in pursuit of learning. Though there were cases of Muslims who were captured and sold as slaves, Muslims were generally immune and safe. They were protected by the reverence for their supernatural powers and found hospitality among fellow Muslims in the commercial communities that developed along the trade routes.

Muslims among the Bambara are known as Maraka, and they consist of two groups: one is made up of those early Soninke Muslims who claim to have migrated from Wagadugu (i.e., old Ghana); the other group were Bambara who had converted to Islam and assumed the identity of Maraka.

In the eighteenth century, when there was an abundant supply of slaves, the Maraka owned more slaves for farming than did the Bambara. Whereas Bambara peasants owned a few slaves who worked in the field together with members of the household, the Maraka owned many slaves who worked in the fields under the supervision of a foreman, himself a slave. The Maraka master was then able to follow his commercial or clerical pursuits. Slave farming became the economic basis for Islamic scholarship. The most elaborated tradition of rural scholarship was developed by the Jakhanke, about whom more will be said in the next chapter.

Islam in the Senegambia during the Eighteenth Century

Islam in the area of present-day Senegal was always somewhat different from other parts of Bilad al-Sudan; it resembled more the Sahara and the Maghrib, particularly in the role of holymen (marabouts). This might be explained by the continuous habitation in the western parts of the Sahara, from Morocco to the Senegal River, where the ocean's influence moderates the harsh desert conditions. In the central parts of the Sahara, on the other hand, the nomads lived only in oases, separated by stretches of inhabitable desert. It was therefore on the lower Senegal River that contacts between the Saharan nomads and black sedentaries were more intensive.

Indeed, in the eleventh century the recently converted Juddala nomads reached the land of the black sedentaries of the Senegal valley, and this might explain the Islamic militancy in Takrur, as described by al-Bakri. Its king, War-Jabi, who pursued an Islamic militant policy, died in 1040, about the time 'Abdallah ibn Yasin first arrived in the southern Sahara. "When 'Abdallah ibn Yasin saw that the Juddala turned away from him, and followed their own passions, he wanted to leave them, and to go to live among the Sudanese, who had already adopted Islam." By that time, therefore, the teaching of Islam had found a fertile ground in Takrur. Labi, son of War Jabi, was an ally of the Almoravids.[61]

Writing in 1286, Ibn Sa'id first noted the distinction between the sedentary Tokolor and the nomad Fulbe, saying that the people of Takrur "are divided into two sections; a section who have become sedentary and live in towns, and a section who are nomads in the open country."[62] Beyond that, there is no information about Takrur, or Futa Toro, as the area is known, except for oral traditions that are difficult to interpret. But toward the end of the fifteenth century, Portuguese sources and the chronicles of Timbuktu converge to throw light on a process of state-building led by a Fulbe warrior by the name of Tengella. He first created a Fulbe state in the Futa Jallon and then moved farther north to Futa Toro. In 1512, after Tengella had been defeated and killed by a Songhay army, the conquest of the Futa Toro was accomplished by his son Koli Tengella, who created the Deniankobe dynasty of Futa Toro.[63]

According to the author of *Tarikh al-Sudan*, a seventeenth-century scholar from Timbuktu, the descendants of Koli Tengella were considered to be good Muslims as the rulers of Mali. Of Koli's second son he says that he was "equal in justice of Mansa Musa of Mali," and of his contemporary Samba Lam, Koli's grandson, who ruled in the first half of the seventeenth century, al-Sa'di says that he "pursued justice and prohibited iniquity."[64] But the Torodbe, the clerics of Futa Toro, viewed the Deniankobe as warrior chiefs. At the interface of the Sahara and the Senegal valley, warriors were in confrontation with Muslim clerics.

The term Torodbe, as the clerics of Futa Toro were known, covered persons of diverse social status and ethnic origin. They spoke Fulfulde and embraced customs of the pastoral Fulbe, but they were sedentaries, and not necessarily of Fulbe origin. The maxim "Torodbe is a beggar" associated them with the mendicant activities of Muslim clerics and students, who lived on charity. The openness of the Torodbe society is expressed in another maxim: if a fisherman pursues learning he becomes a Torodo. In Futa Toro, learning among the Torodbe was at a lower level compared with the scholarship of their Toronkawa brethren, whom we meet later in this chapter in Hausaland. The Torodbe of Futa Toro were an integral part of the peasant society, unlike the Toronkawa of Hausaland, who separated themselves from both the Fulbe pastoralists and the Hausa-speaking peasants. Though the Toronkawa lived in rural enclaves, they cultivated an urban tradition of learning.

The symbiotic relations between the Deniankobe and the Torodbe had first been disturbed in 1673, when the Torodbe joined the militant movement of Nasir al-Din that spilled over from the southern Sahara to the Futa Toro. This jihad was defeated by a coalition of the Deniankobe and the Arab warrior tribes of the Sahara. The nomads of the Sahara, north of the Senegal river, continued during the eighteenth century to disturb life in the Futa Toro. The Torodbe rose again in the 1770s against the Deniankobe that had failed to stop the nomads' raids. This uprising developed into a jihad movement that overthrew the Deniankobe and created an Islamic imamate in the Futa Toro.

Oral traditions connected the history of the Wolof to the Almoravids through the founding king of Jolof, who is said to have been a descendant of Abu Bakr b. ʿUmar.[65] The Grand Jolof was one of the great Muslim states in medieval West Africa. It was for some time a tributary of Mali, but because its marginal position and its own direct commercial relations with the Sahara, Jolof was autonomous culturally and economically. The kingdom of Jolof disintegrated in the sixteenth century under the impact of the Atlantic trade. Kayor, which had been part of Jolof, emerged as the most powerful state of the Wolof, due to its favorable position on the coast and the benefits it derived from the trade with the Europeans. Intensive commercial activities and a process of political centralization enhanced the position of Muslims in Kayor. Early in its history, the son and successor of the first independent king *(damel)* of Kayor, became known as "the clerical *Damel*." He refrained from drinking alcohol and preferred the companionship of clerics. But Islam remained marginal in Kayor, and the growing influence of the Muslims in the court was counterbalanced by the *tyeddo,* the core of the damel's military power, and by the *griots,* the custodians of the traditional heritage.

European visitors since the middle of the fifteenth century were impressed by the role of Muslims in the courts of the Wolof chiefs as secretaries, counselors, and divines. They described the Wolof chiefs as Muslims who observed the prayers, but added that "they render it almost unrecognizable with a multitude of omissions and additions."[66] It is significant, however, that neither in the European sources nor in the oral traditions is there any account of a viable traditional African religion among the Wolof. Oral traditions know no other religion than Islam from the dawn of Wolof history. It seems that most vestiges of organized traditional religion were eliminated under the influence of Islam. Minor cults survived only among women and castes. Muslim clerics took over functions of the traditional priests, and even magic became the prerogative of Muslim clerics.[67]

Most of the clerics In the Wolof courts were of foreign origin—Znaga or Arabs from the Sahara, Tokolor from Futa Toro, and Mandingue-speaking from Mali. The Wolof rulers kept the clerics as an isolated community, not permitted to marry into families of the nobility. Sons of the nobility who took too seriously their Quranic studies and became disciples of a cleric or married his daughter lost whatever rights they might have had to political office. The political and military elite were a warrior class for whom drinking alcohol became a symbol of belonging. We have already referred to the tensions and confrontation between clerics and warriors. The growing influence of the Muslims in the court was counterbalanced by the tyeddo. For the military and political elite, conversion to Islam implied joining the clerical community and change of vocation and lifestyle. The Wolof chiefs therefore rejected demands by Muslim militants to convert.

In the eighteenth century, in the aftermath of the failure of the first jihad, in an attempt at reconciliation, clerics were given, for the first time, territorial chieftaincies. The royal family also sought to cement its relations with the clergy through political marriages. It was expected that by involving the clergy in the political life, the danger of another religious insurgency would be avoided. But in the 1770s, following a successful jihad in the Futa Toro, Wolof cleric collaborated with the militants. They were severely punished, and even sold into slavery, which was a violation of the clerical immunity.

Confrontation with the militant Islamic movements changed political perceptions toward Islam. Whereas earlier European accounts referred to the Wolof as Muslims, later European travelers, from the end of the eighteenth century and throughout the nineteenth century, say that the Wolof were Muslims but their rulers were "pagans." It has been only since the end of the nineteenth century that the whole Wolof society converted to Islam.

☾ ☾ ☾

Further south from Futa Toro and the Wolof, the Portuguese, followed by other Europeans, sailed up the Gambia River, where they were impressed by the number of Muslims on the Gambia. Their numbers increased with the intensification of the Atlantic trade. In 1621, Jobson described Muslim traders on the Gambia who had "free recourse through all places," even in times of war.[68] These were the Jakhanke, who represented the western extension of the Mandingue-speaking trade system. In 1698, Andre Brue found the Jakhanke "confederated in a way that they formed a republic, . . . [with] a considerable town called Conjour, built of stone, where the greatest merchants live, serves as the capital of the marabouts' republic."[69] The near-contemporary author of *Tarikh al-Fattash* confirmed that Conjour was autonomous "under the authority of the qadi and the 'ulama'. No warrior may enter the town, and no tyrant has ever lived there."[70]

The founders of the Mandingue states on the Gambia migrated from the territories of the empire of Mali. They were accompanied by clerics, who played roles similar to those in other states. The Muslim traders on the Gambia carried the slave trade in response to a growing demand by the Europeans on the coast. They controlled also the supply of firearms, bought from the Europeans, which made them an asset but also a potential threat to the rulers.

Islam in Kanem and Bornu

An early trans-Saharan route connected Tripoli on the Mediterranean with Lake Chad in Bilad al-Sudan. Kanem emerged as one of the earliest African kingdoms on the northeastern corner of Lake Chad. Its founders were the Zaghawa nomads of the central Sahara. In the middle of the tenth century, the Egyptian al-Muhallabi described the religion of the Zaghawa in Kanem as divine kingship: "They exalt their king and worship him instead of Allah. They imagine that he does not eat any food. He has unlimited authority over his subjects. Their religion is the worship of kings, for they believe that they bring life and death, sickness and health."[71]

Traits of divine kingship survived at the court of the *mai* (the title of the kings of Kanem and Bornu) long after their conversion to Islam. In the middle of the fourteenth century, Ibn Battuta reports that the king of Bornu "does not appear to the people and does not address them except from behind a curtain."[72]

Kanem became Muslim at the beginning of the twelfth century. Its Saifawa dynasty claimed descent from the legendary Arab hero Sayf b. Dhi Yazan.[73] By the thirteenth century, Islam gained almost universal adherence in Kanem. Its king was "well known for his religious warfare and charitable acts, . . . [with] scholars around him."[74] In the first half of the thirteenth century, the king of Kanem went on pilgrimage; he also built a *madrasa* in Cairo for students from Kanem.[75] About the same time, a devout Muslim king broke with tradition, as recounted in a sixteenth-century chronicle in Arabic: "In the possession of the Saifawa there was a certain thing wrapped up and hidden away, whereon depended their victory in war. It was called Mune and no one dared to open it. Then the sultan Dunama son of Dabale wished to break it open. His people warned him, but he refused to listen to them. He opened it, and whatever was inside flew away."[76] Traditions suggest that this breach of tradition alienated the Bulala clan, of more traditionalist disposition, and in the hostilities that followed, the Saifawa were forced to abandon Kanem on the northeastern corner of Lake Chad. They resettled in Bornu, on the southwestern corner of Lake Chad, in the middle of the fourteenth century. But the Saifawa consolidated their hold over the new country only toward the end of the fifteenth century, with the establishment of the capital at N'Gazargamu.

This was during the reign of ʿAli Ghaji b. Dunama (1476–1503), who is remembered as an exemplary Muslim, a contemporary of other reformist rulers in Bilad al-Sudan, like Rumfa of Kano and Askiya Muhammad of Songhay. He was also the first ruler of Bornu who assumed the title of caliph. The claim to the caliphate might have been in response to a similar claim by Askiya Muhammad. ʿAli Ghaji visited Cairo on his way to Mecca in 1484 and met Jalal al-Din al-Suyuti. It is likely that it was al-Suyuti who obtained the title of caliph from the ʿAbbasid caliph in Cairo.

The Bornu caliphate reached its peak under Mai Idris Alawma (1570–1603), when all the state dignitaries were Muslims and the capital N'Gazargamu was an important center for Islamic learning. Qadis, imams, and teachers were granted privileges and were exempted from taxation. The Shariʿa was considered the law of the state, which is said to have been imposed on the whole population.[77]

Until the sixteenth century, Kanem and Bornu expanded only northward, along the Saharan routes. Bornu did not expand to the lands south of Lake Chad, which were reserved as a hunting ground for slaves. But following the Ottoman annexation of Fezzan in 1577, Bornu turned south because northward expansion was blocked.

About the same time, late in the sixteenth century, the state of Bagirmi emerged in a region that had formerly been raided for slaves. The rulers of Bagirmi became Islamized, but, as late as the middle of the nineteenth century, Barth commented on Bagirmi: "Their adoption of Islam is very recent, and the greater part of them may, even at the present day, with more justice be called pagans than Mohammedans."[78]

The mai of Bornu generously supported scholars and attracted students from far and wide. Scholars from Bornu went to study at Al-Azhar in Cairo, where the madrasa that had been established in the thirteenth century was still in existence in the eighteenth century. The mai issued mahram to encourage the integration of Muslims of different ethnic origins: Fulbe from Hausaland, Tubu from the central Sahara, and North Africans. These privileges gave these foreigners the sense of belonging to Bornu society and a stake in the political economy of Bornu. By the end of the eighteenth century, Islam was deeply rooted in everyday life of the ordinary man, affecting him from the naming ceremony to his funeral.[79] This was admitted even by Muhammad Bello: "Islam was widespread not only among the rulers and ministers, but also among the local people. Indeed there are not to be found in these countries ordinary people more scrupulous than they in reciting the Quran and reading it and memorizing it and writing it out."[80]

But even in Bornu, perhaps the most Islamized of all African states, pre-Islamic elements persisted. The most damaging criticism of the contemporary scene was by a Kanuri scholar Muhammad b. al-Hajj Abd al-Rahman al-Barnawi (d. 1755), known as Hajirmai. He accused the rulers of Bornu of being tyrants and corrupt, and of imposing illegal taxation; the rich, he said, hoarded food at times of famine in the hope of profit; and judges and governors he charged with accepting gifts.

There also were allegations of human sacrifices at the time of the annual flood in the River Komadugu Yobe, and of libations of milk from a black cow before the annual repairs to the city wall.[81] These accusations were echoed by Muhammad Bello as a pretext for the jihad against Bornu: "Their rulers and chiefs have places to which they ride, and where they offer sacrifices and then pour the blood on the gates of their towns. . . . They also perform rites to the river."[82] 'Ulama' who collaborated with the rulers of Bornu were criticized by radical scholars, who withdrew from the centers of political power to establish autonomous religious communities. But even they received mahrams to encourage and sustain the development of Islamic learning in these enclaves of rural scholarship, known as *mallamati*. These communities jealously guarded their autonomy and maintained minimal communications with the state. The mallamati were in fact sufi communities in rural enclaves that performed mystical exercises, including retreats in the bush. Like their contemporary sufis in Timbuktu, they claimed no tariqa affiliation.[83]

Islam in Hausaland before the Jihad

In the whole corpus of Arabic sources for West African history, there is but one reference to the Hausa states; this lone exception is that of Ibn Battuta, who mentioned Gobir (Kubar) as one of the destinations for the export of the copper of Takedda.[84] Because Arab geographers were acquainted only with those regions of Bilad al-Sudan that had commercial relations with North Africa, it follows that Hausaland was not directly connected to the Saharan trade. This is confirmed by the Kano Chronicle, our principal source for the development of Islam in Hausaland.[85] According to the chronicle, it was only in the middle of the fifteenth century that salt caravans came from Air (Asben) in the north and kola caravans came from Gonja in the southwest.

Islam had first been introduced less than a century earlier, at the time of Yaji, king of Kano (1349–1385), when Wangara traders and clerics came from Mali in the west. "When they came they ordered the Sarki to observe the times of prayer, and he complied. . . . The Sarki ordered every town in the country of Kano to observe the times of prayer. . . . A mosque was built beneath the sacred tree facing east, and prayers were made at the five appointed times in it." The chief priest was opposed to the prayer, "and when the Muslims after praying had gone home, he would come with his men and defile the whole mosque and cover it with filth. The Muslim prayed and the Chief of the Pagans was struck blind together with all the pagans who were present at the defilement." The custodians of the traditional religion were defeated on their own ground by a superior magical power. The efficacy of the new religion was tested when the Muslims brought victory to Yeji, the king of Kano, over his most forceful enemy. But when Yeji's son Kanajeji (1390–1410) failed to win a war, he turned back to the traditional priest, who promised his help if the king restored the rites that his father had abandoned. Kanajeji complied, and the traditional priest secured victory over the enemies. Islam temporarily lost ground.

The second generation reverted to the traditional religion, but the third generation turned over completely to Islam. In Kano, as in other African states, kings' sons received elementary Quranic instruction. A few of them went beyond what was expected from princes and became sincere Muslims. 'Umaru, son of Kanajeji (1410–21), was a pupil of the son of one of the Wangarawa who had come in the time of Yaji. When he became king of Kano, his friend Abu Bakr left Kano for Bornu, where he remained eleven years. On his return to Kano, finding 'Umaru still king of Kano, he said to him: "O 'Umaru, you still like the fickle dame who has played you false." He preached to him about the next world, its pains and punishments, and reviled this world and everything in it. 'Umaru said: "I accept your admonition." He called together all the people of Kano and said to them: "This high estate is a trap for the erring: I wash my hands of it." Then he resigned and went away with his friend. He spent the rest of his life in regret for his actions while he had been king. This tradition, once again, demonstrates the built-in contradiction between being a warrior chief and being a Muslim.

The coming of Islam to Kano coincided with the shift of the Saifawa dynasty from Kanem to Bornu, where they became close neighbors of the Hausa states. Though the first Muslim clerics came from Mali in the west, it seems that Islamic influence from Bornu was at least as important.

Islamic learning in Hausaland became upgraded with the coming of the Fulani in the middle of the fifteenth century. They were the so-called "settled Fulani," Torodbe or Toronkawa. They lived in rural enclaves, where they cultivated their tradition of learning. Unlike the urban scholars of Timbuktu, they were not strangers to horsemanship and warfare. They did not render religious services to local rulers and were therefore not involved in non-Islamic ceremonies. They communicated with the rulers, but did not become integrated into the political system. The tensions generated by that mental and physical distance later led to the confrontation and to the jihad.

Islam became integrated into the religious, social, and cultural life of the Hausa without a break with the past. Those who called for a reform were, according to the Kano Chronicle, shurafa', and their leader was 'Abdur-Rahman. He is later identified in the text with Abdu-Karimi, undoubtedly Abd al-Karim al-Maghili, the North African militant scholar, who left his impact both in Kano and in Songhay. He ordered Rumfa, the king of Kano, to cut the sacred tree under which the original mosque had been built which symbolized the symbiosis of Islam and the remnants of the traditional religion. Muhammad Rumfa was the contemporary of the reformist kings of Songhay, Askiya Muhammad, and Bornu, 'Ali Ghaji.

In Kano, as in Bornu, piety and scholarship among the kings peaked in the second half of the sixteenth century. Ramfa's son Abu Bakr Kado (1565–73) did nothing but religious offices. He disdained the duties of king. He and all his chiefs spent their time in prayer. He was the king who made the princes learn the Quran. But then the traditional religion surfaced again at the time of Mohammad Zaki (1582–1618), with the appearance of syncretistic practices, such as the veneration of the Dirki, a Quran covered with layers of goatskin. Facing the recurring attacks by the Kworarafa and Katsina in the seventeenth and eighteenth centuries, the kings of Kano sought relief in rituals and magic from both "non-Muslim" priests and local Muslim clerics. Kano chiefs vacillated between traditional and Islamic rituals, depending on which promised to produce the best results. The cult of *bori* spirits was the most common pre-Islamic survival in Hausaland, mainly among women. Bori spirits were given Muslim names, and Muslim *jinns* (demons) became identified with the bori spirits. Indeed, the fact that the bori spirits became Islamized made it more difficult to eradicate them.

Until the nineteenth century, Katsina, north of Kano, was the most important commercial town in Hausaland. Indeed, the Wangara in Katsina maintained their identity over a period of four hundred years; as late as the middle of the nineteenth century, Barth observed that most of the merchants of Katsina were Wangara.[86] Toward the end of the fifteenth century, the leaders of the Wangara community of Muslim clerics and traders in Katsina felt strong enough to take over political power, and Muhammad Korau, a cleric, became the king of Katsina. Ibrahim Sura (1493–98), the second Muslim ruler of Katsina after Korau, is referred to by al-Suyuti in a treatise addressed to the kings and sultans of Takrur.[87] The general thrust of this treatise indicates that Islam was still relatively a new element in the social and political structure. The Muslim rulers of Katsina were not completely successful in their efforts to turn Katsina into an Islamic state. In the face of strong resistance, they were forced to reach an agreement with the *durbi,* the priest-chief. The outcome was a sort of dual paramountcy, in which the durbi was responsible for choosing the king. Kingship in Katsina took on the characteristics of a sacred traditional kingship.

The reformer of Islam in Katsina was Ibrahim Maje (1549–66). He ordered implementation of the Shariʿa laws of marriage and threatened to arrest those who transgressed the religious prescriptions. The number of scholars in his time increased considerably. Scholars from Timbuktu, who visited Kano and Katsina on their way to Mecca, taught there for some time and contributed to the growth of local Hausa scholarship. During the seventeenth century, scholarship in Katsina was associated with Muhammad b. al-Sabbagh (fl. 1650), known in Hausaland as Dan Marina. He gathered around him a scholarly community that was well versed in all the branches of Islamic learning. Some members of a self-conscious Muslim intelligentsia were employed at the court, but the leading roles in the administration were held by slaves and eunuchs.

One of the last kings of Katsina before the jihad, Gozo (c. 1795–1801), was closer to Islam than many of his predecessors. He built mosques and supported the Shariʿa, but even he was involved in the worship of traditional deities, because the legitimacy of the dynasty continued to be embedded in the traditional belief system. His actions were those of a ruler who was genuinely torn by a dilemma between two systems of religious beliefs. The slaves of the palace opposed the attempts of Gozo to impose the Shariʿa, and they made his successor Bawa dan Gima a tool in their hands.

Scholars who were alienated from the rulers preferred to live on the periphery of Katsina, in towns within a radius of fifteen kilometers from the capital; there, they enjoyed greater autonomy, and the mosques of these towns attracted more people to pray than those of the larger city. It was from these small towns that the supporters of the jihad of dan Fodio came. The rulers ignored them because of their small numbers and their peripheral location, away from the major centers of the population and political power.

The old town of Yandoto, founded by Wangara traders and clerics, prospered with the growth of trade in kola nuts from the Volta basin in the second half of the eighteenth century. This prosperous Muslim community preferred the status quo and opposed the jihad of 'Uthman dan Fodio.[88]

Background to the Jihads

The rise of Islamic militancy in the eighteenth and nineteenth centuries was a radical departure from earlier patterns of relationship between Muslim clerics and scholars, who had been outside the field of political competition, and chiefs, who though not practicing Muslims were not considered unbelievers. This change came about as a result of several factors.

All the jihad movements were carried by Fulfulde-speaking groups, Fulbe pastoralists under the leadership of Torodbe or Toronkawa scholars. Their role should be viewed in the wider context of the expansion of Islam from town to countryside. It is significant that all leaders of the jihad movements in West Africa came from the countryside and not from commercial or capital towns. The challenge to the marginal role of Islam in African societies could not have come from those who benefited from the existing political order—neither from traders who were protected by the rulers nor from clerics who rendered religious services in the chiefly courts.

The new Muslim leaders articulated the grievances of the peasants. In Hausaland, 'Uthman dan Fodio criticized the rulers for killing people, violating their honor, and devouring their wealth. He declared that "to make war upon the oppressor is obligatory by assent."[89] 'Uthman's son, the sultan Muhammad Bello, evoked the wrath of Allah over "the *amir* (ruler) who draws his sustenance from the people but does not bother to treat them justly."[90]

The expansion of Islam to the countryside widened the popular basis for religious teaching and preaching. The dissemination of the knowledge of Islam to the illiterate peasants and herdsmen could have been only in the vernacular languages. Parallel to the transformation of Islam as a popular religion and as a political force, Muslim societies gradually developed a pious literature. The oldest known written texts in Fulfulde date from the second part of the eighteenth century. These poems were written by reformers who sought to reach people of all walks of life. Poems, easily committed to memory and therefore an excellent pedagogical device, became a major vehicle for teaching and preaching (chapters 19 and 23). Vernacular poems were disseminated in handwritten copies among groups of Muslim literati and were then recited in public.[91]

'Abdallah dan Fodio described the role of the vernacular verse: "Then we rose up with the Shaykh, helping him in his mission work for religion. He traveled for that purpose to the east and west, calling people to the religion of God by his preaching and his *qasidas* [poems] in *ajami* [the vernacular], and destroying customs contrary to Muslim law."[92] When the shaykh saw that his community was ready for the jihad, "he began to incite them to arms . . . and he set this in verse in his non-Arabic Qadiri poem *(qasida 'ajamiyya qadiriyya).*" This mystical verse had a hypnotic effect upon devotees on the eve of the jihad.[93]

Muhammad Tukur (d. 1817), a companion of Dan Fodio, composed poems in Fulfulde and in Hausa. One of his poems, "Bringers of Good Tidings," is said to have had such an impact that on the day it was composed, possibly in 1789, "forty persons repented and entered the Sunna of the Prophet."[94] Islamic vernacular literature appeared also—about the same time, in the seventeenth and eighteenth centuries—in East Africa, the Indian subcontinent, and Southeast Asia. Everywhere mystical verse was the earliest and most widespread literary genre. This, one may argue, is because all over the Muslim world there were renewal movements in the eighteenth century, which developed out of restructured and reformed sufi brotherhoods. As already mentioned, there were sufi ideas and practices in Timbuktu and Hausaland in the fifteenth and sixteenth centuries, but there is no evidence of sufi brotherhoods in West Africa before the eighteenth century.

The Qadiriyya brotherhood had first been introduced into the Sahara probably at the end of the fifteenth century. But the Qadiriyya had been loosely organized and rather ineffective until its resurgence, in the second half of the eighteenth century, under the leadership of Sidi al-Mukhtar al-Kunti. He skillfully used his religious prestige to acquire wealth and political influence, as individuals and tribal factions sought his patronage. He reinforced the dependency of these clients by fostering the spiritual chains of the Qadiriyya. His emissaries spread the new branch, known as Qadiriyya-Mukhtariyya, in the Sahara, the Sahel, and as far as Futa Jallon. Sidi al-Mukhtar did not advocate militant jihad, and his son and grandson opposed the jihad of Shaykh Ahmad of Massina and that of Al-Hajj 'Umar. But Sidi al-Mukhtar, the nonmilitant sufi, supported the jihad of 'Uthman dan Fodio: "It was he, according to what we hear, who roused the people to follow what Shaykh 'Uthman said."[95]

In 'Uthman's own career, mystical experiences were of great significance. In 1794, he had a mystical encounter with 'Abd al-Qadir al-Jilani, who girded him with the "Sword of Truth" to draw against the enemies of Allah. Ten years later, in another visionary encounter, 'Abd al-Qadir al-Jilani instructed 'Uthman dan Fodio to perform the pilgrimage to Degel, which was the last stage before the jihad.[96]

Notes

1. Ibn Abi Zayd al-Qayrawani, in Levtzion and Hopkins 1981, *Corpus of Early Arabic Sources for West African History* (hereafter, *Corpus*), 55.

2. al-Bakri, in *Corpus*, 77.

3. al-Zuhri, in *Corpus*, 98.

4. al-Idrisi, in *Corpus*, 109.

5. al-Bakri, in *Corpus*, 81–82.

6. Ibid., 82–83.

7. Horton 1975, 374–75.

8. Ibn Khaldun, in *Corpus*, 322–23.

9. al-Umari, in *Corpus*, 261; *Ta'rikh al-Sudan* (hereafter TS) text 7/translation 13.

10. Ibn Battuta, in *Corpus*, 292–93.

11. Ibn Battuta, in *Corpus*, 296–97.

12. al-Bakri, in *Corpus*, 80.

13. Ibn Battuta, in *Corpus*, 292. Ibn Juzayy, to whom Ibn Battuta dictated his story, added at that point that an ambassador from Mansa Sulayman followed the custom back home and sprinkled dust on his head before the Moroccan sultan. Ibn Khaldun (ibid., 342) also describes the sprinkling of dust by a Malian mission before the Moroccan sultan.

14. Ibn Battuta, ibid., 296.

15. al-Umari, ibid., 268.

16. *Ta'rikh al-Fattash* (hereafter, TF), text 179/translation 314.

17. al-Bakri, in *Corpus*, 79.

18. Ibn Battuta, in *Corpus*, 299.

19. For this date, see Ibn Hajar al-Asklani, in *Corpus*, 358.

20. For this date, see al-Maqqari, in *Corpus*, 321.

21. Leo Africanus 1956, ii, 467.

22. TS 66/91; see also TF 32/56.

23. Ibn Khaldun, in *Corpus*, 334.

24. TS 67/92.

25. TF 51/83–84.

26. Ibid.

27. Ibid., 47–48/78; TS text 16, 28, 61/translation 29, 78, 99–100; Ibn Battuta, in *Corpus*, 287.

28. TS 21/36–37.

29. Ibid., 67/109.

30. al-Ifrani, 75–76.

31. Ibid., 60/116

32. TF 61/117.

33. Baba 1931–32, 218; Hunwick 1996, 186.

34. Hunwick 1996, 181n.

35. TS 83–84/139–40; cf. Hunwick 1996, 190–91.

36. Hunwick 1996, 182; TS 83/138, 109/178; TF 118/216–17.

37. TF 110/202–3.

38. TF 114/209–10.

39. TS 122–30/196–208; the quotation is 129/205.

40. TF 180/315–16.

41. Sartain 1971, 194.

42. Baba 1931–32, 114.

43. Hunwick 1970, 29–30.

44. Levtzion 1997, 153–54.

45. TS 34/55; TF 107, 109/198, 201.

46. *Tadhkirat al-Nisyan* (hereafter TN) 87/141; TS 254/389.

47. Baba 1931–32, 344; TS 39/64.

48. TS 34/56; TF 212–13/222–24.

49. TS, 50–51/82–83.

50. TF 175/308.

51. TS 17–18/31.

52. Ibid., 18/31–32; Hunwick 1996, 187–88.

53. TS 19/34.

54. Roberts 1975, 43.

55. Ibid.

56. Tauxier 1927, 186–92.

57. Ibid., 186–92.

58. Park 1928, 200.

59. Ibid., 195.

60. Gallais 1967, 109–14.

61. al-Bakri, in *Corpus,* 73, 77; Ibn Abi Zar, in *Corpus,* 239.

62. Ibn Sa'id, in *Corpus,* 184.

63. Boulegue 1987, 155–60.

64. TS 77/128.

65. Boulegue 1987, 33–35.

66. Colvin 1974, 593, quoting Durand in 1802, whose report she found at the archives of AOF, Dakar. See also Boulegue 1987, 98.

67. This is convincingly argued by Colvin 1974.

68. Jobson 1932, 17–18, 84, 106.

69. Labat 1728, iii, 335, 371, 338.

70. TF 179–80/314–15.

71. Quoted by Yaqut in *Corpus,* 171.

72. Ibn Battuta, in *Corpus,* 302.

73. *K. al-Istibsar,* in *Corpus,* 138; Ibn Sa'id, ibid., 188.

74. Ibn Sa'id, in *Corpus,* 188.

75. al-Maqrizi, in *Corpus,* 353.

76. Palmer 1936, 184.

77. Ibn Fartuwa 1926, 12–13, 20, 33.

78. Barth 1857, ii, 561.

79. Lavers 1971, 39.

80. Bello 1951.

81. Lavers 1971, 39–42; Bivar and Hiskett, 1/12.

83. Lavers 1971, 32–34.

84. Ibn Battuta, in *Corpus,* 302.

85. The Kano Chronicle, in Palmer 1928, iii, 104–15.

86. Barth 1857, ii, 82.

87. See text in *Tanbih al-Ikhwan,* in Palmer 1914, 407–14.

88. See Bello 1951, 104, on the *mallams* of Yandoto.

89. 'Uthman dan Fodio 1961, 241.

90. Muhammad Bello 1921, 80.

91. Sow 1966, 12–16; Seydou 1973, 184; Hiskett 1957, passim; Brenner and Last 1985, 434.

92. Abdallah dan Fodio 1963, 85.

93. Ibid., 105.

94. Haafkens 1983, 412; Hiskett 1975, 32.

95. Abdallah dan Fodio 1963, 104.

96. Martin 1976, 20; Hiskett 1973, 66.

Bibliography

'Abdallah dan Fodio. 1963. *Tazyin al-waraqat.* Ed. and trans. M. Hiskett. Ibadan: Ibadan University Press.

Abitbol, M. 1979. *Tombouctou et les Arma.* Paris: G. P. Maisonneuve.

Ahmad Baba. 1931–32. *Nayl al-ibtihaj bi-tabriz al-dibaj.* Cairo.

Barth, H. 1857. *Travels and Discoveries in North and Central Africa.* London (reprinted by Frank Cass, 1968).

Bello, Muhammad. 1951. *Infaq al-Maysur.* Ed. C. E. J. Whitting. London.

———. 1971. *Usul al-Siyasa.* Ed. and trans. B. G. Martin. In *Aspects of West African Islam,* ed. D. F. McCall and N. R. Bennet. Boston: African Studies Program.

Bivar, A. D. H. and M. Hiskett. 1962. "The Arabic Literature of Nigeria to 1804," *Bulletin of the School of Oriental and African Studies* 25:104–48.

Bobboyi, Hamidu. 1992. "The 'Ulama' of Borno: A Study of the Relations between Scholars and the State under the Sayfawa (1407–1808)," Ph.D. thesis, Northwestern University.

———. 1993. "Relations of the Borno *'ulama'* with the Sayfawa Rulers: The Role of the *Mahrams,*" *Sudanic Africa* 4:175–204.

Boulegue, J. 1987. *Le Grand Jolof.* Blois: Editions Facades.

Brenner, L., and M. Last. 1985. "The Role of Language in West African Islam," *Africa* 55:432–46.

Colvin, L. G. 1974. "Islam and the State of Kajoor: A Case of Successful Resistance to Jihad," *Journal of African History* 15:587–606.

———. 1987. "The Shaykh's Men: Religion and Power in Senegambian Islam." In *Rural and Urban Islam,* ed. N. Levtzion and H. J. Fisher, 55–65. Boulder, Colo: Lynne Riener.

Ibn Fartuwa, Ahmad. 1926. *History of the First Twelve Years of the Reign of Mai Idris Aloma of Bornu (1571–1583),* trans. H. R. Palmer. Lagos: The Government Printer.

Fisher, H. J. 1973. "Conversion Reconsidered: Some Historical Aspects of Religious Conversion in Black Africa," *Africa* 43:27–40.

Gallais, J. 1967. *Le delta intérieur du Niger.* Dakar: IFAN.

Haafkens, J. 1983. *Chants musulmans en peul: textes de l'héritage musulmane de la communaute mususlmane de Maroua, Cameroun.* Leiden: E. J. Brill.

al-Hajj, M. A. 1968. "A Seventeenth Century Chronicle on the Origins and Missionary Activities of the Wangarawa," *Kano Studies* 1:7–42.

Hiskett, M. 1957. "Material Relating to the State of Learning among the Fulani before Their Jihad," *BSAOAS* 19:550–78.

———. 1973. *The Sword of Truth.* New York: Oxford University Press.

———. 1979. *A History of Hausa Islamic Verse.* London: The School of Oriental and African Studies.

Horton, R. 1975. "On the Rationality of Conversation," *Africa* 45, 3–4:219–35; 373–99.

Hunwick, J. O. 1970. "Notes on a Late Fifteenth-Century Document Concerning 'al-Takrur'." In *African Perspectives,* ed. C. Allen and R.W. Johnson. Cambridge: Cambridge University Press.

———. 1985. *Shari'a in Songhay.* Oxford: Oxford University Press.

———. 1996. "Secular Power and Religious Authority in Muslim Society: The Case of Songhay." *Journal of African History* 37:175–94.

al-Ifrani, n.d. *Nuzhat al-hadi fi akhbar muluk al-qarn al-hadi,* lithographed in Fez.

Jobson, R. 1932. *The Golden Trade.* London. (Reprinted in 1968 by Dawson and Pall Mall).

Kaba, Lansine. 1984. "The Pen, the Sword, and the Crown: Islam and Revolution in Songhay Reconsidered, 1464–1493," *Journal of African History* 25:241–56.

Labat, J. B. 1728. *Nouvelle relation de l'Afrique occidentale.* Paris: G. Cavalier.

Lange, D. 1978. "Progrès de l'Islam et changement politique au Kanem du 11e au 13e siècle: Un essai d'interprétation," *Journal of African History* 19:495–513.

Last, M. 1993. "The Traditional Muslim Intellectuals in Hausaland: The Background." In *African Historiography: Essays in Honor of J. Ade Ajayi,* ed. T. Falola, 116–31. Harlow: Longman.

Lavers, J. E. 1971. "Islam in the Bornu Caliphate," *Odu* 5:27–53.

———. 1987. "Two Sufi Communities in Seventeenth and Nineteenth Century Bornu," paper presented to a workshop at SOAS, September 1987, on Sufism in Africa in the seventeenth and eighteenth centuries.

Leo Africanus. 1956. *Description de l'Afrique,* trans. A. Epaulard. Paris: Adrien-Maisonneuve.

Levitson, N. 1968. *Muslims and Chiefs in West Africa.* Oxford: Clarendon Press.

———. 1986. "Mamluk Egypt and Takrur." In *Studies in Islamic History and Civilization in Honour of David Ayalon,* ed. M. Sharon, 183–207. Leiden: E. J. Brill (reprinted in Levtzion 1994).

———. 1994. *Islam in West Africa: Religion, Society and Politics to 1800.* Aldershot, Hamps.: Variorum.

———. 1997. "Eighteenth Century Sufi Brotherhoods: Structural, Organizational and Ritual Changes." In *Essays on Scripture, Thought and Society,* A Festschrift in Honor of A. H. Johns, ed. P. G. Riddel and Tony Street, 147–60. Leiden: E. J. Brill.

Levtzion, Nehemia, and J. F. P. Hopkins, eds. 1981. *Corpus of Early Arabic Sources for West African History.* Trans. J. F. P. Hopkins. Cambridge: Cambridge University Press.

Martin, B. G. 1976. *Muslim Brotherhoods in Nineteenth-Century Africa.* Cambridge: Cambridge University Press.

Palmer, H. R. 1914. "An early Fulani Conception of Islam," *Journal of the African Society* 13:407–14.

———. 1928. *Sudanese Memoirs.* Lagos: The Government Printer.

———. 1936. *Bornu, Sahara and Sudan.* Rpt. New York: Negro Universities Press, 1970.

Park, Mungo. 1928. *Travels in the Interior Districts of Africa.* London: Bulmer.

Roberts, R. 1975. *Warriors, Merchants and Slaves: The State and the Economy in the Middle Niger Valley, 1700–1914.* Stanford: Stanford University Press.

Robinson, D. 1975. "The Islamic Revolution of Futa Toro," *International Journal of African Historical Studies* 8:185–221.

Sartain, E. M. 1971. "Jalal al-Din al-Suyuti's Relations with the People of Takrur," *Journal of Semitic Studies* 16:193–98.

Seydou, C. 1973. "Panorama de la Literature Peule," *Bulletin de l'IFAN* 35:176–212.

Sow, A. I. 1966. *La femme, la vache, la foi: Ecrivains et pouvoir du Fouta Djalon.* Paris: Julliard.

Tadhkirat al-Nisyan. 1966. Ed. and trans. O. Houdas. Paris: Adrien-Maisonneuve (reprint of the 1913–14 edition).

Ta'rikh al-Fattash. 1964. Ed. and trans. O. Houdas and M. Delafosse. Paris: Adrien-Maisonneuve (reprint of 1912 edition).

Ta'rikh al-Sudan. 'Abd al-Rahman al-Sadi. 1964. Ed. and trans. O. Houdas. Paris: Adrien-Maisonneuve (reprint of 1911 edition).

Tauxier, L. 1927. *La Religion Bambara.* Paris: Paul Geuthner.

'Uthman dan Fodio. 1961. "Wathiqat ahl al-Sudan," *Journal of African History* 2:235–44.

CHAPTER 4

The Juula and the Expansion of Islam into the Forest

Ivor Wilks

The Juula (or Dyula) defy easy identification. The Mandekan word *juula* is of doubtful etymology, but has come to mean "trader" in many dialects.[1] The Juula of this chapter are those who, over several centuries, established networks of trade in the savannah country between the Middle Niger in the north and the forests of the Guinea Coast in the south, and who had a major involvement in the marketing of gold and kola. Their settlements are to be found scattered across the land between the valley of the White Bandama to the west and that of the Oti to the east. Beyond the Bandama, the Juula networks gave way to those of the Jakhanke; and beyond the Oti, to those of the Hausa.

Historically, the origins of the Juula are to be found in the Wangara trading communities of the medieval western Sudan, to which the earliest known reference is that by Abu 'Ubayd 'Abd Allah al-Bakri of Cordoba, in 1068 A.D. He wrote of Yarasna, a town "inhabited by Muslims surrounded by pagans." The former were black, traded in gold, spoke *a'jam,* and were called the "Banu Naghmarata." A minor correction of the Arabic yields "Banu Wanghmarata," presumably to be read as "Banu Wangharata"—the tribe of the Wangara.[2] Al-Bakri's eleventh-century account presciently describes the Juula of the subsequent dispersion. They were and are Muslim, spoke and speak a dialect of Mandekan, and still commonly refer to themselves as "Wangara." They remained deeply involved in the gold (and kola) trades until the beginning of the twentieth century, when they were able to take advantage of the new colonial economies vastly to expand the range of their entrepreneurial activities.

In medieval and early modern times there was an unfailing global demand for gold, and West Africa was a major source of supply. The earliest of its goldfields to be intensively exploited was undoubtedly that of Bambuhu (Bambuk), lying in the region of the headwaters of the Senegal between the Falémé and Bafing Rivers. It is clear from al-Bakri that Bambuhu gold was then entering the world market through Ghana's great Sahelian port, the (excavated) site of which is at Kumbi Saleh. Yarasna, however, was located too far south to have been a center for this trade. It lay on the frontier of the Manden kingdom of Do, and therefore proximate to the Boure goldfields between the Niger and the upper reaches of the Bakhoy.[3] It seems, then, that the eleventh-century Wangara of Yarasna are to be associated not with the older Bambuhu trade, but rather with a developing Boure one. In this context it is significant that the Juula of the southern dispersion universally refer their origins to "Mande Kaba"; that is, the ancient Manden ritual center of Kangaba lying on the eastern fringes of Boure. They also continue to use distinctively Manden patronymics: Bamba, Bagayogo, Jabagate, Kamagate, Tarawiri (Traore), Watara, and so forth. The Boure goldfields of Manden should, then, be regarded as the location within which a distinctive Juula identity emerged.

The history of the early dispersion of Wangara from the heartlands of Mali is at the same time that of the development of new centers of gold production. Settlements were established in the auriferous valley of the upper Black Volta,[4] and, probably in the early fifteenth century, the Juula established a highly lucrative trade with the Akan of the forest country.[5] They obtained supplies of gold from the producers, who washed the rivers and sank pits into the alluvia and lodes. The Juula became, then, the first link in a vast distributive network that extended northward from the goldfields to the greater entrepôts of the western Sudan and Sahel, thence across the Sahara by caravan trails to the Mediterranean littoral, and so into Europe, the Middle East, and beyond. Their activities took them far beyond the outermost fringes of the Muslim world, for the gold producers with whom they did business were *kuffar*, unbelievers.

The Juula settled, most commonly, among 'stateless' peoples, those having systems of authority that seldom extended beyond the level of the village or cluster of villages: among, for example, those broadly referred to as the Bobo, Dagara, Gurensi, Kulango, Lobi, and Senufo. They commonly took wives from the host community and so, in addition to their own Juula dialect of Mandekan, also came to speak its language. The Juula have thus tended to develop secondary identities, as Bobo-Juula, Dagara-Juula, and so forth. Sometimes, however, they established settlements within older centralized kingdoms, most notably perhaps in that of Dagomba; and sometimes, as in the cases of Gonja and Wa, they appear to have been catalysts in the very process of state-formation.[6]

Although the communities of the Juula diaspora originated as parts of a trade network, not all Juula traded all the time, and some did not trade at all. There were those who devoted themselves to learning, others who farmed, and others who were artisans, particularly weavers. And there were still others who were not Juula in the strict sense but who, sharing a common Manden background and using the same patronymics, tended to assimilate to them. These were the *tun tigi* or *sonangui*,[7] the descendants of warriors who, with the decline of imperial Mali, spread into the regions of Juula settlement and sometimes, as well exemplified by the case of Kong, created small Juula chiefdoms.[8] It is the agency of the Juula in the spread of Islam that is of primary concern in this chapter.

On Trading with Unbelievers

It was noted in the reign of Mansa Musa of Mali (c. 1312–37), that when he or his predecessors attempted to extend their sway, and that of the faith, over the gold-mining communities within their dominions, production fell off drastically.[9] Since by that time Mali was within *dar al-Islam* in that its rulers were Muslim, the problem was to do with the terms on which the non-Muslim miners would be "tolerated." The kings, it was reported, "left the gold countries in the hands of their pagan inhabitants, and were content with being assured of their homage and with receiving the tribute imposed on them."[10] The solution was one fully in accordance with Maliki law, then prevalent in western Sudan. In his *Al-Mudawwana,* 'Abd al-Salam Sahnun of Qayrawan (d. 854) reported a *fatwa* given by Imam Malik b. Anas (d. 795) himself. It concerned the correct attitude toward the unbelievers of, in this case, the Fezzan. It was to the effect that war should not be waged against them until they had been given the options, first, of converting, or second, if this was declined, of paying a tribute—the *jizya*—to the Muslim ruler in order to be permitted to retain their own religious customs.[11] The Wangara, then, might quite legitimately do business with the unbelievers of Boure.

The situation was quite different in the south. The Black Volta and Akan goldfields were never brought under the political authority of imperial Mali, and the position of the Juula was that of Muslims living in *dar al-harb;* that is, in lands where the law of Islam was not in force. The status of Muslims in such circumstances was one that had long engaged the attention of North African jurists with particular reference to the trans-Saharan trade with the Bilad al-Sudan. Sahnun's views are evident in a story about him preserved by 'Iyad b. Musa b. 'Iyad al-Sabti (d. 1149). A man asked Sahnun for permission to build a bridge to improve access to his, Sahnun's, house. Sahnun refused, on the grounds that the man's money had been made in trading to the Bilad al-Sudan.[12] The *Risala* of Ibn Abi Zayd of Qayrawan (922/3–996), a manual of Maliki law widely used in western Sudan, has a passage that is much to the point. "Trading to the land of the enemy *(adw)* and to the Bilad al-Sudan is disapproved," wrote Ibn Abi Zayd; "the Prophet (on him be peace!) said: 'Travelling is part of punishment.'"[13] There was in all of this, however, something of a paradox, for the flows of gold from dar al-harb were vital to the well-being of dar al-Islam, and specifically to the economies of Muslim North Africa. One popular way out of the dilemma was simply to deny that it existed; to deny, that is, that there was any real interface between Muslim traders and non-Muslim producers. It was thus that the myth of the "silent trade" was propagated—that the Muslims accomplished their business without ever coming into actual physical contact with unbelievers. Versions of the myth are to be found in, for example, Al-Mas'udi (d. 956), Yaqut (d. 1229), Al-Qazwini (d. 1283), and Al-'Umari (d. 1349),[14] and the topic has been thoroughly reviewed, though in a somewhat different context, by Farias.[15] The serious jurists, however, could not and did not accept this fabrication, but concerned themselves with doctrinal matters.

Michael Brett has drawn attention to two fatwas of a contemporary of Ibn Abi Zayd in Qayrawan; namely, al-Qabisi (935–1012). One of these had to do with Muslims in an unnamed location in Bilad al-Sudan, the non-Muslim ruler of which had appointed a Muslim to supervise the affairs of the faithful, as *nazir*. The matter at issue was whether, in such circumstances, the nazir exercised legitimate authority. Al-Qabisi ruled that he did.

> [S]ince the place . . . was a residence of Muslims who lived and dwelt there, there was no alternative for them but to have someone to supervise their affairs and judge between them, with authority from the ruler of the place to enable him to compel the recalcitrant and carry out his duties. For it is not possible to escape from kings in their power *(sultan)*, and especially not from the power of unbelief *(kufr)* and enmity *('adawa)*. Therefore, if the *nazir* of the Muslims judges them by the laws of the Muslims, his judgement goes, hitting the mark of justice, and binding upon those who have been pleased to enter his jurisdiction *(sultan)* and come under his supervision *(nazar)*, either permanently or in passing.[16]

As Brett comments, al-Qabisi accepted the fact that there are Muslim communities in dar al-harb,[17] recognized that any government is better than no government, and concluded that in such circumstances it becomes necessary to rely on the power of non-Muslim kings to enforce the authority of the nazir and so enable him to apply Muslim law within the community of the faithful.[18]

The views of these Maliki jurists were ones of men securely located in dar al-Islam. In those distant lands where Muslim traders actually lived among, and did business with, unbelievers, the problems were not only ones of legal theory but of daily practice. A critical figure in the determination of what that practice should be was Al-Hajj Salim Suwari, who has been the subject of considerable scholarly interest over the last twenty-five years.[19] He is a greatly revered figure throughout much of West Africa, and particularly among the Juula and the Jakhanke, both of which peoples regard him as the architect of their (similar) ways of life, and as having formulated precepts for the conduct of Muslims living among unbelievers.

Al-Hajj Salim Suwari

Al-Hajj Salim Suwari was a Soninke (Serakhulle). Tradition universally sets the earlier part of his life in Ja (Diakha, Zagha, etc.) in Massina, and has him making the pilgrimage to Mecca seven times. In later life, he resettled at Jahaba (Diakhaba, etc., "great Ja") in Bambuhu. In the seventeenth century it was described as having been "a town of jurists in the interior of Malian territory . . . known as the Town of God." The kings of Mali were said never to enter it, the authority of the *qadi* being supreme.[20] Al-Hajj Salim is the subject of numerous hagiological references in writings that circulate widely among the Juula and Jakhanke. In the *Ta'rikh Jabi,* for example, he is "their Imam and Shaykh of Shaykhs, *wali* of Allah the Highest, maker of many successive miracles."[21] He also figures prominently, as *wali Allah* or "a headman of the Mandinga nation," in traditions to do with Fulani settlement in Futa Jallon.[22] His floruit may be placed in the earlier sixteenth century.[23] Juula tradition numbers Bukari Tarawiri of "Jaraba" and Muhammad Bagayogo of Timbuktu among his followers. The former was qadi of Jenne in the 1570s and 1580; the latter, teacher of the celebrated Ahmad Baba of Timbuktu, was born in 1523/24 and died in 1594.[24]

It is an open question whether any writings of al-Hajj Salim Suwari survive.[25] His teachings, however, were transmitted principally through two of his students; namely, Muhammad al-Buni to the Juula, and Yusuf Kasama to the Jakhanke. A third line, about which less is known, passes through Muhammad Duguri of Koro.[26] Wangara learning was also spreading into Hausaland in the late fifteenth century, when Shaykh 'Abd al-Rahman Zaghaite, a name indicative of Ja or Jahaba connections, moved there with his followers.[27] It may be that the Wangara settlers in Katsina, Kano, and elsewhere carried with them much the same teachings as those of al-Hajj Salim, but a better understanding of the sources is necessary before this can be argued with confidence.[28]

Al-Hajj Salim Suwari established, among Juula and Jakhanke alike, a pedagogical tradition that survives to this day despite the pressures of modernism. It is built around the study of three major works; namely, *Tafsir al-Jalalayn* of al-Mahalli (d. 1459) and al-Suyuti (d. 1505), *Muwatta'* of Imam Malik b. Anas (d. 795), and *Al-Shifa' fi ta'rif huquq al-Mustafa* of 'Iyad b. Musa b. 'Iyad al-Sabti (d. 1149). Of these, the first is, of course, basic. It was completed in Cairo in 1485, and al-Hajj Salim presumably acquired a copy of it in the course of one of his pilgrimages.[29] Al-Suyuti himself referred to the many West Africans who studied with him and obtained copies of his works.[30] In matters of Quranic exegesis, al-Hajj Salim followed al-Suyuti, who was a Shafi'i. He found the latter's relatively liberal attitudes toward non-Muslims congenial: liberal, that is, compared with the harsh pronouncements of his contemporary, Muhammad b. 'Abd al-Karim al-Maghili (d. 1503/4).[31] Nevertheless, in matters of law, al-Hajj Salim identified himself firmly with the Maliki *madhhab.* The sequence of his own teachers extends back through several unidentifiable western Sudanese scholars and is then attached to a well-known North African Maliki line through 'Abd al-Salam Sahnun of Qayrawan and 'Abd al-Rahman b. al-Qasim of Cairo (d. 806/7) to Imam Malik b. Anas.[32]

There is general agreement among *'ulama'* within the Suwarian tradition, whether Juula or Jakhanke, that the principal dicta of al-Hajj Salim had to do with relations with unbelievers. Drawing upon many conversations with learned Juula in the Côte d'Ivoire, Ghana, and Burkina Faso, I believe that the following accurately, if somewhat schematically, represents the Suwarian position on Muslims vis-à-vis unbelievers.[33] First, *kufr*, unbelief, is the result of *jahl*—that is, of ignorance rather than wickedness. Second, God's grand design for the world is such that some people remain in the *jahiliyya*, the state of ignorance, longer than others. Third, true conversion can, therefore, occur only in God's time, and actively to proselytize is to interfere with his will. Accordingly, fourth, *jihad* against unbelievers is an unacceptable method of conversion, and recourse to arms is permissible only in self-defense should the very existence of the Muslim community be threatened by unbelievers. Fifth, Muslims may accept the authority of non-Muslim rulers, and indeed support it insofar as this enables them to follow their own way of life in accordance with the *sunna* of the Prophet. Sixth, the Muslims have to present the unbelievers with *qudwa*, example, and so, when the time for conversion comes, thereby make possible *iqtida*, emulation. And seventh, the Muslims must ensure that, by their commitment to education and learning, they keep their observance of the Law free from error. Al-Hajj Salim Suwari thus formulated a praxis of coexistence such as to enable the Juula to operate within lands of unbelief without prejudice to their distinctive Muslim identity, allowing them access to the material resources of this world without foregoing salvation in the next.[34] His dicta do not at any point conflict with Maliki orthodoxy, but clearly he drew selectively from jurists of the mind of al-Qabisi. Indeed, al-Hajj Salim may well have been acquainted with al-Qabisi's fatwa discussed above, for it was among those that the mufti of Fez, Ahmad b. Yahya al-Wansharisi (c. 1430–1508), included in his massive compilation *Al-Mi'yar al-Mughrib 'an fatawi Ifriqiya wa al-Andalus wa al-Maghrib*.[35]

Al-Hajj Salim Suwari is said to have introduced various ways of affording recognition to achievement in learning: a special turban *('immama)* for those completing the study of the three books, a hooded cloak *(burnus)* for those erudite in the Maliki *madhhab*, and a staff *('asan)* for those skilled in law *(fiqh)*.[36] He, or perhaps his students, also introduced the system of *asanid* (sing. *isnad*) or *salasil* (sing. *silsila*), chains of transmission, from teacher to student, for Tafsir, Muwatta, and Al-Shifa'. The isnad or silsila is at the same time an *ijaza*, or license to teach. Using a sample of some eighty such documents that license Juula teachers either living or recently dead, almost all run back through Muhammad al-Buni to al-Hajj Salim, and for the most part do so in ten to fifteen teaching "generations."[37]

The Juula Dispersion: Traders and Teachers

It is difficult to establish a precise chronology for the early dispersion of the Juula. In the late eleventh century, they were the gold traders, "the tribe of the Wangara," located by al-Bakri in the western Sudanese town of Yarasna. Less than a century later, Abu 'Abd Allah Muhammad al-Idrisi described the inland delta of the Niger as "the country of Wangara" and noted that "its inhabitants are rich, for they possess gold in abundance."[38] By the late fifteenth century, such was the demand for gold that buyers were traveling as far south as the Costa da Mina (Elmina), where the Portuguese knew them as "Mandinguas"; that is, Manden.[39] Much of our knowledge of the period is drawn from European sources. Valentim Fernandes, Pacheco Pereira, and their like were concerned, for practical reasons, to record the growth of the African trade. This was not, however, a matter likely to engage the attention of the Wangara scholars. Their concern was with a kind of frontier history, chronicling the expansion of dar al-Islam and the contraction of dar al-harb (as God had so willed it). Accordingly, the written and oral accounts of those in the Suwarian tradition focus not on those who went to do business in the lands of the unbelievers, but of those who traveled (al-safar) to teach. These were the scholars who sustained the true way of life in the Juula communities and thus at the same time set the example that the unbelievers would in the course of time come to emulate. These themes are well exemplified in the story of the Kamagate of Bighu.

The Juula entrepôt of Bighu (Begho, etc.) was situated on the northern edge of the Akan forest country. Its history has engaged the attention of a number of scholars. The full report of excavations there is awaited, but a provisional reading of the findings suggests that the Juula exercised a commercial sway over the town from the fifteenth to seventeenth centuries.[40] The Kamagate were among the earliest of the Juula to settle there.[41] In the mid-sixteenth century, when central authority in Mali had all but collapsed, a desperate bid was made to secure the southern supplies of gold. A Malian warlord, Nabanga, was sent to occupy Bighu. He did so, but then defected and moved eastwards to found the kingdom of Gonja in the valley of the lower Black Volta. In this venture, the *faqih* Isma'il Kamagate of Bighu and his son Muhammad al-Abyad attached themselves to him. The latter became first imam of the new kingdom. His descendants continued to hold the imamate, and in time founded others in the various divisional towns of Gonja.[42] One of the Gonja imams was Sidi 'Umar b. Suma, who assumed office in 1160 A.H., 1747. He was a great-grandson of the first imam, Muhammad al-Abyad,[43] and an annalist with an impressive command of Arabic. He was, I have suggested, the compiler of the remarkable *Kitab Ghanja,* completed in 1165 A.H., 1751/2. His son and successor in the imamate, 'Umar Kunandi b. 'Umar, was jointly responsible for a version of the chronicle updated to 1178 A.H., 1764,[44] which contains a succinct description of its contents: "It concerns what Allah has brought about from the beginning of Ghanja, the time of Naba' [Nabanga], the faqih Isma'il, and his son Muhmmad al-Abyad; the affairs of the Muslims, the unbelievers, and all the kings of Ghanja to the time of the king, Abu Bakr b. 'Uthman, whose *laqab* is Layu' [Lanyon]."[45] It will be noted that "what Allah has brought about" embraces the affairs of the unbelievers of Gonja as well as the Muslims.

According to the *Kitab Ghanja,* the conversion of the Gonja ruling house occurred in the time of Nabanga's successor, Manwura. Engaged in battle with unbelievers, Manwura could not overcome them. Muhammad al-Abyad walked toward the enemy and planted his staff in the ground. Then, as the writer has it, "by the decree of Allah" the tide turned. Manwura was impressed, converted, and became "devoted to Islam."[46] The rulers of Gonja were probably the first within the Voltaic region to accept Islam.

In 1615 and thereabouts, the Timbuktu jurist Ahmad Baba made several listings of lands of unbelievers; at issue was not so much the matter of trading with them, but of enslaving their people. Gonja does not appear in the lists. Older kingdoms to its west, in the valleys of the White Volta and the Oti Rivers, do.[47] Ahmad Baba's "Dagomba" probably refers to Dagomba proper (Dagbamba) and also to the neighboring and closely related kingdoms of Mamprussi (Mampurugu) and Nanumba, and his "Mossi" describes their northern counterparts, Wagadugu and Yatenga. All five dynasties were founded after the destruction of a more northerly Mossi homeland as a result of Songhay expansion in the course of the fifteenth century.[48] It was not until the second half of the seventeenth century, however, that Islam began to have a significant influence on their ruling houses. The change was brought about by a number of shaykhs who left their towns, Timbuktu among others, to resettle in the southern grasslands.

The history of Dagomba has been the most fully studied.[49] A critical factor was the arrival of Shaykh Sulayman b. ʿAbdallah Bagayogo from Timbuktu. He is said to have proceeded from one to another of the Wangara communities that existed under the protection of non-Muslim rulers: specifically, from Gourcy in Yatenga, to Salmatenga (Kaya) and Mane in Wagadugu. From there he traveled to Dagomba at the request of its king, Na Luro (died c. 1660). He was given land at Sabari, in the Oti Valley, where he built a mosque and opened a school. On his death, his son Yaʿmuru succeeded him. Among Yaʿmuru's students was the young Muhammad Zangina, who was to become, around 1700, the first Muslim Na of Dagomba. He is remembered particularly for opening up his country to trade by encouraging Muslim immigration. Later in the century, a visitor, the Fezzan merchant Sharif Imhammad, described "the Mahometan Kingdom of Degombah." His brief account indicates that a Suwarian tolerance prevailed, for he noted, "that Musselman and the pagan are indiscriminately mixed; that their cattle feed upon the same mountains; and that the approach of evening sends them in peace to the same village."[50]

Across the northern hinterlands of Gonja, from the Black Volta eastward into the Kulkpawn valley, there existed a number of small settlements established, probably in the fifteenth and sixteenth centuries, by warlords of Manden background. Best known of these are, from west to east, Nasa, Visi, and Palewogo.[51] Another Timbuktu shaykh, Abu Bakr b. ʿAli Kunate, is said to have settled first at Kudugu, a Wagadugu town, before continuing south to Visi. His descendants, and those of his companions, were to found many small imamates in the region.[52] Shaykhs Sulayman Bagayogo and Abu Bakr Kunate exemplify what Sanneh describes as characteristic of the Suwarian tradition; namely, "travel or mobility *(al-safar)*. . . the penetration of distant lands for religious purposes."[53] Yaʿmuru Tarawiri belonged to the same category. Of Ja (Dia) origins, he was probably a great-grandson of the later-sixteenth-century *qadi* of Jenne, Bukari Tarawiri, mentioned above as a follower of al-Hajj Salim Suwari. He traveled to Nasa, where a Kunate imamate may already have been established. There he attached himself to a Mampurugu prince in exile, Saliya, and was instrumental in creating the Wa kingdom. Ya'muru's floruit is a late seventeenth and early eighteenth century one. He became the first imam of the new state and his descendants continue to hold the office and most of the lesser imamates created later.[54]

The imamates founded by Isma'il Kamagate in Gonja, Sulayman Bagayogo in Dagomba and Ya'muru Tarawiri in Wa, became hereditary ones. Candidates for the office were chosen from among the descendants of the founder and, in theory at least, had to be approved by the ruler. The incumbent is known to the Juula as *imam al-balad*, imam for the country. He is responsible for the secular affairs of the Muslims; that is, for mediating between them and the ruler under whose authority they come and on whose protection they depend (and in this respect functions not unlike al-Qabisi's nazir). That the three cases related above are all, as it were, success stories, should not obscure the fact that Juula settlers in non-Muslim lands faced major challenges. They seem seldom to have come into conflict with the host communities, but were acutely conscious of their own isolation from major centers of Islamic learning. There was inevitably the danger of backsliding *(ihmal)* and even of apostasy. The Tagara (that is, Tarawiri) of Jirapa, to the north of Wa, are known to have reverted to paganism.[55] So, too, are Sanu in the Bobo country (also listed by Ahmad Baba of Timbuktu as a land of unbelief), who are said to have "stopped praying" for five generations before being reconverted in the later nineteenth century.[56] The Juula accordingly not only placed (and place) much emphasis upon schooling within the community, but also perceived the need for constant renewal *(tajdid)* from without.

The Saganogo as Renewers of Islam

The notion of *mujaddidun,* renewers of Islam, was and is an important one for the Juula.[57] It is firmly associated in their thinking with the celebrated Saganogo shaykhs who impinged upon their world in the eighteenth and nineteenth centuries. Under their influence, a new wave of mosque building began, specifically, of mosques large enough to accommodate whole communities for the Friday prayer. Among them, according to *Al-Jawahir wa al-Yawaqit* by al-Hajj Muhammad Marhaba Saganogo, were those of Kong in 1200 A.H., 1785/6; Buna in 1210, 1795/6; Bonduku in 1212, 1797/8; and Wa in 1216, 1801/2. With the proliferation of mosques went the creation of a new style of imamate. The *imam al-jum'a,* the imam for the Friday mosque, represented the community of the faithful as such. He was chosen by it and assumed responsibility for its spiritual well-being. The office was not hereditary. Quality of learning was all important in the selection of an occupant, and that sons often succeeded fathers reflects only the fact that fathers regularly taught sons.[58] A sadly diminishing number of the striking western Sudanese-style mosques survive in their original form. The imamates, however, still flourish, and for the most part their occupants uphold the liberal tradition of Islam associated with al-Hajj Salim Suwari.

The appendix to this chapter shows *asanid*, teaching chains, for two Juula students and, for comparison, one Jakhanke. Ya'qub b. al-Hajj Sa'id of Wa, Harun b. Baba Watara of Bonduku, and Al-Hajj Muhammad Alfa Silla of Kunting all completed their studies in the mid-twentieth century.[59] The first Juula chain passes through lines of Tarawiri (or "Takari") teachers in Wa and Watara teachers in Buna, and the second through Timite and Konate ("Qunati") teachers in Bonduku. Both, however, will be seen to converge on the figures of 'Abbas Saganogo and his father, Muhammad al-Mustafa b. 'Abbas Saganogo. In this they are typical of Juula chains.[60]

The eastward movement of Saganogo teachers in the second half of the eighteenth century can be dated. The grave of Muhammad al-'Afi, grandfather and teacher of Muhammad al-Mustafa b. 'Abbas, is at Koro, between Odienné and Man in what is now the western Côte d'Ivoire. That of his father, 'Abbas, is at Kani, 95 kilometers to the east, where he is said to have died in 1178 A.H., 1764/65. Muhammad al-Mustafa himself settled in Boron, a further 70 kilometers east. He died there in 1190 A.H., 1776/7 (to select the most acceptable of several dates that appear in Juula writings), and his grave remains the site of local pilgrimage.[61] His teachings were transmitted principally through his son al-'Abbas, who, after the death of his father, moved to Kong, 160 kilometers northeast of Boron, and in time became imam of that town. He died there in 1215 A.H., 1801.[62] Al-'Abbas, according to Saganogo tradition, "brought his brothers to stay there, and then the *'ulama'* gathered around him to learn from him, and the news spread to other places, and the people of Bonduku and Wala came to him, and the people of the land of Ghayagha and also Banda came to study with him."[63] The Wa experience may be used in illustration. Their eleventh imam, Sa'id b. 'Abd al-Qadir Tarawiri, went, according to a local chronicle, "to the town of Pan [Kong] to look for knowledge."[64] In 1964, Imam Sa'id's descendant al-Hajj Siddiq b. Sa'id expanded on this. Long ago, he said,

> all the old men of knowledge *[karamokos]* died. Men of knowledge became few. This continued up to the time of Imam Muhammad b. 'Abd al-Qadir. Then Imam Sa'id, my father's grandfather, went to Kong. He was not then imam, but was sent there. He spent twelve years in Kong. The teacher was Karamoko 'Abbas Saganogo. Sa'id came back from Kong to Wa. He was a *mujaddid*, a reviver of Islam in Wa. Later he was made imam.[65]

The Saganogo achieved a major renewal of learning among the Juula. Most Juula men, if fewer women, were educated to an elementary level by rote learning of the Quran. This is certainly true of recent times and presumably has long been the case.[66] Advanced studies, terminating in the award of the ijaza to teach, were undertaken by relatively few, but it was those few who, as teachers, imams and the like, became responsible for maintaining the quality of the community's religious life. Scholarship tended to become located within specific families, since fathers taught sons and the physical plant that constituted the school—buildings and books—were inherited the one from the other. No *'alim*, however, would teach only his own sons, for the essence of knowledge lay in its diffusion. All such families, for example the Timite of Bonduku, Limamyiri Tarawiri of Wa, Watara of Buna, and Bamba of Banda, regard themselves as *talaba* (students) of the Saganogo. It is the particular imprint of the Saganogo on Juula learning that distinguishes it from that of the Jakhanke, who share the Suwarian legacy but through different lines of transmission.

Windows on the Juula in the Later Eighteenth Century

There are sources that provide useful windows into Juula trading and clerical activities in the second half of the eighteenth century. Some idea of the volume of gold being moved from West Africa to the Maghrib is provided by an item from the trading accounts of al-Hajj Hamad al-Wangari of Timbuku. By the autumn caravan *(al-rkaba al-kharifi)* of 1204 A.H., 1790, bound for Akka in southern Morocco, he sent fifty camels loaded with gum acacia within the skins of which were packed four thousand ounces of "Wangara gold" (specifically, two thousand ounces of gold dust and two thousand ounces of gold bar). These were in payment for a large consignment of Flemish and Irish cloth.[67] We do not know, of course, from which goldfields al-Hajj Hamad was obtaining his supplies, or whether he himself dealt directly with the producers. In such matters as these, we know more about the activities of a contemporary of al-Hajj Hamad—namely, Karamo Sa Watara, a resident of Timbuktu and Jenne.

Karamo Sa Watara was the eldest of five brothers. The second, Idris, was settled at Ja, in Massina; the third, 'Abd al-Rahman, in Kong (where he had married a daughter of Soma 'Ali Watara, ruler of the Nzan province); and the fourth, Mahmud, at Buna (where he, too, married a daughter of its ruler). Only the youngest, Abu Bakr, remained for the time at Timbuktu. As a relatively young man, Karamo Sa did business in Hausaland and Borno and married a daughter of one al-Hajj Muhammad Tafsir, a prosperous merchant (probably of Katsina) who was involved in the Egyptian trade. Early in the 1790s, however, he traveled south to join his brother in Buna. He took with him a number of servants who, to quote from our source, "gathered a quantity of gold for their master; for there is a great deal of gold in that country, from the wilderness down to the river-side [that is, the Black Volta], also from the rocks." Karamo Sa consigned some of the gold to his father-in-law, al-Hajj Muhammad Tafsir, and among the goods he received in return were, apparently, Egyptian silks. We know these details of the life of Karamo Sa from the brief autobiography of his son Abu Bakr al-Siddiq.[68]

Karamo Sa died of fever in the course of his venture into the Black Volta goldfields and was buried in Buna. Five years later, the youthful Abu Bakr al-Siddiq, in the company of his tutor, went to Buna. Abu Bakr was put to school there, to study *tafsir* (exegesis). Among his classmates was his cousin Kotoko Watara, who was later to succeed Soma Ali as ruler of Nzan.[69] The teachers, Abu Bakr reported, were "not natives of one place, but each of them, having quitted his own country, has come and settled there." They included scholars (Jakhanke among them) from as far afield as Futa Jallon and Futa Toro. The head of the school, however, was a Juula, 'Abdallah b. al-Hajj Muhammad Watara. Both 'Abdallah and his father are known independently, from teaching chains. The former is recorded as instructing students from Wa and Bonduku, and has having been taught by his father, Muhammad b. Ibrahim Watara, whose own chain extends back through a line of Saganogo teachers to the revered Muhammad al-Mustafa b. 'Abbas of Boron (and thence, of course, to al-Hajj Salim Suwari himself).[70] Buna retained its fame as an educational center in the mid-nineteenth century, when Henry Barth heard of it as "a place of great celebrity for its learning and its schools, in the countries of the Mohammedan Mandingoes to the south."[71]

It is remarkable that even in the later eighteenth century, there were North African merchants who remained diffident about the morality of doing business with unbelievers. Sidi al-Hajj 'Abd al-Salam Shabayni was a case in point. He was born in Meknes in or about 1743. His father was involved in the West Africa trade, and 'Abd al-Salam accompanied him on one extended visit. They spent twelve years there, from 1757 to 1769, and were resident for the greater part of that time in Timbuktu. Much enriched by their enterprise, they returned to Morocco in or about 1770. 'Abd al-Salam settled in Tetuan. In time he became unhappy about the source of his wealth. "Money gained among the negroes has not the blessing of God on it," he is reported as saying, "but vanishes away without benefit." Later, as a result of a vision, he was to give away all his material possessions and to become a sage and healer *(hakim)* in the Jbala, where his cult survives.[72]

A Window on the Juula in the Early Nineteenth Century

In the mid-eighteenth century, the Juula were deeply involved in the lucrative trade with the Akan goldfields, but seem not to have established a presence in the capital of the kingdom that had, over the previous half century, acquired hegemony in that region—in, that is, Kumase, seat of the powerful Asante kings. In 1750, Asantehene (or King) Opoku Ware died. The *Kitab Ghanja* carried an obituary, penned probably by Imam Sidi 'Umar: "[M]ay Allah curse him and put his soul into hell. It was he who harmed the people of Ghanja [Gonja], oppressing and robbing them of their property at his will. He reigned violently as a tyrant, enjoying his authority. Peoples of the horizons feared him much. He had a long reign of almost forty years."[73] In this case, *kufr*, unbelief, seems to have amounted, even for Suwarian savants, to rather more than ignorance.

But God's inexorable will was in time to reveal itself. By the beginning of the nineteenth century there was a well-established Muslim community in Kumase that regarded the then Asantehene, Osei Tutu Kwame, as "a friend on whom they could always rely for protection."[74] One of its most prominent members was Muhammad Kamagate, known locally as Karamo Togma. He was a son of Gonja Imam Muhammad al-Mustafa, a grandson of Gonja Imam 'Umar Kunandi and a great-grandson of Gonja Imam Sidi 'Umar—Opoku Ware's presumed obituarist. Clearly times had changed.

Karamo Togma, who was a close confidant of the Asantehene, had with him in Kumase at least one section of the *Kitab Ghanja,* and it was presumably he who undertook the compilation of the lost chronicle of the Asante kings.[75] Joseph Dupuis was in Kumase in 1820, as British consul. A knowledge of Arabic enabled him to converse directly with the Muslims there. Although the Asantehene was, they told him, "a misguided infidel, he was yet superior by far, to many other sovereigns, and particularly to the king of Dahomey, his eastern neighbour, who was an infidel of infidels (Kaffar ben al Koufar)."[76]

The fortunate survival of a number of letters from Osei Tutu Kwame's "chancery" provides further insights into the attitude of the Kumase Juula toward their non-Muslim patron. Through Karamo Togma and other members of the Muslim community, the Asantehene maintained an extensive correspondence with the Gonja 'ulama'. He required their prayers for his personal well-being and that of the Asante nation, the two being inseparable. A letter, probably of 1822, from Karamo Togma's paternal uncle, the imam of Gonja, is informative: "Now then, I, Malik, the Imam of Ghanja, ask blessing for your soul and good health, and may you conquer countries. Good health to your son, blessings to your ancestors, to your wives and to your kin. May Allah bless your son and help him conquer the people of the land. Now then, I pray for you, your children, your ancestors, your wives and all the members of your family."[77] Another letter of the same period commences: "O righteous Sultan, benefactor of the Muslims, have mercy upon the Muslims. Allah will give you life, Allah will grant you long life. He will raise you [up] and aid you against all your enemies. Greetings to you, great Sultan."[78] The writer was 'Uthman, son of the imam of the Gonja divisional town of Gbuipe. Two decades or so later he was to become the first imam al-balad of Asante, formally recognized as such by Asantehene Kwaku Dua Panin (1834–67). All subsequent occupants of that imamate have been his descendants.[79]

Had these Juula in Kumase, in making prayers for the well-being of the Asante nation and its non-Muslim king, and even for his ancestors, strayed beyond the limits of what was permitted even within the generous Suwarian concept of coexistence?[80] They were, perhaps, on the very fringes of what was permissible, but they were also very deep in the land of unbelief. Certainly they observed the Suwarian dictates on the importance of education, and it became something of a tradition for Asante imams to receive their education at the prestigious Buna school mentioned above.[81] Certainly, too, their Muslim identity remained quite apparent. The Danish pastor H. C. Monrad, who resided on the Gold Coast near Accra from 1805 to 1809, described the frequent visits of "Moors." They wore Muslim dress, were literate in Arabic, and prayed continuously. Significantly, he remarks that most of them spoke Asante.[82] Monrad had met those Juula still known as Asante Nkramo—Asante Muslims.

The Matter of Jihad

For the Juula, non-Muslim government was regarded as preferable to no government; among other reasons, the former condition was the more conducive to trade. Non-Muslim rulers might convert to Islam, as in Gonja, Dagomba, and Wa, but in other instances Muslim warlords arrived as conquerors, displacing rather than converting earlier rulers. Thus the founder of the appropriately named "Watara States of Kong" was Shehu Watara, who died in 1158 A.H., 1745.[83] A warrior of Manden origins, he first brought the old Juula trading community of Kong under unambiguously Muslim rule.[84] He, his sons, and his brother Famaghan (d. 1163 A.H., 1750),[85] extended their sway—albeit lightly in some places—over a vast area between the Bandama and Black Volta rivers, implanting themselves in positions of power in the lands of Bobo, Kulango, Lobi, and Senufo.[86] They did not, however, attempt the conversion of the rural populations, and in that respect they followed Suwarian precepts.

This was not the case with the movement associated with the name of Mahmud Karantaw, who in the mid-nineteenth century launched a jihad along the higher reaches of the Black Volta. Mahmud Karantaw was educated within the Suwarian tradition, but in the course of his pilgrimage to Mecca he met a Qadiriyya shaykh who convinced him of the propriety of jihad. In the event, Mahmud Karantaw was able to secure the support of Muslim warrior groups in the region, the *tun tigi,* but, with the possible exception of Wa, not of the Juula scholars.[87] Few of the Dafin of the region supported the jihad: enjoying good relations with non-Muslims, they had no wish to fight them and often preferred to emigrate rather than do so.[88] A Saganogo shaykh, Bamori Ja, is said to have met Mahmud Karantaw at Diebougou, and to have persuaded him to end hostilities.[89] The Karantaw jihad was successful, but limited in impact. No more than a few small towns were overrun, their people converted, and mosques and schools built. It would have been at much the same time that, by one report, the Saganogo 'ulama' of Bobo-Dioulasso advised al-Hajj 'Umar al-Futi against jihad.[90] It was also the period in which, in the deep south (as the Juula perhaps perceived it), Asantehene Kwaku Dua Panin formally conferred the Asante imamate on the Kamagate of Kumase.[91]

The Juula of the southern dispersion knew of the radical doctrines of the great *mujaddidun* of the north, of 'Uthman dan Fodio and Ahmadu Lobbo among others. They must have heard of the sack of old Wangara centers in Hausaland such as Yandotu and Kurmin Dan Ranko, whose scholars had refused support for jihad.[92] Nonetheless, the Juula seem to have regarded these distant events as of little relevance to their affairs. As late as the 1870s, for example, in an Asante at war with the British, the Muslims of Kumase continued to work for Asantehene Kofi Kakari, as they had done for his forerunner Osei Tutu Kwame, a half-century earlier. "The

Moorish necromancers and fetish priests," to quote one hostile witness, "continue to be the guiding spirits in Ashantee politics."[93] Word went out, inviting to the capital those willing to support the non-Muslim ruler in Kumase against the Christian one in London. The appeal brought to Kumase, inter alia, Ahmad Batunbuce ("of Timbuktu"), Binafi al-Hawsawi ("the Hausa"), and the Dafin scholar Sulayman b. 'Ali Kunatay.[94]

In 1887, the Zabarima warlord Babatu attacked both Wa and Nasa, destroyed the mosques, and put to death perhaps a hundred of the faithful. His anger had been fueled by the knowledge that Wa Imam 'Uthman Dun (who had studied under 'Abdallah b. al-Hajj Muhammad Watara of Buna) had encouraged the non-Muslim ruler of the Wala, the Wa Na, to oppose the Muslim Zabarima. Specifically, he had "blessed" the Wa Na's gunpowder.[95] The writing was on the wall, but the Juula savants had yet to see it. The very next year, 1888, L.-G. Binger visited Kong and produced a well-informed account of it.[96] Karamoko Oulé, a surviving grandson of Shehu Watara, had been in power for some forty years. The imam was Mustafa Saganogo, who, since he managed a score of schools in Kong, was likened to a minister of public education. He personally taught a class for adults, which Karamoko Oulé and his elders looked in on two or three times a week. There were, Binger thought, few illiterates in the town, and his general observations leave little doubt that the Suwarian tradition prevailed there. He referred to the tolerance and lack of religious fanaticism of the Juula of Kong, and to their "instinctive horror of war, which they consider dishonourable unless in defence of their territorial integrity."[97] He described how one or two Muslim families from the town would settle in an outlying village and establish rapport with the 'fetishist' headman *(roitelet fétichiste),* "securing his confidence and imperceptibly immersing themselves in his affairs."[98] They would open a school and invite the non-Muslim populace to send children to it. The process was, Binger said, one repeated in many villages along the roads running out of Kong—and, we may add, along those of the wider Juula network. Example—*qudwa*—was being put in place; conversion would follow at the appointed time.

The situation in Kong, represented by Binger as almost idyllic, was soon to be disturbed by the appearance on the scene of Almami Samori Ture. In 1885, Samori was consolidating his power in Jamala and Jimini, in what is now the northern Côte d'Ivoire, and his troops were establishing control over a wide belt of country between the Bandama in the west and the Black Volta in the east.[99] One by one, the Juula communities of the region fell under the Almami, who claimed the status of an *amir al-mu'minin,* commander of the faithful. They thus found themselves united for the first time under a common political authority. At the end of 1895, the 'ulama' of Kong sent a letter to those of Buna and Bonduku. Samori did not wish to make war on their towns, it read, but Samori says that obedience is due to him![100] Samori's strength lay not simply in the extraordinarily efficient military machine he had created,[101] but in his intention to use it as an instrument of radical social reform. Conversion was enjoined, and new converts were frequently impressed into the army. Mosques and schools were opened even in small villages, and Islamic law introduced. In the longer term, it seems, agricultural production was to be reformed, and the ancient system of (segmentary) lineage farming was to give way to one based upon plantations.[102]

Person (1975) liked to think of the Samorian movement as a "Dyula Revolution," and wrote of the "profound political and social changes . . . forced on the old structures of Manding society." Many of the developments, however, were perceived as a threat to the traditional Juula way of life. Relations between Samori and the Juula ʿulamaʾ deteriorated rapidly. Samorian soldiers sacked Buna, probably late in 1896. Among those executed for having supported the Buna mansa—regarded as a pagan—was the imam of the Friday mosque, Saʿid Sissay.[103] A few months later, in May 1897, the Almami's troops sacked the town of Kong itself. Forty of the senior ʿulama, who had gathered at the mosque to pray, were taken to the army camp and executed—though, as Muslims, they were afforded proper burials.[104] Marty reported that Samori had been offended by the contempt that Juula scholars had shown for his, Samori's, learning.[105] It may be assumed, conversely, that Samori had found their tolerance of kufr unacceptable. He discovered, moreover, that the Juula of Kong had been in communication with the French. This he regarded an act of treason. This time, though, the Juula had been quick to see the writing on the wall. Under unremitting French pressure, the state that Samori was building collapsed, in 1898, and he himself was taken prisoner in the autumn of that year. The future, as it turned out, lay with Suwarians, rather than Samorians.

Both French and British colonial administrators were to enjoy the close collaboration of the Juula ʿulamaʾ, who had no difficulty in adding Europeans to the list of non-Muslims with whom, over half a millennium and more, they had successfully done business.[106] The story of the Juula under the colonial and postcolonial regimes and governments is beyond the scope of this chapter,[107] but one vignette is offered in conclusion. In the early 1960s, Osagyefo ("Redeemer") Kwame Nkrumah, a (lapsed) Roman Catholic, presided over the affairs of Ghana. Among his personal consultants—indeed, in many respects his imam al-balad—was al-Hajj Sekou. Popularly known as Kankan Nyame, he was, indeed, from Kankan in Guinea. Nkrumah's Ghana Muslim Council drew up its bylaws. Number 8 read: "We should sympathise with every Muslim and non-muslim"; number 11: "We should pray for Osagyefo and the Country on every Friday"; and number 14: "We should always support the Government Party with sincere love for its activities." One may readily recognize, in this later-twentieth-century Ghanaian context, the deeply structured Juula beliefs that al-Hajj Salim Suwari had fashioned some four hundred years earlier. *Plus ça change, plus c'est la même chose.*

Appendix

Juula Teaching Chain	Juula Teaching Chain	Jahanke Teaching Chain
Al-Hajj Salim Suwari, to	Al-Hajj Salim Suwari, to	Al-Hajj Salim Suwari, to
Muhammad al-Buni, to	Muhammad al-Buni, to	Yusuf Kasama, to
Mandi Kuri, to	Mandi Kuri, to	Jibril Kaba, to
'Umar Fufana, to	'Umar Fufana, to	'Uthman Suwari, to
Al-Hajj 'Uthman, to	Al-Hajj 'Uthman Sakanughu, to	Muhammad Fataju, to
Muhammad Tarawiri, to	Muhammad Tarawiri, to	Muhammad Jaghabi, to
Abu Bakr Saghanu, to	Abu Bakr Sakanughu, to	Al-Amin Kajaqi, to
Al-Hajj Muhammad Saghanu, to	Al-Hajj Muhammad Sakanughu, to	Yusuf Darami, to
Imam 'Uthman, to	Imam 'Uthman Sakanughu, to	Muhammad Yaramaghan, to
Al-Hajj Muhammad Saghanu, to	Al-Hajj Muhammad Sakanughu, to	Al-Hajj Kasama, to
Muhammad al-'Afi Saghanu, to	Muhammad al-'Afi Sakanughu, to	Kaba Silla, to
Al-Mustafa b. 'Abbas b. al-Mustafa b. Al-Hajj 'Uthman Saghanu, to his son	Muhammad al-Mustafa Sakanughu, to his son	Muhammad Tanu Turi, to
'Abbas b. al-Mustafa Saghanu, to	Al-'Abbas b. al-Mustafa Sakanughu, to his son	Muhammad Fatim Kasama, to
Yahya b. Muhammad Saghanu, to	Muhammad al-'Afi b. al-'Abbas Sakanughu, to	'Uthman Ghari, to
Ibrahim b. al-Mustafa Saghanu, to his brother	Al-Hasan Qunati, to his son	Al-Hajj Salim Jabi Kasama, to
Muhammad b. al-Mustafa Saghanu, to	Adimuru Qunati, to	Ibrahim Amina Silla, to
Siddiq b. Ibrahim Saghanu, to	'Abd al-Qadir al-Timiti, to	Ibrahim Maryam Silla, to
Muhammad known as Jankira Watara, to	Imam Sa'id b. Muhammad al-Timiti, to his brother	Muhammad Karamba Ba Silla, to
'Abdallah Watara, to	Imam Ibrahim b. Muhammad al-Timiti, to his brother	Shaykh Muhammad Sanusi Silla, to
Sharif b. Madani Tarawiri, to	Imam Isma'il b. Muhammad al-Timiti, to	Muhammad Jurum Silla, to
Imam al-Hajj Sharif b. Imam 'Uthman Takari, to his son	Imam Kunandi b. Malik al-Timiti, to	Al-Hajj Muhammad Alfa Silla
Imam al-Hajj Tamimu b. Imam al-Hajj Takari, to	Abu Bakr Karamoko b. al-Hasan al-Timiti, to	
Ya'qub b. al-Hajj Sa'id	Harun b. Baba Watara	

Notes

1. Delafosse 1955, 2:297–98.
2. Levtzion and Hopkins 1981, 82, 453. Wilks 1982a, 333, but cf. Hunwick 1981, 420–21.
3. I follow Hunwick (1981, 425) in locating Yarasna near the source of the Bakhoy River.
4. Kiéthega 1983, 151–62; Perinbam 1988, 437–62.
5. Wilks 1982a, 339–44.
6. Ferguson 1972, passim; Wilks, Levtzion, and Haight 1986, 13–17, 22; Wilks 1989, passim.
7. Wilks 1968, 164; Launay 1982, 25–34.
8. Green 1984, passim.
9. Gaudefroy-Demombynes 1927, 58–59; Levtzion and Hopkins 1981, 262, and cf. 250.
10. Gaudefroy-Demombynes 1927, 58–59.
11. Brunschvig 1942–47, 120–22.
12. Levtzion and Hopkins 1981, 103, and cf. 61.
13. Levtzion and Hopkins 1981, 55, and see Bercher 1949, 318. The anonymous author of the late-twelfth-century *Siyar al-mashayikh* testifies to the Ibadi concern for the spiritual welfare of those traveling to—and hence presumably trading in—Ghana; see Lewicki 1960, 18–21.
14. Levtzion and Hopkins 1981, 32, 169–70, 177–78, 273.
15. Farias 1974, 9–24.
16. Brett 1983, 433–34.
17. For this, see the testimony of Ibn Hawqal, a contemporary of al-Qabisi, on Muslims in pagan lands, Levtzion and Hopkins 1981, 52.
18. Brett 1983, 435–37.
19. Wilks 1968, 162–97; Hunter 1977; Sanneh 1979.
20. Houdas and Delafosse 1913, 179 (Arabic text) and 314 (translation).
21. Institute of African Studies, University of Ghana, Arabic Collection, IASAR/451, *Tärikh al-Jabi*, otherwise known as *Tärikh al-Madaniyya*.
22. For perhaps the earliest English recension of this tradition, see Reichardt 1876, 319. See further, Sow 1966, 210–11.
23. Wilks 1968, 177–79; Hunter 1977, ch. 2. Sanneh 1979, 23–26, opts for a period three centuries earlier, but this appears incompatible with the burden of the evidence.
24. Wilks 1989, 61–62, 93; Hunwick 1966, 24–25.
25. I have been assured by Juula scholars that such writings do exist, but those works I have seen have turned out to be by the later al-Hajj Salim Kasama of Touba (d. 1836). See, however, Marty 1922, appendix 7, for a reference to al-Hajj Salim Suwari's *Fath al-Aqfal*, perhaps "Opening of the Locks."
26. Wilks 1968, 180.
27. See the Kano Chronicle, in Palmer 1928, 3:104–5, 111; Al-Hajj 1968, 7–42. For the spread of the Wangara into Borgu, see Farias 1996, 259–86.
28. For a tradition linking al-Hajj Salim Suwari and someone of the name Zaghaite ("Diakité"), see de Mézières 1949, 23.
29. Wilks 1968, 179; Hunter 1977, ch. 2.
30. Sartain 1971, 195, citing al-Suyuti's *Tahadduth bi-ni'mat Allah*.
31. Hunwick 1985, 60–95.
32. Wilks 1968, 176–77.
33. Participant observation, and see Ivor Wilks, "Conversations about the Past, mainly from Ghana," field notes on deposit in the Africana Library, Northwestern University.
34. Wilks 1968, 179; Hunter 1977, passim; Sanneh 1979, 2–3, 21–24, 241–47. See further, Curtin 1975, 79–80; Quimby 1975, 604–18; Wilks 1989, 25, 99–100, 202; Owusu-Ansah 1991, 131–33; Launay 1992, 21, 78–81.

35. Brett 1983, 431; Hunwick 1985, 134, 144.

36. Institute of African Studies, University of Ghana, Arabic Collection, IASAR/246: al-Hajj Muhammad Marhaba Saganogo, *Al-Jawahir wa'l Yawaqit fi Dukhul al-Islam fi l-Magharib ma'a 'l-Tawqit.* This work is a recension of earlier writings, and traditions, compiled by al-Hajj Muhammad Marhaba in 1963. For the use of the turban in the Korhogo region, see Launay 1982, 36–37.

37. See, for example, Wilks 1968, 194–97; Wilks 1989, 96–97.

38. Levtzion and Hopkins 1981, 111; McIntosh 1981, passim.

39. Wilks 1993, 4–8.

40. Ibid., 16–22.

41. Levtzion 1968, 8–11; Wilks 1982, 333–49.

42. Wilks, Levtzion, and Haight 1986, 13–15, 36–51, 91–92, 109–10.

43. Ibid., 110.

44. Ibid., 66–71, but cf. 61–66 for Levtzion's differing opinion.

45. Ibid., 89, 108.

46. Ibid., 74, 92–93.

47. I am indebted to Dr. John Hunwick for allowing me to see an early draft of his (and Fatima Harrak's) "Believers and Unbelievers in Seventeenth-Century West Africa: Correspondence on the Legality of Enslavement between Tuwat, Timbuktu, and Southern Morocco" (forthcoming).

48. For a brief account of Mossi origins, see Wilks 1985, 466–76.

49. Wilks 1965, 87–98; Levtzion 1968, 85–123; Ferguson 1972, passim.

50. *Proceedings of the Association for Promoting the Discovery of the Interior Parts of Africa.* 1791, 263–64.

51. Wilks 1989, 85–86.

52. Levtzion 1968, 143–47; Wilks 1989, 53–56.

53. Sanneh 1979, 19.

54. Wilks, 1989, 47–90.

55. Wilks 1968, 195; 1989, 58.

56. Al-Hajj Muhammad Marhaba Saganogo, *Tärikh al-Islam fi Bubu,* and see Wilks, field notes FN/181, 189, interviews with Al-Hajj Muhammad (May 9 and 13, 1966).

57. For the case of the Wa *mujaddidun,* see Wilks 1989, 93–95.

58. Wilks 1989, 109–12.

59. Wilks 1968, 197, and 1989, 97. I am grateful to Dr. Thomas Hunter for supplying me with a copy of the Jakhanke chain.

60. This observation is based upon the sample of eighty Juula *asanid.* Only four follow a different track, to Abu Bakr Jabagate of Jenne, who seems to be a late eighteenth-century figure.

61. Wilks 1968, 173–74. For the grave, see Launay 1992, 220.

62. He died on 8 Dhu 'l-hijja, 1215, after afternoon prayer, according to a marginal note by his son 'Umar, in a work on syntax in the library of al-Hajj Muhammad Marhaba Saganogo in Bobo Dioulasso; see Wilks, field notes, FN/180 (May 8, 1965).

63. *Al-Jawahir wa'l Yawaqit* (note 36).

64. *Ibtida' Din Wa;* see Wilks 1989, 76.

65. Wilks, field notes, FN/53 (July 1, 1964).

66. Wilks 1968, 165–67.

67. Jackson 1820, 347–48.

68. Wilks 1967, 152–69, and *The Life and Times of Abu Bakr al-Siddiq of Timbuktu,* in preparation, which corrects many errors in the earlier account in the light of further data. Inter alia, I have preferred to interpret the "Kara-Mousa" of the text as "Karamo Sa," and Watara *(Weterawi)* as his patronym *(qabila).*

69. Davidson 1839, 124.

70. Wilks 1989, 97 and 216 nn. 16, 17. The reader will readily remark that my interpretation of the text of Abu Bakr al-Siddiq on this point has been a wavering one.

71. Barth 1859, 3:496.

72. Wilks and Ferguson 1970, 35–52.

73. Wilks, Levtzion, and Haight 1986, 86, 104.

74. Dupuis 1824, 250 n.

75. Wilks 1975, 347–52. Wilks, Levtzion, and Haight 1986, 20–21, 202–5.

76. Dupuis 1824, 250 n.

77. Wilks, Levtzion, and Haight 1986, 210–11, 221.

78. Ibid., 210, 220.

79. Wilks 1975, 277–78.

80. I have discussed this issue, in a different context, in Wilks 1989, passim, but especially 202–4. For fuller consideration of the views of the Kumase Muslims, see Wilks 1995, 55–72.

81. Wilks 1975, 315–16.

82. Monrad 1822, 90–91.

83. Wilks, Levtzion, and Haight 1986, 83, 101, 131.

84. The complexities of the situation are examined in Green 1984, 155–217.

85. Wilks, Levtzion, and Haight 1986, 87, 105, 138.

86. Bernus 1960, 242–323; Green 1984, 306–404.

87. Wilks 1989, 100–103.

88. Binger 1892, 1:416, and see 369, 380.

89. Wilks, field notes, FN/186, interview with Al-Hajj Muhammad Marhaba Sagonogo (May 12, 1966).

90. Wilks 1968, 179 n. 2.

91. Wilks 1975, 278.

92. Last 1986, 25.

93. [Maurice, J. F.], *The Ashantee War* (London), 1874, 1:16.

94. Wilks 1975, 238–42.

95. Wilks 1989, 97, 103–8. For the Zabarima intrusion, see Holden 1965, 60–86.

96. Binger 1892, 1:287–334.

97. Ibid., 1:298, 324, 328.

98. Ibid., 1:327.

99. The major study of this phase in the Samorian epic is Person 1975, 3:1537–1993.

100. Marty 1922, 234–35, and annex 13. See also Holden 1970, 97 n. 6.

101. Legassick 1966, 95–115.

102. Holden 1970, 103–5.

103. Ibid., 97–103.

104. Person 1975, 3:1880 and 1900 n. 26.

105. Marty 1922, 188.

106. Launay 1996, 297–318.

107. But see Launay 1982, passim.

Bibliography

al-Hajj, M. A. 1968. "A Seventeenth-Century Chronicle on the Origins and Missionary Activities of the Wangarawa," *Kano Studies* 1, no. 4:7–42.

Allen, C., and R. W. Johnson, eds. 1970. *African Perspectives.* Cambridge: Cambridge University Press.

Barth, H. 1859. *Travels and Discoveries in North and Central Africa.* 3 vols. New York: Harper and Brothers.

Bercher, L. 1949. *Ibn Abi Zayd al-Qayrawani: La Risala.* Algiers.

Bernus, E. 1960. "Kong et sa région," *Etudes éburnéennes* 8:242–323.

Binger, L.-G. 1892. *Du Niger au Golfe de Guinée par le pays de Kong et le Mossi.* 2 vols. Paris: Hachette.

Brett, M. 1983. "Islam and Trade in the *Bilad al-Sudan,* Tenth–Eleventh Century A.D.," *Journal of African History* 24:431–40.

Brunschvig, R. 1942–47. "Ibn ʿAbd al-Hakam et la conquête de l'Afrique du Nord par les Arabes: étude critique," *Annales de l'Institut d'Etudes Orientales* 6:108–55.

Curtin, P. 1975. *Economic Change in Precolonial Africa.* Madison: University of Wisconsin Press.

Davidson, J. 1839. *Notes Taken During Travels in Africa.* London: J. L. Cox and Sons.

Delafosse, M. 1955. *La Langue Mandingue et ses dialectes (Malinké, Bambara, Dioula).* 2 vols. Paris: P. Geuthner.

de Mézières, A. B. 1949. "Les Diakhanke de Banisiraila et du Bondou meridional," *Notes Africaines* 41:20–25.

Dupuis, J. 1824. *Journal of a Residence in Ashantee.* London: H. Colburn.

Farias, P. F. de Moraes. 1974. "Silent Trade: Myth and Historical Evidence," *History in Africa* 1:9–24.

———. 1996. "Borgu in the Cultural Map of the Muslim Diasporas of West Africa." In Hunwick and Lawler 1996, 259–86.

Ferguson, P. 1972. "Islamization in Dagbon: A Study of the Alfanema of Yendi." Ph.D. diss., University of Cambridge.

Gaudefroy-Demombynes, ed. 1927. *Ibn Fadl Allah al-ʿOmari: Masalik el Absar fi Mamalik el Amsar.* Paris: P. Geuthner.

Green, K. L. 1984. "The Foundation of Kong: A Study in Dyula and Sonangui Ethnic Identification." Ph.D. diss., Indiana University.

Holden, J. J. 1965. "The Zabarima Conquest of North-West Ghana, Part. 1," *Transactions of the Historical Society of Ghana,* 8:60–86.

———. 1970. "The Samorian Impact on Buna: An Essay in Methodology." In Allen and Johnson 1970, 83–108.

Houdas, O., and M. Delafosse. 1913. *Tarikh el-Fettach.* Paris: E. Leroux.

Hunter, T. C. 1977. "The Development of an Islamic Tradition of Learning among the Jahanka of West Africa." Ph.D. diss., University of Chicago.

Hunwick, J. O. 1966. "Further Light on Ahmad Baba al-Tinbukti," *Research Bulletin of the Centre of Arabic Documentation* 2, 2:19–32.

———. 1981. "La Géographie du Soudan d'après al-Bakri, troisième lecture." In *Le Sol, la*

Parole, et l'Ecrit: Mélanges en hommage à Raymond Mauny, 416–24. Paris: Société Française d'Histoire d'Outre-Mer.

————. 1985. *Shari'a in Songhay: The Replies of al-Maghili to the Questions of Askia al-Hajj Muhammad.* Oxford: Published for the British Academy by Oxford University Press.

Hunwick, J. O. and N. Lawler. 1996. *The Cloth of Many Colored Silks: Papers on History and Society Ghanaian and Islamic in Honor of Ivor Wilks.* Evanston: Northwestern University Press.

Jackson, J. G. 1820. *An Account of Timbuctoo and Housa.* London: Longman, Hurst, Rees, Orme and Brown.

Kiéthega, J.-B. 1983. *L'Or de la Volta Noire.* Paris: Editions Karthala.

Last, M. 1986. "Reform in West Africa: The *jihad* Movements of the Nineteenth Century." In *History of West Africa,* ed. J. F. A. Ajayi and M. Crowder, vol. 1, 2nd ed. London: Longman.

Launay, R. 1982. *Traders without Trade: Responses to Change in Two Dyula Communities.* Cambridge: Cambridge University Press.

————. 1992. *Beyond the Stream: Islam and Society in a West African Town.* Berkeley: University of California Press.

————. 1996. "*La Trahison des Clercs?* The 'Collaboration' of a Suwarian Alim." In Hunwick and Lawler 1996, 297–318.

Legassick, M. 1966. "Firearms, Horses and Samorian Army Organization (1870–1898)," *Journal of African History* 7:95–115.

Levtzion, Nehemia. 1968. *Muslims and Chiefs in West Africa.* Oxford: Clarendon Press.

Levtzion, Nehemia, and J. F. P. Hopkins. 1981. *Corpus of Early Arabic Sources for West African History.* Trans. J. F. P. Hopkins. Cambridge: Cambridge University Press.

Lewicki, T. 1960. "Quelques extraits inédits relatifs aux voyages des commerçants et des missionaires ibadites nord-africains au pays du Soudan occidental et central au moyen âge," *Folia Orientalia* 2:1–27.

Marty, P. 1922. *Etudes sur Islam en Côte d'Ivoire.* Paris: E. Leroux.

[Maurice, J. F.]. 1874. *The Ashantee War.* 2 vols. London: H. S. King and Co.

McIntosh, S. K. 1981. "A Reconsideration of Wangara/Palolus, Island of Gold," *Journal of African History* 23:145–58.

Monrad, H. C. 1822. *Bidrag til en skildring af Guinea-Kysten og dens Indbyggere, og til en Beskrivelse over de Danske Colonier paa denne Kyst.* Copenhagen: A. Seidelin.

Owusu-Ansah, D. 1991. *Islamic Talismanic Tradition in Nineteenth-Century Asante.* Lewiston: Edwin Mellen Press.

Palmer, H. R. 1928. *Sudanese Memoirs.* 3 vols. Lagos: Government Printer.

Perinbam, B. M. 1988. "The Political Organization of Traditional Gold Mining: The Western Loby (c.1850 to c.1910)," *Journal of African History* 29:437–62.

Person, Y. 1975. *Samori.* 3 vols. Dakar: IFAN.

Proceedings of the Association for Promoting the Discovery of the Interior Parts of Africa. 1791. Association for Promoting the Discovery of the Interior Parts of Africa, London.

Quimby, L. G. 1975. "History as Identity: The Jaaxanke and the Founding of Touba (Senegal)," In *Bull.* IFAN 37, no 3:604–18.

Reichardt, C. A. L. 1876. *Grammar of the Fulbe or Fulde Language.* Church Missionary Society, London.

Sanneh, L. O. 1979. *The Jakhanke.* London: International African Institute.

Sartain, E. M. 1971. "Jalal ad-Din as-Suyuti's Relations with the People of Takrur," *Journal of Semitic Studies* 16:60–95.

Sow, A. I. 1966. *La Femme, La Vache, et la Foi.* Paris: Juilliard.

Wilks, Ivor. 1965. "A Note on the Early Spread of Islam in Dagomba," *Transactions of the Historical Society of Ghana* 8:87–98.

———. 1967. "Abu Bakr al-Siddiq of Timbuktu." In *Africa Remembered,* ed. P. Curtin, 152–69. Madison: University of Wisconsin Press.

———. 1968. "The Transmission of Islamic Learning in the Western Sudan." In *Literacy in Traditional Societies,* ed. J. Goody, 162–97. Cambridge: Cambridge University Press.

———. 1975. *Asante in the Nineteenth Century.* London: Cambridge University Press.

———. 1982. "Wangara, Akan and Portuguese in the Fifteenth and Sixteenth Centuries, 1. The Matter of Bitu: 2. The Struggle for Trade," *Journal of African History* 23, no. 3:333–49, and 23, no. 4:463–72.

———. 1985. "The Mossi and the Akan States (1400 to 1800)." In *History of West Africa,* ed. J. F. A. Ajayi and M. Crowder, vol. 1, 3rd ed., 465–502. Harlow, Essex, and New York: Longman.

———. 1989. *Wa and the Wala: Islam and Polity in Northwestern Ghana.* Cambridge and New York: Cambridge University Press.

———. 1993. *Forests of Gold.* Athens: Ohio University Press.

———. 1995. "Consul Dupuis and Wangara: A Window on Islam in Early Nineteenth-century Asante," *Sudanic Africa* 6:55–72.

———. "Conversations about the Past, mainly from Ghana," field notes on deposit in the Africana Library, Northwestern University.

Wilks, Ivor, and P. Ferguson. 1970. "In Vindication of Sidi al-Hajj ʿAbd al-Salam Shabayni." In Allen and Johnson 1970, 35–52.

Wilks, Ivor, Nehemia Levtzion, and B. Haight. 1986. *Chronicles from Gonja: A Tradition of West African Muslim Historiography.* Cambridge and New York: Cambridge University Press.

CHAPTER 5

Precolonial Islam in the Eastern Sudan

Jay Spaulding

The Early Islamic Centuries

With the fall of Egypt to the Muslims in 641 preparations began at once for the conquest of Nubia, and raiders annually probed the southern frontier. By 652 all was in readiness; a large Islamic force equipped with heavy cavalry and artillery in the form of mangonels invaded the northern Nubian kingdom of Makuria and a memorable battle was fought before the walls of her capital at Old Dongola. The Nubians won decisively. "The Muslims," as one tenth-century Islamic historian put it, "had never suffered a loss like the one they had in Nubia."[1] For most of six centuries thereafter the Nubian authorities were able to impose their own terms upon relations with the Islamic world, an arrangement commonly known among generations to follow as the *baqt*. The baqt exemplified the institutions of administered diplomatic trade through which eastern Sudanic kings normally preferred to conduct their foreign relations; royal emissaries conveyed valuable presents abroad at intervals, and foreign recipients who desired to keep the good will of the donor were expected to reciprocate them. (With the passage of centuries, various Islamic intellectuals, eager to forget the initial Nubian victory, devised increasingly elaborate and fanciful accounts that undertook to construe baqt shipments as payment of tribute.)

The Islamic conquerors, thwarted by Makuria on the Nile, turned their acquisitive attentions eastward toward the Beja. Early border raids were undertaken to impose tribute upon nearby chiefs and to open their country to Islamic merchants. The initial concern of the traders was perhaps primarily safe transit through the desert that separated Upper Egypt from the Red Sea, but they soon found the Beja to be a convenient source of slaves, and a long age of bitter conflict followed as the slaving frontier was gradually extended southward across the Beja homeland. At the height of hostilities a perceptive eleventh-century Persian traveler observed: "The Beja who live in this desert are not bad people, nor are they robbers. It is the Muslims and others who kidnap their children and take them to the towns of Islam, where they sell them."[2]

Muslims who penetrated the Beja homeland soon rediscovered the ancient and long-abandoned mines of gold and precious stones that lined the course of the Wadi al-'Allaqi. The last half of the ninth century witnessed a mining boom that attracted several thousand immigrant Arabs to southern Egypt, and also stimulated a new demand for slaves to serve as miners. The Beja resisted the influx of miners vigorously, and in response the Islamic authorities of the day subsidized in turn a pair of Arab adventurers to mobilize a force of mercenaries against them. The ensuing campaigns revealed that although the Beja were not likely to prevail against a well-ordered conventional army, they were not likely to accept defeat either, and would prove extremely difficult to govern. Since these punitive campaigns also introduced the firm hand of government to the frontier settlements, they alienated many of the very miners the campaigns had been organized to protect; in years to come, as the mining boom gradually faded upon sober reappraisal of the mineral deposits, many immigrant Arabs would be absorbed into the northern Beja lineages with whom they increasingly made common cause. During the tenth century, a few of these bilingual communities of mixed descent were recognized by outsiders as the first Beja Muslims.

Meanwhile on the Nile the ninth-century mineral boom in the Wadi al-'Allaqi threatened the adjoining northern district of Makuria with a new Islamic invasion in the person of traders and miners; worse, it promised to reward any Nubian subject willing to break with tradition by embracing the economic usages of the Mediterranean world. (The fact that some did so may be inferred from the appearance during the ninth century of a Makurian official charged with locating and taxing Nubian traders resident abroad.) In 836, when foreign Muslims asserted their right to buy land within northern Makuria, the Nubian monarch himself journeyed to Baghdad to seek relief from the caliph. Though kindly received, he was not successful; upon his return he was obliged to divide his realm into a northern zone within which intrusive Mediterranean economic principles would prevail, and a conservative southern zone forbidden to private traders on pain of death. In centuries to follow the northerners became Muslims, and in 1174 the zone was reorganized as an officially Islamic province of Makuria under a dignitary entitled Kanz al-Dawla, the head of an elite group of political refugees from Upper Egypt.

As the Beja made the transition from victims to participants in private Islamic commerce, the trading networks of the Red Sea began to impinge upon the large southern Nubian kingdom of Alodia. The capital city of Soba had a quarter for Islamic merchants as early as the tenth century, and by the twelfth the kingdom began to break up; conspicuously, the erstwhile northern riverine province called al-Abwab sponsored a rising international trading entrepôt near the Atbara confluence and conducted a foreign policy that supported the Islamic opponents of Christian Makuria.

Hostilities between the northern Nubian kingdom and the Muslims erupted in 1269, when the Mamluk sultan Baybars rebuffed a Makurian baqt initiative; the Nubians, probably in retaliation, sacked the Egyptian Red Sea port of 'Aydhab in 1272. The Mamluks dispatched exploratory probes up the Nile, and when these indicated that effective resistance was unlikely, in 1276 a major Mamluk force invaded and conquered Makuria. Under the terms of settlement the Nubians were allowed to keep their religion as protected persons under Islamic law and were to be governed via a puppet king to be chosen by the conquerors from among the old royal family. During the century to follow the Nubians tried repeatedly to shake off foreign rule, leading to a renewed series of invasions from Egypt (notably in 1288, 1289–1290, 1315–1317, 1323, 1366, and 1379) with the periodic imposition of Egyptian garrisons to support the puppet kings. During the expedition of 1315–1317 the first Muslim puppet king was imposed, and on 29 May 1317 the great royal palace in Old Dongola was converted into a mosque. In 1324 the Kanz al-Dawla seized the throne from the old dynasty and the country disintegrated into warring factions. The Makurian heartland now became a rich slaving ground for Islamic merchants. "[The Nubians] are Christians and have a hard life," as one fourteenth-century observer from Egypt put it; "they are imported and sold."[3]

As the grasp of the northern and southern Nubian kings faltered, the most conspicuous beneficiaries were the pastoral communities who inhabited the wide lands beyond the irrigated banks of the Nile. The pastoralists of these troubled years sought freedom from the waning Christian state, security from Muslim slave raiders, and a new sense of communal identity through the adoption of Islam; in time the cultivators, who in every century before the twentieth aspired to the pastoral lifestyle, were likely to follow. Just as one great pastoral resurgence a millennium before, perhaps sparked by the introduction of the camel, had brought an end to the ancient state tradition of Kush and Meroe, so the great pastoral resurgence of the fourteenth and fifteenth centuries carved a hiatus through the orderly flow of Sudanese dynastic history at the cusp of transition between the medieval and early modern worlds.

The Islamic African Kingdoms

Renewed centripetal social forces restored royal rule to the Nile in about 1500 and thereafter introduced the state form of government to the western highlands, apparently for the first time, over the century and a half to follow. Legends about the Funj kingdom of Sinnar in the Nile valley and of the realms of Dar Fur and Wadai in the western highlands always characterize the rise of the kings as a triumph for Islam. Close reading, however, reveals that the new kings' defeated opponents also bore conventionally Islamic names; thus the Funj leader 'Amara "Whom One Approaches with Bowed Head" struck down 'Abd Allah "The Gatherer" of the northern riverine communities; Dalil Bahr the Keira son of Ahmad "The Hamstrung" defeated his Tunjur half-brother to create an independent Dar Fur, while 'Abd al-Karim, the founder of Wadai, supplanted his father-in-law Daud after marrying the daughter 'Aysha. In each instance, it would seem that a preliminary conversion had already taken place long before, during the extended struggles among big-men and chiefs that culminated in the imposition of monarchy; by the point when the first kings achieved definitive consolidation of royal authority a pre-Islamic past had already become literally unthinkable. What was different about the new state form of government that emerged during the early modern age was not allegiance to Islam per se, but the finality of society's ideological commitment to the faith and the new uses it would now be expected to serve.

The eastern Sudanic kingdoms were Islamic lands that sought and received recognition as such from their neighbors. They were also feudal societies that postulated a hierarchical social structure preoccupied with differentiations of rank and status, and they accepted as natural and inevitable very wide social distances between the hereditary ruling elite and the polyglot ethnic mosaic of humble commoners. The state ideology of the new kingdoms was structured to serve two aspects of the social dynamic. Islam provided a set of general integrative forms that expressed the corporate unity and excellence of society in its relations with the outside world. The titles of the monarchs themselves as preserved in their charters and letters reveal that a king was expected to enact the role of exemplary Muslim for his community (the kings of Wadai and Dar Fur claimed the caliphal title *amir al-mu'minin;* the kings of Sinnar did not), and the accounts of travelers indicate that many kings took this obligation very seriously. Legend claimed that the sterling Islamic credentials of the first Funj sultan had deterred an invasion of Sinnar by the great Ottoman conqueror Selim the Grim, while by the nineteenth century, as the Turks came to be viewed as fellow-Muslims in an increasingly hostile world, a Dar Fur sultan was said to have tendered formal submission to the Porte. Many kings exercised the royal prerogative of dispatching a *mahmal* of rich presents to the Holy Cities of Arabia and extending charitable donations to other worthy Islamic institutions abroad. Kings were expected to facilitate the passage of pilgrims; indeed, it was not unknown for a ruler to abdicate in order to perform this obligation himself. Visitors with claims to intellectual or spiritual gifts in the Islamic sense were welcomed, and could typically expect to receive generous royal patronage both as privileged courtiers when in the presence of the king and through royal grants of landed estates, groups of subject commoners, and other privileges that established these immigrant holy men as local dignitaries in the countryside. In short, contacts with the outside world were made comprehensible and legitimate to surrounding lands through their conduct in a conventionally Islamic idiom.

The sincere Islamic convictions of eastern Sudanic kings, however, did not preclude considerable flexibility in the conduct of foreign policy. During the sixteenth century, Sinnar resisted Ottoman advances up the Nile and allied herself with Ethiopia to contain Turkish ambitions at their newly annexed Red Sea city-state island outposts of Sawakin and Musawwa'. On the other hand, Sinnar was obliged to repel two major Ethiopian invasions (in 1618–1619 and 1744), and during the later seventeenth century she invaded and annexed the surviving Christian Alodian successor state of Fazughli that controlled important sources of gold near the upper Blue Nile. The two western kingdoms of Dar Fur and Wadai struggled against each other for over a century as each sought to reestablish by force the actual or ostensible unity that was said to have obtained under a dynasty of Tunjur. Toward the close of the eighteenth century, however, a cautious entente was achieved, upon which Wadai directed her expansive energies westward against Baghirmi while Dar Fur began a long and ultimately successful campaign against Sinnar for control of the region of Kordofan that lay between them. No clear pattern of loyalty to specifically Islamic commitments is apparent in the course of political events.

The second set of ideological forms characteristic of the eastern Sudanic monarchies was hierarchical in structure and particularistic in its ramifications; this idiom, drawing heavily upon the lexicon of African kingship, served to justify the authority structure of the state and to rationalize the very great cultural diversities that obtained among the polyethnic class of subjects. Here too the king played a central role, as the ritual initiator of annual cultivation on the Nile or as rainmaker in the west, and everywhere as supreme arbiter over a regime of sumptuary regulations that defined in concrete terms the elaborate social pyramid of rank and status. In Sinnar, for example, (since comparable legal evidence from the western kingdoms is not at hand), the king's law created a carefully defined middle-level social status niche for Islamic holy men. The testimony of a holy man in court was worth less than that of a nobleman but more than that of a commoner; the penalty for killing a holy man was less than that for killing a nobleman, and it was greater if he were a privileged immigrant foreigner than if he were native-born, but in either case greater than the penalty for killing a commoner. In all the kingdoms holy men enjoyed various exemptions from taxation, rights of geographical mobility and personal security, and other privileges that distinguished them from the class of subject commoners.

The Islam of the eastern Sudanic kingdoms was corporate and communal; all obedient subjects of the exemplary Islamic king were Muslims by definition, irrespective of any empirical deviation between their respective lifestyles and the customary usages of the Islamic heartlands. Such discrepancies were often rather wide; pork and beer, for example, were dietary staples in many provinces, while sumptuary laws demanded the exposure of the torso of commoner women and the bare head of commoner men. The Islam of the subject commoners was defined not necessarily through intellectual knowledge about the faith nor through observance of a life-style characteristic of Muslims elsewhere, but through obedence to the Islamic king. Disobedience to the king, conversely, implied rejection of the corporate Islam of the community, and that justified the imposition of severe penalties appropriate to apostasy or unbelief. In practice this onus was borne most commonly by the Islamically controversial southern communities of each kingdom, termed Nuba in Sinnar, Fertit in Dar Fur, and Kirdi in Wadai. They and they alone among the communities of subjects were compelled to discharge their tax obligations to the kings in nonagricultural form, notably in ivory, gold, civet, or slaves, and whoever failed or refused was liable to punitive raids and selective or mass enslavement. Each eastern Sudanic kingdom thus came to possess a bleeding southern frontier along which class conflict manifested itself in the form of a localized but eternal civil war; insecurity was institutionalized, and Islamic status rendered eternally contingent.

The Rise of Middle-Class Interpretations of Islam

A turning point in the history of each of the three great kingdoms of the eastern Sudan came with the decision to open commercial ties with the Ottoman world. In the Funj kingdom this decision was taken in the third quarter of the seventeenth century as Sultan Badi II (1644–1681) established a fixed capital at Sinnar, built an impressive royal mosque, and began to send periodic caravans to Egypt and Sawakin. In Dar Fur the opening came during the last quarter of the eighteenth century as Sultan ʿAbd al-Rahman moved his *fashir* east of the mountains to the site that bears the name today and organized caravans to embark down the Forty Days' Road through the northeastern desert to Egypt. Wadai established significant religious contacts with the Mediterranean milieu when Sultan Muhammad Sharif (1834–1858) became an adherent of the Libyan-based Sanusiyya brotherhood, but because the king was an economic conservative the commercial opening of Wadai had to await the reign of his successor Sultan ʿAli (1858–1874). Increasingly frequent and intimate contact between the African kingdoms and the Mediterranean world could hardly fail to highlight the contrast between the culture of the eastern Sudan and the usages of the heartlands of Islam. While the implications of this critique were similar everywhere, the ultimate consequences became most clearly visible in the case of Sinnar, where a counterculture was given time to gather partisans as the critique ripened.

One index by which the advance of the newly imported critical perspective may be measured lies in the rise of literacy in Arabic, not only among the professionally Islamic classes but also within the government; through written sources such as chronicles, charters, letters, legal documents, hagiography, and poetry the age that followed the opening of the eastern Sudan to the culture of the Mediterranean world would be much more accessible to the historian, albeit through certain admittedly limited perspectives, than what had gone before.

A central preoccupation of the new literature was the professionally Islamic class, by this time no longer necessarily immigrant but rather native sons, and sometimes daughters. Through the corpus of royal charters from Sinnar and Dar Fur, one may observe the process by which the kings endowed holy men with lands, subjects, and an ever-lengthening list of exemptions and immunities that progressively freed them from all residual obligations toward the state and gave them license to reorganize the communities they ruled as they saw fit. The hagiographical literature offers an array of paradigmatic careers through which the holy man may be seen enacting the vocations of healer, teacher, scholar, warrior, merchant, mediator, courtier, judge, mystic, or *pater familias;* perhaps it is significant that the recorded lives of saints who used their powers to defend the interests of subject commoners are considerably longer, on the average, than are those of holy men who merely served as courtiers and judges. The longest hagiographical work, the *Tabaqat* of Muhammad al-Nur b. Dayf Allah, gives fair insight into how the holy men themselves conceptualized their universe. Many holy men, particularly during the earlier generations, thought in terms of Sufism's eloquent elaboration upon the ancient Neoplatonic vision of a cosmos comprising a hierarchy of ascending levels of material and spiritual reality linked through the divine process of creation by a great chain of being. This world view was eminently suited to the society of eastern Sudanic kingdoms, which it mirrored, and it afforded psychedelic visions of unlimited cosmic progress to humble folk who found themselves, by choice or by royal fiat, answerable to a holy man. The *Tabaqat* also reveals, however, that as generations passed interest in the cosmos faded as a second, legally oriented paradigm of society gradually gained in influence.

The literature of private legal documents traces out in exquisite detail precisely how the holy men who led communities gradually transformed them in conformity to the principles and usages of the Islamic heartlands; in the present limited context a few illustrative examples of this complex and highly nuanced process must suffice. The royal grant of free geographical mobility made it possible for individuals of holy status to participate in commerce, and the royal grant of the right to sponsor a market enabled the opportunities of commerce to come to them. The ensuing spread of the money economy made possible a form of speculation in food grains by which many families of cultivators became permanently indebted, though the holy men, who usually preferred political power to monetary gain, were not necessarily the worst of creditors—at least as long as potential markets external to the community itself were few. Within the community of a holy man the concept of private property in land was introduced, and a rudimentary market in real estate was born as the rich began to buy out the poor; conspicuously, the erstwhile traditional landholding rights of women were often extinguished in this way. Holy men relaxed the sumptuary laws regulating bridewealth to encourage competitive bidding for matrimony, a technique that allowed the rich of each generation to consolidate their wealth through corporate marital mergers or for a rising family to convert its newly accumulated wealth into status for its children. The concession to community members of the right to acquire and own slaves carried the potential to transform agriculture fundamentally, but at initial stages a more conspicuous consequence was the introduction of slave concubinage among holy men and the beginning of slave prostitution.

Under the cumulative impact of these institutional changes the status of women within the holy man's community gradually changed; as landholding rights eroded and meaningful participation in production became a marker of low or even slave status, free women urgently sought respectability through evermore-stringent degrees of Islamically sanctioned seclusion. Males compelled to commit substantial resources to competitive bidding for a rich and prestigeous mate embraced the new purdah system wholeheartedly, for it safeguarded their investment. Traditional locally manufactured Sudanese female garments were replaced, by those who could afford them, with more conservative (and more expensive) imported Middle Eastern fashions. In Sinnar, at some point late in the eighteenth century, it was discovered that the female of the species cannot swim—a skill hitherto vital in an agricultural world where cultivated islands were numerous but boats were few. Here as elsewhere the middle-class Islamic institutions and usages pioneered by holy men within the microenvironment of their chartered enclave communities would ultimately become the standard for eastern Sudanic society as a whole.

A second index by which the advance of intrusive Mediterranean institutions may be measured lies in the appearance of towns and the rise of an indigenous urban-based middle class. At early stages of foreign commercial contact visiting merchants were conducted via royal fiat to and from a specially designated entrepôt at or near the capital, and exchanges were confined largely to the court itself. From Wadai comes explicit testimony out of the very first generation during which roads were open to Mediterranean traders from the north to the effect that the people of Wadai bitterly resented the prerogatives lavished upon foreign traders by their king and envied the wealth accumulating in their privileged alien enclave.

In the long run it would prove difficult for Sudanese kings to thwart the desire of their subjects, and not least the provincial authorities who controlled physical access to the realm, to participate in the lucrative new trade with the Islamic heartlands. Wadai resisted throughout her brief half-century of further existence to enter the colonial age as an old agrarian state without cities. Several unruly new towns arose in nineteenth-century Dar Fur, one of which, under the leadership of a holy man, conducted an eleven-year insurrection against the last Keira monarch; meanwhile, the kings auctioned off to rival entrepreneurial consortia of traders and mercenaries the right to conduct the raiding expeditions that supplied a burgeoning nineteenth-century export trade in slaves. But the disintegrative effects of commercial capitalism were most clearly evident in Sinnar, where the number of new eighteenth-century towns approached thirty. The old matrilineal dynasty was overthrown in 1718; the distinctive Funj system of kinship discipline that had united the elite and enforced hierarchy among its members now gave way to the simple sale of titles and offices through competitive bidding among the quarrelsome new warlord patrilineages. In 1762 a clique of middle-class warlords tamed the sultan and imposed one of their own as ruling Hamaj *wazir,* then indulged themselves in half a century of pointless civil war during which each of the new towns was ravaged at least once.

When a society changes, the ideological structures that rationalize it must accommodate to the transformation. The new towns of the late precolonial eastern Sudan housed a variety of lifestyles alien to old agrarian rural society; some typical examples would include the self-made nobleman who purchased his title and bribed his way into office with the profits of speculation on the grain market, the slave who gathered coins for her master through prostitution with itinerant merchants, the mercenary raider who had kidnapped and imported her, the schoolmaster who had taught him to perform calculations of profit and loss, or the respectable free woman who spent her hours of privileged seclusion devising colorful spirit possession cults as an antidote to housewifely boredom. For new townspeople such as these, legally oriented interpretations of Islam imported from abroad encapsulated in handbooks such as the *Mukhtasar* of Khalil b. Ishaq or the *Risala* of Ibn Abi Zayd offered an authoritative and appealing new paradigm of how life should be lived. Empirical conformity to the rules of Islam found in legal texts now became the criterion by which one's status as a Muslim was evaluated. Urban leaders made public prayer compulsory (having provided instruction for those unfamiliar with the requisite formalities), and new urban customs of dress and adornment were established to conform to Middle Eastern usages. In the end the new urban-based middle-class society would claim for itself an entirely new cultural and ethnic identity as Arabs, in support of which bourgeois literati composed appropriately ingenious pedigrees as they chronicled the tumultuous and bloody collapse of the old order. Rural folk, particularly in the southern provinces, were now often denied the status of Muslims in order to legitimize their enslavement.

The Islamic Slavelords

The political vacuum along the Nile created by the victory of middle-class Islam was filled by an invasion of Egyptians in the service of Muhammad Ali and his successors, who conquered Sinnar in 1821 and Dar Fur in 1874. The Turco-Egyptian regime allied itself with the emergent middle classes of Sinnar to introduce or extend Mediterranean institutions such as the money economy and a conventionally Islamic magistracy with which to defend such key principles of the new bourgeois society as private property in land and the right of non-noblemen to own slaves and to conduct private commerce. As the nineteenth century advanced, rural society along the Nile was transformed as slave labor began to replace free in the fields, while trade, moneylending, and cash-cropping elevated new local elites. Historically conspicuous products of this transformation were the *jallaba*, men displaced by poverty and debt from their homes in the irrigated north or drawn by the lure of easy fortune beyond the western or southern Turco-Egyptian frontier. In the wide equatorial lands south of Sinnar and Dar Fur jallaba warlords erected predatory new Islamic slaving regimes to service the demand of the Turco-Egyptian market, while south of Wadai a similar regime arose in response to the arrival of Mediterranean capitalism as mediated by a Libyan Islamic brotherhood, the Sanusiyya.

Along the upper Blue Nile the intrusive northern Islamic jallaba of the late eighteenth and nineteenth centuries were called the Watawit; after several generations of bitter internal conflict a northern Sudanese leader named Khojali Hasan eventually won Ethiopian backing and emerged supreme among them. The Watawit regime differed from its western counterparts in that it mobilized slave labor for the mining or washing of local gold deposits as well as producing slaves for export. Over the century and a half of its existence this slavelord regime succeeded in gradually isolating and decimating the small indigenous communities of the Sudan-Ethiopian borderlands.

Toward the middle of the nineteenth century companies of merchants based in Khartoum succeeded in passing beyond the great equatorial swamps of the White Nile to establish outposts along the rivers of the southern Sudan and on into [modern] Uganda and the Congo. Not all these companies were Islamic; indeed, some of the earliest merchants were European or Egyptian Christians. But all the expeditions and bases of the Khartoumers were staffed largely by northern Sudanese jallaba, and in time the Turkish authorities took steps to drive out the non-Muslims by favoring their Islamic competitors. The motive was not primarily religious scruple but a desire to minimize meddling by foreign powers claiming rights of capitulatory patronage over various classes of non-Muslim Ottoman subjects; the issue was particularly sensitive because, in an age of European abolitionist fervor, slaves were rapidly eclipsing ivory and gum arabic as the major economic preoccupation of the Khartoumers in the south. Thereafter the government in Cairo equivocated between fatally self-contradictory policies of embracing the jallaba slavelords through cooptation or eradicating them through the imposition of direct rule by force. Religion became an overt issue again during the 1870s as the government, bowing to foreign humanitarian sentiments, dispatched European Christians such as Samuel Baker, Romolo Gessi, and Charles Gordon to assert Ottoman control.

Meanwhile the southern frontier had found its organizational genius in the northern Sudanese entrepreneur and slavelord al-Zubayr Rahma Mansur. Upon his arrival in the Bahr al-Ghazal in 1856 he began to build up a network of thirty-one fortified bases from which, when he set forth against Dar Fur in 1874, he could muster 6,400 professional slave troops supported by 9,000 armed jallaba. Zubayr's military machine rested upon a generalized enslavement of the non-Islamic populace; as the resistance of each defeated community was crushed those allowed to survive were given Islamic slave names and assigned duties as cultivators, bearers, soldiers, or concubines—or were sent northward via the jallaba to be exchanged for the firearms and gunpowder upon which the predatory enterprise depended. Zubayr's technique of forcible conversion to Islam through violence and enslavement has remained a compelling precedent for many subsequent Sudanese governments.

At the close of the 1870s the Cairo government stripped al-Zubayr of his conquests through chicannery and force, and many of his outraged minions soon rallied to the cause of the Sudanese Mahdi. One, however, began an independent career of conquest, enslavement, and forced Islamization; between 1878 and 1900 Rabih Fadl Allah carved a broad swath westward from southern Dar Fur. From 1878 until 1891 he occupied the southern frontier zone of Wadai, there building up a force comparable to that of al-Zubayr; then he struck on westward toward the shores of Lake Chad. Upon the departure of Rabih from the southern periphery of Wadai a new slavelord named Sanusi arose to exploit the possibilities of the region;

fed by slave-tended plantations surrounding his capital at Ndele, Sanusi's gunmen extended Islam and servitude across southern Chad and in the northern Central African Republic and exported tens of thousands of slaves northward toward the Mediterranean.

Conclusion

Islam has served to explain and justify four rather different situations in the historical experience of the precolonial eastern Sudan. In some early cases it entered competitive lineage societies during the stage when they were undergoing or resisting the pressures of centralization; there the new ideology apparently followed other valuable, exotic, imported prestige goods down the redistributive networks of the politically consolidating chiefs. In other cases, African kingdoms adopted Islam as state cult. With the opening of these kingdoms to the commercial capitalist usages of the Mediterranean world, Islam provided rationales for a middle-class critique of old agrarian society, and it also defined the essence of the predatory slavelord regimes that arose beyond the nineteenth-century colonial frontier. While today the Islamic rationale for the older two forms of eastern Sudanic society is largely a matter of historical interest, the justifications for the last two remain significant living idioms in the political discourse of the region.

Notes

1. Vantini 1975, 95.
2. Spaulding 1995, 589
3. Ibid., 592.

Bibliography

Adams, William Y. 1977. *Nubia: Corridor to Africa*. Princeton: Princeton University Press.

Bjørkelo, Anders. 1989. *Prelude to the Mahdiyya: Peasants and Traders in the Shendi Region, 1821–1885*. Cambridge: Cambridge University Press.

Carbou, Henry. 1912. *La Région du Tchad et du Ouadaï*. 2 vols. Paris: Leroux.

Cordell, Dennis Dale. 1985. *Dar al-Kuti and the Last Years of the Trans-Saharan Slave Trade*. Madison: University of Wisconsin Press.

———. 1986. "Warlords and Enslavement: A Sample of Slave-Raiders from Eastern Ubangi-Shari." In *Africans in Bondage: Studies in Slavery and the Slave Trade*, ed. Paul E. Lovejoy, 336–65. Madison: African Studies Center, University of Wisconsin.

Cuoq, Joseph. 1986. *Islamisation de la Nubie Chrétienne, VIIe–XVIe siècle*. Paris: Geuthner.

Ewald, Janet J. 1990. *Soldiers, Traders and Slaves: State Formation and Economic Transformation in the Greater Nile Valley, 1700–1885.* Madison: University of Wisconsin Press.

Gray, Richard. 1961. *A History of the Southern Sudan, 1839–1889.* Oxford: Oxford University Press.

Hill, Richard. 1959. *Egypt in the Sudan, 1820–1881.* Oxford: Oxford University Press.

Holy, Ladislav. 1991. *Religion and Custom in a Muslim Society: The Berti of Sudan.* Cambridge: Cambridge University Press.

James, Wendy. 1988. *The Listening Ebony: Moral Knowledge, Religion, and Power among the Uduk of Sudan.* Oxford: Clarendon Press.

Kapteijns, Lidwien. 1983. "Dâr Silâ, the Sultanate in Precolonial Times, 1870–1916," *Cahiers d'études africaines* 92, 23–24:447–70.

———. 1985. *Mahdist Faith and Sudanic Tradition: A History of the Masalit Sultanate, 1870–1930.* London: Routledge & Kegan Paul.

Kapteijns, Lidwien, and Jay Spaulding. 1982. "Precolonial Trade Between States in the Eastern Sudan, c. 1700–c.1900," *African Economic History* 11:29-62.

———. 1988. *After the Millennium: Diplomatic Correspondence from Wadai and Dar Fur on the Eve of Colonial Conquest, 1885–1916.* East Lansing: African Studies Center, Michigan State University.

———. 1991. "History, Ethnicity and Agriculture in the Sudan." In *The Agriculture of the Sudan,* ed. Gillian M. Craig, 84–100. Oxford: Oxford University Press.

McHugh, Neil. 1994. *Holymen of the Blue Nile: The Making of an Arab-Islamic Community in the Nilotic Sudan, 1500–1850.* Evanston: Northwestern University Press.

O'Fahey, R. S. 1980. *State and Society in Dar Fur.* London: C. Hurst.

———. 1994. *Arabic Literature of Africa, Volume 1: The Writings of Eastern Sudanic Africa to c. 1900.* London: Brill.

O'Fahey, R. S., and M. I. Abu Salim. 1983. *Land in Dar Fur: Charters and Related Documents from the Dar Fur Sultanate.* Cambridge: Cambridge University Press.

O'Fahey, R. S. and J. L. Spaulding. 1974. *Kingdoms of the Sudan.* London: Methuen.

Spaulding, Jay. 1985. *The Heroic Age in Sinnar.* East Lansing: African Studies Center, Michigan State University.

———. 1988. "The Business of Slavery in the Central Anglo-Egyptian Sudan, 1910–1930," *African Economic History* 17:23–44.

———. 1995. "Medieval Christian Nubia and the Islamic World: A Reconsideration of the Baqt Treaty," *International Journal of African Historical Studies* 28, 3:577–94.

Spaulding, Jay, and Lidwien Kapteijns. 1991. "The Orientalist Paradigm in the Historiography of the Late Precolonial Sudan." In *Golden Ages, Dark Ages: Imagining the Past in Anthropology and History,* ed. Jay O'Brien and William Roseberry, 139–51. Berkeley: University of California Press.

———. 1994. *An Islamic Alliance: 'Ali Dinar and the Sanusiyya, 1906–1916.* Evanston: Northwestern University Press.

———. Forthcoming. "The Conceptualization of Land Tenure in the Precolonial Sudan:

Evidence and Interpretation." In *State, Land, and Society in the History of Sudanic Africa,* ed. Donald Crummey. Champaign-Urbana: Illinois University Press.

Spaulding, Jay, and Muhammad Ibrahim Aba Salim. 1989. *Public Documents from Sinnar.* East Lansing: Michigan State University Press.

Triulzi, Alessandro. 1981. *Salt, Gold, and Legitimacy: Prelude to the History of a No-Man's Land: Bela Shangul, Wallagga, Ethiopia (ca. 1800–1898).* Napoli: Istituto Universitario Orientale.

Tubiana, Marie-José. 1964. *Survivances préislamiques en Pays Zaghawa.* Paris: Université de Paris.

Tubiana, Marie-José, Issa Hassan Khayar, and Paule Devisse. 1978. *Abd el-Kerim: Propagateur de l'Islam et fondateur du royaume du Ouaddaï.* Paris: CNRS.

Vantini, Giovanni. 1975. *Oriental Sources Concerning Nubia.* Heidelberg: Society for Nubian Studies.

Yusuf Fadl Hasan. 1974. *Kitab al-Tabaqat fi Khusus al-Awliya' wa'l-Salihin wa'l-Ulama' wa'l-Shu'ara' fi'l-Sudan, ta'lif Muhammad al-Nur wad Dayf Allah.* 2nd ed. Khartoum: University of Khartoum Press.

CHAPTER 6

Revolutions in the Western Sudan

David Robinson

Over the course of the eighteenth and nineteenth centuries, a number of West African Muslim scholars and military leaders organized successful movements of reform and state-building. The reform movements they called *jihad;* the regimes, they characterized as Islamic states, under appellations such as imamate or caliphate. These reformers and builders formulated their experience in oral tradition and writing for themselves and future generations, and these accounts had a great impact on their contemporaries in other regions, who were sometimes inspired to follow a similar course. The most prominent scholars and leaders were Fulbe, and over this period they reconstructed their own ethnic identity to fit the dominant role they were playing—or at least thought they were playing—in the Islamization of the region.[1]

During the colonial period, these accounts were reinterpreted by Islamicists and historians and fashioned into an important chapter of West African history. By the 1960s, the subject of the "jihads of West Africa" was a kind of growth industry, overwhelming other less spectacular forms of Islamic practice and Islamization.[2] Since that time, a certain balance has been restored,[3] but these movements merit separate treatment because they constitute an important chapter of the history of the faith in West Africa. They were fundamental to the spread of Islam—often through the agency of Sufi orders—from town and capital to countryside and from elite to common people (as well as from Sunni code to sufi practice). They produced pedagogical systems that provided the tools to understand the faith in its original Arabic form but also in Pulaar (Fulfulde) and other languages.[4] They were instrumental in transforming West Africa into a part of the dar al-Islam.

The movement that led to the creation of the Sokoto caliphate in Hausaland in the central Sudan (today's northern Nigeria and adjacent areas) is by far the best known of these phenomena. It must be understood, however, in its historical and geographical context. It built upon its predecessors and exerted enormous influence upon its successors in the nineteenth century. The fundamental problem faced by all of these movements was the question of legitimation: who had the authority to declare a jihad and to take charge of an emerging Islamic state? The Islamic heartlands were not united under a single authority. The Ottoman sultanate was a distant and declining reality that could not pretend to control the territory much beyond the Mediterranean littoral; Morocco, although independent of Istanbul, maintained fragile claims to territory and influence on the West African fringe. Both regimes were recognized as Islamic authorities, but they were absorbed with European expansion around the Mediterranean, and neither inspired the new leaders of West Africa. In this situation, the West Africans turned to the classical foundations of the faith, to Muhammad and the early Muslims, to create an Islamic authority where, in their judgment, none existed.[5]

At the beginning of the eighteenth century, the West African savanna was a frontier of the faith. The Almoravid movement of the eleventh century had indeed begun with a declaration of jihad, but it did not have a lasting impact in most areas and among most societies. Between the eleventh and eighteenth centuries, when many of the people and ruling classes of the savanna region had a "pagan" identity, there are only fleeting and elusive references to the invocation of jihad.[6] In Sahara and savanna alike, Muslim communities had become accustomed to operating under and alongside non-Muslim authority. Their scholars made much of the corrupting effect of power, and suggested that less injustice was probably committed in the existing order of things than in a specifically "Islamic" regime.[7] This scholarly perspective, related to the Suwarian tradition described in chapter 4, was articulated fully in the eighteenth and nineteenth centuries as a response to the jihadists, who in turn were obliged to delve more deeply into their motivations, conduct, and legitimating authorities.[8] The historical debate, which continues to this day, itself constitutes a major source for the two perspectives.

Interpreting the historical sources constitutes a problem, emerging as they do primarily from the leadership, either as chronicle or theoretical legitimation, or from their critics. Little information was generated by the followers themselves, despite the dramatic spread of literacy, nor by the losers, nor by neutral observers. Europeans began to explore the West African interior in the nineteenth century, and some, such as Heinrich Barth[9] and Eugène Mage,[10] were fascinated by the jihads and Islamic states, but they drew their versions primarily from the scholarly elites. The European explorers and the indigenous elites alike regarded the jihads, the states, and their conspicuous Fulbe leadership as a linked chain and progressive development in West African history.

These sources and movements did not emerge in a social and economic vacuum. Scholars, leaders, and followers were disturbed by the increasing levels of violence, the exploitation by ruling classes, and the enslavement of Muslims. Muslim men, women, and children were often taken with their "pagan" contemporaries, and they might wind up in other African societies, in the Americas, or the Mediterranean area. The impact of the trans-Atlantic slave trade was deeply felt in areas closer to the coast; the trans-Saharan trade touched all the arenas of jihad.[11]

€arly Jihad Initiatives

The earliest link in the "chain" of jihads occurred in the late seventeenth century in the far western portion of the Sahara.[12] This movement, called Sharr Bubba, was occasioned by the spread of Arab nomadic groups, the Bani Hassan, into the far western Sahara. From the fourteenth century on, these groups gradually made their way south, as far as the Senegal River, spreading their version of spoken Arabic (Hassaniyya) and increasingly dominating the indigenous, Berber-speaking inhabitants.

By the 1670s, Nasir al-Din, a Berber scholar and warrior from the southwestern part of present-day Mauritania, rebelled against this domination and fashioned a coalition largely around the indigenous inhabitants. For a few years he succeeded in putting the Hassan on the defensive, portraying them as "bandits" who did not practice the faith, and in establishing an embryonic Islamic state. His entourage of clerics *(zwaya)* recruited disciples in the Wolof and Pulaar-speaking regions of Senegal, and these followers were successful in exploiting local grievances and briefly overthrowing the ruling dynasties of Cayor, Walo, Jolof, and Futa Toro. However, by 1680 the traditional political elites, with some support from French trading interests based in Saint-Louis, had regained power.[13] North of the river, the Hassan not only reasserted their domination but established emirates—confederations of tribes dominated by one "warrior" lineage. The contemporary division of *bidan* society, in which the Hassan dominate the political and military domains while the *zwaya* control religious instruction, adjudication, commerce, and agriculture, and both enjoy the support of various tributaries and slaves, has its origins, or at least its codification, in the final victory of the warrior elite.

South of the river, the reform-minded disciples of Nasir al-Din survived and transmitted their visions of an Islamic society to future generations. They constituted a kind of international reform network in the Senegambia region.[14] Like their counterparts in other parts of the West African savanna, they typically operated at the frontiers or interstices of states. They used their distance from the centers of power to organize and train disciples. In time some of those communities of disciples grew in size and ambition and seized power from the established political elites. These reformers were able to hold on to power and institutionalize at least some of their vision of an Islamic state.

Although it has been claimed that Malik Sy, the founder of the state of Bundu in the 1690s, was the first successful offshoot of Sharr Bubba, not much evidence ties Malik Sy to Sharr Bubba (as Michael Gomez has shown), other than his origins in a village near Podor; nor is there much in his Bundu regime to suggest a commitment to an Islamic society.[15] The next movement in time occurred further south, in the mountainous region called Futa Jalon, in the Guinea Conakry of today. This movement eventually acquired an importance comparable, in many respects, to the Sokoto caliphate, with ramifications through the upper Guinea coast and Senegambia.[16] It is the least studied of all the movements, especially for its origins in the eighteenth century, and it has no obvious connections with the refugees and disciples of Sharr Bubba.[17]

The beginnings of the imamate (or "almamate") of Futa Jalon lie apparently in the growth in population and wealth of a Muslim Fulbe community, with roots in agriculture and pastoralism, and in its increasing conflict with the Jalonke ruling elites and other groups. With support from a Muslim Malinke kingdom to the east, the Fulbe waged a long struggle, over about fifty years. They established their control by about 1780. Two members of one Fulbe family, Ibrahima Sori and Karamoko Alfa Barry, provided the key leadership. They were the progenitors of the Soriya and Alfaya houses that took the title of almamy and alternated in power from the late eighteenth to the late nineteenth century.

Both indigenous and external writers have constructed a history of prosperity and peaceful alternation in power of the two ruling houses. On the issue of prosperity, they have it right: prosperity was rooted in the country's location, enormous potential in agricultural and pastoral production, and the regime's ability to use slave labor and to supply excess labor capacity to slave traders, especially those tied into the trans-Atlantic system out of the Rio Nunez and Rio Pongo. Futa was even able to adjust to the gradual abolition of the Atlantic system.[18] More perhaps than any other Fulbe-dominated regime, the political economy was based on a thorough integration into the internal and Atlantic slave trades. There was a heavy accumulation of slave labor; indeed, slave labor freed up the Fulbe for the political, religious, and educational tasks to which they gave priority.[19] But the political scene was different—and anything but peaceful. The two ruling houses fought frequently over control of the federation, and both in turn struggled with the regional barons, most particularly the Alfa mo Labe, ruler in Labe, throughout the nineteenth century. Under French colonial rule in the twentieth century, regional and national leaders retained their positions and some influence.[20]

Despite the insecurity, and assisted by the prosperity, Fulbe scholars in Futa Jalon gave serious attention to the interpretation of their revolution and to the development of a specifically Pulaar pedagogy for teaching and spreading the faith. These scholars were especially visible in the Labe region, under the patronage of the Alfa mo Labe, and they have left a heritage almost as remarkable and extensive as the literature of legitimation created by 'Uthman dan Fodio and his contemporaries in Sokoto. The Labe literature was primarily in Pulaar, not Arabic; much of it was designed for recitation and the edification of the women, slaves, and other less literate members of the population. Free Fulbe women could acquire positions as teachers and pedagogues, but they were contained within a very patriarchal framework.[21] For a vast surrounding area, including the Muslim communities of the

Freetown peninsula and other parts of the upper Guinea coast, teachers in Futa Jalon provided the models of Islamic learning and drew aspiring scholars to their schools.[22] This intellectual heritage made it important for Shaykh 'Umar, the leader of the last major Fulbe effort in the nineteenth century, to sojourn for a number of years in Futa Jalon.

Reformers in Futa Toro, the middle valley of the Senegal River, were the next to lead a movement in favor of an Islamic state.[23] In their case, the connections to Sharr Bubba are clear. Key leaders studied in schools connected to the earlier movement, most notably at Pir in southern Cayor.[24] They were closely connected by marriages contracted in the late seventeenth or early eighteenth century, an indication that their ancestors were active participants in the earlier reform. By the 1760s, they had constituted themselves as a group, the Torodbe, or "seekers," and begun to sharpen their criticism of the reigning dynasty in Futa Toro, the Denyanke. But in this case the rulers were also Fulbe, and the reformers put the accent even more clearly on their religious, as distinguished from ethnic, identity.[25]

Like the construction of the founding of the almamate of Futa Jalon, the history of reform in Futa centers on two figures. The first, Sulayman Bal, prepared the way. He delivered sharp critiques of the Denyanke, because of their failures to promote the faith and to mobilize the population against famine and raids. The Hassan, supported by contingents from Morocco, raided with impunity in the valley throughout much of the eighteenth century.[26] Bal died in one of the battles, and his abrupt departure threw the embryonic Torodbe regime into a quandary; they had no obvious leader of stature, learning, and connection to take his place.

After a period of probably several years, the Muslim community secured the services of a kinsman, a graduate of Pir who had been teaching in relative isolation on the border with Bundu. Abdul Qadir Kan was well connected to the *torodbe* and to the Sharr Bubba tradition. He had studied and taught across the region of southern Mauritania and northern Senegambia. After his inauguration as imam, or almamy,[27] he instituted a series of religious and political innovations. To encourage literacy and the practice of the faith, he established mosques, schools, and courts in the villages, a fact that, more than any other, has made the Futanke, under their Senegalese appellation Tokolor, leaders in the processes of Islamization in the region. To provide protection, he strengthened or founded settlements at the key river fords; his policy was to stop the Hassan raids at the river, rather than actively to encourage settlement on the north bank.[28] Finally, Almamy Abdul passed treaties with the French, the dominant European trading partner along the river. The 1786 agreement spelled out the "customs" that the French should pay for the right to trade in and through Futa with the upper valley, and made it clear that Muslims must not be the victims of the slave trade.[29]

Almamy Abdul maintained a strict and personalized control over events and relations in Futa. Over time he came into conflict with his first allies, powerful regional lords or "electors." These men came from Fulbe families who were closer to the older traditions of pastoralism and autonomy and did not share the commitment to Islamization. They bridled at the strict application of the shari'a. By the early 1800s, they were ready to revolt.[30]

The internal dissension ultimately converged with strong pressures from outside. Initially, Abdul had enjoyed great success on the external front: he engineered a successful campaign against the Hassan leader 'Ali Kowri, who, as head of the Trarza confederation and ally of Moroccan forces in the Sahara, had made frequent exactions among the Fulbe of the middle valley; Abdul then resumed the aborted mission of Sharr Bubba, and as the patron of militant Muslim minorities in the Wolof areas, he imposed his will on the ruling dynasties.[31] But when Damel Amary Ngone resisted his demands, Abdul mobilized a huge force and marched into Cayor: the Damel filled the wells in front of the approaching army, destroyed his weakened foes, and took Abdul prisoner.[32]

With Abdul imprisoned in Cayor, the electors and reformers in Futa were forced to choose an interim leader. Abdul later returned and resumed command, but his authority was seriously diminished, and the influence of his electors had increased. He tried nonetheless to impose his will to the east, over Bundu and the upper valley. In the process, he treated members of the royal family of Bundu brutally and lost the support of some of the most prestigious Muslims of the region. Mukhtar wuld Buna, a zwaya scholar who had praised the victory over Eli Kowri, had this to say:

> As for me, I was disgusted with the religion of the Moors and came among the Blacks to learn their religion and abandoned the thinking of people who don't believe at all. But you, you have convoked this man [the Almamy of Bundu] in the name of Islam [and sentenced him without hearing his testimony and then killed him]. Why have you acted in this way?[33]

The overextension to the east led directly to the downfall and death of Almamy Abdul. The Bamana state of Kaarta, overtly non-Muslim in a period of conflicting religious identities, had become the patron of one of the royal factions of Bundu. The Bamana king eagerly mobilized an upper-valley coalition, coordinated his activities with the internal dissidents, including the grand electors, and killed Abdul in 1807.[34]

The death of Almamy Abdul marked the end of strong central government in Futa Toro. Electors and other regional leaders dominated the political life of the regime for the rest of the nineteenth century, even though almamies were chosen until the French established colonial rule in 1890–91. The effect of the fundamental reforms did survive, however. The Futanke preserved a strong sense of Islamic identity, education, and commitment to jihad, and maintained ties with militant Muslim communities across Senegambia. They played major roles in reform movements throughout the region in the nineteenth century, and they were critical to the success of the holy war of their compatriot 'Umar Tal.[35]

These "far western" movements are often dismissed as precursors to more fundamental changes of the nineteenth century, but this judgment is primarily the product of limited research, the abrupt end to the experiment in centralization in Futa Toro, and the overwhelming attention of scholars to the Sokoto caliphate. At the fundamental levels of Islamization—spreading literacy and building a consciousness of a dar al-Islam—it would be hard to overestimate the importance of the two Futas and of their influence over the vast region stretching from southern Mauritania to Sierra Leone. By their "success" in at least establishing regimes that could lay claim to an Islamic identity, they "solved" the great problem of legitimation. It is nonetheless true that these Islamic revolutions did not generalize their results to the larger world of the West African savanna, nor did they seriously engage the scholarly partisans of the older tradition of avoiding the military and political domains.

The Emergence of the Sokoto Caliphate

The next movement in the "chain" begins with 'Uthman dan Fodio, who grew up in a Fulbe community in the northwestern part of Hausaland in the late-eighteenth century.[36] He came from a distinguished scholarly lineage that had migrated from the west, probably from Futa Toro, some centuries before, and he soon distinguished himself as student, teacher, preacher, and author.

Amid growing violence, wars, and raids between and within states, and periods of drought,[37] 'Uthman sharpened his message of reform. By the 1780s, he had acquired a considerable following, drawn especially from the Fulbe of Hausaland but also including some Hausa and Tuareg. He exercised considerable influence at the court of the sultan of Gobir, but by the 1790s his community was perceived as a threat to established interests. In 1804, a Gobir force actually attacked and killed several members of the 'Uthmanian group, whereupon 'Uthman and his forces fled, proclaimed themselves an Islamic state, and declared war on Gobir. They framed this in the classical Muhammadan pattern of *hijra* and *jihad*, more clearly than most of the other reformers described in this chapter.

The Gobir phase of the jihad culminated in the capture of the sultan's capital in 1808 and in the construction of a new town, Sokoto, the following year. Sokoto became the principal residence of 'Uthman and his entourage. He was ably assisted by his brother 'Abdullah, his son Muhammad Bello, his daughter Nana Asma'u, and Nana's husband Gidado, who was the *wazir*, or chief minister. Bello, who increasingly took over the direction of military and political affairs, succeeded 'Uthman when he died in 1817. Bello became the first caliph. 'Abdullah, with some bitterness against his nephew, moved to nearby Gwandu and became the ruler over the lesser, western dominions of the emerging state.[38]

The second phase of the military campaigns began shortly after 1804, when members of the 'Uthmanian community took "flags" of justification back to their home areas in Hausaland and summoned the Hausa sultans to convert and obey the new Islamic authority. When the sultans refused, the 'Uthmanians declared jihad and, in most cases, succeeded in toppling the old dynasties and replacing them in the old palaces and cities of Hausaland. Within a few years, in a third phase, communities attached to 'Uthman pushed east, south, and west to establish domination over peoples who were neither Hausa nor Fulbe.

They faced their stiffest military and intellectual challenge on the eastern frontier. Muhammad al-Amin al-Kanemi, a scholar who had taken over the old kingdom of Bornu, retorted in a correspondence with 'Uthman and Bello in the 1810s that his people might be sinners but they had not rejected Islam, and that consequently the jihad was not justified in that region. He combined his highly defensible argument with successful defensive mobilization against the jihadic forces.[39]

In their two decades of watching over the domains of the vast new confederation, Muhammad Bello and Wazir Gidado established the main features of Sokoto administration.[40] Most power lay in the emirates, where the bearers of 'Uthman's flags and their descendants held sway. Despite the goal of simplifying administration and ending uncanonical taxation, the new regimes soon adopted the broad outlines of the old Hausa bureaucracy. Through intermarriage with Hausa women, the new ruling families came to speak Hausa more fluently than Fulfulde. But much of the 'Uthmanian vision of a deeper and wiser practice of Islam was put in place. Mosques and schools multiplied, in rural as well as urban areas, and Qadiriyya sufi practices were encouraged to support the process of Islamization. In most years, the emirates sent military contingents to wage a collective jihad on the northwestern frontier, near Sokoto and the frontiers of resistance. They recognized the contribution of 'Uthman and the primacy of his family throughout the nineteenth century.

On the economic front, the lands of the Sokoto caliphate, and particularly its hubs in Hausaland, prospered as perhaps never before. Agricultural and artisan production grew under the impetus of an expanding supply of slaves from, in particular, the smaller societies to the south.[41] The surplus in cereals, animals, and manufactured goods attracted even more traders from the trans-Saharan, savanna, and forest networks; they had confidence in the relative security of routes in most directions, and appreciated the oversight exercised by the emirates and Sokoto.

One of the most signal achievements of the caliphate was a vast literature of apologetics. More than any other set of leaders of the reform movements, the 'Uthmanians were inveterate writers.[42] While most key narratives and interpretations were composed in Arabic, many of the pedagogical works were written in Hausa and Fulfulde, and were designed for recitation to the less literate—women, slaves, farmers, and pastoralists. The key texts were copied and circulated to other parts of the savanna and helped to create what I have called elsewhere the "Sokoto model" of jihad.[43] Sokoto became a place to visit and study, for the likes of the Kunta of the Niger Buckle and 'Umar Tal.

One of the most vital contributions to the apologetic literature was made by Nana Asma'u, 'Uthman's daughter. With encouragement from her father, brother, and husband, she developed a pedagogy and organization to reach the women of the Sokoto region. She hoped gradually to displace the dependence on the ancient *bori* practices of healing, divination, and social reproduction. By her poetry in Ful-fulde, Hausa, and Arabic, and by her training of teachers, she probably accomplished more thoroughgoing Islamization in the northwestern part of Hausaland than anyone else in the calpihate.[44]

At the end of the century, British, French, and German interests competed for the territory of the caliphate. In 1903, the British won out, occupying all of the critical cities and settled zones, including Sokoto and the biggest commercial hub, Kano. The French took some of the northern and western zones, where Niger, Burkina Faso, and Benin lie today, and the Germans obtained the eastern fringe in today's Cameroon. All of the colonial powers were slow to alter the hierarchies of the precolonial era, including the subordination of women and the practice of slavery upon which the whole society had come to depend.[45] Under Frederick Lugard, the British developed their system of indirect rule, keeping much of the emiral structure in place. In some respects, this policy made the Hausa-speaking 'Uthma-nians more powerful than before and put the political and military elites of the northern part of Nigeria in a position to play a dominant role after independence in 1960.[46] As recent events have shown, these elites remain powerful and cohesive in contemporary Nigeria.

The Middle Niger and the Caliphate of Hamdullahi

After 1804 and the creation of the apologetic literature, Sokoto became the model of militant Islam for many West Africans. Its flags of authorization definitively "solved" the problem of legitimating jihad in the West African savanna. Seku Amadu, the founder of the Islamic regime in Masina, the middle delta of the Niger, was no exception.[47]

The movement led by Seku Amadu Bari (Cisse) was marked by a strong rural bias against the corruption of the city. For Amadu, this meant the practices of Jenne, the old trading and production center of the middle delta, and the domination of a foreign "pagan" power, the Bamana state of Segu.[48] Amadu studied and taught in the countryside not far from Jenne, and he became acutely aware of the compromises of the urban *'ulama'*, the influence of the large scholarly and commercial network maintained by the Kunta of Arawan and Timbuktu, and the capacity for intervention of Segu, which lay just to the southwest. In the second decade of the nineteenth century he began to mobilize his Fulbe followers, secured a flag of legitimation from 'Uthman, and organized resistance to Segu's incursions.

In 1818, Amadu won a major battle against Segu. In subsequent years he inaugurated a new regime, dropped the link to Sokoto,[49] and established a new and "incorruptible" capital at Hamdullahi ("Praise be to God.") He created a small council of advisers, a larger council of about one hundred leaders, and the most centralized regime of any of the Muslim Fulbe entrepreneurs. He and his councilors regimented the lives of people in city and countryside alike. They settled pastoralists in designated areas and established transhumant paths for their flocks.

Amadu and his most trusted adviser Shaykh Nuh Tayru, who had been educated within the Kunta network, then took their most ambitious step: they declared Amadu the twelfth caliph, predicted from the time of Askiya Muhammad's pilgrimage at the end of the fifteenth century. His accession was announced in letters to Muslim communities across the Sahel, Sahara, and North Africa.[50] This bold invention was probably designed to compensate for dropping the link to the Sokoto caliphate and to justify the exercise of power in Timbuktu and the Niger Buckle, where the old traditions of Songhay held sway. It also helped as Masina extended its influence, in political and cultural terms, to the east, into Liptako and other Fulbe areas of today's Burkina Faso.

Hamdullahi quickly came into conflict with the dominant religious and commercial network of the region, the Kunta. Sidi Muhammad and Ahmad al-Bakkay, son and grandson respectively of Sidi al-Mukhtar, contested Amadu's claims and considered his severe interpretations of Islamic practice to be wrongheaded—the product of a very limited experience in Islamic education and practice.[51] The Kunta also objected to Hamdullahi's ban on the sale and consumption of tobacco, a product in which they had a very profitable interest, and to the strict regulations of movement, which made their Middle Niger networks harder to maintain.

Hamdullahi had its share of internal problems as well. Seku Amadu reigned for almost three decades. He did not clearly designate a successor, and when he died in 1845 there were a number of candidates, especially the oldest brother, Ba Lobbo, and the oldest son, Amadu II. The council chose the son, and Ba Lobbo became the leading general in the army. The dissension became more pronounced when Amadu II died in 1853 and the succession passed to his son Amadu mo Amadu (Amadu III). This Amadu had had a more traditional Fulbe socialization, and he did not maintain the strict traditions of his predecessors in Islamic education and control. By the late 1850s, when an external threat surged on the horizon, the disaffection, especially among the older generation and the better educated, was very great indeed.[52]

The Jihad of Al-Hajj Umar

The threat to Hamdullahi came from a native son of Futa Toro. Umar Tal, with an ambition borne of the experience in the two Futas and of sojourns in Sokoto and Hamdullahi, sought to unite the western Sudan in a confederation comparable in scale to the Sokoto caliphate. More than any other individual, he provides the linkages among the jihads.

Umar came slowly to this vision. Born at the end of the eighteenth century,[53] he grew up in the Podor region of Futa Toro at a time when the almamate was in full decline. He studied in Futa Jalon for several years in the early 1820s, having become a practitioner of the Tijaniyya, the sufi order based in Algeria and Morocco but new to West Africa.[54] (See chapter 20.) The founder had claimed direct revelation from the Prophet and from God, and some followers used his charisma to promote the superiority of the order over other sufi allegiances. Over time, Umar Tal became the principal agent of the Tijaniyya in West Africa. He used his authority to challenge the Kunta and other leaders of the older Qadiriyya establishment, and in later life he linked the order to the military struggle against non-Muslims.

In the 1820s, the Tijaniyya was very active in Mecca and Medina. 'Umar decided to make the pilgrimage, an unusual commitment at the time for West African Muslims and one that none of his "jihadic" predecessors had accomplished. He spent the years 1828–30 in Mecca and Medina, performing the pilgrimage each year, and obtaining a commission for spreading the Tijaniyya in West Africa—a designation fundamental to the rest of his career. En route to and from Mecca, he visited the Hamdullahi and Sokoto caliphates.

On his return, he spent some six years in Hausaland, most of it (1831–38) at the court of Muhammad Bello. He made a strong impression as teacher, scholar, adviser, and military leader. When he departed, he left behind a small but prestigious Tijaniyya community, and took with him one of Bello's daughters.[55] The Tijaniyya presence produced tense relations with the local court and the Kunta patrons of the Qadiriyya.

'Umar spent most of the 1840s in Futa Jalon. He received a positive reception from one almamy and settled in the village of Jegunko. There he formed another important Tijaniyya Muslim community, including adepts from as far away as Futa Toro in the north and Freetown in the south.[56] He completed his major work, *al-Rimah,* which today is still a major resource for Tijaniyya followers.[57] In 1846–47, 'Umar traveled through Senegambia to Futa Toro to test reactions to a possible relocation. Returning south, he moved his following beyond the eastern edge of Futa Jalon to a relatively open area in the small Mandinka kingdom of Tamba.

From hereon, 'Umar emphasized not writing or teaching but waging the military struggle. He linked Tijaniyya affiliation to this effort. The jihad, launched in 1852 against the king of Tamba, quickly moved on to more ambitious targets: the two Bamana kingdoms that had emerged in the eighteenth century around a very conscious non-Muslim identity.[58] Segu controlled the middle Niger and was the principal adversary for the caliphate of Hamdullahi; Karta developed in the Sahelian space northeast of the upper Senegal, where it intervened decisively in the Senegal River valley and (as shown above) against Almamy Abdul of Futa Toro. 'Umar made the destruction of these outstanding "pagan" regimes, which threatened the emerging dar al-Islam of West Africa, his particular calling.[59] He recruited his armies in the "west," among the Muslim and especially the Fulbe populations of Futa Jalon, Bundu, Futa Toro, and other parts of Senegambia. He secured European firearms, powder, and artillery from French and British sources at the coast; this gave him a superiority in weaponry over his more landlocked foes to the "east."

In 1855, 'Umar marched into Nioro, the Kaarta capital. In 1861, he seized Segu and staged a public ceremony of destruction of fetishes from the palace. At this juncture 'Umar's prestige knew no bounds; he received letters and delegations of congratulation from all over the African Muslim world. Muhammad Akansus, a well-placed Tijaniyya leader in Morocco, put this achievement in flowery terms:

> Our ears have been delighted by this good news about you and your
> majesty. . . . It is news of victory and conquest, the news of clear glory, a
> great victory, a source of much joy. In truth this is a glory for the Muslim
> nation, a victory through a road that had previously been blocked, it is a joy
> for the saints of God who repeat it standing and sitting. I pray that the
> swords of truth will strike the foreheads and cheeks of the evil people.[60]

'Umar had designed a movement that differed significantly from its predecessors: it was a movement not to reform or overthrow his native land but to spread the
faith by the destruction of "pagan" regimes.[61] In the destructive task he succeeded
admirably. The dar al-Islam of the western Sudan was a reality, or so it seemed, and
Muslim scholars of many persuasions recognized the achievement.

'Umar gave little attention to the construction of the Islamic state. This was due
in part to the constraints of war mobilization. Once he decided to challenge the
"pagan" regimes, especially the aggressive Bamana ones,[62] he had to devote his energies to massive recruitment and military strategy. His sons and potential successors were quite young. The eldest, born during his sojourn in Hausaland, were just
reaching their mid-twenties as he undertook the Segu campaign, and it was only
then that they left the family center of Dingiray to gain experience in the arts of war
and administration. Indeed, the biggest deficiency was 'Umar's own inexperience
and lack of interest in establishing courts, schools, mosques, and the other institutions of an Islamic state—institutions that might have brought the Bamana and
other subject populations into suitable Muslim practice.[63] This neglect separates
him in many respects from the founders of the regimes discussed above.

Another reason for 'Umar's inattention to these matters was his determination
to settle a conflict with the Muslim Fulbe state of Masina. Hamdullahi, and its new-
found Kunta ally Ahmad al-Bekkay, had provided critical assistance for Segu's resistance to conquest; 'Umar found incriminating letters from Amadu III and the
Kunta in the Segu palace. For 'Umar, this support was unforgivable; it constituted
evidence of apostasy. In 1861–62, he demanded that Hamdullahi acknowledge the
error of its ways and surrender the Bamana king, who had taken refuge there. Hamdullahi refused,[64] and 'Umar embarked on a military campaign during the hot dry
season of 1862. His arguments are contained in a long, bristling, and carefully documented treatise, the *Bayan Ma Waqa*. The treatise was eloquent, but it probably
did little to persuade most West African scholars of the legitimacy of the campaign.[65]

The 'Umarian forces were initially victorious; they controlled Masina for about
a year. But the Masinanke, with the help of Bekkay, organized a successful revolt
and siege in 1863, defeated most of the Futanke forces, and killed 'Umar in February 1864. 'Umar's nephew Ahmad al-Tijani, who escaped the siege, then mobilized
the traditional enemies of the Masinanke to the east and began an arduous, bloody,
but ultimately successful "reconquest" from his base in Bandiagara. The toll of conquest, revolt, and reconquest was enormous in terms of lives lost and prosperity de-

stroyed. The struggles damaged the unity and practice of Islam and diminished the prestige of the Kunta and Ahmad al-Bakkay, the leader from the anti-jihadic tradition who died waging jihad against jihad.[66] *family Sufi order*

After the catastrophe of Masina, the 'Umarians began to lose their leading role in the spread of Islamic practice and of Tijaniyya affiliation in West Africa. Ahmad al-Kabir, who following his father's death presided over the 'Umarian dominions from Segu, struggled to maintain control within the family and against numerous external foes.[67] Al-Tijani gave him no recognition in Bandiagara as he sought to reclaim the ravaged plains and rivers of Masina. Several brothers who lived around Nioro, the key staging area for 'Umarian recruits and weapons on their way to Segu, rejected Ahmad's authority in the early 1870s and again in 1885.[68] The Bamana and other subjects were in frequent revolt; Samori cut him off from Dingiray and diminished his influence in the south; and the French steadily intruded into his domain. When the French took the capitals of Segu, Nioro, and Bandiagara between 1890 and 1893, they destroyed the last vestiges of the 'Umarian state and laid the foundations for the colonial territory of the Soudan.[69]

In the late-nineteenth century, the mantle of holy war and Islamic state was carried by a variety of leaders and peoples. It ceased in any sense to be the preserve of the Fulbe. In the upper Niger there was the Mandinka leader Samori, as well as his precursors and rivals.[70] The Futa Jalon was the scene of a number of reforms, often greeted with hostility by the almamate, which had become the establishment. In similar ways, Senegambian reformers took on the abuses of the so-called Islamic states as well as the *anciens régimes,* and challenged all states to live up to their responsibilities toward their subjects. And anti-jihad scholars, from the Kunta, Fadiliyya, and Sidiyya, for example, used the excesses and violence of the nineteenth-century movements to bolster their argument that all power was corrupting.[71]

'Umar Tal helped to provide the transition to a new understanding of Islamic obligation in the late-nineteenth century: as resistance to European intrusion. In his confrontations with Faidherbe and the French along the Senegal River in the 1850s, 'Umar did not clearly call for holy war against the Europeans. He did, however, mobilize an embargo, attack a few isolated outposts,[72] and call into question *muwalat,* "friendship" with the Europeans. By the late 1850s, when it was obvious that he could not dislodge the French from the Senegal valley, he called for hijra, massive emigration, from the region.[73] It was this call that Ahmad al-Kabir subsequently used to attract Senegambian militants to the 'Umarian capitals of Nioro and Segu late in the nineteenth century. He made his own hijra in 1893, when he departed Bandiagara for the east—just ahead of the armies of Colonel Louis Archinard.[74] Many other Muslims reacted in similar fashion to the European intrusion into West Africa at the end of the century. They typically moved to the east, toward the Sudan of the Mahdi and the holy lands of Islam, or to the north, toward today's Mauritania or Morocco, which was not yet under French domination.

☾ ☾ ☾

The holy wars of the eighteenth and nineteenth centuries mark an important phase in the history of Islam and Islamization in West Africa. They heightened the sense of belonging to the dar al-Islam. They made the practice of the faith more attractive to many. They also sharpened the use of Islamic practice as a criterion for distinguishing between slave and free, provided relatively few opportunities for women beyond marriage and the household, and increased the level of violence throughout the region. The Fulbe, as the ethnic group that furnished most of the leadership, emerged from this period with a heightened sense of their own Islamic preeminence.

It is important not to forget the less spectacular contributions of Muslim teachers who stuck to more traditional and less "jihadic" ways. In fact, the overwhelmingly Muslim identity of the savanna region today may be more a product of their efforts, and of the desire of West Africans to affirm a recognizable identity in the face of European colonial rule. This striking Islamization has proceeded despite the destruction of the Islamic states—with the partial exception of the Sokoto caliphate—established by jihad in the eighteenth and nineteenth centuries.

Notes

1. In particular they established a genealogy that linked them to ʿUqba ibn Nafiʿ, the Arab conqueror of parts of the Maghrib in the seventh century C.E., and developed a tradition whereby their language, Pulaar, or Fulfulde, was second only to Arabic in the estimation of the Prophet. Robinson 1985, chapter 2.

2. Symbolized in Curtin 1975.

3. See the critique of the "jihadic" emphasis expressed in Searing 1993.

4. See Brenner 1985 and Robinson 1982. The spread of literacy in Arabic and its ability to survive the multiple vicissitudes of slavery can be seen in the experience of Muslim slaves in the United States and Jamaica. See Gomez 1994.

5. This can be seen most conspicuously in the interpretations of ʿUthman dan Fodio, ʿAbdullahi, and Muhammad Bello in the Sokoto-Gobir case in the early nineteenth century. See Last 1967. But it is also present in the other movements, some of which preceded the Sokoto development. See Robinson 1985, chapter 2.

6. The most visible case was the flirtation of Askiya Muhammad of Songhay with the prospect of jihad and Islamic government around 1500. See Hunwick 1985 and Willis 1989.

7. See Brenner 1988.

8. For some instances of this related to the career of al-Hajj Umar, see Robinson 1985, 44, 121–22, 354–55.

9. Barth 1857–58.

10. Mage 1868.

11. For a discussion of the preferences for women slaves in West African societies, see Klein and Robertson 1983, Klein 1972, and Robinson 1985, 55, 63–65, 114, 179, 245–46, 303. For Muslims in the British colonies and the United States, see Gomez 1994.

12. Sharr Bubba, or Shurbubba, may mean "Babba's war," "Cry out assent!" or something else. I draw my basic view from Ould Cheikh 1990 and 1985. For a more standard interpretation,

see Stewart 1972. For other relevant material and the larger context of relations between Saharan Muslims, who typically understood themselves as "white," with Muslims in the Sahel and the savanna, who were identified as "black," see Brenner 1988; Stewart 1976a; Webb 1995.

13. This is the interpretation offered by Barry 1972 and Ritchie 1968. The French traders preferred to work with the warrior groups, who were less likely to impose conditions on the commerce in gum. See Ould Cheikh 1980. For a study of the importance of this to the later successful Islamic revolution in Futa Toro, see Robinson 1975.

14. For example, centers such as Pir, in the southern reaches of Cayor, or Coki, in the northern part, which often operated independently of the throne. See Boulègue 1987 and Robinson 1975.

15. In Gomez 1993.

16. These follow a more conventional definition of Senegambia, such as the one formulated by Curtin 1975, rather than the one that embraces Futa Jalon in Senegambia; see Barry 1988. The most complete account of the Islamic movement in Futa Jalon is still Rodney 1968 and Person's article in vol. 2 of Ajayi and Crowder, eds. 1985. See also McGowan 1975 and Diallo 1972.

17. The one scholar working on the subject actively is Botte 1990, 1991, 1994.

18. Bruce Mouser 1973a, 1973b, and Rodney 1968.

19. See the Botte articles (1990, 1991, 1994) and Balde 1975.

20. Harrison 1988. But the French eventually undermined the influence of the ruling elite.

21. See Botte 1990. Botte also indicates that the *ajami* system of pedagogy began even before the military revolution and that the ruling classes specifically refused to allow the non-Fulbe to become Muslim. The pedagogical materials, especially those produced by the Labe scholars, and particularly Cerno Muhammad Samba Mombeya, are accessible in the Fonds Vieillard at IFAN in Dakar. They have been exploited primarily by Alfa Ibrahima Sow 1965, 1968, and 1971.

22. See, for example, Harrell-Bond et al. 1978. The Muslim scholars of Futa included some Mande-speaking scholars as well, such as the Jakhanke of Touba. See Sanneh 1979.

23. The most complete article on this subject is still my "Islamic Revolution" (1975). See also Kane 1973.

24. Pir occupies an important place in the historiography of Islamization in Senegal; Boulègue 1987. The reformers were also linked to Coki.

25. For the best recent statement on the emergence of the different social classes and categories in Futa Toro, see Kyburz 1994.

26. Curtin 1975; Webb 1995.

27. Traditionally placed in 1776. Almamy Abdul and his contemporaries seem not to have left a written record comparable to that of the other Fulbe-led Islamic movements (nor did they accumulate slaves on a scale comparable to that of Futa Jalon). More Arabic documentation may come to light, however, with the publication of the French translation of Kamara 1998.

28. Many of the lineages of the central region of Futa have had a fairly continuous occupation of the right bank. See Leservoisier 1994. The issue of land and rights on the north bank of the Senegal has become a heated debate in the last decade, fueled by the disputes and killings in Mauritania and Senegal. Most of the occupation of the north bank by *haal-pulaar* goes back to the early twentieth century.

29. In the search for African resistance to the practice of enslavement and slave trade, historians have often seized upon this instance in the career of Almamy Abdul. The sovereign was not, however, expressing opposition to the slave trade and slavery as institutions—only to the victimization of Muslims in them. See Barry 1988, 156.

30. In particular, 'Ali Dundu Kan, the elector of Dabiya in Bossea, and 'Ali Sidi Ba, the elector of Mbolo 'Ali Sidi, in Yirlabe. For an oral tradition of this encounter, see Kane and Robinson 1984, 53–63.

31. He used the Maliki formula, an invitation, usually in the form of a diplomatic mission, to "convert" and swear allegiance to the new Islamic regime of Futa Toro. This provided his potential enemies with more ample opportunity to organize resistance. It is likely that the other reformers mentioned in this chapter, all of whom came from traditions of the Maliki school of law, followed the same practice. See Seed's (1995) demonstration of the impact of this Maliki practice on Spanish practice in the Iberian peninsula and the Americas.

32. Abdul's fortunes in Cayor are a favorite subject of the oral traditions of Senegal, and the perspective taken is typically that of the Damel. See Roger 1829 for the conflict between the Muslims of Njambur and the Cayorian king, and for the Futanke intervention, see Robinson 1975.

33. Soh 1913, 46.

34. For a Futanke perspective on this signal event, in which Almamy Abdul is portrayed as a martyr against the forces of reaction, see Kane and Robinson 1984, 65–71. For a Bundu perspective, which regards Abdul's death as a liberation from foreign domination, see Gomez, 1993, 31–35.

35. The 'Umarian phenomenon is treated later in this chapter. Futanke or Tokolor origin was virtually a prerequisite for "reform" identity in nineteenth-century Senegambia: Ma Ba Diakho, Amadu Bamba, and Malik Sy all claimed Futanke origins. For other reform movements in Senegal, see Klein 1972; Robinson, "An Emerging Pattern of Cooperation between Colonial Authorities and Muslim Societies in Senegal and Mauritania," in Robinson and Triaud 1997; Barry 1988.

36. The best available source on 'Uthman and the Gobir phase of his movements is still Last 1967. A very useful biography of 'Uthman, with numerous examples of his work in Arabic, Fulfulde, and Hausa, is Hiskett 1973.

37. On the economy and environment, see Baier and Lovejoy 1975.

38. See Stewart and Adeleye, "The Sokoto Caliphate in the Nineteenth Century," in Ajayi and Crowder, eds. 1985, vol 2.

39. See Brenner 1973 and 1992.

40. The most succinct treatment of the caliphate in the nineteenth century is still Adeleye 1971. See also Hogben and Kirk-Greene 1996.

41. The Sokoto region was probably as dependent on slave labor as was Futa Jalon in the nineteenth century. It is hard to compare Sokoto's slave exports into the Saharan and trans-Saharan trade with Futa's more fully documented exportation into the Atlantic trade. On questions of slavery, slave trade, and slave resistance, see Lovejoy 1986.

42. For a list of the main works of the Sokoto leadership, see Last 1967, 236ff.

43. Robinson 1985, 76–77, 365–70.

44. It seems unlikely that her example was duplicated either in other parts of the caliphate or in the other movements described in this chapter. We now have a biography and complete set of her works: see Boyd 1989; Boyd and Mack 1997.

45. See Hogendorn and Lovejoy 1992, 1993.

46. Last, "The 'Colonial Caliphate' of Northern Nigeria," in Robinson and Triaud 1997; Sani Umar 1997.

47. Stewart 1976.

48. Research on the caliphate of Hamdullahi or Masina developed rapidly through the 1970s but has developed little in the last two decades. The principal contributions were made by Amadou Hampate Ba, a Masinanke, with Daget 1955; Brown 1969; Sanankoua 1990; Johnson 1976.

49. Stewart speculates that Amadu's success, combined with the death of 'Uthman and dissension between his son Muhammad Bello and his brother 'Abdullahi, led to this declaration of "independence"; Stewart 1976.

50. Amadu and Nuh made changes in the copies of the *Tārikh al-Fattash*, one of the two major "Timbuktu" chronicles that forms the cornerstone of Songhay and much West African his-

tory. See Levtzion 1971. Some of the documents can be found at the Fonds Gironcourt at the Institut de France in Paris.

51. We are fortunate to have, from the early 1850s, the observations of Heinrich Barth on Hamdullahi and the Kunta. Barth was the guest in Timbuktu of Ahmad al-Bakkay and was threatened several times by the forces of Hamdullahi as he traveled in the Middle Niger. (Barth 1857–58, 3:321ff). See also Robinson 1985, 99–112, 282–91.

52. For the internal dimensions, the best source is still Ba and Daget 1955, 1:72, 248ff., 285–86. There was also a Tijaniyya community in Hamdullahi, the product of 'Umar's passage there in 1838, but it is difficult to estimate its role in the weakness of the regime in the 1850s. See Robinson 1990.

53. The date is uncertain—between 1794 and 1797. I have adopted the date of 1797. For narrative and analysis on 'Umar Tal and his movement, see Robinson 1985; Ly-Tall, 1991. For works that focus on the intellectual and sufi contributions of 'Umar, see Dumont 1971; Willis 1989.

54. See Abun-Nasr 1965. Sufism was not, however, the only path to Islamization in nineteenth-century West Africa; many learned, devout, and charismatic Muslims continued to practice in the older patterns. See, for example, the study of the Tagant region: Villasante-de Beauvais 1995.

55. Controversy surrounds the identity of this person. What likely happened is that Muhammad Bello gave his daughter Mariam to 'Umar just before his death and that she died shortly thereafter. A second daughter, perhaps named Ramatullah, was then given to 'Umar, and she became the mother of Habib and Mukhtar. Seydu Nuru Tall claimed to be a descendant of Ramatullah. See Ly-Tall 1991, 127; Robinson 1985, 105–6.

56. The Freetown Muslims actually remember Dingiray as the place where they studied. Robinson 1985, 115–17.

57. The full title is *Kitab Rimah Hizb al-Rahim ala Nuhur Hizb al-Rajim;* it was published in the margins of Harazim 1963–64. It deals with his pilgrimage, authorization, and some aspects of his stay in Sokoto.

58. For Bamana identity, see Amselle 1990.

59. This interpretation is fully developed in Dumont 1971.

60. Hanson and Robinson 1991, 68.

61. The contrast is developed more fully in Robinson 1991, chapter 9. There is tantalizing evidence that 'Umar in 1861–62 envisaged continuing to wage war against the remaining "pagan pockets" of West Africa.

62. Kaarta had dominated the upper Senegal and played the key role in the downfall of Almamy Abdul, the "martyr" and centralizer of the Futa Toro experiment, while Segu had dominated the Middle Delta region and made life difficult for the Hamdullahi regime; 'Umar was perceived by many as a liberator from the pagan yoke. Ibid., 320–29.

63. Ibid., chapter 9.

64. 'Umar was certainly aware of the decline in Islamic practice in Hamdullahi, especially under the regime of Amadu III, and the animosity between communities of Tijaniyya and Qadiriyya allegiance. The Tijaniyya in Masina were a sturdy minority committed to reform. But it is difficult to imagine 'Umar undertaking an ultimatum and military campaign simply to reform Islamic practice or spread the Tijaniyya. Ibid., chapter 8.

65. See the careful translation and commentary completed by Mahibou and Triaud 1984. It is a good example of the debates that the jihad of the sword generated during this time and that are referred to in note 8 above.

66. Robinson 1985, 305–16.

67. For translations of documents and commentary organized around the reign of Ahmad, see Hanson and Robinson 1991.

68. Hanson 1996.

69. For the French penetration and destruction, see Kanya-Forstner 1969.

70. See ibid. and Person 1968–75.

71. Kanya-Forstner 1969.

72. Most notably at the unsuccessful siege of Medine in 1857. For the confrontational period, see Robinson 1985, chapter 6; also, Hanson and Robinson 1991, 106–11.

73. Hanson 1996.

74. On Ahmad al-Kabir's emigration and the general problem for Muslims, see Robinson 1987.

Bibliography

Abun-Nasr, Jamil. 1965. *The Tijaniyya: A Sufi Order in the Modern World.* Oxford: Oxford University Press.

Adeleye, Remi. 1971. *Power and Diplomacy in Northern Nigeria (1804–1906).* London: Longman.

Ajayi, J. F. Ade, and Michael Crowder, eds. 1985. *History of West Africa.* 3rd ed. 2 vols. London: Longman.

Amselle, Jean-Loups. 1990. *Logiques métisses: Anthropologie de l'identité en Afrique et ailleurs.* Paris: Payot.

Ba, Amadou Hampâté, and Serge Daget. 1955. *L'Empire Peul du Macina.* Dakar: IFAN.

Baier, Stephen, and Paul Lovejoy. 1975. "The Desert-side Economy of the Central Sudan," *International Journal of African Historical Studies* 8:551–81.

Balde, Mamadou. 1975. "L'esclavage et la guerre sainte au Futa Jalon." In *L'Esclavage en Afrique pre-coloniale,* ed. C. Meillassoux. Paris.

Barry, Boubacar. 1985. *Le Royaume du Waalo: Le Senégal avant la conquête.* Paris: Karthala.

———. 1988. *La Senégambie du XVe au XIX siècle: Traité Négière, islam et conquête coloniale.* Paris: L'Harmattan.

Barry, Ismael. 1992. "Le Fuuta Jaloo face à la colonisation: Conquête et mise en place de l'administration en Guinée." Thèse de doctorat en histoire. University of Paris 7.

Barth, Heinrich. 1857–58. *Travels and Discoveries in North and Central Africa (1849–55).* 3 vols. New York and London: Longmans, Groen and Co.

Botte, Roger. 1990. "Pouvoir du Livre, pouvoir des hommes: La religion comme critère de distinction," *Journal des Africanistes* 60, no. 2:37–51.

———. 1991. "Les rapports Nord-Sud, la traite négrière et le Fuuta Jaloo à la fin du 18e siècle," *Annales ESC* 46, no. 6:1411–35.

———. 1994. "Stigmates sociaux et discriminations religieuses: L'ancienne classe servile au Fuuta Jaloo," *Cahiers d'Etudes Africaines* 133–35:109–36.

Boulègue, Jean. 1987. "La participation possible des centres de Pir et de Ndogal à la révolution islamique sénégambienne de 1673." In *Contributions à l'histoire du Senegal.* Paris.

Boyd, Jean. 1989. *The Caliph's Sister: Nana Asma'u (1793–1865): Teacher, Poet, and Islamic Leader.* London: Cass.

Boyd, Jean, and Beverly Mack, eds. 1997. *The Collected Works of Nana Asma'u.* East Lansing: Michigan State University Press.

Brenner, Louis. 1973. *The Shehus of Kukawa.* Oxford: Clarendon Press.

———. 1985. *Reflexions sur le savoir islamique en Afrique de l'ouest.* Bordeaux: CEAN.

———. 1988. "Concepts of *Tariqa* in West Africa: The case of the Qadiriyya." In *Charisma and Brotherhood in African Islam,* ed. Donal Cruise O'Brien and Christian Coulon. Oxford: Oxford University Press.

———. 1992. "The *Jihad* Debate between Sokoto and Borno." In *People and Empires in African History: Essays in Memory of Michael Crowder,* ed. J. F. Ade Ajayi and J. D. Y. Peel, 21–43. London.

Brown, William. 1969. "The Caliphate of Hamdullahi (c. 1818–64)," Ph.D. thesis, University of Wisconsin.

Curtin, Philip. 1971. "The *Jihads* of West Africa: Early Relations and Linkages," *Journal of African History* 2:11–24.

———. 1975. *Economic Change in Pre-Colonial Africa. Senegambia in the Era of the Slave Trade.* Madison: University of Wisconsin Press.

Diallo, Tierno. 1972. *Les institutions politiques du Fouta Dyalon au XIXe siècle.* Dakar: IFAN.

Dumont, Fernand. 1971. *L'Anti-Sultan, ou Al-Hajj Omar Tal du Fouta, combattant de la Foi (1794–1864).* Dakar: Nouvelles Editions Africaines.

Gomez, Michael. 1993. *Pragmatism in the Age of Jihad.* Cambridge: Cambridge University Press.

———. 1994. "Muslims in Early America," *Journal of Southern History* 60:671–710.

Hanson, John. 1996. *Migration, Jihad, and Muslim Authority in West Africa.* Bloomington: Indiana University Press.

Hanson, John, and David Robinson, eds. and trans. 1991. *After the Jihad: The Reign of Ahmad al-Kabir in the Western Sudan.* East Lansing: Michigan State University Press.

Harazim, Ali. 1963–64. *Kitab Jawahir al-Ma'ani wa Bulugh al-Amani.* Cairo: 1383AH/1963–64.

Harrell-Bond, Barbara, Allen Howard, and David Skinner. 1978. *Community Leadership and the Transformation of Freetown (1801–1976).* The Hague: Mouton.

Harrison, Chris. 1988. *France and Islam in West Africa (1860–1960).* Cambridge: Cambridge University Press.

Hiskett, Mervyn. 1973. *The Sword of Truth.* Oxford: Oxford University Press.

Hogben, S. J., and A. Kirk-Greene. 1966. *The Emirates of Northern Nigeria.* Rev. ed. Oxford: Oxford University Press.

Hogendorn, Jan, and Paul Lovejoy. 1992. "Revolutionary Mahdism and Resistance to Colonial Rule in the Sokoto Caliphate (Northern Nigeria and Niger)," *Journal of African History* 32:217–44.

———. 1993. *Slow Death for Slavery: The Course of Abolition in Northern Nigeria (1897–1936).* Cambridge: Cambridge University Press.

Hunwick, John. 1985. *Shari'a in Songhay*. Oxford: Oxford University Press.

Johnson, Marian. 1976. "The Economic Foundations of an Islamic Theocracy: The Case of Masina," *Journal of African History* 17:481–95.

Kamara, Shaikh Musa. 1998–. *Zuhur al-Basatin, ou Histoire des noirs musulmans*. Trans. and commentary, 4 vols. Paris: CNRS and ORSTOM.

Kane, Oumar. "Les Maures du Futa Toro au XVIIIe siècle," *Cahiers d'Etudes Africaines* 14.

———. 1973. "Les unités territoriales du Futa Toro," *Bulletin de l'IFAN*, series B.

Kane, Moustapha, and David Robinson. 1984. *The Islamic Regime of Futa Toro*. East Lansing: African Studies Center, Michigan State University.

Kanya-Forstner, Sydney. 1969. *The Conquest of the Western Sudan*. Cambridge: Cambridge University Press.

Klein, Martin. 1972. "Social and Economic Factors in the Muslim Revolution in Senegambia," *Journal of African History* 13: 419–41.

Klein, Martin, and C. Robertson, eds. 1983. *Women and Slavery in Africa*. Madison: University of Wisconsin Press.

Kyburz, Olivier. 1994. "Les hiérarchies sociales et leurs fondements idéologiques chez les *haalpulaar* en Sénégal," Thèse de doctorat en ethnologie, University of Paris 10.

Last, Murray. 1967. *The Sokoto Caliphate*. London: Humanities Press.

Leservoisier, Olivier. 1994. *La question foncière en Mauretanie*. Paris: L'Harmattan.

Levtzion, Nehemia. 1971. "A Seventeenth-century Chronicle by Ibn al-Mukhtar: A Critical Study of the *Tarikh al-Fattash*," *Bulletin of the School of Oriental and African Studies* 34: 571–93.

Lovejoy, Paul. 1986. "Fugitive Slaves: Resistance to Slavery in the Sokoto Caliphate." In *In Resistance: Studies in African, Afro-American, and Caribbean History*, ed. G. Okihiro. London.

Ly-Tall, Madina. 1991. *Un Islam militant en Afrique de l'ouest au XIXe siècle*. Paris: L'Harmattan.

Mage, Eugène. 1868. *Voyage dans le Soudan occidental (1863–66)*. Paris.

Mahibou, Sidi Mohamed, and Jean-Louis Triaud. 1984. *Voilà ce qui est arrivé: Le Bayan Ma Waqa' d'Al-Hajj Umar*. Paris: CNRS.

McGowan, W. F. 1975. "The Development of European Relations with Futa Jalon and the Foundation of French Colonial Rule (1794–1895)." Ph.D. thesis, London: SOAS.

Mouser, Bruce. 1973a. "Trade, Coasters and Conflict in Rio Pongo from 1790 to 1808," *Journal of African History* 14:45–64.

———. 1973b. "The Nunez Affair," *Bulletin des Séances de l'Academie Royale des Sciences d'Outre-Mer* (Brussels) 19:697–742.

Ould Cheikh, Abdel Wedoud. 1985. "Nomadisme, islam et pouvoir politique dans la société maure précoloniale." Thèse de doctorat en sociologie, University of Paris 5.

———. 1990. "Herders, Traders and Clerics: The Impact of Trade, Religion, and Warfare on the Evolution of Moorish Society." In *Herders, Warriors, and Traders: Pastoralism in Africa*, ed. John Galaty and Pierre Bonte. Boulder, Colo.: Westview.

Person, Yves. 1968–75. *Samori, une revolution dyula*. 3 vols. Dakar: IFAN.

Ritchie, Carson. 1968. "Deux textes sur le Sénégal (1673–1677)," *Bulletin de l'IFAN,* series B: 30:289–353.

Robinson, David. 1975. "The Islamic Revolution of Futa Toro," *International Journal of African Historical Studies* 8:185–221.

———. 1982. "Fulfulde Literature in Arabic Script," *History in Africa* 9:251–61.

———. 1985. *The Holy War of Umar Tal.* Oxford: Clarendon Press.

———. 1987. "The Umarian Emigration of the Late Nineteenth Century," *International Journal of African Historical Studies* 20:245–70.

———. 1990. "Yirkoy Talfi et le Masina au XIXe siècle: Un propagandiste de la Tijaniyya 'umarienne," *Islam et Sociétés au Sud du Sahara* 4:143–8.

Robinson, David, and Jean-Louis Triaud, eds. 1997. *Le Temps des marabouts: Itineraires et strategies islamiques en Afrique Occidentale Francaise, v. 1880–1960.* Paris: Karthala.

Rodney, Walter. 1968. "*Jihad* and Social Revolution in Futa Jalon in the Eighteenth Century," *Journal of the Historical Society of Nigeria* 4:269–84.

Roger, Baron. 1829. *Keledor, histoire Africaine.* Paris.

Sanankoua, Bintou. 1990. *Un empire peul au XIXe siècle: La Dina du Massina.* Paris: Karthala.

Sani Umar, Muhammed. 1997. "Muslims' Intellectual Responses to British Colonialism in Northern Nigeria, 1903–45." Ph.D. thesis, Northwestern University.

Sanneh, Lamin. 1979. *The Jakhanke.* London: International African Institute.

Searing, James. 1993. *West African Society and the Slave Trade.* Cambridge: Cambridge University Press.

Seed, Patricia. 1995. *Ceremonies of Possession in Europe's Conquest of the New World (1492–1640).* Cambridge: Cambridge University Press.

Soh, Sire-Abbas. 1913. *Chroniques du Fouta senegalais.* Trans. and ed. M. Delafosse and H. Gaden. Paris: E. Leroux.

Sow, Alfa Ibrahima. 1965. *La femme, la vache, la foi.* Paris: Julliard.

———. 1968. *Chroniques et récits du Fouta Djalon.* Paris: Klincksieck.

Sow, Alfa Ibrahima, with Lilyan Kesteloot. 1971. *Le Filon du bonheur éternel.* Paris: Armand Colin.

Stewart, Charles. 1972. "Political Authority and Social Stratification in Mauritania." In *Arabs and Berbers,* ed. Ernest Gellner and Charles Micaud, 375–93. London: Duckworth.

———. 1973. *Islam and Social Order in Mauritania.* Oxford: Clarendon Press.

———. 1976a. "Frontier Disputes and Problems of Legitimation: Sokoto-Masina Relations (1817–37)," *Journal of African History* 17:497–514.

———. 1976b. "Southern Saharan Scholarship," *Journal of African History* 17:73–93.

Tall, Umar. 1963–64. *Kitab Rimah Hizb al-Rahim.* Published in the margins of Ali Harazim, *Kitab Jawahir al-Ma'ani wa Bulugh al-Amani.*

Villasante-de Beauvais, Mariella. 1995. "Solidarité et hierarchie au sein des Ahl Sidi Mahmud: Essai d'anthropologie historique d'une confédération tribale mauritanienne, XVIII–XXème siècles." 4 vols. Paris.

David Robinson

Webb, James J. 1995. *Desert Frontier: Ecological and Economic Change along the Western Sahel (1600–1850)*. Madison: University of Wisconsin Press.

Willis, John Ralph. 1989. *In the Path of Allah, the Passion of Al-Hajj Umar: An Essay into the Nature of Charisma in Islam*. London: Cass.

CHAPTER 7

The Eastern Sudan, 1822 to the Present

John O. Voll

Islam and modern state structures are closely related in Sudan. Muslim movements and concepts have provided important foundations for the development of a centralized state and have been crucial to the definition of the modern Sudanese political system. However, Islam does not provide the basis for an effectively inclusive Sudanese national identity. Instead, it represents an alternative basis for organizing state and community and is, as a result, often a cause of disunity and conflict.

The movement begun by Muhammad Ahmad, when in 1881 he proclaimed his mission as the Mahdi or divinely guided leader, provided Sudan with a locally created ideal of a centralized state system. Although some later Sudanese nationalists viewed this as the creation of the first "Sudanese" state, it was not a nation-state. It was a political system based on Islam, not an awareness of an explicitly Sudanese identity. Similarly in the nineteenth century, there were a number of Islamic organizations that joined together people from different regions and ethnic groups. The broader sense of communal identity created by these groups was Islamically defined and not related to a sense of national identity.

From the time of the Mahdiyyah to the era of the National Salvation Revolution of the 1990s, Islamic conceptualizations of state, political processes, and community identity have played an important and sometimes crucial role in Sudanese politics and society. Islamic concepts and institutions in Sudan are operating within a complex, pluralistic society. As a result, Islamic ideals of a centralized state and Muslim communal ties divide rather than unify. The diversity within the boundaries of the modern Sudan makes it impossible for Islam to provide the final basis for the definition of a Sudanese *national* identity or a Sudanese nation-state.

State and Diversity in Sudan

The areas included in Sudan during the twentieth century were brought together into a single unit only during the nineteenth century. Before the conquest of the region in the 1820s by the armies of Muhammad Ali, the Ottoman governor of Egypt, "Sudan" did not exist as a single unit, either in political or historical terms. The period of Turko-Egyptian rule followed by the government of the Mahdiyyah confirmed the organization of much of contemporary Sudan as a unit controlled by a central state, but this did not mean that there was a single, clearly "Sudanese" identity that had emerged.

Turko-Egyptian conquests and rule defined an administrative area that included much of modern Sudan. However, the central state created as a result was a foreign structure bringing together a number of different societies. It was only with the Mahdiyyah that this central structure of rule gained a local identity. Discontent with Turko-Egyptian rule intensified during the 1870s. Rulers in Cairo began to recruit a variety of non-Muslim Europeans to administer Sudanese territories and the administrative bureaucracy was viewed as corrupt and oppressive by many. Egypt attempted to extend the abolition of slavery and the slave trade to Sudan and this created discontent among the wealthy and powerful groups involved in the slave trade.[1] There was also at this time a growing sense of apocalyptic expectation among Muslims in the Sudanic regions just south of the Sahara.[2] The conditions were prepared for the successful revolution to oust the Turko-Egyptian rulers in the name of a messianic Islam under the leadership of Muhammad Ahmad, a popular local religious teacher with a reputation for austere piety.

Muhammad Ahmad preached a message that the rulers were impious and oppressive and that "the people were intent in agreement on illegitimate innovation and love of the things of this world."[3] He called upon people to fight against the Turks who, because of their impiety and oppression, were unbelievers. The Mahdi proclaimed that war against the Turks was a necessary jihad.[4] He rapidly gained a large following and won a series of major military victories. By the time of his death in 1885, Mahdist forces controlled most of the northern Sudan and had begun to establish a centralized state based on principles of rule defined by the Mahdi. While this was a state that established rule by Sudanese as a result of a victory over non-Sudanese rulers, there was nothing in the ideology or organization of the Mahdist state that could be considered "national."

When the Mahdi died, his successor, Khalipha 'Abdallahi, faced the "dual task of consolidating the gains of the revolution in the Sudan by building a state on the primitive Islamic model, and of waging the universal jihad beyond the borders of the Sudan."[5] The Mahdist state continued as the central government in the northern Sudan until 1898, but the "conditions of the late-nineteenth century were inimical to the maintenance of an independent Islamic state in a part of Africa exposed to the rival imperialisms of the European powers."[6]

The experience of the Mahdist state set a firm foundation for the idea of an independent state in Sudan. However, the basis for that state was not a sense of national identity; it was an Islamic tradition of rule. The followers of the Mahdi, the Ansar, did not disappear when the Mahdist state was conquered by an Anglo-Egyptian army in 1898–99. In the twentieth century, they emerged as the largest single organized group within the boundaries of Sudan as established by the British. The Mahdi both strengthened traditions of centralized state rule in Sudan and added a new element of diversity to the Sudanese sociopolitical environment.

When the Mahdist state was defeated and destroyed by the "Anglo-Egyptian Reconquest" in 1898, the British created the system of the Anglo-Egyptian condominium. Under this system, there was, in principle, a sovereignty shared by Egypt and Great Britain, but in practice the British ruled Sudan. The British diplomatic victory over the French in the Fashoda affair in southern Sudan in 1898 guaranteed that the territories of the upper Nile valley that had been part of the old Turko-Egyptian empire and some other areas in equatorial Africa would be included in the territories ruled by the British-controlled central government in Khartoum.

Imperial diplomacy and military action created a Sudan that extended from Egyptian Nubia in the north to the rain forests of central Africa, and from the Red Sea through the regions of the old sultanate of Darfur in the west. Sudan became the largest state in Africa, and it crossed many geographical and cultural borders. The result was a society that contains a high degree of diversity and pluralism. In broader, continental terms, it has been described as a region of "multiple marginality,"[7] being on the boundaries between a number of distinctive African regions.

In specifically Islamic terms, modern Sudan is a "frontier" society. People in the Nile valley south of Egypt have been in contact with Muslims since the very earliest days of Islam, following the Arab-Muslim conquest of Egypt. However, Muslims did not represent a significant proportion of the population in the northern part of the territory of the modern Sudan until the sixteenth century. The processes of Islamization were relatively slow and had virtually no impact before the nineteenth century in the southern regions of the contemporary Sudan. The result of this was that the Sudan that was established at the beginning of the twentieth century clearly spanned the border between the Islamic and non-Muslim societies in Africa. The overwhelming majority of people in the northern two-thirds of the country were Muslim and spoke Arabic, although many were part of non-Arab ethnic groups. In the southern one-third of the country, most people were part of major distinctive communities, like the Dinka, Nuer, Shilluk, and Azande, and they were neither Muslim nor Arabic-speaking. British rule reinforced this division, and as the southern Sudanese became educated, many of the leaders also became Christian since the major educational institutions in the south were established by Christian missionaries.

Sudan at the beginning of the twentieth century was thus basically an administrative unit. It had central state institutions that had some foundations in nineteenth-century history. The society, in contrast, was a complex collection of different language and ethnic groups brought together by military conquest and political expediency. The Nile provides some important connections and was the core of the territories of the central state, but there were few interregional cultural connections.

In this context, Islam provided the basis for some of the most important connections that went beyond local groupings. During the nineteenth century, a few major regionwide associations were established in the Muslim areas. The most important of these were the Khatmiyyah *tariqa* led by the Mirghani family and the organization of the followers of the Mahdi, the Ansar, which survived the destruction of the Mahdist state. In addition, smaller brotherhoods also had influence and significance beyond the local level. Groups like the Idrisiyyah, Majdhubiyyah, and Hindiyyah tariqas had followers in a number of areas, although not on the "national" (that is to say, northern Sudanese) scale of the Ansar and the Khatmiyyah.

The central state established by the British at the beginning of the twentieth century thus controlled a highly diverse collection of peoples. Increasingly, the southern one-third of the country was effectively isolated from the north and maintained its character of being distinctive in terms of language, ethnic identity, and religion. In the north, a sense of political community was emerging. When early British intelligence reports spoke of the possible development of nationalism, for example, this was largely conceived in terms of the northern Sudan and northern Sudanese, even though in the early days a number of people with southern background were active in the early expressions of nationalism. The "nationalist" leader in the uprising in 1924, ʿAli ʿAbd al-Latif, "belonged to a class of individuals whose forebears had been slaves" and was of Dinka background.[8] However, the theater of operation of the White Flag League that ʿAli ʿAbd al-Latif led was the north, and it had little direct relationship to any events or developments in southern Sudan. Development of state institutions and political awareness were thus initially largely northern phenomena, and as a result were strongly affected by the Islamic dimensions of Sudanese life.

State and Society in the Condominium

The British were strongly influenced, in the early years of the condominium, by the memory of the rapid and effective rise to power of the Mahdi. They made major efforts to control "potential Mahdis" by swift and punitive responses to any local Muslim teacher who showed the potential for leading an antigovernment movement. In addition, the British were diligent in identifying those Muslims who could be considered major leaders of local opinion and who were also unlikely to revolt. Such leaders were often publically consulted and associated with policies that were of special interest to the Muslim population.

British policy gave special influence to the leaders of the larger Muslim associations. Initially, this policy involved a close cooperation with the Khatmiyyah tariqa, especially with Sayyid ʿAli al-Mirghani, who emerged both as the leader of the brotherhood and a person recognized by the British as a leading representative notable who could speak for the Sudanese. This process worked in two important ways: government support strengthened the position of Sayyid ʿAli and the Khatmiyyah, and the cooperation of the Khatmiyyah gave a certain aura of Islamic legitimacy to British rule.

A similar process helped to define the position of the other large Muslim association, the Ansar. Initially, the British had attempted to eliminate all potential symbols for mobilizing Mahdist activity. The tomb of the Mahdi was bombed, and recitation of the special prayers and ritual developed by the Mahdi ("The Ratib" of the Mahdi) was prohibited. Important leaders in the Mahdi's family were killed in a series of military actions and the remaining members of the family were kept under close surveillance. The utility of these actions from a security perspective was borne out by the fact that there was a series of Mahdi-like movements that arose in a number of areas. Some of these raised the banner of revolt and British military intelligence believed that such apocalyptic movements had the potential of becoming a major security problem. The last of such revolts of any significance was in Nyala, in western Sudan, in 1921. After that, the security concerns of British intelligence concentrated on potential nationalist movements.

Mahdism was transformed by the leadership of a son of the Mahdi, Sayyid ʿAbd al-Rahman al-Mahdi. His activities were carefully controlled in the early days of British rule, but it soon became clear that he was not going to lead a messianic revolt. Instead, he set out to restructure the Ansar as a more modern Muslim association, although still well within the traditions and attitudes of popular Islam in Sudan. Gradually, Sayyid ʿAbd al-Rahman came to be included in the lists of those notables whose views were requested, and he became, as the leader of the largest single Muslim association in the country, a highly visible and influential personality. He was among those figures who called upon Muslims in Sudan not to answer the call of the Ottoman sultan to rise in jihad against the British during World War I, and he was a highly visible figure in the delegation sent to London at the end of the war to congratulate the king on the British victory.[9]

Other Muslim notables also were involved in this British policy, and the list of members of the delegation at the end of World War I includes the leaders of the largest Muslim organizations of the day. However, by the 1920s, the political skills and adept leadership of Sayyid ʿAli al-Mirghani and Sayyid ʿAbd al-Rahman al-Mahdi meant that these two sayyids came to be the most important and visible political figures in Sudan. Their prominence reinforced the importance of Islam as a factor in shaping the development of political attitudes and institutions.

In this context, the Muslim leaders came to be viewed as representing the voices of Sudanese society. Major tribal leaders were also consulted, but they spoke for more specific and local groupings. The voice of the larger community was Muslim rather than tribal or ethnic. It was clear, however, that this larger community was not seen as a "national" political community, even though it may have operated as a form of civil society within the context of the imperialist central state, creating an institutional zone of mediation and power brokerage between the foreign rulers and the broader society.

The emergence of the two sayyids and their organizations as major features of the political society in the 1920s does not represent the rise of a nationalist movement. Instead, they were in a balanced and interacting power relationship with the imperial state. They neither challenged the central state nor its foreign controllers. They worked to achieve a maximum advantage from the political system as it was developing.[10] This was in a number of ways a reflection of the continuing disjunction between the central state in Sudan and Sudanese society.

At the same time, there was the beginning of a more standard style of nationalist sentiment in Sudan among the small professional and modern-educated class that had begun to develop by the 1920s. The new nationalists were directly opposed to foreign rule and sought, in the simple sense of classic antiimperialist nationalism, to take control of the central government. Although Sudanese nationalist theory was not fully articulated, it is possible to argue that there was an assumption that the control of a central state by a nationalist movement would, in fact, result in the creation of a "nation-state."

"The two most distinctive features of this first phase of Sudanese nationalism" are the "secular outlook and modern methods of organization and agitation."[11] Small associations opposed to imperial rule were organized, the most important being the White Flag League and the League of Sudanese Union, and occasional small demonstrations took place. These developments reached a climax in 1924 when the British governor-general of Sudan, Sir Lee Stack, was murdered by an Egyptian nationalist in Cairo. Local nationalist demonstrations in Sudan and a major mutiny of Sudanese soldiers resulted in severe suppression of any expressions of opposition to British. In the aftermath, there was little effective nationalist activity. The modern-educated Sudanese withdrew from political affairs but began a major effort of intellectual definition of societal identity.

In the early nationalist pronouncements, there was little to identify the movement(s) as specifically Islamic. Instead, there was some explicit mention of a "Sudanese Nation." In the early groups, a significant number of visible leaders came from the communities in Omdurman who were southern in origin and from families of former slaves in the military. "It is, therefore, no accident that many of the so-called black officers who became active in the nationalist movement were of Dinka origin."[12] While most of these people may have been Muslim, they had little association with the major northern Muslim organizations.

In contrast to the development of the Wafd Party and nationalism in Egypt, the White Flag League was not successful in establishing a movement with mass support. This failure, in the view of Abdin, "was due to the fact that the League neither sought nor indeed wished to ally itself with tribalism or religious sectarianism, the two reservoirs of mass following in the country."[13]

Sudanese intellectuals and professionals again attempted to establish a nationalist movement that did not depend upon the more "traditional" social structures of clan and sect. In 1938, they formed the Graduates Congress, which, while not opposed to religion or the religious associations, attempted to establish a "nonsectarian" base for emerging nationalist politics. In this they, too, failed, and a key event in that failure was the rejection in 1942 by the British of the congress's demands for Sudanese self-determination, on the grounds that the congress was not a representative, mass organization. Relatively rapidly after that, political parties were formed and their leaders either sought the patronage of the sayyids or were in some way related to the two largest Muslim organizations.

The failures of the White Flag League and the Graduates' Congress to develop a national sense of identity reflected the more fundamental diversity of the country inside the borders drawn by imperialism at the beginning of the twentieth century. There was no "nation" to which the leaders of these groups could appeal. One-third of the country (the south) was almost completely outside of the developing political arena, and many of the people in the northern two-thirds of the country already were part of well-organized mass associations that could negotiate on their behalf with the political powers. Since these associations were Muslim in their identity, Islam was a major force in this process of emerging political sensitivity.

State, Society, and Independence

When mass movements calling for an end to imperial rule developed in the 1940s, it was natural under the conditions of the time that the movements would also be identified with the Ansar and the Khatmiyyah. The special structure of the condominium meant that there were two "nationalist" options. One viewed the British as the primary enemy and worked with Egyptian nationalists in forming a movement advocating the "Unity of the Nile Valley." These unionists gained the support of Sayyid 'Ali al-Mirghani and the Khatmiyyah, who had maintained close ties with Egypt since the nineteenth century. Sayyid 'Ali had an added incentive because Sayyid 'Abd al-Rahman and the Ansar provided the major support for the other "nationalist" option: an independent Sudan. Many believed that an independent Sudan would be politically dominated by the Ansar, and it was natural for their sectarian rivals to support the unionist cause.

The basic unit with which these emerging "nationalist" movements identified was not a unified and clearly identifable "nation." In some ways, this was not unique to the Sudanese situation: many nationalist movements were developing within political units that had been created by imperialist powers. In that context, the major task literally was "nation-building," and a minimal sense of a truly national identity could be encouraged by leaders like Kwame Nkrumah in the Gold Coast (the future Ghana).

What was relatively distinctive about the Sudanese situation was the close correlation between developing the "nationalist" organizations and programs and the already existing and well-organized mass associations, which were not representative of a "national" Sudanese identity. There was a sharp difference between the central-state orientation of a nationalist vision and the existing and political powerful Muslim associations that did not depend upon a state for their existence. The distinction between state and society, or between central state structures and societal institutions, is one of the most important features of the relationship between Islam and the "modern nation-state" in Sudan in the twentieth century.

Other organizational formats existed in the middle of the twentieth century and they had the potential for political significance. However, in the competition for power as Sudanese "nationalism" developed and as Sudan gained independence, it was the sectarian format for political organization that dominated the "national" political system.

There were two other older, societal, non-national styles of association that had and continue to have some importance. The Ansar and the Khatmiyyah are not the only Muslim organizations in Sudan. For centuries, Muslim life in Sudan has been associated with local teacher-leaders who established schools and local centers of devotions. These "holy families" are an important part of Muslim life in Sudan, and their family centers and tombs are a major feature of Sudanese society.[14] Leaders of these families often associated with state activities during the condominium, and as nationalist movements developed, notables from these families were often active in political affairs. However, the brotherhoods that these notables led did not directly participate in the political process as associations. Members of the family of Yusuf al-Hindi, leader of the Hindiyyah tariqa early in the twentieth century, became prominent in unionist political organizations and continued to be active in leadership positions in the politics of the 1990s. However, the Hindiyyah tariqa did not, as an association, provide a mass base for any political party.

The local Muslim teacher always has the potential for an important political role, as the rapid rise of the Mahdi showed at the end of the nineteenth century. In the first quarter of the twentieth century, such teachers were, as a class, a visible politico-military force, although militarily they were rapidly defeated by the British. These teachers and their centers remained a very important societal force, even as their military and political impact faded. Centers like the tomb complex at Umm Dubban gradually evolved into more modern marketing and educational centers. Brotherhoods like the Idrisiyyah, Majdhubiyyah, and Isma'iliyyah are important in both urban and rural life in Sudan and represent a style of active societal structures that are relatively independent of the political processes directly associated with the central state. These associations may be in competition with the Ansar and Khatmiyyah for societal influence, but they did not emerge as an alternative mode of political mobilization.

The second older societal, non-national style of organization was the "tribal," or larger ethnic or kin-based associations. Throughout Sudan, both north and south, there are major groupings of people who are identified by a shared sense of historical identity, often defined in terms of a common ancestor and sometimes reinforced by a distinctive language. The largest such group in Sudan is the Dinka, representing possibly as much as 10 percent of the total population of Sudan. In the early days of the condominium, the British identified the leaders of these groups, along with the Muslim notables, as significant forces. In the 1920s, there was a conscious effort to create a structure of "native administration," in which these tribal notables were given recognition. The transformations of society and economy that were taking place reduced the importance of tribal affiliations and the tribal leaders became increasingly dependent upon the state structure for their authority.

In the late 1940s, it was thought by many people that the tribal notables represented a viable political alternative to the sayyids. In 1951, a party, the Socialist Republican Party (SRP), was organized by a number of these notables and moderate intellectuals, and it was seen as a potentially important political force. However, in the 1953 elections for the first self-governing parliament, the SRP won only three seats and was soon disbanded. Although family loyalties and clan identities remain important in the north, it is only in the southern Sudan that the larger ethnic group identity maintains political significance.

More modern-style organizations also developed in the middle of the twentieth century and played roles of some significance. Similar to most modern institutions, these organizations tended to assume the existence of a central state system, conceived as a nation-state. Social and economic organizations like labor unions and professional associations (lawyers, doctors, and so on) often were politically active, and when they were it was in this context—working to influence or gain control of the central "national" state. Political parties not identified with a sectarian organization also acted within such a conception. The Ashiqqa' Party was formed at the end of World War II as a nationalist party opposed to British rule. However, it was gradually absorbed into the sectarian-supported political system; it was dissolved in 1952 and its members became part of the Khatmiyyah-supported National Unionist Party (NUP). In the first era of parliamentary politics (1953–58), the NUP was led by Isma'il al-Azhari, who became the first prime minister when the self-governing parliament voted for the creation of an independent Sudan in 1956. Al-Azhari came into conflict with the Sayyids and for a time there was the Ansar-supported Ummah Party, the Khatmiyyah-supported People's Democratic Party (PDP), and the NUP. However, the NUP rapidly integrated itself into the sectarian political pattern, working with the Ummah and PDP in opposition during the first period of military rule (1958–64), and by the end of the second era of parliamentary politics (1964–69) the NUP joined the PDP in forming the Democratic Unionist Party (DUP).

The only significant modern-style political organizations that were not integrated into the sectarian-style political system were the Sudan Communist Party (SCP) and the Sudanese Muslim Brotherhood. In the first years of independence, neither of these had any significant following other than the students and the modern-educated professional groups. In the 1960s, the SCP became one of the largest Communist parties in Africa, but it still had no mass following. The SCP was the first Sudanese political party to open its membership to women, and it supported the establishment of the Women's Union (WU), which became one of the most effective women's political organizations in Africa in the 1960s, but its fortunes followed that of the SCP.[15] The Communists gained their strongest political position when the second military takeover of the state occurred in 1969. The new leader, Ja'far Numayri, initially followed a leftist style politics and members of the Community Party had important roles in the new military government. The party was effectively destroyed following an unsuccessful leftist coup attempt in 1971.

The Issue of National Unity

In all of the political activity of the first two eras of parliamentary politics and the first military regime (led by Ibrahim Abboud), the southern Sudanese were essentially marginal. In the 1950s, there had been talk of establishing a federal system that would give some recognition to the special character of the southern Sudan, but little came of this. The sectarian parties had little place within their structure for non-Muslims and the political organizations of the southerners had little impact on political developments in the northern-dominated central government. This central government was not a national government.

Southern resistance to northern domination had already begun in 1955, the year before independence, when southern troops mutinied. By the time of the first military regime, southern resistance became better organized and a civil war developed that became increasingly violent. After the fall of the Abboud regime, there were major efforts to negotiate an end to the civil war, but they failed. The fighting increased in intensity, and it was not until the Numayri era that negotiations brought an end to the fighting. The Addis Ababa agreement of 1972 recognized special southern autonomy within the Sudanese political system, under a framework of a central state that was national in scope but not nationalist in imposing a common identity of language or culture. For all practical terms, this meant an agreement by leaders in the north not to impose either Arabization or Islamization on the south. Viewed in another way, in principle, the agreement involved the redefinition of "Sudan" as a pluralistic society operating within the framework of a federal state. In other words, the Addis Ababa agreement was a recognition that "national" unity in Sudan means that Sudan cannot be a "nation-state."

The Addis Ababa arrangement collapsed by the early 1980s, when Numayri acted unilaterally to make significant changes in the political system. He attempted to change the definition of the autonomous unit in the system from a united southern region into three separate regions. This was rejected by most southern leaders and fighting began again. The level of violent opposition to central government control increased dramatically in 1983, when Numayri promulgated the "September Laws." These proclamations ordered the implementation of the shari'a (Islamic law) as the law of the land, replacing the existing legal system. While many northern Muslims opposed these laws, one important effect of their promulgation and attempted enforcement was to bring religion to the forefront in the north-south conflict.

The new civil war emerged as a conflict between a central state that defined itself in explicitly Islamic terms and an opposition that rejected that definition. The strongest opposition came from the newly created Sudan Peoples Liberation Army

(SPLA) led by John Garang. The SPLA program specifically advocated a united Sudan and opposed southern separatism. However, the fact that most of the SPLA leaders were southerners and the SPLA military actions were in many ways a continuation of earlier fighting in the south meant that for many, both inside and outside Sudan, the SPLA was viewed as a "southern" movement. Garang's program presented the basic alternative to an Islamic central state. He called for the unity of Sudan with recognition of distinctive local autonomy, and an absolute separation of religion from politics. No political party should have a religious identification. In the SPLA vision, the only path to a united Sudan was a purely secular state.

Thus the basic development of politics in Sudan created what Francis Deng has called the "war of visions."[16] In these conflicting perspectives, Islam was a factor of disunity rather than unity, and in neither view was it possible to envision a "national" identity for Sudan in which religion would play the role that it commonly plays in creating a sense of "nationhood." Instead, during the 1980s there was a growing sense of societal identities that were sometimes in tension with the interests of the central state. Although there were significant transformations in the nature of society (and societies) in Sudan, there was a significant continuity of the older format of a discontinuity between societal operations and the central state.

The Old and New Politics of the 1980s and 1990s

The Numayri regime faced growing opposition on many different fronts by the mid-1980s. Demonstrations early in 1985 created a high level of instability, and military leaders ousted Numayri in April, promising a rapid return to civilian parliamentary politics. The transitional regime of 1985–86 fulfilled its promise: elections were held and a new parliament was established.

The third era of parliamentary politics was remarkably similar to the first two. Garang refused to recognize the new system established during the transitional regime. He continued to fight against the central government at a time when virtually all northern groups were participating in the new political system. This emphasized the southern nature of the SPLA, the continuation of the north-south division, and the continued marginalization of southerners in the politics of the central state.

The largest parties were again the parties sponsored by the two major Muslim organizations: the Ummah Party supported by the Ansar and led by Sayyid Sadiq al-Mahdi (who had been a prime minister in the 1960s) and the Democratic Unionist Party supported by the Khatmiyyah and led by Sayyid Muhammad ʿUthman, the son of Sayyid ʿAli al-Mirghani. The politics of the central state continued to be the politics of northern Muslim organizations and interest groups.

The political life of the new parliamentary era shows the continuing strength of the societal institutions of the northern Sudan. There had been many changes in the economic system and significant numbers of people had migrated to the cities. Numayri had made a conscious effort for more than fifteen years to eliminate the influence and power of the old institutions and to replace them with "more modern" types of associations and interest groups. However, society remained in important ways independent of the activities of the central state, and the continuing salience of the older identities was shown by the power politics of the third parliamentary era.

One important new element was the emergence of a significant nonsectarian but still Islamic grouping: the Muslim Brotherhood led by Hasan al-Turabi. The brotherhood began as a student organization in the 1940s and 1950s and had some following among urban intellectuals and professionals. It advocated a formally Islamic constitution for Sudan and participated in politics through "united fronts" like the Islamic Charter Front of the 1960s. While visible, it had little direct impact and it was not the most important force opposing the sectarian parties and advocating a new type of political system. During the 1960s, the best-organized political group advocating an alternative to sectarian politics was the Sudan Communist Party (SCP). However, with the collapse of the SCP in the early 1970s, the Muslim Brotherhood emerged as the most visible advocate of an alternative system, although it usually worked closely with the older parties in opposition to Numayri.

Within the brotherhood in the 1970s there was a major debate over strategy, with one group advocating the idea of keeping the brotherhood as a small, elite, and potentially revolutionary group, while others, led by Hasan al-Turabi, advocated the reformation of the brotherhood as a popular, potentially mass, political association.[17] Turabi and his allies won this debate. They first opted to cooperate with Numayri when Numayri issued a call for national reconciliation in 1978. With the new openings that this provided, the Muslim Brotherhood laid the foundations for the National Islamic Front (NIF) and the emergence of the Islamists as an effective, if still relatively small, political force. Although NIF leaders disagreed with specifics of the September Laws, they agreed in principle.

Numayri suppressed the NIF early in 1985. It reemerged as an active force in the elections of 1986, when it received almost 20 percent of the vote. Even though the old sectarian parties received the vast majority of votes, their proportion of the total was significantly smaller than it had been in the final elections of the 1960s. The NIF vote represented the emergence of a nonsectarian, Islamist political group that was still relatively small but now no longer confined to the constituencies specially reserved for "graduates." It had emerged as a major political force. The NIF made significant efforts to organize women and had a strong appeal among female students in the universities during the 1980s. One scholar noted that women "are the nexus of the NIF in a number of ways. They are the most active and *visible* organizers."[18] In the third parliamentary era (1985–89), the two women who were elected to parliament were both members of the NIF.

In this political situation, there was no "national" party. Garang attempted to build a national, secular party based on the SPLA: the Sudan Peoples Liberation Movement. But the nonparticipation of the SPLM in elections and the continued fighting in the south meant that it had no possibility of emerging as a truly national party. As for the NIF and the old sectarian parties, both groupings were organizationally unable to bring in sufficient southern, non-Muslim support to be considered national. Essentially, the old situation continued: political organizations active in the central state represented preexisting societal identities and structures, maintaining the old distinction between state and society.

The NIF State and Society

To conclude: The third era of parliamentary politics was brought to an end by a military coup in June 1989 led by 'Umar Hasan al-Bashir in what came to be called officially the National Salvation Revolution. Although the leaders in the Revolutionary Command Council were relatively unknown, the new government soon became identified with the NIF, and Hasan al-Turabi became as the major articulator of the ideology and programs of the new regime.

The Bashir government actively suppressed all opposition and worked to defeat the SPLA militarily. The record of the regime on human rights has been widely condemned, and a major coalition of opposition forces in exile, the National Democratic Alliance, was organized. The record of the National Salvation Revolution is open to substantial criticism. However, in the broader context of the relationship between Islam and "nation-state" structures in Sudan, two important aspects of continuity should be noted: (1) there continues to be a discontinuity between central state and society, and the NIF experience appears both to confirm this and to work within the framework of that kind of social structure; (2) Islam continues to be a factor of disunity rather than unity, making it impossible to create a "modern nation-state" in Sudan.

Sudanese Islamist strategies as they developed in the 1970s and 1980s reflect a broader style of Islamic resurgence programs: the emphasis is on transforming and Islamizing society rather than attempting to take control of state structures. This is an emphasis on the "bottom-up" form of religious resurgence, not a "top-down," imposed revival.

The opportunities provided by cooperation with military rulers, however, have made NIF strategies more complicated and possibly confused. The September Laws of 1983 were clearly an effort to impose Islamic law by a state rather than being the product of an advanced stage of Islamic revival in society. However, the NIF did not feel it could oppose, in principle, the effort to implement Islamic law, and in practice came to accept the idea that the September Laws represented a first step, however imperfect they might be, in the Islamization of society.

The National Salvation Revolution (NSR) provides the opportunity for a more coherent and thorough Islamization program. Turabi remained officially outside the government for a number of years, but took the position of Speaker of the national assembly as the political system became more clearly defined. The formal political structure that has been created by the NSR is a synthesis of old statism and "societal transformationism." The official structure of the central state involves a formal decentralization of state action through local and regional consultative councils and a more federal system of small provinces. There is thus at least an official effort to define a state system that involves less of the central-state control aspect and more of a system that would give formal place to local and regional autonomy. It is not clear that in practice this represents any significant reduction of the power of the central state, but there is at least some recognition of the old problem.

In addition, the NIF system involves the creation of clearly societal structures that are in contrast to the official structures of the state. To a remarkable degree, the NIF regime has created military militias separate from the army of the central state and a popular police separate from statal police; and major sectors of the economy that were previously part of state enterprise have now passed into "private" hands. In a number of ways, it is possible to argue that the developing NIF system represents an institutionalization of the old state-society discontinuity.

Such a system in principle might provide a recognition of regional and local autonomy that could resolve the issues of national unity. Some observers see this potential in the agreement signed between the central government and a number of southern organizations (but not with Garang's SPLA) in April 1997. However, the close association of the system with an explicitly Islamic identity makes it difficult for the non-Muslim Sudanese to accept it.

Islam has provided important foundations for the establishment of central-state systems both in eras of parliamentary politics and military rule. However, such an Islamically identified state, whether led by mass sectarian parties or generals, does not provide an effective foundation for a truly national identity in Sudan. In this sense, Islam is an obstacle to the creation of a "modern nation-state" in Sudan. In the long run, "national" unity—if that is what is to be—will depend upon the success of the Sudanese in reconceiving their identity, transcending the current "war of visions," and building a society and state system that transcends the demands imposed by remaining tied to concepts—possibly outmoded concepts—like the nation-state.

Notes

1. A comprehensive analysis of the causes of the Mahdiyyah can be found in Holt 1970, introduction and chapter 1.

2. See, for example, the analysis in Biobaku and al-Hajj 1966.

3. Letter of the Mahdi, no. 19; in Salim 1990, 1:88. This letter provides a presentation of the Mahdi's basic message in the early days of his mission.

4. Ibid., letter 42, 1:151–54.

5. Holt 1970, 264.

6. Ibid., 266.

7. Mazrui 1971.

8. Deng 1995, 106–7.

9. See the analysis in two important articles—Ibrahim 1979, 1980.

10. See, for example, the discussion in Woodward 1990.

11. Abdin (n.d.), 111.
12. Ibid., 84.
13. Ibid., 112–13.
14. An important discussion of these families and their roles can be found in Holt 1973.
15. See Hale 1996, 165–79.
16. Deng 1995.
17. Descriptions of these discussions can be found in el-Affendi 1991 and al-Turabi 1991.
18. Hale 1996, 217.

Bibliography

Abdin, Hasan. n.d. *Early Sudanese Nationalism (1919–1925)*. Khartoum: Khartoum University Press.

el-Affendi, Abdelwahab. 1991. *Turabi's Revolution: Islam and Power in Sudan*. London: Grey Seal.

Biobaku, Saburi, and Muhammad al-Hajj. 1966. "The Sudanese Mahdiyyah and the Niger-Chad Region." In *Islam in Tropical Africa*, ed. I. M. Lewis, 425–41. London: Oxford University Press.

Deng, Francis M. 1995. *War of Visions: Conflict of Identities in the Sudan*. Washington, D.C.: Brookings Inst.

Hale, Sondra. 1996. *Gender Politics in Sudan*. Boulder, Colo.: Westview.

Holt, Peter M. 1970. *The Mahdist State in the Sudan (1881–1898)*. 2nd ed. Oxford: Clarendon.

———. 1973. "Holy Families and Islam in the Sudan." In *Studies in the History of the Near East*. London: Cass.

Ibrahim, Hassan Ahmed. 1979. "Mahdist Risings against Condominium Government in Sudan (1900–1927)," *International Journal of African Historical Studies* 12:440–71.

———. 1980. "Imperialism and Neo-Mahdism in the Sudan: A Study of British Policy towards Neo-Mahdism (1924–1927)," *International Journal of African Historical Studies* 13:214–39.

Mazrui, Ali A. 1971. "The Multiple Marginality of the Sudan." In *Sudan in Africa*, ed. Yusuf Fadl Hasan. Khartoum: Khartoum University Press.

Salim, Muhammad Abu, ed. 1990. *Al-athar al-kamilah li al-Imam al-Mahdi* [The Complete Works of Imam al-Mahdi]. Khartoum: Khartoum University Press.

al-Turabi, Hasan. 1991. *Al-harakah al-islamiyyah fi al-sudan: Al-kasb, al-tatawwir, al-manhaj*. Cairo: Dar al-Qari' al-Arabi.

Woodward, Peter. 1990. *Sudan (1898–1989): The Unstable State*. Boulder, Colo.: Lynne Rienner.

CHAPTER 8

Islam in Africa under French Colonial Rule

Jean-Louis Triaud

The colonial period played a decisive role in the history of Islam in French–speaking Africa: it was the period of the greatest expansion of the Muslim presence in Africa. This paradox should be borne in mind when, on the scale of the millennium, one draws the balance of this significant period, which extends essentially from the mid-nineteenth century to 1960.

At the summit of its empire, France prided itself in being a "major Muslim power," due to its possessions in the Maghrib, Black Africa, and the Middle East. This expression was ambiguous, for, under the pretext of recognizing its Muslim subjects, France's interests lay rather in competing with the British Empire by symbolically vying for control over the territory of Islam.

Yet it is precisely the comparison with France's great British rival that permits one to better emphasize the existence of French specificity in Islamic matters. In Africa—for example in the Sudan and Nigeria—under the doctrine of Indirect Rule, the British delegated local powers of jurisdiction to the holders of Islamic legitimacy, albeit under British control. France, for its part, even when it made use of the mediation of the Islamic brotherhoods, always refused to invest them with a recognized legal power. This was not merely a question of different conceptions of colonial policy but also concerned a particular representation of Islam. One thus cannot comprehend French policy in its sub-Saharan Muslim domain without going back to older determinants.

The French Fear of Islam

There is an anti-Islamic dimension inherent and recurrent in French political and administrative thought that merits study and inquiry. Although there have been authors, and periods, manifesting interest and sympathy for the Muslim world, French culture has maintained strong continuity in its negative view and fear of Islam.

The strictly religious sources that nourished a mutual spirit of a holy war between Islam and Christianity for several centuries are well known. But there are more recent ones. The hostility to Islam in France also has roots—and this is something that has been recognized less well—in the direct heritage of the French Revolution and the republic; namely, in the spirit accompanying the separation between church and state. Both republicans and radical secularists, who had waged an unfettered struggle against the Roman Catholic Church—denouncing it as obscurantist, feudal, and authoritarian—believed that they were encountering the same adversary again on the other side of the Mediterranean, but that this time it bore Islamic features. Their struggle against the Islam that dominated life beyond the Mediterranean was thus a direct extension of their confrontation with the Catholicism that dominated on the near side of the Mediterranean. The cult of democracy, science, and progress was not able to accommodate itself to a reactionary and dogmatic clergy that taught ignorance to the faithful.[1] The administrative reports deriving from the colonial period bear witness to the permanent action against Muslim institutions.

In contrast to British colonialism, which had other points of reference and other forms of practice, French colonialism always experienced the Muslim presence in the guise of a counterrevolutionary conspiracy. Writing of the "French secular tradition," Cholvy (1991) says, "It invites the religious to be silent." And when religion is not silent—which was the case in the conquered Muslim countries—this is perceived as an intolerable attack on the secular religion of "progress."

The Model of the Secret Society

Fifteen years after the conquest of Algiers, French observers discovered the Muslim brotherhoods. These were immediately likened to their presumed European counterparts, in particular to the Jesuits, who were a "secret society" par excellence, being conspiratorial and subversive in the eyes of the republicans of the epoch.

In 1845, de Neveu, captain at the staff headquarters and a member of the scientific commission of Algeria, published a small volume in Algiers that was to become the required model of all approaches to the phenomenon of the Muslim brotherhood. His *Les Khouans, ordres religieux chez les Musulmans d'Algérie* was the first of a long series of works published in Algeria (by, for example, Brosselard, Rinn, Depont, and Coppolani). The brotherhoods were presented therein as secret societies that menaced the colonial power. From that time on, the colonial administration did not cease to investigate the connections between insurrections and the *"Khouan"*—the "brothers" affiliated to these orders. A generation later, in the 1880s, which were the years in which the republic was established in France, the same models were still very much in evidence. They were applied, for example, by the scholar Duveyrier to the brotherhood of the Sanusiyya.[2]

Initially adopted in Algeria, the classificatory scheme that was applied to all Muslims according to brotherhood affiliation, at times contrary to the evidence, passed from Algeria to south of the Sahara at the end of the century. Alfred Le Chatelier, an officer and orientalist who later became a professor at the Collège de France, traveled from Algeria to West Africa at the end of the 1880s to study sub-Saharan Islam. Twelve years later, when he published his results, he explained how much he had been influenced by this schematic grid, although it was poorly adapted to the local realities. Despite these reservations, the brotherhood remained one of the foundations of colonial administrative taxonomy up to independence. From 1840 to 1960, both to the north and south of the Sahara, human groups and individuals were classified according to ethnic entities, tribes, and brotherhoods.

To French observers who made a fetish of this structure, the brotherhood ensnared the minds of Muslims in bonds of obscurantism and rural superstition. For the republicans especially, the brotherhood was a form of *chouannerie*.[3] For them, the religious community was one more example of those medieval holdovers that hindered the separation of church and state, the preeminence of science over superstition, and the superiority of bureaucratic organization over local "feudal systems." Periodically, therefore, republican and anticlerical discourse together nourished and legitimized the struggle against Muslim institutions.

Islam in the Evolutionary Chain

To the "social Darwinism" of the age, on the scale of civilizations, Islam, because it had a written culture, was considered midway between barbarism and progress. In the context of the Maghrib, what was emphasized and denounced above all was the perception that Islam blocked progress. Islam was the vector and the sign of backwardness, as compared with the industrial societies. In the context of Black Africa, the place it occupied was different and more complex. Islamic culture was judged, on the one hand, to lag behind Western civilization; but on the other, it was seen to be in advance of sub-Saharan societies designated as "fetishistic." This evolutionary perspective explains why, for a while, particularly under the governorship of Faidherbe in Senegal in the mid-nineteenth century, Islam was credited by the administration with this positive "differential":

> The Muslim propaganda is a step toward civilization in West Africa, and it is universally recognized that, with respect to social organization, the Muslim peoples of these regions are superior to the populations that have remained fetishistic.

> We cannot claim to make it possible to climb in one sole generation, or even in five or six, the rungs of a ladder whose summit the old Western world cannot yet see, even after hundreds of years. One should remember that Nature does not make any leaps and that it is if not impossible at least dangerous for the Black to pass abruptly from his semi-barbarous state to the

highly advanced state of our social development. One should also remember that Islam bears an indisputable de-brutalizing force and moral value.[4]

However, after World War I, the fear of Islam and of a conspiracy that would take its orders abroad, in Germany and in Turkey, finally overrode all other considerations. Paul Marty, the great French specialist on Muslim affairs in West Africa, expressly warned against the view that "the stage of Islamic evolution is necessary in order to elevate the fetishistic natives to French civilization."[5] French conquest of and progressive contacts with more southerly, animistic peoples produced a reevaluation of the place of these societies in the overall scale of human development. With this, the Islamic "stage," far from being an opportunity to move forward, seemed more and more to be blocked. Professional ethnographers such as Marcel Griaule, who appeared on the Africa scene in those years, now privileged non-Islamized societies, in the name of African authenticity, and in so doing, they constructed a model of isolated cultural entities that is the object of considerable doubt today. They agreed with their predecessors on one detail: the Islamic branch of the human species was a sterile bough, an impasse in the evolutionary chain, from which one could not expect any progress.

These variations in the order of discourse illustrate the fluid character of an Islamic policy whose formulation depended on the dominance of given ideological and conceptual references, on agents in the field, and on local and regional conjectures. The intensive use of polemical anti-Islamic literature, which was sometimes obsessive, created a common "culture of Muslim affairs" with which a large number of civil and military functionaries became permanently infused.

Variations of Time and Space

Beyond this common fear of Islam, one should not, in defining the objectives of French Muslim policy in Africa, retrospectively construct a scheme that is too linear. The administrator Mouradian (under the name of Gouilly), speaking from close acquaintance with the field, measured these variations in official viewpoints: "France, like the other powers that have colonized West Africa, has never had a Muslim policy, properly speaking. Administrative and political measures that are clearly directed against Islam have been pronounced, others have been taken in its favor, sometimes on the same point of territory, at the same time, and by the same authority. Thus, in matters of this kind one should avoid generalizations and systems constructed after the fact."[6] Any reconstruction that does not take into account the multiple levels of decisions and execution and their occasional contradictions risks being artificial.[7]

Given these reservations, it is possible to sketch a convenient periodization that distinguishes four phases: the time of conquest and occupation; the official defiance from 1906 on; the accommodation that occured between the two world wars; and the recent decolonization.

The Time of Conquest: The Algerian Model

From the beginning, the French conquerors south of the Sahara were interested in Islam. Algeria was then the only recent model of colonization available, and with Islam one was on known ground, in contrast to what was known of the "fetishistic" cultures; they were regarded as disquieting and barbaric.[8]

Faidherbe, a pioneer and administrator of the colony of Senegal (1854–65), was a good representative of this tendency in the mid-nineteenth century. During his time, a Muslim court, Franco-Arab schools, and a unit of Senegalese *tirailleurs* were created, following the Algerian model. Faidherbe implanted the Arab tradition of the *burnus* in Senegal, where previously it was unknown. This hooded cloak was given to native chiefs as a sign of investiture and the power to govern.[9] Thus, a generation later, Le Chatelier would criticize this orientation violently: "Saint-Louis was . . . , before the period of Muslim policy inaugurated by Faidherbe, a town of merchants who were indifferent in religious matters. Today it is an Islamic center, learned, devout, and restless."[10] However, this favorable attitude toward Islam, which was accompanied by the building of mosques, remained ambiguous.[11] Faidherbe himself was conscious of the danger involved in disseminating the Arabic language to the detriment of French. There was also not an undifferentiated recognition of Islam. The "enemy" was Tijani, first to be found in the person of al-Hajj ʿUmar, then his successor Ahmadu, and so it remained for a long time (see chapter 18). (Some have seen at the time the effects of a "Tijani league" in the religious resistance of the second half of the nineteenth century in Senegambia.)[12]

The benevolent attitude toward Islam by Faidherbe and others was thus accompanied by a clear demarcation, following the Algerian model, between "good" and the "bad" brotherhoods. This favorable predisposition, selective as it was, and determined partly by vested interests, never commanded the support of all the agents of French colonialism. In particular, it was not shared by some members of the army, hostile to a policy favoring the Muslims, in the Sudan at that time. However, the support given by the notables of Saint-Louis and by Shaykh Sidiyya Baba and Shaykh Saad Buh in the conquest north of the Senegal River lent weight to this pro-Islamic orientation. Coppolani (1902–5) conducted a systematic policy in Mauritania of using religious figures as a network of domination. Here, however, as in Senegal, and in contrast to Algeria, the Qadiriyya and the Tijaniyya were cast in reverse roles. In contrast to Algeria, it was the Tijaniyya who were known for their intolerance and the Qadiriyya were seen as decked out in all the virtues.

The Path to War: Suspect Islam

The years from 1905–1914 witnessed a mounting danger. German claims to Morocco and other parts of the continent and the constant fear of an alliance between pan-Germanism, pan-Arabism, and pan-Islam, in the terms of the time, caused disquiet. French colonial officials thought it was no longer the time to make concessions to the Muslims, who were suspected of clearing a path for the external enemy. At the same time, the assassination of Coppolani (May 1905) and the resistance of Ma' al-'Aynayn in the northwest Sahara, caused tensions to mount.

This also was the period when the separation of church and state (1905), a powerful moment in the struggle against "Catholic clericalism," created a political environment that reinforced established patterns of treating Islamic institutions. Governor General William Ponty (1907–15), in the militant discourse of republican secularism,[13] denounced Islam as being a feudal and enslaving system. His circular of 1912 strongly illustrates this: "The Marabou propaganda is a hypocritical facade, behind which egotistical desires of old privileged groups reside. The Marabou is the last obstacle to the complete triumph of our civilizing work based on respect of justice and human liberty. This Marabou will disappear completely the day when all its unmasked militants, under close surveillance, will no longer be able to pass through the mesh of the vast net which surrounds them in the whole extent of our African West."[14] In the same period, specialists abandoned the schematic grid of the brotherhood to adopt the concept corresponding to maraboutism[15]—an Islam structured according to clienteles around local personalities. In colonial literature, the theme of "Marabou feudal systems" from then on occupied pride of place and will be constantly drawn upon.

More important and lasting in its effects is the concept of "Black Islam" that emerged at the same time and that was to have a long career. In 1906, a Service of Muslim Affairs, charged with specialized surveillance, had been created in the government of French West Africa. The first head of this service was Robert Arnaud, a close friend of Coppolani and the author of a work that still marks in its contents the clear predominance of Mauritania in the treatment of the Muslim question in French West Africa.[16] However, progressively, in the international context of the age, specialists advanced the idea that, under the condition that it be separated from the Islamic Mediterranean, the source of all danger, "Black Islam" could be recovered! For Quellien, "Sudanese Islam . . . has the advantage of tending to lose its fanatical character in measure of the increase in the black color."[17] Arnaud developed the same position in his manual of Muslim politics (1912): "In West Africa Islam is virtually separated from the influence of the political turbulence that is elsewhere modifying its traditional aspect. Because West African Islam was increasingly mixed with fetishism, its way of life is particular to it and acquires an individuality that allows it to have its particular evolution, beyond the ideas professed by the social transformers of Egypt, Turkey, and Persia." And further: "We have a considerable interest in seeing a purely African Islam continue and evolve in West Africa. . . . It would be desirable for us not to be indifferent to the formation of a Muslim Ethiopianism in the Western part of this continent."[18] Enclosed within communities infused with "fetishism," "Black Islam" would lose by this all its power of causing harm. It would be ethnicized and tribalized. It would cease to be a historic agent while waiting for its final assimilation to civilization.

Paul Marty, who succeeded Arnaud at the head of the Service of Muslim Affairs and was the author, between 1913 and 1930, of nine major regional syntheses issuing directly from dossiers of service, provided further dimensions to this policy of "Black Islam." In particular, he made of this the theoretical basis of a reconciliation of the administration with Mouridism, a "sort of new religion born of Islam."[19] The theory of "Black Islam" would have contradictory effects. In the administration, it appeased the fear of Islamic danger, but it placed the communities under constant surveillance.[20]

World War I represented the hour of truth. With the exception of the rims of the Sahara, the Muslims of French West Africa remained impervious to subversion. Muslim troops proved their courage and their loyalty. Throughout French West Africa, prominent Muslims, upon being duly solicited, officially took positions in favor of the French war effort and supported military recruitment.[21] The "Islamic danger" thus seemed to have been dispelled. The fear had been great in all of the central Sahara, in the form of an old imaginary adversary—the Sanusiyya brotherhood—that had become very real with time.[22]

An essentially Maghribi brotherhood, the Sanusiyya was based in Cyrenaica; thus, it occupied a marginal position in the Sahel-Sudanese territory. However, it was against this brotherhood that French troops achieved the conquest of Chad in 1913, ending ten years of recurrent war between France and the Sanusi in this area. By transforming itself into a political and military force, the Sanusiyya subsequently became one of the inspirations for the uprisings that took place in the Sahara during World War I. Tuareg detachments, led by Sanusi agents, occupied the town of Agades for three months, from December 1916, imperiling the fragile French apparatus in the eastern end of French West Africa. Throughout the Sahara, the French perceived the Sanusiyya in particular and Islam in general as the force motivating the resistance. Revenge and repression were directed especially toward the men of religion. In 1917, the marabou of Agades, who had sought refuge in the Great Mosque, and those of Abeche, who were gathered in the town, were massacred with machetes, although they were innocent of the accusations levied against them of conspiracy and of being an armed movement; at least the systematic crushing of resistance in the Sahara created a certain euphoria in the victorious colonial apparatus.

Between Two Wars: Domesticated Islam

Because Islam no longer inspired fear, for French colonial officials it became from now on a matter of reducing its significance. This reduction of the dramatization of the Islamic question was accompanied by a resurgence of criticism of those who had privileged Islam. This reaction found its most developed expression in Jules Brevié, whose *Islamisme contre "naturisme" au Soudan français,* a work with academic pretensions, was published in 1923. The work had a preface by Maurice Delafosse, the pioneer of French Africanism, who found in Brevié's work ideas that he himself defended later.[23]

Brevié—a future governor general of French West Africa—reversed the old priorities: the fetishist was seen as perfectible, but not the Muslim, who remained frozen in a "moral impasse." On the other hand, Brevié dramatized what he presented as the secular confrontation between Islam, a foreign religion, and the traditional African cultures, and he called into question the strength and the progress of Islam. Brevié praised William Ponty's circular and, supported by Delafosse, deplored French ignorance of the African cultures and languages. No doubt Brevié's work should be seen as an exercise on style; in any event, the idea of a "secular struggle" between Islam and what Delafosse called animism would from now on be a part of the administrative conceptual tools. These were the last flames of the burning debates on Islam. Everything, or almost everything, had been said.

Behind the conceptual polemics, complicity in the field was confirmed. In Senegal, the talents of the Mourid brotherhood, which corresponded to the needs and the demands of the administration, won quasi-immunity for the brotherhood in the French colonial system. Elsewhere, the networks of Muslim merchants, particularly the Juula, thanks to their role as intermediaries along the railway routes and the trails, benefited from the protection of an administration with vested interests.[24] Muslim elites and the French administration found the terms for a lasting compromise, albeit one that was at times disturbed by fits of mistrust. Under the Popular Front, de Coppet, the socialist governor general of French West Africa, renewed links with "Islamophile" practices close to the British style, including attending the major Muslim feasts, subsidizing Islamic institutions, and giving instructions in this vein to the administrators. This movement to redress the balance in the opposite direction was not to have lasting effects.

There was, also, an important exception to this atmosphere of compromise and cooperation; namely, the situation with Hamallism. It was called thus after the name of its founder Shaykh Hamahullah, or Hamallah (approx. 1882–1943). Hamallism, or Hamawiyya, is a branch of the Tijaniyya that had come to refuse the monopoly of the 'Umarian family in the name of a particular transmission of charisma (chapter 18). Minor divergences bearing on ritual only served to sanction this conflict of legitimacy. The splendid isolation of the shaykh, the turbulence of his partisans, and the hostility of the 'Umarian family provoked terrible repression in 1940. The believers were deported and sent to internment camps. Shaykh Hamallah died in Montlucon (France) in 1943 after having been deported first to Mauritania, then Côte d'Ivoire, and then Algeria. This not only repressed Hamallism: the strike was also of pedagogic value for all those who may have doubted the determination of the French administration to prevent Islamic leadership from passing beyond its control.

After 1945: The Twilight of Muslim Affairs

The 1950s represent a period of "happy colonization": there was a conjunction of prospering agriculture, an administration from now on more committed to economic development, and progressive political liberalization. However, the fear of Islam, which was reactivated by conflicts in the Near East and in the Maghrib, remained alive. The administration fortified itself on the theory of "Black Islam," trying by all its means to cut the Muslims off from their Arab fellow believers. The brotherhood policy continued, above all in Senegal.

The perceived enemy at this moment was the real or supposed Wahhabism imported by young preachers, emerging from the world of the Mandenka and the Juula, educated at al-Azhar, and wanting to reform and purify their communities upon returning to their country from their studies abroad.[25] Confrontations between traditionalists and newcomers for the control of the mosques and their communities took place in the 1950s at Bamako, Sikasso, Kankan, and Bouake. The administration, which took resolute action against these reformers, saw in them the sign of a conspiracy emanating from the Near East (it was the period of Nasser, then of the Algerian War). Yet times had changed and repression did not pass the stage of bureaucratic maneuvers.

In fact, the horizon of decolonization profoundly modified the relations of power. The government desks of Muslim Affairs grudgingly recognized that Islamization had taken an irreversible leap forward in three generations and that the means at their disposal did not permit them to control the movements that were taking place. When local autonomy was instituted in 1956, it was the end of the system.

The Major Lines of French Policy

The colonial order was an authoritarian system imposed on Muslims and non-Muslims alike, and the administrators did not always distinguish among their subjects in the field. The ideological discussions on Islam thus remained limited to the sphere of the decision makers and policymakers, and the variations of opinion among them did not always weigh on colonial realities in decisive ways.

In this landscape painted in half-tints, major lines of French Muslim policy nevertheless remained, and they fixed the contours in lasting ways. First of all, the policy of the brotherhoods that was begun in Algeria and put to work by Coppolani was developed with success in Mauritania, Senegal, and Gambia. Leaders of sufi brotherhoods opted for cooperation with the colonial system: among these were counted Sidiyya Baba (d. 1924) for the Qadiriyya, Saad Buh (d. 1917) for the Fadiliyya, al-Hajj Malik Sy (d. 1922) and 'Abdullahi Niasse (d. 1922) for the Tijaniyya, and, after a "bad start," Amadou Bamba (d. 1927) for the Mourid brotherhood. The preeminent symbol of this spirit of cooperation was Seydou Nourou Tall (d. 1980), a descendant of al-Hajj 'Umar, the son-in-law of Hajj Malik Sy. His life spanned this whole period and he served all the regimes, combining service to the colonial regime and the defense of the interests of the Tijaniyya and of his lineage with skill and discretion.[26] With the exception of Seydou Nourou Tall, all these major figures died in the years closely following World War I. The system, however, composed of services rendered, obtained either from coercion or complicity, was firmly established and the colonial administration could congratulate itself by the end of the war on its successes.

Another policy that issued from the Algerian model and that was acclimatized with much more difficulty south of the Sahara was that of the Madrasa; that is, Franco-Arab educational institutions under French control. The goal was to form future Muslim elites in schools controlled by the administration. The first *madrasas* were created at Saint-Louis and Jenne in 1906 and Timbuktu in 1910. This approach did not meet with unanimous approval in the administration and it had difficulty taking hold in the population.[27] The idea was taken up again in the 1930s in Mauritania (Boutilimit 1930; Timbedra 1933; Atar 1936), but the results never matched up to aspirations. The administration ran up against an obstinate "refusal of school" on the part of the Muslim elites, including those of the brotherhoods and the allied families, who were determined not to deliver their children up to an education governed by infidels.[28] The last attempts focused on the creation of a "Franco-Arab college" at Abeche in 1952, conceived as providing a counter to a reformist local madrasa,[29] and an institute of Muslim studies at Boutilimit in Mauritania in November 1953, aimed at discouraging African students from studying at al-Azhar.

The Persistence of Conspiracy Theory

Despite its successes, the administration had never lost its feeling of an Islamic peril. Persons and brotherhoods well known for their loyalty were subjected to the meddling surveillance of bureaucrats. This fear of the Islamic peril also took the form of a conspiracy theory that periodically was resuscitated. The three main sources of this French fear were those raised by the Sanusiyya before World War I, by the Hamawiyya between the two wars, and by the Wahhabiyya in the 1950s.[30] In all three cases, Islamic leaders were accused of organized conspiracy against the colonial order and became the objects of campaigns or stern repression. Viewed with detachment, the accusations levied seem disproportionate, even fabricated. The goal of the government to distinguish between "good" religious movements and "bad" ones, and the repression of the latter, reminded Muslims of the realities of domination.

A Policy Key: The Geographical Diversity

Muslim Africa—from Senegal to Chad—is diverse in its historic and sociological heritage. It is possible to distinguish several geographical cleavages in the interior of this vast space. French observers had very early been sensitive to a historical dynamic that flowed from the north to the south. The progress of Islam had been perceived as a "descent" from the north to the south, whose advance it was necessary to block. This representation in terms of transversal belts, from the more to the less Islamized, was one of the keys to French Muslim policy. It thus distinguished, from north to south, Mauritania, the Sahel countries, the southern Savannah, and the countries of the forest. In each of these regions, with time, a differential strategy was applied that was a function of the proportion of Muslims in each of them.

Mauritania, which was completely Muslim and had an Arabic-speaking majority, had a distinct position. The strategic importance of this territory in the Sahara, whose economic value was mediocre, forced a compromise at a very early point. The government in Paris never contested this specificity, and merely attempted, with some success, to win part of the Muslim elite to its cause. In the Sahel countries, a majority adhered to Islam (but not to Arabic). Despite periodical fits of mistrust, the administration ratified the fait accompli and again sought to profit from the cooperation of the religious elites. In the 1920s, the Sahel was recognized as Islamic territory, and Christian missions were not encouraged there. Conversely, the countries of the forest, following Ponty and Brevié, were considered as protected territory, where Islamic propaganda had to be forbidden, using all means. However, and this was an internal contradiction in the system, economic logic reinforced the penetration of the Juula and introduced the ferment of local Islamization in the south. The most sensitive area thus became the southern savanna, which was largely animistic at the beginning of the century. There, from the point of view of the administration, exposure to Islam had to be firmly combated.

Yet this division into north and south according to religious criteria was not the only form of geographic cleavage. In the literature on Muslim Affairs and in specialist academic writing afterwards, it all seems as if there were a Senegalese and Mauritanian bloc that alone occupied the whole stage and served as the principal, if not unique, reference. Thus one can speak of a western "Marabou arc," stretching from Trarza (Shaykh Sidiyya Baba) to Kankan (Shaykh Muḥammad Cherif Fanta-Madi, 1874–1955). It is there, in effect, that one finds the larger part of information and documentation; it is there that one finds the major emblematic figures. This primacy, which reflects the apparatus of colonial power (with Senegal placed at the center), creates a disequilibrium in observation.

Independent of the Senegambian "laboratory," one finds in the rest of French West Africa a certain number of experiences whose results can be compared with those more classical ones of Senegambia. Thus the space of the Kunta provides an example of the cleavage between men of religion and warriors, the former being more favorable to an entente with the colonial power. One of their most brilliant representatives is Bay al-Kunti, the great grandson of Sidi al-Mukhtar al-Kunti, resident in the Adrar of the Ifoghas, whose role was decisive in the final rallying to France of Musa ag-Amastan, the *amenokal* of Hoggar, and the vanquished Tuareg fighters at the end of World War I. In the Air, north of the Niger republic, Malam Musa also provides the example from the 1940s of a brotherhood "reconstruction," under the sign of the Khalwatiyya. It evoked the relief of the warriors by the brotherhoods and cooperation with the administration, as could be observed in Senegal.[31]

Finally, the vast world of the Juula, which is more discreet in the religious context, is one of the principal stages of the remarkable numerical leap forward that characterizes West African Islam in the colonial situation.[32] A readjustment is thus necessary between the sparkling facade of the western arc and the less mediated developments of the interior.

A Historical Balance

The decolonization of French-speaking Africa (1956–60, excluding Djibuti) and the progressive affirmation in the Muslim population of a strongly Islamic identity from the 1970s on have orientated contemporary historiography toward an appreciation of the value of the Islamic historical legacy. This is presented, sometimes without nuances, as the essential foundation of what became the political, military, and cultural resistance to French colonization. There is no doubt about the existence of Islamic resistance. It is still necessary to distinguish regions, periods, and actors. After having been crushed in the 1890s (the conquest of Segu, the capture of Samori) in the region of the Sudan, it continued up to World War I in the Saharan regions (Ma' al-'Aynayn, Sanusiyya).

The failure of armed resistance led to the emergence of religious leaders who, from one end to the other of the Sudanese-Sahel band, tended to continue the cause of the defeated aristocracies and to establish their own hegemonies. Convinced that any armed resistance was in vain, these elites advanced a peaceful strategy based on the recognition of the colonial authorities and cooperation with them. Presenting themselves as intermediaries between the believers and the administration, they thus consolidated the base of their own power. The principal emblematic figures engaged in this type of strategy have already been named.

The Judicial Debates in the Muslim Community

With regard to jurisprudence, Islam under colonial protection was confronted with a completely unforeseen situation. In general, scholars could invoke the precedent of the Muslims of Granada, after 1492, who were authorized by the qadi of Oran to practice mental restriction and dissimulation *(taqiyya)* while waiting for liberation by the Ottomans. However, for the literate and the learned, who were used to a mode of reasoning based on the shari'a, the question had to be posed in more technical terms. In the first period of conquest, several positions confronted each other. Some, such as Ma' al-'Aynayn, espoused the obligation to emigrate *(hijra)* and practice holy war. Others, conscious of the unfavorable relations of power, supported passive and silent resistance. Still others, finally, spoke openly of collaboration *(muwalat)*[33] in the name of the overriding interests *(maslaha)*[34] of the community. A concept rarely used by the Sunnis, *taqiyya* (legal dissimulation) covered various forms of accommodation. Cooperation subsequently took on a quasi-structural form—that of an entente between French power and the Muslim establishment.

All those who now positioned themselves outside this dominant alliance were repressed unmercifully. Their existence must, however, be remembered. Apart from the Hamallists, one should name the local "Mahdi" figures. The extent of this dispersed dissidence of the Mahdi type merits investigation to a greater degree than has hitherto been the case.[35] Thus, as late as 1941, a handful of Muslims attacked the

Hotel Dalet in Bobo-Dioulasso and killed several Frenchmen, despite the total opposition of the Muslim heads of the town.

Cooperation with the colonial authorities was highly beneficial to the official Islamic movement. The colonial power, whether it repressed Islam, suspected Islam, or favored Islam, in every case accorded a particular status to the religion, which in the end added to Islam's authority. This phenomenon of Islamization in the French colonial situation does not have, I contend, an equivalent in the rest of the world (including the rest of Africa). Above all, the remarkable malleability and adaptability of the African Muslim world must be recalled, one that was capable of utilizing cooperation and compromise with a *kafir* (non-Muslim) power to its ultimate benefit. Certainly, French colonization gained some advantages from this (finding, for example, in the Mourid or Tijani hierarchy in some places the framework for an indirect management of the believers), but it never succeeded in making of West African Islam a "Black Islam" or a "French Islam" other than in a conjectural fashion. The desolate cries of the administration in the 1950s bear witness to both this failure and the success of the strategy of compromise.[36]

Profiting, simultaneously, from its positions of power in the colonial apparatus, its close links to the commercial networks,[37] and its implicit dimension as a "culture of resistance" in the eyes of the Sudanese population, Islam has strongly consolidated its positions. Even today, in contrast to North Africa, African opinion does not reproach the elites for having cooperated with the colonial power. This collaboration, which was a source of power for the families involved, could even be viewed as a proof of the charisma of their members, who had established themselves as the interlocutors of the colonial power and had served as "links" to the rest of the population.

The Disadvanatages of the Muwalat

A more nuanced presentation remains to be made for this period. At the moment of independence, the religious elites were ousted lastingly from their politically determining positions by elites who had a French education.[38] They were left behind by the new state of the game, just as the colonial power itself had been. They also suffered, in varying degrees, the policy of undermining the Islamic culture fostered by French colonialism, which had discouraged the opening of Quranic schools and had controlled and diverted newspapers and books in Arabic by means of the postal service. Their intellectual production—beyond the major figures of the brotherhoods and the savants, such as Shaykh Musa Kamara[39]—responded to the needs of the colonialists, and was limited. The French regime contributed to a certain isolation of the communities. In the 1950s, contacts with the Arab world permitted the opening of reformist sectors of the Ibn Badis school, like the Muslim Cultural Union in Senegal[40] and the neo-Wahhabis in the Juula world. These disputed expressions were, however, of limited extent. There is thus a contradiction for the period under consideration between a spectacular numerical upsurge and a substantial defensive conservatism, or stagnation, of thought and intellectual reflection.

Material remains for investigation concerning the precise relations that existed between the representatives of the Islamic communities and French power in the colonial period. In the French-speaking context, "collaboration" and "resistance" have an echo that is out of all proportion—relating to events that France experienced in World War II; the term *collaboration* becomes defamatory, and apologists are anxious to find the virtues of resistance in those who have chosen the path of compromise (*silent resistance, passive resistance,* and so on). We might enlarge a concept that research in English has used for a long time: *accommodation.* The accommodation in question here encompasses all those attitudes that, without necessarily leading to open ideological collaboration, manifest the concern to adapt in various ways to new relations of power.[41] Political collaboration is included here, but it represents only an extreme variant. Thus, the contours of a vast movement are revealed between *collaboration* and *resistance,* and it resists being systematically and definitively classified. This is the "period of the Marabou," a short period (hardly more than three generations) that witnessed the emergence of new religious entrepreneurs, of new brotherhoods, and of a new leap forward of the African Islamic frontier.

Notes

1. In the eighteenth century, the authors of the Enlightenment readily saw in Islam the deistic and natural religion that was capable of advantageously opposing Christian "obscurantism." With the development of European imperialism in India, the Mediterranean, and Africa, there was no longer any question of this taking place.

2. In 1883, with respect to the Sanusi, Duveyrier speaks of "their experience of the world," of "a political sense comparable with that which one can observe in the Jesuit order," and of the "intrigues of the Senousiya, that is of a secret, religious, and political society." The references are quoted in Triaud 1995.

3. The reference is to the followers of the Breton Chouan, royalist peasants who opposed the French Revolution.

4. Quellien (a functionary in the colonial ministry) 1910, 100, 128–29.

5. Marty 1917, 261–62.

6. Gouilly 1952, 248–49.

7. A good example of this is the way in which the Sanusi question was treated in Chad in 1900–1902. Destenave, who had come as the successor of Emile Gentil at the head of the "Lands and Protectorates of Chad," decided to attack the closest Sanusi *zawiya* of Bir Alali. This broke with the policy pursued by Gentil and contravened the instructions of the government. See Triaud 1987a.

8. "Far from going to war with Islam, we should use it, we should profit from the social progress which it has brought to the fetishistic peoples. . . . The enemy, the only one, the real one, is fetishism." See Villamur and Richaud 1903. One finds the same Islamophile tone in Binger 1906, which attempts precisely to refute the idea of an Islamic peril in West Africa.

9. Pasquier 1974, 263–84.

10. Le Chatelier 1989, 348.

11. This tendency was not limited to Senegal. One finds the effects of this, with a chronological delay, in other colonies, such as Côte d'Ivoire. Marty thus notes, "One encouraged the construction of a mosque at Tiassalé and Clozel, the governor, contributed 250 francs towards the expenses (1904). . . . The administration encouraged the construction of a mosque at Toumodi in 1904. It cost 2,000 francs and Clozel, the governor, subsidized it with 200 francs." Marty 1922, 48, 51.

12. Militant leaders on the Senegal and the Gambia Rivers were influenced by the Umarian jihad or by the *toorodo* model: Ma Ba Jaaxu, south of the Senegal river (1861–67); Cerno Brahim (defeated in 1869); Amadu Seexu, leader of the Madiyankoobe, who was killed by French troops in Futa in 1875; and Mamadu Laamin Daraame, at the juncture of today's Senegal and Mali, who was killed in 1886. None of these were Tijani.

13. See Johnson 1978, 127–56.

14. William Ponty, governor general of French West Africa, circular on the surveillance of Islam, Dec. 26, 1912.

15. Delafosse 1911, 81–90.

16. Arnaud 1906.

17. Quellien 1910, 111–12.

18. Arnaud 1912, 6, 128–29.

19. Marty 1917, 261–62.

20. One notes that this policy does not exclusively concern sub-Saharan Africa, even if it has the effect of establishing a split between Maghrib and Mediterranean Islam. See Laroui on this subject, with respect to the policy followed by the French administration in Morocco: "One attempted to encourage even the most abstruse particularisms in order to give popular religion a local, naturalistic, and primitive character." Laroui 1975, 116.

21. See the testimonies published in the *Revue du Monde Musulman* (1915), "Les Musulmans francais et la guerre." Here one finds all the major names of the period, among them Shaykh Sidiyya Baba, al-Hajj Malik Sy, and al-Hajj Abdullahi Niass.

22. On the theory of conspiracy applied to the Sanusiyya, see Triaud 1995.

23. Delafosse 1922.

24. Such an administrator writes in 1933, with respect to the Juula: "One should also not neglect to accord this faction of Islam the importance which it bears, and to consider it as the most reliable political agent among populations given over to the roughest mysticism." Touladjian, head of the subdivision of the Toumodi (Côte d'Ivoire), in a certificate delivered to Seydou Nourou Tall while he was on tour. National Archives of Senegal, 19 G 57 (108).

25. Kaba 1974.

26. See Garcia 1997. Seydou Nourou Tall's major tours in French West Africa in the 1930s exhibited this entente between the administration and the Umari heir in a magnificent and very ostentatious way.

27. On the question of the Medersa, see Harrison 1988, 62–65, 101–2, 183–86; and Brenner 1991.

28. Issa Hassan Khayar 1976.

29. Gardinier 1989.

30. One can add here more localized cases such as the affair of the Wali of Goumba (1909–12), in Guinea, well documented by Sanneh 1987; Harrison 1988, 68f.

31. On Malam Musa, see Triaud 1983.

32. On the Juula world, see Launay 1997.

33. On the concept of muwalat and the debates that it gives rise to, see Mahibou and Triaud 1983, 107–32 (for al-Hajj Umar); Quick 1993, 7–33 (for Sokoto), and Mbaye 1993, 504–5.

34. See the presentation of the debate among the Mauritanian *'ulama*. Wuld Bara 1997; also Adeleye 1968.

35. Little has been written about the insurrectional Mahdism of West Africa. One can consult Hodgkin 1970; Le Grip 1952; al-Hajj 1967; and Biobaku and al-Hajj 1966 and 1969.

36. "One should not nurture any illusion: French West Africa is already too involved in the path to Islam, and the disequilibrium of power has already developed too far for our action to be able to expect anything other than a delaying effect" (Centre des Archives d'Outre-Mer, Aix-en-Provence, Aff. Pol. 2256, d. 4, governor general of French West Africa to the French Overseas Ministry, 7 July 1950).

37. The opening of paths of communication (roads, railways) and the existence of the colonial order facilitate the installation of Muslim colonies in the southern regions where they had hitherto been absent (such as Côte d'Ivoire).

38. On the relations between the colonial administration and the Marabou and on the debates of 1958 to 1962 in Senegal, see Coulon 1981.

39. On Shaykh Musa Kamara, see several articles in vol. 7 of the journal *Islam et sociétés au sud du Sahara* (1993).

40. Loimeier 1994.

41. Robinson (1997) has reconstructed the stages of compromise between the elites and the authorities in Senegambia.

Bibliography

Adeleye, R. A. 1968. "The Dilemma of the Wazir: The Place of the *Risalat al-Wazir ila ahl al-ilm wa'l-tadabbur*," *Journal of the Historical Society of Nigeria* 4:285–311.

Arnaud, Robert. 1906. *Précis de politique musulmane 1: Pays maures de la rive droite du Sénégal.* Algiers.

———. 1912. *L'Islam et la politique musulmane française en Afrique Occidentale française.* Paris: Comité de l'Afrique Française.

Bernus, Edmund. 1993. *Nomades et commandants: Administration et sociétés nomades dans l'ancienne A.O.F.* Paris: Karthala.

Binger, L. 1906. *Le Péril de l'Islam.* Paris: Comité de l'Afrique Française.

Biobaku, S., and M. A. al-Hajj. 1966, 1969. "The Sudanese Mahdiyya and the Niger-Tchad Region." In *Islam in Tropical Africa,* ed. I. M. Lewis, 425–38. London: Oxford University Press.

Brenner, Louis. 1991. "Medresas au Mali: Transformations d'une institution islamique." In *L'enseignement islamique au Mali,* ed. Bintou Sanankoua and Louis Brenner, 65–68. Bamako: Editions Jamana.

———. 1997. "Becoming Muslim in Soudan Français." In Robinson and Triaud 1997, 65–68.

Brevié, Jules, 1923. *Islamisme contre "naturisme" au Soudan français: Essai de psychologie politique coloniale.* Paris: Leroux.

Brosselard, L. 1859. *Les Khouan: De la constitution des ordres religieux musulmans en Algérie.* Algeria.

Cholvy, Gérard. 1991. *La religion en France de la fin du 18ème siècle à nos jours.* Paris: Hachette.

Coulon, Christian. 1981. *Le marabout et le prince (Islam et pouvoir au Sénégal).* Paris: Pedone.

Cruise O'Brien, Donal. 1967. "Towards an 'Islamic Policy' in French West Africa (1854–1914)," *Journal of African History* 8:303–16.

Delafosse, Maurice. 1911. "Les confréries musulmanes et le maraboutisme dans les pays du Sénégal et du Niger," *Bulletin du Comité de l'Afrique Française, Renseignements Coloniaux*, no. 4:81–90.

———. 1922. "L'animisme nègre et sa résistance à l'islamisation en Afrique occidentale," *Revue du Monde Musulman*.

Depont, Octave, and Xavier Coppolani. 1897. *Le confréries religieuses musulmanes*. Algiers.

Garcia, Sylvianne. 1997. "Al-Hajj Seydou Nourou Tall 'grand marabout' tijani: L'histoire d'une carrière (c.1880–1980)." In Robinson and Triaud 1997, 247–75.

Gardinier, David. 1989. "Muhammad Awuda Oulech at Abeche: A Reformist Islamic Challenge to French and Traditionalist Interests in Ouaddai, Chad (1947–1956)," *Islam et Sociétés au sud du Sahara* 3:159–85.

Gouilly, Alphonse [Mouradian]. 1952. *L'Islam dans l'Afrique occidentale française*. Paris.

Griaule, Marcel. 1938. *Masques dogons*. Paris: Institut d'Ethnologie.

al-Hajj, M. A. 1967. "The Thirteenth Century in Muslim Eschatology: Mahdist Expectations in the Sokoto Caliphate," *Research Bulletin* (Ibadan) 3:100–115.

Hames, Constant. 1983. "Cheikh Hamallah ou qu'est-ce qu'une confrérie islamique (tariqa)," *Archives de Sciences Sociales des religions*.

———. 1997. "Le premier exil de Shaikh Hamallah et la mémoire hamalliste (Nioro-Mederdra, 1925)." In Robinson and Triaud 1997, 337–60.

Harrison, Christopher. 1988. *France and Islam in West Africa (1860–1960)*. Cambridge University Press.

Hodgkin, Thomas. 1970. "Mahdisme, messianisme, et marxisme dans le contexte africain," *Présence Africaine* 74:128–53.

Issa Hassan Khayar. 1976. *Le refus de l'école: Contribution á l'étude des problèmes de l'éducation chez les Musulmans du Ouaddai (Tchad)*. Paris: Maisonneuve.

Johnson, Wesley G. 1978. "William Ponty and Republican Paternalism in West Africa." In *African Proconsuls*, ed. L. Gann and P. Duignan, 127–56. New York.

Joly, Vincent. 1993. "L'administration du Soudan français et les événements de Nioro-Assaba (aout 1940)." In Edmund Bernus et al., 49–60.

———. 1997. "La réconciliation de Nioro (septembre 1937): Un tournant dans la politique musulmane au Soudan français?" In Robinson and Triaud 1997, 361–72.

Kaba, Lansiné. 1974. *The Wahhabiyya: Islamic Reform and Politics in French West Africa*. Evanston.

Klein, Martin. 1968. *Islam and Imperialism in Senegal*. Edinburgh.

Laroui, Abdalla. 1975. *L'Histoire du Maghreb*, vol. 2. Paris: François Mapero.

Launay, Robert. 1997. "Des infidèles d'un autre type: Les réponses au pouvoir colonial dans une communauté musulmane du Côte d'Ivoire." In Robinson and Triaud 1997, 415–30.

Le Chatelier, Alfred. 1989. *L'Islam en Afrique occidentale*. Paris: Steinheil.

Le Grip, P. A. 1952. "Le Mahdisme en Afrique noire," *L'Afrique et Asie* 18:3–16.

Levtzion, Nehemia, and H. J. Fisher, eds. 1986. *Rural and Urban Islam in West Africa*. Special issue of *Asian and African Studies* vol. 20, no. 1.

Levtzion, Nehemia, and H. J. Fisher, eds. 1987. *Rural and Urban Islam in West Africa*. Boulder, Colo.: Lynne Reinner.

Loimeier, Roman. 1994. "Cheikh Touré: Du réformisme à l'islamisme, un musulman sénégalais dans le siècle," *Islam et sociétés au sud du Sahara* 8:55–66.

Mahibou, Sidi Mohammed, and Jean-Louis Triaud. 1983. *Voilà ce qui est arrivé*. Paris: CRNS.

Marty, Paul. 1917. *Etudes sur l'Islam au Sénégal*. 2 vols.

———. 1922. *Etudes sur l'islam en Côte d'Ivoire*. Paris: Leroux.

Mbaye, El Hadji Ravane. 1993. "La pensée et l'action d'El Hadji Malick Sy: Un pôle d'attraction entre la sharia et la tariqa." Université de la Sorbonne Nouvelle (Paris 3), thèse de doctorat d'Etat. 4 vols.

Pasquier, Roger. 1974. "L'influence de l'expérience algérienne sur la politique de la France au Sénégal (1842–1869)." In *Mélanges Hubert Deschamps*, 263–84. Paris: Publications de la Sorbonne.

Quellien, Alain. 1910. *La politique musulmane dans l'Afrique occidentale*. Paris: Larose.

Quick, Abdullah Hakim. 1993. "The Concept of Muwalat in the Sokoto Caliphate and the Resulting Dilemma at the Time of British Conquest," *Islam et sociétés au sud du Sahara* 7:17–33.

Rinn, Louis. 1884. *Marabouts et Khouan*. Algiers.

Robinson, David. 1988. "French Islamic Policy and Practice towards Islam in Late Nineteenth Century Senegal," *Journal of African History* 29.

———. 1997. "An Emerging Pattern of Cooperation between Colonial Authorities and Muslim Societies in Senegal and Mauritania." In Robinson and Triaud 1997, 155–80.

Robinson, David, and Jean-Louis Triaud. 1997. *Le Temps des marabouts. Itinéraires et stratégies islamiques en Afrique occidentale française (v. 1880–1960)*. Paris: Karthala.

Rocaboy, Joseph. 1993. "Le cas hamalliste: Les événements de Nioro-Assaba (août 1940)." In Bernus et al. 1993, 41–48.

Sanneh, Lamine. 1987. "Tcherno Aliou, the Wali of Goumba: Islam, Colonialism, and the Rural Factor in Futa Jallon (1867–1912)." In Levtzion and Fisher 1987, 73–102.

Savadogo, Boukary. 1996. "La Tijaniyya Hamawiyya au Moogo central," *Islam et sociétés au sud du Sahara* 10:7–23.

Soares, Benjamin F. 1997. "The Spiritual Economy of Nioro du Sahel: Islamic Discourses and Practices in a Malian Religious Center," Ph.D. diss., Northwestern University.

Traore, Alioune. 1983. *Islam et le colonisation en Afrique: Cheikh Hamahoullah, homme de foi et résistant*. Paris: Maisonneuve et Larose.

Triaud, Jean-Louis. 1974. "La question musulmane en Côte d'Ivoire (1893–1939)," *Revue française d'histoire d'Outre-Mer*, 61, no. 225:542–71.

———. 1983. "Hommes de religion et confréries islamiques dans une société en crise: L'Air aux 19ème et 20ème siècles: Le cas de la Khalwatiyya," *Cahiers d'Etudes Africaines* 23:239–80.

————. 1986. "Le thème confrérique en Afrique de l'ouest: Essai historique et bibliographique." In *Les Ordres mystiques dans l'Islam. Cheminements et situation actuelle,* ed. A. Popovic and G. Veinstein, 271–82. Paris: Editions de l'EHESS.

————. 1987a. *Tchad 1900–1902: Une guerre franco-sanûsî oubliée?* Paris: L'Harmattan.

————. 1987b. "Les études en langue française sur l'Islam en Afrique noire: Essai historiographique," *Lettre d'Information de l'Association Française pour l'Etude du Monde Arabe et Musulman,* no. 2: Aix-en-Provence, 65–80.

————. 1992. "L'Islam sous le régime colonial." In *L'Afrique occidentale au temps des Français, colonisateurs et colonisés (c. 1869–1960),* 141–55, ed. Catherine Coquery-Vidrovitch and Odile Georg. Paris: La Découverte.

————. 1995. *La Légende noire de la Sanûsiyya: Une confrérie musulmane saharienne sous le regard Français (1840–1930),* vol. 1: 11–12. Paris: Editions de la Maison des Sciences de l'Homme.

Villamur, Roger, and Léon Richaud. 1903. *Notre colonie de la Côte-d'Ivoire.* Preface L. Binger. Paris: Challamel.

Wuld Bara, Yahya. 1997. "Les théologiens mauritaniens face au colonialisme français: Etude de fatwas de jurisprudence musulmane." In Robinson and Triaud 1997, 85–117.

CHAPTER 9

Islam in West Africa: Radicalism and the New Ethic of Disagreement, 1960-1990

Lansiné Kaba

This chapter examines the origins and forms of the current Islamic vitality in the Francophone states of Guinea, Mali, and Côte d'Ivoire in West Africa since their independence, with special attention to new attitudes. A broad attempt at reflection on religion and politics, the chapter is based on information gleaned from archival research and gathered from oral interviews with both reform and nonreform Muslims between 1985 and 1995. It analyzes the Muslim leaders' perceptions of their roles in modern societies and their concerns, in the words of a respected imam, as "people of God committed to peace and development."[1]

Unlike in the post–World War II decades, when numerous African territories achieved independence from European colonial powers, and when the Marxist interpretation of history and society, with its neglect of religion's significance, dominated the intellectual discourse, religious movements and thoughts have received, since the 1980s, more attention from scholars and policy makers. For example, as shown in chapter 7, Islam has emerged in many areas as a force both in national and international politics. In some West African countries, Muslims have exulted in the resurgence of religious fervor. This spirit seems to indicate a success over the benign indifference that characterized the first decades of independence. From the campus of the university of Dakar-Fann in Senegal, with a large student body formerly committed to socialism and militancy, to the mosque of the Riviera in the plush Cocody section of Abidjan in Côte d'Ivoire, which symbolizes an Islamic fervor unusual in a modernizing bourgeoisie, Quranic preachers urge their brethren to abide by the traditions of the Prophet Muhammad *(sunna)*, the foundation of Islamic orthodoxy (sunnism), and to ensure its triumph. Although Muslim leaders remain apprehensive for the future of politics in their respective countries, their confidence in the prospects for further growth, bolstered by the spread of orthodoxy, remains steadfast. They have acquired a greater awareness of the worldwide Islamic community *(umma),* due in part to their travels, in part to the activities of the World Islamic League and the Organization of Islamic Conference (OIC). The situation has not been easy, however.

Islam Marginalized

The first form of reform in contemporary West Africa was waged in the 1950s by the graduates of al-Azhar University in Cairo and other Near Eastern schools.[2] Commonly called Wahhabi or Subbanu or Arabicists, they sought to reform—that is, to purify—the practice of Islam. They decried the worship of sainthood *(walaya)* and other uncanonical devotional practices. Calling themselves "the people of *sunna*" (*sunna-mo,* in the Mandinka language), they refused to bow to any authority other than that of orthodoxy and rejected existing institutions and concepts of society. Unlike other Muslims who prayed with their arms along each side of the body, they worshipped with their hands crossed on their chest, thereby receiving the nickname of *bras croisés* in the French colonial reports (*bolo-minalalu,* in Mandinka). Recognizable by their beards and Middle Eastern types of clothing, they favored the loose-fitting, long-sleeved, ankle-length, light-cotton shirts *(chemises arabes)* with collar and cuffs instead of the wide, West African caftan *(pipao)* and bulky, sleeveless, ceremonial damask gowns *(boubou).* They thought that their style, by requiring less fabric, was more suitable to modern life and conformed to the Islamic ideals of simplicity and modesty. The new style amounted to a revolutionary statement, signaling the wearer's adherence to a different interpretation of the Islamic doctrine and ethos.

These Subbanu of the 1950s appeared as "radical" social reformers in that they introduced new attitudes about the family and marriage. They claimed that "a proper, non-complacent reading of the Quran and of the *sunna* of the Prophet Muhammad might not endorse polygamy," although the same texts seem to allow its practice. Arguing that "no man, if he married more than one wife, could treat all his wives equally," they attacked the Islamic establishment on this ground. The Quran, a prominent Wahhabi teacher often reminded, "forcefully rejects polygamy, but in an indirect way."[3] Subbanu followers tended to practice monogamy. From this practice emerged a concept of social reform and an ethical viewpoint that gave Islam a human voice and enjoined the faithful to strive for justice.

Unlike Jean-Claude Froelich who claimed that the French promoted the spread of Islam during the colonial era, I would argue that this process rather indicated the internal vitality of the Muslim community. The role of the Mande traders *(juula)* who controlled local trade, transportation, and Islamic affairs must be stressed, in particular.[4] The advance of Islam also went hand in hand with political militancy.

The Subbanu were the first proponents of fundamentalism; that is, a literal interpretation of the scriptures calling for an involvement in politics as a means to establish a Muslim-centered government. To achieve the integration of this community, they sought to have their own Friday mosques and secure greater autonomy for their actions. The early stage of their expansion from Bamako to neighboring countries witnessed various forms of conflicts, sometimes violent and bloody, fought against the leaders and followers of sufi brotherhoods. To extend the discussion beyond the middle Niger River Valley area, the Tijani also acted as religious reformers in Nigeria. The attainment of independence from colonial rule and the subsequent fear of the new states' coercive power put an end to the religious confrontation.[5]

To appreciate fully the issue of Islam in West Africa, we need a historical perspective see chapter 3). In many areas, the dynamics of contemporary Islam continues a historical process consistent with the tradition of accommodation that characterized the medieval Ghana and Mali empires. Until the era of the jihad in the nineteenth century (chapter 6), conversion was achieved mostly through trade and other peaceful means. Two major shifts have occurred since the end of the colonial era. The first, primarily educational and mystical, marked the decline of Mauritania and the Maghrib as places to go for attaining higher education and leadership in the two main brotherhoods, the Qadiriyya and the Tijaniyya.[6] The Western Sahara and the Maghrib lost their aura as main sources of Islamic education. The yearly collections of gifts for the Mauritanian sufi masters came to an end as the number of West African students in Egypt and the Middle East increased. The second shift has involved a change in the way in which Muslim leaders have behaved in the postindependence political arena, at times defying the secular power and at times showing respect and even despondency to the political elite.[7]

Independence was won in West Africa without a war of liberation, except in Guinea-Bissau. In the former French colonies, the *Rassemblement démocratique africain* (RDA), which was then the strongest nationalist party, operated as a mass-based movement, stretching from the cities into the remote rural communities.[8] The success of such a mobilization required the politics of a united front cutting across ethnic and religious boundaries. Thus, Muslim and Christian leaders alike— for example, Sékou Touré in Guinea, Léopold S. Senghor in Senegal, and Félix Houphouët-Boigny in Côte d'Ivoire—sought support from their Islamic communities. In the countries with a large Muslim merchant group, Islamic concerns played a determinant role in political mobilization. The Muslim clerics (*marabouts,* in French; *mori* in Mandinka), who were under police surveillance, and the merchants, who had little access to long-term bank credits, continued to hold grievances against the colonial administration. The image of Islam as a non-European belief system, coupled with its role in the precolonial resistance movements, also served as a catalyst for mobilization.

Despite the common front, the alliance between anticolonial and Islamic radicalisms came to an abrupt end after independence, as the new elite in control of power opted for a secular order. The idea of an Islamic state, even in the countries in which the Muslims were a dominant majority, was rejected, although Islam remained a main component of the local culture. These leaders considered religion a sectarian system difficult to control politically, whose goals were incompatible with those of national integration. Islam became marginalized, perhaps except in Senegal, where Senghor's political interests converged with, and depended on, those of the influential Tijani, Qadiri, Murid, and Layenne brotherhoods.[9] The pressure by the student movement, including the Muslim Association of Black African Students (*Association musulmane des étudiants d'Afrique noire,* AMEA), which focused on national liberation and pan-Islamism, also forced Senghor to be responsive to the demands of the Muslim community.[10]

Elsewhere—in Guinea, for example—the first years of independence witnessed a politics that appeared "anti-marabout" and "anti-fetish." President Sékou Touré, a Muslim, restricted the freedom of any association whose legitimacy lay outside his *Parti démocratique de Guinée* (PDG). To create the young wing of the party, in March 1959 he suppressed the voluntary associations, including the Islamic ones.[11] Later, the Muslim associations reemerged, but under strict party control. Friday's sermons were expected to deal only with issues consistent with the PDG's official ideology. Muslim clerics were forbidden to organize evening lectures and make collections, and workers were advised not to use religion as a justification for their lateness or absence. The Roman Catholic bishop of Conakry, Mgr. de Milleville, was expelled from Guinea, and his church was excluded from all educational activities.[12] Many who questioned the wisdom of these moves wondered whether Touré was "instigating a religious war";[13] others interpreted his religious policy as a "struggle in the very name and interest of Islam against mystification and uncanonical practices."

In any case, Muslims who criticized the government were afraid of its security forces and felt they were bound by the doctrine of the duty of obedience, the cornerstone of the Muslim attitudes to power and authority. This principle lies in the Quranic verses: "O ye who believe! Obey God, and obey the Apostle, and those charged with authority among you."[14] The Muslim communities acquiesced and did not call for the overthrow of the government; in fact, they suffered from a lack of unity and appropriate leadership to express their outcry. Many individuals in private disagreed with the government's policy and suspected Touré of Freemason (antireligious) tendencies. Guinean Muslim leaders practiced, in the words of al-Hajj Kabiné Diané, a "politics of distance and proximity" *(ma-tankali)* that involved cooperation without compromising the doctrine or endangering individual safety.

Subsequently, in October 1959, the PDG political secretary, Saifoulaye Diallo, spelled out the party's Islamic policy in a document known as "Memorandum 81 of the Politburo." He exhorted the PDG sections to wage a vigilant war against Muslim associations and leaders because of their "political anti-conformism." The politburo feared that "the evolution of the religious phenomenon would result in a dictatorship based on fanaticism, intolerance, sectarianism, and other obscurantist conceptions with many risks for the state in its policy making, its conception of society, and its authority." To the PDG leadership, Islamic fundamentalism appeared dangerous not because of its puritanism but rather its political implications. To ward off this danger, Guineans were asked to "war against the hustlers and swindlers licensed as 'marabouts'; against fanaticism, which is a sedition-monger and destroys brotherhood and solidarity; against charlatanry, and other forms of mystification and exploitation linked to these obscurantist entities." The document concluded with a surprisingly strong denunciation of pan-Islamism, pan-Arabism, and other forms of religious extremism because of their "reactionary, racist, and dangerous tendencies." "'Demarabutization,' demystification and deintoxication of the masses thus became the official religious policies."[15]

The party also later initiated a vast campaign against fetishism and sorcery, destroying sacred groves and other secret worship places, mainly in the Forest region. It also canceled a pan-Islamic convention scheduled to be held in Conakry on December 25, 1959 by the Muslim Cultural Union (*Union culturelle musulmane,* or UCM), an organization known for its radical stand on social and cultural issues. The government's uneasiness with fundamentalism belonged to Sékou Touré's fear of an ideology that could legitimize protest movements at a time when France had isolated Guinea in Africa and had attempted to disrupt Guinean economy and political stability.[16]

By April 1960, the relations between the PDG and Muslim groups further worsened with the news of a plot against the regime, and the execution, for treason, of al-Hajj Lamine Kaba, imam of the Korontee quarter in Conakry. Touré also opposed the construction of a reformist mosque in Conakry by al-Hajj Mamadou Fofana, a former PDG chief treasurer who would later serve years in prison for conspiracy. The Guinean leadership was also determined to eradicate the non-Muslim cult of land deities and to control fundamentalism. Later, al-Hajj Chérif Nabaniou, a prominent political figure who headed the National Islamic Council (*Conseil national islamique*), was arrested.[17]

The attempt to curtail the influences of fundamentalism in the early 1960s cut across national boundaries. In Mali, Modibo Keita attacked all associations deemed dangerous, including the Muslim reformist organizations. He abolished the UCM and placed its schools under state control, thereby reducing the Arabic teachers' influence. In Upper Volta (Burkina Faso), Maurice Yaméogo viewed the Muslim associations as "potential problem-makers" and thus included few Muslims in his government. In Niger, Hamani Diori's politics, too, aimed at containing Islamic organizations. In Côte d'Ivoire, Muslims, despite their demographic and economic importance, felt themselves second-class citizens as compared with the minority Roman Catholic community; they had little access to the media, and many of their holidays were ignored. Houphouët never lost sight of the risk of a Muslim revolt, in the urban areas especially, positioning himself against the politics of pan-Islam advocated by Egypt's Gamal Abdel Nasser. He developed, however, strong personal relationships with nonreformist leaders, showering funds on them and their associations.

A Renewed Vigor and Radicalism

Islam, though marginalized, did not decline; it could not be eclipsed. The Muslims everywhere displayed a "modernizing initiative"; that is, a will to participate in social and economic activities as members of a "God-inspired community." In the tradition of the Juula, they took advantage of newer trade, real-estate, and transportation opportunities and hence acquired more influence. The politics of cultural nationalism and the growth of the informal economy, with a significant participation by women, further strengthened their creed and their social position. This process in general, and the reform doctrine in particular, also benefited from the perception of Islam by many Africans as the religion par excellence that best fitted their milieu and ethos. Islam therefore experienced an unprecedented growth in the region. The 1970s witnessed, to borrow J. Vatin's words, "a regeneration of culture, a profound renewal of religiosity, and an exploitation of the Islamic ideology and vocabulary"[18] by ordinary people seeking greater participation in the Muslim-dominated urban life, and by secular leaders eager to reinforce their legitimacy and their power.

Because the Mandinka Muslim clerics welcomed this development, they seldom spoke of "pure" and "less pure" forms of Islam. Rather, they viewed the growing acceptance of Islam as a challenge to provide more education to their followers. Many political leaders, too, would feel compelled to reconsider their attitudes under the pressure of their domestic and foreign policies. Sékou Touré, for example, went a step further, imposing an Islamic character on his party. He established Islamic councils parallel to the PDG branches; Islamic meetings were held weekly on Fridays, and his speeches abounded in Islamic themes. To bolster his image as a Muslim leader, he authored a book on Islam and revolution—a work that received a $100,000 award from a Saudi foundation in 1978.[19] The growing religiosity resulted in an improvement in the general level of education. Mosques and voluntary associations developed extensive adult-education programs in Arabic and African languages.

In this politico-religious context lay the new manifestation of Islamic radicalism. The "new" reform remained radical in its puritanism and its strict obedience to the traditions of the Prophet. Unlike in the 1950s, however, reform has been more inward looking and less confrontational, in part because of the involvement of an urban middle class of businessmen and civil servants who have been drawn to the quest of orthodoxy and spiritual perfection by, among various considerations, the reaction to secularization, the presence of new opportunities, and what is known in Mandinka as the "fear of God" *(Allah nya-silanni)*. Regardless of their doctrinal differences, the participants in the adult-education program have demonstrated an eagerness to follow, in peace, the Sunni tradition and to get involved in community services, prayer meetings, group recitations of hymns *(dhikr)*, and other supererogatory rituals.

This movement of popular learning and piety witnessed a growing presence of women in Muslim affairs, individually and collectively in their associations. House-wives and professionals alike volunteered their services and skills for "the sake of God." The lettered women engaged in adult literacy, complementing their blend of puritanism and modernity, and thus fulfilling a much-needed task. The rise of women as a strong Muslim force reflected their demographic importance as well as their involvement and success in the informal economy, including long-distance trade. Many housewives have now become true businesswomen (*femmes d'affaires* in French; *juula-mosso* in Mandinka). They have emerged as the main breadwinners in many households.

Among those who perform the yearly canonical pilgrimage (*hajj*), the number of businesswomen has risen. And the small pilgrimage, *'umra,* which may be per-formed at any time of the year and involves trade, has been often described as the "women's pilgrimage." Travel agents have reported that, without businesswomen, "no airline would operate the route from Conakry to Jeddah."[20] The popularity of 'umra has testified to the rising status of women in West African societies. In their associations (called *dahira* in Senegal) both Western-educated professionals and un-educated housewives have devoted much time to prayers and learning the Quran, preaching to other women, and performing voluntary services. Notably, they have gone bare-faced and have argued for women's education and full participation in modern life. In conversation, Hajja Oumoun Sanankouwa, an engineer and a chief financial analyst in Abidjan, reminded me that these women's commitment to Islam is a modern interpretation of the ideal Muslim womanhood and that it is consistent with the tradition of social engagement reminiscent of that of the Prophet's wives.[21]

Islam and Recent Politics: A Synopsis

The evolution of Islamic affairs during the decade from 1963 to 1973 coincided with the growth of Arab-African diplomatic ties. This process was in part related to the history of precolonial contact and the setting in 1963 of the Organization of African Unity. Although inter-African relations for a long time were determined mostly by politics rather than religion—that is, the cleavage between the so-called radical and conservative regimes—in the long run, Islamic concerns affected African diplomacy.

For example, African attitudes toward Israel were first influenced "more by the political orientation of the regime than the weight of Islam."[22] However, by the time the Arab countries and Israel fought the wars of 1967 and 1973, as Victor Levine and Timothy Lake have examined, Islam had become an instrument of diplomatic rapprochement among Muslim states. Guinea broke off diplomatic re-lations with Israel in 1967. In 1969, Chad, Mali, Senegal, and Guinea joined the Is-lamic summit in Rabat that initiated the Organization of the Islamic Conference (OIC).Pan-Islamism, or the ideals of Islamic brotherhood and cooperation, played a role in their policies toward the Middle East. Chad, Niger, and Mali severed their ties with Israel in 1973. The politics of Libya's Colonel Mu'amar al-Qadhafi, who began to champion the Arab cause in Africa through diplomacy, economic assistance, and military subversion (plus the oil crisis in 1973) accelerated this process. These factors resulted in, to borrow Colin Legum's expression, "the political avalanche of October/November 1973,"[23] as most African states broke diplomatic relations with Israel. Arab leaders capitalized on religion to boost their diplomacy.

More and more, Africans now wonder whether the level of Arab investments in sub-Saharan Africa has been commensurate with the diplomatic support given, notwithstanding the creation of the Islamic Development Bank in 1975 and the Arab Bank for Economic Development in Africa, with headquarters in Jeddah and Khartoum respectively. Whatever the case might be, the resurgence of Islamic fervor in West Africa has been partly associated with this growing contact with the center of the Islamic world.

In general, the post-1973 period saw a close tie between the religious domestic context and the formulation and implementation of foreign policy. Islamic leaders influenced their countries' foreign policies by representing their values as those of the majority population, and by forcing on their governments the links that they had established with religious figures or organizations in the Middle East. For example, the visits made by the imams of Mekka, Madina, and al-Azhar University to Guinea and other countries in the 1960s and 1970s stemmed in part from the local marabouts' acquaintance with these Arab men of religion. The visits ushered in a new stage in Arab-African relations. The visitors' interpretation of the canon, and their praying style, tended to legitimize the Wahhabi position. In countries with a dominant Muslim population and a Muslim establishment close to the ruling elite, religion, by arousing people's convictions, compelled many political leaders not only to show greater respect to the heads of Muslim associations but also concrete evidence of their support.

The 1967 and 1973 Arab/Israeli wars also influenced Islamic affairs in West Africa by increasing business opportunities. Saudi Arabia, Kuwait, and other Arab countries created banks and other financial institutions in joint partnership with various African states. In Guinea and Mali principally, a vigorous Middle Eastern connection has emerged, first led by Wahhabi businessmen and fueled by the exportation of tropical fruits independent of the already-established Levantine merchants. This commerce has played a critical role in the renewal of religiosity, as evidenced by the attendance at the Friday prayers and the great number of new mosques often built with Arab assistance. Moreover, as the Muslim community became a power to reckon with, the Islamic code (the *shari'a*) was adapted in several countries to become one of the bases for the legal system.

Many Muslim spokesmen expected a strong regeneration of religiosity because of Islam's undeniable mark on local value systems, and the connection assumed to exist between creed and color. Although the subject is complex and arguable, in this view it is thought that to be a Mandinka, a Wolof, a Fulah, a Hausa, or even any kind of black person implies an "innate" association with, and loyalty to, Islam. "Africanity (or blackness) and being a Muslim go together" (*fada-finn ya ni missil-*

iminn ya ye wala i nyon fe, as it is said in Mandinka). Ethnicity and "Muslim-ness" have been so closely identified and have interacted so thoroughly that they have become inseparable components of identity in many communities. The role of African languages in Islamic education and the indigenous nature of the Muslim leadership in Mali, Senegal, Guinea, or Niger have further reinforced this process. This might explain why Guinea's former prime minister, Dr. Louis Béavogui, and President Bernard Bongo of Gabon changed their first names to Lansana and Omar, respectively. They converted to Islam and gave themselves an Islamic image in the late 1960s. During the heyday of the single-party system, no government wished to rouse the wrath of the Muslims for fear of an uprising and hence endangering the financial relations with the oil-rich Arab countries.

☾ ☾ ☾

An overview of the politics and deeds of some African statesmen will illuminate these issues. By 1984, when President Sékou Touré died, he was recognized as a "dedicated Muslim leader." With his extensive involvement in the Organization of Islamic Conference (OIC), the World Islamic League, and other religious organizations, historical materialism disappeared from his speeches and writing. After the aborted Portuguese invasion of Guinea in November 1970, to show his gratitude to Allah he instituted the practice of reciting the opening chapter of the Quran *(al-fatiha)* at all public gatherings, and he regularly gave extensive lectures on Islamic politics and the Islamic nature of his party. The national radio network and television extended the daily coverage of Muslim activities.

Sékou Touré instituted Islamic councils and a Ministry of Islamic Affairs, making Sunni Islam a foundation of his regime. Imams were granted monthly salaries and other stipends as public servants; Guinean officials were urged to perform the hajj, and citizens known for their impeccable political commitment were rewarded with free transportation to Mekka. A member of the OIC executive board, Touré performed the ʿumra and convened numerous Islamic conferences in Conakry. In sum, he used Islam to legitimize his regime, "politicizing Islam and Islamizing his politics,"[24] thereby depoliticizing the question of fundamentalism. His era witnessed a phenomenal growth of Islam.

During Touré's time, Wahhabi and sufi groups alike enjoyed support in the National Islamic Council. The reform movement made great strides in the cities and the diamonds fields in the Forest. Al-Hajj Mamadi Kébé, a businessman and an in-law of the president,[25] financed the construction in Coleah-Conakry of a mosque that became the main center of radical reform under the leadership of al-Hajj Kabiné Diané, a World Islamic League representative. On many issues, including relations with the Arab world, Touré sought the advice of this imam. In Upper Guinea and the Forest, the reform movement benefited from the philanthropy of the new, fortunate class of Guineans, the diamond dealers, who built mosques and financed other religious activities. Except in Futa Jallon, which until the early 1980s experienced little reformist activity, there was little dispute over the establishment of these new mosques: the Islamic council imposed cooperation and order.

☾ ☾ ☾

In other countries, Muslim clerics exercised a great deal of influence as politicians of all religious persuasions competed for their support. Since winning their blessings became a signal feature of political life, their concerns could not go unheeded. The national media increased coverage of all Muslim public affairs, including the Friday prayers. To reduce sectarianism, Senghor and Houphouët, who were known for their steadfast Roman Catholicism, gave utmost attention to Islamic affairs. According to Christian Coulon and others, Senghor's relations with the heads of brotherhoods whose backing determined the outcome of the elections in Senegal not only encouraged tolerance in the body politic but also increased consensus and unity within the Islamic community. Through the semiofficial *Fédération des associations islamiques du Sénégal,* his government dealt with all the Muslim groups, including the UCM, and UCM representatives broadcast an Islamic program on the national radio network. To respond to the Muslims' expectations, a French/ Arabic curriculum was offered in primary schools and classical Arabic in secondary schools, along with Latin. With little sectarian strife, these processes blossomed into Islam's peaceful new age in Senegal; there were countless new mosques, Muslim associations, and publications.

In Côte d'Ivoire, Muslims formed more than half of the total population. During the colonial era, their massive migration to the south in search of economic gains destroyed the old geographical cleavage, without bringing about any significant conversion among the southerners. As Islam remained the religion of the savannah peoples, the ethnic and religious cleavage sharpened in the country. Houphouët-Boigny, to win Muslim support, built a large mosque in Yamoussokro, his hometown, and another in Abidjan-Riviera. He befriended the marabouts. Yet his regime feared the renewal of religious violence as a steady Muslim migration from neighboring countries in the 1970s fostered the conditions for a large-scale radical Islamic movement.

By 1990, the reformist organizations had spread, giving Islam the image of a modern religion—with telegenic spokespersons, new facilities, and a growing number of European-educated followers. This development reached secondary-school students, who at summer camps and conventions, held with Houphouët's financial assistance, were galvanized into religious fervor.[26] To minimize the risk of conflict within the Muslim Juula communities who had been among his first backers in the 1940s, Houphouët established an Islamic Superior Council (the *Conseil supérieur islamique,* or CSI). The CSI branches were supervised by the Imams' Superior Council (the *Conseil supérieur des imams,* or COSIM), and sought to integrate the Muslim groups, reformist and nonreformist alike, in order to formulate an Islamic agenda in harmony with the government's policies.

Economic concerns, coupled with political frustration, partly explain why the growth of Islamic radicalism became a problem. By 1985, with the abrupt end of the economic boom that Côte d'Ivoire had sustained since its independence—the "Ivoirian miracle"—the crisis had cut the incomes of civil servants, businessmen, and rich Akan coffee and cocoa farmers. Strikes by students and unions were followed by riots, the government no longer being able to subsidize the economy. In 1989, the situation became critical. The discontent spread, creating great pressure on the ruling party, from both inside and outside. This conflict soon prompted the emergence of a multiparty system mostly based on ethnicity, which heightened the crisis. To contain it, in October 1990 the government devised an electoral scheme to force the opposition parties to gear their energies toward political mobilization rather than protest. It thought that it could easily win reelection because of its political experience and its considerable electoral funds.

However, the Muslim vote, which had been crucial for the ruling party in the north and the urban areas, was no longer certain. Business in general, and especially transportation and urban real estate, had nosedived. Scores of businessmen complained that the treasury, unable to honor its vouchers, was defaulting on its obligations, including paying rent for properties and other services they rendered to the government. The revenues of many well-to-do Muslim families were slashed, and from being merely discontents, these groups soon became Houphouët's opponents. Muslim students and other dissidents also criticized Houphouët for the construction, at a cost of about $400 million, of a basilica, Notre Dame de la Paix, which is larger than Saint Peter's in Rome and can seat the whole Roman Catholic community of Yamoussokro. According to these critics, this monument, much more so than the cathedral built earlier in Abidjan Plateau, "symbolized the official status and power of the Catholic church." It confirmed the paramountcy of the ruler's religion, according to the doctrine *cujus regio, ejus religio* (whoever rules determines the religion) and hence challenged Islam's dominant position. No conflicts erupted between Christians and Muslims, but the issue of the separation of state and church had been raised.

Some critics thought that the president's role in religious affairs should come under scrutiny. They also alleged that the basilica amounted to an "unwise and unneeded extravaganza to be paid for by the whole nation," which he denied. The Christian and Muslim communities continued to tolerate each other, however. The lack of a common front among the opponents improved the government's prospect for success. The imams' support, coupled with the absence of a meaningful contact between the Muslims and the main opposition party, assured Houphouët's bid for reelection on October 28, 1990. He defeated the historian Laurent Gbagbo, who headed the Ivoirian Popular Front (*Front populaire ivoirien*). A month later, on November 25, the government won another victory, with 163 seats out of a total of 185, in the general election.

Houphouët's death in December 1993 brought about a contest between the then-interim president, Henri Konan Bédié, and a former prime minister, Alhassane

Ouattara. Bédié, a Roman Catholic from the Akan/Baule ethnic group, served as a finance minister for many years before becoming the Speaker of the national assembly. Ouattara, a Muslim from the northern border region near Burkina Faso, headed the Central Bank of West African States in Dakar before assuming the prime ministership in 1990. At the time of Houphouët's death, according to all reporters and informants, Bédié considered Ouattara as his most formidable contender, despite the latter's lack of strong political backing and experience (this fear might explain why Bédié promptly declared himself interim president, instead of waiting for the national assembly's validation). The political question took on a religious and ethnic dimension: a mostly Christian and animist Akan south confronted a predominantly Muslim Juula north. The creation of a breakaway faction of the ruling party by Ouattara's partisans, an issue of power and influence, symbolized the rift within the nation, thereby exacerbating the crisis.

By the time Houphouët's state funeral was held at the basilica in February 1994, Bédié had firmly consolidated his grip over the state apparatus and had received official recognition from France and other great powers. Many of Ouattara's followers were harassed and arrested. Although Bédié enjoyed the support of the official Islamic establishment,[27] many Muslims feared that his policies would tear the country apart along religious and ethnic lines. They thought that the purge of Juula officers from the army and civil servants from key government posts, the incarceration of journalists and students, and the campaigns of intimidation against opponents raised doubt about Bédié's commitment to unity and democracy. As the repression intensified, some Muslims argued that the country was in an "undeclared state of war." *Plume libre,* a Muslim monthly, ordered that the community "recite *al-fatiha* for the Muslims held at Abidjan's main prison."[28] Amnesty International in its 1995 annual report criticized the government for its human-rights abuses. An anonymous Muslim critic compared "Bédié's Côte d'Ivoire to a pressure cooker filled with volatile ingredients and manipulated by an inept kitchen staff."[29] Indeed, Bédié took no chances over his election as president. In 1994, he rammed through the parliament a citizenship bill that barred from elective office anyone, even those born in Côte d'Ivoire, whose two parents were not "100 percent Ivoirian," and who had not lived in the country during the five years preceding the race. The law was directed both at Ouattara, who had spent most of his career outside the country, and his supporters of Juula origins, whose parents belonged to the Mande world stretching beyond Côte d'Ivoire's northern borders.

Implicitly, the legislation created a dual system of citizenship favorable to the Christian southerners—deemed "pure Ivoirians." The northerners, recognizable by their clothes and surnames, were now liable to be confused with alien residents: identification cards were checked at random by the police, even near the mosques. The security forces in frequent roundups in the poor sections of Abidjan and other southern cities often humiliated the northerners and tore their identity cards. The new bill was portrayed in the opposition papers as the law of "Ivoirity and mediocrity." Many Ivoirians of Christian background also denounced it, calling it wrong legislation in the context of a multiethnic country. The ruling party lost its cohesion.

The attempt by Bédié and Ouattara to use the Muslim organizations to bolster their campaigns splintered the leadership of the Islamic movement into two factions. A new national organization—the National Islamic Council (*Conseil national islamique,* or CNI), funded in 1993 by various individuals and voluntary associations—contested the authority of the government-controlled Superior Islamic Council. The CNI was led by a national executive board headed by al-Hajj Idriss Koundouss Koné, a bank executive. Idriss Koné escaped several attempts made on his life because of his political leaning toward Ouattara.[30] The leaders of the opposition denounced the permanent "conspiracy" led by the government against the Muslim community and its lawful leaders. The CNI included many educated members, some of them Arab-university graduates, all united by commitment to Sunni Islam, whereas the CSI has been perceived as a tool designed by the government to divide and weaken the juula community. Its chief, Al-Hajj Diaby "Koweit," belonged to President Bédié's inner circle of advisers.

The establishment of CNI branches throughout the country alarmed the regime. CNI members railed at Bédié's "religious and tribal bigotry." But, unlike its rival the CSI, the organization could not receive any funds from the government to conduct its activities; moreover, to meet legal requirements, the CNI board had to include a CSI representative in its official deliberations. For many, the issue was how the Muslims would fare under the regime. Ouattara, whose father was born in Burkina Faso, removed his candidacy, and the other opposition leaders boycotted the presidential contest in October 1995. Bédié's election reinvigorated the Muslims with more will to spread their creed and defend their rights. By 1994, Islam had become a powerful vehicle of political opposition in the Côte d'Ivoire.

☾ ☾ ☾

In Mali, the coordination of Islamic organizations has been a major concern for the authorities. The UCM and other organizations reappeared after the overthrow of Modibo Keita in 1968. President Moussa Traoré's ruling party, the Malian People's National Union (Union nationale du peuple malien), used its prerogatives to create a Muslim umbrella organization, the Malian Association for Islam's Unity and Progress (*Association malienne pour l'unité et le progrès de l'Islam*). The party firmly controlled the association and used it to quell intra-Muslim confrontations and reinforce Islam's position in Malian society. Religious unity was considered essential: the country had experienced many disputes and mosque riots in the 1950s. Although the doctrinal differences have persisted, Muslims in Bamako and elsewhere now pray at the nearest mosque, without consideration of the imam's denomination.

However, small groups of new reformists, consisting primarily of petty traders and craftsmen, have emerged within the fringe of the Wahhabi circles, displaying a greater radicalism in their outlook and behavior. Unlike the mainstream Wahhabi reformers, these new puritans practice a strict gender separation, abstain from shaking hands with women, and describe Western-type education as the "scourge of modern evil." Their wives and daughters wear the veil and other "Islamic garments" considered not sexually enciting—loose-fitting dark clothes, from head to toe. In the judgment of this group, veils for women and beards for men are Quranic imperatives (an arguable viewpoint). Undoubtedly, these fundamentalists represented a minority community whose members opposed what the Mandinka have called the "new age" *(tele kuda);* that is, the era marked by modernization, gender equality, and women's full participation in society. To other Muslims, this new puritanism symbolizes a "backwardness contrary to local social traditions."

Lightening Up—A New Ethics of Disagreement (Sanankun-ya)

The concept of "radical Islam" in many Muslim communities in West Africa, and particularly among the Mandinka, has taken on a new meaning that is concealed below the layers of the rivalry characteristic of the 1950s. Radicalism has lost part of its violent and sectarian connotations, conveying more and more the idea of the "original" creed—that is, the practice by the first generations of Muslims. A consensus has grown among the different groups about the normativeness of this orthodox tradition for every Muslim, regardless of his affiliation. The new meaning of radicalism denotes a struggle, first fought against oneself and then within one's community, whether it is a brotherhood's lodge *(zawiya)* or a Wahhabi circle, to improve adherence to the fundamentals of the faith.

This goal has become "ecumenical" in that it cuts across brotherhoods and organizations to promote cooperation. To be a "good Muslim"—that is, a follower of the sunna—involves foremost a total commitment to orthodoxy, whether transmitted by a sufi shaykh or a Subbanu teacher. Among the Mandinka, regardless of individual ideological preference or state's leadership, Islam has emerged as a significant political factor.

According to two prominent leaders, al-Hajj Kabiné Diané and al-Hajj Kabiné Kaba, the "prayers and humility needed to please God and to improve the human condition may be attained in a brotherhood *[tariqa].*" Hence, a brotherhood is not "in itself a condemnable organization."[31] This culture of tolerance implies a determination to challenge atheism, associationism, and alienation. The sufi leaders, too, have stressed the quest for orthodoxy and tolerance *(entente religieuse cordiale)* for the sake of God, the Prophet, and the community. In Kankan, for example, the former imam al-Hajj Siddik Kaba and other renowned teachers, including those of the well-known and influential Chérif family, have criticized sectarianism and violence, thereby underscoring spiritual growth as a "key to salvation."[32]

Praying styles and identification with a saint or a mosque have lost a good deal of their significance, too. In Senegal—the land of powerful brotherhoods—the caliph of the Muridiyya order, al-Hajj Falilou M'Backé, enjoined his adepts to abide by the canonical precepts. He ordered especially the Bayy-Fal, who had long been known for their conspicuous "demonstration of unorthodoxy"[33] and their commitment to menial work instead of spirituality, to pray and regularly practice other rituals. Developing a modus vivendi and a common front with others for the success of Islam emerged as a strategy in this media-oriented world in which no single Islamic organization has arisen to dominate the landscape alone.

Thus, a new ethic of disagreement has emerged, not unlike in other religious movements in the world. According to this doctrine, the enemy resides within oneself, and the Muslims must act on the basis of their unity rather than differences. Mutual respect and congeniality have replaced inflammatory statements and personal attacks in the debates over doctrine. Old adversaries now know how to articulate jointly their needs within their government-sponsored umbrella organizations in order to get concrete results for their communities. In the area of education, reformist schools operated by native reformers, or Azharists, have coexisted and cooperated with the zawiya-operated ones. These instructors have been mostly interested in providing a modern program capable of competing with secular education in French. Hence, Quranic schools have improved their appearances with tables, blackboards, chalk, and other modern equipment; the curriculum, even in the more traditional schools, covers elementary geography and science. Wahabbi and sufi teachers have learned how to perceive each other as members of the same team dedicated to the spread of Islam.

This new spirit of tolerance has been embodied in a system of playful interaction, known as *tolonn* in Mandinka. Tolonn entails joking relationships comparable to those of *sanankun-ya* among Mande patronymic clans:[34] as "kinsmen," reformers and traditionalists enjoy their brotherhood and differences; once foes, they become joking "cousins" who laugh together, respect one another, and solve their disputes through peaceful means. Sanankun-ya assumes equality among partners and recognizes each one's identity in his defined group and role. By lowering the tensions in the community, it has encouraged a free expression of ideas and promoted a general sense of brotherhood—regarded as a cardinal value.

By prohibiting religious violence and giving greater visibility to Friday prayers and other Muslim activities, African rulers have indirectly contributed to Islamization. The "Muslim Hours" program, broadcast regularly on television and radio, has brought about a change in religious discourse and the general perception of the religion. Muslim spokesmen, some of whom are known for their telegenic qualities, have "modernized" their appearances and languages in societies that have continued to value Western clothing and oratorical styles. They don suits and explain liturgical points in one of the African languages; they answer questions from audiences in "plain language" instead of (to use their Westernized critics' words) "mystifying the listeners with Arabic phrases." As a result, the Muslim programs have become lively and attractive. To have even greater impact on the literate public and reach the rural world, Muslim organizations have printed newspapers in French and published audio and video cassettes in African languages.[35]

As a consequence, a newer type of Islamic leadership has emerged. It has been much engaged in missionary and conversion activities—and described this as jihad. Since 1980, a Guinean-born educator, al-Hajj Muhammad Lamine Chérif-Haïdara, has embodied this new type of cleric. Nicknamed Islam's "traveling salesman" *(pigeon voyageur)*, he has plied through the villages and hamlets in the Senegal-Niger Rivers region. He has commanded respect because of his simple life and his habit of telling the truth to political leaders. In his demeanor, Chérif-Haïdara combined the sufi's detachment from material gains with the lifestyle and open-mindedness of an affable Wahhabi preacher. His grounding in the Mandinka culture, combined with his eloquence and mastery of Islam, has appealed to villagers in Guinea, Mali, Burkina Faso, Sierra Leone, and the Côte d'Ivoire. Merchants and ordinary people have thronged his sermons, delivered in a Mandinka oratory that skillfully blends history, religion, morals, and current affairs. He has also made extensive use of cassette recording. Other itinerant reformers, too, have applied modern technological communication skills, and as a result the Mandinka language in which they communicate their thoughts (the Mandinka-Mori idiom of Kankan in particular) has expanded. One development along these lines has been that Al-Hajj Fodé Souleymane Kanté and his Wahhabi disciples have translated the Quran and other Islamic texts in Nko script.[36]

Such fervor has shattered the commonly held assumption that religion would decline under the pressure of modernization and secularism. Religious consciousness in West Africa has shown amazing resiliency. Guinea, Senegal, Mali, and other modern states have identified themselves culturally with Islam, despite their political leaders' fear of revolt in the name of God. Islamic radicalism must be appreciated within the general framework of competition for power. And with the fervor Islam has instilled in its followers, it has appeared as a living religion that believers can use according to their own needs.

Since the 1980s, radicalism has reflected a Muslim reaction to the three-decade-long crisis that has sapped the foundations of African economy and has resulted in distrust of government. Pervasive cultural values from the West have exacerbated the malaise, spreading a climate of gloom and uncertainty. With this as context, the new radicalism may represent a search for an Islamic solution to the crisis. This should give the creed prominence. Al-Hajj Abdelrahman Konadi Koné, an Ivoirian, has argued that Muslims in Africa should rely more on the quality of their doctrine, their numbers, their educational and organizational skills, and their external connections, primarily in the Middle East, to effect change.[37]

Underscoring this point, numerous Muslims known for their association with the reform movement have received important political appointments.[38] They have assumed their duties with the awareness that the dream of "salvation in the hereafter," conditioned by the need for a decent and successful life here on earth, calls for participation in politics. A result has been that the heads of Islamic movements have lent their support to such candidates—those with strong signs of Muslim identity and commitment to the welfare of Muslims, with little sectarianism. As a blend of theology and politics, Islamic radicalism has come to express the quest for Muslims' peaceful survival.

Notes

1. Al-Hajj Kabiné Diané, imam of the Coléah mosque in Conakry, May 1990.

2. See Kaba 1974.

3. Conversations with al-Hajj Kabiné Kaba, Bamako, and Kankan, July 1986 and August 1991.

4. Froelich 1963, 84–85.

5. Cohen 1969.

6. See chapters 6 and 8. Also Le Chatelier 1899 and Gouilly 1982.

7. Religious leaders often avoid taking positions on heated issues. By saying *"naʿam"* or *"innsh-Allah"* ("yes" or "May God will"), they do not always mean an affirmative answer. This courtesy may be a form of self-protection.

8. Morgenthau 1964.

9. Coulon 1981 has aptly examined this complementarity; see also Sy 1969; Behrman 1970; Cruise O'Brien 1971.

10. See Bathily, Diouf, and Mbodj 1995.

11. Rivière 1971; Kaba 1995.

12. Vieira 1992.

13. Discussions in September 1960 with Cheikh Sékou Chérif, a close assistant to President Sékou Touré and former ambassador to the Soviet Union in the early 1970s.

14. Sura 4 (*Nisaʾ*, [The women]), verse 59, in Yussuf-Ali 1934, 198.

15. Rivière 1971.

16. Guinea achieved independence "without and despite France" by voting "no" to General de Gaulle's referendum on Sept. 28, 1958. See Pompidou 1972; Chaffard 1964, 218; Kaba 1989.

17. Nabaniou Chérif, an Arab university graduate, made a name for himself as a school principal and a PDG political organizer in Boké.

18. Vatin 1982.

19. Touré 1978.

20. Al-Hajj Ibrahima Diané, manager of Umra Voyage Co./Saudi Airline, Conakry.

21. Conversation in August 1995 with Hajja Oumoun Sanankoua, who works at the African Bank of Development and is very active in women's Islamic affairs. Similar views have been expressed by other professional women elsewhere in the region.

22. Levtzion 1979, 35.

23. Colin Legum, quoted by Levtzion, ibid.

24. Discussions with Cheikh Sékou Chérif, Paris, July 1994.

25. Al-Hajj Mamadi (Muhammad) Kébé (called "Petit Kébé") belongs to the Kébé family of Kankan, whose members settled in Côte d'Ivoire during the colonial era. He married Touré's niece Passy.

26. Discussions with various Muslim figures in Abidjan, Bouaké, Daloa, and Yamossokro, July 1991. The most active Islamic organizations include the Union culturelle musulmane (UCM), the Association des étudiants et élèves musulmans de Côte d'Ivoire (AEEMCI), the Association des femmes musulmanes de Côte d'Ivoire (AFMCI), and the Cercle d'études et de recherches islamiques en Côte d'Ivoire (CERICI). The range of many more organizations is limited to a town or a section of a town. Although a dynamic expression of the Muslim community, this pluralism raises a problem of efficiency because it breeds competition among the leaders.

27. See, for example, "Les imams prônent la paix," *Fraternité matin,* no. 9245 (Aug. 9 1995).

28. *Plume libre* (June 1994). *Al-fatihah*, the first sura of the Quran, is recited publicly to acknowledge and ward off crises.

29. Report from a Conseil national islamique meeting held in Daloa, Apr. 1995.

30. Coulibaly 1995.

31. In August 1992, these two Islamic figures (respectively in Conakry and Kankan) confirmed again their Wahhabi positions. They also revealed their willingness to revisit and criticize their own past, and especially "the force of their words" instead of "the power of their arguments" during the initial years of the reform movement in the late 1940s and early 1950s. Al-Hajj Kabiné Kaba was the most outspoken of the four Azharists who introduced the Wahhabi tradition in Bamako in 1946; he died in Kankan in 1992. Al-Hajj Kabiné Diané, a scholar who translated the Quran into French and an entrepreneur who organized many hajj by truck, served as imam in Bouaké, Côte d'Ivoire, in the 1950s and in Conakry until his death in March 1993.

32. Conversations with various Islamic leaders, Kankan, June 1995.

33. The Bayy-Fall organization was set up by Shaykh Ibra Fall, a prominent disciple of Shayk Ahmadu Bamba, the founder of the Muridiyya. In the words of D. B. Cruise O'Brien and other students of the brotherhood, "the eccentric beliefs and conduct of the Bayy-Fall members placed them at the limits of the world of Islam." Cruise O'Brien 1971, 141.

34. For an appreciation of joking relations in the Mande world in general, and among some social groups in northern Côte d'Ivoire in particular, see Launay 1977.

35. The Muslim papers include in the Côte d'Ivoire *Allahou Akhbar* (Revue ivoirienne de formation et d'information islamiques) and *Plume libre* (Mensuel islamique ivoirien d'informations générales). In Senegal, *Wal fajir* has become almost an institution.

36. Kanté has published various works on different subjects in the Nko script, including Kanté 1962, and Kanté and Diané 1995. For an appreciation of Nko's significance, see Vydrine 1995.

37. Koné 1982. Ibrahima Doukouré, an Azharist and businessman, has shared his French copy of this work with me.

38. The ambassadors appointed to the Arab countries have been actively involved in Islamic affairs. For example, al-Hajj Abou Doumbia, a banker member of the Riviera mosque and the ruling party's politburo, was appointed ambassador to Saudi Arabia in 1992. See *Allahou Akhbar*, no. 15 (Dec. 1995).

Bibliography

Allahou Akhbar. 1990, 1995. Journal musulman d'information, Abidjan, Côte d'Ivoire.

Bathily, Abdoulaye, Mamoudou Diouf, and Mohammed Mbodj. 1995. "The Senegalese Student Movement from its Inception to 1989." In *African Studies in Social Movement and Democracy,* ed. Mahmood Mamdani and Ernest Wamba-dia-Wamb, 369–406. Dakar: Codesria.

Baulin, J. 1961. *The Arab Role in Africa.* New York, Penguin.

Behrman, Lucy C. 1970. *Muslim Brotherhoods and Politics in Senegal.* Cambridge. Harvard University Press.

Brenner, Louis. 1993. *Muslim Identity and Social Change in Sub-Saharan Africa.* Bloomington: Indiana University Press.

Chaffard, Georges. 1964. *Les carnets secrets de la décolonisation.* Paris: Calman-Lévi.

Clark, Peter B. 1982. *West Africa and Islam.* London, Arnold.

Cohen, Abner. 1969. *Custom and Politics in Urban Africa: A Study of Hausa Migrants in Yoruba Towns*. Berkeley: University of California Press.

Coulibaly, Tiémoko. 1995. "Démocratie et surenchères identaires en Côte d'Ivoire," *Politique africaine* 58 (June): 146.

Coulon, Christian. 1981. *Le marabout et le prince (Islam et pouvoir au Sénégal*. Paris: Pédone.

Cruise O'Brien, Donald. 1971. *The Mourides of Senegal: The Political and Economic Organization of an Islamic Brotherhood*. Oxford: Clarendon.

———, and C. Coulon, eds. 1988. *Charisma and Brotherhoods in African Islam*. London: Oxford University Press.

Dessouki, A., ed. 1982. *Islamic Resurgence in the Arab World*. New York: Praeger.

Fraternité-matin. 1990, 1995. Quotidien d'information. Abidjan.

Froelich, Jean-Claude. 1963. *Les musulmans d'Afrique noire*. Paris: Éditions de l'Orante.

Gouilly, Alphonse. 1982. *L'Islam dans l'Afrique française*. Paris: Larose.

Harrison, Christopher. 1988. *France and Islam in West Africa (1860–1960)*. Cambridge: Cambridge University Press.

Haynes, Jeff. 1994. *Religion in Third World Politics*. Boulder, Colo.: Lynne Rienner.

Kaba, Lansiné. 1974. *The Wahhabiyya: Islamic Reform and Politics in French-Speaking Africa*. Evanston: Northwestern University Press.

———. 1974. "Islam's Advance in Tropical Africa," *Africa Report* 21, no. 2:37–41.

———. 1989. *Le "non" de la Guinée au général de Gaulle*. Paris: Chaka.

———. 1995. *Lettre à un ami sur la politique et le bon usage du pouvoir*. Paris: Présence africaine.

Kanté, al-Hajj Fodé Souleymane. 1962. *Nko kodo-yidalan fasarilan hama kodofolan [Dictionnaire Nko en langue mandingue commune]*. Kankan.

———, and Mamadi Diané. 1995. *Kurana kalanke dalamidaden [Le saint Coran, traduit en langue commune du Manding, Nko]*. Kankan.

Koné, Al-Hajj Abdelrahman Konadi. 1982. "L'Islam et les musulmans de Côte d'Ivoire." Ph.D. diss., al-Azhar University.

Launay, Robert. 1977. "Joking Slavery," *Africa* 47:413–21.

———. 1982. *Traders without Trade: Response to Change in Two Dyula Communities*. London: Cambridge University Press.

Levine, Victor, and Timothy Lake. 1979. *The Arab-African Connection: Political and Economic Realities*. Boulder, Colo.: Westview.

Le Chatelier, A. 1899. *L'Islam dans l'Afrique occidentale*. Paris: Steinhall.

Levtzion, Nehemia. 1973. *Ancient Ghana and Mali*. London: Methuen.

———, ed. 1979. *Conversion to Islam*. New York: Holmes & Meier.

———. 1979. *International Islamic Solidarity and its Limitations*. Jerusalem: Magnes Press, Hebrew University.

Lewis, I. M., ed. 1966. *Islam in Tropical Africa*. London: Oxford University Press.

Little, Kenneth. 1972. *African Women in Towns: An Aspect of Africa's Social Revolution.* London: Cambridge University Press.

McKay, V. 1965. "The Impact of Islam on Relations among the New African States." In *Islam and International Relations,* ed. J. M. Proctor. New York: Praeger.

Monteil, Vincent. 1963. *L'Islam noir.* Paris: Seuil.

Morgenthau, Ruth S. 1964. *Political Parties in French-Speaking West Africa.* London: Oxford University Press.

Plume libre. 1992–1995. Mensuel islamique ivoirien d'informations générales. Abidjan.

Pompidou, Georges. 1972. "Déclarations au cours du voyage officiel au Togo," *Marchés tropicaux 1413* (Dec. 8).

Rivière, Claude. 1971. *Mutations sociales en Guinée.* Paris: Rivière.

Robinson, David, and Jean-Louis Triaud, eds. 1997. *Le Temps des marabouts: Itinéraires et stratégies islamiques en Afrique occidentale française (v. 1880–1960).* Paris: Karthala.

Sy, C. Tidiane. 1969. *La confrérie sénégalaise des Mourides.* Paris: Présence Africaine.

Touré, Sékou. 1978. *Révolution et religion.* Conakry: Editions Patrice Lumumba.

Trimingham, James Spencer. 1959. *Islam in West Africa.* London: Oxford University Press.

———. 1968. *Influence of Islam upon Africa.* London: Longmans.

Vatin, J. 1982. "Revival in the Maghreb." In *Islamic Resurgence in the Arab World,* ed. A. Dessouki, 246–47. New York: Praeger.

Vieira, Gérard. 1992. *Sous le signe du laïcat: L'église catholique en Guinée, 1 (1875–1925).* Dakar.

Voll, John Obert. 1982. *Islam: Continuity and Change in the Modern World.* Boulder, Colo.: Westview.

Vydrine, Valentin. 1995. "Sur le dictionnaire Nko." Manding Studies Association papers. Leiden.

Wal fajir. 1989–1995. Journal musulman. Dakar.

Yussuf-Ali, Abdullah, trans. 1934. *Glorious Qur'an.* Cairo: Dar al-Kitab al-Masri.

Zuccarelli, F. 1988. *La vie politique sénégalaise (1940–1988),* vol. 2. Paris: CHAM.

CHAPTER 10

Religious Pluralisms in Northern Nigeria

William F. S. Miles

Fewer than one-half of Nigeria's people are Muslim, yet the country has far more adherents to Islam—around 45 million—than any other country in sub-Saharan Africa.[1] The demographics, moreover, fall short in explaining the significance of Islam in this, Africa's most populous nation. The intertwining of religion and politics throughout the history of Nigeria's colonial and postcolonial periods epitomizes many of the tensions pitting Islam against state in much of Africa.

In this chapter we focus on Islam's difficult relationship with the ideal—however imperfectly realized—of Nigerian pluralism. We also highlight the recent upsurge in Muslim-motivated resistance to political authority. Both phenomena have roots in the colonial era.

Religious pluralism encompasses more than the relationship between Muslim and non-Muslim Nigerians. Islam in northern Nigeria is itself multiple and multistranded: it comprises contrasting organizational and theological tendencies, and thus we must pluralize the very paradigm of pluralism for present-day northern Nigeria.

Islam under the British

When Lord Lugard "pacified" the major Islamic emirates of Kano and Sokoto in 1903, Nigeria did not yet exist as a consolidated colony.[2] From the 1880s on, private British interests had, through the Royal Niger Company, attempted to exercise influence both north and south of the Benue and Niger Rivers. It was only with the liquidation of the company in 1900 and its takeover by the Crown that colonization as a state enterprise proceeded systematically. Yet it was far from inevitable that the Colony and Protectorate of Southern Nigeria would be amalgamated with the Protectorate of Northern Nigeria. When this merger did occur, in 1914, it gave Nigeria much the form it has today, and created a colonial entity that was much more religiously diverse than otherwise would have been the case.

From this perspective, Nigeria resembles Sudan (chapter 7): a nation whose north is Muslim but whose south is anything but.[3] As with southern Sudan, southern Nigeria was composed of various groups practicing animism, and under the pressures and enticements of colonial and missionary education, these people gradually became Christianized. Although a significant minority of Yoruba were, or became, Muslim, by and large they, together with the Igbo, have come to constitute the bulk of Nigerians indiscriminatingly lumped together as "southern Christians." Though less starkly than in the Sudan, which was wracked by civil war along religious lines, fault fissures in Nigeria also follow this "northern Muslim vs. southern Christian" dichotomy.

One hundred years prior to Lugard's conquest of northern Nigeria, the forces of the Fulani shaykh ʿUthman dan Fodio had captured and subdued much the same territory that Lugard was to inherit. (The most important exception was the kingdom of Kanem-Borno, which under Muhammad al-Kanemi successfully fought off the Fulani assaults.) Although imperialism may also have been one motif of the ʿUthmanian revolution, the surface casus belli was jihad—a war for Islam. Chapter 6 explains why (if we use the Quranic account as model) the revolution of ʿUthman dan Fodio was the most "classic" of jihads. The fact that probably most of the urban populations, and virtually all of the indigenous Hausa leaders, already practiced Islam (even if nominally) by the time of the jihad does not detract from the theologic of the ʿUthmanian revolution. (Borno-Kanem resisted the ʿUthmanian jihad by defending the legitimacy of mixed Islam; that is, religion that combined Quranic principle with pre-Islamic practices.)

ʿUthman dan Fodio and his followers did not merely attempt to purify Islam as a religion; they also wished to rationalize the administration of law and justice under their expanded jurisdictions. They therefore consolidated the hitherto loosely federated Hausa emirates into a much more centralized empire, with Sokoto—seat of the ʿUthmanian dynasty—as the capital. It was this Sokoto caliphate, to which the lesser Hausa-Fulani emirates owed fealty, that constituted both Lugard's test and prize.

The caliph of Sokoto (the "Commander of the Faithful" Sarkin Musulmi) at the time of the British invasion was Attahiru dan Ahmadu. It was in the name of Islam that, in 1902, Caliph Attahiru rejected Lugard's initial overtures for bloodless accommodation: "From us to you. I do not consent that any one from you should ever dwell with us. I will never agree with you. I will have nothing ever to do with you. Between us and you there are no dealings except as between Muslims and unbelievers, war, as God Almighty has enjoined on us. There is no power or strength save in God on high."

But the caliphs wielded more spiritual than military power. When Kano fell in January 1903, it was only a matter of months before Sokoto, too, succumbed to the British. Caliph Attahiru fled eastward, claiming he had begun a *hajj* (pilgrimage to

Mecca), though his movements more resembled *hijra* (flight from infidels). British forces pursued him and his entourage and at Burmi forced a one-sided battle in which Attahiru was killed. At the coronation of the successor to the caliph (now retitled sultan), Lugard expressed both political magnanimity and religious toleration: "The Fulani in old times under Dan Fodio conquered this country. They took the right to rule over, to levy taxes, to depose kings and to create kings. . . . All these things . . . do now pass to the British. . . . [But] all men are free to worship God as they please. Mosques and prayer places will be treated with respect by us. . . . You need have no fear regarding British rule, it is our wish to learn your customs and fashion."

This conciliatory spirit of conquest on the part of the British overlords made it easier for the newly constituted Muslim leadership to adopt a policy of *taqiyya*. Although *taqiyya* is literally translated as "dissembling," it more accurately describes a strategic combination of outward submission to superior physical force with continued inner fealty to Islam. Outright resistance, as practiced by the caliph of Sokoto, was renounced—although in 1906 the Mahdist (violently millenarian) Malam Isa and his followers at Satiru virtually wiped out a British detachment. Ironically, as we shall see below, Islamic-based resistance to supposedly unjust authority in Nigeria has been more prominent after the colonial era than during it.

If Hausaland was a model of Islamic jihad for 'Uthman dan Fodio, northern Nigeria presented an ideal type of British administration for Lord Lugard. Under the rubric of "indirect rule," indigenous rulers (i.e., sultans, emirs, district heads, and chiefs) would preserve most of their traditional prerogatives as leaders while carrying out the mildly reformist programs instigated by the British. In the early years of colonial rule, this mainly entailed ending the slave trade and instituting a less predatory system of taxation. By the 1950s, a more developmental mandate was conferred to the Native Authorities (the indigenous body responsible for carrying out British policy), the aim being to improve medical, educational, and agricultural facilities and services. Abuse and corruption on the part of indigenous elites persisted throughout the colonial era, even if British colonial sovereignty conveyed a veneer of supervision over the institution of chiefly authority.

The accommodations between colonialism and traditionalism had important implications for Islam. No less than in the aftermath of the 'Uthmanian revolution, traditional rulers gained legitimacy through their public display and knowledge of Islam. Emirs were not merely political or administrative figures; they were spiritual leaders as well. Side by side with a British-style legal system for criminal law, Islamic courts had wide jurisdiction in private and family law. Christian proselytizing, in contrast, was discouraged. Familiarity with and respect for a quasi-monarchical system of government and a well-established, codified judicial system disposed the British more positively to the religion and institutions of the north than to the diverse, helter-skelter systems operating in the south. Preexisting Islamic networks of formal, literate education also impressed the colonial rulers, who preferred grafting secular subjects onto traditional schooling rather than replacing Quranic schools with European ones. British colonialism in northern Nigeria conferred a stamp of legitimacy on Muslim leadership and Islamic governance and culture.

Colonial rule did not merely preserve the role of Islam in Nigeria; it also indirectly strengthened it. The Pax Britannica facilitated the formal and informal missionization by Muslim clerics and others in areas that previously, on account of warfare or banditry, had been no-go zones. Transportation infrastructure and mass-media networks also made it easier to spread the message of Islam among neighboring "pagan" peoples. Out of expediency, the British sometimes extended Muslim rulership and shari'a (Islamic law) to non-Muslim pockets of northern Nigeria.

Although preserving the cultural and political autonomy of northern Nigeria strengthened Islam there, among some non-Muslims and southerners it fomented distrust. Religious antagonism was muted as long as the British retained ultimate sovereignty; but with prospects of independence looming in the 1950s, the religious factor in Nigerian politics grew in importance. Which group would lead the country into independence—and at whose expense?

Late-colonial politics in northern Nigeria was dominated by the Northern People's Congress (NPC), founded in the late 1940s, largely in response to youth movements and nationalist parties. The NPC was led by Ahmadu Bello, a high-ranking Muslim official in the Sokoto caliphate with the title of sardauna (war minister). Bello and the NPC strove to preserve the integrity of the Islamic emirates of the north, both internally and vis-à-vis the more reformist southern parties. To do so, the NPC embraced a vision of gradual modernization, stressing the education and economic development that it felt was indispensable to northern success. Other prominent northern politicians were Abubakar Tafawa Balewa and Aminu Kano. Kano broke with the NPC, in the belief that true progress for the north could never occur under the hegemony of emirs and traditional chiefs; as a class, he felt, they were fundamentally reactionary and feudalistic. His opposition to this northern political establishment and its corrupt, self-serving brand of Islam took the form of an opposition party, the Northern Elements Progressive Union (NEPU).

The constitution that ushered Nigeria into national sovereignty in 1960 administratively divided the country into three regions: Northern, Western, and Eastern. Each region was headed by a premier. In the case of Northern Nigeria, this was the sardauna of Sokoto. On the national level, the demographic superiority of the north ensured an overall NPC victory in elections to the house of representatives. Tafawa Balewa became prime minister of all Nigeria. Coalition with the Igbo-dominated National Council of Nigerian Citizens (NCNC) of the Eastern Region forestalled—but did not prevent—Christian and minority fears of Muslim domination. In 1966, a military coup of (mostly Igbo) middle-ranking officers assassinated Bello, Balewa, and high-ranking northern officers. One of the few non-Muslim casualties was the (Yoruba) premier of the Western Region, who had allied his party with the NPC. Coup leaders moved to undo the constitutional structure of Nigerian regionalism and replace it with a centralized system of governance.

The 1966 coup (which incited violence against Igbo Christians residing in the north, particularly in Kano) not only spelled the end of Nigeria's First Republic. It stimulated a countercoup by northern officers and sowed the seeds for greater northern-southern/Muslim-Christian violence, especially the catastrophic Biafran civil war.

Intra-Muslim Cleavages: Sunnis, Sufis, and Mahdis

Islam in Northern Nigeria, as in the rest of Bilad al-Sudan, is Sunni Maliki. Early influences of the Ibadiyya disappeared by the eleventh century, and Shi'ite influences never crossed the Sahara.

Islam in Northern Nigeria, however, carries the burden of the heritage of the jihad of 'Uthman dan Fodio. The ambiguity of this heritage stems from the fact that the original radical ideology which ignited the 'Uthmanian revolution had to be accommodated over the years to the exigencies of government. The victory of the jihad resulted in the creation of the Sokoto caliphate and of the Fulani emirates, all committed in principle to the ideals of Islam as articulated by 'Uthman dan Fodio and his companions. But the successors of the revolutionaries, those who ruled the emirates for almost a century before the coming of the British, were unable to practice themselves all that their ancestors had preached to the rulers before the jihad. The Fulani rulers, heirs to the leaders of the jihad, accommodated even further when they continued to hold power also under Christian-British rule.

The gap between ideals and practice in North Nigerian Islam created recurring tensions, between those among the 'ulama' who continued to adhere strictly to the ideals of the jihad, and others, the majority, who fulfilled the traditional roles of 'ulama' in Muslim states, namely providing legitimacy to the government. These tensions were under control, but could also erupt to cause instability in the Sokoto caliphate or in one of the major emirates.

In the twentieth century intra-Muslim tensions found expression first in the rivalry among the sufi brotherhoods, when one of them was identified with the established regime, and the other articulated radical ideas claiming to represent the original spirit of the jihad. Both sufi brotherhoods, however, soon encountered the criticism of the purists among the 'ulama', who led an anti-sufi movement.[4]

The Brotherhoods: Qadiriyya and Tijaniyya

The two most important sufi brotherhoods in Nigeria are the Qadiriyya and the Tijaniyya. Qadiriyya is the older of the two and its lineage can be traced to Baghdad in the twelfth century. It was established in the north of what is now Nigeria in the early seventeenth century and may very well have counted 'Uthman dan Fodio among its "brothers," becoming most important in the Sokoto caliphate. It long remained associated with conservative, "establishment" Islam in Nigeria, and in the run-up to independence, this linkage translated into Qadiri support for the NPC and the sardauna of Sokoto.

The Qadiriyya was originally subdivided into five different branches (Ahl al-Bayt, Kuntiyya, Shinqitiyya, 'Usmaniyya, and Sammaniyya). In the late 1930s and

1940s, Malam Nasiru Kabara led a campaign to consolidate, reinvigorate, and popularize the Qadiriyya, which was in part animated by competition from the rival Tijaniyya brotherhood.

The Tijaniyya spread to and through northern Nigeria in reaction to the perceived elitist bent of the Qadiriyya. Kano became an important center for the brotherhood during the colonial era. This stemmed in large part from its being embraced by 'Abbas, the emir of Kano, around the time of World War I. Ibrahim Niass of Senegal took over as West African Tijaniyya leader from a Kano scholar in 1938; Tijani Usman and Emir Muhammad Sanusi of Kano, however, remained important figures in the brotherhood. It was only after the colonial period that Tijanis managed to overtake the Qadaris in numbers; they did, however, represent a viable, preindependence challenge to conservative Sokoto hegemony. Aminu Kano succeeded in tapping the Tijaniyya support base for partisan NEPU objectives.

Nigerian Sunnis and Anti-Sufism

Not all northern Nigerian Muslims identified with either of the above brotherhoods. Neither Qadiriyya nor Tijaniyya ever made much headway in the successor states to Borno-Kanem, and in rural Hausaland the brotherhoods have never been as important as in the cities. A self-conscious school of radical Sunni Islam in northern Nigeria came to reject the sufi manifestations that arose in its midst, reacting especially against the rapid expansion of the two brotherhoods in the 1940s and 1950s. Anti-sufi critics lumped together the brotherhoods within a larger social structure corrupted by British colonialism, collaborationist emirs, co-opted Quranic schools, and pseudo-Islamic customs.

As forerunner to organized anti-sufism, the northern nationalist Saad Zungur singled out the veneration of saints as a typically illegitimate practice of sufism.[5] Abubakar Gummi, grand kadi of the north, subsequently became the most outspoken advocate of Sunni Islam in northern Nigeria. More than his theological critique of the improper "innovativeness" of the brotherhoods, Gummi's translation of the Quran into the Hausa vernacular advanced the idea of restoring sunna to the people.

In the context of northern Nigeria, Islamic reform as represented by Gummi is paradoxically at once both modernizing and fundamentalist. By rejecting the West African brotherhoods as imperfect and anachronistic deformations of the Faith, Gummi and the group strongly associated with him, the Yan Izala, wished to bring Nigerian Islam in line with the idealized way of the forefathers *(salaf)*. At the same time, the militancy with which he (and Yan Izala) advocated reform and called for a greater role for Islam in the Nigerian state echoed the Islamic fundamentalist agenda as spearheaded by Iran. Whereas Yan Izala is populist, the Muslim Students Society (MSS) provided Gummi with university-level support.

Usmaniyya refers to the transbrotherhood movement spearheaded by the sardauna of Sokoto. Sir Ahmadu Bello viewed the brotherhood networks as divisive and antithetical to the goal of establishing (northern) regional unity based on straightforward Islam. As the name implies, the movement's driving ethos was the common northern Nigerian legacy of 'Uthman dan Fodio's jihad. Usmaniyya as a self-conscious movement did not survive the Sardauna's assassination in 1966: however, one of the major organizations set up in its wake—Jamaatu Nasril Islam (JNI—the Society for the Victory of Islam)—did remain.

Mahdiyya

Violent eruptions of the tensions in Northern Nigerian Islam found expression in movements that sometimes became known as Mahdist movements. They may be considered successors to the late nineteenth-century Mahdiyya movement of the Sudan, as described in chapter 7. All these movements share harsh criticism of the established social and political order, and the belief that they carry a universal message of lasting justice.

❨ ❨ ❨

Such a cursory examination of the major tendencies within northern Nigerian Islam does not do justice to underlying schisms and nuances within them. Within the major brotherhoods, for instance, there are "reformed" varieties of Tijaniyya and Qadiriyya in contrast to the "traditional" ones. But the above summary illustrates the plurality of paths within Islam as it is practiced in northern Nigeria.

Nigerian Islam since Independence: A National Perspective

If colonialism prompted the interaction of members of different groups, independence accelerated it. Paradoxically, these interactions have both created a more coherent sense of Nigerianhood while sowing the seeds for Nigerian civil strife. Islam has been far from absent in this process.

Longstanding bases of cleavage in Nigeria are economic (oil-producing states versus revenue-dependent ones); political (military versus civilian elites); class-based (traditional hierarchy versus meritocratic achievement); and geographic and ethnic (Hausa-Fulani in the north/Yoruba in the west/Igbo in the east). Surveying the entire period of independence, however, one can argue that the most increasingly salient cleavage is religion.

Religious overtones to the Biafran conflict were relatively muted during the civil war itself. From the Biafran side, the war was fought on the basis of self-determination, not preservation of Christianity. National unity, not jihad, is how the (northern-based) federal government justified its forcible retention of the southeast as part of the Nigerian republic. Nigerians of both sides were congratulated after the war for their spirit of reconciliation. Ironically, newly based animosities are infusing even the Biafran war with a religious dimension that it did not overtly possess at the time.[8]

Since independence, Nigeria has experienced Muslim (although not necessarily Islamic) domination in national leadership, civilian as well as military. Nigeria's first and sole prime minister (Tafawa Balewa, 1960–66, of the First Republic) was a Hausa Muslim. The first elected president to hold office (Shehu Shagari, 1979–83; Second Republic) was a Hausa-speaking Fulani Muslim. M. K. O. Abiola, who was elected to be president of the ill-fated Third Republic in 1993 but was barred from taking office by a military junta (and subsequently imprisoned until his death in 1998) was a Muslim from Yorubaland, in the southwest. Five of Nigeria's eight military rulers (Murtala Muhammad, Muhammadu Buhari, Ibrahim Babangida, Sani Abacha, and Abdulsalam Abubakar) have been Muslims from the north. The last four of those five ruled Nigeria from 1984 to 1999, when retired General (and former head of state) Olusegun Obasanjo—a non-Muslim—was elected president.

Whereas First Republic regionalism facilitated an overtly Islamic agenda among the northern-based national leadership, post-1966 state creation has diminished it. Within the current thirty-six-state structure, twelve states—all in the far north—are predominantly Muslim;[9] another eleven combine substantial Muslim with Christian populations.[10] Nevertheless, the stamp of northern Muslims on Nigerian national politics continues. Two of the most volatile issues in recent years have concerned Nigeria's relationship to the Organization of the Islamic Conference (OIC) and a proposal (alarming to non-Muslims) to (re)introduce shari'a into the Nigerian legal system.

Shari'a Redux

As Nigeria prepared to reestablish a democratic polity in the guise of the Second Republic (1979–83), the most contentious constitutional issue concerned a matter of Islamic law and procedure. In an effort to rationalize the parallel judicial system of Quranic law, a subcommittee of the Constitutional Drafting Committee recommended that there be a Federal Sharia Court of Appeal (FSCA). The FSCA was to be the highest level of adjudication in matters of civil law between Muslims; its jurisdiction lay between the shari'a court of appeals in individual states and the nation's supreme court. The reasoning was as follows: No shari'a court had previously existed at the national level, and states of the east and southeast, with few Muslim residents, had no need of one. But a Quranic court of appeal for the north alone—which had existed under the British and during the First Republic—would have vitiated the administrative breakup of the country; and Nigeria had been intentionally deregionalized.[11]

Debate of the proposal in the constituent assembly was vociferous. Opponents—mostly Christians—feared that FSCA betokened the Islamization of the Federal Republic. Opposition was interpreted by Muslim advocates as stemming from anti-Islamic prejudice. The conflicting views represented antagonistic perceptions of "'neo-jihad' versus 'Christianization',"[12] and Doomsday parallels were drawn in the press and in the assembly between FSCA polarization and strife in Lebanon, Northern Ireland, and South Africa. In the end, conflict was avoided (the subcommittee withdrew the FSCA provisions) and Quranic law disappeared as a major issue in national politics[13]—a fortuitous outcome attributed by David Laitin to the moderating role played by Yoruba members of the assembly.[14] Nevertheless, the shari'a controversy did expose potential explosiveness within Nigeria.

The OIC Controversy

The defusing of the shari'a issue on a national level may be attributed to the ethos of compromise that democratic process tends to instil. Resentment may not be so easily resolved when unchallengeable military rulers are suspected of religious favoritism—to wit, Nigeria's somewhat stealthy joining of the Organisation of the Islamic Conference while under the leadership of a Muslim general.

The OIC was established in 1971 with the mission to "strengthen the struggle of all Muslim people with a view to safeguarding their dignity, independence and national rights."[15] Nigeria had observer status in the OIC for several years; but when President Ibrahim Babangida unexpectedly announced (March 1986) that Nigeria had become a full OIC member, denunciation from non-Muslim Nigerians was vehement. One university campus demonstration against this purported Islamization of Nigeria resulted in at least fifteen deaths (May 1986).[16] When Babangida subsequently established a presidential committee to investigate possible ramifications of Nigerian OIC membership, the committee itself split along religious lines.

Although Abuja announced its withdrawal effective 1991, the OIC continues to list Nigeria as a full member. Opponents, with a mixture of resignation and futility, tend to treat official Nigerian Islamization as a fait accompli. Nevertheless, given that Nigeria had long been a member in the International Islamic Organization and the International Islamic Federation of Student Organizations (as well as several other transnational Islamic associations) without controversy, the volatile reaction to OIC membership speaks to the increasing apprehension about the official role of Islam in the country. When the widening of Nigeria's profile as an Islamic state is perceived to occur under a succession of military dictators of northern origin, the potential resentment among non-Muslims (and non-northerners) is all the greater.

Toward a Christian Countercoup?

In April 1990, a coup was attempted against the Babangida government. Foiled coups are a periodic staple of Nigerian political life, but this one was distinctive for two reasons: it was hatched by a civilian figure, not the military; and there were explicitly religious overtones to it.

Behind the coup was Great Ogboru, a multimillionaire, born-again Christian of the Household of God Fellowship Church, a Pentecostal denomination. The takeover was announced on radio by a military man, Major Gideon Orka, who in a prepared text used both political and fundamentalist rhetoric: Babangida's administration, he claimed, was "dictatorial, corrupt, drug baronish, evil . . . sadistic, deceitful, homosexually-centred, [and] prodigalistic," not to mention "unpatriotic."[17]

One of the goals of the coup leaders was to oust five northern states—the five most homogeneously Muslim ones—from the federal republic.[18]

Ironically, Ibrahim Babangida, the target of this coup, displayed less religious favoritism than his predecessor, President (Major-General) Muhammadu Buhari, had done. Under Buhari (January 1984 to August 1985), the government took over several schools run by Christian denominations and delayed permits for church construction; at the same time, the building of mosques intensified.[19] In contrast, Babangida—whose usurping of power from Buhari was in part a "corrective" measure designed to mollify non-Muslim apprehensions, and perhaps forestall an anti-Muslim coup—had actually been quite ecumenical, at least in his public pronouncements (Christianity and Islam "are in fact remarkably similar," he declared in 1988, "in that they have the same ideas about what is right and what is wrong").[20]

However, in the eyes of skeptical southerners, simply the holding of Muslim identity by national leaders is no less threatening than overt enactment of Islamic policy.[21] Suspicion, of course, is not limited to the south. Northern leaders may suspect even their own people. Such at least seemed to be the case with Sani Abacha, when the late general and president began replacing the (Muslim) heads of the military branches with loyalist Christians from minority groups of the Middle Belt.

Conflicts within Northern Nigeria

We have discussed tensions at the national level (the OIC issue; FSCA; the foiled Christian countercoup). But there has also been continuing religious volatility at a regional level, particularly in the north. This may be discussed under two rubrics: Christian-Muslim relations and Muslim-Muslim divergences.

Reconciliation over the Biafran war has ironically recreated conditions of Christian-Muslim conflict in northern Nigeria. As southerners have returned to cities in the north, the predominantly Christian neighborhood of Kano (the *sabon gari,* or "new town") has reacquired its pre-1966 vitality. More problematic has been an upsurge in Christian evangelism and missionary activity, perceived as an affront to the northern Islamic establishment.[22]

Since the early 1980s, there have been periodic clashes between Christians and Muslims in both urban and rural areas of northern Nigeria. In 1982, Kano was the first scene of a destructive rampage against a number of churches when it was announced that a new church was to be built within the traditional walled part of the city. Five years later, in Kaduna state, YMCA offices, more than 150 churches, and a university chapel at Ahmadu Bello University (ABU), Zaria, were burned down. Five mosques were destroyed in retaliation; at least nineteen people died. The 1987 rioting was touched off by anti-Islamic comments attributed to a Christian preacher, a recent convert. His remarks, at the Teachers College in Kafanchan, were challenged by a female Muslim student and MSS members fought students from the Fellowship of Christian Students. A year later, student-council elections at ABU degenerated into pitched battles between Christian and Muslim students, resulting in one death and more than a hundred wounded.

An impending (but eventually cancelled) visit by a Christian fundamentalist preacher from Germany touched off more rioting in Kano in 1991. A year later, clashes broke out against Christians of the Kataf minority and Muslim Hausas in Zangon-Kataf. Fighting spread throughout Kaduna state and hundreds of deaths were reported.

Explanations for heightened "interfaith antagonism"[23] range from economic frustration to political entrepreneurship. Whatever the cause, Christian-Muslim conflict is an increasing worry for those concerned with Nigerian unity.

Intramural Muslim Conflicts

Conflict between Muslims and Christians has not stopped struggles within competing camps of Islam itself. Indeed, intra-Muslim violence in northern Nigeria is more deeply rooted than is Christian-Muslim strife.[24]

Interbrotherhood friction flared up in the late-colonial period. Beginning with the 1949 demolition of Tijani mosques in Sokoto Province at the order of the sultan of Sokoto, tensions between Tijaniyya and Qadiriyya periodically erupted into violence throughout the 1950s and 1960s. A 1956 riot in two districts of Sokoto resulted in four deaths, including that of a Qadiri imam. In 1965, again in Sokoto Province, clashes attributed to Tijaniyya-Qadiriyya disputes resulted in the deaths of eleven policemen. As in Mali (see chapter 9), a potent symbol of (and perhaps pretext for) interbrotherhood antagonism remains the posture of arms during prayer: Tijanis cross their arms over the chest *(kabalu)*, whereas Qadaris keep their arms straight at their sides. The Qadiris regard kabalu as heretical.[25]

Another intra-Muslim conflict has been anti-sufi: Yan Izala and other Sunni "fundamentalists"[26] (notably MSS and JNI) have attacked brotherhoods across the board, rhetorically as well as physically. Following reports that Gummi had preached against ʿUthman dan Fodio and the founder of the Tijaniyya brotherhood at the beginning of 1979, there were yearlong clashes throughout most of northern Nigeria.[27] In 1988, followers of Gummi and Dahiru Bauchi (Tijaniyya) fought over control of a mosque in Zuru; three persons died and the mosque had to be destroyed.[28] Fundamentalist calls for an Islamic state, however ambiguously couched, worry not only Christians but also Muslims who embrace Nigerian nationalism (among the latter are a small but vocal group of Islamic socialists, including the Muslim Committee for Progressive Nigeria and the intellectual Usman Bala). However, there is factionalization within the antibrotherhood camp itself: splits have been reported in the Muslim Students Society between pro-Saudi (Daʿwah) and pro-Iranian (Ummah) elements.[29]

Yan Izala have been linked to northern Nigeria's most explosive movement of the 1980s, that of the millenarian Yan Tatsine, follower of Alhaji Muhammadu Marwa (Maitatsine). The heretical Maitatsine declared himself greater than the Prophet Muhammad, and it is debatable whether to classify him within the history of Nigerian Islam. Emerging from a Muslim tradition of Mahdist rebellion, however, the Maitatsine movement undeniably resulted in monumental intra-Muslim conflict. Maitatsine inveighed against the corruption of Nigerian Islam, Nigerian society, and the world at large. As his entourage began taking over urban neighborhoods, security forces stepped in. Upwards of five thousand people, including Maitatsine followers (young Muslim mendicants from the countryside), bystanders, and security officers, died in riots between 1980 and 1984. The worst violence occurred in Kano in 1980, when Maitatsine himself died. Thereafter, his followers fomented hysteria and violent crackdowns in Maidugari, Kano, Yola, and Gombe.[30] In 1993, clashes in Funtua between yet two other sects, the Kalakato and Almajiri, resulted in scores of deaths, including those of two policemen.[31]

Since the death of Gummi in 1992, the lightning rod of Islamic fundamentalism has become Sheikh Ibrahim al-Zakzady. Leading a group called the Muslim Brothers and appealing to the same population as did Maitatsine, Zakzady—whom the Western press unfailingly reports to be Shi'ite—challenged the "secular" government of Sani Abacha and reputedly encouraged his followers to take over mosques in his hometown of Zaria. Zakzaky was taken into custody in September 1996. Ensuing confrontations between his followers and security forces left more than a dozen people dead in the state of Kaduna in 1996 and perhaps another ten in Kano city in early 1997. Following President Abacha's sudden death, Zakzaky was released from detention in late 1998.[32]

In northern Nigeria, the historically strong association between traditional leadership and Islamic faith has been another cause of violent intra-Muslim incidents. Perceived insults to the emir of Kano by the governor of that state provoked riots and arson of state buildings in 1981. The government's overriding of the religious establishment's preferred choice for sultan of Sokoto with Ibrahim Dasuki led to fatal clashes (ten persons killed) in 1988. In 1996, Dasuki was deposed and finally replaced by Muhammadu Maccido, eldest son of Dasuki's predecessor, Sultan Abubakar Saddiq III.

☾ ☾ ☾

Future treatments of Nigerian Islam will have to focus on the political and economic ramifications of the inexorable and irrepressible process of globalization. Here we cannot sufficiently explore the global dimension; nor can we examine the impact of events in Iran, Palestine, Bosnia, Saudi Arabia, India, Kosovo, and elsewhere in the Muslim world on Islamic thought and action in northern Nigeria. We cannot even summarize the economic dimension,[33] other than to say that even the most traditional and conservative expressions of Islam there are being affected by—if only in reaction—globalization, whether or not they are conscious of it.

Looking beyond the most recent return to civilian governance, we conclude by confirming not only the pluralities of Islam in northern Nigeria but the increasing salience of religion in the Nigerian polity. Religious resurgence—Christian as well as Islamic—will continue to challenge not only the viability of democracy in Nigeria but the very relevance of Nigeria as a unified, secular, and constitutionally based federal republic. Reconciling northern Islam to Nigerian democracy remains a formidable test in this much vaunted symbol of African nationhood.

Notes

1. The second edition of Donald Morrison's handbook of black Africa (1989, 45–46) estimates the number of Nigerians identifying with Islam in 1980 to be 45 percent. This is 4 percent fewer than the number identifying with Christianity, and 5 percent fewer than the estimated number of Nigerian Muslims in 1960. Using various data sets (Miles 1990, 218) I came up with a slightly higher proportion: 47 percent, closer to that advanced in *The Statesman's Yearbook (1995–96)* (48 percent). Until the census of 1991, Nigeria's population was generally reported at upwards of 100 million. Were that so, Nigeria might have been the most populated Muslim nation in all of Africa. The 1991 census, however, yielded a total of 88 million Nigerians, of whom no more than 42 million were probably Muslim. That would place Nigeria behind Egypt, whose Muslim population in 1992 was estimated in *The Statesman's Yearbook* to be 50.4 million.

2. This section distills seminal research as found in Crowder 1962, 1968, Hiskett 1973, 1984, Hogben and Kirk-Greene 1966, Last 1967, Muffet 1964, Paden 1973, Smith 1960, 1978, and Whitaker 1970.

3. "Islam accounts for about 70 percent of the population of the old Northern Region and about 20 to 30 percent of the population of the southern regions." Gambari 1992, 86.

4. See Paden 1973.

5. See Umar 1993.

6. Muhammad Ahmad, the self-styled Mahdi (Messiah) from the Sudan, announced an impending Islamic apocalypse and was killed fighting the British in 1885.

7. Belief in the Mahdi. Mahdiyya refers to a specific group of Mahdists.

8. See Soyinka 1996.

9. Sokoto, Zamfara, Katsina, Kano, Jigawa, Bauchi, Gombe, Yobe, Borno, Adamawa, Kebbi, and Niger.

10. Kaduna, Plateau, Nassarawa, Taraba, Benue, Kogi, Kwara, Oyo, Oshun, Ogun, and Lagos.

11. For a thorough treatment of the FSCA, see Laitin 1982; also Ubah 1990.

12. Latin 1982, 413.

13. Clarke and Linden 1983, 81–92.

14. Laitin 1982, 424–30.

15. *The Yearbook of International Organizations 1986–87* (Munich: Saur, 1986).

16. *African Research Bulletin. Political, Social and Cultural Series* 23, no. 6 (1986): 8121.

17. Quoted in Ibrahim 1991, 134–35.

18. Sokoto, Borno, Katsina, Kano, and Bauchi.

19. Gargan 1986.

20. Quoted in Ibrahim 1991, 117.

21. John Hunwick notes the perception that Babangida began to jettison his erstwhile (Christian) Middle Belt power base in favor of Sokoto support. "Among other things General Babangida has been accused of dropping Christians from his government in favor of Muslims and of replacing senior public servants who are Christians with Muslims." Hunwick 1992b, 6, 9 n.

22. See Opeloye 1989.

23. The term—at least in the present context—is Hunwick's (1992).

24. A major exception to good preindependence relations between Christians and Muslims in the north occurred in Kano in 1953, when twenty-one southerners were killed. See Paden 1973, 321.

25. Clarke and Linden 1983, 45; Paden 1973, passim.

26. See Clarke and Linden 1983, 75–76, for a discussion of the appropriateness of the term *fundamentalist* as applied to Yan Izala and Alhaji Abubakar Mahmud Gummi.

27. Clarke and Linden 1983, 80.

28. Ibrahim 1991, 123.

29. Ibid.

30. For deeper analysis of the Maitatsine phenomenon, see Lubeck 1981, 1985, and Hiskett 1987.

31. *Africa Research Bulletin* (Jan. 1993).

32. Andersson 1996, A9; *Africa Research Bulletin* (Feb. 1997 and Dec. 1998).

33. See Miles 1986, 1990.

Bibliography

Andersson, Hilary. 1996. "Two Branches of Islam Clashing in Nigeria," *New York Times,* Oct. 11, A9.

Barkindo, Bawuro. M. 1993. "Growing Islamism in Kano City since 1970." In Brenner 1993.

Bidmos, M. A. 1986. "The Islamic Approach to Religious Dialogue: With Special Reference to Nigeria." *Journal [of the] Institute of Muslim Minority Affairs* 8:22–27.

Bienen, Henry. 1986. "Religion, Legitimacy, and Conflict in Nigeria." *Annals of the American Academy of Political and Social Science* 483:50–60.

Brenner, Louis. 1993. "Muslim Representations of Unity and Difference in the African Discourse." In *Muslim Identity and Social Change in Sub-Saharan Africa,* ed. Louis Brenner. Bloomington: Indiana University Press.

Clarke, Peter. 1979. "The Religious Factor in the Developmental Process in Nigeria: A Socio-Historical Analysis." *Genève-Afrique* 17:46–62.

———. 1982. *West Africa and Islam.* London: Edward Arnold.

———. 1988. "Islamic Reform in Contemporary Nigeria: Methods and Aims." *Third World Quarterly* 10:519–38.

———, and Ian Linden. 1983. *Islam in Modern Nigeria: A Study of a Muslim Community in a Post-Independence State (1960–80).* Mainz, Germany: Gruenewald.

Crowder, Michael. 1962. *A Short History of Nigeria.* New York: Praeger.

———. 1968. *West Africa under Colonial Rule.* Evanston: Northwestern University Press.

Gambari, Ibrahim. 1992. "The Role of Religion in National Life: Reflections on Recent Experiences in Nigeria." In Hunwick 1992b.

Gargan, Edward A. 1986. "A Burst of Moslem Fervor in Nigeria: The North Stirs and the South Frets," *New York Times,* Feb. 21, A8.

Gilliland, Dean. 1986. *African Religion Meets Islam: Religious Change in Northern Nigeria.* Lanham, Md: University Press of America.

Hiskett, Mervyn. 1973. *The Sword of Truth: The Life and Times of the Shehu Usuman Dan Fodio.* Oxford: Oxford University Press.

———. 1984. *The Development of Islam in West Africa.* London: Longman.

———. 1987. "The Maitatsine Riots in Kano, 1980: An Assessment." *Journal of Religion in Africa* 17:209–23.

Hogben, S. J., and A. H. M. Kirk-Greene. 1966. *The Emirates of Northern Nigeria: A Preliminary Survey of Their Historical Traditions.* London: Oxford University Press.

Hunwick, John. 1992a. "An African Case Study of Political Islam: Nigeria." *Annals of the American Academy of Political and Social Science* 483:84–92.

———. 1992b. Introduction to *Religion and National Integration in Africa: Islam, Christianity, and Politics in the Sudan and Nigeria,* ed. John Hunwick. Evanston: Northwestern University Press.

Ibrahim, Jibrin. 1990. "The Politics of Religion in Nigeria: The Parameters of the 1987 Crisis in Kaduna State." *Review of African Political Economy* 45/46:65–82.

———. 1991. "Religion and Political Turbulence in Nigeria." *Journal of Modern African Studies* 29:115–36.

Laitin, David. 1982. "The Sharia Debate and the Origins of Nigeria's Second Republic." *Journal of Modern African Studies* 20:411–30.

Last, Murray. 1967. *The Sokoto Caliphate.* London: Longman.

Lubeck, Paul M. 1979. "Islam and Resistance in Northern Nigeria." In *The World System of Capitalism,* ed. Walter Goldfrank. Beverly Hills: Sage. Publications.

———. 1981. "Islamic Networks and Urban Capitalism: An Instance of Articulation from Northern Nigeria." *Cahiers d'Etudes Africaines* 81–83:67–78.

———. 1985. "Islamic Protest under Semi-Industrial Capitalism: 'Yan Tatsine Explained." *Africa* 55:369–87.

Mazrui, Ali. 1988. "African Islam and Competitive Religion: Between Revivalism and Expansion," *Third World Quarterly* 10:499–518. Contains special reference to Nigeria.

Miles, William. 1986. "Islam and Development in the Western Sahel: Engine or Brake?" *Journal [of the] Institute of Muslim Minority Affairs* 7:439–63.

———. 1990. "Islam and Development in West Africa." In *West African Regional Cooperation and Development,* ed. Julius Okolo and Stephen Wright. Boulder, Colo.: Westview.

Morrison, Donald. 1989. *Black Africa: A Comparative Handbook.* 2nd ed. New York: Paragon.

Muffet, D. J. M. 1964. *Concerning Brave Captains: Being a History of the British Occupation of Kano and Sokoto and of the Last Stand of the Fulani Forces.* London: Deutsch.

Nicolas, Guy. 1984. "Métamorphose de l'Islam Nigérian." *Le Mois en Afrique* 223–24, 225–26.

Nyang, Sulayman S. 1988. "West Africa." In *The Politics of Islamic Revivalism,* ed. Shireen Hunter. Bloomington: Indiana University Press. Contains special reference to Nigeria.

Ohadike, Don. 1992. "Muslim-Christian Conflict and Political Instability in Nigeria." In Hunwick 1992b.

Opeloye, Muhib B. 1989. "Religious Factor in Nigerian Politics: Implications for Christian-Muslim Relations in Nigeria," *Journal [of the] Institute of Muslim Minority Affairs* 10:351–60.

Paden, John N. 1973. *Religion and Political Culture in Kano.* Berkeley: University of California Press.

———. 1992. "Religious Identity and Political Values in Nigeria: The Transformation of the Muslim Community." Paper delivered at the Center for International Affairs, Harvard University, Africa Seminar Series on African Identities in a Time of Change.

Smith, M. G. 1960. *Government in Zazzau (1800–1950).* New York: Oxford University Press.

———. 1978. *The Affairs of Daura: History and Change in a Hausa State (1800–1958).* Berkeley: University of California Press.

Soyinka, Wole. 1996. *The Open Sore of a Continent: A Personal Narrative of the Nigerian Crisis.* New York: Oxford University Press.

Tangban, O. E. 1991. "The Hajj and the Nigerian Economy (1960–1981)." *Journal of Religion in Africa* 21:241–55.

Ubah, Chinedu N. 1990. "The Historical Roots of the Shariah Question in Nigeria." *Journal [of the] Institute of Muslim Minority Affairs* 11:321–33.

Umar, Muhammad Sani. 1993. "Changing Islamic Identity in Nigeria from the 1960s to the 1980s: From Sufism to Anti-Sufism." In Brenner 1993.

Voll, John. 1992. "Religion and Politics in Islamic Africa." In *The Religious Challenge to the State,* ed. Matthew Moen and Lowell Gustafson. Philadelphia: Temple University Press. Contains special reference to Nigeria.

Whitaker, C. S. Jr. 1970. *The Politics of Tradition: Continuity and Change in Northern Nigeria (1946–66).* Princeton: Princeton University Press.

Part III

Eastern and Southern Africa

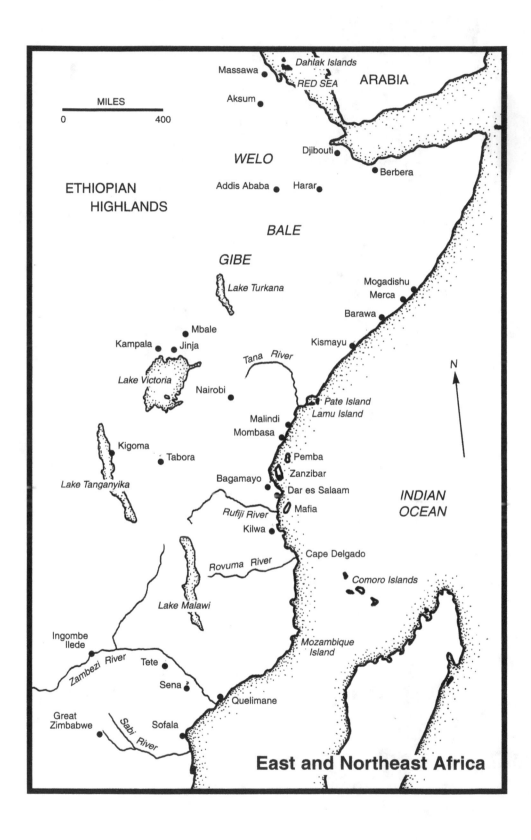

East and Northeast Africa

CHAPTER II

Ethiopia and the Horn of Africa

Lidwien Kapteijns

From its emergence in the seventh century, Islam has formed an integral part of the history of what are today Ethiopia, Eritrea, Djibouti, and Somalia. The old notion of Ethiopia as "an island of Christianity in the sea of Islam"[1] has been abandoned, for recent scholarship has shown that the history of Islam and Muslims within the Ethiopian state is inextricably interwoven with that outside of its (changing) borders, and that it is equally as old, as complex, and as significant. This chapter tells that story.

Political History—the Seventh Century through Colonial Rule
Muslims, Trade, and State Formation before 1800

The nature of the available sources (local chronicles and religious writings, accounts by Arab geographers and travelers, and some oral traditions) allows insight into only a limited set of historical themes. Prevalent among these is Islam's articulation with processes of state formation, foreign interventions and alliances, and shifting patterns of long-distance trade.

The sources show two kinds of early communities of Muslims: first, groups of protected Muslim traders inside the Christian state of Aksum (and then Ethiopia); and second, a string of trade-based Muslim principalities along trade routes leading inland from Zeila. From the fourteenth century on, a power struggle developed between the latter (individually and in coalition) and the Christian state of Ethiopia. The fighting culminated in the conquest of large parts of the Ethiopian state by the Muslim coalition under Imam Ahmad b. Ibrahim (1529–43). Although the Muslim victories were short-lived, the consequences of the war, which included laying the land open to the large-scale migrations of the Oromo people of the southwest, were long-lasting. The Oromo migrations drove a wedge between the two warring parties. Not until the eighteenth century, the sources indicate, did they themselves become major actors in the history of Islam in Ethiopia.

☾ ☾ ☾

[1] The emergence of Islam coincided with the decline of the kingdom of Aksum. Although early Muslim refugees from persecution in Mecca found asylum at the Aksum court in 615 C.E., the first communities to adopt Islam were associated with trading centers frequented by Muslim merchants. The latter conducted their trade under royal protection, but did not enjoy full freedom of worship or the right to proselytize.[2] The Dahlak Islands, a significant outlet for Ethiopian trade in this early period, embraced Islam in the eighth century and was in regular contact with the center of the Islamic state in Baghdad.

With the rise of the Fatimid dynasty in Egypt and the revival of the Red Sea trade in the late tenth century, the process of Islamization in the Horn intensified, with the Fatimids posing as protectors of Muslims inside the Christian state. After 1270, when the new Solomonic dynasty moved the heart of the Ethiopian state southward, Zeila eclipsed the Dahlak archipel and became both the major outlet for trade from its Ethiopian hinterland and a central point of diffusion of Islam into the interior. By then, there were many Muslim communities in the Christian highlands, and a series of Islamic principalities had risen along the long-distance trade routes from the coast to southern Amhara and Shewa in the north and to the Rift Valley lakes in the south. Fourteenth-century Arab geographers knew these principalities as "the country of Zeila."[3]

The oldest documented Muslim polity inland was the sultanate of Shewa, whose dynastic family, the Makhzumis, claimed to have originated in 896 C.E. They ruled until 1295, when they were deposed by the Walashma dynasty of Yifat, or Ifat (1285–1415), once Shewa's easternmost district. On the coast further south, Mogadishu, founded perhaps as early as the eighth or tenth century, blossomed into a sultanate in the twelfth century, as did Brava and Merca; the latter, presented by the twelfth-century geographer al-Idrisi as a center of the Hawiya Somalis, was the first city-state unambiguously associated with the Somali people. A later, long-lived example of state formation among the Somali was the Islamic Ajuraan confederacy (1500–1700) in the hinterland of the Benadir coast.

There is little doubt that, in addition, by the thirteenth century many of the nomadic peoples of the region, which did not form part of any state, and included the Afar (first mentioned by the thirteenth-century geographer Ibn Said as "Dankal"), the Somali (first mentioned by the twelfth-century geographer al-Idrisi as "Hawiya"), as well as groups no longer extant (such as the Gabal and Warjih), had become Muslims.[4] The population of the leading principality of Yifat included some of these Cushitic-speaking nomadic groups as well as sedentary agriculturalists of Semitic speech, such as the no-longer-extant Hararle and the Harari (whose language has survived in the city of Harar).[5] Reports by the Arab geographers about the religious affiliation of the Beja (straddling the modern Sudanese-Eritrean border) in the north were contradictory; yet by the thirteenth and fourteenth centuries, some Beja had become Muslim, as had the inhabitants of the Red Sea coastal towns of Aydhab and Sawakin.[6]

As the Ethiopian state under the Solomonid dynasty set out on a course of southward expansion, it clashed with the Muslim principalities, especially Yifat, over control of the long-distance trade routes. A major war erupted in 1332. The temporary Muslim league that Yifat headed against the Ethiopian state led by Amda-Syon (ruled 1314–44) met with defeat and Yifat became tributary to Ethiopia. The virulent invective of the Ethiopian chronicles describing these events bears testimony to the bitterness of the struggle. Thus Amda-Syon refused to end his campaigns "as long as these hyenas and dogs, sons of vipers and seed of evil ones who do not believe in the Son of God keep on biting me."[7] Racked by internal political rivalries, Yifat weakened further, and in 1420 it was overtaken by its easternmost region and former member of its league, the sultanate of Adal (1420–1560).

Ruled by a branch of the same Walashma dynasty, Adal occupied the whole Afar plain from Sawakin to the Shewa and Chercher mountains, including a significant part of northern Somalia. Between 1400 and 1450, the fighting between Adal and the Ethiopian state went back and forth, with the latter often, but always only temporarily, victorious.[8] As Adal appears to have adopted the policy of drawing on Somali fighting power, it is probably not an accident that it is in this period that the name Somali first occurs in Ethiopian documents.[9] Indicative of future developments was the ability of one of Adal's Walashma rulers, Ahmad Badlay (r. 1432–1445), to organize a Muslim coalition that included Mogadishu in the south and Bait Mala (of northern Eritrea) in the north, and that sought support from Mamluk Egypt.[10] Ethiopia's continuous military campaigns, which targeted the permanent settlements, enhanced the influence of the only partially governed nomadic groups and drove the mercantile and agricultural communities into the arms of what emerged in their midst as the war party.[11] The latter, guided by a series of charismatic leaders who adopted the title of imam, defined their goals in Islamic terms, side-stepped the Walashma aristocratic establishment (the peace party), and declared holy war against Christian Ethiopia. This movement reached its apogee under Imam Ahmad b. Ibrahim al-Ghazi of Harar (called Grañ by the Ethiopians, Guray by the Somalis), who conquered and ruled most of the Ethiopian state from 1529 to 1543.

Imam Ahmad's jihad occurred at a strategic moment for the Muslim coalition. The Ethiopian state was weak, for during its rapid expansion south, it had overextended itself and had failed to integrate the new areas organizationally or ideologically. Internationally, Muslim sentiment had been aroused by Portuguese successes in the Red Sea and the news of a Portuguese mission to the Ethiopian king. Imam Ahmad moreover had the moral and military support of the Ottomans, who had taken control of Egypt in 1517 and the Yemen in 1525. In 1529, Imam Ahmad crushed the army of the Ethiopian king; from then until his death in 1543, he conquered one region after another, from Bale in the south to Tigray in the north, at an incredible cost in property and lives. In the conquered areas, the conquerors briefly established themselves as a small new military elite ruling and extracting tribute through the existing elites. The arrival of a small contingent of well-armed Portuguese soldiers strengthened the Ethiopian king and led to a final round of fighting. In an engagement in 1543, Imam Ahmad was felled by a Portuguese bullet. Having had no time to consolidate its rule, the Islamic imamate of Ethiopia collapsed like a house of cards. Although Adal, inspired partly by Ahmad's widow Bati Del Wanbara,[12] organized several more raids, by 1555 the Ethiopian state had restored its pre-jihad boundaries.[13] The consequences of the jihad were nevertheless far-reaching.

Among these consequences the enormous loss of life and destruction of Christian Ethiopia's religious cultural heritage ranked first. Second, more people had become Muslims, even in the highlands. As the Ethiopian reconquest did not immediately entail massive revenge on Muslims, Islam continued to grow until the reign of Yohannes I (1667–82). In c. 1630, the Portuguese missionary Manoel d'Almeida believed that one-third of the population of the Ethiopian state was Muslim.[14]

A third consequence of the jihad was that the imperialist appetites of the Portuguese and the Ottomans had been only whetted; in the decades to come, the Ethiopian state had to rebuff both of these powers: the Portuguese sought to replace the Coptic creed of the Ethiopian church with Roman Catholicism, and the Ottomans (in 1555 and 1576) took a course of direct territorial invasion. A further consequence of jihad, following the weakening of both the Christian state and the Muslim principalities, was that the land was laid wide open to the mass migrations of the pastoral Oromo people, who, from their homeland in northwest Borena, now moved into the fertile highlands. In the next two centuries, they were to transform the political, religious, and ethnic make-up of the whole region, including the Ethiopian state. By inserting themselves between the Muslim principalities and the Christian state (and by overwhelming both), the Oromos disrupted the hostilities between them. It was not until the eighteenth century that the Oromo themselves became central actors in the history and expansion of Islam in the region.

By 1600, the Oromo had taken over all areas south of Shewa and had established themselves on the eastern edge of the highlands. Adal had disintegrated, while the city of Harar, twice devastated, survived as a center of commerce and Islamic learning by working out a precarious coexistence with the surrounding Oromo peasantry. Yet the trade routes were often disturbed, partly because similarly tense relations prevailed between Zeila (taken over by the Ottomans in 1620) and the surrounding Somali nomads.

Eyewitness accounts of European travelers such as Charles-Jacques Poncet allow some insights into the status of Muslims in the Ethiopian state in the last quarter of the seventeenth century. Yohannes I (1667–82) convened a council that ordered Muslims to live separately from Christians in villages and town quarters of their own. In Gonder, this meant that several thousands of Muslims moved down to the riverbank, where they still live. Muslims could not usually own land, and for this reason they took up commerce and craft activities and often resided in towns, where they could rent church lands. While Muslims served the state as royal envoys and leading merchants, Christian Ethiopians would not eat with them, drink from cups they had used (unless purified by a man of religion), or eat meat slaughtered by Muslims. They greeted Muslims with the left hand—a sign of contempt—and called them, pejoratively, *naggade* (merchant), or *eslam*. (A respectful name for the indigenous Muslims of the northern and central Ethiopian region was that of Jabarti.)[15]

The period 1769 to 1855—called the *mesafint* or "era of the princes," as regional lords completely overshadowed the emperor and central state—again witnessed a further growth of Islam. It is possible and probable that some Oromo settlers in the highlands had adopted Islam before the seventeenth century.[16] However, it was during the eighteenth century that some Oromo groups became central actors in the expansion of Islam in the highlands. The chiefly families of the Qallu, Rayya, and Welo Oromo had embraced Islam, given patronage to Muslim clerics, appointed Islamic judges, and made Islam an increasingly integral part of the lives of their subjects. In Welo, where there were six Muslim dynasties, the ruling elite of the Warra Himano Oromo, in particular, articulated the legitimacy of their rule, their expansion, and their efforts at regional integration in Islamic terms. Like Harar in the south, Welo became a center of Islamic learning.[17] It was also during the mesafint that the Tigre-speaking nomadic peoples of the north, whose ruling families had been Christian, began to convert to Islam.[18] However, by the middle of the nineteenth century the economic, religious, and political situation in the Red Sea and Indian Ocean had dramatically changed.

Nineteenth-Century Imperialism: Islamic Reform and Militance

The history of Islam in the nineteenth century (in particular 1820–80) was interwoven with European expansion and the development of local expansionist centers of capitalist enterprise and territorial aggrandizement such as Egypt and Zanzibar. Coinciding with—and to some extent in response to—these changes was the set of movements often referred to as "the Islamic revival." The revival expressed itself in attempts to deepen Islamic piety and knowledge among rulers and commoners alike, efforts to convert non-Muslims (especially adherents of indigenous religions) to Islam, the composition of many works of Islamic scholarship, teaching, and devotion, the introduction of innovative forms of social organizations (such as the Somali *jamaa,* or religious settlement), and the adoption of militant stances against both the Christian Ethiopian state and the European colonizing powers.

The period 1880 to 1918 was characterized by an Islamic militancy that had its roots in the preceding period: militancy against lax Muslims and local non-Muslims, against the expanding Ethiopian state under Menilik, and against the Christian colonial powers in the area. The era of World War I, which witnessed a pan-Islamic alliance forged between representatives of the Ottoman cause and Muslim leaders in the region, represented the culmination of the Islamic reform movement, as well as its political failure.

℘ ℘ ℘

In the early nineteenth century, two territorially and economically expansive powers had a pervasive influence upon the history of Islam in northeastern Africa. In Egypt, Muhammad 'Ali (1805–49), drawing on European capital and personnel, pursued a domestic program of industrial capitalist transformation in combination with a foreign policy of colonial expansion. Apart from occupying the Sudan (1820–85), where it set into motion an intensive private trade in slaves, Egypt expanded into the Red Sea and beyond, occupying Zeila in 1870 and Harar in 1875. Its invasion of Ethiopia in 1875–76 met with defeat, and in 1885, after the defeat at the hands of the Mahdi in Sudan, its northeastern African empire was dissolved. The second expansive power was Zanzibar, whose economy was dominated by a partnership between the Omani sultans, Indian and Arab money lenders and merchants, and European entrepreneurs in search of cheap, tropical raw materials.

The expansion of Egypt and Zanzibar, themselves under increasing pressure from western European (and American) powers and markets, led to an intensified exploitation of their vast hinterlands and an upsurge in the trade in slaves.[19] In parts of this hinterland, such as the Benadir coast of southern Somalia, this led to large-scale, slave-based agriculture and the increased importation and local use of slaves. Other areas of the region, such as the nonstate societies of the south and southwest of the Ethiopian region, were forced to supply increasing numbers of slaves. The latter consisted of Oromo, Sidama, and Agew-speaking communities, adhering to indigenous religions.[20] Muslims and Christians participated in, and profited from, this increased trade in slaves, but in the capital-intensive, long-distance transport and sale of slaves, Muslim merchants had an advantage and were prevalent.[21]

These developments of course shaped the history of Islam and the patterns of Islamization in this region. In a pioneering attempt to theorize this impact, Levtzion distinguished two patterns: Firstly, when Muslim traders obtained slaves from across the border separating Muslim lands from areas inhabited by adherents to indigenous religions, these areas were not deeply influenced by Islam[22]—a pattern that may have obtained in the stateless societies of the south and southwest, which remained non-Muslim. We do not know whether local people turned away from Islam as the religion of the slave traders; nor do we know whether the local traders, who often collected the slaves at their source and handed them over to local rulers or long-distance traders,[23] became Muslims. The second pattern obtained when Muslim traders "opened up new regions for exploitation far from their base,"[24] and this may help explain the expansion of Islam in the Gibe area, part of the southwest of the Ethiopian region, west of the Rift Valley. There, between 1800 and 1830, at the terminus of many trade routes from the coast, five Muslim Oromo states emerged: Jimma, Gumma, Limmu Enarya, Gomma, and Geru. Influenced by

Muslim merchants and sufi teachers, the first to embrace Islam were kings and nobility, legitimizing their rule in its name, but by the 1860s, Islam had also become
part of the lives of the common people.[25] However, more research is needed, for, as
exemplified by Kaffa, some of the principalities of the south deeply involved in the
slave trade did not become Muslim; they preserved their indigenous religions until
the conquest by Menilek and beyond.

☾ ☾ ☾

Although it is essential to understand the nineteenth-century history of Islam
in the context of changes in political economy and trade relations, as important was
the religious reform movement known as "the Islamic revival."[26] Its most relevant
aspect in Ethiopia and the Horn was the emergence of new brotherhoods founded
by students of Ahmad ibn Idris (1785–1837), together with an intensification of the
activities of existing orders. The reformist agendas of the new orders encompassed
all areas of life, from intellectual, theological, and political thought to religious and
sociopolitical practice. They emphasized religious devotional practices that avoided
sensual stimulation (through coffee, *qat* [*catha edulis*, a mild intoxicant], dancing,
or drumming) and rejected *tawassul*, the belief that deceased or living "holy men"
could intercede with God for the common believer. Many reformists adopted militant and uncompromising stances toward both Christians and those who practiced
local indigenous religions. Although the older orders such as the Qadiriyya (in
Harar, perhaps established as early as 1500) played a central role in the revivification
of Islam among kings and commoners alike, it was the reformist orders that, as the
century wore on, led the struggle against European colonial rule.

In Welo, the Qadiriyya was introduced by Shaykh Muhammad Shafi b. Askari
Muhammad (1783–1806); the Sammaniyya came via al-Hajj Bushra Ay Muhammad
(d. 1823).[27] Both orders were instrumental in the Islamic revival, and many sufi
teachers interacted closely with the heads of the Welo Oromo dynasties, often receiving grants of land to sustain themselves and their followers. At times, the secular rulers supported a shaykh in his forceful expansion of Islam, as when Shaykh
Muhammad Shafi of Qallu raided neighboring villages to convert them to Islam.[28]
Religious leaders who criticized the local rulers are even better remembered. In the
1830s or 1840s, at a religious celebration in Qallu, a shaykh translated into Amharic
a tradition that declared the marriage contract of wine-drinking men void and their
children illegitimate. The ruler, Berru Lubo, who was present, took offense, and the
shaykh was exiled for his trouble.[29] The religious leaders also took a hard line
against ordinary believers who were lax in their observance of Islam. They criticized
the drinking of wine and the ritual slaughter of livestock at funerals (involving the
sprinkling of blood on the participants).[30] They also attempted to put an end to the
customary *wayyane* ritual feuds—"periodic inter-ethnic or individual fights primarily intended to test courage and sharpen fighting skills"—by threatening to refuse to
perform the proper funeral prayers for the victims.[31] Islamic education was central

to the activities of the sufi shaykhs. The centers they established served as institutions of higher learning, spiritual training, and devotional practice, and they made written contributions to the Islamic scholarship of their era.[32]

While the Muslim teachers of Welo were part of the Islamic revival radiating out from the Hijaz, they were also radicalized by local conditions. In 1855, the Ethiopian emperor Tewodros (ruled 1855–68) set out to restore and reunify the kingdom by emphasizing its Christian identity and suppressing regional autonomy. In Welo, this policy led to a series of devastating campaigns that aimed both at breaking the power of the local Oromo dynasties and the elimination of Islam. Tewodros's successors—Yohannes of Tigray (ruled 1872–89) and Menelik of Shewa (ruled 1889–1913)—continued the military campaigns, after having promulgated the compulsory conversion of Welo Muslims (and later those of Gonder and Shewa) at the council of Boru-Meda in 1878. These forced conversions, the obligation to build churches, pay church tithes, and provide quarters for the state's soldiers, and the execution of thousands of Muslims who refused to give up Islam, in the 1880s inspired some religious leaders like the Oromo Shaykh Talha b. Jafar (c. 1853–1936) to take up arms against the Christian state. Resistance, however, elicited more destruction, which was followed by a devastating famine (1888–92). Other shaykhs moved to Harerghe and the Gibe region, where they contributed to the revitalization of Islamic devotion and learning. In the 1880s, the small state of Jimma had eighty *madrasas*.[33]

In the Gibe region, the religious orders played a role both in the adoption of Islam as an ideology of state by the local rulers and in the deepening and mainstreaming of Islamic belief and practice among the common people. By the 1860s, the Oromo commoners fasted, began to use Islamic rather than customary law in marriage and inheritance, paid the *zakat* levied by the kings, circumcised their sons at an age earlier than before, used the Islamic calendar next to the Oromo one, and went on pilgrimage to Mecca.[34] There were nevertheless resilient communities of non-Muslims, too, as is evident from songs of this era collected by Cerulli in 1927 and 1928. In these songs, non-Muslims ridiculed Muslims by calling them "bottom-rinsers" (a reference to their ritual ablutions) and comparing the muezzin to the leader of a troop of monkeys who would create a loud racket at the approach of danger.[35]

The Qadiriyya was the oldest and most popular order, but the Tijaniyya and Ahmadiyya also had a presence. Rulers appear to have vied with each other in their patronage of men of religion, who often received grants of land to establish religious centers. From the late 1860s onward, Gumma in particular experienced a strong religious fervor; its kings conducted a jihad first against non-Muslim neighbors who belonged to stateless societies and, after 1882, against the occupation armies of the Ethiopian emperor Menilek.[36]

In Eritrea, the revitalization of Islamic belief and practice among the Bani Amir and the Tigray-speaking nomadic peoples of modern Eritrea was associated with the Qadiriyya and the Mirghaniyya. The latter was introduced in Massawwa in 1860 by Shaykh Hassan al-Mirghani, son of the order's founder, and became the dominant order in the area. The conversion to Islam of the Habab, Marya, and Bayt Asgede, Trimingham reports, dates from the 1820s, coinciding with Egypt's conquest of the Sudan.[37]

In Somalia, long before 1800 religious leaders had played central roles in the multiethnic (or multi-clan) Muslim principalities of southern Somalia such as the sultanate of Mogadishu, the Ajuraan confederacy (c. 1500–1700), and the Geledi federation (after 1750). Moreover, the Qadiriyya may have been established in the coastal cities of Massawa, Zeila, and Mogadishu, as well as in Harar, as early as the late-fifteenth century. However, the influence of the brotherhoods in the interior appears to date from the early 1800s, for the Qadiri shaykhs credited with the popularization of the order in Somalia all lived in the first half of the nineteenth century.[38] Thus Shaykh Uways Muhammad Muhyi al-Din (1847–1909) founded a *tariqa* settlement (called *jamaa* by the Somalis) in Biyole, along the upper reaches of the Juba River,[39] Shaykh Abd al-Rahman b. Abdallah al-Shashi (d. 1919), better known as Shaykh Sufi, had a center in Mogadishu,[40] and Shaykh Abd al-Rahman al-Zaylai (1820–82) had a jamaa at Qulunqul in the Ogaden.[41] The Qadiri shaykhs were known for their insistence on a humble, pure Islamic lifestyle, for their miracles, and for their commitment to the teaching of Islam and Arabic (the latter as a tool toward teaching the former). Like the heads of other orders, they, moreover, sought to promote a communal identity defined in Islamic rather than kinship terms; in their religious settlements, Somalis of various clan backgrounds lived together as *ikhwan* (brothers), jointly engaged in cultivation, livestock husbandry, and religious study and worship. Shaykh al-Zaylai had women students *(muridat)*, and his daughter Shaykha Fatima became a religious figure in her own right.[42]

The brotherhood that developed into the Qadiriyya's most important rival was the Salihiyya, established in Mecca by Muhammad Salih (1854–1919) as an offshoot of the Rashidiyya founded by Ibrahim al-Rashid (d. 1874). In Somalia, the Salihiyya was introduced by Shaykh Muhammad Gulayd (d. 1918), who took it to the Jowhar area.[43] Its most famous representatives were Shaykh Ali Nairobi (d. 1920), who established a jamaa along the middle Juba,[44] and Sayyid Muhammad Abdallah Hassan (1856–1920), whose reformist program included purifying the country from the Ethiopian and European "unbelievers."

The antagonism between the Salihiyya and Qadiriyya came to a head during Sayyid Muhammad's jihad, which began in 1898. By then, the Qadiriyya in Somalia had become associated with the colonial status quo and was prepared to collaborate with the Christian European entrepreneurs and administrators. It also stood for a longer established, mystical, less puritanical form of Islam; it accepted popular belief in intercession by holy men and engaged in devotional practices that promoted a heightened sensual awareness and ecstatic absorption. The Qadiriyya may also have had a more inclusive attitude toward the religious participation of women and their presence in public. The Salihiyya, on the other hand, at least as interpreted by the Sayyid, insisted on militancy and holy war against both the Christian invaders and their Muslim associates. It was against tawassul, puritanical and sober in its religious worship, and intolerant of anything that could be considered a corruption of or cultural accretion to Islam. It appears to have followed a harder line against the association of male and female believers.[45]

In the period 1880 to 1918, the three forms of Islamic militancy referred to above—that against adherents of indigenous religions and lax Muslims, that against the expanding and intolerant Christian Ethiopian state, and that against the colonizing powers from Christian Europe—became interconnected and fueled the pan-Islamic sentiments roused by Ottoman participation (and defeat) in World War I. In the Gibe region west of the Rift Valley lakes, militant reform movements that had targeted non-Muslim neighbors and backsliding Muslims channeled their energies after 1882 into vain attempts to stem Menilek's southward expansion.[46] In Welo, the targets of Shaykh Talha's revolts (1884–95) were the same. The shaykh was moreover in contact with the Mahdist state in the Sudan, the Italian invaders of northern Ethiopia, the leader of the Somali jihad, and, after 1913, indirectly with the pan-Islamic movement.[47] The *trait d'union* between the seething discontent of the Muslim victims of the Ethiopian and European expansion and the pan-Islamic cause promoted by the Ottoman Empire was Emperor Lij Iyasu (1909/13–1916). Lij Iyasu, who was Menilek's grandson and successor, was also the son of that very Welo Oromo leader who in 1878 had been forcibly converted to Islam. When he, as head of state, openly adopted Islam and began to court his Muslim subjects, the nobility and church elite combined to excommunicate and depose him.[48]

In Somalia, the jihad of Sayyid Muhammad (1898–1920) targeted local colonial collaborators, the tax raiders of Menilek's expansionist state (overrunning western Somalia after the occupation of Harar in 1887), and the colonial administrations of British and Italian Somaliland. In many ways, the Sayyid was like the Islamic leaders described above. He was a shaykh of the puritanical Salihiyya, founder of a jamaʿa, a teacher and author of theological treatises, a jihad leader, and an advocate of communal definition in terms of Islam rather than clan affiliation.

The Sayyid resembled the Oromo militant clerics further west, even when he appealed to both the "religious impulse and cultural nationalism" of his fellow Somalis—asking, "If the land is your land, why aren't you its government? If Islam is your religion, why submit to infidel overlords?"[49] The Sayyid, however, was also unique. First, he was uniquely contradictory; thus, he both sought to overcome Somali clan divisions and at the same time intensified, perpetuated, and embittered them. Second, while he strove to purify Islam, his strategies (including the taking of Muslim lives and his at times vicious and obscene polemic poetry in Somali) were incompatible with Islamic ideals. Third, and perhaps most unique, was the Sayyid's political ambition—that of establishing an independent Islamic state for Somalis, together with his exceptional ability to articulate his goals. In his poem *Dardaarran* ("Parting Words of Wisdom"), the Sayyid, faced with defeat, argued:

> There is no remedy if you expect a good reward from the Christian foreigners. Once you let down your guard, the infidel will ensnare you. The money

he squanders [on you] now, will come back to haunt you. First he will rob you from your firearms, as if you are women. Then he will brand you like cattle. Next he will order you to sell the country [to him], and then he will put loads on your backs as on donkeys.[50]

The Islamic reform movement found both its nadir and its culmination in the Sayyid's movement. The destruction of Somali life and property in the name of Islam represents its lowest point, while the Sayyid's attempt to found an independent Muslim state can be seen as its climax. After his defeat, the sayyid looked back on his career:

Although I failed to have a flag flown for me from here to Nairobi, did I not gain religious honor in victory and defeat? Although I failed to obtain the luscious grazing of the 'Iid and the Nugaal as pasture, did I not successfully ride my steed out to war? Although I failed to get people to show me sympathy and acknowledge their kinship with me, did I not gain God's mercy and [the reward of seeing] the Prophet's countenance?[51]

Islam and the Establishment of Colonial Rule after 1885

In the last two decades of the nineteenth century, Britain, France, and Italy established colonial rule over parts of the region. In British, French, and Italian Somaliland, the colonial powers were mostly neither defenders nor promoters of Islam. Administering their colonies by direct rule, they limited the application of Islamic law and based policy on the conviction that kin-based realities and relations were the most truly traditional and authentic ones. They promoted certain representatives and representations of Islam over other ones, appointing functionaries (and with them, values) who were often middle-class and foreign, imported from Muslim colonies in which colonial dominion was old and well-established (India, Egypt). In their attempts to make local Muslims "upgrade" their Islam, colonial rule divided local Muslims along emerging class lines and to some extent undermined the latter's confidence in their own rich devotional life and religious knowledge. Only Italy, after its invasion of Ethiopia in 1935–36, promoted Islam and Muslims explicitly, with the objective of both defeating the Ethiopian state and suppressing resistance against the Italian occupation. This policy was reversed after Haile Selassie regained the Ethiopian throne.

☾ ☾ ☾

The attitudes and policies of the European colonial powers toward Islam were complex. Trimingham was at least partly correct when he criticized them for favoring "both the consolidation of orthodox Islam and its spread among pagan peoples." As the colonial administrations undertook to introduce written legal codes, as in Europe, he argued, "they seized upon the *shari'a,* as a ready-made code to regulate the religious and social life of any people who could, however superficially, be called Muslim."[52] Thus the British, who had excluded Christian missionaries from the northern (but not southern) Sudan since their conquest in 1898, after 1909 also refused any missionary body entrance to British Somaliland. However, the French in Djibouti and the Italians in Eritrea and Italian Somaliland did allow missionaries to operate, even if they did not share missionary optimism that uneducated Muslims were necessarily "superficial" ones.

All in all, the colonial powers in the region were not defenders or promoters of Islam. First, all colonial administrations in the area established direct rule, concentrating vast administrative and judicial powers in the hands of governors who were often directly accountable to a specific metropolitan minister. Islamic and customary law, while accepted as a source of law in the colony, could only be applied if (in the case of the Italian colonies) it were compatible with Italian law, or if (in the case of the British protectorate) it were not "repugnant to justice, equity and good conscience" or inconsistent with any written law in force.[53] Second, while the colonial governments, especially the British, indulged the Islam of the collaborating, "useful," local elite (such as Shaykh Mattar of Hargeisa), they based administrative policies on the firmly held conviction that kin-based (clan or subclan) relationships were the relevant and authentically traditional communal realities. When the colonial administrations of the area recognized Islamic-cum-customary laws as one of the sources of the colony's laws, they did not distinguish between the two. Thus *qadis* were expected to administer customary as well as Islamic law, in particular in regard to marriage and child-support payments. In British Somaliland, the power of Islamic judges was moreover restricted to a limited number of enumerated civil issues, "marriage, including divorce and maintenance, guardianship of minors and family relationship, wakf [*waqf*], gift, succession and will."[54] Although in Italian Somaliland qadis had wider judicial powers, as they until 1958 administered penal law,[55] there, too, the administration continually balanced Islamic and customary law against each other, without an explicit acknowledgment of their contradictions or a reasoned systematic subordination of one to the other. The result was, as Trimingham observed,[56] that non-Islamic "tribal" customs that were unacceptable to colonial administrations when encountered among non-Muslim populations were accepted when practiced by Muslims.

Colonial administrations also influenced the development of Islam by authorizing *some* representatives and representations of Islam, while undermining the legitimacy of others. In Somaliland and Sudan, where the British confronted militant Islamic resistance, the colonial authorities were eager to present themselves to the Muslim population as closely allied with the most authoritative and prestigious sources and representatives of Islam. The British willingness to help local Muslims "upgrade" their Islam was aimed at creating goodwill for the administration and delegitimizing anticolonial Muslim militants; it also served to undermine the confidence of local Muslims in their own, culturally specific, interpretations of Islamic belief and practice. Thus the British, while courting those members of the local Islamic elite who were willing to cooperate, appointed Islamic qadis and imams who had been educated abroad (for example, in Aden or Egypt), who were initially often foreign-born, and who had been exposed to a strong and seasoned colonial British administration. For example, to counteract the pan-Islamic enthusiasm for the Ottoman cause during World War I, the British sent a group of Somali notables, including the major religious leaders, to Egypt, where they could be dazzled by British military and political power and experience Egyptian Muslim support for the Allies.[57]

While making some room for Islamic law and legal experts in the apparatus of colonial rule and indulging the leading brotherhood shaykhs, the British administration showed little interest in mystical Islam and the rich devotional life of Somali Muslims. Preoccupied with the Somali clan structure as the key to understanding Somali society and maintaining law and order, officials were always more interested in genealogies and secular political poetry than in praise-songs for the Prophet and *qasidas* (poems) for the *awliya*. When feasible, the French in Djibouti and the Italians in their colonies of Eritrea and Italian Somaliland also allied with existing political and religious elites. However, their legitimizing ideologies appear less designed to hide the iron fist in the colonial glove, less concerned with creating formal legal rationales articulated in terms of "authentic tradition," and less obsessed with wresting approval and admiration for their justice from the colonized than the British.[58]

In Ethiopia, Italy changed its policy toward Islam only in the context of its invasion and occupation from 1936 to 1941. First, Italy, then under Fascist rule, enlisted many Muslims from northeast Africa in its army of invasion. As many as thirty-five thousand Muslims from northern Ethiopia as well as forty thousand Somalis were reported to have joined the Italian armies, and others served as guides, spies, and informants.[59] After the conquest, Italy counted on the support of Ethiopian Muslims (whom they estimated as numbering about six million, or one half of the population) to contain the old ruling class, in particular the Amhara resistance. The Italians therefore posed as the great champions of Islam. In Ethiopia, they immediately granted Muslims full freedom of religion and undertook an active program of mosque building. Apart from the "gratitude" mosque in Addis Ababa, they built and restored mosques (with mosque schools) wherever there were Muslims.[60] In Harar and Jimma, they planned higher institutes of Islamic learning and introduced Arabic in all Muslim schools. Newspapers now had Arabic sections, and there were radio broadcasts in Arabic. In Harar, Arabic became the official language. In Muslim areas, the Italians replaced Amhara judges with qadis; they appointed new Muslim chiefs, and created two new governorships (Harar and Oromo-Sidama) to bring Muslims together administratively. They facilitated the pilgrimage to Mecca for collaborating chiefs and allowed Muslims to proselytize among the Arussi and Christian Oromo.[61]

The End of Colonial Rule and the Disintegration of Ethiopia's Christian State

Italian rule over Ethiopia was short-lived. In June 1940, Italy declared war on the Allies; by April 1941, British troops had put an end to Italy's East African empire, and soon thereafter Haile Selassie was restored to the throne of Ethiopia.[62] Haile Selassie not only turned the clock back by restoring discriminating practices against Muslim Ethiopians, but he also took punitive action against them for having sided with the enemy.

While Haile Salassie's regime did not openly or actively hinder Islamic worship, it undermined Islam and Muslims through purposeful and systematic disregard. In official rhetoric, the country belonged to all, with religion a mere private affair. In reality, state and nation were defined in terms of Christianity, with Muslims excluded from land ownership and higher government service. As a result, the economically most successful and wealthy Muslims continued to be engaged in commerce or the crafts.[63] The Ethiopian church was heavily subsidized, as was religious (Christian) education in state schools, where Amharic was imposed and Arabic banned. Muslim employees had to work on Fridays and observe Sunday as a holiday. Foreign missionaries were allowed to proselytize in Muslim areas.[64] The civil code of 1960 regulated marriage, divorce, and family property in ways that conflicted with Islamic law and practice. No Muslim experts were consulted, and while the draft code had included a section on provisions regarding Muslims, this was missing in the final text. While Haile Selassie allowed Muslim courts to operate, he neither acknowledged or legalized them. As late as 1974, just before Haile Selassie's fall, Ethiopian Muslims were still officially referred to as "Muslims residing in Ethiopia."[65]

The range of Muslim grievances is evident from the list of demands they submitted to the new regime that took power in 1974. Muslims petitioned for the organization of independent Islamic courts with their own budgets; for the right to establish religious organizations, to own land, and to work in administration, justice, and the military; for the teaching of Islam in all schools and via the national media; and for the official observation of Islamic holidays.[66] For several years, Muslims made great gains, with Muslims even serving as members of the highest organ of state, the Darj.[67] However, as the Darj gradually turned against all forms of religion, its relationship with Muslims soured. The government's move against wealthy merchants as enemies of the people harmed Muslim wholesalers (as well as Christians), and its abolition of land tenancy drove Muslim tenants in the north off the land. The fall of the Darj in May 1991 again led to a temporary improvement in the position of Muslims,[68] not least as a result of the new freedom of the press (curbed again in 1992).[69]

Haile Selassie's regime, which had presented Ethiopia abroad as a Christian country, had carefully kept two secrets: the size of the nation's populations of Muslims and Oromos. On the basis of the first census of 1984, the authors of *Ethiopia: A Country Study* estimated Ethiopia's 1991 population at 51.7 million people; of these, 40 percent were believed to be Oromo, 50 percent to be Muslim.[70] In neighboring Eritrea, the population, estimated in 1984 at 2.7 million, was approximately evenly divided between Muslims (largely in the coastal cities and lowlands) and Christians (in the highlands).[71] As in Ethiopia, social prejudice existed in the Eritrean highlands as well and wealthy Jabarti traders and poor tenant farmers often lived segregated from Christians. However, in Eritrea, economic inequalities (such as serf status) and ethnic conflicts did not coincide with religious dividing lines.[72] Religious identity indeed partly shaped political stances; however, neither Christians nor Muslims succeeded in creating an internal consensus about any of the large political issues of the 1940s and thereafter—whether this was about the political fate of Eritrea after the end of British military rule or about the Eritrean war of independence (1960–91). In the early 1990s, however, in the context of the intensification of Islamist activities in all of northeastern Africa, some of the opposition to the newly independent government of Eritrea (1993) mobilized support in exclusively Islamic terms.[73] In Somalia, a number of Islamist movements, most of them with headquarters abroad, have emerged since the 1970s and 1980s, when they played a significant role in opposing Siyad Barre's regime.[74] It is unclear, however, whether the quasi-Islamic kangaroo courts of Mogadishu and northern Somaliland, which have imposed and executed Quranic sentences in the midst of cheering crowds, are formally related to these organizations.[75] In some inland areas (such as Hudur), morally irreprehensible leaders, with long-standing religious prestige, have succeeded in recreating some sense of community through appealing to the common bond of Islam, without formal ties to international Islamist organizations.

In all the countries under study here, the late 1980s and early 1990s witnessed important developments in the ways Muslims lived and gave expression to their faith. Individuals and groups were drawn to what they defined as a lifestyle of greater personal piety and a stricter adherence to the tenets of Islam, and they did so as part of (and in response to) a wider international movement for the revitalization of Islam. Often the energies flowing from these new commitments and from the financial support provided by organizations in Saudi Arabia, Iran, and elsewhere were directed toward local communal development projects, charity, and education. Side by side with this socioreligious movement, and not always easily distinguishable from it, a variety of political movements have emerged that have used international Islamist aid to become major political players locally. Who sets the agenda of these movements and what impact they will have both on the political power struggles of the area and on the nature of Islamic belief and practice remains to be seen.

The History of Islamic Learning and Devotion

Of the three legal systems *(madhhabs)* represented in the region, the Shafi'i school, associated with influence from Arabia, is most common, particularly among the Somalis and Oromos. In Eritrea, the Maliki school is influential, indicating a common history with neighboring Sudan. The Hanafi school is represented mainly in the coastal towns, where it was introduced by the Ottomans.[76] Of the oldest Islamic principalities, only the town of Harar is still functioning as a center of Islamic learning, although part of its Islamic heritage has passed to the modern population centers such as Dire Dawa and Djibouti, heirs to the ancient city of Zeila.

The kinds and levels of learning historically pursued in Harar is evident from the work of Drewes, who described the library of the amir who ruled Harar from 1856 to 1875.[77] Shafiʿi legal texts figured prominently in this library, which also included Qurans and Quranic commentaries, hadith collections, texts on Islamic history, including the life of the Prophet, and collections of *mawlids* and praise-poetry for the Prophet. Given the scarcity of data on the roles of women in the history of Islam in the region, it is noteworthy that the manuscripts the amir inherited from his aunt Gisti Amat Allah constituted the beginnings of his library.[78]

The oldest memories of the history of Islam in the region are memories of Islamic holy men such as Shaykh Husayn of Bale, Aw Yusuf Barkhadle, and Shaykh Umar Abadir al-Bakri of Harar.[79] It is significant that oral memory does not explicitly associate these earliest teachers of Islam in the region with a particular brotherhood, as it does in regard to the holy men who lived after 1800. Instead, they are associated with the old city-states. Thus, in Lewis's words, Shaykh Husayn presents "the spiritual residue, so to speak, of the ancient Muslim state of Bale," as Aw Barkhadle, the ancestor of the founder of the Walashma dynasty, represents "the spiritual legacy of the Islamic state of Yifat/Adal."[80] A second group of early, pre-sixteenth-century holy men are remembered not in relation to the city-states but as founding fathers of various Somali clans.[81]

However, most of the holy men whose tombs Muslims of the region still visit, whose birthdays they still celebrate, and whose intercession they actively seek out, are the sufi leaders associated with the early nineteenth-century Islamic revival. These truly shaped some of the specific features of Islam in northeastern Africa. The communities they founded set three significant precedents: they experimented with new forms of social organization, undertook organized political and military action, and constituted centers of Islamic learning, teaching, and devotional practice throughout the region.

The nineteenth-century Somali jamaʿas, mentioned above, represented a radically innovative form of social organization in two ways. First, they sustained themselves through settled cultivation, even in areas where pastoralism was more common and more prestigious. Second, they brought together individuals of various clan backgrounds, even members of the agricultural riverain groups who were excluded from the "noble" Somali clan genealogies and therefore had low social prestige. Hersi, who gives an overview of the jamaʿas, referred to "the flocking of servile classes to the settlements" in the south of the early nineteenth century.[82] Late-nineteenth-century European visitors to the northwest (such as the Swayne brothers) noted the large numbers of sick, old, and disabled individuals present in the settlements.[83] Some of the jamaas became the nuclei for towns; thus Baardheere on the Juba flourished as a small city-state in the 1830s, while the colonial town of Hargeisa in the northwest had developed around the jamaʿa of Shaykh Mattar.

Many of the political and militant movements of the region articulated their motivation and goals in Islamic terms, were led by sufi shaykhs, and sometimes originated from the social frame of the jamaa. Thus in the early 1840s, the jamaa of Baardheere conducted military campaigns in and around the towns of Brava and Luuq, against whose economic and religious practice it objected. Economically, it opposed the trade in ivory, the product of a ritually unclean animal, the elephant. Religiously it took offense at the indulgence of the senses during worship, against dancing, and the social mixing of men and women.[84] The shaykhs of the tariqa settlements that the Swayne brothers encountered in northwest Somalia in the late 1880s were politically quietist, friendly to European visitors, and in complete disarray because of Menelik's tax-raiding parties and armies.[85] As they perceived it, the Europeans who set up administrations in Somalia in the mid- and late-1880s not only failed to offer help against Ethiopia but also scrambled to divide Somalia among themselves.

It was in this context that the formidable Sayyid Muhammad founded his humble jamaʿa at Qoryaweyn and then proceeded to set the country afire with his jihad against Ethiopians, Europeans, and Somali collaborators alike.[86] As late as 1936, some of the tariqa leaders of British Somaliland led a militant protest movement against the introduction of a primary-education system based on Somali, rather than Arabic, as the language of instruction. After the arrogant but well-meaning director of education had narrowly escaped death by stoning in Burʾo, Somali was dropped and Arabic triumphed. Taking their cue from Kenya, where Somalis, as Muslims, struggled to be classified with the Asians rather than the Africans, British Somalis, too, objected to a policy that seemed to underplay their Islamic identity.[87]

The educational mission of the sufi orders and their local representatives was permanent and universal. The most significant religious centers (and most areas had at least one) served as seats of higher learning, of teaching, and of devotional practice. Here gathered the leading Islamic scholars who were not only conversant with the kinds of texts the amir of Harar had in his library but also wrote their own commentaries and treatises. The treatise on theology and law by the Oromo shaykh Jafar b. Talha (1853–1936) of Welo was a relatively late example, written, probably for pedagogical reasons, in Amharic in Arabic script. Shaykh Talha also translated the Quran, wrote a multivolume manuscript biography of the Prophet, and prepared a religious manual in Arabic.[88] Other examples of theological and jurisprudential argumentation are Arabic prose polemics exchanged by, for example, the Salihi shaykh Sayyid Muhammad and his Qadiri opponents. The sufi shaykhs also taught the Arabic language. Thus Sharif Yusuf Barkhadle is remembered for having devised a system of notation for Arabic short vowels for Somali-speaking students.[89]

Many men of religion studied with several of the leading teachers and eventually settled down to found their own network of schools. Apart from serving as institutions of religious scholarship and higher education, the sufi centers also were at the heart of the devotional practice of Islam in the region. As they were the seats of both contemporary sufi shaykhs and the sites of the tombs of deceased holy men, Muslim men, women, and children from throughout the region would seasonally make a pilgrimage (lit., *ziyara,* "visit") to these centers. The annual celebration of the birthday of the Prophet or the holy man associated with the shrine attracted the largest numbers of believers. All came to celebrate their faith and devotion, but many came with a special purpose as well, asking the holy man to intercede for them with God and the Prophet for solutions to specific problems such as illness, infertility, poverty, thwarted love, or drought. During the festivals, the pilgrims participated in a range of devotional acts. They held *dhikr* and *hadra* sessions for the ritual mentioning of God's name. They recited the *mawlid al-nabi,* the epic poem about the Prophet's family background, birth, and life; they recited praise-poetry for God and the Prophet *(madih;* Somali: *nabi ammaan);* they sang qasidas and recounted oral or written legends *(manqabas)* extolling the virtues and miraculous deeds of the deceased holy men of the order.[90] Many of the devotional songs of the Oromo of Gimma, like their Somali and Amharic counterparts, deal with death and the tomb. The following song, collected by Cerulli, addresses Shaykh Husayn of Bale:

> *When my soul is about to depart*
> *and the angel will examine it*
> *and tell it to "think about your life"*
> *When my fate will be discussed*
> *Mercy, oh Shaykh Husayn.*[91]

In Somalia, women organized women-only prayer groups to sing hymns, called *sittaat,* to the leading women of early Islamic history, from Eve to Fatima. Through the sittaat, women praised the heavenly women and asked them for assistance, especially when giving birth. As men believed that they could bring about the spiritual presence of the Prophet through the recital of the mawlid al-nabi (at which women were present but not central participants), women believed that the sittaat would bring Fatima into their midst: "Madaad, madaad, Fatima, daughter of the Chosen One, madaad, madaad, Fatima, daughter of the Prophet, give us that for which we call upon you."[92] Also, although it was (and is) frowned upon as a non-Islamic (or pre-Islamic) practice by most Muslims of the region, the therapeutic trance-dance called *zar* continued to be performed at some Islamic centers and saints' tombs as recently as 1982.[93] Thus the sufi centers seasonally became a microcosm of all the believers and forms of worship of the whole region.

Islam in northeast Africa has been characterized by two traditions, an exuberant mystical and a sober reformist one. To help them attain spiritual absorption, many common believers—and not only Qadiris—engaged in exuberant forms of devotional practice. They burned incense, doused themselves with perfume, and tied fragrant herbs into their clothing. They drank coffee, chewed qat, sang hymns, and danced to the rhythm of the drums.[94] However, equally integral to the Islamic tradition of the region is belief in more sober devotional practices that avoid the ritual indulgence of the senses and exuberant mystical Islam of the common believers.

Today, the adherents of this tradition are called fundamentalists or Islamists. Rather than seeing themselves as heirs to a local reformist tradition, they appear to have turned their backs on the rich and complex historical legacy of Islam in northeastern Africa and to focus instead exclusively on the new international religious and politico-religious agendas of the Middle East.

Notes

1. Quoted in Ahmed 1985, 777.
2. Tamrat 1972, 50. For Ethiopia's relations with Fatimid and then Mamluk Egypt, see Ehrlich 1994, 23–25, and Cuoq 1981, 93–114, 177–96.
3. Tamrat 1977, 139.
4. Ibid., 136–39
5. Braukämper 1977, 22–38.
6. Ibid.
7. Demoz 1972, 9.
8. Tamrat 1977, 143–49; Braukämper 1977; Abir 1965, 19–28.
9. Tamrat 1977, 154.
10. Ibid., 155; Ehrlich 1994, 27.
11. Abir 1965, 33; Martin 1975, 376.
12. Trimingham 1965, 91.
13. For accounts of the Imam's movement, see Tamrat 1977, 164–81; Abir 1965, 69–107; Ehrlich 1994, 29–40.
14. Trimingham 1965, 101.
15. Ibid., 103. Also A. Ahmed 1992, 102–16; H. Ahmed 1992, 20, 29–30.
16. Hassen 1992, 77; Ahmed 1989, 17; 1990, 62; Marcus 1994, 50.
17. Ahmed 1985, 122–87. Trimingham 1965, 193–98.
18. Trimingham 1965, 112–13.
19. Abir 1985, 129–33; Fernyhough 1989, 107 ff.; Sheriff 1989, 161.
20. Abir 1985, 128–30; Sheriff 1989, 175.
21. Abir 1985, 127; Fernyhough 1989, 112.
22. Levtzion 1985, 192.
23. Fernyhough 1989, 108.
24. Levtzion 1985, 193.
25. Hassen 1990; Trimingham 1965, 199–205; Cerulli 1933, 2:191.
26. Trimingham 1965, 114; Hersi 1977, 244.
27. Ahmed 1985, 188–251; 1990, 63–65.
28. Ahmed 1989, 14.
29. Ahmed 1985, 282.
30. Ibid., 273.
31. Ibid., 283.
32. See below.
33. Ahmed 1985, 323–63; 1989; Hassen 1992, 89–96.
34. Hassen 1990, 156–58.
35. Cerulli 1933, 2:192.

36. Hassen 1990, 159–60.

37. Trimingham 1965, 113, 239, 245.

38. Hersi 1977, 246.

39. Ibid., 250; Samatar 1992a, 48–74.

40. Trimingham 1965, 241.

41. Martin 1992, 11–32.

42. Ibid., 14–15, 22.

43. Hersi 1977, 255; Trimingham 1965, 243.

44. Trimingham 1965, 243.

45. Martin 1976, 200.

46. Hassen 1990, 160–61.

47. Ahmed 1989; Hassen 1992, 96.

48. Marcus 1994, 104–15; Trimingham 1965, 130–31.

49. Sheik-Abdi 1992, 205; quotation from 211.

50. Ciise 1974, 127–28; Sheik-Abdi 1992, 180. My translation.

51. Ciise 1974, 293; Sheik-Abdi 1992, 175–76. My translation.

52. Trimingham 1965, 277.

53. Noor Muhammad 1972, 117.

54. Ibid., 117.

55. Ibid., 89–90, 97.

56. Trimingham 1965, 277–78.

57. Public Record Office, London, Colonial Office Records on Somaliland, vols. 42, 43, 140.

58. Kapteijns, unpublished 1996.

59. Sbacchi 1985, 162; Lewis 1965, 111.

60. Sbacchi 1985, 163.

61. Ibid., 162–64; Trimingham 1965, 137.

62. Marcus 1994, 130–63.

63. Ahmed 1995, 776–79; Markakis 1990, 73–74.

64. Markakis 1990, 74.

65. Ahmed 1995, 776–78.

66. Ibid., 780–81.

67. Ibid., 784, 788.

68. Ibid.

69. *Africa South of the Sahara*, 379.

70. Ofcansky and Berry 1993, 71. Cf. *Africa South of the Sahara* (375, 384): 39,868,501 in 1984; 49,947,400 in 1991. Of these, 45 percent were estimated to be Muslim and 40 percent Ethiopian Orthodox.

71. Markakis 1990, 60.

72. Ibid., 60–62.

73. *Africa South of the Sahara*, 369, 371.

74. Aqli 1993.

75. Amnesty International 1994; Watson 1994.

76. Trimingham 1965, 232, reports that in 1931 65 percent were Maliki, 26 percent Hanafi, and 9 percent Shafii.

77. Drewes 1983, 68–79; Cerulli 1971 published Harar's historical chronicles.

78. Drewes 1983, 71.

79. Trimingham 1965, 249–51; Lewis 1980, 409–14; 1966, 75–81; 1955–56.

80. Lewis 1980, 412.

81. Lewis 1955–56; Hersi 1977, 18, 121–23; Trimingham 1965, 251; Tamrat 1972, 138.

82. Hersi 1977, 249.

83. Swayne 1985, 101, 260.

84. Cassanelli 1982, 135–46; Hersi 1977, 249–50. It is uncertain whether Baardheere was a Qadiri or a Ahmadi/Salihi settlement.

85. Swayne 1985, 91, 101, 129, 202–3.

86. Lewis 1965, 65–85; Jaamac Cumar Ciise 1976.

87. Kakwenzire 1976, 543–55; Lewis 1965, 103–4.

88. Ahmed 1989.

89. Lewis 1966, 75.

90. Ahmed 1990; Andrzejewski 1974a; Trimingham 1965, 247–56.

91. Cerulli 1933, 1:95.

92. Kapteijns 1995.

93. Ahmed 1990.

94. Mekouria 1988, 583, reports that the fourteenth-century amir Sabr al-Din boasted that he would conquer the capital of Christian Ethiopia to plant qat there.

Bibliography

Abir, Mordechai. 1964. "Trade and Politics in the Ethiopian Region (1830–1855)," Ph.D. diss., School of Oriental and African Studies, University of London.

———. 1965. *Ethiopia and the Red Sea: The Rise and Decline of the Solomonic Dynasty and Muslim-European Rivalry in the Region.* London: Cass.

———. 1968. *The Era of the Princes: The Challenge of Islam and the Re-unification of the Christian Empire.* New York: Praeger.

———. 1978. "Ethiopia and the Horn of Africa." In *The Cambridge History of Africa,* vol. 4, *From c. 1600 to c. 1790,* ed. Richard Gray, 537–77. Cambridge: Cambridge University Press.

———. 1985. "The Ethiopian Slave Trade and Its Relation to the Islamic World." In Willis 1985, 123–36.

Africa South of the Sahara. 1995. London: Europa.

Ahmed, Abdussamad. 1992. "Popular Islam in Twentieth-Century Africa: The Muslims of Gondar (1900–1935)." In Samatar 1992, 102–16. Trenton: Red Sea.

Ahmed, Hussein. 1985. "Clerics, Traders and Chiefs: A Historical Study of Islam in Wallo (Ethiopia), with Special Emphasis on the Nineteenth Century," Ph.D. diss., University of Birmingham, England.

———. 1989. "The Life and Career of Shaykh Talha b. Jafar (c. 1853–1936), *Journal of Ethiopian Studies* 22:13–30.

———. 1990. "Two Muslim Shrines in South Wallo." In *Proceedings of the Fifth Seminar of the Department of History,* Debre Zeit, Jun. 30-Jul. 3, 1989, 61–73. Addis Ababa: Addis Ababa University.

———. 1992. "The Historiography of Islam in Ethiopia," *Journal of Islamic Studies* 3:15–46.

———. 1995. "Islam and Islamic Discourses in Ethiopia (1973–93). In *New Trends in Ethiopian Studies*. Papers of the Twelfth International Conference of Ethiopian Studies, Michigan State University, Sept. 5–10, 1995, ed. Harold Marcus and Grover Hudson, 775–801. Lawrenceville, N.J.: Red Sea.

Amnesty International. 1994. "Somalia: Amnesty International Protests Cruel Punishments." Amnesty Intnl. News Service bulletin 284/94.

Andrzejewski, B. W. 1974a. "The Veneration of Sufi Saints and Its Impact on the Oral Literature of the Somali and Their Literature in Arabic," *African Language Studies* 15:15–53.

———. 1974b. "Shaykh Hussein of Bali in Galla Oral Traditions," *IV Congresso Internazionale di Studi Etiopici*, 33–34. Rome.

———. 1975. "A Genealogical Note Relevant to the Dating of Shaykh Hussein of Bale," *Bulletin of the School of Oriental and African Studies* 38 (pt. 1):139–40.

Aqli, Abdirisaq. 1993. "Historical Development of Islamic Movements in the Horn of Africa," paper presented to the First Conference of the European Association of Somali Studies, London, School of Oriental and African Studies, Sept. 23–25.

Braukämper, Ulrich. 1977. "Islamic Principalities in Southeast Ethiopia between the Thirteenth and Sixteenth Centuries (Part One)," *Ethiopianist Notes* no. 1, 1:17–57; 2:1–43.

Cassanelli, Lee V. 1982. *The Shaping of Somali Society: Reconstructing the History of a Pastoral People (1600–1900)*. Philadelphia: University of Pennsylvania Press.

Caulk, Richard. 1972. "Religion and State in Nineteenth-Century Ethiopia," *Journal of Ethiopian Studies* 10:23–41.

———. 1977. "Harar Town and Its Neighbors in the Nineteenth Century," *Journal of African History* 18:369–86.

Cerulli, Enrico. 1933. *Etiopia Occidentale: Dallo Scioa alla Frontiera del Sudan, Note del Viaggio (1927–1928)*. Roma: Sindicato Italiano Arti Grafiche.

———. 1971. *L'Islam Di Ieri e Di Oggi*. Roma: Istituto per l'Oriente.

Ciise, Jaamac Cumar. 1974. *Diiwaanka Gabayadii Sayid Maxamad Cabdulle Xasan*. Muqdisho: Akadeemiyaha Dhaqanka.

———. 1976. *Taariikhdii Daarawiishta iyo Sayid Maxamed Cabdulle Xasan*. Muqdisho: Akadeemiyaha Dhaqanka.

Crummey, Donald. 1969. "Tewodros as Reformer and Modernizer," *Journal of African History* 10:457–70.

Cuoq, Joseph. 1981. *L'Islam en Ethiopia des origines au XVIe siècle*. Paris: Nouvelles Editions Latines.

Demoz, Abraham. 1972. "Moslems and Islam in Ethiopic Literature," *Journal of Ethiopian Studies* 10, 1:1–11.

Drewes, A. J. 1983. "The Library of Muhammad b. Ali b. Abd al-Shakur, Sultan of Harar (1272–92/1856–75)." In *Arabian and Islamic Studies: Articles Presented to R. B. Serjeant*, ed. R. L. Bidwell and G. R. Smith, 68–79. London: Longman.

Ehrlich, Haggai. 1994. *Ethiopia and the Middle East*. Boulder, Colo.: Lynne Rienner.

Fernyhough, Timothy. 1989. "Slavery and the Slave Trade in Southern Ethiopia in the Nineteenth Century." In *The Economics of the Indian Ocean Slave Trade in the Nineteenth Century*, ed. William Gervase Clarence-Smith, 103–30. Totowa, N.J.: Cass.

Hassen, Mohammed. 1990. *The Oromo of Ethiopia: A History (1570–1850)*. Cambridge: Cambridge University Press.

———. 1992. "Islam as a Resistance Ideology among the Oromo of Ethiopia: The Wallo Case (1700–1900)." In Samatar 1992, 75–101. Trenton: Red Sea.

Hersi, Ali Abdirahman. 1977. "The Arab Factor in Somali History: The Origins and the Development of Arab Enterprise and Cultural Influences in the Somali Peninsula," Ph.D. diss., University of California, Los Angeles.

Kakwenzire, Patrick K. 1976. "Colonial Rule in the British Somaliland Protectorate (1905–1939)," Ph.D. diss., University of London.

Kapteijns, Lidwien, with Mariam Omar Ali. 1995. "Sittaat: Somali Women's Songs for the 'Mothers of the Believers.'" Boston University African Studies Center, Working Papers in African Studies, no. 25. (Also forthcoming in Kenneth W. Harrow, ed., *The Marabout and the Muse: New Approaches to Islam in African Literature* [Portsmouth, Maine: Heinemann, 1996, 124–41.].)

Kapteijns, Lidwien. 1996. "Women and the Struggle Over the Law in Colonial British Somaliland (1905–1950)," paper presented to the Symposium on Colonialism, Gender, and the Law: Comparative Perspectives, Wellesley College, April 12–13.

Levtzion, Nehemia. 1985. "Slavery and Islamization in Africa: A Comparative Study." In Willis 1985, 182–98.

Lewis, I. M. 1955–56. "Islamism in Somaliland: A Study in Tribal Islam," *Bulletin of the School of Oriental and African Studies* 17:581–602; 18:145–60.

———. 1965. *The Modern History of Somaliland: From Nation to State*. New York: Praeger.

———. 1966. "Sharif Yusuf Barkhadle: The Blessed Saint of Somaliland." In *Proceedings of the Third International Conference of Ethiopian Studies*, 75–81. Addis Ababa: Institute of Ethiopian Studies.

———. 1980. "The Western Somali Liberation Front (WSLF) and the Legacy of Shaykh Hussein of Bale." In *Modern Ethiopia from the Accession of Menilek II to the Present*, ed. Joseph Tubiana, 409–14. Rotterdam: Balkema.

———. 1983. "The Past and the Present in Islam: The Case of African 'Survivals.'" In *Temenos: Studies in Comparative Religion* 19:55–67.

Marcus, Harold. 1994. *A History of Ethiopia*. Berkeley: University of California Press.

Markakis, John. 1990. *National and Class Conflict in the Horn of Africa*. London: Zed.

Martin, B. G. 1969. "Muslim Politics and Resistance to Colonial Rule: Shaykh Uways B. Muhammad Al-Barawi and the Qadiriya Brotherhood in East Africa," *Journal of African History* 10:471–86.

———. 1975. "Arab Migrations to East Africa in Medieval Times," *International Journal of African Historical Studies* 7:367–90.

———. 1976. *Muslim Brotherhoods in Nineteenth-Century Africa*. Cambridge: Cambridge University Press.

———. 1992. "Shaykh Zaylai and the Nineteenth-Century Somali Qadiriya." In Samatar 1992, 11–32.

Mekouria, T. T. 1988. "The Horn of Africa." In *General History of Africa,* vol. 3, *Africa from the Seventh to the Eleventh Century,* ed. M. Elfasi and J. Hrbek, 558–74. Portsmouth, Maine: Heinemann.

Noor Muhammad, Haji N. A. 1972. *The Legal System of the Somali Democratic Republic.* Charlottesville, Va.: Michie.

Ofcansky, Thomas P., and LaVerle Berry, eds. 1993. *Ethiopia: A Country Study.* Washington: Department of the Army.

Samatar, Said S. 1992. *In the Shadow of Conquest: Islam in Colonial Northeast Africa.* Trenton: Red Sea.

———. 1992a. "Shaykh Uways Muhammad of Baraawe (1847–1909): Mystic and Reformer in East Africa." In Samatar 1992, 48–74.

Sbacchi, Alberto. 1985. *Ethiopia under Mussolini: Fascism and the Colonial Experience.* London: Zed.

Sheik-Abdi, Abdi. 1992. *Divine Madness: Mohammed Abdulle Hassan (1856–1920).* London: Zed.

Sheriff, A. M. H. 1989. "The Slave Mode of Production Along the East African Coast (1810–1873)." In *The Economics of the Indian Ocean Slave Trade in the Nineteenth Century,* ed. William Gervase Clarence-Smith, 161–81.

Somaliya: Antologia Storico-Culturale, no. 3. Muqdisho: Ministero Publica Istruzione, 1967.

Swayne, H. G. C. 1985. *Seventeen Trips through Somaliland: A Record of Exploration and Big Game Shooting* [1885 to 1893]. London: Rowland Ward.

Tamrat, Tadesse. 1972. *Church and State in Ethiopia (1270–1527).* Oxford: Oxford University Press.

———. 1977. "Ethiopia, the Red Sea, and the Horn." In *The Cambridge History of Africa,* vol. 3, *From c. 1050 to c. 1600,* ed. Roland Oliver, 98–118. Cambridge: Cambridge University Press.

Trimingham, J. Spencer. 1965. *Islam in Ethiopia.* London: Cass.

Watson, Paul. 1994. "On stoning in Somalia," *Toronto Star,* Dec. 10.

Willis, John Ralph, ed. 1985. *Slaves and Slavery in Muslim Africa,* vol. 1, 123–36 and 182–98. Totowa, N.J.: Cass.

CHAPTER 12

The East African Coast, c. 780 to 1900 C.E.

Randall L. Pouwels

The Swahili of East Africa have one of the most venerable Islamic traditions in sub-Saharan Africa. Much as elsewhere on the continent, Islam made its first impressions through commercial exchanges between Africans and Muslims, though jihad never became the important instrument of conversion or enforcement in East Africa that it was in other places. Following the first conversions on the northern coast, the tenth through the fifteenth centuries was a time of steady and peaceful expansion southward in the wake of developing trade. By 1500, and as early as 1200 in a few locations, Islam had become the majority religion of coastal peoples. Arab, Persian, and even Indian immigrants played their parts in this process, yet it is false to see the emergence of Islam in East Africa as an extrinsic phenomenon. Rather, these were centuries when Islam was adopted, adapted, and internalized, as a coastal "African" religion. By 1500, Islam had become central to Swahili society and identity everywhere.[1]

The truth of the last statement is most apparent in the primacy given to religion in the Swahili struggle against Portuguese attacks in the middle period of coastal history, 1500 to 1800. Not only did coastal Muslims succeed in driving out their Christian nemeses, they renewed and added new foundations to their faith. Ties with the Middle East were strengthened, literacy assumed an unprecedented position, and Arabizing fashions began at this time. Most of these new developments again radiated southward from the northern coast, where the Pate region had become the focal point of Swahili culture and religion during these centuries.

Such tendencies were both augmented and changed in the nineteenth century when the Zanzibar sultanate gave new luster to everything "Arab." In addition, all the sultans, especially Barghash b. Said, evinced a greater interest in enforcing more control over religion and law by appointing *qadis,* while maintaining closer ties with the heartlands of Islam. More people went on pilgrimage. More 'ulamā' sought training at the feet of scholars in Arabia, Mombasa, Lamu, and Zanzibar. The tariqas appear also to have played a greater part in many coastal people's religious practices, which contributed to local religious tensions. Yet, by the end of the century the first encounters with European colonialism strengthened the sultanate and the position of Zanzibar as the new fount of coastal religion.

Foundations, c. 780 to 1500

The earliest and most detailed evidence so far discovered of an Islamic presence in East Africa has been at Shanga in the Lamu archipelago. Horton there excavated a mosque and Muslim burials dated between 780 and 850 C.E.[2] From the time of its original construction to its abandonment early in the fifteenth century, this mosque went through twenty-five refurbishments, evolving from a tiny, "tent-like" structure, built from impermanent materials pegged to posts, to one made of a timber and daub, then to a porites coral-and-mud building, and finally to a substantial edifice made of coral rag and lime plaster. Continual reconstructions were done to correct the qibla line and to enlarge the mosque for a community whose Muslim population was growing.

From slightly later, archaeologists have found evidence of Muslim settlement of Pemba and Zanzibar. At what might have been Qanbalu (Ras Mkumbuu), Horton has excavated a large Friday mosque dated to about the tenth century. Dating from the tenth and eleventh centuries, mixed Muslim and non-Muslim burials have been unearthed at nearby Mtambwe Mkuu, while twelfth-century mosques bearing Kufic inscriptions have been discovered at Tumbatu Jongowe and Kizimkazi.[3]

Likewise, numismatic findings have provided clues to the earliest appearance and spread of Islam on the coast, and again the evidence is strikingly rich. Ninth-century silver coins have been exhumed at Shanga, bearing inscriptions of local Muslim rulers. Others of the later-tenth and eleventh centuries from Shanga and Mtambwe Mkuu strongly resemble Fatimid currencies, attesting to the later influences of the Red Sea region on the coast. Testifying to Kilwa's later prominence, large numbers of Islamic coins minted there in the twelfth to fifteenth centuries have been unearthed at many locations.[4]

So far, this dating sequence suggests that Islam materialized on the northern coast late in the first millennium, then spread southward with the direction of later commercial development. The earliest mosque at Kilwa dates to the thirteenth century, but like Shanga it underwent continual expansion and renovation thereafter.[5] Mosques and Islamic burials remained relatively few until the thirteenth century, but dramatic proof of the expansion and growth of Islam is provided at locales like Shanga and Kilwa, which saw continual augmentations and improvements to existing mosques, as well as new additions. By the fourteenth century, it is estimated, there were more than thirty communities that had at least one mosque, many with several. Furthermore, Islam had extended to the Comoro Islands and Madagascar sometime during this period, perhaps as early as the eleventh century.[6]

Here it is appropriate to inquire into the nature of early Islam on the coast and ask what changes it underwent. First, there is little doubt that it was a by-product of the growing incorporation of East Africa into the world of the western Indian Ocean, a process that had begun centuries before the Islamic era but that reached its greatest development between 1000 and 1500. This encompassed many peoples, some as far away as the headwaters of the Congo River and the fringes of the Kalahari Desert. The crucial vehicle of this process was trade. While many scholars in the past recognized this fact, they viewed Islamization in East Africa as solely the result of Arab commercial initiative, which included the founding of coastal sites like Shanga, Mombasa, Kilwa, and others. Contacts with other peoples of the Indian Ocean did play an important part in the mechanism of change; however, it is important now to recognize that to understand the conversion of coastal peoples and the nature of coastal Islam, the broader context of cultural and religious change among Africans has to be taken into consideration.

By the time the earliest Swahili settled locations like Shanga late in the first millennium C.E., their Eastern Bantu–speaking ancestors already had experienced centuries of steady expansion and migration from the Western Rift region of East Africa, where they originally dwelt. Moreover, change through cross-cultural borrowing was not new to them. Their ancestors had established contacts with neighboring eastern and central Sudanic and Southern Cushitic-speaking societies, and they had been exposed to a wide range of physical environments. Though originally a Neolithic people who lived from a subsistence tradition that included hunting and planting in well-watered areas, they had habituated to the drier conditions of East African savannas by learning livestock-breeding, cereal cultivation, and iron-making techniques.[7] Significantly, most of these skills had been acquired from non-Bantu-speaking neighbors. Arriving on the coast c. 100–350 C.E., their descendants the Proto-Northeast-Coastal Bantu-speakers (PNEC) merely continued the already ancient habits of cultural adaptation to new conditions. Through the normal process of dialect and language formation, between 350 and 650 C.E., the PNEC-speakers split into three major language communities, including the Proto-Sabaki (PSA). Finally, between 650 and 1000 C.E., the PSA cluster split into five dialects, including the ancestors of the Swahili, the Comorians, the Mijikenda, the Elwana, and the Pokomo. Throughout this entire period, as PNEC gave rise to PSA, and as PSA gave rise to Proto-KiSwahili (PSW), the long-familiar pattern of adapting their cultures to new surroundings—this time to a coastal environment—continued. The dynamics of this process emerge clearly from the kinds of lexical innovations introduced into PNEC, then PSA, then finally into the Proto-Swahili between 100 and 1000 C.E., as shown in table 1.[8]

Especially noteworthy is that the number of innovations increased with time, indicating that the pace and extent of environmental adaptation accelerated.

It must also be emphasized that these Africans' acculturation to the coast was not restricted to their physical surroundings, but included the human environment as well. Cultural vocabulary from other Bantu- and Cushitic-speaking communities continued to be borrowed, but for the first time in their experience their environ-

Table 1

PNEC (100–350)	PSA (350–650)	PSW (650–1000)
God	Doum palm	a free person
rice	Borassus palm	slave (two terms)
island	*water pot	*barbarian
short rains	coconut leaf	*lady (bibi)
cloth	coconut juice	*gentleman (bawana)
*mush (ugali)	shark	seagoing ship
	*steel	ship mast
	*fishing net	*fortified place (boma)
	*rope	*canoe
		*fishing net
		*cuttlefish
		*oyster
		rock cod
		fish weir
		*incense

ment included exogenes. Therefore, some early innovations, indicated in the table by starred items, originated in Persian and Indian languages, suggesting that even before the Islamic era, coastal Bantu-speakers' experience of their surroundings included significant foreign components. It is important here to note that, though these components were extrinsic, their inclusion was intrinsic to the larger processes of adaptation and change that coastal Africans had experienced for many centuries. The Islamization of the Swahili-speaking peoples was innate to their emergence as a distinct culture.

ꞁThat conversions to Islam occurred early in the emergence of a Swahili civilization comes as no surprise, a fact demonstrated by Horton's discovery of a late-eighth-century mosque at Shanga. For starters, Ehret's evidence suggests that the Swahilis' Eastern Bantu ancestors (1000–500 B.C.E.) already had a concept of a Supreme God; however, the focus of their daily religious "observance" was on spirits that were considered to be nearer than this Creator God.ꞁThe innovation of a new term for God (mulungu) in Northeast-Coastal Bantu further suggests that shifting to a new religion in which God played a central role would have demanded relatively little intellectual change—something closer to a reorientation of spiritual solemnization than to a conceptual shift.

Reorientation, of course, did not require wholesale abdication of ancient beliefs and rituals. As in other parts of the continent, for centuries coastal settlements harbored "mixed" populations of believers and unbelievers, while Muslims themselves continued honoring the ancestors and fearing malevolent forces, both Muslim and non-Muslim.[9] Verification of the appearance, mixing, and enlargement of Muslim communities from archaeology has been cited already. Arab sources reveal how gradually mixed populations gave way to communities in which the majority had converted. In the tenth century, Masudi was the first to register the presence of Muslims among the coastal "Zanj" population, and it was only at Qanbalu that Muslims seem to have had a majority by that time. Even in Qanbalu, though, Muslims and "infidels" lived side by side, and where they had the majority, they remained surrounded by non-Muslim neighbors (in the significantly named *ard al-zanj*, land of the zanj—blacks—the East African equivalent of the Sudanic Bilad al-Sudan) against whom they sometimes waged jihad, as reported by Ibn Said in the thirteenth century and Ibn Battuta in the fourteenth.

Coastal Islam developed its own distinctive flavor right from the beginning, one that mixed local with universal practices. The Shanga mosque provides exquisite archaeological detail about how this happened.[10] First, not only were the early mosques quite small, but, as Horton's evidence strongly documents, their appearance was entirely within a context rooted in a non-Muslim, presumably Bantu-speaking, past, situated as it was in a Mijikenda-like central enclosure that appears to have been restricted to community, clan, and ritual (including non-Islamic) use. Even long after they had become the majority, Shanga's Muslims continued building their mosques and tombs in their own style and from natural local materials like coral, coconut by-products, and a particularly sticky form of mud *(kinyokae)*. Only after the eleventh century did foreign influences creep into some details of mosque architecture at Shanga, Kizimkazi, and Tumbatu. Also, Arabic and European notices attest that local Islam continued to include practices that had non-Muslim origins both before and after 1500. Ibn Battuta observed scarification among Muslims at Kilwa, for example, and Figueroa mentioned seeing uncircumcised Muslims at Kilwa. Santos was only the first of many who observed widespread coastal practice of sorcery, and in the seventeenth century Dapper reported that the sultan of Malindi relied on Muslim advisers *(walimu)* who employed necromancy.[11] Even today, practices similar to these remain common among African Muslims everywhere (see chapter 21).

Were there foreign influences on early coastal Islam? Certainly there were, especially in the great commercial centers like Mogadishu (see chapter 11), Mombasa, and Kilwa, as well as at secondary locations like Shanga, Mozambique, the Comoro Islands, and Madagascar. Archaeologists have found many varieties of imported pottery, particularly at northern sites in the earlier phases (to 1100), then at southern sites later. Among these are pre-Islamic Sassanian and post-Islamic Sassanian-Islamic, lead-glazed, monochrome, and sgraffiato wares from the Persian Gulf; several kinds of Indian pottery and glass beads; and post-thirteenth-century black-on-yellow wares from Yemen. The testimonies of local traditions that tell of "Shirazi" and "Debuli" immigrants provide echoes of this early era of dominance of the coastal trade by merchants from Siraf and Sind.[12] The inclusion of Indian and Persian loanwords in PSA and PSW lends support to the evidence. Arab influences came later, after the eleventh century, when Fatimid initiatives reinjected energy into the Red Sea trade eastward to India and the East Indies, and northward to Byzantium and the Mediterranean. On the coast, evidence of this development was found by Horton in the Fatimid-like coins minted at Shanga and Pemba, cited above. However, the most enduring Arab Islamic influences came from Yemen after the thirteenth century, the hallmark of which was black-on-yellow pottery. This also was an age conspicuous for the first of three major waves of migrations of *shurafā* families from Yemen and the Hadhramaut that would occur in subsequent centuries. The most important of these migrants was the Mahdali clan, who eventually founded the Abul-Mawahib dynasty at Kilwa and reigned over that city's rise as an influential center of trade and Islam in the fourteenth century.

A case already has been made for the essentially local flavor of early coastal Islam, but there were influences from foreign Muslims, particularly immigrants. There is evidence, much as in the western Sudan, that some minority forms of Islam were exported to East Africa in the early centuries. An eighteenth-century account tells of a putative migration of the Ibadi Julanda family from Uman to the coast in the eighth century following their defeat at the hands of the Umayyads. Horton believes he has found evidence that Ibadis were present at Tumbatu, and Wilkinson has discovered clues that Ibadis were present at Kilwa and engaged in proselytizing among the local population.[13] Other clues suggest that Shiʻis also found their way to the coast. It appears unlikely they ever managed to become a majority anywhere, though testimonies of their presence lingered well after 1500.

Barros tells of the "Emozaidi," a Fiver Shiʻi sect of Yemen who, he claims, emigrated to the coast and eventually settled inland among the "Baduys." Dapper specifically cites Malindi as a Zaidi stronghold.[14] Elsewhere, he alludes to other Shiʻi groups who settled the coast after being driven from their lands because they were of the "cult of Hali [*sic*]." Santos claims that many coastal Muslims of the sixteenth century followed the "Persian" sect, who were said to have been "at great variance" with the official sect of the "Turks."[15] Given the prominence of Oman, Siraf, Kish, Yemen, and Fatimid Egypt in the early coastal trade, the likelihood that heterodoxy existed in these regions at that time seems high; therefore, these accounts have some ring of truth about them. On the other hand, it seems likely that some Portuguese confused local traditions of "Shirazi" origins with sectarian differences, or they simply could have misunderstood the local Islamic practices to be manifestations of Ibadism or Shiʻism. Whatever their truth, the long-term effects of early Ibadism and Shiʻism on coastal Muslims are nebulous.

The decline of heterodoxy in the Islamic heartlands after 1100 and the continued importance of the Red Sea, Yemen, and the Hadhramaut in the commerce of the western Indian Ocean, however, helped assure the conversion of most coastal Muslims to Shafiʻi Islam. (Sind might have been an early orthodox influence on the coast, also, since by the ninth century Daybul appears to have become a source of "official" religious propaganda.)[16] When Ibn Battuta visited the coast in 1331, he mentioned encountering only Shafiʻis, and in the sixteenth century Santos observed that many followed "the Xaphaya sect."[17] If Shiʻi Islam established a presence on the coast and hung on for several more centuries, it appears that Shafiʻi Sunnis had a lasting influence on the major commercial centers. The early connection Islam had with trade in East Africa clearly continued after 1200. At Shanga, for example, as Horton has suggested, the piety of the commercial classes lay behind the construction of two new neighborhood mosques in the fourteenth century.[18] The emergence of a wealthy and influential commercial class contributed to the proliferation of neighborhood mosques all along the coast and to the popularity of the Shafi'i *madhhab*. It was trade that attracted clans like the Mahdali to the major entrepôts, and because clans like the Mahdali demonstrated an ability to bring prosperity wherever they settled, the example they set of lives devoted to pious Shafi'i observances would have greatly influenced many coastal Africans and explains why they were given dynastic titles like "The Father of Gifts (Abul-Mawahib)."

What was the nature of this influence? Aside from creating prosperity, the merchant-sultans of Mogadishu and Kilwa assumed responsibility for constructing and expanding community religious buildings like the Friday mosque at Kilwa. From Ibn Battuta's account, both cities had sultans who governed by Sunni principles by including *wazirs*, qadis, and *muhtasibs* in their court entourages. Abu al-Muzzafar Hasan, the Mahdali sultan visited by Battuta, was noted for his many charitable gifts, as well as his veneration of "holy men" who frequented his court from as far away as the Hijaz and Iraq. Several from Kilwa's ruling family personally received training in the religious sciences. They waged jihad against the "infidels" of the mainland opposite the island community, and we are told by the author of the Kilwa Chronicle that one of the sultans was "martyred" in such a raid.[19]

The paucity of evidence makes it is difficult to comment extensively on the level of scholarship before the eighteenth century; however, the few indications available point to its relative superficiality. At least in the major commercial centers, ulama apparently could be found. Mogadishu achieved an early reputation as a center of learning, and Ibn Battuta reported that many "lawyers" resided there, where disputes were settled by qadis according to the Shari'a. At Kilwa, he encountered numerous 'ulama' and shurafa' who were revered and patronized by the sultans. Abu'l-Mahasin mentioned a qadi from Lamu whom he described as "a man of great erudition in the law according to the Shafi'i rite."[20]

Our sources are equally inconclusive concerning the extent to which Arabic was understood and used prior to the eighteenth century. It was understood by a few, perhaps as a second language, at Kilwa, Malindi, and Mogadishu, while religious texts were known and prized among the ruling classes.[21] On the other hand, spoken and written Arabic was hardly known even among the elite in remote locations. General illiteracy is what one would expect since KiSwahili was not yet a written language, and religious instruction seems to have been available only for those who could manage a voyage to Arabia.[22] When some could go, their primary purposes were for trade or pilgrimage *(hajj)*. It is impossible to speculate knowledgeably even about this, although Abul-Mahasin's qadi comes to mind since he was met while on the hajj, and it should be remembered that the sultans of Kilwa took advantage of their pilgrimage for instruction. Nothing in any sources prior to the eighteenth century mention locally available forms of religious tutelage.

A very telling indicator of Arabic literacy is that there was no significant borrowing of Arabic loanwords into the Swahili language before at least the seventeenth century. According to Nurse and Hinnebusch, this was true not only for cultural taxonomy, where Arabic later made an impact—that is, for terms relating to law, literature, and religion—but was especially the case involving basic vocabulary.[23] One is forced to draw the conclusion that, to whatever extent Arabic was known, until the seventeenth century it remained confined to first-generation immigrants and to the few who obtained religious tutelage abroad. It appears that Arabic and Swahili coexisted by performing parallel roles: for most, Swahili remained the language of daily discourse, while Arabic, as a "canonical" language, remained confined to religion and correspondence.

The Middle Period: 1500 to 1800

When without warning Vasco da Gama appeared off the East African coast in 1498, he came as the representative of a king and people who were interested in commerce and religious crusade, in that order. With a view to raking profits from the fabled gold trade, Sofala, Mozambique, and Kilwa were subjugated and fortified in 1505. The expected riches failed to materialize, so in 1511 Mozambique and Kilwa were abandoned, and almost the entire focus of Portuguese commercial attention shifted to India and the Far East. As for crusade, initially most of the coast was affected but little. However, coastal Muslims and Portuguese Christians immediately assumed positions of mutual distrust, and the Portuguese, following practices that long had existed between Muslims and Christians of the Mediterranean, perpetrated several acts of egregious brutality. In one notorious episode, they attacked and scuttled an entire shipload of Muslim pilgrims.[24]

Wherever soldiers and sailors went, missionaries accompanied them in the global Christian effort to outflank Islam. In the fleet of 1500, eight Franciscan friars made the crossing to India, and the first church was built at Cochim in 1503.[25] Several religious orders established mother houses in Goa with a view to bringing the sign of the cross to Indian Ocean peoples, and Mozambique became a host to Jesuit and Dominican friars who soon began proselytizing among Muslims and non-Muslims of the southern coast and the Zambezi River valley. They largely ignored the northern coast until the late sixteenth century, except for sporadic attacks on Mombasa, Ozi, and Pate. However, in 1516 Sultan Selim ("the Grim") captured Egypt for the Ottomans, and Suleyman the Magnificent's Muslim counteroffensive in the Red Sea and the Indian Ocean began in the 1520s. Against this background, the situation on the coast played itself out and preordained a determined Christian riposte.

A problem for the Portuguese was their failure to capture Mogadishu, Zeila, and Aden. Combined with the extension of Ottoman sovereignty over Egypt, the Red Sea, and the Hijaz, this gave heart to the coastal people's tendency to seek new champions and sources of reassurance from the religious epicenters of the Red Sea and Arabia during the dark, humiliating centuries of "infidel" rule. Many who op-

posed the "infidels" naturally considered themselves to be the subjects of the Ottoman sultans and said the *khutba* in their names. Throughout much of the sixteenth century, numerous bloody, closely fought battles on land and sea blazed
between Muslims and Christians from Ethiopia to Goa. By midcentury, especially
with the defeat of Ahmad Gran's jihad in Ethiopia, it seemed that the Portuguese
and their Ethiopian coreligionists had seized the high ground. However, between
the 1540s and 1560s, fleets from the Red Sea region attacked Ormuz, Calicut, and
Malabar.[26] The east coast seems not to have been directly involved in this fighting;
however, the threat to the Portuguese remained throughout the century, and twice,
in 1588 and 1592, the Ottomans attempted forays against Pate and Mombasa; they
were, however, defeated.

Pivotal developments resulted from these occurrences. First, the old links with
southern Arabia and the Red Sea were sustained, extending northward from Madagascar, Angoche, and Grand Comoro Island as far as the Straits of Mecca (the Red
Sea). Besides the Swahili (from the "coast of Malindi"), apparently "Arabs from
Mecca" played an important part in this linkage, and for this reason, according to
Portuguese accounts, Islam and coastal civilization were making new inroads everywhere in the sixteenth and seventeenth centuries.[27] The slave trade from Madagascar and the southern coast seems to have grown, a crucial fact because enslavement
for Africans often meant their transportation to Arabia and conversion to Islam.[28]
For this reason, in 1620, the Inquisition tried to stop Arab and Swahili merchants
from trading in slaves.[29]

The importance of these commercial ties was, if anything, augmented because
they assumed a new significance with the decline of Kilwa Kisiwani as a commercial
and religious center. Pate stepped in as one of the key elements in the chain linking
the coast, via Mogadishu, and the Red Sea. Situated just off the northern coast of
present-day Kenya, Pate was a natural way station of the coastal trade, and its
friendly ties with powerful mainland peoples added greatly to its middleman position in the supply of ivory and other animal by-products, most of which were supplied by Oromo and Aweera hunters. These amicable relations also permitted
residents to farm extensively in mainland areas in relative safety, producing grains
like rice and millet in exportable quantities. This made Pate not only a major fun-
nel of the slave trade, but a substantial consumer of slaves as well. This dual status
both as a producer and as a crucial link in the coasting trade, which put it in direct
contact with the southern coast on the one hand, and the Red Sea and Southern
Arabia on the other, made Pate inviting for immigrants.

Probably beginning after the defeat of the jihad of Ahmad Gran in 1542, and extending into the next century, Pate became the new home for various, high-profile
Muslims who, besides having trade connections throughout the Indian Ocean as far
as Java, strongly adhered to the Alawi tariqa of the Hadhramaut. Among these were
a number of *sharif* clans and others noted for their learning and piety, the most
noteworthy of whom were the al-Husayni, the Jamal al-Layl, the Abu Bakr bin
Salim, and the al-Masila Ba Alawi clans. Many of these undoubtedly arrived directly

from southern Arabian homelands, while others, according to Martin, arrived on the coast after having fought unsuccessfully in the jihad of Ahmad Gran.[30] Not only, therefore, were they active in the slave trade, according to Portuguese accounts, but they introduced the militancy of Gran's holy war to Islamic resistance to the Portuguese Christians in East Africa. In Pate, these clans settled in their own quarters, one of which was significantly named Inati, after the Hadhrami town of their origins. In 1569, Barreto already alluded to the presence of a Muslim "priest" at Pate whom he reported to have already achieved the status of being the "principal one" for the entire coast. The significance and activities of Pate's shurafa, however, were articulated with the greatest precision by Father Thomas do Domingos in 1630: "Ships come to this island of Pate, on their way from Mecca to the Island of San Laurenco [Madagascar], with *sharifs [Xarifos]* who are their *qadis [Cassizes]*, who go there to spread their faith and to obtain many Malagasy, native Gentiles, to take to Mecca and to make them Muslims *[Mouros]*."[31]

The Portuguese religious offensive began in 1560 during the height of the Muslim attacks against their Persian Gulf and Indian bases. Pope Paul created the See and Archbishopric of Goa, and Cochim and Malacca each became bishoprics, and two inquisitors accompanied the fleet of 1559–60.[32] Augustinians shouldered the task of leading the offensive, establishing monasteries at Tana, Cochim, Chaul, Malacca, Macao, Isfahan, Muscat, Bassein, Goa, and Ormuz.[33] On the East African coast, the response was a little delayed, but in 1598 they established the convent of Santo Antonio near the new stronghold (Fort Jesus) they were building in Mombasa.[34] Soon, three new *residencias* followed in Faza, Pate, and Zanzibar, and the brethren were occupied in "converting many to the faith of our Lord." Initially, successes were few, but in time the friars claimed to have had a mixed congregation at Mombasa of four thousand, and moderate success among the neighboring, non-Muslim population.[35]

The fact that a few Muslims (mostly women) numbered among the converts was not the only vexation the Augustinian and Dominican brothers caused.[36] At Pate, the Augustinian residencia was forced on the city in 1598, very much over the pleadings and objections of its sultan, and one can easily imagine that they were no more welcome elsewhere. Even their allies, the sultans of Malindi, complained numerous times of interference by missionaries, probably not unlike the intolerant behavior exhibited by Father dos Santos at Mozambique.[37] By the 1620s, it appears that inquisitors and "Pais do Christaos" from India were active on the coast to shore up laxity among Christians and to take action against the Muslim slave trade. Local fear of the inquisitors was high enough that guarantees against them were added to a treaty between the Portuguese and the citizens of Pate, Lamu, and Siyu in 1636.[38]

According to Dapper, coastal Muslims "everywhere" revolted and "made every effort to put themselves under the protection of the Turk" because the Portuguese would not allow them freedom of religion.[39] Above all, it appears that the shurafa of Pate were at the center of this resistance, and Pate itself remained a major thorn in the side of the Portuguese throughout the seventeenth century. The church there was subject to occasional clandestine desecrations, and priests were surreptitiously poisoned; some of these victims were forced to return to Goa to expire.[40] From Pate, resistance spread elsewhere. Ave-Maria presents an entire list of Augustinian padres who died, many of them murdered, at Zanzibar between 1649 and 1694.[41] At both Pate and Zanzibar, the churches were attacked and eventually had to be abandoned. Apparently, only the ones at Mombasa and Faza remained beyond 1650.

It is important to note that the nature and extent of leadership by the Hadhrami immigrants were not expressed only in the form of resistance: indeed, after 1600 the beginning of a religious renaissance blossomed in the Lamu archipelago. Thanks especially to the shurafa', a scholarly tradition in the advanced religious sciences was established locally for the first time, though this remained an avocational path closed to most ordinary Swahili until the nineteenth century. An even more momentous Hadhrami contribution was their origination of a written coastal literature. At first, religious didactic and artistic works were written in their native Arabic, but as they became indigenized, coastal scholars of Hadhrami background began writing in KiSwahili; consequently, the earliest written poetry from the coast dates from the middle of the seventeenth century.[42] One by-product of this was the development of a handicraft industry that produced copies of religious texts of very high quality at Pate, Lamu, and especially Siyu in this period.[43]

Thanks chiefly to the Hadhramis, the Lamu archipelago thus became the religious and cultural heartland of the coast between 1550 and 1800, and the influence of the Lamu region and the Pate shurafa' became widespread. After having settled in Pate and its immediate neighbors for several generations, sharif families further migrated to other parts to the south, taking their spiritual charisma and scholarly traditions with them wherever they relocated. By the 1700s, new 'Alawi ruling houses appeared all along the coast—at Ozi, Vumba Kuu, Tumbatu, Zanzibar, Kilwa, the Comoro Islands, and elsewhere—all claiming to have connections with Pate.[44] Nurse and Hinnebusch have found further evidence of this: according to their monumental study of the history of the Swahili language, the dialect of the Pate-Lamu region had a large preponderance in the southern coastal dialects at that time—indicating a southward migration of a "large or prestigious group of [northern] immigrants" from the Pate region.[45]

The Nineteenth Century

The final expulsion of the Portuguese from the coast north of Mozambique in 1728 brought yet another new era of Arabization and religious developments to East Africa. In some respects, it continued changes that had been occurring over the previous two centuries, especially those involving the intellectual and religious importance of the northern coast and migrants from southern Arabia (another significant migration occurred in the 1800s). Above all, the Arabization of Swahili culture and religion was the hallmark of the nineteenth century. Of course, in some respects this had begun earlier, perhaps even as early as the fourteenth century, and certainly by the seventeenth century. Yet it seems to have been the arrival of the Omanis in the eighteenth century and the establishment of the Zanzibar sultanate in the 1820s that really made the difference.

Prior to the (effective) relocation of the sultanate of the al-Busaidi from Oman to East Africa, the observation of strict religious practices and the administration of the shari'a appears to have been fundamentally an informal and haphazard affair in the majority of coastal centers. In most instances, local 'ulama' and other persons variously educated in law and theology (for example, *wanazuoni*) served in merely advisory capacities; local rulers reserved for themselves the actual rights of adjudication.[46] This situation changed gradually under the first three Busaidi sultans.[47] While the sultans retained the right of final appeal, in a growing number of instances through the nineteenth-century heyday of their rule, adjudication was delegated to court-appointed qadis. The first two sultans, Sayyids Said (1832–56) and Majid (1856–70), appointed two official court qadis, one Ibadi, for their Omani subjects, and one Shafi'i, for the Swahili majority. There also appear to have been other 'ulama' present at their courts who served in other advisory capacities. Official qadis like Shaykh Muhammad b. Juma al-Barwani and Shaykh Muhyi ad-Din al-Qahtani al-Wa'il sometimes were required to undertake diplomatic commissions.

Elsewhere, as in Mombasa, local elders were permitted to nominate their qadi, who then was officially confirmed in office by the sultan. The third sultan, Barghash (1870–88), extended and strengthened the religious leadership of the sultanate in coastal life far beyond that of his predecessors. Disposed temperamentally more toward religious idealism than to pragmatism, in the early years of his rule Sayyid Barghash displayed a much greater tendency to follow the exhortations of his 'ulama' and to take an independent line from the "advice" of the British consul. By 1875, however, circumstances had forced him to rely on British support. That, and a desire to augment and streamline his governing apparatus, led him to appoint many more officials throughout his East African dominions, including additional religious functionaries not only in Zanzibar but in all the major coastal towns. Besides local *walis*, Barghash and his successors directly appointed qadis for Lamu, Mombasa, Bagamoyo, Lindi, and Kilwa. Perhaps most important, Sayyid Barghash provided annual passage to Mecca for indigent pilgrims, a fact that won for him the accolade of the "Harun al-Rashid" of East Africa.[48]

The practice started by Sultan Barghash became established under his successors. Naturally, the colonial administrations added their own wrinkles. While German rule lasted, they directly appointed administrators (among them, the qadis) and limited their authority. The British preferred indirect rule: they tried to preserve local customs and judicial institutions as much as possible—wherever they were consistent with "civilized" behavior. In Zanzibar and the coast, for the most part this meant support for the existing system of qadis courts.[49] However, there were changes. For one, the authority of the qadis courts was gradually curtailed to extend only to matters of domestic and family law; the more serious criminal matters were left to secular administrators, including *mudirs*, who were appointed either directly by the colonial authorities with the approval of the sultan (in Kenya and Tanganyika), or by the sultan with the approval of colonial authorities (in Zanzibar). There were also higher tribunals to handle the most serious matters and to act as courts of appeal: these were "mixed" courts, consisting half of Muslim judges and half of British jurists, and they administered versions of the Indian civil and penal regulations.

The more important aspect of the colonial system is that it further institutionalized the formal nature of the system started by Barghash. While some 'ulama' refused positions and refused to cooperate with this application of *kafir* regulation, many others continued to go along with it actively and accept positions whenever they were offered. Thus, for example, the British formalized the positions of chief qadi for Zanzibar and Kenya, and an entire procession of Mazrui *shaykhs* was none too proud to accept the pay of their colonial masters for serving them in this capacity.

But it was not only the sultanate that transformed religious life at Zanzibar. The new merchant and landowning class, wealthy from the plantation and trading economy of the coast, contributed to the religious revival of the nineteenth century. As documented by Berg and Walter (1968) and Sheriff (1992), the era saw a dramatic increase in the number of mosques, mosque officials, Quran schools, and religious endowments. It was the new "bourgeoisie" who were responsible for this "unofficial" expansion of Islam, driven as they were by piety and a desire to leave named memorials and endowments for their descendants.[50] Though many of the new mosques were built by Ibadis principally for their use, Zanzibar and other locations seem to have enjoyed a pervasive atmosphere of sectarian liberality, and often Shafi'is were allowed by their Arab and Indian builders to enjoy the use of these new religious monuments. Moreover, powerful clans like the Barwani and the Harthi could afford to employ their own religious advisers, thus increasing the number of opportunities for employment among the learned class.

The older, established centers had more than their quota of wanazuoni and 'ulama', but Zanzibar nevertheless attracted some of the ablest scholars of Mombasa, the Lamu region, the Comoro Islands, and the Benadir towns. Mombasa was home to the distinguished Mazrui 'ulama', mostly from the line of Shaykh 'Ali b. 'Abdallah Mazru'i. The Comoro Islands contributed many scholars, the most notable of whom were scions of Hadhrami clans who had migrated there from Pate or directly from Arabia. The most noteworthy of these was Sayyid Ahmad b. Abu Bakr bin Sumayt, who served as the qadi al-qudat for all the sultans from the time of Barghash until his death in 1925, as well as Sh. Hasan b. Yusuf Mngazija and Sh. 'Abdallah b. Wazir Msujini. From Lamu came Sh. 'Abdallah Bakathir, Sayyid Ahmad's contemporary; Barawa and other Benadir towns contributed several distinguished 'ulama', among them Sh. Muhyi ad-Din, Sayyid Said's first Shafii court qadi, and 'Abdul-'Aziz b. 'Abdul-Ghani al-Amawi. The greatest source of information on the Shafii 'ulama' of East Africa over the past 175 years, Sh. 'Abdallah Salih Farsy, provides biographic information on more than 170 individuals, most of whom were connected with Zanzibar at some time in their lives.[51] Prosperity and the chance of finding employment made Zanzibar an attractive destination for religious scholars from all over the region.

Given these conditions, throughout the century the standard of religious education and scholarship continued to wax higher. Quran schools offered basic instruction to anyone who desired it, and most 'ulama' offered advanced training in some specialized science. The quality of religious education benefitted especially from men like Sh. 'Ali b. 'Abdallah Mazru'i, Sayyid Ahmad bin Sumayt, and Sh. 'Abdallah Bakathir who traveled to southern Arabia and the Hijaz to receive training that they then passed on to students. Unfortunately for a wider dissemination of advanced teaching, in most cases the shaykhs of "Arab" families such as the Mazrui, bin Sumayt, Maawi, Husayni, and Mandhiry offered higher-level lessons only to select scions of "Arab" clans. They provided such classes in the privacy of their homes and only at special hours. Little or no such instruction was given to women; once women had been trained to memorize the Quran, no further efforts were made to include them in the private classes—though one catches a glimpse in Farsy's work of an occasional exceptional daughter of a shaykh who managed to learn a lot through eavesdropping.

The texts these shaykhs taught were for the most part, as observed by Becker, the standard Shafi'i legal and theological works that formed part of the "Indian Ocean corpus." Most of these were produced in Cairo, the Hadhramaut, Yemen, and Java, and for the most part they were based on Nawawi, Ibn Hajar, Ghazali, and Ba Fadhl.[52] But these scholars also authored religious tracts of their own: Sh. Muhyi ad-Din composed a theological work (on *tawhid*, proofs of God's singularity), a commentary on Nawawi's *Minhaj al-Talibin,* and a short work on Arabic morphology. Perhaps the largest corpus of locally written work was that of Sh. 'Abdul-'Aziz b. 'Abdul-Ghani, whose writings dealt with a variety of subjects, among them tawhid, Arabic grammar, and rhetoric. Interestingly, he seems to have avoided anything on law *(fiqh).*[53]

Not only did the nineteenth century see growing depth to local standards of literacy and scholarship, but in some respects the new standards became more popular and widespread. This was due to the more significant part the tariqas had begun to play. For several centuries, beginning with the era of the Hadhrami immigrations after the sixteenth century, the 'Alawiyya already had made contributions toward this end; however, that sodality being unusually devoted to venerating the shurafa', it tightly restricted religious education only to descendants of the Prophet and a few other families. In the Benadir towns and the Comoro Islands, on the other hand, the Qadiriyya and the Shadhiliyya orders had grown popular over the previous centuries, so when 'ulama' from those places turned up in growing numbers in East African locations, these religious orders arrived with them. The end of the nineteenth century and the early decades of the twentieth thus witnessed the appearance of a new type of missionary and teacher in East Africa: this new breed devoted themselves to the spiritual and educational needs of disadvantaged Muslims and non-Muslims. Most, but not all, were members of the two brotherhoods named above, the most noteworthy being Shaykh ʿAbdul-ʿAziz b. ʿAbdul-Ghani and Shaykh Uways b. Muhammad al-Qadiri from Somalia, Shaykh Yahya b. ʿAbdallah (Sh. Rumiyya) of Bagamoyo, Sayyid ʿAbdur-Rahman b. Ahmad al-Saqqaf of Siyu, and Habib Salih b. ʿAlawi Jamal al-Layl of Lamu.[54] Tariqa shaykhs like Shaykh Rumiyya and Shaykh Uways, through their efforts to spread the teachings of their religious orders, aided in the conversion of neighboring non-Muslim peoples to Islam. But more important, all these men trained a new class of Swahili shaykhs for whom any education in the religious sciences would have previously been unobtainable.

The coming of the popular tariqas had two other results: it helped to popularize Islam and it contributed to the ethnic tension and conflict that was characteristic of the colonial era; it still echoes today in East Africa. Most of the adherents of the tariqas managed to get some degree of advanced education; thus, today one hears of many Swahili and non-Swahili *wanazuoni wakatikati, wanazuoni wadogo,* and *walimu*—"middle-level" and "little" ʿulamaʾ of former times whose religious education, though sometimes considerable, did not quite rival the scope of that of the "great" shaykhs. Many of them mixed elements of literacy with related sciences such as amulet-making, numerology, and *falak* (Islamic divination). This "Africanization" of popular Islam even extended to changing perceptions of the prophet Muhammad, who was seen by some as black. Such opinions and practices, along with public, and frequently noisy, performances of their *dhikrs,* aroused the opprobrium of the ʿulamaʾ. Because most ʿulamaʾ who opposed the popular orders were from the traditionally trained, immigrant clans, rivalries between "orthodoxy" and "heterodoxy" became an expression of a kind of class conflict. Later, in the postcolonial era, these rivalries took on an ethnic appearance that pitted "Africans" against "Arabs"; in similar fashion, the race for sinecures in the new administrations produced competition between scions of "Arab" families (for example, the Mazrui, the bin Sumayt, and the Bakathir) and the prized Swahili pupils of men like Sh. Ahmad al-Saqqaf and Sh. Ramiyya.

In other ways, as Zanzibar became the new focal point of the cultural and religious life of the coast in the nineteenth century, coastal Muslims of all sects came to look to the Arabs, the sultans, the sultans' courts, and the new Zanzibar ʿulamaʾ and their schools as the new cynosures of Islamic probity and prestige. The old term for a civilized or cultured person, *uungwana* (literally, a freeborn, city person), thus gave way to *ustaarabu,* "to be Arab-like," and it was between 1650 and 1900 that most of the Arabic loanwords presently in the language were absorbed. In the 1800s, the Zanzibar dialect, Kiunguja, replaced that of the Pate-Lamu archipelago as the prevalent dialect of KiSwahili.[55] These changes in the Swahili language itself reflected the escalating cultural and religious prestige of the Arabs and Zanzibar.

This growing trend toward greater literacy and attention to the written law had other consequences. Landownership, family inheritance practices, and the general status of women underwent subtle changes, as Caplan, Strobel, and others demonstrate.[56] Prior to the nineteenth century, Swahili clansmen and clanswomen in most locations shared equal rights of land use—rights that derived solely from principles of kinship. And, for the most part, it appears that locally born and reared elders, sultans, and even qadis conformed to local property-rights customs. Beginning with the Mazrui arrival in Pemba in the 1700s, but much more so in the 1800s under Busaidi rule, land that previously had been used to grow food crops for local consumption was converted to cash cropping. As subsistence practices rapidly yielded to a cash-based and mercantile economy, in locations like Pemba, Zanzibar, and the Malindi and Lamu regions especially, rights to land use rapidly yielded to rights of land ownership. Customary inheritance rights and practices concerning such land gradually were replaced literally by the letter of the shari'a.

The imposition of stricter standards and the appointment of walis, mudirs, and qadis to apply those standards by the sultans, and later by their colonial masters, extended their reach into other areas of family law all over the coast. For all women, but especially for those of the upper class, this meant both a decline in personal status vis-à-vis male family members and in their share of inherited property. Indeed, ironically in certain respects women of slave or lower-class status, and women living in the shrinking areas into which the written law was not yet applied (the so-called underdeveloped areas), fared better than their wealthier, upper-class sisters: they were left with rights that the more prosperous lost.

☾ ☾ ☾

The long march of Islam in subequatorial Africa had its beginnings in, and for many centuries remained largely confined to, the coast of East Africa. The latest evidence indicates that it permanently established itself in the region earlier than it did in any other part of sub-Saharan Africa. But it was extremely slow in making headway beyond its coastal foothold.

The twelve-hundred-year-long history of Islam on the coast produced a civilization that was as rich as it was deep in its tradition—a tradition that therefore proved to be exceedingly resilient in times of crisis. Conversion to Islam in the early centuries proceeded slowly and unevenly, but by the time the first Europeans arrived to challenge Islamic civilization in East Africa, the faith already had achieved majority status in the coastal towns, which by then existed by the dozens.

The Islamic tradition, rooted in both its African and Islamic past, proved to be highly adaptable, and this characteristic assured its survival against determined efforts by European missionaries to subvert it. Under Arab and British rule in the nineteenth and twentieth centuries, moreover, when coastal Islamic civilization moved away from its robust African underpinnings toward one displaying significantly greater foreign influences, it was not undermined. The new influences somewhat altered the character of East African Islam, making it more literate and outward-looking than before. But like many African religions, coastal Islam not only managed to survive, absorbing and adapting powerful outside trends, it thrived.[57]

Notes

1. Mazrui and Shariff 1994, 25.

2. Horton 1996, chapters 9–10.

3. Horton 1991; Flury 1922.

4. Horton et al. 1986; Horton 1996; Freeman-Grenville 1971.

5. Chittick 1974, 34.

6. Wright 1992, 1986; Couto 1778–88, 311; Barros 1945, 9.

7. See Ehret 1998, 171 passim.

8. Most of this information and the data are taken from Nurse and Hinnebusch 1993, 288–97.

9. See Pouwels 1987, 63–97.

10. Horton 1996, chapters 9–10.

11. Devic 1975, 86–87; Figueroa 1974, 592; Santos 1891, 1:427–31; Dapper 1686, 401.

12. See Khan 1969; Kirkman 1983; Whitehouse and Williamson 1973; Whitehouse 1974; Whitehouse 1977; Whitcomb 1975.

13. Badger 1871, 18; Wilkinson 1975; Wilkinson 1981; Horton 1992.

14. Barros, in Freeman-Grenville 1962, 83; Dapper 1686, 401.

15. Dapper 1686, 396; Santos 1891, 1:381.

16. See Abdul-Ghafur 1966.

17. Ibn Battuta, in Freeman-Grenville 1962, 31; Santos 1891, 1:381.

18. Horton 1996, 62.

19. Ibn Said, quoted in Guillain 1856, 268–69; "Ibn Battuta and the 'Kilwa Chronicle,'" in Freeman-Grenville 1962, 28–32, 39–42.

20. For Ibn Battuta and Abu'l-Mahasin, see Freeman-Grenville 1962, 28–30, 33. For evidence on Mogadishu, see Ibn Said, in Ferrand 1903, 322–23.

21. Trindade claimed that Arabic was spoken "widely" at Kilwa, and Barbosa reported that the sultan of Kilwa possessed "books of the Alcoran." At Malindi, Lopes reported that the king corresponded in Arabic. See Trindade 1866, 2:8; Stanley 1866, 11; Lopes 1812, 106, 168.

22. Gois reported that most people at Kilwa spoke only "gibberish" *(algaravia);* that is, the vernacular that probably was not initially understood by the Portuguese. Gois 1978, 148.

23. Nurse and Hinnebusch 1993, 286, 328. For a more recent discussion of the possible early impact of Arabic on Swahili, see Hinnebusch 1996.

24. See Rezende [n.d.].

25. Ibid., fl. 1.

26. Ibid., 23–32; Barros, 22.

27. Many so-called Moorish towns, built in the style of the coast, were mentioned by Barros (9). On the "Arabs of Mecca," see Dapper 1686, 398–99; Trindade 1866, 43. On the trade with the Red Sea, see Santos 1891, 1:288.

28. At the Madagascar town of Mafialage, according to Faria e Sousa, "the Moors used to buy boys whom they sent to Arabia to serve their lust." Faria e Sousa 1971, 266. For more on the slave trade, see Correa 1975, 665.

29. Fernao de Albuquerque to the king, 14 Feb., 1620, in *Os Livros das Moncoes,* Torre do Tombo (National Archives, Lisboa), 22B, fls. 438–40; *Os Livros das Moncoes,* 17, fl. 10; Strandes, 1961, 243.

30. Martin 1974; Pouwels 1987.

31. Barreto de Rezende, in Theal 1898, 216. For the quotation, see Espirito Sancto 1630, 13.

32. Rezende [n.d.], 31–32.

33. Alonso 1988, 29.

34. This and most of the following information on the Augustinians is based on Alonso 1988 and Hartman 1967.

35. Felix of Jesus, in Hartman 1967, 59ff. Also, Ave-Maria 1948.

36. Strandes 1961, 175.

37. Q.v. Santos 1891, 2:242–46.

38. On the Pais dos Christaos, see the regimento of the king to the viceroy, Feb. 27, 1568; also, Fernao de Albuquerque to the king, 14 Feb., 1620, both in *Livros,* (note 29), vol. 22B, 438–40; and vol. 40, 260, 267, 272, 272v. Also, Strandes 1961, 210, 243.

39. Dapper 1686, 401.

40. "Index Parochiorum," in Alonso 1988, 245; and Hartman 1967, 60. The so-called Pate chronicles provide numerous evidences of the shurafa leadership during this period.

41. Ave-Maria 1948, 473, 500, 508, 521, 537, 571, 664.

42. E.g., Knappert 1979.

43. Allen 1981.

44. See Pouwels 1987, 138ff. Given the Hadhrami migrations of the thirteenth century, however, some coastal ʿAlawi dynasties might have pre-dated the seventeenth century. The Pate Chronicles also allude to supposed conquests of mainland areas, including the *jumbeates* of the Mrima coast. Quite possibly, given that there is no evidence of any such actual conquest by the ruling Nabahani of Pate, these would more likely refer to the influence Pate would have wielded over these southern ports.

45. Nurse and Hinnebusch 1993, 30, 328–29.

46. Much of this material is discussed in greater detail in Pouwels 1987, 63–96.

47. Ibid., 97–144.

48. Farsy 1989, 107–8.

49. See Anderson 1970, xi, 61–67; Pouwels 1987, 163–90.

50. Berg and Walter 1968; Sheriff 1992.

51. Farsy 1989.

52. Becker 1968; Pouwels 1997.

53. Farsy 1989, 43–44. Many of these works can be found in the library of the East African Centre for Research in Oral Traditions and African National Languages (EACROTANAL) in Zanzibar.

54. All these are discussed at length in Pouwels 1987, 158–62 and 196–201. See also Martin 1976, 164–69; Nimtz 1973; Zein 1972; Lienhardt 1959.

55. Nurse and Hinnebusch 1993, 328–31.

56. Caplan 1982, 29–44; Strobel 1979, 43ff.

57. The author wishes to thank the Research Council of the University of Central Arkansas, the American Philosophical Society, and the National Endowment for the Humanities for financial support toward the research and writing of this chapter.

Bibliography

ʿAbdu'l-Ghafur, M. 1966. "Fourteen Kufic Inscriptions of Banbhore, The Site of Daybul," *Pakistan Archaeology* 10: 65–90.

Allen, James deV. 1981. "Swahili Book Production." In *Kenya Past and Present,* 13:17–22.

Alonso, Fr. Carlos. 1988. *Los Agustinos en la Costa Suahili.* Valladolid: Estudio Agustiniano.

Anderson, J. N. D. 1970. *Islamic Law in Africa.* London: Cass.

Ave-Maria, M. de. 1948. "Manuel eremetico de congregacao de India Orientale dos eremitas de N. P. S. Agostinho." In *Documentaca para a historia das missoes do padroado Portugues do Oriente,* ed. A. de Silva-Rego, 12:160–73. Lisbon: Agencia Geral do Ultramar.

Badger, G. P. 1871. *History of the Imams and Sayyids of Oman from A.D. 661 to 1856.* London: Hakluyt Society.

Barros, J. dos. 1945. *Asia: Dos feitos que os Portugueses fizeram no decobrimento e conquista dos mares e terras do Oriente,* Dec. 2. Lisbon: Agencia Geral das Colonias.

Becker, C. H. 1968. "Materials for the Understanding of Islam in German East Africa," *Tanzanian Notes and Records* 68, trans. and ed. B. G. Martin: 46–51.

Berg, F. J., and B. J. Walter. 1968. "Mosques, Population, and Urban Development in Mombasa," *Hadith* (ed. B. A. Ogot; Nairobi) 1:47–100.

Caplan, A. P. 1982. "Gender, Ideology, and Modes of Production on the Coast of East Africa." In *Paideuma 28: From Zinj to Zanzibar, in Honour of James Kirkman,* ed. J. de Vere Allen and T. H. Wilson, 29–44. Wiesbaden: Steiner.

Chittick, H. N. 1974. *Kilwa: An Islamic Trading City on the East African Coast.* London: British Institute in Eastern Africa.

Correa, G. 1975. *Lendas da India,* vol. 1. Oporto: Lello e Irmao.

Couto, D. de. 1778–88. *Decadas da Asia.* Lisbon: Regia Officina Typografica.

Dapper, O. 1686. *Description de l'Afrique.* Amsterdam: Wolfgang, Wassberge, Boom, & van Someren.

Devic, L.-M. 1975. *Les pays du Zendj, ou la cote Orientale d'Afrique.* Amsterdam: Oriental.

Ehret, Christopher. 1998. *An African Classical Age: Eastern and Southern Africa in World History (1000 B.C. to 400 A.D.).* Charlottesville: University Press of Virginia.

Espirito Sancto, Fr. Thomas do Domingos. 1630. *Breve relacao das Christandades que os religiosos de nosso Padre Sancto Agostinho teem a sua conta nas partes do Oriente e do fruyto que nellas se faz.* Lisbon: Imprensa dos Padres de Sancto Domingos.

Faria e Sousa. 1971. *The Portuguese Asia,* vol. 3. Farnborough, U.K.: Gregg International.

Farsy, Shaykh ʿAbdallah S. 1989. *The Shafiʿi ʿUlama of East Africa (1820 to 1970): A Hagiographic Account.* Ed. And trans. Randall L. Pouwels. Madison: University of Wisconsin African Studies Center.

Ferrand, G. 1903. *Relations du voyages et textes géographiques Arabes, Persans, et Turcs relatifs a l'Extrème Oriente de VIIIe au XVIIIe siècles.* Paris: Leroux.

Figueroa, M. F. de. 1974. "Chapters Relating to East Africa in the Account of Martin Fernandez de Figueroa." In *Documentos sobre os Portugueses em Mozambique e na Africa Central,* vol. 3. Lisbon: Centro de Estudos Historicos Ultramaronos.

Flury, S. 1922. "The Kufic Inscriptions of Kizimkazi Mosque, Zanzibar, 500 A.H. (A.D. 1107)," *Journal of the Royal Asiatic Society* 21:38–46.

Freeman-Grenville, G. S. P. 1962. *East African Coast, Select Documents.* London: Oxford University Press.

———. 1971. "Coin Finds and the Significance for East African Chronology," *Numismatic Chronicle* 11:283–301.

Gois, D, de. 1978. *Cronica de Dom Manuel.* Vol. 1. Lisbon: Edicao Amigos do Livro.

Guillain, Charles. 1856. *Documents sur l'histoire, le géographie, et le commerce de l'Afrique Orientale,* vol. 1. Paris: Bertrand.

Hartman, Fr. A. 1967. "The Augustinians in Golden Goa, According to a Manuscript by Felix of Jesus, O.S.A." In *Analecta Augustiniana* 30:5–167.

Hinnebusch, T. J. 1996. "What Kind of Language is Swahili?" AAP no. 47: *Swahili Forum* 3 (Sept.), ed. R.-M. Beck et al.

Horton, Mark. 1991. "Primitive Islam and Architecture in East Africa," *Muquarmas* 8:103–18.

———. 1992. "Archaeology and the Early History of Zanzibar." Paper presented at the International Conference on the History and Culture of Zanzibar (Dec.).

———. 1996. *Shanga, The Archaeology of a Muslim Trading Community on the Coast of East Africa.* London: British Institutute in Eastern Africa.

Horton, Mark, et al. 1986 "The Mtambwe Hoard," *Azania* 21:115–23.

Khan, F. A. 1969. *Banbhore: A Preliminary Report on the Recent Archaeological Excavations at Banbhore.* Lahore: Dept. of Archaeology and Museums.

Kirkman, J. 1983. "The Early History of Oman in East Africa," *The Journal of Oman Studies* 6:41–58.

Knappert, J. 1979. *Four Centuries of Swahili Verse.* London: Heinemann.

Lienhardt, Peter. 1959. "The Mosque College of Lamu and Its Social Background," *Tanganyika Notes and Records* 53:228–42.

Lopes, Thome. 1812. "Navegacao as Indias Orientes." In *Colleccao de noticias para a historia e geografia das nacoes ultramarinas que vivem nos dominios Portugueses.* Lisbon: Academia Real das Sciencias.

Martin, B. G. 1974. "Arab Migrations to East Africa in Medieval Times," *International Journal of African Historical Studies* 7:367–90.

———. 1976. *Muslim Brotherhoods in Nineteenth Century Africa.* Cambridge: Cambridge University Press.

Mazrui, A. M., and I. N. Shariff. 1994. *The Swahili: Idiom of an African People.* Trenton, N.J.: Africa World History.

Nimtz, A. H. 1973. *The Role of the Muslim Sufi Order in Political Change.* Ph.D. diss., Indiana University.

Nurse, Derek, and Thomas Hinnebusch. 1993. *Swahili and Sabaki, a Linguistic History.* Los Angeles: University of California Press.

Pouwels, Randall L. 1987. *Horn and Crescent: Cultural Change and Traditional Islam on the East African Coast (800–1900).* Cambridge: Cambridge University Press.

———. 1997. "Islamic Law and Theology." In *Encyclopedia of Sub-Saharan Africa.* New York: Scribner's.

Rezende, P. Barreto de. [n.d.]"Breve Trotado e Epilogo Todos os Visoreys que tem travido no Estado da India." Bibliothèque Nationale de Paris, Manuscripts Portugais no. 1.

Santos, dos J. 1891. *Etiopia Orientale.* Lisbon: Biblioteca de Classicos Portugueses.

Sheriff, A. H. M. 1992. "Mosques, Merchants, and Landowners in Zanzibar Stone Town," *Azania* 27:1–20.

Stanley, H. E. J. 1866. *Duarte Barbosa: A Description of the Coasts of East Africa and Malabar in the Beginning of the Sixteenth Century.* London: Hakluyt.

Strandes, Justus. 1961. *The Portuguese Period in East Africa.* Trans. J. Wallwork. Nairobi: East African Literature Bureau.

Strobel, Margaret. 1979. *Muslim Women in Mombasa (1890–1975).* New Haven: Yale University Press.

Theal, George M. 1898. *Records of South-eastern Africa: Collected in Various Libraries and Archive Departments in Europe.* Vol. 3. London: Government of the Cape Colony.

Trindade, Paulo de. 1866. *Conquista espiritual do Oriente.* Lisbon: Centro dos Estudos Historicos Ultramarinos.

Whitcomb, D. 1975. "The Archaeology of Oman: A Preliminary Discussion of the Islamic Periods," *Journal of Oman Studies* 1:123–57.

Whitehouse, D. 1974. "Excavations at Siraf," *Iran* 12:12–30.

———. 1977. "Maritime Trade in the Arabian Sea: The Ninth and Tenth Centuries A.D." In *South Asian Archaeology (1977),* ed. Maurizio Taddei, 865–88. Naples: Instituto Universitario Orentale.

Whitehouse, D., and A. Williamson. 1973. "Sasanian Maritime Trade," *Iran* 11:29–49.

Wilkinson, J. C. 1975. "The Julanda of Oman," *Journal of Oman Studies* 1:97–108.

———. 1981. "Oman and East Africa: New Light on Early Kilwan History from Omani Sources," *International Journal of African Historical Studies* 1:272–305.

Wright, H. T. 1986. "Early Communities on the Island of Maore and the Coast of Madagascar." In *Madagascar, Society and History,* ed. D. P. Kottak et al., 53–88. Durham: Carolina Academic Press.

———. 1992. "Early Islam, Oceanic Trade, and Town Development on Nzwani: The Comorian Archipelago in the Eleventh to Fifteenth Centuries A.D.," *Azania* 27:81–128.

el-Zein, A.-H. 1972. *The Sacred Meadows, a Structural Analysis of Religious Symbolism in an East African Town.* Ph.D. diss., University of Chicago.

CHAPTER 13

The Coastal Hinterland
and Interior of East Africa

David C. Sperling

with additional material by Jose H. Kagabo

Although Islam has been present on the East African coast for more than twelve centuries (chapter 12), in assessing the extent of Islamic influence we need to distinguish between the Swahili towns, centers of Islam on or near the coast, and the neighboring rural areas of the coastal hinterland, which remained untouched by Islam until relatively recent times. Arabic, Chinese, and Portuguese references to the indigenous peoples of the coast are scanty, but they say enough for us to conclude that prior to the nineteenth century the influence of Islam in the immediate hinterland and the interior was negligible, hardly extending beyond the outskirts of the coastal towns.[1]

In this chapter, we look at the way Islam spread, beginning in the nineteenth century, among the peoples of the coastal hinterland, behind a stretch of the East African coast extending for some five hundred miles (eight hundred kilometers), from the Tana River-Lamu archipelago region in the north to the Rufiji River delta region in the south. This stretch, known as the Swahili coast, can be divided into two sections. The sections are dissimilar but roughly equal in length, running 1. from the Lamu archipelago south as far as Tanga (in whose hinterland the Usambara Mountains rise); and 2. from Tanga south to the Rufiji River. The dissimilarities stem from a combination of geographical, historical, and economic factors.

North of Tanga, the coastal hinterland is relatively narrow, extending only fifteen to twenty miles inland, and in some places less, before one enters dry, inhospitable scrubland, known to the Swahili as the Nyika (*nyika* being the Swahili word for "desolate barren country"). South of Tanga, the hinterland is habitable further inland and the interior beyond is more easily accessible. This southern section of the

East African coast, from Tanga south to the Rufiji River, has long been called the Mrima coast, or the Mrima, a term used in this chapter to distinguish it from the Swahili coast north of Tanga.

To these topographical features can be added the differences in proximity to the island of Zanzibar, and the ensuing different economic and political relations with the Omani Busaidi sultanate whose commercial empire in East Africa came to be centered on that island. The Mrima coast (such towns as Pangani, Saadani, and Bagamoyo) experienced varying degrees of Busaidi political control, or interference, and the full force of the interior caravan trade emanating from the commercial expansion that took place in the nineteenth century. In contrast, although the main towns of the coast north of Tanga felt the political impact of Busaidi conquest and rule, many smaller Muslim settlements were quite independent from Zanzibar throughout the nineteenth century, and the northern coast was less directly affected by the caravan trade into the interior. Berg points out that, for example, Mombasa's economy was a "slave-absorbing and grain-producing" component of the Zanzibar system, and most of the town's direct trade was confined to the Arabian Sea.[2]

The differentiation that concerns us here is that related to the ways in which distinct local or regional settings affected contacts between Muslims and non-Muslims, since to a large extent the key to understanding the beginnings of Islamization, if not its subsequent course, lies in the nature of relations between Muslim and non-Muslim. Thus, for example, to attribute the spread of Islam to trade and traders is correct only in a certain sense. Trade facilitated contacts between Muslim and non-Muslim parties, but any ensuing process of Islamization worked itself out within the tissue of relations between those parties, subject to many and varied circumstances.

In this chapter we also examine the penetration of Islam into the interior of East Africa, as far west as the Great Lakes region, in the area corresponding roughly to present-day Kenya, mainland Tanzania (north of the Rufiji River), Uganda, Rwanda and Burundi, and the eastern Congo. The differences noted above between the southern and northern parts of the coast come to be reflected to some extent in the interior, where, for example, by the 1820s, Muslim traders had already reached the region of Tabora (180 miles south of Lake Victoria), whereas the first Muslim traders to reach the Wanga region (northeast of Lake Victoria) arrived only some forty or fifty years later.

Two questions come to mind: Why, in spite of the Islamic character of the coastal towns, did they for so many centuries exert so little religious influence over the rural hinterland of the coast? And what was it that, beginning in the nineteenth century, brought about the spread of Islam among indigenous Africans of the coastal hinterland and the interior? The beginnings of the answer to these questions lies in the nature of the relations between the Muslim inhabitants of the towns and the hinterland peoples in the early nineteenth century.

The Coast in the Early Nineteenth Century

For the century after 1729, once the Portuguese had withdrawn from Mombasa to Mozambique, we have few documentary sources of information about the East African coast north of the Ruvuma River. One of the few is the journal kept by Acting Lieutenant James Emery of the British Royal Navy during his twenty-three-month residence in Mombasa, from August 1824 to July 1826. Emery records numerous details about relations between the town dwellers of Mombasa and the neighboring hinterland peoples, then called the Wanyika (the people of the Nyika), but known today as the Mijikenda. (The contrast between hinterland peoples and town Muslims was less pointed than the words *rural* and *urban* might imply: though the Swahili of the eighteenth and nineteenth centuries were "town-dwellers," they correspond *mutatis mutandis* to Weber's "semi-peasant urbanite" who had a parcel of land that fed him.[3] Many Swahili settlements are better described as villages or "semi-rural" towns. For example, the Swahili who lived on the island of Mombasa had farms on the mainland where they grew their own food.)

Emery's journal gives a first-hand account of life in Mombasa, which he described as "entirely Mohammedan," and of related Mijikenda activities: the Mijikenda would capture runaway slaves and be paid to return them; when the occasional dispute arose among the Mijikenda, the Swahili would mediate; the Mazrui *liwali* (governor) of the town occasionally consulted with Mijikenda chiefs about matters of mutual interest, and at one point the Mijikenda elders were called to Mombasa to be informed that the liwali no longer had authority, since the town had been handed over to the British; the Mijikenda would be given cloth as presents or be paid their "annual" payment. In a general assessment, Emery speaks of the Swahili as being united with the Mijikenda "in closest alliance."[4]

Of the various transactions that brought town and country into contact, by far the most frequent was trade. The pattern of trade was remarkably uniform and constant. Innumerable entries in Emery's journal refer to the Mijikenda bringing goods into town; he uses such phrases as, "a great many Whanekas came into town with fruit and vegetables" and "the Whanekas are daily coming into town with articles of trade." The Mijikenda supplied Mombasa with their own produce (ivory, gum copal, grain, cassava, and other fruits and vegetables) and goods they obtained from the interior—from the Kamba and, to a lesser extent, from the Orma (Galla)—(ivory, rhinoceros horn, and skins). Swahili and Arab traders resident in the town went into the hinterland only very occasionally. Only once during his two years in Mombasa does Emery mention the townspeople going into the hinterland to look for trade goods (in this case ivory), and this was at a time of year (September) when dhows were about to sail north and did not have enough cargo. The townspeople of Mombasa must have known of the rural Mijikenda markets, but since those markets traded in relatively bulky goods—goods that were being brought to them and could be obtained easily in Mombasa—there was no reason to frequent them.

Among the numerous Mijikenda visitors to Mombasa, there must have been those who took up residence there; how many we cannot be sure. Emery noted that there was "constant intermarriage" between the Swahili and the Mijikenda—that is, Swahili men marrying Mijikenda women. Though Emery makes no mention of Mijikenda Muslims, some Mijikenda had undoubtedly adopted Islam by this time. Mijikenda women married to Swahili would have become Muslim, as did some urbanized Mijikenda men. Twenty-five years later, Erhardt, an early Anglican missionary at Rabai, wrote of "Islamised Wanika workmen" from Mombasa.[5]

Mijikenda who accepted Islam were, by and large, persons who had opted out of their own society and been assimilated into town life. There is no evidence that Muslims propagated Islam among the Mijikenda in any way, and there were few adherents of Islam living within Mijikenda society. During extensive travels among the Giriama in the hinterland in the 1840s, another observer, Johann Ludwig Krapf, came across only one such person "who many years ago had turned Mohamedan and who lives since among his clansmen, not with a view to bringing them over to the Mohamedan persuasion for the latter sits very loosely upon him."[6] Islam was an entirely urban phenomenon, and the very process of Islamization was centered on the towns—what we might call "urban Islamization." Relations between the Mijikenda and the Muslims of Mombasa, peoples living apart with distinct social and cultural traditions, gave little scope for the penetration of Islam into the rural hinterland, where the Mijikenda continued to follow their own religious beliefs and practices.

In 1850, Krapf took a "coasting voyage" south from Mombasa and left an account that reveals similar relations between Swahili Muslims and rural peoples on the coast south of the Pangani River:

> The Wasegua [Zigua] reside south of Pangani [town], these as well as all the other tribes which I shall name are heathen. The Wasegua [extend] south as far as the village of Sadani [Saadani], a Suaheli village opposite Zanzibar . . . the Wadoye [Doe], the Waseramu [Zaramo], the Watumbi [Matumbi]. . . . All the villages on the immediate seashore are Suaheli Mohamedans and governed by chiefs under the influence of the Imam [of Muscat and Zanzibar] . . . all the pagan tribes situated at a small distance from the coast have constant intercourse with the Suaheli . . . [who] find it in their interest to keep good terms with the pagans on whom they are so much dependent concerning their trade and intercourse with the interior of Africa.[7]

The limited evidence available does not allow us to reach firm conclusions regarding the whole East African coast, but Emery's and Krapf's descriptions give a general idea of prevailing circumstances and of relations between the Swahili towns and the rural areas of the hinterland. Trading activity dominated these relations and was the main occasion for contacts between Muslims and non-Muslims, but evidently trade in itself, extensive and regular as it was, did not create conditions conducive to the spread of Islamic influence among the non-Muslim peoples of the coastal hinterland.

Nineteenth-Century Growth of Hinterland Trade and Agriculture

Early in the nineteenth century, the prevailing pattern of trade on the East African coast began to change under the influence of two related phenomena. The coast was being incorporated, in varying degrees and ways, into the growing commercial and political empire of the Omani Busaidi Arabs centered at Zanzibar. At the same time, the East African economy was expanding, as external economic forces created an unprecedented demand for such goods as ivory, slaves, gum copal, and grain.[8] The quantity of these goods reaching the towns was insufficient to meet regional and international demand. As a result, there occurred a virtual "economic invasion" of the hinterland and the interior by Muslim traders, who were no longer content simply to receive trade goods from rural peoples as in the past, but sought rather to increase their supply, and profit, by venturing inland in search of goods at their source. Emery had noticed something similar in the 1820s in the hinterland of Mombasa: a last-minute quest for ivory before dhows made their seasonal voyage north. Indeed, it is possible that the incident he observed was an instance of incipient change and the beginning of the trend that was to persist and increase for the next half century.

Economic growth was accompanied by Busaidi political expansion. The concerted effort by the Busaidi Arabs to dominate the northern Swahili coast—more specifically, the Busaidi takeover of Lamu (1813), Pemba island (1822), Pate (1824), and Mombasa (1837)—displaced many Muslims and caused them to emigrate from island towns to the rural mainland, where they undertook the foundation of new settlements. From Pate, those displaced were Nabahany Swahili and their supporters, who settled at Ozi in the Tana River delta area.[9] In the case of Pemba and Mombasa, those emigrating were for the most part Mazrui and their Swahili and slave followers. The Mazrui formed new settlements at Takaungu north of Mombasa and at Gasi to the south.[10] Guillain estimated that some fifteen hundred persons took part in the move from Mombasa.[11] The Tangana Swahili from Pemba settled on the coastal plain south of Mombasa in the area of Mtongwe.[12] As a result of this widespread redistribution of population, Muslims found themselves living far closer to non-Muslim rural peoples (the Pokomo south and west of the Lamu archipelago; the Mijikenda north and south of Mombasa; the Segeju in the Vanga region), and the potential for contacts between Muslims and non-Muslim Africans on the northern coast was substantially increased. On the Mrima coast, the existing Muslim settlements generally accepted a form of Busaidi overlordship, and no similar displacement of population took place.

By the 1840s, trade on the coast had entered fully into a period of expansion. More often than not, the growth of the East African economy during the middle decades of the nineteenth century is viewed in terms of the long-distance caravan trade into the interior.[13] Less evident, but no less important for contacts between Muslims and non-Muslims, was short-distance trade and other commercial ventures, including agriculture, in the rural hinterland near coastal towns. Hinterland trade and agriculture were important, for example, in the main caravan towns of Bagamoyo and Pangani on the Mrima coast. The Bagamoyo hinterland was particularly rich in good-quality gum copal, for which there was high international demand.[14] According to W. T. Brown, gum copal (from the coastal hinterland) and ivory (from the interior) were the two main articles of trade from Bagamoyo during the 1860s and 1870s; slaves constituted only a small percentage of total exports.[15] As the town grew in size, surrounding land (for which the neighboring Zaramo were compensated) was brought under cultivation to provide food for both consumption and export. As the number of caravans leaving for the interior from Bagamoyo increased, the Swahili of the town (known locally as the Shomvi) negotiated an agreement with the Zaramo chiefs by which caravans made payment for the privilege of passing through their territory.[16] Evidence for hinterland trade at Saadani, another Mrima town, is limited. By 1857, when Burton visited the town, it was still a small village.[17] As Saadani developed into an important caravan terminus in the 1860s, its hinterland trade seems to have been largely overshadowed by the caravan trade into the interior, in which Zigua chiefs successfully participated.[18] Farther north, at the town of Pangani, Muslims had been engaged in short-distance trade into the hinterland since the early nineteenth century.[19] Later in the century, Arab settlers developed large sugar plantations, using slave labor, in the hinterland along the Pangani River.[20]

Evidence for the hinterland trade of some of the northern towns (Takaungu, Mombasa, Gasi, Vanga, and Tanga) is more detailed. Krapf finds Muslims frequenting the villages of the Mombasa hinterland "in the business of trade," and in some villages Muslim traders built houses for residence during their "trading tours." Krapf also noted the monopoly that "the Mohamedans of Mombas" had on the trade of gum copal, which he described as "a very valuable article of trade" in the hinterland forests.[21] Muslim traders also began to settle near Mijikenda villages. Krapf left a description of one of these settlements, Magombani, near the village of Jibana:

> I insisted on being conducted to Djibana [hill], at the foot of which Magombani has been erected. . . . The tract of country where the hamlet Magombani has been built by some Mohamedan speculators of Mombas is egregiously well chosen, since it is but 4–5 miles from the bay, and as they are able on this spot to secure to themselves the advantageous monopoly of copal which the forest of Djibana produces; besides they cultivate much rice and maize, and make use of the fine timber, which the forest presents, for boards used by the Arabic [sic] boat-builders.[22]

In 1848, Rebmann found Muslims trading at another Mijikenda settlement, Chonyi, which he described as a village of "about 1,500 inhabitants in the midst of a forest . . . [a] Wanika town in which we saw a small market, kept up by Mohamedans."[23] Other traders moved deeper into the hinterland in search of ivory, into an area inhabited by the Giriama people, some fifteen miles inland. When visiting the village of Mikomani, described by Krapf as the largest of Giriamaland, he came across the "Mohamedan Sheikh of Keriama," who had erected "a cottage in which he resides on his trading tours . . . all the Muhamedan passengers [travelers] spend a night in that house."[24] In 1861, Thornton found a Muslim trader residing some twenty miles inland at a large village beyond Kwale.[25] Von der Decken described the same Muslim trader as "Nasoro, a Swahili and caravan leader."[26]

Expansion of hinterland trade was accompanied by a corresponding increase in agricultural production in response to the demand from Arabia, Pemba, and Zanzibar for grain. In the case of the latter two islands this was to feed the large numbers of slaves working on the clove plantations.[27] Muslims expanded their own farms and also established commercial agricultural plantations, particularly on the Shimoni peninsula, around Gasi, on the mainland north and south of Mombasa, and in the Mazrui-dominated areas between Takaungu and Msabaha.[28] In addition to increasing their own agricultural production, Swahili and Arabs in the coastal towns intensified trade in grain (millet, maize, sesame, rice) with their rural African neighbors. By the 1860s, the Digo of the Tanga region were important suppliers of grain. Erhardt described them as "the cultivators of the land . . . they are the rich. . . . Almost all the semsem [sesame] and guinea corn [maize] imported at Zanzibar comes from them. . . . If the Wadigo do not choose to bring their productions to the market, the Islams have nothing to eat."[29] Further north, Malindi prospered as a plantation town, as vast tracts of land in the uninhabited rural hinterland were brought under cultivation; in 1877, Kirk described fields of millet extending ten to fifteen miles inland.[30] There was also a general increase in agricultural production on the mainland coast of the Lamu-Tana River area.

Agriculture was so important to the Swahili that New, who worked as a Methodist missionary at Ribe from 1863 until his death in 1875, described it as "one of their chief pursuits." He noted: "Every man of any position has his shamba, or plantation, whence he derives his chief support. The labor is done by slaves."[31] As a result, the hinterland around Mombasa came to be surrounded by plantations:

> The land on all sides is very fertile, and is largely cultivated. Kisauni to the north, Changamwe to the north-west, Mtongue and Lakone to the south are all covered with thriving plantations. The produce they send to the town adds largely to its wealth and importance. They are the market-gardening districts of Mombasa. All kinds of fruits, vegetables, pulse and cereals, grow in abundance. . . . Sesamum is cultivated largely, and is an important article of commerce. These districts are backed by the Wanika-land, which supplies rice, Indian corn, and millet to an almost unlimited extent.[32]

As agriculture prospered in the 1850s and 1860s, more slaves were needed. According to Guillain, who visited Mombasa in 1848, the population on the island of Mombasa was between twenty-five hundred and three thousand, and the population of the "dependencies" of Mombasa (by which he means the mainland agricultural villages) was six thousand, of whom some forty-five hundred were slaves.[33] Soon after reaching Mombasa in 1863, New estimated: "The population of Mombasa cannot be less than 15,000. It has greatly increased of late years, chiefly, however, through the importation of slaves."[34]

Some plantation owners lived in Mtwapa or Mombasa, from where they periodically visited their plantations. Other owners stayed in small agricultural villages near their plantations. Owners created separate residential villages for their slaves, who came under Islamic influence in varying degrees. Ahmad Stambuli, a plantation owner at Shariani (south of Kilifi), had his slaves build a mosque in which he would pray with them when he visited, but many agricultural villages had no mosque. The Muslim owners would go there mainly to supervise agricultural work, and although some built small prayer-houses (Swa., *misala;* sing., *msala*), for Friday prayers they would go to town.[35]

Although most slaves on the East African became at least nominal Muslims, the practice of Islam by slaves is not well documented. Morton argues that whereas the adoption of Islam gave slaves a sense of superiority over unbelievers, rigid class barriers usually prevented them from rising above their inferior status.[36] Cooper states that slaves were taught the Quran, but this would have been true mainly of domestic slaves living in town.[37] Friday was usually a day of rest for slaves. Some prayed, but others would pray only when their master was present—behavior perhaps reminiscent of that of schoolboys with regard to their teachers. The varying attitudes of slave owners toward religion often determined the religious practice of slaves: Muslims who were religiously inclined might sell off slaves who did not pray, but Muslims for whom religion was unimportant would not even give their slaves time off for prayer. Islam among slaves was much attenuated by the low standard of Islamic education available to them. Illiteracy was high, opportunities for learning few, and knowledge of the faith rudimentary. Slave villages had no Quran schools, and slaves, and the children of slaves, had little chance to learn about their faith. Slaves who lived in town had better access to education, and sometimes studied to quite high standards. For example, one of the teachers of the last liwali of Mombasa, Shaykh Mbarak bin 'Ali al-Hinawi, was a slave.[38] But even slaves without a solid grounding in Islamic doctrine acquired a veneer of Muslim attitudes and practice. New described how slaves "sometimes learn by rote sufficient of the Koran, though in an unknown tongue to them, to take part with their betters in the religious exercises of the mosque."[39]

☾ ☾ ☾

The presence of Muslims in rural areas thus grew in several ways: the emigration of Muslims from established towns to found new rural settlements; greater initiative on the part of Muslim traders, who began to frequent and in some cases even settle in the rural hinterland; and the general expansion of agriculture by Muslims into areas that bordered on or intermingled with non-Muslim peoples. These developments affected different parts of the coastal hinterland in varying ways, but the net overall effect was to bring Muslims and non-Muslims into closer, more frequent contact with each other and to increase the number and kinds of transactions between them. More subtle, and less easy to evaluate, is the evidence that the nature of contacts between Muslims and non-Muslims was beginning to change. As Muslim entrepreneurs sought out reliable trading partners, relations that had previously been group-oriented came to be more personal and individual. Krapf made a reference to the existence of such direct personal links between Muslims and Mijikenda: "The Mohamedan guide . . . will introduce you to that Wanika with whose interests those of his own are connected."[40]

Throughout this period, urban Islamization continued, and probably increased, if for no other reason than because new Muslim settlements attracted immigrants. There is also evidence that the increase in contacts between Muslims and non-Muslims in the hinterland attracted larger numbers of non-Muslims to visit the towns. Thus, the number of non-Muslim Africans adopting Islam may have been increasing, but most of these would have still gravitated to urban life. In spite of closer and more frequent contacts between Muslims and non-Muslims, there is little evidence that Islam had begun to take hold among peoples in the rural hinterland before the second half of the nineteenth century. Indeed, Krapf's assessment of relations between Mombasa and the Mijikenda in 1844 was remarkably similar to Emery's: "The secular interests of the Wonicas are intimately connected with those of the people of Mombas [*sic*]. Both live in peace with each other, except that the latter look on the Wonicas as infidels."[41] And on the Mrima coast in 1857, Burton was still able to refer to the Zaramo of the hinterland of Bagamoyo as a "barbarian maritime race" who go to the Luguru mountains to worship.[42]

The Beginnings and Growth of Rural Islam

By the third quarter of the nineteenth century, there is evidence that some non-Muslim Africans had adopted Islam and continued to reside in their rural villages—the beginnings of what we might call "rural Islamization." This change marked a significant turning point in the spread of Islam. Previously, the emigration of Islamized Africans away from their own people to settle in Muslim towns had removed elements that might otherwise have proved innovative, if not disruptive, to their own societies. Now, the presence of indigenous African Muslims in rural villages created new circumstances and the potential for change. Rural Islamization first began in those places where non-Muslims developed particularly close relations with Muslims, as a result either of Muslim agricultural expansion into rural areas or of prolonged and intense trade with Muslims. Rural Islamization also occurred in another quite different way: by remigration—that is, the return of Muslim Africans from residence in towns to their original rural homes.

Some of the earliest evidence we have for rural Islamization comes from the

Vanga-Shimoni area (near the present-day border between Kenya and Tanzania), where Muslim influence was already spreading among the Segeju people indigenous to the area before 1850. In 1854, Erhardt reported that the Segeju "have become mostly Mahomedans."[43] The Segeju had especially close contacts with the Vumba Swahili of Wasin Island, who established farms on the mainland peninsula (known today as Shimoni) opposite the island. Land was plentiful on the peninsula, and the Segeju are said to have allowed the Vumba to settle there.[44] Most Vumba continued to reside on the island (and in Vanga town), and farmed on the mainland seasonally, but some settled near or in Segeju villages, took Segeju wives, and became permanent mainland residents. Eventually the whole Shimoni area came to be regarded as joint Vumba-Segeju land.[45] The children of Vumba-Segeju marriages were brought up as Muslims, and other Segeju, not related to the Vumba by marriage, must have been attracted to Islam. The Islamizing role of the Vumba is corroborated by Segeju traditions, which state that the coastal Segeju (as distinguished from the Segeju, who were settled inland at Bwiti and Daluni) were converted to Islam by the Vumba. Thus, the Segeju came to be among the first indigenous African people of the coastal hinterland to adopt Islam on a large scale, and this was not so much because of trading contacts but as a result of close relations arising out of interspersed settlement and intermarriage. They were also the first to build their own mosques, in such villages as Kibiga, Kirau (Kidimu), and Hormuz (Ormuz), in the third quarter of the nineteenth century. Later in the nineteenth century, Segeju teachers contributed to the spread of Islam among the Mijikenda, particularly among the southern Digo of Tanga.[46]

Relations developed somewhat similarly between the Digo south of Mombasa and the Tangana Swahili who settled at Mtongwe. The Tangana began to cultivate land near the Digo and to marry Digo women. By 1860, the Tangana and Digo were collaborating in many ways. Some Digo had taken up residence among the Tangana for purposes of trade or to work, and the Tangana elders knew and met regularly with their Digo counterparts. By the 1870s, some of the Digo of Mtongwe had begun to adopt Islam, and from then on the number of Digo Muslims increased, gradually but steadily. These early converts to Islam, while continuing to live in their villages, would go to pray in neighboring Tangana mosques. They seem to have had no difficulty leading their traditional way of life and at the same time responding to the demands of their new religious faith.[47] In 1915, the year the Digo Muslims built their own mosque at Mtongwe, Dundas was able to write: "Although many Wadigo have become converted to the Moslem faith, this can scarcely be described as their only or true religion. Side by side with Mohamedan practices they continue their tribal religious observances, none of which have been displaced by Mohamedanism. Most of their wives and women folk are pagans and their husbands do not seem to consider it necessary for them to be anything else."[48]

On the Mrima coast, in the area of Saadani, there is early evidence for intermarriage between Swahili and Zigua women of the hinterland. Bwana Heri bin Juma, who was the autonomous ruler of Saadani from the 1860s until the German occupation, is said to have been born of a Swahili father and a Zigua mother.[49] We can postulate, too, that as the Shomvi Swahili expanded to settle and farm in the outlying areas of Bagamoyo town, they came to develop comparably closer relations with the neighboring Zaramo. In all these instances we can perceive a general pattern. As Muslims settled to live and farm closer to non-Muslims, the two came to reside so near to each other, indeed often interspersed, that their lives intermingled and they shared the same concerns of daily life. In this way, Islam came to have a direct presence and particularly strong influence among non-Muslim rural peoples.

Krapf observed this influence at Mwakirunge (in the coastal plain north of Mombasa), where he was received by Sheikh Ibrahim, a Muslim who had "flourishing plantations of rice, cassava, maize, etc." and was "much respected by the few pagan families which have fixed their huts around him." Krapf commented: "It is surprising how the Mahomedans [*sic*] encroach upon the Wonica land in this direction. They erect small hamlets . . . people them with their slaves, and secure the good will of the Wonicas by trifling presents which they give them. . . . In the course of time new settlers arrive carrying with them a Sheikh who superintends their religious wants and ensnares the infidels whenever he can."[50]

Turning to look at Islamic influence arising out of trading relations, we find that as the trading initiative shifted to town centers, not only did the presence of Muslim traders in the hinterland increase, but the direction and focus of trade changed as well. Whereas the town constituted a single marketplace attracting the surrounding hinterland peoples without distinction, the town trader viewed the rural hinterland selectively, and sought above all to establish contact with those places nearest to him or that represented the largest prospective market and source of supply. Thus, the areas of the hinterland that were more accessible or that had a larger and more densely settled population were especially attractive to Muslim traders.

In this regard, non-Muslims in the immediate hinterland of the towns, within a distance of ten to twelve miles, seem to have been the object of constant and regular visits by local Muslim traders. The hinterland peoples of the Mrima (the Zaramo, Zigua, Doe, Bondei, and Digo) all came under steady Islamic influence in this way. The degree of influence seems to have been proportional to the distance from town. For example, by 1890, the Zaramo near Dar es Salaam and as far as ten miles inland were already adopting Islam, whereas farther inland, at Kisarawe (twenty miles from the coast) and Maneramango (fifty miles southwest of Dar es Salaam), the Zaramo had had little contact with Muslim traders.[51] Similarly, Digo elders in the coastal plain immediately south of Mombasa had begun to adopt Islam in the 1860s and 1870s, and by the end of the nineteenth century had built three mosques, whereas the Digo in the sparsely populated Kwale hills fifteen to twenty miles inland began to adopt Islam only some forty years later, and did not build their first mosque until after World War I.[52] Further south, in the hinterland of Tanga, the Digo were said to be "becoming Muslim" in the 1890s, and by 1911 more than twenty Digo villages had mosques.[53]

Further north, in the Tana River area, remigration was responsible for the beginning of Islamization among the upper Pokomo. In the 1880s, a number of young men from upper Pokomo migrated to settle at Chara in lower Pokomo country, where they began trading with Muslim traders at Kau. Under the influence of these traders, some of the men became Muslim. Had they continued to reside at Chara, they might have remained nothing more than a community of Islamized immigrants, but in 1910 they began to return to their upper Pokomo homeland, where together with Muslim traders, who were then entering upper Pokomo country for the first time, they began to spread Islam.[54]

By the end of the nineteenth century, most Africans in the immediate coastal hinterland had experienced the impact of Islam in one way or other. They may not have formally adopted Islam—in particular, far fewer women than men had become Muslim—but some of their kinsfolk would have done so, and the presence of Islam had permeated into many rural villages. A high proportion of the first African converts were village elders and chiefs, and by all accounts many of them were men of forceful character and prestige, like Kibasila, the Zaramo chief of Kisangire (south of Dar es Salaam), who in 1905 refused the offer of a Lutheran mission school since he already had a Quran school in his village, and Abdallah Mwapodzo, the *mwanatsi* (senior elder) of Diani (south of Mombasa), who is said to have been the first Muslim Digo in the area and to have been instrumental in bringing other Digo elders into Islam.[55]

By this time, too, other forces had begun to strengthen Islam in the coastal region. The Qadiriyya and Shadhiliyya were both active, particularly along the Mrima coast, where they had spread from Barawa via Zanzibar, and numerous Quran schools had been started in rural villages, mainly for the children of the first generation of African Muslims.[56] Further north, in the hinterland of Mombasa, the Qadiriyya spread among African Muslims at least fifteen or twenty years after it had begun on the Mrima coast. The Qadiriyya attracted some new converts, but its greatest impact seems to have been to encourage African Muslims, including second-generation Muslims, to live their faith more enthusiastically and with greater conviction.[57]

The Caravan Trade and the Spread of Islam into the Interior

By the 1830s and 1840s, caravans were traveling regularly into the East African interior. Arabs, Swahili, and sometimes Indians trekked inland in search mainly of ivory and slaves and the lucrative gains to be obtained from such trade. The growth of the caravan trade, during this period and the ensuing half century, is best understood in the context of two related factors: a steady rise in international demand for ivory and slaves, and the monopoly control that came to be exercised over trade in the region by the Omani sultanate based in Zanzibar. Indeed, it was the trading expansion inland that assured Zanzibar of its key position in the commerce that linked East Africa with the larger world. East Africa produced high-quality ivory, much in demand in international markets, as well as slaves, which were sought by the expanding plantation economies, on the coast itself, and on the islands of Zanzibar, Pemba, and Mauritius, which produced cloves, sugar, and grain for export. The reverse movement of manufactured products (cloth, guns, beads, and ironware) from India, America, and Europe was also channeled through Zanzibar. To control this trade, the Zanzibar sultans established a strong and effective administration. They do not, however, appear to have desired formal political control beyond the coast and islands. Doubtless, they possessed neither the means nor the human resources to achieve a true colonization of the region; nor is there any indication that they harbored any religious agenda for the coast, much less for all of East Africa. Nevertheless, the caravan trade marks the beginning of a substantial movement of new peoples and ideas, including those of Islam, into the interior.

Much of the trading initiative before the 1820s came from inland peoples like the Kamba (in the northern interior) and the Nyamwezi (in the central interior), who brought trade goods to the coast and who in so doing pioneered routes that were later used by Muslim traders from the coast. The first caravans moving from the coast into the interior entered the region south and southeast of Lake Victoria (present-day central and western Tanzania). Only later did caravans begin traveling into the northern interior (present-day central and western Kenya). By the 1850s and 1860s, caravans were the main source of supply of ivory, and only small quantities of ivory made their way to indigenous markets at the coast.

Evidence for the first decades of the caravan trade is sparse, and much of our knowledge has been pieced together from accounts of early travelers (Burton, Speke, Stanley), who recounted events they were told about but did not witness. The earliest travelers from the coast into the interior are said to have been two Indian Muslim brothers, Sayan and Musa Muzuri, who departed the coast around 1825 with more than fifteen tons of pearls and textiles that were credited to the account of the Omani liwali of Zanzibar. Sayan died en route; Musa, after suffering a large loss of merchandise, settled for several years in the Lake Victoria region. His business prospered, especially at Tabora and Karagwe, where he appears to have been one of the most successful traders of the mid-nineteenth century. Later, he was joined by an Arab, Ahmad bin Ibrahim, whose parents had immigrated to Zanzibar sometime before Sayyid Said, the Sultan of Oman, decided in 1840 to reside there more or less permanently. Ahmad is said to have been one of the first traders to make his way to the kingdom of Buganda on the northern shores of Lake Victoria.[58]

The trade routes have been well studied and described in various sources.[59] Three routes concern us here. Two were from the Mrima coast: the so-called central route (used mainly by caravans from Dar es Salaam, Bagamoyo, and Saadani) running through Ugogo,[60] then on westward to Tabora in Unyamwezi and Lake Tanganyika; and the so-called northern route (used mainly by caravans from Pangani, Tanga, and Vanga) going from the northern Mrima coast, inland along the Pangani

River to Kilimanjaro and Maasailand. The third route was further north (used mainly by caravans from Mombasa), traveling across the Nyika and then to the Kilimanjaro region or into Kamba country, thence westward across the Rift Valley toward Lake Victoria. Descriptions of the continent's interior by later European travelers suggest the risks that must have been encountered by the Muslim traders who preceded them. The routes, hardly more than tracks, presented numerous obstacles: "muddy streams, quagmired rivers, deep ravines, thick forests, sheer rocks, marshes." As Burton noted, "streams of water that could easily be forged during the dry season often became dangerous torrents when the rains began."[61] In addition to such natural hardships, the routes were riddled with other obstacles: not only was there the levying of tribute and pillaging of goods, but "wars or conflicts between tribes . . . often blocked the way."[62]

The geographical details of the routes are of less importance to our study than an understanding of their common characteristics. In general, the routes passed through low-lying areas, avoiding mountainous terrain. Thus, for example, as the central route entered the country west of Uzaramo, it avoided the Luguru hills, traveling instead through the lower arid plains. Muslim traders thus had regular contact with the Luguru of the plains but almost no contact with the more densely populated hill country. The population distribution of Uluguru in the late 1950s reflected this early influence: in the highland region of Mgeta, 4 percent of the population was Muslim and 86 percent was Christian; in the lower regions of Uluguru, such as Mililingwa and Malela, the Muslim population was more than 70 percent.[63] When Christian missions first began their work among the Luguru, they established stations in the highlands, where they found less Islamic influence. A similar example of lowland travel can be found on the northern route, which passed through the lower southern sections of Usambara and Upare, avoiding the mountains.

Trade from the East African coast into the interior, which came to be totally dominated by Muslims, was instrumental in bringing Muslims into places where none had ever been before. Although the hamlets built by traders along the routes were potential conduits for the spread of Islam, most African peoples felt little, if any, Islamic influence. As Muslims sought to dominate trade routes that had been pioneered by Africans (bringing goods to the coast from the interior), intense trading competition arose, and the relations of Muslim trader-settlers with indigenous non-Muslims were not always cordial.

The number of settlements established by Muslims was few in relation to the vast area through which the caravans passed; moreover, the population of the settlements was generally low. In large parts of the interior—in Usukuma south of Lake Victoria, for example, where ivory was scarce—no settlements or trading centers were established at all. Caravans did their best to avoid or pass quickly through other areas, such as Ugogo, dry, difficult country, where no ivory was available and the people were considered to be generally hostile. Traders established one trading post at Mpwapwa on the southeastern boundary of Ugogo, but the main focus of relations there concerned the right of passage and provision of supplies. Overall, there was limited contact between Muslim traders and the Gogo, and there is no evidence of Muslim proselytization among them.[64]

The reasons for establishing settlements or trading centers were varied; for example, it might have been to secure a strategic or convenient location, or because of the availability of trade items or provisions, or the political influence of a particular chief or leader. Before the 1860s, Swahili traders were frequenting Upare, where their main trade was in ivory. They established a permanent base for this trade in Ugweno in northern Pare, the only part of Upare with a supply of ivory rivaling that of the Kilimanjaro area. Today, Ugweno is the place in Upare that has the strongest Muslim influence.[65] In Usambara, Muslims were attracted to the town of Vugha, the old center of Kilindi power in the highlands. When Erhardt stayed in Vugha for three months in 1853, he found there a strong Muslim presence, including several Muslim scribes and "sorcerers," and that one of the king's sons had become a Muslim.[66] Though Usambara did not generally become Muslim, Kilindi power came to be associated with Islam during the nineteenth century. In 1911, Becker noticed "a large Muslim community" and the presence of a Muslim teacher among the Shambaa people at Mlalo, near Vugha.[67] Even today, the main center of Muslim influence in Usambara is at Mlalo-Mhelo.[68]

Where only one or two Muslim traders were residing alone in the interior, they seem to have had little impact on the general population, and in some instances may themselves have been influenced by local circumstances. When Rebmann reached Machame, in Chagga country, in January 1849, he met "Maigni Wasiri," called Nasiri by the Chagga, a Swahili from Pangani who had been living among the Chagga for some six years and was employed by Mamkinga as "his physician and sorcerer." Nasiri came to visit Rebmann, who described him as "now from his long residence in Chagga rather a heathen than a Mahomedan [*sic*]. He wears his clothes like the Chagga and it is said that the king obliged him to eat such flesh as is declared 'haram' to the Moslems."[69]

Trade routes sometimes changed—in response to conflict, refusal of African chiefs to allow passage, or general insecurity. For example, in the 1870s raiding parties led by Mirambo in northern and northwestern Unyamwezi made the Karagwe route to the west of Lake Victoria unsafe, and traders were forced to shift to what became known as the "Lake route," through Usukuma to the southern shores of Lake Victoria, where Kageye became the terminus port, handling goods coming and going across the lake. When Henry Morton Stanley arrived at Kageye in 1875, he found only one coastal trader, Songoro Tarib, in residence. Songoro is said to have been absent much of the time, doing business in Ukerewe and arranging transport for ivory to Tabora. His and his successors' influence on the Sukuma, with whom they had little interaction, was minimal.[70] All this is not to say that there was no Islamic influence arising out of the caravan trade, but the proportion of inland African peoples affected was small.

❨ ❨ ❨

It was at Tabora and Ujiji in the central interior that the greatest Muslim settlements developed. Ujiji, located on the eastern shores of Lake Tanganyika, was an
important staging point for trade across the lake; Tabora, some 180 miles south of
Lake Victoria and 200 miles east of Lake Tanganyika, was strategically located in a
well-watered fertile region at the crucial junction where the central trade route split
into two branches, one proceeding west to Ujiji, the other north, around the western shores of Lake Victoria, to terminate in Buganda.

To ensure the smooth operation of their affairs, the Arab and Swahili merchants sought to forge solid alliances with local rulers. The rulers expected their
coastal allies to supply them with the firearms they needed to defend themselves
from the attacks of hostile neighbors or to help them organize the conquest of new
territory. In turn, the providers of firearms benefited by sharing the booty seized in
battle: prisoners of war or stocks of ivory. These alliances were sometimes sealed by
the marriage of a trader to the daughter of an influential elder or chief. Such marriages took place at both Tabora and Ujiji.

In the 1840s at Tabora, the trader Muhammad bin Juma, a Muslim of mixed
Omani and African descent, married a daughter of Fundikira I, the *ntemi* (ruler or
chief) of Unyanyembe, one of the two main chiefdoms of Unyamwezi. The Arab-
Swahili community helped Fundikira I in several armed clashes with his neighbors.
By the 1860s, Tabora had grown into the most important of the Muslim settlements
of the central interior, and the local liwali, the official representative of the sultan,
had established his residence there. However, Islamic influence at Tabora was mitigated by various circumstances, and Muhammad bin Juma's marriage to Fundikira's
daughter had no broad repercussions on Nyamwezi society. In 1858, it was overshadowed by the violent conflict that broke out between the Arabs and Mnywa
Sele, Fundikira's successor.[71] The Nyamwezi, who were themselves trading competitors of the Arabs and the Swahili, kept the Muslims confined to Tabora town,
where few Nyamwezi were resident.

The rise to power in the late 1860s of another Nyamwezi chief, Mirambo, who
was hostile to Unyanyembe and opposed to the presence and influence of the Muslim traders there, changed the circumstances of much of Unyamwezi. Mirambo's
raiding campaigns severely disrupted trade and constrained the activities of many of
the coastal traders. Unsympathetic to the Zanzibaris, the redoubtable Mirambo
(called by some a "black Napoleon") knew how to play to his advantage the rivalry
between them and the Christian missionaries, who first arrived in the Tabora region
in 1879. According to a description of the town in the 1880s, there were no
Nyamwezi living within three miles of Tabora, where the Arabs and Swahili stayed
with their Islamized Manyema slaves, and the town had become as much a plantation as a trading settlement.[72]

To all these circumstances must be added a further, less tangible and definable, factor—the apparent general lack of interest among most Muslim traders in spreading their religion. Few local Africans seem to have adopted Islam, and those who did generally numbered among the immediate entourage of Arab and Swahili merchants: their wives and sometimes the relatives of their wives, retainers or porters, and slaves. European observers were struck by the absence of places of prayer and religious instruction. Though undoubtedly these practices were going on unobserved—in particular, the Zanzibaris are said to have preferred praying in the privacy of their homes—it is difficult to gauge their extent. Because of the limitation of our sources and consequent lack of knowledge, the history of Islam necessarily lies hidden behind the secular and commercial activities whose details are so much better known.

The trading center at Ujiji seems to have benefited from the change of circumstances in Unyamwezi. Whereas in 1860 Ujiji had not achieved even the size or importance of Kazeh or Msene (two of the hamlets that made up Tabora), by 1880 it was home to seven or eight thousand inhabitants. When Stanley visited Ujiji in 1872, he described "the vigorous mingling of regional and long-distance trade taking place there."[73] The town's resident merchant colony was governed by a Swahili chief, Mwinyi Mkuu, whose brother Mwinyi Kheri had married the daughter of the king of Bujiji. After acquiring the status of a chief under the king of Bujiji, Mwinyi Kheri came to control most of the trade that passed between Ujiji and Uvira on the western shore of Lake Tanganyika. The Europeans who met him about 1880 found him in possession of 120 slaves, eighty rifles, and nine canoes.[74] Christian missionaries described Ujiji as "the most populous Arab center in Tanganyika, where arrive all the slave caravans taken from the interior and sent to Zanzibar. It is there that all the half-castes gather to decide among themselves from which direction and in which region they would direct their forays."[75] Images drawn of the scene suggest that coastal peoples had established themselves there quite permanently:

> Imagine then a tangle of trees, of palms, of banana trees, of mango trees: here and there heaps of refuse and debris; huts scattered without pattern along winding paths which open their way with difficulty through this wild vegetation favored by a humid, stifling climate. Here and there arise the tembes of the Arabs,[76] massively heavy buildings . . . with reddish walls and narrow windows. . . . A veranda extending the length of the facade of the tembe, which accommodates Arabs and their guests during the day, for the Arabs spend their whole lives outdoors. . . . Around the tembes there are scattered without order the huts of the slaves and the dwellings of somewhat well-off people who are able to build in brick. The tembe is to these huts what the chateau is to the village houses of Europe. In ordinary times, Oujiji can hold seven or eight thousand inhabitants. Twelve dozen pure-blooded Arabs at most are to be found there, but each of these Arabs has hundreds, and some even a thousand, slaves.[77]

Ujiji also served as a base for the commercial penetration of the region west of Lake Tanganyika, then known as Manyema (now the eastern region of Congo-Kinshasa). The expansion of trade into Manyema is synonymous with the name of Hamed bin Muhammad Tippu Tip, the most famous of the Swahili interlacustrine merchants and the son of Muhammad bin Juma, who had settled at Tabora. Tippu was initiated into commerce by his family at just twelve years of age, when he began going on local trading trips in the coastal hinterland. At the age of eighteen, his father took him to Tabora and on to Ujiji, from where he crossed the lake. This was his introduction to Manyema country, where he was to spend much of the rest of his life.

On his third journey into Manyema (1870–82), Tippu cleverly managed to pass himself off as the grandson of a paramount ruler of the Batetela. Previously, a daughter of the Tetela ruler had been taken to Zanzibar, and the family had been waiting many years for news of her. Thus, Tippu Tip claimed his part of the inheritance according to local custom, which privileged the maternal line in matters of succession. Kasongo Rushi, the Tetela chief, moved at finding his "grandson," presented Tippu to the crowd that had gathered for the occasion: "This is your chief Tippu Tip! I no longer have any stake in the chieftainship; bring all the tusks (of ivory) to him."[78] During the twelve years that he remained in his inherited land, Tippu used his prerogative as Kasongo's grandson to organize and control local trade in ivory and slaves. During the years leading up to the Scramble, he became the only local notable to negotiate with the Europeans who had come to explore the immense territory that King Leopold II coveted. Even when Europeans used the cover of the antislavery campaign to seize African possessions, Tippu's knack for being the right person in the right place held true. He received numerous emissaries from the Belgian sovereign, as well as explorers and missionaries, to whom he supplied porters and protection all the way from western Tanganyika to Manyema. Fearing a Mahdist invasion from the Sudan,[79] and from his French rivals on the western bank of the Congo River, Leopold II used the Arabs and the Swahili to occupy "his" territory. In 1887, he designated Tippu Tip as his governor at Stanley Falls (present-day Kisangani), the first outpost of the new Congo Free State.

All the years of activity of Tippu Tip, and other traders, in Manyema had singularly little consequence for the spread of Islam. Some Manyema made their way to Tabora and Ujiji, more often than not as slaves, and became Muslim there, but little permanent residue of Islam remained in Manyema once the slave trade was declared illegal and suppressed by the Belgian colonial government. Beyond the western bank of Lake Tanganyika, Muslim traders appear to have been even less concerned with spreading their religion than they were in Ujiji or Tabora. Several theories have been advanced to explain this: for example, their lack of political ambition, or their contempt for local nonbelievers. Indeed, the coast men did think themselves superior to the inhabitants of the far interior, to whom they regularly applied the Swahili term *washenzi* ("barbarians"), and who were discovering for the first time the technological superiority of firearms and other products of the industrial revolution. It is equally pertinent to remember that many of the Swahili and

descendants of Omani immigrants may have had little religious instruction themselves, and the general temper of the age in which they lived did not stress that Muslims had an obligation to spread their religion to other peoples.

The northern interior, along the route inland from Mombasa, experienced the
impact of trading caravans later and to a lesser degree than had happened in the central interior further south. By the 1850s, early Muslim traders had probably found
their way as far as Lake Baringo, which became an important outpost and supply
point, but regular caravans began traversing this route only in the late 1860s and
1870s. We have far less evidence for trade in this region, since European travelers
and explorers, whose accounts give so many details about trade in the central interior, did not enter the northern region until the 1880s.

The main Muslim settlement in the northern interior was the one established
among the Wanga people (the present-day area of Mumias in northwestern Kenya).
The first Muslim traders were welcomed by Shiundu, the traditional *nabongo* (ruler)
of the Wanga, who saw in them a potential ally in his struggle against hostile neighbors, in particular the Bukusu. Shiundu's son, Nabongo Mumia (after whom the
present town of Mumias is named), became a Muslim, as did a number of other
members of the royal Abashitsetse clan. The traders were given Wanga women in
marriage, and by the 1890s, on the eve of colonial rule, a small but thriving Muslim
trading community had been consolidated at Mumias. Muslim traders also founded
trading and supply centers along the main trade route at such places as Kitui,
Machakos, Baringo, and Eldama Ravine,[80] but the settlements were small and unstable and had few residents. They had little Islamizing influence on the societies
around them.

Islam and the Kingdom of Buganda

Of all the places in the interior of East Africa that felt the influence of Islam
during the nineteenth century, Buganda must be considered preeminent, not just
because it was the most prosperous and highly centralized kingdom of the region,
but also because its rulers took a singular interest in the religion of Islam.

Oral traditions and written accounts agree that Islam was first taken to
Buganda by Muslim traders coming from the southeast through Karagwe during
the reign of Kabaka Suna (c. 1832–56). The number of traders reaching Buganda at
this time was small, however, and few of these are known to have attempted to
spread Islam.

Among the first Muslims to arrive was Ahmad bin Ibrahim, who was known
particularly for his proselytizing, an unusual trait not often mentioned in accounts
about traders. According to European sources, his efforts at converting local
Baganda to Islam were a result of his "Wahhabist" sympathies. Ahmad, who was
treated as a friend and protégé of Suna, held discussions with the kabaka about the
Quran, Muslim theology, and law. Suna is said to have learned several chapters of
the Quran by heart, and manuscript pages from the Quran were discovered in his

house after his death.[81] Despite this, there is no evidence that Suna ever seriously intended to adopt Islam. On the other hand, it is known that he encouraged Ahmad to extend the teaching of Islam to his subjects as well as to neighboring Karagwe. In Karagwe, Ahmad warehoused quantities of merchandise, especially firearms and cotton goods—items he traded or sold for livestock, slaves, and elephant tusks, which the kingdom provided in abundance. When Stanley met him in 1876, he possessed "150 head of stock, 100 slaves, and 450 ivory tusks."[82] Details of his life (see, for example, the narratives of Stanley and Burton) draw a picture similar to those of other great merchants of the era who traversed the Zambezi Valley and the regions that later formed part of the "Arab empire of Manyema."

Suna's son and successor, Kabaka Mutesa, is said to have exhibited an even keener interest in Islam than his father. One of the first Muslim traders to visit Mutesa is said to have been Ali Nakatukula, who came in the late 1850s or early 1860s. Ali left a Swahili servant to teach Mutesa, who quickly learned to read and understand Arabic, to the extent that he was able to render portions of the Quran from Arabic into Luganda, his mother tongue. After having studied the Quran for some time, he summoned all his chiefs and started to teach them about Islam, and ordered all his subjects to learn about it as well. He built a large mosque at his palace in Nakawa and appointed a number of his pages as guardians of the mosque, where he arrived to pray every Friday with a large contingent of chiefs. He decreed that his chiefs and subjects should perform daily ritual prayers and use Arabic or Swahili forms of greeting, and he introduced Muslim forms of attire at his court. Mutesa first observed Ramadan, the month of fasting, in 1867, and continued the observance for the next ten years. More interestingly, he made the practice of fasting obligatory for all his subjects. Mutesa is even said to have sent a mission, though unsuccessfully, to the neighboring kingdom of Bunyoro in the hopes of convincing Kabarega to adopt Islam. Thus, whereas under Suna the spread of Islam had been confined mainly to the court and its immediate surroundings, under Mutesa the influence of Islam began to spread into the countryside. Indeed, during these years, Islam became a kind of "state" religion.[83]

Stanley's visit to the kabaka's court in 1875, followed two years later by the arrival of the first Christian missionaries in Buganda, marked a turning point in Mutesa's perception of Islam, and indeed in the history of Islam in Buganda. By this time, the kabaka felt that his kingdom was threatened from the north by the Anglo-Egyptian expeditions into the Sudan. Sir Samuel Baker, an English officer who had been appointed governor of the Sudan in 1869 by Khedive Ismail, had proclaimed the annexation to Egypt of "the regions south of the Gondokoro," extending nearly to the southern border of present-day Uganda.[84] Mutesa's interest in Islam continued, as did his open admiration of the culture of the sultans of Zanzibar, but his relations with Muslims came to be exercised within the context of contemporary political circumstances. The kabaka seems to have had an overriding interest in obtaining guns from whomever he could, from the well-armed coastal Muslims, who frequented his realm, and from the Roman Catholic and Protestant missionaries and other explorers, who visited him and spoke of the omnipotence of their God and the power of Europe.[85]

During the period between 1877 and 1884, the year of Mutesa's death, the Muslim position in Buganda deteriorated, as the Christian missionaries succeeded in arousing doubts and weakening Mutesa's practice of the Muslim faith. If one considers further the tolerant attitude of Mutesa toward the Christian sects, whose supporters at his court sought his favor, the eminently political dimension of his interest in Islam and Christianity cannot be ignored.

The kabaka aimed to maximize his political options while maintaining control of the foreign visitors at his court. He continued to advocate the practice of Islam, while refusing to undergo circumcision and frequently neglecting to pray, both of which were considered by Muslims to be critical indicators of a true Muslim. He welcomed European explorers and missionaries with the same honors he bestowed on Muslim visitors. At the same time, he affirmed his friendship with the sultan of Zanzibar, Sayyid Barghash. Tired of this maneuvering, the Protestant missionary Mackay concluded that the kabaka "has no other desire in his heart than the satisfaction of his passions and the desire for wealth."[86] Father Nicq, of the White Fathers, accused him of being "as touchy, as greedy, as despotic, as savage as anyone."[87] Yet, he also recognized his shrewdness and political genius.[88] The Protestant missionary Pearson wrote in his diary, after having learned that a certain Rashid bin Surur had obtained five hundred rifles for the king, "Now that this Arab has brought so many rifles, Mutesa will choose Islam."[89]

The years immediately following the death of Mutesa are often referred to by historians as the period of the "wars of religion," during which the forces of Islam, Christianity (in its two forms, Protestant and Catholic), and traditional religion vied for power and control. The Baganda who had adopted Islam under Mutesa occupied many important posts, and their influence was such that they were able to set Prince Kalema on the throne against Mutesa's designated successor, Mwanga. For a while, Kalema prevailed and ruled as a Muslim kabaka (1888–89), but in 1890 the arrival in Buganda of agents of the Imperial British East Africa Company helped to turn the tide irreversibly against Islam.[90]

Islam and Colonial Rule

The steady growth of a European presence in East Africa during the 1870s and 1880s, culminating in the imposition of colonial rule, had decisive consequences for Islam in the region. The course of Islam during the colonial period came to be influenced, not so much by a clearly defined colonial policy toward Islam—no such policy seems to have been elaborated by the colonial powers, except in the broadest terms (chapter 8)—as by diverse precolonial circumstances, and various ad hoc measures taken by colonial governments as they sought to establish their administration.

In some instances, the impact of colonial policy had rather abrupt and immediate consequences for Islam. For example, in two short years, by the treaties of 1890 and 1892, Lugard, acting in the name of the British East Africa Company, succeeded in influencing the religious composition of the traditional Buganda hierarchical structure. Of the ten chieftainships, six were assigned to the Protestants, covering in Lugard's own estimate 60 to 70 percent of Buganda, three (the smallest) to the Muslims, and one to the Roman Catholics. Within another year, two of the three chieftainships had been removed from the Muslims and reallocated to the Protestant and Catholic parties, leaving the Muslims with only one. This arrangement, which marked the institutionalization of Christian dominance in Buganda, was confirmed by the Uganda Agreement of 1900, which strengthened the privileged position of the Christians and the hegemony of the Protestants at the very center of power. Official correspondence from Sir Harry Johnston, who negotiated the Uganda Agreement on behalf of the British government, leaves no doubt that he was concerned about the political consequences of the spread of Islam, and applied a criterion of inequality in religious matters.[91]

Notwithstanding this inequity, the British unintentionally fostered the spread of Islam into other areas of Uganda (outside Buganda). One of the consequences of the loss of influence by Muslims in the court and government of Buganda was the emigration of Baganda Muslims, "for the new Buganda was in theory Christian and it was impossible to have status without a Christian name."[92] Baganda Muslims sought their fortunes elsewhere, going to neighboring areas, like Busoga, Toro, and Bunyoro, and a large group of Muslims from Buganda was also given refuge by the ruler of Ankole. These refugees are known to have been instrumental in disseminating their faith among the peoples who received them. Baganda Muslims were also recruited by the British as administrative agents, interpreters, and chiefs in such places as Lango, Teso, and Bukedi, where they used their influence to spread Islam. And the Sudanese (Nubian) soldiers placed by the British in their main administrative centers imparted a permanent Muslim character to the towns in which they lived. Though not numerous, descendants of the soldiers, many of whom were later absorbed into civilian life, form Muslim communities in most of these areas to this day. Notable, and exceptional, among these communities are the Muslims of Aringa County of the West Nile District in northwest Uganda, where some 80 percent of the population is Muslim. This is the only part of East Africa where the Maliki school of law *(madhhab)* prevails, a lasting testimony to the Islamic influence from the north.[93]

Initially, the process of establishing and consolidating colonial rule, in British East Africa and German East Africa, offered Muslims an unprecedented occasion for expansion throughout the interior. The military conquest preceding the establishment of colonial rule was carried out in large part by Muslim soldiers, many of whom were then stationed in the new administrative centers they had helped to create. On retirement from military service, soldiers were offered land by the colonial government, and many decided to settle permanently in the areas in which they had served.

During the early years of colonial administration, both the British and the Germans relied on Muslims to occupy key positions as chiefs, headmen, clerks, and tax collectors. Beginning in 1892, the German colonial government established its first educational institutions at the coast (at Tanga, Dar es Salaam, and Lindi), and most of the African administrative staff trained there were coastal Muslims. These junior civil servants are known to have been instrumental in spreading Islam to such places as Mahenge, Kondoa, Irangi, Singida, and Musoma. By the time of World War I, Christian missionary leaders in German East Africa were voicing open criticism of what they saw as the pro-Islamic policy of the German colonial government.

The significance of the precolonial trading centers established in the interior during the nineteenth century becomes evident under colonial rule. Not only do many of the centers survive, with a continuity of Muslim presence, but some of them expand and take on added importance in another guise, when the German and British colonial governments develop them into administrative centers. To give just one example: beginning in 1891, Tabora became the German military and administrative headquarters in central German East Africa, thereby even increasing its Muslim character, since the numerous government officials who came to Tabora were mostly Muslim. In 1911, Becker called Tabora "the citadel of Islam in the interior."[94] By 1902, its population was thirty thousand, and still growing. With the arrival of the central railway line (and major railway workshops) at Tabora in 1912, new opportunities for employment were created, and the Nyamwezi of the surrounding hinterland migrated to the town in large numbers, where they came under Muslim influence, in a local upcountry version of urban Islamization. Though details are not yet known, the increase in the number of urbanized Nyamwezi Muslims in Tabora was followed, or possibly accompanied, by rural Islamization among the Nyamwezi in the hinterland of the town. By 1957, Abrahams finds Islam "of importance in the rural areas around Tabora where many villages have predominantly Muslim populations."[95] Not all nineteenth-century trading centers come to have such a profound Islamic influence as Tabora during the colonial period, but the Muslim presence in these towns, dating back to the caravan days, remains, and in many places has become significant only in recent times.

Colonial governments also founded new administrative centers in the interior in places untouched by the earlier caravan trade. These centers attracted an influx of Muslim traders (Arab, Swahili, Somali, Indian, and Ismaili) seeking the opportunities and newly established security provided by the colonial presence. Thus, communities of immigrant Muslims came to live and settle in areas that had previously been closed, unsafe, or only partially accessible to Muslims, and in the midst of non-Muslim societies with little or no previous exposure to Islam.

The influence of Islam was generally strongest among those peoples who were living nearest to administrative centers (and therefore to the Muslim communities of the centers) or who developed special relations with resident Muslim traders. The Muslim inhabitants of the centers often married local African women and attracted African employees from the surrounding countryside, some of whom became Muslim, to settle in these new colonial towns. Thus there occurred a process of urban

Islamization, not unlike what had happened in the Swahili towns during the early centuries of Islam on the East Africa coast. By the time of the First World War, Muslim communities existed in or near most colonial administrative centers. Most of these communities inherited the dominant attributes of Swahili Islam (Sunni and the Shafi'i school of law), and they came to exhibit common underlying characteristics derived from Swahili coastal culture, notably Swahili cuisine, dress, dances and songs, and the use of Swahili as the language of Islam, though they continued to speak their vernacular language in daily life and in dealings with their non-Muslim fellow Africans.

As the period of colonial rule progressed, the pervasive presence of Christian missions had a signal effect on Islam. The arrival of a small but growing number of Christian missionaries in the 1860s and 1870s had presaged the gradual spread of Christian missions throughout most of the interior, facilitated by colonial policies generally favorable to Christianity. During the early years of colonial rule, there occurred a steady expansion of missionary enterprise, evangelization, and education. Eventually, almost all peoples of East Africa, except those who were already thoroughly Islamized and the less accessible pastoral peoples, came under the influence of one or more Christian missions and had a chance to acquire formal Western education.

In this regard, precolonial circumstances played a significant role in defining the future of Islam (and Christianity). In areas where Islam had already taken root or was on its way to doing so, for example, in many parts of the coastal region and in such places as Kigoma and Ujiji, the work of Christian missions either proved to be sterile or was eventually abandoned, or in some cases simply did not begin. In areas where Islam had gained an initial but insecure foothold, Christian missionary work usually acted as a counterinfluence and had an adverse impact on the growth of Islam. In places where no Muslim influence was present, Christian missionary work for the most part proceeded unimpeded, though not without difficulties and setbacks. There were exceptions to these general trends, however. The deportation of large numbers of missionaries from German East Africa after World War I weakened Christian influence. For example, the Christian chief of Maneromango, in Uzaramo, became a Muslim, as did other Zaramo Christians, after the German missionaries left.[96] During the years immediately after World War I, there was an increase in Muslim influence, particularly in areas where Islam was already present, but in the 1920s the new British colonial government of Tanganyika came out in strong support of missionary work, and there followed a big expansion of Christian education.

By the 1920s, Christian influence was rapidly outstripping the Muslim. In spite of the early impetus given to the spread of Islam with the creation of colonial administrative centers in the interior, the fact that by and large Islam remained confined to the immediate vicinity of these centers greatly restricted its growth. Christian missions, on the other hand, systematically spread throughout the rural areas. As the twentieth century progressed, many Africans acquired literacy and formal Western education (and became Christian), while Muslims, who continued to follow their traditional Islamic system of education, had less access and opportunity for formal education. Since Muslims tended to avoid going to mission schools or were excluded from them, Christians came to have a "privileged position" in society.[97] With the rise of a class of literate Africans, Muslims became less important to the colonial administration, and Muslim communities tended to become marginalized from the modern economic sector. The imbalances created by these unequal colonial circumstances make up much of the legacy being experienced by the Muslim peoples of East Africa to this day.[98]

Notes

1. Quite different circumstances led to the earlier penetration of Islam farther south in the coastal hinterland and interior of present-day Mozambique; see chapter 15.

2. Berg 1971, 8.

3. Weber 1966, 70–71.

4. Emery 1833, 283.

5. Erhardt to Venn, Sept. 22, 1852, Church Missionary Society (CMS), CA/09/9.

6. Krapf's journal, Aug. 19, 1845, CMS, CA5/ML/676.

7. "Dr. Krapf's Journal Descriptive of a Voyage," 1850, CMS, CA5/M2.

8. Sheriff 1987, 87–110; Nicholls 1971, 324–75.

9. Ylvisaker 1979, 121–30.

10. Koffsky 1971, 5–20.

11. Guillain 1856, 2:236.

12. Sperling 1988, 62–65.

13. Lamphear 1970, 75–101; Berg 1971, 225–35; Glassman 1994, 55–78.

14. Sheriff 1987, 96, 129.

15. W. T. Brown 1971, 119–21, 246.

16. Ibid., 100–104, 140–44.

17. Burton 1872, 2:267–70.

18. Glassman 1994, 64–68.

19. Sheriff 1987, 172–73.

20. Glassman 1994, 96–106.

21. Krapf to the lay secretary, Aug. 13, 1844, CMS, CA5/016/26 and Sept. 15, 1844, CMS, CA5/ML/492.

22. Krapf to the lay secretary, Sept. 25 , 1844, CMS, CA5/016/28.

23. Rebmann's journal, Feb. 11, 1848, CMS, CA5/024/52A.

24. Krapf's journal, Feb. 17, 1845, CMS, CA5/016/168; Krapf to the lay secretary, Aug. 26, 1845, CMS, CA5/016/44.

25. Thornton's journal, entry for Jun. 30, 1861, Royal Geographical Society, Thornton MA file.

26. Von der Decken 1869–79, 235.

27. Sheriff 1987, 54–55.

28. Cooper 1977, 98–103.

29. Erhardt to Venn, Oct. 27, 1854, CMS, CA5/09/14.

30. Cooper 1977, 85.

31. New 1873, 62.

32. Ibid., 54–55.

33. Guillain 1856, 2:235, 239.

34. New 1873, 54.

35. Sperling 1988, 85.

36. Morton 1976, 101–13.

37. Cooper 1977, 215.

38. Sperling 1988, 85–86.

39. New 1873, 58.

40. Krapf's journal, Feb. 17, 1845, CA5/016/168; Krapf to the lay secretary, Aug. 26, 1845, CMS, CA5/016/44.

41. Krapf to W. K. Fletcher, Sept. 15, 1844, CMS, CA5/ML/491.

42. Burton 1872: 2: 256.

43. Erhardt to Venn, Oct. 27, 1854, CMS, CA5/09/14.

44. "Notes on the Wasegeju of Vanga District," 1923, Kenya National Archives (KNA), DC/KWL/3/5; Hollis 1899.

45. McKay 1975, 154–57.

46. Sperling 1988, 46–47.

47. Ibid., 62–64.

48. File memo by C. Dundas, 1915, Political Record Book, KNA, DC/MSA/8/2.

49. Glassman 1994, 65–66.

50. Krapf to the lay secretary, Sept. 25, 1844, CMS, CA5/016/28.

51. Swantz 1956, 67.

52. Sperling 1988, 110–11, 120, 125–30.

53. Bethel Mission Archives, M/IL/1.5, Johanssen to Kandidatenkonvict, Tanga, Jul. 31, 1892, and M/IL/1. I 1, Uberblick uber besuchte Digodorfer, Feb. 27, 1911.

54. Bunger 1973, 57–79.

55. Kimambo 1996, 14; Sperling 1988, 147.

56. Nimtz 1980, 4–20.

57. Sperling 1988, 104–5.

58. King, Kasozi, and Oded 1973, 2–3.

59. Iliffe 1979, 40–52; Sheriff 1987, 172–79.

60. The prefix U- is used as the locative in Swahili. This usage is adopted for this chapter.

61. Stanley 1890, 65; Burton 1862, 293–94.

62. Burton 1862, 293–94.

63. Young and Fosbrooke 1960, 73–74.

64. Rigby 1966, 271–72.

65. Kimambo 1969, 21–24.

66. Erhardt to Venn, Dec. 27, 1853, CMS, CA5/09/11.

67. Becker 1968, 42.

68. Thompson 1983, 185–94.

69. "Account of a Journey to Madshame," by Rev. J. Rebmann, March/April 1849, CMS, CA5/024/54.

70. Itandala 1983, 221–224.

71. Bennett 1971, 25–29.

72. The description comes from the records of the White Fathers Mission at Kipalapala, six miles from Tabora, during the years 1883–1889, cited in Nolan 1977, 99–107.

73. Iliffe 1979, 67.

74. B. Brown 1971.

75. Alexis 1989, 153–54.

76. These were houses constructed from materials used in Nyamwezi buildings, but modified into the rectangular form of the traditional coastal dwelling. Similar structures were found wherever coastal peoples settled inland, as, for example, on the shores of Lake Malawi. See chapter 14.

77. Coulbois 1901, 68–69.

78. Murjebi 1974, 70–71.

79. See chapter 7.

80. "Political History of Baringo and Eldama Ravine Districts." KNA, PC/RVP, 8/1-A; Abdallah 1971; Mohammed 1983–84.

81. Oded 1974, 49–51.

82. Stanley 1890, 288.

83. Oded 1974, 65–81.

84. Gray 1961, 202.

85. King, Kasozi, and Oded 1973, 7–10; Oded 1974, 226–50.

86. Mackay 1890, 613.

87. Nicq 1884, 342.

88. Ibid., 343.

89. Pearson CMS 6/019. 618.

90. Kasozi 1974, 146–53.

91. Johnston 1902, 108–10.

92. Kasozi 1974, 176.

93. King, Kasozi, and Oded 1973, 31–48.

94. Becker 1968, 67.

95. Abrahams 1967, 80. Though published in 1967, Abrahams's survey is based on information he recorded in the 1957–60 period.

96. Kimambo 1996, 9–11.

97. Chande 1998, 6–8.

98. The authors gratefully acknowledge the help of Joel Pouwels, who kindly translated the material provided by Jose Kagabo from French into English.

Bibliography

Abdallah, M. A. 1971. "Some Aspects of Coastal and Islamic Influences in Mumias from the Late Nineteenth Century to the Early Twentieth Century." B.A. thesis, University of Nairobi.

Abel, A. 1960. *Les musulmans noirs du Manyema.* Brussels: Centre pour l'étude des problèmes du Monde Musulman Contemporain.

Abrahams, R. G. 1967. *The Peoples of Greater Unyamwezi.* London: International African Institute.

Alexis, M. G. 1989. *La traite des nègres et la croisade africaine.* Liege.

Alpers, E. A. 1975. *Ivory and Slaves in East Africa.* London: Heinemann.

Anciaux, L. 1879. *Le problème musulman dans l'Afrique Belge.* Brussels: Institut Royal Colonial Belge.

Ashe, R. P. 1894. *Two Kings of Uganda*. London: Low.

Baker, E. C. 1949. "Notes on the History of the Wasegeju." In *Tanganyika Notes and Records* 27:16–41.

Baker, S. W. 1979. *Ismailia: A Narrative of the Expedition to Central Africa for the Suppression of the Slave Trade*. London: Macmillan.

Becker, C. H. 1968. "Materials for the Understanding of Islam in German East Africa." In *Tanzania Notes and Records* 68, trans. B. G. Martin, 31–61.

Bennett, N. R. 1971. *Mirambo of Tanzania (1840-1884)*. Oxford: Oxford University Press.

Berg, F. J. 1971. "Mombasa under the Busaidi Sultanate: The City and Its Hinterland in the Nineteenth Century." Ph.D. diss., University of Wisconsin.

Bethel Mission Archives. M/II/1.5 and M/II/1.11.

Brown, B. 1971. "Muslim Influence on Trade and Politics in the Lake Tanganyika Region," *African Historical Studies* 4:617–30.

Brown, W. T. 1971. "A Pre-Colonial History of Bagamoyo: Aspects of the Growth of an East African Coastal Town." Ph.D. diss., Boston University.

Bunger, R. 1973. *Islamization among the Upper Pokomo*. Syracuse.

Burton, R. F. 1862. *Voyage aux Grands Lacs de l'Afrique Orientale*. Paris: Hachette.

———. 1872. *Zanzibar: City, Island, and Coast*. 2 vols. London: Tinsley.

Burton, R. F., and J. H. Speke. 1858. "A Coasting Voyage from Mombasa to the Pangani River," *Journal of the Royal Geographical Society* 28.

Ceulmans, P. *La question arabe et le Congo (1883–1892)*. Brussels: Académie Royale des Sciences Coloniales.

Chaltin, L. 1894. *La question arabe au Congo*. Brussels.

Chande, Abdin. 1998. *Islam, Ulamaa, and Community Development in Tanzania: A Study of Islamic Trends in Tanzania, East Africa*. San Francisco: Austin & Lawrier.

Church Missionary Society Archives (CMS). CA5 series.

Constantin, F. 1987. "Le saint et le prince: Sur les fondements de la dynamique confrérique en Afrique orientale." In *Les Voies de l'Islam en Afrique orientale*, ed. F. Constantin, 85–109. Paris: Karthala.

Cooper, F. 1977. *Plantation Slavery in East Africa*. New Haven: Yale University Press.

Coulbois, F. 1901. *Dix années au Tanganyika*. Limoges.

Emery, [James]. 1833. "Short Account of Mombas and the Neighbouring Coast of Africa," *Journal of the Royal Geographical Society* 3:280–83.

Fouquer, R. P. 1966. *Mirambo*. Paris: Nouvelles Editions Latines.

Glassman, J. 1994. *Feasts and Riot: Revelry, Rebellion, and Popular Consciousness on the Swahili Coast (1856–1888)*. London: Heinemann.

Gray, J. 1947. "Ahmed ben Ibrahim: The First Arab to Arrive in Buganda." In *Tanganyika Notes and Records* 11/12:80–97.

———. 1961. "Ismail Pacha and Sir Samuel Baker." In *Tanganyika Notes and Records* 25/2:199–213.

Guillain, C. 1856. *Documents sur l'Histoire, le Géographie, et le Commerce de l'Afrique Orientale.* 3 vols. Paris: Bertrand.

Hansen, H. B. 1984. *Missionary, Church, and State in a Colonial Setting: Uganda 1890–1925.* London: Heinemann.

Hollis, A. C. 1899. "The Wasegeju," Rhodes House, MSS. Afr. s. 1272 a,b.

Iliffe, John. 1979. *A Modern History of Tanganyika.* Cambridge: Cambridge University Press.

Itandala, A. Buluda. 1983. "A History of the Babinza of Usukuma, Tanzania, to 1890." Ph.D. diss., Dalhousie University.

Johnston, Harry H. 1902. *The Uganda Protectorate.* London: Hutchison.

Kagabo, J. H. 1987. "La formation des 'walimu' au Rwanda." In *Les Voies de l'Islam en Afrique orientale,* ed. F. Constantin, 73–83. Paris: Karthala.

———. 1988. *L'Islam at les Swahili au Rwanda.* Paris: Editions de l'Ecole des Hautes Etudes en Sciences Sociales.

Kagwa, A. 1947. "Extracts from Mengo 4," *Uganda Journal* 11/12:110–22.

———. 1971. *The Kings of Buganda.* Kampala: East African Publishing.

Kasozi, Abdu B. 1974. "The Spread of Islam in Uganda (1844–1945)." Ph.D. diss., University of California, Santa Cruz.

Kavulu, D. 1969. *Uganda Martyrs.* Kampala: Longmans of Uganda.

Kimambo, I. 1969. *The Political History of the Pare of Tanzania (c. 1500–1900).* Nairobi: East African Publishing.

———. 1996. "The Impact of Christianity among the Zaramo: A Case Study of Maneromango Lutheran Parish." Conference paper. Reprinted 1999 in *East African Expressions of Christianity,* ed. T. Spear and I. N. Kimambo, 63–82. Athens: Ohio University Press.

King, N. Q., A. Kasozi, and A. Oded. 1973. *Islam and the Confluence of Religions in Uganda, 1840–1966.* Tallahassee: American Academy of Religion.

Kiwanuka, M. S. M. 1971. *A History of Buganda, from the Foundations of the Kingdom to 1900.* London: Longmans.

Koffsky, P. L. 1971. "History of Takaungu, East Africa (1830–1896)." Ph.D. diss., University of Wisconsin.

Lamphear, J. 1970. "The Kamba and the Northern Mrima Coast." In *Pre-Colonial African Trade,* ed. R. Gray and D. Birmingham, 75–101. London: Oxford University Press.

Lodhi, A. Y. 1973. *The Institution of Slavery in Zanzibar and Pemba.* Uppsala: Scandinavian Institute of African Studies.

Mackay, A. 1890. *A. M. Mackay: Pioneer Missionary of the Church Missionary Society in Uganda.* New York: Armstrong.

McKay, W. F. 1975. "A Pre-Colonial History of the Southern Kenya Coast." Ph.D. diss., Boston University.

Mohammed, H. K. 1983–84. "Some Aspects of Islam in Kitui (c. 1890–1963)." Dept. of History, University of Nairobi: Staff Seminar Paper.

Morton, R. F. 1976. "Slaves, Fugitives, and Freedmen on the Kenya Coast, 1873–1907." Ph.D. diss., Syracuse University.

el-Murjebi, Hamed M. 1974. *Maisha ya Hamed bin Muhammed El Murjebi, Yaani Tippu Tip, Kwa Maneno Yake Mwenyewe.* Nairobi: East African Literature Bureau.

New, C. 1873. *Life, Wanderings, and Labours in Eastern Africa.* London.

Nicholls, C. S. 1971. The Swahili Coast: Politics, Diplomacy and Trade on the East African Littoral, 1798–1856. London: Allen and Unwin.

Nicq, A. 1884. *Le Père Simeon Lourdel de la Société des Pères Blancs et les premières années de la mission de Ouganda.* Maison Cance: Imprimerie des Missionaires d'Afrique.

Nimtz, A. H. 1980. *Islam and Politics in East Africa: the Sufi Order in Tanzania.* Minneapolis: University of Minnesota Press.

Nolan, F. P. 1977. "Christianity in Unyamwezi (1878–1928)." Ph.D. diss., Cambridge University.

Oded, A. 1974. *Islam in Uganda: Islamization through a Centralized State in Pre-colonial Africa.* New York: Wiley.

Pères Blancs, Les. 1884. *A l'assaut des pays nègres: Journal des missionaires d'Alger dans l'Afrique équatoriale.* Lille.

———. 1885. *Près des Grands Lacs.* Paris.

Pouwels, R. L. 1987. *Horn and Crescent: Cultural Change and Traditional Islam on the East African Coast (800–1900).* Cambridge: Cambridge University Press.

Rigby, P. J. A. 1966. "Sociological Factors in the Contact of the Gogo of Central Tanzania with Islam." In *Islam in Tropical Africa,* ed. I. M. Lewis, 268–90. Oxford: Oxford University Press.

Sheriff, Abdul. 1987. *Slaves, Spices, and Ivory in Zanzibar.* London: James Currey.

Sperling, D. C. 1988. "The Growth of Islam among the Mijikenda of the Kenya Coast (1826–1933)." Ph.D. diss., University of London.

Stanley, H. M. 1890. *In Darkest Africa.* 2 vols. London: Low.

Swantz, Lloyd. 1956. "The Zaramo of Tanzanyika." M.A. thesis, Syracuse University.

Thompson, G. 1983. "The Merchants and Merchandise of Religious Change: The New Orthodoxies of Religious Belief amongst the Shambaa People of Mlalo, North East Tanzania." Ph.D. diss., Cambridge University.

von der Decken, C. Claus. 1869–79. *Baron Carl von der Deckens Reisen in Ost-Afrika in den Jahren 1859 bis 1865.* Leipzig & Heidelberg: C. F. Winter.

Weber, Max. 1966. *The City.* Trans. and ed. Don Martindale and Gertrud Neuwirth. New York: Free Press.

Ylvisaker, M. 1979. *Lamu in the Nineteenth Century: Land, Trade, and Politics.* Boston: African Studies Center, Boston University.

Young, R., and H. Fosbrooke. 1960. *Smoke in the Hills: Land and Politics among the Luguru of Tanganyika.* London: Routledge & Kegan Paul.

CHAPTER 14

East Central Africa

Edward A. Alpers

Historically, East Central Africa stands at the margin of the Islamic world. Although Arab traders probably introduced Islam to the coast of modern Mozambique no later than the thirteenth century and a small community of Muslims existed in the Zambezi valley during the fifteenth and sixteenth centuries, Islam did not begin to take root in the interior of East Central Africa until the nineteenth century. In the last hundred years, however, Islam has steadily increased the number of its adherents in the region, (precise numbers are not available and estimates vary widely, depending on the source). Moreover, while Muslims remain a minority, they are a distinct grouping that is increasingly becoming a force to be reckoned with on the national level in Malawi and Mozambique. How and why this has come about is the focus of this chapter.

Specifically, the chapter explores the history of Islamic expansion and the development of Islamic communities in East Central Africa from the end of the fifteenth century to the present. At the same time, however, it analyzes the way in which the attitudes and policies of both the colonial regimes and independent governments of Malawi and Mozambique, as well as the wider Islamic world, have affected and continue to affect these Muslim communities; it also connects this history to the wider experience of Islam in eastern and southern Africa. The scope of the chapter includes northern Mozambique and Malawi, with brief reference to Zambia and Zimbabwe, whose much smaller Muslim communities are closely bound up with those of, in particular, Malawi.

Early History

The early history of Islam in East Central Africa is intimately linked to the extension of Muslim trading communities along the coast and offshore islands of the western Indian Ocean. At the end of the fifteenth century, when the Portuguese intruded into this trading complex, the most important of the southern coastal communities was Sofala, which was subordinate to Kilwa. In the early sixteenth century, Gaspar Correa recorded that the ruling Moors of Sofala "were native Kaffirs who turned Moors owing to their dealings and friendship with foreign Moorish merchants who came to Sofala to trade," and Duarte Barbosa noted that some Muslims spoke Arabic.[1] By the end of the third decade of the century, the Portuguese had effectively driven out most Muslims from this once thriving commercial outpost, leaving only very small communities around Sofala and south as far as Bazaruto Island. Yet even under these reduced circumstances, Islam apparently survived with enough vitality for a local saint's tomb and mosque, dedicated to one Mwinyi Muhammad, to have flourished in the late sixteenth century on an island opposite the Portuguese fort at Sofala.[2]

Representatives of this Muslim maritime commercial community settled the coast of northern Mozambique later than they populated Sofala. They came probably during the fifteenth century, as a consequence of the reorientation of the gold trade from the southern plateau of Zimbabwe, for which Sofala and related ports were natural outlets, toward the Zambezi valley, to which towns like Mozambique Island, Angoche, and Quelimane gave readier access. When Vasco da Gama visited Mozambique Island in 1498, he observed that its inhabitants were "of the Mahommedan sect and speak like Moors" (presumably a way of saying they spoke Arabic). He noted further that the sultan of Mozambique sent "as ambassador a white Moor" and "while we were here there came a Moor . . . aboard one of our ships saying he would come with us because he was from the neighbourhood of Mecca and had come here to Mozambique as a pilot on one of the ships of these lands."[3] Two decades later, Barbosa observed that the sultan himself was a *sharif*, although the governor of Mozambique reported from the same time that there was no Muslim there who could read a letter written (presumably in Arabic) to him from Sofala.[4] Here is certain evidence of significant links to the wider Islamic world. At mid-sixteenth century, the Portuguese still maintained some dialogue with the local Muslim community. A few years later, tensions between Muslims and Roman Catholics came to a head, and with official consent, a Franciscan friar "pulled down a mosque in the village where the Mozambican Moors dwell."[5]

The only indication that Islam penetrated the interior during this era comes from the Zimbabwe plateau—the source of the gold upon which the trade of Kilwa and Sofala was based, where we know Muslim traders, whether Arabs, Swahili, or Islamized Shona, were well-established until the arrival of the Portuguese. Beach, however, suggests that their number probably never exceeded fifteen hundred to two thousand. As Portuguese presence up the Zambezi and on the Zimbabwe plateau increased during the first three-quarters of the sixteenth century, Muslim presence declined, although a Muslim sharif was granted title to a small territory by the Mutapa in the 1630s, and a sharif (perhaps the same individual) was involved in the Torwa civil war of the 1640s that occasioned the killing of many Muslims. Those

Muslims who remained on the plateau subsequently became "more and more ab-sorbed into the Shona world, to become the Lemba groups scattered across the Plateau, groups that retained little more than fragments of the Islamic faith and cul-ture."[6] Indeed, the Lemba, who are often lumped together with other Muslims as *mwenye*, "claim that their ancestors descended from Muslim Arabs or at least had direct contact with them."[7] Although the Lemba, whose clan names indicate Arab influence, apparently observed certain social practices that showed the influence of Islam, they did not follow the faith until they were discovered by local Asian Mus-lims in 1961; the Asians have since initiated a program of "re-Islamization" among the Lemba. The fact remains, however, that by the mid-seventeenth century, Islam was generally not a factor of any significance in the interior.

Coastal northern Mozambique remained distinctly Muslim—Swahili at its northern extreme toward Cape Delgado, and shading off into Makua-speaking communities toward Angoche. We know virtually nothing about Islam in these communities during this period, although it is safe to state that they maintained communication among themselves and beyond Cape Delgado by way of coastal trading, and also remained firmly embedded in the commercial networks of the Mozambique Channel through trade with the Comoro Islands and the Muslim ports of northwestern Madagascar. Muslims lived interspersed with their Makua-speaking neighbors, with whom they no doubt established marriage ties and from whom they probably attracted occasional converts, but who generally maintained their own ancestor-based religion. There is no evidence whatsoever during this pe-riod that Islam particularly flourished or sought to extend the *umma*, which seems to accord with what we know from eastern Africa in general.

Beginning in the early eighteenth century, there are some indications that Islam may have begun to experience a slow revival. In the 1720s, the Portuguese imposed a flurry of economically motivated restrictions on Muslim Indians at Mozambique Is-land. This was followed in 1736 by a viceregal order from Goa against "the [Indian] Moors and Gentiles [that is, Hindus] preaching their laws to the Cafres." Several years later, the archbishop of Mozambique lamented Muslim success in conversion when compared with the failure of the church. He noted their easy access to Quelimane, So-fala, and Inhambane, citing especially the latter for the free exercise of the Muslim re-ligion. Not surprisingly, soon he argued against Muslims exercising their beliefs at all.[8] In 1750, new restrictions on Muslims owning slaves were imposed because Muslim owners indoctrinated the slaves with "their damned Mohammedan faith."[9] Although there is no mention of Muslim proselytizing activity in the vicinity of Mozambique Is-land, in 1759 five Indian Muslims were returned to the colonial capital from Inham-bane, where they had organized Muslim schools for the local Africans.[10] About the same time, the lieutenant-general of the Rivers complained bitterly that Muslim traders from Sanculo, a small polity on the mainland just south of Mozambique Is-land, were both trading illegally and zealously preaching Islam among the Africans around Murambala, north of the Zambezi and east of the Shire rivers from Sena.[11] Whether the evidence we possess reflects actual Muslim proselytization or Portuguese

Catholic rhetoric in a struggle to control trade is difficult to determine; at the very least, however, it suggests that there may have been a gradual increase in Muslim presence inland in conjunction with the rise of Arab-Swahili commercial expansion in the eighteenth century.

The Long Nineteenth Century: From Busaidi Zanzibar to Colonial Conquest

The revival of Islam in East Central Africa coincided with the rise of the Busaidi sultanate of Zanzibar. In this sense it paralleled the initial growth of Islam during the pre-Portuguese period, with commercial expansion linked to wider dissemination of the faith. For not only was Zanzibar the commercial center of East African trade, it became also the center for a rejuvenated Sunni Islam, which paradoxically flourished under the Omani Ibadite rulers. The penetration of Islam closely followed the trade routes linking coast to interior, the most important locus being Kilwa, with Angoche a secondary point of entry for Islam. Despite its commercial significance, Mozambique Island was an inhospitable environment for Islam. Slave raiding among the Makua of the Mozambique hinterland may have compounded the situation, for the routes connecting that section of the coast to the interior seem not to have provided a viable entry point for Islam at this time; and when the Portuguese abolished slave trading in the mid-nineteenth century, that seems to have precipitated closer commercial and political alliances between coastal Muslims, or Swahili, and some of their Makua neighbors, providing fertile ground for conversion to Islam.

There is some evidence, however, that as early as the 1770s there may have been an initial expansion of Islam in Macuana, the immediate hinterland of Mozambique Island, that coincided with the first significant period of Swahili slave trading in the interior. One Portuguese governor complained in 1772 that Muslims had introduced circumcision in the region and built mosques.[12] One strategy that reflects commercial collaboration was for important coastal Muslims to marry the daughters of Makua chiefs, although, since Makua culture was strongly matrilineal, it is not at all clear that such marriages ought to be considered as part of a pattern of Islamic conversion. A well-informed source in 1789 observed of Angoche that the Muslims who journeyed through the interior were "diligent missionaries" for their faith.[13] If the reported estimates at the beginning of the nineteenth century (fifteen thousand Muslims in the Cape Delgado region; twenty thousand in the coastal hinterland of Mozambique Island) are even remotely correct, then it may be safe to assume that at least some of these Muslims were Makua converts.

During the first half of the nineteenth century—though we lack details—it appears that influences from the Zanzibar sultanate had permeated northern coastal Mozambique and invigorated both Muslim commerce and religious activity. The first solid indication we possess of the latter comes from oral traditions reported about the youth of Musa Momadi Sabo, who later would become a major economic and political figure at Angoche known as Musa Quanto. The young Musa accompanied a relative of his—a man who was a sharif and a *hajji*—on an extended proselytizing mission deep into the interior, as far as the north bank of the Zambesi and the valley of the Lugenda River. Upon his return to the coast, he traveled to Mozambique Island, Zanzibar, the Comoros, and northwest Madagascar, before returning home in the mid-1850s. Whether or not Musa Quanto's efforts from 1862 to 1877 to extend the Angoche sultanate militarily can be described as a jihad is doubtful; but there can be little question that his entire project was embedded in the Islamic networks of the Mozambique Channel, and thereby of the western Indian Ocean.[14] Musa Quanto is usually the central figure of this story, but it is his relative, whose only goal was reportedly "to convert barbarians and infidels to belief in the Prophet," who interests us here. According to one source, his efforts reached as far as the Yao, some of whom by that time would have already migrated into the Shire valley.[15] If there were others like him at this time they remain unknown to us, but his journey was a harbinger of things to come a generation later.

A report by the governor of Mozambique in 1852 refers to "the extraordinary Muslim advance, its infiltration into the interior, and respective miscegenation."[16] This advance appears to have been uneven, however; according to Livingstone's Arab guide at Cape Delgado in 1866, no attempt was made to convert the Makonde, although Makonde slaves at the coast had become Muslims. When Elton traveled in the coastal hinterland of Mozambique in 1875–76, Islam was well-established in specific localities, and some Makua chiefs sported Arab garb, even if they were not themselves Muslims. By the early 1890s, according to a survey of the new Nyasa Company territories, many Makua were reported to have adopted Islam, "thanks to their relations with Arab and Indian Muslims." Others had taken to wearing Muslim dress, as was also the case among a number of Makonde chiefs.[17] A different example from the Mozambique hinterland of the way in which Islamic and indigenous forms of belief were gradually being mediated was the practice of judging one's innocence by "eating without vomiting an uncooked ball of rice flour in which is written a phrase from the Quran."[18]

As for the Yao of northwestern Mozambique and southern Malawi, whose very identity is today bound up with Islam, although they had traded to the coast since at least the early seventeenth century, their conversion also dates to no earlier than the nineteenth century. Individual Yao from up-country may have adopted Islam in the past, or at least assumed its practices for as long as they remained at the coast, but the first regular appearance of Islam farther inland seems to have been the Muslim traders and scribes who accompanied coastal caravans as they penetrated the interior during the first decades of the nineteenth century. Kubik suggests that Chief Makanjila Banali, who is generally regarded as the first Yao convert to Islam, in about 1870, visited Zanzibar as early as 1830 and may have converted sooner than previously thought.[19] Coastal attire became fashionable among the Yao, and Yao chiefs consciously sought to implant coastal style at their towns. By the mid-1880s, most major Yao chiefs had embraced Islam, and their towns were centers for Muslim proselytization and Quran education. For example, Roman Catholic missionaries reported in 1891 that there were twelve Quran schools, each with its own *mwalimu,* at Mponda's important Yao town at the confluence of Lake Malawi and the Shire River. At about the same time, Coutinho records meeting Yao caravan chiefs at Quelimane who "say they are Muslims, and some, in fact, carry the Quran religiously wrapped up in a fold of their cloth," although he goes on to note that some Muslims ridiculed their claim and said they practice fetishism.[20] The conversion of Yao chiefs at this time after so long an association with the coast without conversion can be explained by a complex set of factors including closer association with Muslim trading partners at the coast and increased coastal prestige, particularly deriving from the Busaidi regime at Zanzibar; the desire for the ability to correspond in writing with the coast; the consolidation of chiefly authority with the support of Islam as an ideology of governance; the role of Swahili scribes and traders, not least for their knowledge of Islamic charms, which had particular salience during this stressful half century; and resistance to encroaching colonial rule.

Parallel with these developments, two small but influential Swahili communities were established on the shores of Lake Malawi. The earlier and more robust was at Nkhotakota around 1840, where Salim b. 'Abdulla established a trading town on the western shore, converted his mainly Chewa followers to Islam, and established indirect rule over neighboring Chewa chiefs. He and successive Jumbes of Nkhotakota cultivated their ties to Zanzibar; according to oral tradition, "to promote the chiefs' loyalty they encouraged them to send their sons and nephews to Zanzibar where they underwent Islamic rites and instruction." A much smaller Muslim community was established by a Swahili *shaykh* from southern Tanzania around 1880 at Karonga, at the north end of the lake, under the political protection of the coastal Arab trader Mlozi.[21]

After centuries of lethargy, the Portuguese finally began to assert their paper claims to northern Mozambique, while the British sought to bring what was to become Malawi under effective control. The effect of this combined assault was to sharpen Muslim identities in opposition to European, Christian, and anti-slave-trading imperialism. This confrontation also yields the first coherent body of evidence on grassroots Islam in East Central Africa, as Europeans finally left the relative security of coastal outposts and struck inland. According to a Roman Catholic missionary at Quelimane in 1893, although most African Muslims had only adopted "certain exterior practices" of the religion, Arab proselytization was active and effective among the Africans of the Licungo River and Maganja da Costa, north of Quelimane. Five Arabs had established a school at the mouth of the Moniga River, about one hundred miles north from Quelimane, where they lived very simply, recruiting their disciples and students mainly along the coast.

> When a child enters that school, the first condition that is imposed on him
> is to embrace the religion of Muhammad, then the father of the child ac-

cepts the obligation to furnish a domestic servant to the Arabs as a slave when the child has completed his studies.

These studies are ordinarily completed in three years, during which time the child is taught to read and write in Arabic, not Portuguese; a little medicine is also taught; on completion of his studies the disciple takes the name of *Malimu* [*mwalimu*] and is *doctor*. Upon fulfillment of payment by his father, he then returns to his kin and his people and exercises his art among them, taking little advantage from his knowledge.[22]

Here for the first time we have solid evidence of a missionary strategy for the propagation of Islam in East Central Africa.

Islam Takes Off: Shaykhs and Sufis (c. 1890s–1960s)

The Portuguese conquest of northern Mozambique was difficult and protracted; for the Portuguese it also assumed the character of a modern crusade against the combined forces of Islam and paganism. Not surprisingly, the Portuguese found the success of Muslim proselytization worrisome, especially when contrasted with the miserable failure of Roman Catholicism in gaining converts. They feared Muslim alliances with African chiefs in opposition to Portuguese rule and influence and specifically attacked Muslim strongholds in their campaigns to establish effective colonial domination. At the very beginning of the century, the region of Angoche is reported to have supported fifteen mosques and ten Quran schools. "Nearly all the *monhés* [a term applied to mixed Afro-Muslims, as opposed to Swahili, i.e., coastal, Muslims] know to write their language in Arabic characters. On the island of Angoche, there are even numerous Swahili women who know how to read and write."[23] This was a specter the Portuguese could not bear, and in 1903 they sacked the town of the sultan of Angoche, destroying its houses and mosques.[24] Nevertheless, during the first decade of this century, Muslim communities with Quran schools are reported to have been a growing force in the coastal hinterland. According to a 1905 report on education and missions, Islam was spread peacefully by Muslim traders, on the one hand, but also by "the *manlimos* [*walimu*] and charifos [*sharifs*], with their religio-magical knowledge," and "the innumerable *mafundi* (masters) in the villages, in any hut, on a verandah, or under the shade of a tree as school, [who] teach children Swahili . . . the lingua franca from the coast to Zambezia," which it was feared created "a community of thought across extensive regions" and facilitated opposition to Portuguese influence.[25] On the mainland north of Ibo, the most influential individual at the beginning of the century was a wealthy Muslim named Haji Musa b. Yusufu. Quirambo island was noteworthy for "a tomb venerated because it is said to contain the remains of a holy sharif who came from Angoche a long time ago."[26] Clearly, Islam was alive and well along the coast.

Around Lake Malawi, there are further signs of greatly increased Islamic activity during the period of colonial conquest, which although it ended for those

Africans who came under British hegemony in 1899, persisted for those who found themselves in Portuguese territory until 1912. In practice, Muslim proselytization paid little attention to these borders, although the lingering armed struggle by Yao chiefs against Portuguese domination surely reinforced the emerging Yao sense of cultural distinctiveness as an increasingly Muslim people. According to Greenstein, "*Pax Britannica* permitted a freedom and security of movement that enabled the *'ulama'*, and would-be *'ulama'*, to travel peacefully in their 'shaykh-seeking' endeavours."[27] Perhaps even more significantly, the British alliance with conservative Yao Muslim chiefs in the aftermath of the Chilembwe Rising of 1915 caused the colonial regime in Nyasaland to refuse to allow Christian missionaries to establish stations and schools in the villages of Muslim chiefs unless they were invited to do so, which created an environment in which Islam could grow and flourish.[28]

The quintessential member of this class was Shaykh 'Abdallah b. Haji Mkwanda (c.1860–1930), the son of a prominent ivory trader (and probable slave trader) who was born at the town of the important Yao chief Makanjila. Greenstein considers 'Abdallah "undoubtedly the individual most responsible for Muslim expansion in Malawi." He began his studies as a boy at Kilwa in about 1870 and was instructed in all the major Islamic texts of the day, including works on law and the preparation of amulets and talismans. He returned to the lake in about 1884 and spent the rest of his life propagating the faith throughout the lake region and pursuing his business interests. Many young men studied with him to earn their *ijaza* and themselves become Muslim teachers, including Shaykh Issa Chikoka, "who had great influence on Muslim activities on the Mozambique side of the lake."[29] Shaykh 'Abdallah's most famous disciple was Shaykh Thabit b. Muhammad Ngaunje (c.1880–1959), a second-generation Muslim born near Mtengula, Mozambique, whose importance in spreading Islam among the Yao of southern Malawi is confirmed by Thorold's informants.[30]

Men like these regularly worked both sides of the colonial border during this era, as they also regularly traveled to Lindi, Mikindani, and Kilwa on the southern Tanzanian coast, and in some cases as far as Zanzibar and Mombasa for additional study or to obtain religious literature. To take one more example, the most prominent apostle of Islam among the Yao of northwestern Mozambique was Shaykh Mzee Chiwaula, who studied at Nkhotakota, where one of the leading shaykhs was a Mozambique-born Yao, before returning to the Lichinga plateau and converting the Yao masses to Islam.[31] In addition to this local leadership, Islam was also propagated in some communities by African Muslims from the coast and the Tanzanian interior, but the enduring connection was always Zanzibar. It should not surprise us, then, to be reminded that for the Muslims of East Central Africa, Zanzibar and its sultan, generically referred to by variations on the name of Sultan Barghash b. Sa'id (1870–88) throughout this period, symbolically represented the center of Islamic learning and prestige.

Between the last few years of the nineteenth century and the middle of the following decade, the two major sufi *tariqas* in East Africa, the Shadhiliyya and the

Qadiriyya, were implanted at Mozambique Island, which became a focal point for the expansion of Islam inland during the following decade. By 1920, the Qadiriyya was also gaining adherents around Lake Malawi, though its reference point remained primarily the Tanzania coast, rather than that of Mozambique.

The Shadhiliyya took its lead from Shaykh Muhammad Maʿruf b. Shaykh Ahmed b. Abi Bakr (1853–1905). A Hadrami sharif, he joined the Yashruti branch of the tariqa while in Zanzibar, returning to his home in Moroni, Ngazidja, the largest of the Comoro Islands, to preach its message—a process of religious revivalism that often put him in conflict with established Muslim authorities, who were probably members of the rival Alawiyya. His most famous khalifa, Shaykh Husayn b. Mahmud, established an important school at Kilwa that attracted students from as far afield as Mozambique. In 1896, Shaykh Amir b. Jimba of Moroni, also a member of the Yashrutiyya and a trader based at Zanzibar, settled at Mozambique from Madagascar. A year later, Shaykh Maʿruf visited Mozambique Island for a month and, after granting ijaza to two individuals, he left them as joint leaders of his particular branch of the tariqa Shadhiliyya Yashrutiyya.[32]

Whatever Maʿruf's reasons for acknowledging these men rather than Shaykh Amir as his khalifas, the latter succeeded in asserting his control over the local tariqa. The contest for power was serious enough that the following year, Shaykh Maʿruf's brother was sent to Mozambique to adjudicate its resolution. The details of leadership are less important than the recognition that from the very beginning of its establishment at Mozambique, the tariqa became an object of significant local struggle and, eventually, of division along lines that reflected socioeconomic divisions rather than the sectarian questions that masked these differences. Eventually, these manifested themselves in a great scission in 1924–25 that led to a new branch of the order, the Shadhiliyya E'Madhania, that was established by direct intervention from the mother house of the order at Medina. A decade later, in 1936, another group broke away from the Yashrutiyya to form a new order called Itifaque.[33] Thorold suggests that the Shadhiliyya, which Greenstein indicates was especially strong in parts of southern Malawi, such as Makanjila, entered the lake region from Mozambique. This makes sense in view of the close connections between Makanjila and Quelimane and the more general set of Islamic relationships linking Mozambique, Angoche, and the Comoros (referred to above), although it is possible that Shaykh Husayn's well-established school at Kilwa was influential in its dissemination to Malawi.

The Qadiriyya had many branches in eastern Africa, two of which are important for East Central Africa. The most important branch was established by Shaykh ʿAli Msemakweli, a khalifa of Shaykh Husayn b. ʿAbd Allah al-Muʿin and a Yao, who spread the order to Kilwa, Lindi, and thence inland to northwestern Mozambique and Malawi. Shaykh Husayn's branch of the order preceded the better-known branch of the Bravanese Shaykh Uways b. Muhammad by about a decade at Zanzibar, taking root in the mid-1870s. In the mid-1920s, Shaykh Mtira, a khalifa of the important branch established at Bagamoyo in 1905 and vigorously led by its first khalifa, Shaykh Yahya b. 'Abd Allah, known as Shaykh Ramiya (d. 1931), took this branch of the Qadiriyya to Malawi. A branch of the Qadriyya known as Sadate was also established at Mozambique in 1904, when Shaykh Isa b. Ahmad arrived at the island from Zanzibar.[34] In 1925, Shaykh Isa returned to Zanzibar, delegating authority to his khalifa Momade Arune, who was also a court official in the colonial regime.

About this time, a subordinate branch of the Qadiriyya Sadate was founded at Angoche. After Momade Arune's death in 1929, however, the tariqa was split by rivalries for leadership, which ultimately led to the formation of a new branch in 1934 (Qadiriyya Bagdad). Scarcely a decade later, new tensions caused a further rift, and in 1945 the Qadiriyya Jailane was established on the island, while in 1953 yet another split from the Bagdad branch resulted in the creation of the Qadiriyya Bagdad Hujate Saliquine. Finally, following the assumption in 1963 of leadership of the Sadate branch by Haji Mahamudo Selemangy, a descendant of Daman Muslims whose origins were in Gujarat and a resident of the mainland, disaffected members on the island broke away to form a fifth branch of the Qadiriyya in Mozambique, the Macheraba. By the 1930s, we also know that Mecufi, south of Pemba in Cabo Delgado, was an important center of Qadiriyya activity and teaching under the leadership of Abdul Magid.[35]

There are few published sources for Mozambique that provide details of how the tariqas spread to the interior or even along the coastal hinterland. Carvalho notes that for the first two decades of the twentieth century, the two tariqas restricted their activities to the immediate coastal hinterland. But beginning in the second decade, three developments combined to facilitate the expansion inland of Islam and the tariqas: the presence after 1916 of more than six thousand British colonial troops, most of them Muslims; the advance of Muslim Indian commerce beyond the coast; and the construction of the railroad inland from Lumbo, on the mainland opposite Mozambique Island, from 1913. This general expansion of Islam caused the tariqas at Mozambique "to create branches in the principal settlements of Nampula and Cabo Delgado, constructing mosques with local materials for the men and *zawiyas* (enclosed spaces) for the women." Each location had a representative of the tariqa from the island. Carvalho attributes the segmentation of the tariqas to this expansion, and indeed growth may have been a precipitating factor; but he is closer to the mark, I think, when he observes that "the brotherhoods were, in fact, great political and religious constituencies of the different factions of local society."[36]

Turning to the lake region, most of the individuals who brought the message of the two tariqas to the interior were second-generation young men who had been initially trained by the pioneering shaykhs discussed above. Individually and separately, they generally made their way to the coast and after a few years of study returned, in the 1920s and 1930s, to introduce their tariqas to their homelands. Most of Greenstein's evidence concerns those who embraced the Qadiriyya at Zanzibar, since that order became the most popular in Malawi, but he includes information on at least one individual who obtained his Shadhiliyya ijaza at Dar es Salaam.

It is especially noteworthy that Shaykh Mtumwa bt. 'Ali b. Yusufu, "the most important woman in Malawi Islamic history," introduced the Qadiriyya at Nkhotakota in 1929, having studied and received her ijaza at Zanzibar. Her leadership and teaching brought many women into an active role in the revitalized umma through the use of tariqa banners, *dhikr,* and occasions for collective religious celebration.[37] Although there seem not to have been any parallels to her leadership or evidence that there was an increase in women's participation in Islam as a result of the spread of the tariqas in Mozambique, there are a few indications that women may have experienced greater visibility and agency in the umma through the tariqas than previously obtained.

Islam challenged historical cultural practices, particularly with respect to kinship and inheritance, among the matrilineal societies of East Central Africa. The strongly patrilineal social order of Islam provided the first Yao chiefs to convert with a patrilateral means by which to attach slave women and children to their own matrilineages, and sons of chiefs figure prominently among the first generation of young men sent to the coast for religious training. Nevertheless, customary law and matrilinearity prevailed among the Yao throughout the colonial era. Similarly, an important feature of Islam that emerged during this period was the partial Islamization of pre-Islamic religious practices among the Yao. Indigenous boys' initiation ceremonies involving partial circumcision became transformed into *jando,* deriving from the coast, which introduced them into Islam and entailed full circumcision. Feasts associated with the end of mourning and those connected with ancestor veneration became known as *sadaka* and were supervised by a Muslim authority.[38]

This situation was paralleled among the Makua, where the tension between indigenous matrilineal social principles and the patrilineal order of Islam may have been more pronounced. For example, when in 1940 ʿAbdul Kamal-Megama succeeded his matrilineal uncle as *mwene* of his lineage in Chiure, Cabo Delgado Province, he abandoned his positions as shaykh and mwalimu in the Qadiriyya, although he certainly continued to practice his religion and made the pilgrimage in 1963.[39]

One of the most interesting aspects of tariqa-dominated Islam during the colonial period was the emergence of a major dispute between the *twaliki* and *sukuti* in both Malawi and northwestern Mozambique; that is to say, primarily among the Yao, although Nkhotakota was also involved. The twaliki (derived from tariqa) celebrated funerals and other religious celebrations by performing dhikr (called *sikiri* by the Yao) with drumming and loud chanting and waving tariqa flags; the sukuti (from Swahili *sukutu,* "be silent") opposed such vocal displays and argued strenuously for a more dignified, quietist approach to such ceremonies, and to Islam in general. So heated did this dispute eventually become that in 1949 the British colonial government invited Sharif ʿAbdul Hasan b. Ahamed Jamali Laili, a respected scholar from Zanzibar, to visit Nyasaland to arbitrate. He held meetings attended by thousands at Mangochi, among the Yao, and at Nkhotakota, though in the end he was unable to get them to resolve their differences.[40] In 1968 and 1972, the same dispute surfaced at Angoche over proper demeanor at funerals. The disagreement was sufficiently serious in the former instance to require Shaykh Momade Saide Mujabo of Mozambique Island, who was widely respected for his "independence and moderation of conduct," to issue what amounts to a compromise *fatwa* determining that funerals should be celebrated "in a normal voice"—neither shouting nor in silence.[41] Earlier interpretations of this struggle over the character of Islam in East Central Africa suggest that it reflected either a division within the Qadiriyya over practice or differences between the Qadiriyya and the Shadhiliyya; however, Thorold argues persuasively that in fact this dispute reveals an internal reformist tendency opposing sufi practices, especially dhikr.

Whereas British colonial policy toward Islam in Malawi was marked by relative restraint and tolerance, such was not the case with the Portuguese in northern Mozambique, where hysteria and paranoia often ruled the day. The Portuguese never abandoned the spirit of Roman Catholic crusade that characterized their self-delusionary "civilizing mission," and these fears had real consequences for their policy toward Islam. Such fears were sustained by the fact that Mozambican Muslims looked to Zanzibar as the regional center of Sunni Islam and a major source of Islamic publications; to its sultan as their spiritual protector (notwithstanding his own nonconformist beliefs as an Ibadi, calling upon his name during the *khutba* at Friday prayers); and to the fact that the leader of the Qadiriyya Sadate at Mozambique Island from 1929 to 1963 referred to himself as the sultan's representative to Mozambique, while a late 1960s survey of Islamic leaders throughout the entire colony found that 176, all from the north, recognized the sultan of Zanzibar as their imam, even though this was theologically impossible.[42]

In this context, Portuguese fears were accordingly exacerbated by incidents like the "Mecca letter" scare of 1908, which mobilized anticolonial sentiment among East African Muslims, and the defense of Ethiopia letters that circulated in both Cabo Delgado and Mozambique Districts in 1937. In the latter instance, because they believed these letters to have been circulated by Muslim traders, in March 1937 the colonial authorities took action against "the promoters of Islam," closing Quran schools and mosques in the major coastal towns of both districts under the pretense of "not having legal 'licenses,'" even though there were no other schools in the region. In September 1938, however, common sense prevailed and the ban was lifted.[43]

By 1960, the isolation that had characterized Islam in Mozambique was being eroded. This trend worried the Portuguese sufficiently that the colonial regime commissioned a confidential investigation that discovered Muslims were seeking education beyond what was available locally by traveling to Tanzania and Arabia for study. It identified a broad range of Islamic publications available in Mozambique from publishers in Cairo and Bombay, together with widespread interest in acquiring literacy in Arabic. Radio Cairo broadcasts were awakening local consciousness, as were Arab and Islamic phonograph records from Egypt. In this context, reports that Yao

Muslims looked to Baghdad and coastal Muslims to Oman for religious leadership were even more worrying. African nationalism was reported to be gaining strength among Mozambique's Muslims, as well, and was linked to anti-Portuguese propaganda entering the colony from Arab sources. The report warned of a looming "phase of open war" with Islam growing out of the enduring Portuguese "spirit of anti-Islamic Crusade." It proposed a campaign of church construction to combat the existence of mosques throughout the region, and radio programs in Makua "to dissuade listeners from foreign and anti-national broadcasts." The report recommended, moreover, that "it is imperative to avoid unnecessary friction with Islam."[44] There is also some indication that clandestine Islamic associations may have been formed in the 1950s.[45]

For very different reasons, Muslims in both Malawi and Mozambique were denied access to Western education during this period. In the case of Malawi, the permissive attitude of the British colonial authorities toward Islamic self-determination, combined with the close linkage of Western education to Christian missions and religious instruction in Christianity, resulted in very few Muslim children receiving Western secular education. Islam provided an alternative social and educational hierarchy that insulated the community from the modernizing tendencies associated with Western education and secularization, in general. Malawi Muslims were consequently almost completely shut out of good jobs and positions of territorial influence at independence.[46] Compared with Malawi, where Western education was widely available for those who accepted its conditions, northern Mozambique was an educational wasteland. Quran education was accordingly the only alternative to traditional education for most children.

Independence, Armed Struggle, and Islamic Revival

Independence came to Malawi and Mozambique through very different political processes that in both countries had profound repercussions for the course of Islam. In the case of Malawi, the process of nationalist organization and decolonization progressed through democratic elections that led to the granting of independence under the leadership of Hastings Kamuzu Banda and the Malawi Congress Party in 1963. As part of the nationalist project, explicit efforts were made to include Muslims in the new nation and, in particular, to open up secular education to their children. In Mozambique, on the other hand, colonial intransigence when confronted with the stirrings of African nationalism provoked an armed liberation struggle lasting from 1964 to 1974 that played itself out in the northern half of the country and stimulated a colonial policy designed to win the support of the Muslim community against the forces of Frelimo, the Mozambique Liberation Front.

The 1961 manifesto of the Malawi Congress Party pledged: "The party when in power will pay special attention to those parts of the country like the Muslim areas . . . where education has been deplorably neglected."[47] True to its pledge, at independence the new government eradicated denominationalism in education and exhorted Muslim parents to send their children to school. President Banda personally (and eventually publicly) paid the school fees for a son of a respected shaykh.[48]

The results of this campaign (notwithstanding the cabinet crisis of 1964 that led to reprisals against some Yao Muslim communities) laid the foundation for a new, Western-educated generation of young Muslims who would form the social basis of Islamic reform in Malawi in the 1970s. Bone demonstrates that these individuals quickly established themselves in the national salariat and became role models for their juniors. Literacy in English enhanced their access to Islamic literature so that "Islamic knowledge, once the monopoly of the ʿulamaʾ, is now widely available and in a form uninfluenced by local tradition." This new class of Malawi Muslims made contact with world Islam through study abroad and attending conferences. At university, they organized themselves as the Muslim Students Association, and by the mid-1980s the first generation of this leadership had occupied most of the executive positions in the Muslim Association of Malawi (this body evolved from a central Board for Muslim Education in about 1950).[49]

These developments did not occur in isolation. Islamic revivalism in Malawi owed its origins to the Asian Muslim population, which in the early 1960s experienced an influx of Tabligh Jamaats from India, Pakistan, and South Africa. By the late 1970s, cooperation between reform-minded African and Asian Muslims was beginning to be achieved; it was limited, but it included financial support for community projects. The most significant event for the opening up of Malawi Islam was a visit to Malawi in April 1977 by a representative of the Muslim Youth Movement of South Africa, which resulted in a delegation of Malawi Muslims attending the first Southern Africa Islamic Youth Conference at Gaborone, Botswana. In 1981, the Muslim Association of Malawi hosted the third of these conferences at Blantyre, and in 1984 it hosted the African Zone Conference of the World Assembly of Muslim Youth.[50]

By now securely located in the wider Islamic world, Malawi Muslims have received significant funding for mosque and madrasa construction from charitable organizations like the African Muslims Committee based in Kuwait. Directing these monies through the Muslim Association of Malawi, some thirty "spectacularly minareted" mosques were built in the 1980s, which "has given Islam a striking visible presence in Malawi," even if they are sometimes located where there is no significant Muslim population. Similarly, the number of madrasas was dramatically increased nationally, although there were more schools than qualified teachers. Bursaries for students were also increased, some for study abroad, "usually specialising in dawa . . . principally in Sudan." In 1982 came the opening of the Blantyre Islamic Mission, again built with funding from the African Muslims Committee and staffed by expatriate Muslims, and two years later an Islamic health clinic began operation, as did an Islamic bookstore in Blantyre that helped disseminate a much wider range of Islamic literature, including work from South Africa, than had previously been available.

Beginning in 1986, the Islamic Development Bank provided scholarships to undergraduates studying medicine and engineering in Pakistan. Meanwhile, the Muslim Students Association worked actively to promote *da'wa;* in 1987 it produced a syllabus for Muslim education to help those who had not attended madrasa.[51] Thorold attributes this reformist activity among the Yao, who still constitute the vast majority of Muslims in the country, to "a kind of internal logic of Islamic transformation" that is "scripturalist in the extreme" and represents something entirely different from the reformist notions of the sukuti movement. As a popular slogan of the Muslim Students Association proclaims: "'No Qadiriyya! No Sukutiyya! Islamiyya!'"[52] There is no question that reformist Islam challenges deeply held beliefs among many Malawi Muslims, as it also caused some concern to Banda's authoritarian regime. But though it still represents a minority within a minority, it appears to be a force that will continue to flourish with support from regional and international pan-Islamic organizations.

With the election in 1994 of Bakili Muluzi, a Muslim, as president of Malawi, Islam seems likely to become a more significant issue in national political life. Indeed, certain tensions have manifested themselves, as when President Muluzi stated in 1996 that a meeting had occurred at the Bible Society of Malawi "to plot religious unrest by burning down mosques for political gains," to which came the retort that "although a meeting took place to discuss allegations about the burning of Bibles by Moslems, the meeting never discussed the burning of mosques."[53] While most Malawians regard their president as a politician first and a Muslim second, it is clear that Malawi Muslims will no longer remain as much on the periphery of national life.

During the colonial period, Islamic communities also established themselves in both Zambia and Zimbabwe. In Zambia, where the main mosque in Lusaka is known locally as "the Indian Church," there is also a very small community of African Muslims composed of immigrants from Malawi, Somalia, and the Congo. Their orientation is more toward South Africa than East Africa. The situation in Zimbabwe, where Yao labor migrants constitute the majority of African Muslims, is especially closely linked to Malawi. The Yao in Zimbabwe formed a tightly knit religious and social community, but over time they have established a complementary relationship with the local Asian Muslim community, from whom they received financial support for mosque building as long ago as the early 1960s, despite their differences in legal schools. The Zimbabwe Islamic Mission was founded in 1977 by Shaykh Adam Moosa Makda, who in addition to stimulating the umma in that country, toured Malawi to promote the faith. Finally, the role of Muslim youth in spearheading Islamic reform nationally, which dates to 1953 but had a discontinuous history until the 1980s, parallels the situation in Malawi and provides a further example of the significance of the linkages to South Africa's Muslim community.[54]

Clearly, conditions were entirely different in northern Mozambique during this period, not discounting the Second Chimurenga in Zimbabwe. The armed liberation struggle caused tremendous economic, social, and political upheaval throughout this vast region, spilling over into southern Malawi and Zimbabwe as Mozambican refugees flowed across borders many had crossed during the colonial period. The Portuguese strategy to defeat Frelimo included a specific campaign to win the hearts and minds of Muslim leaders throughout the entire colony. From 1965 to 1968, the colonial government conducted a comprehensive counterintelligence operation to determine the communication links that existed among the Islamic leadership so that this network could serve as "the interlocutor of the Administration." More to the point, Frelimo was believed by the Portuguese to have alienated many Muslims, whereas "our actual policy to capture the Muslim masses . . . through their religious chiefs" was thought to be appreciated by many Muslims. What this meant in northern Mozambique was working through the tariqas, which were regarded as a conservative, local force against more radical, international organizational forms of Islam and political subversion, a role they apparently fulfilled from 1967 to 1974.[55]

The Portuguese identified twenty-one key territorial leaders, most of them from the north, where the overwhelming majority of Muslims lived, through whom they sought to subvert the radical, anticolonial tendencies of these networks by exploiting the close connections among tariqa and indigenous political leadership. The external orientation of southern Mozambique, where Asian Muslims of the Hanafi school predominated and with which we are only marginally concerned here, was toward Durban and Karachi; in the wake of the Zanzibar revolution of 1964, however, northern Mozambique, where Africans of the Shafii school predominated, looked outward to the Comoro Islands and Saudi Arabia. Capitalizing on these connections, and reminiscent of the British strategy for resolving the twaliki/sukuti dispute a generation earlier, in 1972 the Portuguese brought in the mufti of the Comoros, Sayyid Omar b. Ahmad b. Abu Bakr b. Sumayt al-ʿAlawi, to resolve differences regarding forbidden practices among the eight tariqas at Mozambique Island. When the mufti decided in favor of the tariqas, the Portuguese immediately sought to build on their successful intervention by enlisting the support of these twenty-one leaders in publishing an official, Portuguese-language version of Muhammad ibn Ismail al-Bukhari's extracts from the hadith, "as a political instrument, to promote the diffusion of Portuguese among the Islamized strata of the Province."[56] In November 1972, the colonial government also produced a special number of the official *Moçambique em Imagens* that illustrated the signing of the "declaration of agreement" by many of these Muslim dignitaries for inclusion in the translation of the hadith.[57] Although this strategy represented a dramatic change of direction from the earlier colonial period, when Islam was demonized by the Portuguese administration and the church in Mozambique, it reflects a wider conservative alliance across Africa by which "colonial authorities tried either to co-opt or control Muslim leadership."[58]

When in 1975 Mozambique gained its independence under Frelimo, which was secularist and moving toward its 1977 redefinition of itself as a Marxist-Leninist political party, the umma therefore found its leadership discredited, and the new government banned some Muslim associations in August 1976. Moreover, whatever the contributions of individual Muslims to the liberation struggle, and they were not insignificant, Frelimo rejected the colonial policy of alliance with organized religion that had produced the intimate relationship between the colonial state and the Roman Catholic Church. There were, to complicate matters, mixed messages for Muslims from Frelimo during the first years of independence.

In 1980, Mozambican Muslim students in exile in Dar es Salaam denounced the repression of Islam at home,[59] and by the early 1980s, as destabilization of the government through the agency of Renamo gathered steam, Mozambique found that its treatment of Muslims provided reason for both Saudi Arabia and Oman to send supplies to Renamo. Evidence also indicates that South Africa used the Comoro Islands as a conduit for supplying Renamo from 1983 to 1989.[60] At the end of the 1990s, however, we remained woefully uninformed about either the actual role Muslim leadership played during the terrorist war waged by Renamo in northern Mozambique or the impact of the war on the Islamic community.

At the end of 1982, recognizing the state's need for allies against Renamo, President Samora Machel created an opening for organized religion, including Islam, and in 1983 Frelimo officially recognized a new national Council of Muslims of Mozambique (CISLAMO).[61] By the end of the 1990s, in addition to securing economic benefits, Mozambique had become a member of the Organization of the Islamic Conference. Most of the reformist activity associated with this opening to the principal Islamic states, such as hosting the fifth Southern African Islamic Youth Conference in 1987, appears to have been concentrated in Maputo, far away from the mass of Muslims north of the Zambezi. Indeed, tensions between the sufi leaders of the majority of Muslims in the north and the more radical reformers based in the south have caused the former to split off from CISLAMO and form their own organization, the Congresso Islâmico.[62] Nevertheless, whatever the future holds for Islam in the republic of Mozambique, the large Muslim community of the north is likely to come under increasing pressure from the prevailing currents of Islamic revival.

The end of the war with Renamo, the jettisoning of socialism by Frelimo, and the latter's narrow victory in the multiparty democratic elections of 1993 created an entirely new political context for organized religion in Mozambique. No longer holding absolute power, in May 1996 the transformed Frelimo government—motivated by the fact that a majority of citizens in the Muslim zones of the country voted against Frelimo—sought to gain the support of the umma against Renamo and other political forces by passing a law that recognized the Islamic holy days of 'Id al-Adha and 'Id al-Fitr as national holidays. And though this political gambit was soon declared unconstitutional by the supreme court, in political terms it accorded Islam equal footing with other religions in its relations with the state and marked the end of the Catholic hegemony in Mozambique.[63] It thus seems that, across East Central Africa, Islam is poised to assert itself as a major force in the religious, social, and political life of its citizens.[64]

Notes

1. Theal 1898 2:37; Barbosa 1918, 1:6, 8.

2. Santos 1901, 351–52.

3. *Documents* 1962, 19, 23.

4. Barbosa 1918, 1:16.

5. *Documents* 1971, 376–79; *Documents* 1975, 62–63.

6. Beach 1980, 107–8; 78, 129, 175, 200, 284, 213.

7. Mandivenga 1983, 30–34; Mandivenga 1985.

8. Alpers 1975, 92–94; British Library, Additional Manuscript 20,890, fl. 67–68, the king to Marquês de Louriçal, Lisboa occidental, May 3, 1741; Ferraz 1973, 1:281, 286.

9. Biblioteca Nacional de Lisboa, Pombalina 742, fl. 8–9, *bando* (official decree), Marquês de Távora, Mozambique, Aug. 4, 1750.

10. Andrade 1955, 97.

11. Arquivo Histórico Ultramarino, Lisbon, Caixa Moçambique 9, Marco António de Azevedo Coutinho de Montaury to the king, Sena, Jul. 19, 1762.

12. Arquivo Histórico Ultramarino, Lisbon, Caixa Moçambique 19, Baltasar Pereira do Lago to the king, Mozambique, Aug. 10, 1772.

13. Andrade 1917, 120.

14. Machado 1920, 63. For the wider context of this history, see Alpers 1999b.

15. Lupi 1907, 183; Coutinho 1935, 10–11.

16. Monteiro 1989, 69.

17. Livingstone 1874, 1:23–24, 28; Elton 1879, 171, 178, 197; Coutinho 1893, 40, 42, 44; cf. Stevenson-Hamilton 1909, 525–26.

18. Camizão 1901, 6; cf. Reis 1962, 35–37; el-Tom 1985, 414–30.

19. Kubik 1984, 24, cited in Thorold 1987, 22–23.

20. Linden 1974, 27; Coutinho 1893, 46.

21. Bone 1982, 126–27; Mwafulirwa 1984.

22. Desmaroux 1895, 680–81.

23. Neves 1901, 17, quoted in translation by Pelissier 1984, 1:208, n. 167.

24. Pimental 1905, 75.

25. Ibid, 158; Lupi 1907, 176–77; for the 1905 report, Amorim 1908, 74.

26. Vilhena 1905, 10–11, 234–35.

27. Greenstein 1976/77, 14.

28. White 1984; Vail and White 1991, 168–73.

29. Greenstein 1976/77, 14–17.

30. Thorold 1987, 24.

31. Amaral 1990, 379; Greenstein 1976/77, 22.

32. Nimtz 1980, 60; Nimtz 1973, 77. But note that the standard life of Shaykh Maruf specifically states that he did not leave the Comoros at this time, for which see Alpers 1999b.

33. Carvalho 1988, 61–63.

34. Nimtz 1980, 59; Nimtz 1973, 81, 75.

35. Carvalho 1988, 63–64; João 1990, 139–40.

36. Carvalho 1988, 60–61; cf. Caplan 1975, 94–96.

37. Greenstein 1976/77, 19, 21, 23, 24, 26, 32; cf. Constantin 1987.

38. Alpers 1972, 179–80; Thorold 1987, 24–25; Thorold 1993, 84–85; Msiska 1995, 70–80; cf. Eile 1990.

39. João 1990, 140.

40. Anderson 1954, 169–70; Greenstein 1976/77, 35.

41. Monteiro 1993a, 90–91, and 101–3 for the complete text of the fatwa, which is dated Moçambique, Aug. 1968; Anderson 1954, 169; Mitchell 1956, 51–52; Greenstein 1976/77, 19, 34–35; Thorold 1993, 79–80, 85–87.

42. Monteiro 1989, 73–79. For Islamic literature in Arabic and Swahili introduced to Mozambique, see Peirone 1967, 89–126.

43. Departamento de História 1993, 49; Arquivo Histórico de Mozambique, Maputo, Fundo Governo Geral, Caixa 2450, 1:56–57.

44. Pedro 1961.

45. "Islam" 1969, 50.

46. Bone 1987a, 28–30; Bone 1987b, 1–7. Perhaps concern over educational isolation in 1960 prompted the colonial authorities to invite Shaykh 'Abdallah Salih Farsy, later chief qadi of Kenya, to tour Muslim schools in Malawi and report to the chief secretary for education. Shaykh 'Abdallah was also a vigorous proponent of the *sunna* and against the innovative practices of tariqas. As a consequence of his visit, a number of Malawians studied under him and returned home to renew Islam in their country. See Bone 1987c, 23 n. 37; Sicard 1994, 114.

47. Quoted in Bone 1987c, 13.

48. Bone 1987a, 30; Bone 1987b, 8.

49. Ibid, 9–10.

50. Panjwani 1979–80, 166–67; cf. Bone 1987c, 14.

51. Ibid, 15–17; Bone 1987b, 14–17; cf. Matiki 1991.

52. Thorold 1993, 79, 88, 87.

53. Malawi News Online 11 (Jul. 14, 1996), item 10; 22 (Jan. 10, 1997), item 3, available at <http://spicerack.sr.unh.edu/~llk/mwupdate.html>.

54. Mandivenga 1983, 39–44, 47–49, 54–64; cf. Mandivenga 1989, 507–19; Bone 1987c, 14–15.

55. Monteiro 1989, 80–81, 84; Monteiro 1993a. For the full account of this campaign of psychological warfare, see Monteiro 1993b. For a wider perspective on the interlocutory role played by tariqas, see O'Brien 1981. For a more complete discussion of this historical episode, see Alpers 1999a.

56. Monteiro, 1989, 83. For a different perspective on these issues, see Cahen 1998.

57. Monteiro 1993b, 352, anexo no. 6.

58. Hunwick 1996, 235; cf. Coulon 1987, 130–31; Iliffe 1979, 370.

59. Constantin 1983, 89–90; "Islam" 1981.

60. Finnegan 1992, 33–34; Vines 1991, 67–68, 110; Verin 1994, 214–16.

61. *Tempo* 1982; Constantin 1983, 93.

62. Siefert 1994. My thanks to Liazzat Bonate for sharing this essay with me and to Dennis Laumann for translating it.

63. "NotMoc-Noticias de Mocambique," 75 (Mar. 31, 1996), electronic newsletter <wenke@adam.uem.mz>; "NotMoc-Noticias de Mocambique," 94 (Jan. 10, 1997).

64. I am grateful to David S. Bone and François Constantin for providing me with materials, as well as for their comments, and those of Alan Thorold, on the first draft of this chapter. Thanks also to L. Lloys Frates for invaluable research assistance in its preparation, which was supported by a grant from the Council on Research of the Academic Senate, UCLA.

Bibliography

Alpers, Edward A. 1972. "Towards a History of the Expansion of Islam in East Africa, the Matrilineal Peoples of the Southern Interior." In *The Historical Study of African Religions,* ed. T. O. Ranger and I. N. Kimambo, 171–201. London: Heinemann.

———. 1975. *Ivory and Slaves in East Central Africa: Changing Patterns of International Trade to the Later Nineteenth Century.* London: Heinemann.

———. 1999a. "Islam in the Service of Colonialism? Portuguese Strategy during the Armed Liberation Struggle in Mozambique." Forthcoming in *Lusotopie: Enjeux contemporains dans les espaces lusophones* (Paris).

———. 1999b. "A Complex Relationship: Mozambique and the Comoro Islands in the Nineteenth and Twentieth Centuries." Paper presented to the Colloque Marquant le XXème Anniversaire de la Création du CNDRS, Moroni, R.F.I. des Comores, January 26–28.

Amaral, Manuel Gama. 1990. *O Povo Yao-Subsidios para o Estudo de um Povo do Noroeste de Moçambique.* Lisbon: Instituto de Investigação Científica e Tropical.

Amorim, Pedro Massano de. 1908. *Districto de Moçambique-Relatorio do Governador (1906–1907).* Lourenço Marques: Imprensa Nacional.

Anderson, J. N. D. 1954. *Islamic Law in Africa.* London: H.M. Stationery Office, Colonial Research Publications, no. 16.

Andrade, António Alberto de. 1955. *Relações de Moçambique Setecentista.* Lisbon: Agencia Geral do Ultramar.

Andrade, Jerónimo José Nogueira de. 1917. "Descripção do Estada em que Ficavão os Negocios da Capitania de Mossabique nos Fins de Novembro de 1789 com Algumas Observaçoens, e reflecçoens sobre a causa da decadencia do Commercio dos Estabelecimentos Portugueses na Costa Oriental da Affrica." In *Arquivo das Colónias* (Lisbon) 1:75–96, 115–34, 166–84, 213–35, 275–88.

Barbosa, Duarte. 1918–23. *The Book of Duarte Barbosa.* Trans. Mansel Longworth Dames. London: Hakluyt Society. 2nd series, 44 and 49.

Beach, David N. 1980. *The Shona and Zimbabwe (900–1850).* London: Heinemann.

Bone, David S. 1982. "Islam in Malawi," *Journal of Religion in Africa* 13, no. 2:126–38.

———. 1987a. "The Muslim Minority in Malawi and Western Education." *Religion in Malawi* (University of Malawi, Zomba), 28–31.

———. 1987b. "Modernists and Marginalisation in Malawi." Seminar paper, Department of Religious Studies, Chancellor College, University of Malawi.

———. 1987c. "The Development of Islam in Malawi and the Response of the Christian Churches (1940–1986)," *Bulletin on Islam and Christian-Muslim Relations in Africa* 5, no. 4:7–13.

Cahen, Michel. 1998. "L'Etat nouveau et la diversification réligieuse au Mozambique, 1930–1974." Draft article, Bordeaux, France, February–June, with minor revisions 12 November.

Camizão, António. 1901. *Indicações geraes sobre a Capitania-Mór do Mossuril.* Moçambique: Imprensa Nacional.

Caplan, Ann Patricia. 1975. *Choice and Constraint in a Swahili Community: Property, Hierarchy, and Cognatic Descent on the East African Coast.* London: Oxford University Press.

Carvalho, Alvaro Pinto de. 1988. "Notas para a História das Confrarias Islâmicas na Ilha de Moçambique." *Arquivo* (Maputo) 4:59–66.

Constantin, François. 1983. "Mozambique: Du colonialisme catholique a l'état marxiste," *Les communautés musulmanes d'Afrique orientale* (Pau) 1:84–93. Travaux et Documents du CREPAO. Centre de Recherche et d'Etude sur les Pays d'Afrique Orientale, Université de Pau et des Pays de l'Adour.

———. 1987. "Condition feminine et dynamique confrérique en Afrique Orientale," *Islam et sociétés au sud du Sahara* 1:58–59.

Coulon, Christian. 1987. "Vers une sociologie des confréries en Afrique orientale." In *Les voies de l'Islam en Afrique orientale*, ed. François Constantin, 111–33. Paris: Karthala.

Coutinho, João de Azevedo. 1893. *Do Nyassa a Pemba.* Lisbon: Typographia do Companhia Nacional Editora.

———. 1935. *As Duas Conquistas de Angoche.* Lisbon: Agência Geral das Colónias.

Departamento da História, Universidade Eduardo Mondlane. 1993. *História de Moçambique*, vol. 3, *Moçambique no auge do colonialismo (1930–1961).* Maputo: Universidade Eduardo Mondlane.

Desmaroux, Félix. 1895. "Informações acerca da situação moral e religiosa e dos usos e costumes dos povos no meio das quais a Missão dos Santos Anjos é destinada a exercer a sua influência (Zambezia)," *Boletim da Sociedade de Geografia de Lisboa* 14:679–88.

Documents on the Portuguese in Mozambique and Central Africa (1497–1840). 1 (1962); 7 (1971); 8 (1975). Lisbon: Centro de Estudos Históricos Ultramarinos and National Archives of Rhodesia and Nyasaland.

Eile, Lena. 1990. *Jando—the Rite of Circumcision and Initiation in East African Islam.* Lund Studies in African and Asian Religions 5. Lund: Plus Ultra.

Elton, J. Frederic. 1879. *Travels and Researches among the Lakes and Mountains of Eastern and Central Africa.* Ed. H. B. Cotterill. London: J. Murray.

Ferraz, Maria de Lourdes Esteves dos Santos. 1973. *Documentação Histórica Moçambicana*, 1. Lisbon: Junta de Investigações do Ultramar.

Finnegan, William. 1992. *A Complicated War: The Harrowing of Mozambique.* Berkeley: Univerrsity of California Press.

Greenstein, Robert. 1976/1977. "*Shaykhs* and *Tariqas:* The Early Muslim *'Ulama'* and *Tariqa* Development in Malawi (c. 1885–1949)." Seminar paper, History Department, Chancellor College, University of Malawi.

Hunwick, John. 1996. "Sub-Saharan Africa and the Wider World of Islam: Historical and Contemporary Perspectives," *Journal of Religion in Africa* 26, no. 3:230–57.

Iliffe, John. 1979. *A Modern History of Tanganyika.* Cambridge: Cambridge University Press.

"Islam in Mozambique (East Africa)." 1969. In *Islamic Literature* 15, no. 9:547–55.

João, Benedito Brito. 1990. "Abdul Kamal-Megama (1892–1966): Pouvoir et religion dans un district du Nord-Mozambique," *Islam et Sociétés au sud du Sahara* 4:137–41.

Kubik, Gerhard. 1984. "Report on Cultural Field Research in Mangochi District." *Baraza* 2. Cited in Thorold 1987.

Linden, Ian, and Jane Linden. 1974. *Catholics, Peasants, and Chewa Resistance in Nyasaland (1889–1939)*. Berkeley: University of California Press.

Livingstone, David. 1874. *Last Journals*. Ed. Horace Waller. London: J. Murray.

Lupi, Eduardo do Couto. 1907. *Angoche*. Lisbon: Typographia do Annuario Commercial.

Machado, Carlos Roma. 1920. "Mussa-Quanto o Namuali (O Napoleão de Angoche)," *Boletim da Sociedade de Geografia de Lisboa* 38, nos. 1–2:54–70.

Mandivenga, Ephraim C. 1983. *Islam in Zimbabwe*. Gweru: Mambo Press.

———. 1985. "The History and 'Re-conversion' of the Varemba of Zimbabwe," *Journal of Religion in Africa* 19, no. 2:98–124.

———. 1989. "The Migration of Muslims to Zimbabwe," *Journal [of the] Institute of Muslim Minority Affairs* 10, no. 2:507–19.

Matiki, Alfred J. 1994. "Problems of Islamic Education in Malawi," *Journal [of the] Institute of Muslim Minority Affairs* 12, no. 1:127–34.

Mitchell, J. Clyde. 1956. *The Yao Village–A Study of the Social Structure of a Nyasaland Tribe*. Manchester: Manchester University Press.

Monteiro, Fernando Amaro. 1989. "As comunidades islâmicas em Moçambique: Mecanismos de comunicação," *Africana* (Porto) 4:63–89

———. 1993a. "Sobre a actuação da corente 'Wahhabita' no Islão Moçambicana: Algumas notas relativas ao período 1964–1974," *Africana* (Porto) 12:85–111.

———. 1993b. *O Islão, o poder, e a guerra (Moçambique 1964–1974)*. Porto: Universidade Portucalense.

Msiska, Augustine W. C. 1995. "The Spread of Islam in Malawi and Its Impact on Yao Rites of Passage (1870–1960)," *Society of Malawi Journal* 48, no. 2:49–86.

Mwafulirwa, Yaulungu A. H. 1984. "Islam in Karonga District." Seminar paper, History Department, Chancellor College, University of Malawi.

Neves, F. A. da Silva. 1901. *Informações á cerca da Capitania-Mór de Angoche*. Moçambique: Imprensa Nacional.

Nimtz, August H. Jr. 1973. "The Role of the Muslim Sufi Order in Political Change: An Overview and Micro-analysis from Tanzania." Ph.D. diss., Indiana University.

———. 1980. *Islam and Politics in East Africa: The Sufi Order in Tanzania*. Minneapolis: University of Minnesota Press.

O'Brien, Donal Cruise. 1981. "Le filière musulmane: Confréries soufies et politique en Afrique noire," *Politique Africaine* 1, no. 4:16–28.

Panjwani, Ibrahim A. G. 1979–80. "Muslims in Malawi" *Journal [of the] Institute of Muslim Minority Affairs* 1, no. 2, and 2, no. 1:58–68.

Pedro, Albano Mendes. 1961. "Influências politico-sociais do Islamismo em Moçambique (Relatório Confidencial)." Typescript dated May 31.

Peirone, Frederico José. 1967. *A Tribo Ajaua do Alto Niassa (Moçambique) e Alguns Aspectos da Sua Problemática Néo-Islâmica*. Lisbon: Junta de Investigações do Ultramar.

Pelissier, René. 1984. *Naissance du Mozambique.* Orgeval: Pelissier.

Pimental, Jayme Pereira de Sampaio Forjaz de Serpa. 1905. *No Districto de Moçambique-Memorias, Estudos e Considerações (1902–1904).* Lisbon.

Reis, Diogo da Câmara. 1962. "Os Macuas de Mogovolas," *Boletim da Sociedade de Estudos de Moçambique* 31, no. 131:9–37.

"Repression of Muslims in Mozambique." 1981/1982. In *Al Islam, The Quarterly Journal of the Islamic Foundation* (Nairobi).

Santos, João dos. 1901. *Ethiopia Oriental* (1609). In *Records of South-Eastern Africa,* George McCall Theal, 7:1–370. London: W. Clowes.

Sicard, Sigvard von. 1994. "Islam in Malawi," *Journal [of the] Institute of Muslim Minority Affairs* 14, nos. 1 and 2:107–15.

Siefert, Sakia. 1994. "Muslime in Mosambik-Versuch einer Bestandsaufnahme." Bielefeld: Forschungsprogramm Entwicklungspolitik: Handlungsbedingungen und Handlungs-Spielräume für Entwicklungspolitik, nr. 36, Universität Bielefeld, Fakultät Soziologie.

Stevenson-Hamilton, J. 1909. "Notes on a Journey through Portuguese East Africa, from Ibo to Lake Nyasa," *Geographical Journal* 34:514–29.

Tempo. 1982. "Une-nos o amor à patria: Presidente Samora Machel aos dirigentes religiosos," *Tempo* (Maputo) no. 637 (Dec. 26): 24–29.

Theal, George McCall. 1898. *Records of South-Eastern Africa,* vol. 2 London: W. Clowes.

Thorold, Alan. 1987. "Yao Conversion to Islam," *Cambridge Anthropology* 12, no. 2:18–28.

———. 1993. "Metamorphoses of the Yao Muslims." In *Muslim Identity and Social Change in Sub-Saharan Africa,* ed. Louis Brenner, 79–90. Bloomington: Indiana University Press.

———. 1985. "The Yao Muslims: Religion and Social Change in Southern Malawi." Ph.D. diss., Churchill College, Cambridge University.

el-Tom, Abdullahi Osman. 1985. "Drinking the Koran: The Meaning of Koranic Verses in Berti Erasure," *Africa* 55, no. 4:414–30.

Vail, Leroy, and Landeg White. 1991. "Tribalism in the Political History of Malawi." In *The Creation of Tribalism in Southern Africa,* ed. Leroy Vail, 151–92. Berkeley: University of California Press.

Verin, Pierre. 1994. *Les Comores.* Paris.

Vilhena, Ernesto Jardim de. 1905. *Companhia do Nyassa-Relatorios e Memorias sobre os Territorios pelo Governador.* Lisbon: Typographia da "A Editoria."

Vines, Alex. 1991. *Renamo: Terrorism in Mozambique.* University of York: Centre for Southern African Studies; London: James Currey; Bloomington and Indianapolis: Indiana University Press.

White, Landeg. 1984. "'Tribes' and the Aftermath of the Chilembwe Rising," *African Affairs* 83:511–41.

CHAPTER 15

Islam in Southern Africa, 1652-1998

Robert C.-H. Shell

Ideas follow trade routes, but not necessarily voluntarily. This was the case when the first Muslim, Ibrahim van Batavia, a slave, splashed ashore in Table Bay in the second half of the seventeenth century, shipped to southern Africa by an unlikely agent of Islam—the Dutch East India Company.[1] Islam arrived in southern Africa as a coincidence of geography, colonization, slavery, and the geopolitics of mercantile commerce. A new society emerged, "where the South Atlantic joins the Indian Ocean, and Calvinist Christianity with Roman law bobbed, uneasily, at the confluence of a sad human sea that flowed as much from the Muslim East Indies as from the tip of Africa."[2] The number of South Africa's Muslims grew until, by the last census of 1996, there were nearly 504,000 of them (in a population of some forty-one million).

South African Muslims can boast one of the highest rates of *hajj* outside of the Middle East; however, while the study of Islam in North, West, and East Africa has been well documented, the topic of Islam in southern Africa is still in its infancy. After more than three centuries at this southern tip, South African Muslims afford fertile ground for further study: they comprise a well-documented, highly urbanized set of minority communities in a plural, modernizing society.

The First Phase of Immigration

The Cape of Good Hope, which served the Dutch East India Company (hereafter the DEIC) primarily as a refreshment station for its fleets plying the Far East trade, simultaneously functioned as an effective place of exile for political leaders whom the company had dethroned in its eastern possessions. Most of these political exiles were Muslims, sometimes accompanied by a following of coreligionists.

Some two hundred spent time at the Cape between 1652 and the end of company rule in 1795. The arrival in 1682 of Makasserese political prisoners of state rank, including army officers and "three Makasserese princesses," marked the DEIC decision to neutralize all Muslims at the Cape by isolating them on outstations. Sometimes, families were split apart.[3]

Among these early political exiles to the Cape was Shaykh Yusuf, a man widely regarded as an Islamic saint and a person who embodies the Cape exile experience.[4] Yusuf, born at Maccassar (on Sulawesi, in modern Indonesia) in 1626, was a relative of the king of Goa, the ruling dynasty of Sulawesi. Converted to Islam, he went on hajj at eighteen. He studied for several years at Mecca, but who his teachers were is not known. Yusuf then established himself at the court of Sultan Ageng of Bantam, in western Java, where in 1646 he married one of the sultan's relatives and became the leading religious authority. Regarded as a man of great piety and culture, he spent many years teaching the sultan and his court about Islam. Some have argued he was a Shafii sufi.[5]

On 1 May 1680, Sultan Ageng, by then the last independent sultan in the archipelago, was forced off the throne by his son, Sultan Haji, one of Yusuf's pupils.[6] This palace revolution was probably engineered by the DEIC, who now held a controlling hand over the new, young, sultan. In 1682, the old sultan tried to engineer a countercoup, forcing his son to appeal to the Dutch at Batavia for help, who gladly seized this chance of crushing the Bantamese power. Shaykh Yusuf, however, continued the struggle in a protracted guerrilla operation, until, more than a year later, he was persuaded to give himself up on the promise of a pardon.[7] This promise was never honored by the DEIC, and following Yusuf's imprisonment in Batavia and exile in Sri Lanka, the company resolved to send him to the Cape. In 1694, Yusuf, now sixty-eight years of age, arrived in the DEIC flute *De Voetboog* with his two wives, family, twelve disciples, friends, slaves, and followers. In all, there were forty-nine Muslims.[8]

The DEIC had not forgotten Yusuf's revolutionary background, and the authorities at the Cape were given orders that Yusuf "was to be located at a distance from the roadstead in Table Bay so that he would not be able to get in touch with any adherents of the old regime." With this in mind, the DEIC carefully interned Yusuf and his followers twenty miles from the roadstead, on the farm of a Dutch Reformed minister, the Reverend Petrus Kalden, at Faure. At this isolated spot on the False Bay coast, Shaykh Yusuf and his followers erected a few sparse dwellings. According to Jeffreys, this spot soon proved a rallying point for fugitive slaves and other easterners and "thereby brought the exiles into disrepute with the local authorities."[9] This seems to be the first evidence that Islam was being established and spread among the slaves at the Cape.

Yusuf's home near the Maccassar Downs became a gathering spot for Muslims and runaway slaves until his death in May 1699.[10] Reporting on Shaykh Yusuf's death on 23 May 1699, the local officials uncharitably stated that they "welcomed" the death of the shaykh as a relief from financial expenditure and also from the anxiety of guarding against his escape. They concluded their dispatch by describing the situation at Faure: "These Mohammedans are multiplying rapidly and increasing in numbers. However, Joseph is now dead and we therefore ask you to find a proper method by which to release us from his adherents and their heavy expense, and also that we may in future be exempted from such people."[11]

Yusuf was the author of several *kitabs* (religious writings) that are now housed in Leyden University. These works are today again being used by Cape Muslims. Yusuf is regarded as the founder of Islam in South Africa, although he seems not to have been the first Muslim to arrive there.[12]

The Bandit Imams

Nearly three thousand convicts *(bandietten)* arrived at the Cape to work in gangs on the fortification and harbor works of Cape Town. Of all enforced labor groups, they suffered the highest mortality, but they were free if they survived their sentences. Most came from the Indian subcontinent and the Indonesian archipelago; some were from Java (the bulk of whom were of Chinese descent), but a few came from the Middle and Near East. The DEIC had trading stations at Gamron (Bandar Abas) in Iran and at Mokka on the Red Sea coast. Among these convicts were some exiled *imams.*

As early as 1725, these holy men were making their moral presence felt at the Cape, in the following case outside the notorious company brothel—the Lodge. Jan Svilt, a bookkeeper on a DEIC ship, *de Geertruijd,* provides the first commentary on the Islamic moral presence at the Cape:

> Near us stood an elderly Moslem, from Persia I believe, who had been watching while our shipmates taunted us. . . . He pointed at the sailors swaying in line waiting for the whores, and said: "You Dutch Christians preach to us of your superior religion. The Calvinists are, to hear them, the salt of the earth with God-given morals." He pointed to the line of drunken sailors: "Look at how you really are. You behave like swine, like drunken, whoring pigs. I would never allow my daughter to marry a Dutchman. I would break her neck first. Now you have the better ships, the bigger guns, and you make us your slaves. But one day Allah will be revenged." I could not reply. The old man walked away. Bandino, whose mother had been a Bug[a]nese slave and a Moslem, was much upset by the old man's harangue—Oh Christ, how different is your ideal world from the vile existence that surrounds me and my shipmates? That evening aboard our ship, little Bandino asked me to read to him a portion of the Bible which touched on the punishment for sinners who do not tread the narrow path of righteousness. I read him a sermon by St. Paul, which we both took to heart.[13]

Most early Cape Muslim leaders like the one mentioned here came from the ranks of the freed convicts rather than from the political exiles on the colony's outstations *(buitenposten)*, such as Robben Island. The bandiet imams, in contrast to the isolated exiles, trickled into the hurly-burly of Cape Town throughout the eighteenth century. Among them were men such as Sapoer (n.d.); ʿAbdul Radeen (n.d.); Abdullah van Batavia (n.d.); Joudaan Tappa Santrij (mentioned in sources in 1713) (*santrij* = scholar; he is known as "the free Javanese Pope"—the first Muslim martyr at the Cape); Fortuijn Aloewie Saʿid van Mokka (1744) and Hajjie Mattavaan (1744) (these two Muslim "priesters" were chained together to work; Hajjie Mattavaan died the next year and Saʿid Alowie was allowed to work in Cape Town a few years later as a policeman);[14] imam Fakirij van de Negerij Niassinna, (1746);[15] Agmat, a prince from Ternate, and Al Jina ʿAbdullah (these two were banned on the same day in October 1766);[16] Noriman van Cheribon (1767) (he ended his servitude in the slave lodge);[17] imam ʿAbdullah (1780); imam Noro (1780); imam Patrodien (1780); imam ʿAbdullah, Prins van Ternate (1780) (also known as Tuan Guru); and an imam simply recorded as Achmat (1795) (he, too, ended his sentence in the slave lodge). All these men were listed as *"Mahometaanse priesters"* or Muslim leaders in the voluminous *bandietrollen* (convict censuses). By no means all convicts were Muslims, but the convict population remained a source of Muslims. After the Dutch occupation ended (1795), the Reverend William Elliot, in charge of Christian evangelical activity to Muslims, was surprised to find, in 1829, that "[t]here are at present eighty-three convicts lodged in the battery, about half of whom are Mahometans."[18]

Convict imams provided the core of the Cape's early *ʿulamaʾ* (Muslim clergy) and also much of their genetic stock until the twentieth century.[19] Such imams represent a spectacular example of colonial status inversion: in settler eyes they were convicts, but in the eyes of the autochthonous, slave, and free black populations they became leaders of an alternative culture.

Slaves and Their Religion

The Cape was a growing colony starved of labor. The autochthonous people were too independent to be enslaved, although there were several attempts to enslave them. Since the DEIC was forbidden from slaving on the west coast of Africa by the Dutch Estates General, the company and the early Cape colonists turned to the Indian Ocean for slaves. Some sixty-three thousand slaves were landed in South Africa between 1652 and 1807; then Britain abruptly abolished the oceanic slave trade.

The Indian subcontinent supplied more than a quarter of early South Africa's formal slaves, and the Indonesian archipelago supplied another quarter, or slightly less. A little more than half of the slaves came from Madagascar, the Mascarene islands of the Indian Ocean, and the east coast of Africa. The Muslim sympathies of these groups were first noticed in the 1770s by the English explorer George Forster, who mentioned that a few slaves "weekly meet in a private house belonging to a free Mohammedan, in order to read, or rather chaunt, several prayers and chapters of the Koran."[20]

The institution of slavery generated multiple pathways to Islamic conversion. The colony was ostensibly Christian, and in Dutch Reformed Christianity, baptism—which replaced the Old Testament rite of circumcision—was the key both to the religion and to society.[21] The DEIC had an unwavering policy of baptizing its own slaves born at the Cape, but among the slaves owned by the settlers (the overwhelming majority) neither company, church, nor settlers engaged in significant Christian proselytization. Owners who evangelized among their slaves were bound by Dutch Reformed precept—though not by law—to bring them into the realm of legal and social equality. Most important, the right of an owner to sell a fellow Christian was circumscribed, and by 1799 most slave owners believed they would lose the right to sell their slaves if the slaves became Christian. In 1822, W. W. Bird, the comptroller of customs, reported that it was a frequent answer of a slave, when asked his motive for turning to Islam, that "some religion he must have, and he is not allowed to turn Christian."[22] By 1830, Christian conversion by slaves was at a standstill.

Interestingly, Christian and Muslim slave owners were both under similar precepts—the former from the Bible, the latter from the Quran. Both religions derived the stricture about not selling coreligionists from the example of Abraham, who had to circumcise all his household, including his slaves. Neither Christians nor Muslims could keep a fellow religionist in slavery. An imam named Muding explained to a British official in 1824 that "[a] Mahometan who has purchased a slave is forbidden by the principles of his faith to sell him, and they are never sold. If they embrace the faith, they [and their children] are enfranchised at the death of their owner."[23] But as Achmat Davids has observed there were several cases where even revered imams did not manumit their slaves at their death. For example, two of Tuan Guru's slaves remained the property of his heirs until emancipation in 1834; another of his slaves purchased his freedom from the family nine years after the Tuan's death in 1807.[24] Whatever the case, the several hundred male slaves who bought their freedom or received it as a gift from their owners did not then turn to Christianity or its missionaries, whom they saw as having rejected them, but to Islam and to the open arms of the Cape imams.

The Muslim free blacks used their relative prosperity to free their own slaves and set a dramatic example by manumitting others, including Christian slaves. The Christian missionary John Philip noticed in 1831 with some poignancy that many slaves once owned by Muslims had been freed: "I do not know whether there is a law among the Malays binding them to make their slaves free," he wrote, "but it is known that they seldom retain in slavery those that embrace their religion, & to the honor of the Malays it must be stated many instances have occurred in which, at public sales, they have purchased aged & wretched creatures, irrespective of their religion, to make them free."[25] Few such acts of piety for their fellow religionists could be found among the Christian slave owners.

The Reverend James Laing, from the Glasgow Missionary Society, noticed the zeal of the Muslims in the rates of conversion,[26] and the Anglican Arabist William

Elliot pointed out a powerful, but little discussed, anticolonial motivation for Islamic conversion: converts to Islam owed no intellectual inspiration to the European presence; every Muslim knew his or her religious identity was autonomous. A Muslim convert, *ipso facto,* was no Uncle Tom. In short, conversion to Islam may be seen in part as a cultural payback for the miseries of the colonial slave regime.

By the early nineteenth century, wine had come to dominate the Cape economy. This, too, opened an avenue for Islamic conversion. Owners of wine estates preferred their overseers and wagon drivers to be Muslim since they did not drink wine. W. W. Bird sums up this attitude: "It is made a question, still with worldly considerations only, whether the Muhammedan slave makes not a better servant than the Christian. His sobriety, as it is affirmed, makes amends for some ill-habits attendant on Muhammedanism. Christians, slaves as freedmen, blacks no less than whites, are, it is lamentable to say, drunken."[27]

Under these conditions, Islam spread quickly among slaves and former slaves at the Cape. Christianity, on the other hand, lost—and decisively lost—this vital constituency. This era might be considered the golden age of Islam in Southern Africa in terms of numbers of converts.

Mardyckers and the Public Toleration of Islam

Islam was finally propelled from the private to the public sphere by a shortage of military manpower at the Cape and the concomitant emergence of what may be called the Cape Mardyker tradition.

The Portuguese word *meredika* was derived from the Sanskrit *maharddhika,* meaning "great man." François Valentijn, the Dutch traveler and peripatetic Dutch Reformed minister of the seventeenth and early eighteenth centuries explained how the term had changed: "*Mardijcker* was derived from Ambon, where there is a hamlet called *Campon-Meredhika* [*Kampung* = village; lit., village of Mardijckers] inhabited by strangers who first arrived with the Portuguese from the Molluccas proper and were employed to help in strengthening the latter against the Amboinese."[28] Thus, in the archipelago, the new Malayo-Portuguese word *merdeka* came to have a meaning quite different from its Sanskrit roots: it now meant slaves who had been freed for defensive purposes.[29] The concept was used in the Cape and can be said to have been responsible for the era of religious toleration following 1804. In that year, the Cape Muslims were enrolled in two artillery units in preparation for the invasion of the British. In return, they were given the right to worship publicly. After slavery they were obliged to fight in "the war of the axe" against the amaXhosa (1846–47), and many of those veterans elected to stay in the new frontier town of Port Elizabeth.[30]

Prize Negroes

After the formal abolition of the oceanic slave trade, the British acquired a new problem and the colony a new element in the population. What was to be the lot of slaves aboard ships the British navy intercepted at sea? The British Admiralty argued that such persons (who came to be called Prize Negroes) could not be returned to their homeland for the logical—but still somehow perverse—reason that they would run the risk of being re-enslaved. Consequently, two depots for these spectacular casualties of fate were established, one at Sierra Leone and one at Cape Town. Cape Town was doubly convenient as a dumping ground for Prize Negroes since its winter port of Simonstown had become the new South Atlantic base for the Royal Navy—in effect, the Gibraltar of the Indian Ocean rim.

While landing Prize Negroes at the Cape had begun as a philanthropic and liberty-affirming gesture, an ironic problem quickly arose: what was to be the extent of their freedom? The navy and the army could not employ all of them, and soon some were given out to individuals, with conditions of service being stipulated.[31] When resistance from the new "employers" was encountered, a compromise was worked out: fourteen years of apprenticeship would have to pass before these slaves could be "free." It also must be noted that some Prize Negroes' children, aged from five to eighteen, were folded into the remaining slave population by unscrupulous beneficiaries of this scheme.[32]

According to Saunders, approximately five thousand such slaves were landed at the Cape between 1808 and 1856, a population (not counting offspring) equivalent to all the 1820 British settlers. In 1822, Bird observed that they were distributed throughout the colony as far afield as Farmerfield and Grahamstown in the Eastern Cape, but remained concentrated in the Cape district.[33] The navy even built houses for the Prize Negroes in Blacktown, as that part of Simonstown became known.[34]

It was not to the faith of their Christian benefactors that many of these landed slaves now turned. Despite some official sympathy for them, there was to be no Christian assimilation. Bird recalled in 1822: "A former governor was desirous of having a cargo of prize slaves baptised as they landed, great and small, old and young; but, upon being asked by the clergyman, who disliked the proceeding, whether he would undertake the office of general godfather . . . it was declined."[35] It was to the Muslim community that the Prize Negroes turned. By the early nineteenth century, Muslim tailors from Cape Town (specializing in naval uniforms) had established themselves in the small but growing naval base, and they became the source for the slaves' religious inspiration.

Just after the inception of the Prize Negroes scheme officials remarked for the first time on a rapid spread of Islam in the colony. On 4 February 1808, the Earl of Caledon, the first civilian governor of the colony, wrote to Viscount Castlereagh, the British secretary for war: "The imported slaves are mostly from Mozambique, arriving here in total ignorance, and being permitted to remain in that state, they, for the most part, embrace the Mahomedan faith."[36] Imam Muding suggested in 1823 that at least "half" of the Muslims in the Cape colony were Prize Negroes.[37] Gray, the Anglican archbishop, wrote in 1848 that "there are a very great number of Mahometans in and around Cape Town; their converts are made chiefly from among the liberated Africans."[38] In the same year, Gray's colleague Archdeacon

Merriman learned from a Cape farmer friend, a Mr. Maynier, "that the native families who had settled on his son-in-law's . . . [Versveld's] estate were all of Mozambique origin, and were, of course, heathen, but that all of them had at least nominally joined the Mohammedans and loved to be considered as Malays."[39] Among the Prize Negroes, religious conversion was unambiguously alloyed with an expressed need for a new ethnic identity.

The Prize Negroes, then, crossed what turned out to be a most convoluted cultural gangplank when they came ashore in dusty Simonstown. In 1864, De Roubaix, a French émigré, put an end to the Prize Negro period. When a Muslim slaving crew from Zanzibar was put ashore in Simonstown by the Royal Navy and treated as Prize Negroes, the crew turned to de Rouxbaix for help. Two years later, he returned them to Zanzibar at his own expense and wrote letters to the British Parliament to stop further shipments.

Doctrinal Disputes

It is usually affirmed that the Cape Muslims were of the Shafi'i school of law. The basis given for this is that the Shafi'is were firmly imbedded in the Indonesian archipelago, and it was from there that all Cape "Malays" originated (it must be noted, however, that several contemporary sources questioned what "Malay" really meant in the Cape context).

There is only scant evidence for a Shafi'i orthodoxy in the Islamic theological kaleidoscope of the early Cape; there is also little evidence on the origins of the slaves themselves. Whatever Islam brought to the early Cape it was not a Shafi'i uniformity. Recent research has shown that a number of slaves imported to the Cape came from India, in particular from Bengal.[40] In Bengal, the Shafi'i orthodoxy had disappeared in the fourteenth century (to be displaced by the Hanafi school, and some Shi'ites).[41] However, as Achmat Davids has pointed out, there were Shafi'i communities on the Malabar and Coromandel coasts. Still, since so many of the early Muslim slaves and later indentured servants were from the Bengal province, one might well dare ask whether the Shafi'i "roots" of Cape Islam may not have been boosted in the historical literature in an attempt to maintain the embattled yet persistent "Malay" identity for the Cape Muslims.[42]

Frank Bradlow, a writer on Islam at the Cape, has already suggested this reasoning in respect of the large number of slaves and important "chief priests" from the province of Bengal, such as Frans van Bengal (chief imam in 1806). Bradlow wrote: "There is little doubt however that the immigrants from Bengal, whether they came as slaves, freemen or servants of Company officials . . . were the most important and influential of the people who established Islam in the Colony."[43] There is also the statement of John Mayson, a visiting English army officer: "The ancestor of the present chief Imam ["Abdul Roof," 1854] came from Bengal, at the request of Mahometans at the Cape, and was by them elected to that important office."[44] Is it not natural that Indian Muslims in the early Cape, wanting reassurance about the authority of their precepts, should have sent for one from their homeland? Would a Shafiʿi "Malay" congregation have sent for an imam from Bengal?

Mayson was aware only of "orthodox sect[s]" of Sunnis and the Shiʿites in Cape Town. Of them, he wrote: "Few of them are aware of the existence of any phase of Mahometanism than that which is familiar to the confraternity. Differences which prevail among them have not originated in any doctrinal diversity, but in the claims of ecclesiastical candidates, and in the personal quarrels of imams."[45] In the late 1860s, doctrinal differences had resulted in a situation in which Muslim "relatives and other parties had been living in enmity for nearly a century."[46] Such differences can firmly be traced back to at least 1824, when an imam told how one congregation, led by an imam named Jan [van Boegies], "was not recognised by us" because of a separation. Moreover, in the same interviews, each imam told of different mosque disciplines. One congregation flogged disorderly people with canes *(rattans)* and "excommunicated" them; another only "excommunicated" offenders.[47] There were certainly many such disputes throughout the nineteenth and twentieth centuries.

Links with the Outside World of Islam

By the 1790s, free Muslims were numerous enough to form a small, but self-assured, mercantile community in Cape Town, described by both travelers and colonists with approval. In 1799, Mirza Isfahani Abu Talib Ibn Muhammad Khan, a Persian visitor to the Cape, recalled that among the people of Cape Town he had "met with many pious good Mussulmans, several of whom possessed property. I had the pleasure of forming an acquaintance here with Sheikh ʿAbdullah, the son of ʿAbd al ʿAziz, a native of Mecca, who having come to the Cape on some commercial adventure, married the daughter of one of the Malays, and settled there. He was very civil, introduced me to all his friends, and anticipated all my wishes."[48] Imam Muding in 1824 told the Cape authorities that Cape "Arab" imams who had been at Mecca had imposed a limitation of two wives on the Cape congregations and implied that only such high authority could mandate such a reformulation of the traditional Muslim restriction of four wives.[49]

James Backhouse, a Christian missionary writing in the early 1830s, provides a clue about the routes of the first hajjis: "Their priests wore turbans, and garments of various colors; some of them made pilgrimages to Mecca, going to Arabia by way of Mauritius."[50] On the early pilgrimages along this well-sailed Cape slave route, these hajjis would have met other leaders of their faith. But there were other connections with the East African coast. For example, Mayson even tells of a state visit: "In 1820 and 1821, a number of distinguished Arabs from the island of Johanna, in the Mozambique channel, visited the colony. They were kindly received by the government, and were hospitably entertained by the Malays, whom they further instructed in the faith and practice of Islam, and with whom they have since constantly corresponded, sending them also supplies of the Koran and other books."[51] Even the sultan of the island visited in 1834, as is independently recorded: "Abdola, Sultan of the Island of St. [*sic*] Johanna," staying at 61 Bree Street.[52]

Johanna (a.k.a. Anjouan), the most frequented island in the Comores group in the Mozambique channel, was long subject to Muslim influence and was also a slave entrepôt. The local dynasty was founded in 1506 by Muslims from Shiraz in Iran. The DEIC had contact with Anjouan from 1706, when they incurred a debt. The Dutch visited again from time to time and there was talk of rerouting the Ceylon fleets via Anjouan, but nothing came of this plan. One visit in 1773 by a Cape slaver—*de Snelheid*—resulted in a cordial exchange of letters in Arabic between the Cape and Anjouan.[53] According to James Armstrong, a historian of Cape slavery, the Johannese leaders remembered all the previous DEIC visits to their "ancestors" and looked forward to renewed contact (and also politely never mentioned the debt). Armstrong also mentions the possibility that the Arabic interpreter on board was Tuan Guru, who clearly identified himself as the "oppressed Imam, Abdallah ibn al Mazlum Qadi 'Abd al Salam al Taduri, a Shafi'i by religious rite, and Ash'ari by conviction." This Johannese connection did not die away: elsewhere Mayson mentions that in the 1850s "their Johanese friends" still provided the older Muslims with Areca nuts and Betel leaf.[54] Max Kollisch, a late nineteenth-century orientalist, confirmed the continuation of the Johannese connection.[55]

The Sultan of Johanna may have been responsible for having initiated something of a religious schism in the hitherto orthodox Sunni Muslim community of the Cape (orthodox, that is, by the lights of the dress of the Cape Muslims). According to Mayson, "the white turban is the distinguishing mark of the Sonnites [i.e., "Sunni"]; the red turban that of the rival sect of Shi'ites."[56] Muslims wearing either the white or red turban are portrayed in many of the paintings and watercolors of the early Cape.

By the late nineteenth century, Meccans knew of the existence of Muslims at the southern extremity of Africa and called them *Ahl Kâf* (the people of the Cape), as the peripatetic Dutch scholar C. Snouck-Hurgronje recalled from his secret visit to Mecca in 1884–85 disguised as a Muslim:

> A class of Jâwah [Javanese] who dwell outside the geographical boundaries but who in late years have made regular pilgrimages to Mecca are people from the Cape of Good Hope. They are derived from Malays, formerly brought to the Cape by the Dutch, with a small mixture of Dutch blood. Some words of their Malay speech have passed into the strange, clipped-Dutch dialect of the Boers. On the other hand they have exchanged their mother tongue for Cape Dutch, of course, retaining many Malay expressions. Taking into consideration the genuinely Dutch names of many of these *Ahl Kâf* (as they are called in Mecca) one is tempted to believe that degenerated Dutch have been drawn by them into their religion, and many types among them increase the probability of this suggestion. Separated from intercourse with other Moslims they would scarcely have had the

moral strength to hold to their religion, had not eager co-religionists come to them from abroad. When and whence these came is not known to me; however this may be, the mosques in [the] Cape Colony have been more fervently supported in the last twenty years than ever before, more trouble is taken in teaching religion and every year some of the *Ahl Kâf* fare on pilgrimage to the Holy City.[57]

The Reverend Thomas Fothergill Lightfoot pointed out in 1910 that the opening of steamship passages to Zanzibar had "rendered the pilgrimage to Mecca more practicable."[58] He added that "there are now in Cape Town many followers of Islam who have obtained a knowledge of their creed [*sic*] some at Mecca and Zanzibar."[59] Muhammad Salieh Hendricks, who had grown up in rural Swellendam, had gone to Mecca to study in 1888. On his return to the Cape in 1902, he stayed in Zanzibar for almost a year, acting in various religious capacities.[60] Gustav Gerdener, a theologian from Stellenbosch who worked among the Cape Town Muslims, confirmed the continuing importance of the East African links in January 1915, noticing that "Zanzibar has been a source of inspiration on more than one occasion, as when a [Cape] deputation visited that quarter some years ago on behalf of a Mohammedan college [the Tafalah Institute] then in building at Claremont, and as when a deputation of three priests [i.e., imams] visited Zanzibar a few months ago to settle a certain dispute."[61] George Bernard Shaw, en route to South Africa in 1934, stopped in Mombasa and interviewed the resident Muslim scholar, Maulana Mahomet Abdul Aleem Siddiqui. This was of such interest to the Cape Muslims that they reprinted the ensuing debate in its entirety.[62] One may conclude that the Cape Muslims enjoyed a wide range of contacts with the other Muslims on the East coast of Africa, contacts maintained in part by the pious obligations of the hajj.

From Slavery to the Era of Emancipation

During slavery, Islam's authentic universalism had a powerful appeal. Even a humble slave or a convicted felon could be a leader in the Cape Muslim religious community. In this status inversion, in a sense the entire Muslim community could, if not ignore, then bypass the demeaning European-imposed quotidian status categories. But such demonstrations of universalism proved short-lived. Even in the decades before emancipation, the Cape ʿulamaʾ had started becoming a hereditary class. Numerous examples of father-son relationships exist in the nineteenth- and twentieth-century ʿulamaʾ.[63]

Religious leadership in any Islamic community necessarily goes to the most qualified and learned. While it is easy to see how the most qualified might well be the son of an imam, it is also clear that once leadership became the automatic consequence of genealogy, Islam could no longer lay claim to an authentic universalism. The legitimacy of any ʿulamaʾ is vexed, as Jeppe has pointed out.[64] The endless succession disputes—by no means peculiar to the Cape—must have qualified Islam's appeal among other groups over the long term, as did analogous differences in Christian congregations. These led to numerous succession squabbles and sometimes summary exclusions of interlopers. Muslim scholars like Davids and de Costa thus have suggested that litigation became a pattern of virtually all Cape mosque succession disputes: nearly twenty cases were heard in the Cape Supreme Court between 1860 and 1900.

But it would seem churlish to detract from the achievements of these busy and remarkable holy men. They were the first Cape Muslims to go on hajj; they were the first to write religious and other manuscripts—including *Azimats*—in the new Arabic-Afrikaans; they established *madrasas* (schools); manumitted slaves; ran congregations; conducted marriages; performed funerals, and, for the most part, successfully interlocuted with the colonial authorities. As Peter Brown described the functions of the holy men of another monotheistic faith, those of Christian antiquity: "It was through the hard business of living his life for twenty-four hours in the day, through catering for the day-to-day needs of his locality, through allowing his person to be charged with the normal hopes and fears of his fellow men, that the holy man gained the power in society that enabled him to carry off the occasional *coup de théâtre*."[65] But emancipation subtly changed this body of holy men. The immediate effect of the emancipation of slaves was a double religious revival: slaves deserted the rural areas and flocked to the towns and the open arms of the imams or the eager embrace of Christian missionaries. It was a defining moment for all religions in the colony.

The Muslims were most vulnerable on their rites. The magical/mystical Muslim ceremony of *ratiep* or *kalifa* had caused an outcry from Cape Town's Christian population, who considered spectacles like the ritual of flashing sabers passing across unharmed living human flesh to be luring many away from Christianity. One person had been accidentally killed in 1813 by an overly enthusiastic Prize Negro convert.[66] Finally, in 1855, after many complaints from Christian commentators, the Cape Town police attempted to ban the kalifa. For their part, the imams conceded that there was considerable dispute among the various congregations about the appropriateness of this ceremony. The imams used the opportunity to complain that the Cape Muslims had never had any missionaries sent out to them, unlike the other peoples of the Cape. Thus was begun an extraordinary effort to petition Queen Victoria to send a Muslim missionary to Cape Town, on the grounds that the Muslims were taxpayers but, unlike other inhabitants, had never had any missionaries.[67] It was the first step to orthodoxy, and the beginning of the end for the erstwhile free-wheeling Cape Islam.

After a seven-year delay, the unlikely event of a Muslim missionary sponsored by Queen Victoria came to pass: a Kurdish scholar, Shaykh Abu Bakr Effendi, was sent out to the Cape Muslims in 1862 to teach them the true path.[68] However, despite Abu Bakr's pioneering scholarly efforts in learning the world's newest Indo-European language—Afrikaans—and introducing Muslim education for girls and women, he was not popular. That he was "Aryan"—to use Van Selms's shibboleth—

must have come as a shock. His efforts by 1888 had resulted in only one congregation and one school in Cape Town, funded among others by Barney Barnato, a Jewish mining magnate whom Abu Bakr supported in an election.[69] Perhaps because of his failure in Cape Town, he turned to other mission fields. He established theological seminaries at Kimberley, Port Elizabeth, and at Lourenço Marques (Maputo). His single orthodoxy was the banning of the eating of crustaceans, especially the popular Cape lobster *(kreef)*. This doomed his mission: the issue was even debated in Mecca.

Despite a subsequent domestic scandal, his congregation backed the Kurdish imam, but his preeminent position was now lost—to the relief of his competitors, the nearly eclipsed Cape Town ʻulamaʼ. Thereafter, he and his family fitted into the Cape Muslim scene as just another schismatic element.

Still, Abu Bakr's short-lived influence had permanently refocused all Cape Muslims onto the wider world of Islam outside of South Africa. The Turkish *fez* now replaced the *toerang* and the handkerchief, the traditional headdress of Cape Muslims. When an Australian troopship on its way to the Dardanelles stopped in Cape Town during World War I for coal, a few Australian crewmen, coming across Cape Muslims wearing fezzes, concluded that the Turks had occupied the port, and were thoroughly disconcerted. A new, albeit minor, Turkiya had definitely come to Cape Town.

The kalifa, and along with it much of the "magic," went out of the religion as Abu Bakr laid the foundations for the modernizing of Cape Islam. But the appeal of the religion was also reduced by the dead hand of orthodoxy. Conversion to Islam slowed. Gone were the days when Cape imams converted all and sundry. Gone, too, it seems, was the open door to Africans like the Prize Negroes. Further growth of Islam in South Africa had to await another overseas migration of Muslims and a completely new chapter in the history of Islam in South Africa.

The Second Phase of Immigration

After slavery was finally abolished in the British empire in 1838 (following a four-year period of apprenticeship), British colonies founded after that date had to devise alternative labor systems, because wage labor was still beyond the capacity of most fledgling colonies. Such was the case when the British and the Voortrekkers attempted to colonize Natal on South Africa's East coast in the 1830s, '40s, and '50s. Since the local Zulus were unwilling to work in the Europeans' sugarcane fields or in their coal mines, Indians were brought in, with the permission of the British, as indentured servants to form the last component of Natal's triracial population. Between 1860 and 1868 and again from 1874 to 1911, some 176,000 Indians of all faiths were brought to Natal. Approximately 7 to 10 percent of the first shipment of Natal Indians was Muslim; then 80 to 90 percent of the second, but smaller, shipments (termed Passenger Indians, because they paid their fares) was Muslim.

Indentured labor from India was supplemented by African labor from Zanzibar. British interest in the island had increased throughout the nineteenth century, partly as a continuing effort to end the oceanic slave trade. This interest culminated in a British protectorate over the islands of Pemba and Zanzibar in 1890. Before the protectorate, between 1873 and 1880, the Royal Navy had brought some hundreds of "Zanzibari Arabs" to the British naval base in Durban to work as stokers. In that city they were obliged to establish their own mosque as they were not embraced by the already established Indian Muslims. The Zanzibari Arabs appear as a named group in the Population Registration Act of 1950. Proclamation R123 of 1968 refers to "Other Asiatics including Zanzibari Arabs" as one of the seven subsections of the statutory "Coloured" community. These curious categories suggest that they were not assimilated, or zealous apartheid clerks were intent on finding ethnic differences even among the tiny Muslim community of Natal.

Islam in Natal

Islam in Natal also boasted its founding fathers. The first Shaykh Ahmad (popularly known as Majzoob Bdasha Peer) arrived with the indentured Indians of the 1860s and was reputed to be a miracle worker and charismatic. Like the Cape's founding father Shaykh Yusuf, he was also rumored to be a sufi. After an early release from his indentures, he sold fruit and vegetables in Durban until his death in 1886. The second founding father, Shah Ghulum Muhhad Soofie Siddiqui (popularly, Soofie Saheb) established a more lasting tradition. He arrived in 1895 and discovered Shaykh Ahmad's grave. Since impoverished Natal Indian Muslims were always at risk of being absorbed into the Hinduism of the other Indians among whom they lived, he demarcated special Islamic folk festivals to lure the undecided; he also established Muslim orphanages and several madrasas.

After serving their indentures, the Natal Muslims were free, and a significant number spread into the interior of South Africa during its mining revolution (1867–1948) in a countrywide Muslim diaspora that included many entrepreneurial Cape Muslims from most South African ports. Some Indian Muslims from Natal went to Cape Town, where they set up a separate mosque as early as 1892. Some even made their way to Botswana, traveling the old missionary road.[70] Most made their way to Kimberley or the Witwatersrand. The British and Cape governments cited the "unfair treatment" in the Transvaal Republic of a sizeable group of migrating Indians ("citizens of the British empire") as one of the British "grievances" in their ultimatum leading to the Anglo-Boer War (1899–1902).

Despite this diaspora and some intermarriage, the Muslims of the Cape remained separated by geography, doctrine, class, history, and language until well into the twentieth century. The Natal Indian Muslims spoke Urdu, Gujerati, Tamil, Sindhi, and English, and their congregations were based on powerful mosque committees, dominated by merchants; the Cape Muslims, on the other hand, spoke creole Dutch, or Afrikaans;[71] their congregations were controlled by a wide variety of artisans, working-class people, and only a small merchant group.

The Transvaal Fatwa

The twentieth century revealed three regional Muslim communities: in the Cape, in Natal, and a third (derived from internal migration) in the inland republic (later, the colony) of Transvaal. There were no Muslims in the Orange Free State because of draconian legislation against "Asian" settlers. John Voll has drawn attention to the 1903 Transvaal *fatwa* (authoritative legal opinion) and called it "one of the famous documents of early Islamic modernist thought."[72] A Transvaal Muslim, al-Hajj Mustafa al-Transvaali, submitted three questions to Muhammad Abduh, the grand mufti of Egypt, that—it turned out—were of great importance to all Muslims in a modernizing world. It represents a classic case of what Muslims experience when they are a minority, and it also ventilated some of the profoundest problems of the South African Muslims. The questions hinged on issues of dress codes, the offense of slaughtering of animals by axe, and, finally, prayer procedures. The responses were liberal and inclusive and generated considerable debate throughout the Muslim world. Voll is quite right, though, in insisting on seeing the Transvaal fatwa in its South African context.

Johannesburg after the mining revolution and the Anglo-Boer War was the most modern of South Africa's cities and was the first site where a significant number of Hanafi and Shafii Muslims had to live together. The Natal and Cape Muslims were the most urbanized groups in South Africa throughout its colonial history, but they first came together in the Transvaal. The fatwa responses did little, however, to unite the Muslim groups.

During the Bubonic plague of 1901, the government had placed "Indians" in isolation camps, which prompted Muslim fears. Following the Anglo-Boer War, the South African Moslem Association (SAMA) launched a preemptive program to recruit all "Dutch-speaking Malays" against possible government attempts to create "locations" for them. Curiously, "Indians, Arabs and Afghans" were not allowed to join SAMA; hence, under the simultaneous burdens of ethnic and linguistic division, any seeds of a pan-Islamist movement could not germinate. Names of subsequent Muslim organizations seemed designed to exclude others. For example, in 1920, the Cape Malay Association and in 1923 the South African Indian Moslem Congress represented clear evidence of the geographical and ethnic divisions that continued to divide Natal and Cape Muslims. Some intermarriage of leading families softened, but failed to remove, the gulf between Cape and Natal.

Secularization

But the biggest division was not geographical. The main challenge to Islam in twentieth-century South Africa was secularization. One does not have to be versed in the various Muslim disputes to know that there are two competing visions of the past: some Muslims try to restore strength and sincerity to their convictions by seeking in the Quran and hadith the authority for norms appropriate to modern needs and situations, in the belief that in scripture those needs and situations had been, if not foreseen, then at least provided for. In other words, change is both good *and* Islamic, or can be rendered so. Other Muslims, equally sincere and idealistic, have wished instead to reproduce exactly the patterns of a past period of human life—a period deemed to be ideal, usually that of the Prophet's own lifetime and of that of his companions. Change, in this view, has been for the worse, and should be reversed. Muslim debate in twentieth-century South Africa has seesawed over these ancient alternatives.

This basic difference may be perceived at the level of personalities: on the one hand, there were modernists, people like ʿAbdullah ʿAbduhuraman (1872–1940), who promoted both secular and Muslim education; on the other hand, there were traditionalists, like Shaykh Muhammad Salieh Hendricks (1871–1945), who, while promoting education, also wished to protect Muslim women from modern influences and made them cover their *aurahs* and wear *hijab*. It is a tribute to the closeness of the Muslim community that these men (both from the rural Cape) were brothers-in-law.

The basic defense against secularization is recognition of religious authority. It is therefore not surprising that the first such recognition should be in the Transvaal, the origin of the fatwa concerning secularization. The first organization of the South African ʿulamaʾ, the Jamiʿat al-ʿUlamaʾ, was founded in that province in 1923.[73] In 1940, the most important secular leader of the Muslims, Dr. Abduhuraman, died. In his wake, in February 1945, near the end of World War II, imams and religious leaders in Cape Town gathered to establish an organization to represent the specific religious needs of local Muslim imams and to consider the means to protect Islamic customs. They named their association the Moslem Judicial Council (MJC). It became the platform for the voice of the ʿulamaʾ of the city and constituted itself as the only legitimate representative of Muslims and of Islam to the state. The equivalent Natal Jamʿiat al-ʿUlamaʾ, was launched in 1952. While the MJC was certainly a rational innovation, it remained dominated by the Cape shaykhs, who according to certain critics were too conservative and sometimes arbitrary in their exclusionary tactics.

The conservative character of the South African MJC was challenged by the growing inequalities and iniquities of the apartheid state (1948–1994). The death of Imam ʿAbdullah Haron while in police custody in 1969 radicalized his congregation and sent shock waves throughout the South African Muslim world (although not a shaykh, he sat on the MJC). He had, among several pioneering activities, helped form the Nyanga Muslim Association in the African township of the same name. He also had a large influence on the Muslim youth. Before Steve Biko was killed in custody in 1977, the Muslims had an equivalent martyr.

In 1990, a historic national Muslim conference took place. Delegates from Muslim organizations throughout the country came together to consider their response to the new situation. This resulted in the formation of the Muslim Front. While the Muslim Front canvassed for the ANC in 1994, some Muslims formed alternatives—

the African Muslim Party and the Islamic Party. Both failed to return any seats. That same year, the ANC appointed Abdullah Omar, a committed Muslim, to the portfolio of justice in the government of national unity. The influential and scholarly Muslim youth movement, which from time to time still politely challenges the moral authority of the quietist MJC, is bound to inherit a broad Islamic resurgence in the new South Africa.

Islam in the South Africa of the year 2000 could enjoy an awakening in the light of persistent failures of the secular state to provide a spiritual home for the people of South Africa. But there are problems at the community level. The state's failure to resolve basic law-and-order issues that are close to the heart of all concerned citizens—Muslim and non-Muslim alike—have led, among Muslims, to the creation of grassroots organizations like PAGAD (People against Gangsterism and Drugs), whose members model themselves (at least, in terms of dress) on Middle East Muslims.

Ethnic tensions in the 1990s have run high. There was, for example, a resurgence of "Malay" identity after 1994 as trade and cultural links with Malaysia increased. In 1997, a few extremists vented their fury against a Jewish bookshop owner on the eve of Cape Town's bid for the Olympic Games. Muslims denounced this regrettable episode as an unfortunate perversion, but to some it was a mini *kristalnacht*. Women were excluded from appearing on one Muslim radio station. The combination of these developments did not endear the Muslims to the jittery country at large.

☾ ☾ ☾

There has been a strong, but understandable, tendency in liberal South African history up to 1994 to document the intricate dovetailing of the evils of colonialism, the class system, or "the Boerewors curtain"—apartheid. This historiography of guilt assumed that everything divisive in South Africa derived from the same poisoned well—Europe.

This guilty, intently Eurocentric vision has had several unintended effects. First, it has intimidated (or excused) local communities from critically interrogating their own pasts, thereby cheating communities of essential self-knowledge. Second, too little attention has been paid to the *longue durée* of sustained autonomous cultural achievement of such "oppressed" groups and all the inspiration to be found in such histories. Third, one may tentatively suggest that internal divisions are not always derived from colonialism and apartheid, although the hidden injuries of those systems may at first blush seem endless. The divisions that continue to split the Muslim communities of South Africa are relics of quite ancient fissiparous tendencies—largely independent of the colonial order—that continue operating to divide ordinary people of the same faith from one another. In this case, one of South Africa's oldest, and indeed most independent of communities, has been intramurally divided for most of its distinguished and sometimes glorious history—and, let it be said, by the same issues of privilege, language, ethnicity, and gender that have bedeviled their European compatriots.

Still, when one considers the entire history of Islam in South Africa, one can only conclude that the history of all Muslim cultural achievements began at the community level. It is that community ethos that now has to be recovered historically for all groups. From the martyrdoms of Joudan Tappa (1713) to that of imam Haron (1969), from the *azimats* of the eighteenth century to the FM radio stations of 1998, the voice of Islam has always been heard in South Africa with authority, fidelity, and even, sometimes, tolerance.

Notes

1. Muhammed Haron provides access to most of the sources consulted in this chapter. The secondary works on the subject of South Africa's Muslims—especially those of M. Ajam; Adil Bradlow and Frank Bradlow; S. Brandel-Syrier; Margaret Cairns; Yusuf da Costa; Suleman Essop Dangor; Achmat Davids; Kate Jeffreys; Shamil Jeppie; Samuel Abraham Rochlin, and Abdulkader Tayob—have provided useful background. I am especially grateful to the late Achmat Davids, Muhammed Haron, Shamil Jeppie, Laura Mitchell, Sandy Rowoldt, Christopher Saunders, and Michael Whisson for reading this chapter and providing additional material and references.

2. I am grateful to Peter Brown for permission to use this quotation.

3. Böeseken et al. 1957, 54–55.

4. Dangor is the only full biography. See also *Dictionary of South African Biography* (hereafter *DSAB*), s.v. "Van Selms," 893–94; Cense 1950, 50–57.

5. Dangor 1982, 4.

6. Theal 1964, 3:261.

7. *DSAB*, 1:894.

8. Dangor 1982, 3 (section 4):123; 5:47ff. "*zyn Sappa (of uitgekaaude pinang) die by wagwierp, als een heilighed eerbiedig opgeraapt, bewaard.*" Also, Du Plessis 1972, 4.

9. Jeffreys 1939, 195.

10. Cape Archives Depot (hereafter CAD) "*Extract uijt de Generale Resolutien,*" C 424 (30 Oct. 1699): 449–59, 453.

11. Jeffreys 1939, 196.

12. Dangor 1982.

13. Agnos 1993, 82–83.

14. Sleigh 1993, 386; CAD CJ 3318, "Bandiette Rolle" (1744): 324–25; Hajji's death, 355, 526.

15. CAD CJ 3318, "Bandiette Rolle" (1746): 488.

16. CAD CJ 3318, "Bandiette Rolle" (Oct. 1766): 579.

17. CAD CJ 3318, "Bandiette Rolle" (1767): 551, 579, 582, 589.

18. Convict estimate from Armstrong, Jun. 1995; SOAS, Council for World Mission Archives, LMS Series, South African Correspondence, box 11, folder 3, jacket A, Elliot to Miles (1 Jan. 1829).

19. Those who undertook a course of study in the Middle East were termed *shaykhs,* those who only completed the pilgrimage *hajjis,* while those who could not afford to go to Mecca remained ordinary imams; cf. Jeppie 1996, 139–62.

20. Forster 1777, 2:60–61.

21. Shell 1997, 268–85.

22. Bird 1823, 349.

23. "Evidence of Two Mahometan Priests," in *Papers Relative,* 208.

24. Personal communication with the author.

25. SOAS, Council for World Mission Archives, LMS Series, South African correspondence, box 12, folder 4, jacket B, Philip to the directors, LMS (14 Jan. 1831).

26. Cory Library, MS 16,579: Laing's journal (28 Jan. 1831). I am grateful to Sandra Rowoldt for this reference.

27. Bird 1823, 349–50.

28. Aspeling 1883, 4.

29. Massleman 1963, 63 and note 18, 77.

30. Shell 1995, 3–20; Davids 1997, 12–16.

31. Public Record Office, CO 414/6 12285, "A Return of the Negroes Imported into the Colony Since 1808" (12 Feb. 1822), folio 45, p. 500 (Kew enumeration).

32. Theal 1903, "Report of John Thomas Bigge upon the Finances" (6 Sept. 1826) 27:493.

33. Bird 1823, 360, s.v. "Apprentices."

34. Whisson 1985, 153.

35. Bird 1823, 76.

36. Theal 1903. Letter, Earl of Caledon to Viscount Castlereagh (4 Feb. 1808), 6:271.

37. *Papers Relative,* 207.

38. Gray 1876, 1:169.

39. Merriman 1957, 8–9.

40. Shell 1994, 11–39.

41. Hardy n.d., 7:390–404.

42. Jeppie 1988.

43. Bradlow 1981, 12–19.

44. Mayson 1861, 16.

45. Ibid., 17–18.

46. Kollisch 1867, 6.

47. *Papers Relative,* 207, 209, 210.

48. Khan 1810, 1:72–73.

49. *Papers Relative,* 208.

50. Backhouse 1844, 82–83.

51. Mayson 1861, 12.

52. *South African Directory and Almanac for the Year 1834,* 206.

53. Armstrong 1982.

54. Mayson 1861, 27–28.

55. Kollisch 1867, 13.

56. Mayson 1861, 12.

57. Snouck-Hurgronje 1931, 216–17.

58. Lightfoot 1900, 39.

59. Ibid., 43.

60. de Costa 1994, 106–7.

61. Gerdener 1914, 55. For the Tafalah Institute, see *DSAB,* s.v. "Abdurahman, Abdullah" [by Thelma Shifrin].

62. *Shavian Meets a Theologian.*

63. *Papers Relative,* 207; Jeppie 1996, 139–62.

64. Jeppie 1996, 139.

65. Brown 1982, 105.

66. CJ 805: folio 825, no. 12 (2 Sept. 1813).
67. De Lima 1857.
68. *DSAB* 1:4–5.
69. *Cape Argus* (2 Nov. 1888), p. 4, col. 3.
70. Parratt 1989, 71–82.
71. Malayu was heard in mosques as late as the 1930s.
72. Voll 1996, 27.
73. Naudé 1982, 23–39.

Bibliography

Agnos, Peter, ed. 1993. *The Queer Dutchman: True Account of a Sailor Castaway on a Desert Island for "Unnatural Acts" and Left to God's Mercy.* New York: Green Eagle. Reprint of 1762 edition.

Armstrong, James C. 1982. "Two Comorian Letters of 1773." Association Historique Internationale de L'Ocean Indien. Table Ronde de Saint Denis (Jun. 25–28).

Aspeling, Eric. 1883. "The Cape Malays: An Essay." Cape Town.

Backhouse, James. 1844. *A Narrative of a Visit to the Mauritius and South Africa.* London: Hamilton, Adams.

Bird, William W. 1823. *State of the Cape of Good Hope in 1822.* London: John Murray, 1966 facsimile reprint, Cape Town: Struik.

Böeseken, Anna J. 1977. *Slaves and Free Blacks at the Cape (1658–1700).* Cape Town: Tafelberg.

Böeseken, Anna J., et al., eds. 1957. *Suid-Afrikaanse Argiefstukke: Resolusies van die Politieke Raad.* Cape Town: Cape Times.

Bradlow, Frank. 1981. "Islam at the Cape of Good Hope," *South African Historical Journal* 13:12–19.

Brown, Peter. 1982. "The Rise and Function of the Holy Man in Late Antiquity." In *Society and the Holy in Late Antiquity,* ed. Peter Brown. Berkeley: University of California Press.

Cense, A. A. 1950. "De Verering van Sjaich Jusuf in Zuid-Celebes," *Bingkisan Budi* (Aug. 1):50–57.

de Costa, Yusuf. 1994. "From Social Cohesion to Religious Discord: The Life and Times of *Shaykh* Muhammad Salih Hendricks." In *Pages from Cape Muslim History,* ed. Yusuf de Costa and Achmat Davids, 103–14. Pietermaritzburg, South Africa: Shuter & Shooter.

Dangor, Suleman Essop. 1982. *Shaykh Yusuf.* Mobeni: IQRA. Research Committee.

Davids, Achmat. 1997. "The Early History of Islam in Port Elizabeth," *Boorhaanol* 32,4:12–16.

———. Forthcoming. "The South East Asian Roots of the Mystical Practices and Shari 'Ah-centric Piety of the Cape Muslims." In "Slaves, Sheikhs, Sultans, and Saints: The Kramats of the Western Cape," MS in process.

Dictionary of South African Biography. 1968–. Pretoria: HSRC.

Du Plessis, Izaak D. 1972. *The Cape Malays.* 3rd ed. Cape Town: Balkema.

Forster, George. 1777. *A Voyage Round the World in His Britannic Majesty's Sloop, Resolution, Commanded by Captain James Cook during the Years 1772, 1773, 1774, 1775.* 2 vols. London: White.

Gerdener, G. B. A. 1914–1915. "Mohammedanism in South Africa," *South African Quarterly* 1:53–56.

Gray, Robert. 1876. *Life of Robert Gray, Bishop of Cape Town and Metropolitan of Africa.* 2 vols. ed. Rev. Charles Gray (his son). London: Rivingtons.

Hardy, Peter. "Islam in South Asia," *Encyclopedia of Religion,* ed. Mircea Eliade. New York: Macmillan.

Haron, Muhammed. 1997. *Muslims in South Africa: An Annotated Bibliography.* Cape Town: South African Library.

Jeffreys, Kathleen M. 1939. "The Kramat at Zandvliet, Faure: Part 2: 'Sheikh Joseph at the Cape,'" *Cape Naturalist* 1,6 (Jul.):195–99.

Jeppie, Shamil. 1988. "I. D. du Plessis and the 'Re-Invention' of the 'Malay' (c.1935–1952)." Paper given at Department of Economic History, University of Cape Town, Sept. 8.

———. 1996. "Leadership and Loyalties: The Imams of Nineteenth Century Colonial Cape Town, South Africa," *Journal of Religion in Africa* 26:139–62.

Khan, Mirza Isfahani Abu Talib ibn Muhammed. 1810. *The Voyages of Mirza Abu Taleb Khan in Asia, Africa, and Europe in the Years 1799, 1800, 1801, 1802 and 1803, written by himself in the Persian Language.* Trans. Charles Stewart. 2 vols. London: Longman, Hurst, Rees, and Orme.

Kollisch, Max. 1867. *The Musselman Population at the Cape of Good Hope.* Constantinople: Levant Herald Office.

Lightfoot, Thomas F. 1900. "The Cape Malays." In *Sketches of Church Work and Life in the Diocese of Cape Town,* ed. Alan George Sumner Gibson. Cape Town: S.A. "Electric."

De Lima, Joseph Suasso. 1857. *The Chalifa Question: Documents Connected with the Matter.* Cape Town: Van de Sandt & de Villiers.

Massleman, George. 1963. *The Cradle of Colonialism.* New Haven: Yale University Press.

Mayson, John S. 1861. *The Malays of Cape Town.* Manchester: Galt.

Merriman, Nathaniel J. 1957. *The Cape Journals of Archdeacon N. J. Merriman (1848–1855).* Cape Town: Van Riebeeck Society.

Naudé, J. A. 1982. "The Ulema in South Africa, with Particular Reference to the Transvaal Ulema," *Journal of Islamic Studies* 2:23–39.

Papers Relative to the Condition and Treatment of the Native Inhabitants of Southern Africa within the Colony of the Cape of Good Hope, part 1 (Mar. 18, 1835).

Parratt, Saroj N. 1989. "Muslims in Botswana," *African Studies* 48,1:71–81.

Shavian Meets a Theologian (1934), A. 1960. Athlone Islamic Publications Bureau, series no. 7.

Shell, Robert C.-H. 1994. "The 'Tower of Babel': The Slave Trade and Creolization at the Cape (1652–1834)." In *Slavery in South Africa: Captive Labor on the Dutch Frontier,* ed. Elizabeth Eldridge and Fred Morton 12–39. Boulder, Colo.: Westview.

————. 1995. "The March of the Mardijckers: The Toleration of Islam at the Cape (1633–1861)," *Kronos* 22:3–20.

————. 1997. "Between Christ and Muhammad: Conversion, Slavery, and Gender in the Urban Western Cape." In *Christianity in South Africa: A Political, Social, and Cultural History,* ed. Richard Elphick and Rodney Davenport, 268–78. Berkeley: University of California Press; Cape Town: Philip.

Sleigh, Dan. 1993. *Die Buiteposte: VOC-buitposte onder Kaapse bestuur, 1652–1795.* Pretoria: Haum.

Snouck-Hurgronje, C. 1931. *Mekka in the Latter Part of the Nineteenth Century.* Leyden: Brill.

South African Directory and Almanac for the Year 1834. 1833. Cape Town: Greig.

Theal, George M. 1903. *Records of the Cape Colony.* 36 vols. Cape Town: Government Printers.

————. 1964. *History of African South of the Zambezi.* Facsimile edition, 11 vols. Cape Town: Struik.

Valéntyn, François. 1724–26. *Oud en Nieuw Oost Indien.* 5 vols. Dordrecht.

Van Selms, A. "Yussuf, Sjech." In *Dictionary of South African Biography,* 1:893–94.

Voll, John O. 1996. "Abduh and the Transvaal Fatwa: The Neglected Question." In *Islam and the Question of Minorities,* ed. Tamara Sonn, 27–39. University of South Florida, Scholars Press.

Whisson, Michael. 1985. "Water and Workers: Meeting the Needs of the Royal Navy in Simon's Town," *Simon's Town Historical Society Bulletin* 13,3:151–54.

CHAPTER 16

Radicalism and Reform in East Africa

Abdin Chande

The emergence of Islamic radicalism in East Africa in recent decades is fired by a vision of the universal *umma,* the commonwealth of all believers over time and space. This radicalism is in some sense an attempt to recover this community vision of Islam. It is motivated by an impulse to influence other Muslims, as well as to reform their practices to bring them in line with scriptural Islam. This desire for reform to reconstruct local understanding of Islam has caused a massive internal struggle against the accepted or ingrained popular mind-set. It reflects both Islam's entrenchment in the region and tensions within the Muslim community that in fact mark the end of the period of religious tolerance of local Islam.[1]

The three East African countries have witnessed intensive preaching activity in recent decades—a phenomenon connected with Islamic mobilization of the community. The preachers, trained locally or (in many cases) in Saudi Arabia, appeal to young people to become agents for renewal and reform. Some, especially in Uganda, espouse a radical understanding of Islam of the "fundamentalist"/Islamist variety.[2] This type of Islam has been influenced by trends in the Islamic world where political pressure is exerted for the implementation of Islam in the wider area.

❮ ❮ ❮

Discussion of this topic has to be set in the context of developments during the colonial era. The problems that East African Muslims face (and that make Islamic resurgence or activism possible) to a large extent stem from that period. More specifically, it was the colonial educational system (dominated by Christian missions) that structured the social order. The outcome was that education was and has continued to be a source of Muslim grievance. The educational structure perpetuated the existing social and economic divisions in East African societies, thus privileging certain ethnic groups with the longest and deepest contacts with Christian missions. Muslim efforts to mobilize their communities for educational opportunities have progressively over time contributed to a growing Islamic consciousness.

In the case of Kenya, a political dimension clearly has been involved in this growing Muslim awareness. The process of colonization, moving from the coast to the interior, underlaid the shift in power that, to the present day, continues to favor up-country ethnic groups. Most high positions in government fell to non-Muslims educated in the up-country Christian mission schools. This was why, during the period of colonial rule and agitation for independence, coastal Muslims, fearing unfair treatment by the dominant ethnic groups, launched the Mwambao movement to fight for autonomy (the ten-mile coastal strip they sought was theoretically part of Zanzibar), whereas other Muslims (including most in up-country areas) joined the dominant African political parties such as Kanu and Kadu.

The process of marginalizing Muslims continued during the postcolonial period, at first through Kenyatta's privileging of ethnicity and then through Moi's privileging of both ethnicity and religion.[3] In a new era of multiparty politics, with Kenya's political marketplace having thus been ethnically defined, Islamic interests came to be voiced in the 1990s by the Islamic Party of Kenya (IPK) and Shaykh Balala. Thus in Kenya (the subject of the next section) Islamic resurgence has taken different forms and has manifested in different arenas.

The Islamic Reform Movement in Kenya

The reform movement in East Africa has its origins in developments in the Middle East in the eighteenth and nineteenth centuries. The ideas of Muslim thinkers such as Afghani, Muhammad Abduh, and Rashid Rida (the latter had Wahhabi sympathies) began to filter into the East African coastal region in the 1920s and 1930s.

Shaykh al-Amin Mazruʻi, the chief *qadi* of Kenya until his death in 1947, emerged as the leading champion of reform against "religious innovations" *(bidʻa)*. A popularizer, through lectures in mosques and in his newspapers *(al-Islah* and *al-Sahifa)*, Mazruʻi championed modernist reformist ideas. He sought both to promote a stricter form of Islam (in opposition to the local popular version) and to suggest ways in which Kenyan Muslims on the coast could respond to the changes brought about by colonialism.[4]

Mazruʻi's crusade was continued by a former student of his, Shaykh ʻAbdalla Saleh al-Farsy, who became chief qadi of Kenya in 1968. Shaykh al-Farsy opposed local practices such as saint veneration, costly *khitmas* (mourning rites), and the lavish celebration of *mawlid.* Born in Zanzibar, where he lived until 1967, when he moved to Mombasa, he died in 1982. (The best-known representative of the traditional ʻulamaʼ group in these years was Sayyid Ali Badawi Jamalil-Lail (d. 1988), who was based in Lamu.) Farsy, the main advocate and popularizer of reformism in East

Africa, had access to radio and other forums. He also gave sermons and public lectures in mosques, and his many writings, which were widely read, included the first complete translation of the Quran in KiSwahili.[5]

Farsy inspired a whole generation of young Muslims. The new group of scholars (both locally- and foreign-trained) represented by him are motivated by an impulse to restructure the local understanding of the Muslim faith along strict Salafi lines. Those who espouse reform (i.e., a return to a stricter form of Islam in line with scripture and the prophetic model) refer to themselves as Salafi. In other words, these reformers call for a return to the religion of the salaf, the ancestors, who followed the original principles of the faith. Their activities have both heightened Islamic awareness and precipitated a major struggle within their communities.

Islamic Radicalism in Kenya

Radicalization of the Muslim community in Kenya has its basis in three factors: the rise of a new ʿulamaʾ group; the heightened awareness created by the success of the Islamic revolution in Iran; and the rising number of Muslims who are being exposed to secular education at Kenya's four local universities.[6] The new ʿulamaʾ include Shaykh Ali Shee (currently *imam* of the Jamia mosque in Nairobi), Shaykh Nasoro Khamisi (who delivers mosque-lectures in Mombasa, continuing the work of al-Farsy), and Shaykh Ahmad Msallam. A considerable number of young Muslims who have been educated at Islamic centers of learning, most notably the university of Madina, have returned as reformers and as pan-Islamists (that is to say, those with a much more global understanding of Islam than that of most local ʿulamaʾ). A good number have also had the opportunity to combine Islamic with secular education; they have been exposed to the political Islamist writings of scholars Sayyid Qutb, Muhammad Qutb, and others. This makes them uniquely qualified to relate their sermons to the problems of the day and thus raise Muslim political consciousness.[7]

Muslims were especially exercised over Kenya's controversial law of succession.[8] This issue came up in the late 1970s and 1980s, at a time when Muslims were better prepared than before to mount a united opposition. Shaykh ʿAbdillahi Nassir, a Muslim activist committed to socioeconomic and political reform of society, played an important role in mobilizing Muslim opinion against the proposed law (as did the current chief qadi, Shaykh Nassor Nahdi, and others). Nassir, well-known in Kenya for his sympathies for the Iranian revolution and for writings and talks on Shiʿism, became a controversial figure in Kenya's predominantly Sunni Muslim community. Through concerted efforts and diplomacy, Muslims persuaded the Moi government in 1990 not to apply the controversial laws of succession, marriage, and divorce,which were seen as undermining the shariʿa. Another sensitive issue has been the wearing of head scarves in secondary schools: Muslim girls have been suspended from school for donning *hijab*. In a number of cases, however, the courts have ruled, based on the Kenyan constitution, in their favor.

(((

Muslims make up between 20 and 30 percent of Kenya's population,[9] yet for long they have felt effectively excluded from the power-sharing process. Although the rise of multiparty politics provided Muslims with opportunities to voice grievances against the ruling Kanu party, the government has proved reluctant to deal with issues of land, employment, and educational opportunities.[10] The Muslim organization known as the Supreme Council of Kenya Muslims (Supkem—established in 1973) has been as ineffective as its equivalent, Bakwata, in Tanzania (Christian organizations—for instance, NCCK in Kenya—have been far more effective and more vocal on political issues).

From modern Kenya's beginnings, Muslims have had little political power. Kenyatta's cabinet contained no Muslims—although during his era it was not religion that was the governing factor: Kenyatta was much more swayed in his political decisions by ethnic considerations (in distribution of positions of power, access to foreign aid, resettlement plans, and other economic opportunities and privileges, his policies tended to favor his kinsmen). Moi was the first to make religion a factor in Kenya's national politics (his weekly attendance at church is given wide coverage in the media). Moi's cabinet, like Kenyatta's, did not include a single Muslim; then the abortive coup attempt of 1982, which he survived due to the loyalist forces led by general Mahmoud Muhammad, a career soldier of Kenyan Somali origin, led to the general's younger brother being appointed a cabinet minister. However, in a political system riddled with patronage and sectional/ethnic lobbying, Muslim politicians (Moi loyalists) did little to promote the interests of the Muslim masses.[11]

In January 1992, in an atmosphere of growing Islamic political awareness, the Islamic Party of Kenya (IPK) was founded by young, educated Muslims Omar Mwinyi and Abdulrahman Wandati.[12] By the middle of the year, the head of the IPK was a young activist, Shaykh Khalid Balala, a University of Madina graduate and self-employed businessman who had traveled extensively in the Middle East, the Far East, Europe, and Africa, preaching and advancing Islamic scholarship.[13] President Moi, fearing that such an Islamic party would erode Kanu's support in Muslim areas, was quick to dissuade Muslims from associating with "Islamic fundamentalism,"[14] but what was in fact at stake (even Muslim public figures within Kanu admitted this) was the discriminatory practices of the government toward Muslims.[15] When the IPK successfully capitalized on the general feeling of alienation among coastal Muslims, the government predictably denied it official recognition,[16] and with tensions running high in Mombasa, on 19 and 20 May 1992 there was a rampage by Muslims. In the aftermath, some Muslim preachers who were critical of the government were arrested at a public rally. This sparked a two-day riot (cries of "Allahu Akbar" were heard in the city). Four Muslims were shot dead by the police.[17]

Muslim grievances included low representation in government/public institutions; discrimination in applications processed by government ministries; fewer educational institutions set up in the coastal region, and no university; lack of equal time for Muslims on government-run radio and television; up-country Christian Africans (Kikuyus and Kalenjin) being given the lion's share of jobs and profits from tourism and hotels on the coast; and the lack of developmental projects (other than in tourism) in the coastal towns.[18] Shaykh Balala, delivering impassioned speeches to Muslim crowds, called on them to press their demands; if the demands were not met, Muslims should, he said, advocating active Muslim confrontation with the secular power, take their destiny into their own hands.[19] When Shaykh Balala was arrested, the ensuing one-day strike paralyzed Mombasa.

The riots propelled the IPK into prominence, garnering support in the Muslim community. Ali Mazrui, who was denied permission to give a public lecture a few days later, took the case of the plight of Muslims to the international press corps; a leading Kenyan Muslim intellectual also spoke out against anti-Muslim discrimination;[20] and the stand-off continued. The police stormed a mosque in Mombasa and the government later apologized; President Moi, speaking at annual Madaraka Day celebrations, in Muslim eyes insulted them by equating Islam with slavery.[21]

Tensions simmered through 1995 and 1996. Violent raids erupted in August 1997 at Likoni and continued on Kenya's southern coast in September and October. These were aggravated by (but not necessarily caused by) unemployed Muslim and non-Muslim youths at the coast who were alienated at the sight of wealth and prosperity all around them.[22] Moi subsequently instigated the formation of an association called the United Muslims of Africa (UMA)—an attempt to divide coastal Muslims along ethnic lines. UMA (headed by Masumbuko) was presented as the party of "African" Muslims, as against the IPK, which was painted as a party of "Arabs." Balala, forced to flee to a European country, had his passport cancelled; the Moi government claimed he had a Yemeni passport and forbade his return to the country.

In the run-up to the 1997 elections, amid Muslim unrest and dissatisfaction with Kanu, the opposition parties attempted to secure the Muslim vote by promising power-sharing if elected, and the IPK failed to achieve broad national support. The party, which declared an alliance with the National Democratic Party (as it had done with Ford-Kenya in 1992) exerted minimal influence on Kenyan Muslims. The result reflected the success of Moi's politics of divide and rule, and the ongoing challenge to the different ethnic communities to forge unity.[23]

Relations between the Kenyan Muslims and the Moi government continued to deteriorate, especially following the bombing of the U.S. embassy, on 7 August 1998, one of the consequences of which was the banning of Muslim NGOs—a cause of much anger among Kenyan Muslims. Through legal representation, however, Muslims were later successful in having the ban lifted against these NGOs which had been de-registered, though without justification, by Kenya's Non-governmental Organizations' Coordination Board.

The Contemporary Islamic Movement in Uganda

Uganda's political history is a tale of competition between Islam and Christianity and between Roman Catholics and Protestants—struggles that are charged by numerous issues, historical, political, and socioeconomic.

Islam arrived in southern Uganda (Buganda) from the East African coastal region by 1840. The religion also reached the country from a northerly direction with the stationing of Sudanese soldiers in northern Uganda under the command of Emin Pasha. Due to developments in northern Sudan in the era of the Mahdi, these Muslims eventually settled in Madi and parts of West Nile. Nevertheless, although Islam reached the country three and a half decades before the arrival of Christianity, it lost out to the latter because the British colonial authorities saw Islam as a potential threat to their interests. In the bitter rivalry and religious wars of the 1880s, Muslims were defeated. Thereafter, the spread of Christianity, aided by the school system, was encouraged to check the diffusion of Islam.

The outcome of these developments in the colonial era was that positions of influence in the country eventually fell into the hands of missionary-educated African Christians. Lacking Western education, Muslims ended up as traders, butchers, taxi or bus drivers, and petty shopkeepers.[24] In Uganda as in Kenya, Muslim activism in the contemporary Uganda therefore can be seen in large measure as a response to the economic and social inequalities that developed in the colonial and postcolonial period.

In Uganda, however, the political strength of Muslims bears no relation to their numerical strength, which is between 10 and 15 percent of the population. In the political struggles between the Democratic Party (DP), which drew its support from the Catholic areas, and the Uganda People's Congress (UPC), which was identified as the party of the Protestants, Muslims were courted by the UPC—and the UPC was successful in its bid for power.

The endemic leadership struggles within the Muslim community (which go back to the early decades of this century in Buganda), have been exploited by successive regimes in Uganda to split the Muslim community by supporting one rival leader against another.[25] Milton Obote (UPC), through the efforts of his cousin al-Hajj Nekyon, a cabinet minister, created the National Association for the Advancement of Muslims (NAAM) in 1965 as a support base for his party in Buganda in opposition to a Mulangira Muslim faction, with ties to the Buganda monarchy. With the overthrow of Obote's government in 1971, Idi Amin banned NAAM and other Muslim organizations. Amin created a central body, the Uganda Muslim Supreme Council (UMSC). It was provided with *awqaf* (property endowments), which included some buildings belonging to Asian Muslim *jama'at* (community organizations with religious or social functions). The regime also appointed qadis in each district (although they operated only on the periphery of society).

Clearly, Muslims came into prominence in the 1970s under Amin, a Muslim military leader. The Amin regime established closer relations with some Arab states, and thus Ugandan Muslims were able to pursue Islamic education at the Islamic University of Madina. Uganda also became a member of the Organization of the Islamic Conference (OIC) and received petro-dollars to finance projects such as the construction of Islamic schools, the Islamic University of Mbale, mosques, and clinics. But Idi Amin lacked a political constituency beyond his tiny Kakwa ethnic group, which only enjoyed a strategic base in the Uganda army. Amin's ouster from power in 1979 raised the fears of Muslims, especially in the wake of atrocities committed against Muslims, particularly Nubis (reprisals for the brutalities of the Idi Amin regime). There were reports of mosques being transformed into nightclubs in eastern Uganda, and of the mass flight of Nubis as refugees to Sudan.[26]

The Reformist Movement in Uganda

Throughout the 1970s and 1980s, several hundred Ugandan Muslim students studied at the Islamic University of Medina. On their return to Uganda, they preached a stricter form of Islam that until then had been unknown in Uganda. The influence of reformist trends strengthened the international network linking Ugandan Muslims to the major centers of Islam for the first time. Pan-Islamic activism, associated with the Salafi movement, coincided with a growing Islamic awareness worldwide. This activism was eventually to turn in a political direction, a development not new to Uganda, where religion and politics have often interacted, notably with state attempts to control the institutions of civil society.

By the mid-1980s, the emerging divisions between the young Salafis and the traditional 'ulama' of popular religion had begun to harden. Ugandan Muslim society divided along generational lines, with the youth *(vijana)* on one side and the elders *(wazee)* on the other. In most major towns, and to a certain extent in villages, too, in the southern, eastern, and even Western parts of the country one today finds that young people tend to frequent mosques run by the Salafis while the elders attend the mosques of traditional 'ulama'.

The Salafi reputation rests on their scholarly activities and the challenge they pose (given their skills in the Arabic language) to the monopoly on religious education held by traditional scholars. Their efforts have made Islamic education more accessible.

The Tabligh Movement in Uganda

The 1970s and 1980s also witnessed growing activism by the international Jama'at Tabligh.[27] This movement originated on the Indo-Pakistan subcontinent. Considered to be the largest missionary organization in the world, its *da'wa* (missionary efforts) are directed toward fellow Muslims. It purposes to revive faith at the individual level. In Uganda, the leading proponent of Jama'at Tabligh is Shaykh Marmazinga. Some leading Salafis (for example, Shaykh Sulaiman Kakeeto) reportedly began their missionary activities with the Jama'at Tabligh then later parted company with it to set up their own version of the movement. The two cofounders of the first Salafi organization (Spidica—the Society for Preaching and Denouncement of Qadianism and Atheism, which split off from the parent organization), Shaykh Muhamad Ziwa Kizito and Hussein Musa Njuki (both graduates of Islamic law in Pakistan), disagreed over priorities: the former was interested in first constructing a mosque; the latter insisted upon setting up a shariʿa newsletter to propagate Islam.[28]

The catalyst that transformed the Salafis from a reformist group to a full-fledged radical Islamist movement was the decision by Uganda's supreme court on 19 March 1991 to rule in favor of Shaykh Ibrahim Luwemba as the mufti of Uganda.[29] The Salafis opposed both Luwemba's leadership and the leadership of the Uganda Muslim Supreme Council (UMSC), which they blamed for taking an issue involving Muslims to a non-Islamic court for adjudication. It was unacceptable to them that Luwemba's position be decided by a "kafir" court, and in protest they took matters into their own hands. On 22 March 1991 they attacked the UMSC building (which houses the old Kampala mosque) and took it over. In the ensuing confrontation, four policemen and one Salafi were reported killed, and in the aftermath, an estimated 434 Muslims were rounded up and charged with murder.[30] The charges were later dropped; apparently money was sent by a Saudi philanthropist to the Tabligh to cover the youths' legal expenses. A row developed within the group over this money, straining relations between the militant Jamil Mukulu and Kakeeto (accused by the former of misuse of these funds).[31]

Some top leaders of Tabligh, including one Shaykh Muhammad Kamoga, fled the country; others, among them Mukulu,[32] went to prison. Kakeeto was elected as the group's national leader—that is, the one who gives *fatwas* (religious rulings and decisions on problems posed by Muslims).[33] He quickly charted a new course for the group, denouncing the use of violence and setting up the Tabligh movement as an autonomous religious group with its own mosque.[34]

Mukulu, upon release from Luzira prison, denounced Kakeeto's policies and in August 1992 established the more radical wing of the Tabligh movement (the Salaf Foundation), which drew most of its membership, at least initially, from the youths who had been in prison with him. Its main objectives were to disseminate correct Islamic belief and practice and to work for the establishment of an Islamic social, moral, and political order guided entirely by shariʿa principles. They also sought to construct mosques, hospitals, schools, and orphanages to form a support base for realizing the group's goals. Their main center (which included a hostel) was the famous Masjid Noor Mosque on William Street where Mukulu was the main preacher from 1986 to 1992, with considerable success at converting non-Muslims (Christians) to Islam. The group's radical message—plus its diagnosis of Uganda's ills in purely political Islamist terms, with a clear program for change, and its activist stance by highly motivated individuals (some of whom have trained in the use of firearms)—has attracted committed young people, especially in the eastern part of the country.

Shaykh Mukulu's militancy and preaching style has antagonized non-Muslims and the wider Muslim community, further creating division within the Salafi movement between strict Salafis and the moderate but larger wing headed by Kakeeto. For instance, Kakeeto does not forbid his followers from associating with those who perform mawlid and other rituals labelled as religiously unsanctioned. He believes that it is through wise preaching and dialogue, rather than the use of harsh language, that such Muslims can be educated to give up their old practices. He has thus succeeded in appealing to some Muslims of the older generation.

In the early 1990s, Shaykh Mukulu's young activists engaged in what other Ugandans saw as divisive preaching; they eventually began to defy what they considered to be kafir (infidel) authority. By the beginning of 1995, Mukulu was reported to have fled the country for England. Around the same time, the Uganda Muslim Liberation Army (UMLA) was formed to champion the rights of Muslims against what they saw as the Museveni government's disregard for their rights and interests. They accused the Museveni government of attempting to undermine their religion and their community by converting mosques into offices as part of a policy to return several properties formerly under the control of UMSC to their former Asian owners.[35]

Socioeconomic forces were clearly at play here: when Muslims, as a minority, call for the establishment of an Islamic government to replace the "kafir" one, they are seeking the rights and privileges of "full citizenship" that they feel they have been denied. This community response to the failure of national institutions to provide social services and so on, is rooted in religious identity. In this interpretation, one can therefore say that the Salafi assault on popular practices has not only been directed against local "religious innovations"/devotional aberrations, but also against government authority. Such authority itself is seen as an aberration.

The Museveni regime, conscious of Muslim frustrations and unfulfilled aspirations (especially with the reversal of fortunes following the ouster of Amin) has maintained Uganda's links with some Arab countries. In the hope of gaining some benefits, Museveni has retained Uganda's membership in the OIC. He has also (unlike the Moi government in Kenya) included several Muslim ministers in his cabinet. Yet Museveni (like Obote before him) has also exploited leadership struggles within the Muslim community—for example, by supporting Luwemba; his vice-president has also thrown his weight behind Shaykh Kakoza, the main rival and leadership contestant.

In view of the radical stance of the Salafis and, more importantly, their opposition to UMSC, Luwemba (as official mufti) distanced himself from the Tabligh movement. Following attacks on police stations in 1995, for instance, he used the occasion of the Id-ul fitr celebrations to attack a "clique" in the Muslim community that, he said, since 1991 had been fighting the government under the guise of fighting religious wars against him.[36] Luwemba's death recently has not ended Uganda's Muslim leadership woes.

The Tabligh movement itself has become weaker: Mukulu's flight robbed the Salaf Foundation of his dynamic leadership, and the moderate Shaykh Kakeeto has been warming to the government, as evidenced by the receipt of a pickup truck as a present from President Museveni, a Mnyankole like himself. Uneasy relations with the government continue, however, as indicated by the flight of a radical member of the movement: Abdul Karim Sentamu left the country to avoid apprehension by the authorities. The bombing of the U.S. embassies in Nairobi and Dar es Salaam in August 1998 further strained these relations, especially following indiscriminate arrests of Ugandan Muslims for investigation. Jama'at Tabligh groups from India and Pakistan have since been banned from entereing Uganda. There have been, moreover, reports of human rights abuses and mysterious disappearances of Muslims in Museveni's attempts to deal with rebel groups belonging to ADF (Allied Democratic Front), which has Muslim fighters.

☾ ☾ ☾

The main programmatic objective of the Salafis has been, as we have seen, to establish an Islamic society in which Islam would be purged of local customs; hence the emphasis on the role of *fiqh* to redress social and economic ills. In their efforts to promote their cause, the Salafi have challenged not only popular Islam but on occasion the central authority as well. Conflict over such critical issues was in fact bound to develop into such a confrontation. Some have resorted to armed training (as in the case of some of Mukulu's followers) and in the western part of the country this has led to clashes with the security forces. The Museveni regime—seeking to restrict elements whose agitation was provoked by the pressures of nationalism and the politics of secular modernization (groups labeled "fundamentalist")—is strongly concerned about confirming its authority over a population divided along ethnic and religious lines. Islam, for its part, has clearly been reasserting itself as a political force.

Islamic Reform in Tanzania

We noted above that the Zanzibari-born Shaykh al-Farsy (qadi of Zanzibar, later appointed the chief qadi of Kenya) was the main popularizer and leading proponent of reformist ideas in East Africa in the 1960s and 1970s. His reformist crusade is being championed today by his former students in Zanzibar and, especially, in Dar es Salaam. There Shaykh Sa'id Musa, through his writings, is the leading critic of popular Islam in the country. Here are also some Muslim youth organizations (such as the Ansaar Sunna of Tanga, some of whose members have been exposed to Wahhabi teachings or Saudi-based education) that have attempted to recast the Islamic discourse along scripturalist-traditionalist lines. Young people have thus introduced controversy over "true" Islam by their insistence on strict adherence to Quran and Sunna as the only sources of guidance and practice for Muslims.

Such groups have opened their own mosques to propagate their ideas unhindered. Their Arabic-language skills have provided them with the means to challenge the traditional ʿulamaʾ. Yet, it should be noted that religious reformism is still in a state of gestation; it is not a major element in the evolving ideology and identity of Tanzanian Muslims as a whole. And for most Muslim youth organizations, reformism is not their main platform or orientation; they tend more toward Islamic activism, whose goal is partly to redress existing imbalances in society and partly to establish an Islamic social order.

Islamic activism in Tanzania, while it has a history of its own, is exemplified today by Warsha, which appeals to students and seems to enjoy the sympathy of a good segment of the urban Muslim population. Warsha attempts to get this segment involved in issues of concern to the Muslim community, and in this is consistent with Islamic movements led by university students elsewhere. There is, however, one significant difference, which has to do with demography. Warsha, which is far more limited in resources and manpower (it is not a mass movement or even an unofficial party like the IPK in Kenya), has behaved more as a Muslim pressure group that catalogues Muslim grievances than as a group set on contesting power with the government.

As noted earlier, the increasing politicization of Islamic groups has its roots in colonial developments in the nineteenth and twentieth centuries. Political and economic changes brought about then created conditions for regional and national-level politics and awareness. In Tanzania, this was also the period when Islam, in its diffusion and consolidation in the interior of the country, became an integrating factor for the identity of Africans who were involved in anticolonial struggles. Some of this anticolonial resistance became channeled into organizational activities by Muslim groups responding to the socioeconomic inequalities. The next section deals with this political challenge.

The Political Challenge of the Tanzanian Revival

The first important Muslim involvement in an oppositional role during the colonial period was during the Maji Maji war (1905–7), when rural followers of the *tariqas* (the Qadiriyya in particular) were among those involved in the struggles against the Germans. With the onset of British rule after World War I, when indirect rule was established, urban Muslims were at the forefront of organizational attempts to bring about changes in the territory.

These efforts led to the establishment of, first, the Tanganyika Territory African Civil Service Association (TTACSA) in Tanga in 1922 to fight for the privileges for African civil servants. Martin Kayamba, head clerk in the Tanga District Office, was the president of the society.[37] During the same decade, the Tanganyika African Association (TAA), TTACSA's successor, was set up in Dar es Salaam. It had a special appeal for clerks and teachers and was particularly attractive to Muslim townsmen.[38] After World War II, the TAA became increasingly political and began to develop into a national movement with branches in different parts of the country. It began to attract traders and farmers. In 1954, the Tanganyika African National Union (Tanu) was established to succeed TAA as a national political organization. Tanu was most successful in Muslim areas of the country; for instance, in Bagamoyo followers of the Qadiriyya order threw their support behind the nationalist movement and got involved with the party.[39] Muslim trader-politicians in many urban centers of the country (Tanga, Tabora, Dar es Salaam) were especially active in Tanu.[40] By joining Tanu, Muslims hoped to be able to contribute to policies aimed at redressing imbalances in society.

Concern for Muslim advancement in education and government jobs led other Muslims to organize independently of Tanu. In 1957, the All-Muslim National Union of Tanganyika (AMNUT) was formed. AMNUT attracted some conservative coastal leaders, elderly TAA activists, who were its founders. It tended to act as a Muslim pressure group in the nation's capital.[41] In 1959, it urged the British government to delay independence until Muslims acquired sufficient education to be able to share equitably in the fruits of independence.[42] AMNUT was roundly denounced by Muslim leaders who were strong supporters of Tanu. Nevertheless, when elements within Tanu itself put forward "Muslim" demands, the party reacted quickly by providing an Elders Section within Tanu.[43] The elders wing of the party was dominated by the coastal and Islamic branches of Tanu based in Dar es Salaam and Tanga. In 1958, Shaykh Sulaiman Taqdiri was expelled from Tanu because he made religiously based demands. At a mawlid festival (attended by Nyerere), Taqdiri pointed out that Muslims were not getting a fair deal. More seriously, he complained that there were not enough Muslims on the Tanu election slate. Nyerere had him expelled from the party because he had mixed religion with politics.

In the postcolonial period (October 1963), a Muslim society known as Daawa al-Islamiyya was established to promote unification and advancement of Muslims—for instance, by expanding the number of Muslim schools. It sent a letter to all bishops and religious leaders complaining about the lack of parity in educational matters between Muslims and Christians; it expressed frustration at government indifference toward Muslim attempts to set up schools.[44] The society was in fact arguing that Muslims needed special help from the government since they did not have institutions on a par with church missions. Shortly after the release of the letter, Khamis J. Abedi, president of the society, and Abdillahi S. Plantan were sent to detention camps in Mnulu and Chunya "in the interests of security."[45]

The above examples reveal a nationalist Tanu strongly reacting to pressure from Muslim groups. Nyerere was apprehensive that the highly emotional subject of Muslim educational backwardness might create dissension and disunity in the country; therefore, to keep Muslim demands at bay, he kept on insisting that Tanzania's politics knows no religion. Religious issues, particularly involving Islam and Muslims, were considered too sensitive for public discussion. The Nyerere regime wanted the Muslims not to be alarmed at the slow pace of their community's educational progress; that they be patient and trust the government to change conditions that promoted inequality in the country.

Accordingly, in keeping with its policy first announced in 1961 to provide free education for all, the government took over a few selected church mission and other private schools, including Muslim ones. Secondary schools and seminaries were not affected. In 1969–70, following the Education Act of 1969, Tanu assumed control of the primary-school system as a way of ending differential access to education by virtue of religion, geographical origin, class, or ethnicity, and also as a way of promoting education for social development. This, however, did not solve the problem: the policy of education for social development, or *ujamaa,* which among other things, aimed at enhancing education of less-privileged groups, had not had "the desired effects when applied to selection for secondary schools, an area where there was considerable scope for patronage and nepotism."[46]

From the mid-1940s onward, the Muslim community was led by the East African Muslim Welfare Society (EAMWS), which mobilized Muslims for educational opportunities. EAMWS was pan-Islamic and nonsectarian. Its activities were felt all over East Africa, and for this reason it was capable of unifying Muslims, especially coastal elements, into a bloc that could pose as a threat to Tanu. In 1968, however, the society became involved in a minor religious dispute (between the national headquarters and the Bukoba branch of the society) that eventually ripped the society apart. The dispute (over whether or not the prescribed noon prayers should be offered in addition to the Friday prayers that occur at the same time) was transformed from a mere theological argument into a serious ideological dispute and leadership contest. Confused by ideology and power dynamics, the conflict encouraged the intrusion of politics, and as a result the Nyerere government got involved in the Muslim crisis. Pan-Islamists were pitted against ujamaa supporters within EAMWS and the conflict was exploited to bring Muslims under control in a new pro-government Muslim council known as Bakwata. Tanu and the ujamaa regime banned the EAMWS and gave speedy recognition to Bakwata.[47]

Despite being closely associated with Tanu, or CCM (Chama cha Mapinduzi) as it came to be known later, Bakwata itself was later involved in trouble—the seminary dispute of 1981–82, when two of its secondary schools (one in Dar es Salaam and the other in Tanga) were converted into what can be known as Muslim seminaries.[48] Bakwata's Kinondoni school in Dar es Salaam was run by Islamic activists belonging to Warsha (a young Muslim writers' workshop). These youths had come under the influence of Muhammad Malik, a secular teacher (originally from Pakistan) who during his free time taught young people who wanted to learn more about Islam. He played a crucial role in the evolution of a broader Islamic outlook among young Tanzanian Muslim students, exposing them to the teachings of Sayyid Qutb and Mawlana Maududi. Clearly the Nyerere government was afraid that these schools run as seminaries might become a seedbed for Islamic activism.

The dynamism of Warsha's activities (producing textbooks for the seminaries, contributing to Bakwata's monthly newsletter *Muislamu*) captured the attention of Muslims as they sought to expand the role of religious institutions and scope of religious practice. It was a situation that could lead to the mixing of religion with politics. As a result of intrigues that followed within Bakwata, the secretary general of Bakwata, Shaykh Muhammad Ali al-Buhriy, was forced to resign and Warsha was expelled from Bakwata.

The above examples illustrate TANU/CCM's cynical attempts to squash institutions of civil society in its efforts to eliminate sources of potential opposition to the regime and the one-party ujamaa policies. The nature of this state control over civil society, and of popular perceptions of that control, lies at the center of Muslim groups' dealings with the government.

In the period of Mwinyi's presidency, Islamic activism became much more pronounced. For instance, Warsha continued to make its presence felt in the country through its writings, including widely circulated letters around Friday mosques. It has particularly appealed to people aged between their late teens and the late thirties.[49] Its emphasis has been on a renewed commitment on the part of Tanzanian Muslims to the establishment of an Islamic social order. It has in fact influenced other youth Muslim organizations, including MSAUD (Muslim Student Association of University of Dar es Salaam—which is closely linked to Warsha) and Uvikita (Union of Muslim Youths, also known as Ansaar Sunna in Tanga) in urban centers such as Tanga and Mwanza.

Among many Muslim groups that share this activist stance are the Union of Muslim Preachers (Uwamdi—whose videos and cassettes have been available for sale) that has been involved in confrontations with Bakwata;[50] the Islamic Propagation Center (IPC), which is an off-shoot of MSAUD and publishes a newsletter known as Annur; Baraza la Walimu wa Kiislamu Tanzania (the council of Tanzanian Muslim/Islamic teachers—mainly made up of former University of Madina graduates); Balucta (the council for the promotion of the Quran in Tanzania), which promotes Quranic recitals in public (it was involved in the "pork" episode discussed below); and Aboud Jumbe's Bamita (the council of Tanzanian mosques), which has been weak since Jumbe's fall from political grace in 1984. Even Bakwata, which is generally timid and ineffectual, has felt the activist pressure and on occasions has organized public lectures on Islam and made statements asking the government to reestablish Islamic courts.

This rise in Islamic activism was the result of a number of factors, among them the collapse of the one-party system, which allowed Muslims to organize and to speak freely in the new multiparty environment (although no party based on ethnic or religious affiliation was to be allowed to function); the activities of external Islamic organizations, including Muslim embassies (in sympathy with Muslim aspirations) in financing new mosques, schools, scholarships, dispensaries, and so on;[51] and the significance of the Iranian revolution. My impression from discussions with Tanzanians both in Tanzania and North America is that in the 1980s and 1990s these Muslim youth organizations have had an impact on the youth that far exceeds their resources and numerical strength. For instance, the older people (rather than the youth) in some parts of the country are much more likely to be involved with the tariqas (Qadiriyya and Shadhiliyya). (The same observation can be made about

Kenya and Uganda, where tariqas never had much influence to begin with). Tabora, in Tanzania, had been one of the strong centers for tariqa activities, yet even there, according to Mohamed ʿAbdul Ghani, whose grandfather was a tariqa leader in that town, its influence has declined.[52]

The 1980s and 1990s also witnessed public interfaith debates in which Tanzanian Muslim missionaries (Uwamdi) addressed public rallies and engaged Christians in Bible-based discussions on the divinity of Christ. These discussion (which led to some Christians converting to Islam, including a few clerics) have often angered the Christian clergy. Hence the ruling party's attempts to curb such exchanges: they have banned them and ordered that audio/video tapes of such discussions be surrendered to the government.[53] The debates, however, have continued.

In March 1993, Muslim scholars of the Bible (though not involved in the attack on pork shops in the Ndungumbi area of Dar es Salaam, where Muslims complained that non-Muslim butchers had sold them pork knowingly) were among the first to be arrested, as were a number of shaykhs, including Shaykh Kassim b. Juma. Tapes were also confiscated in what was seen as an attempt to stamp out Islamic "fundamentalism."[54] Further action by Augustine Mrema, the then minister of home affairs, included expelling three Sudanese teachers (in the belief that through foreign contacts Islamic activism was being fostered). The important point to note is that in the 1990s (contrary when Nyerere was president) Muslim issues such as the above were being discussed in newspapers and in the ruling party and state institutions. The Muslim factor had resurfaced in Tanzanian politics again, with Muslim groups urging the Mwinyi government to take special steps to promote the number of Muslims in government positions and in higher institutions of learning. This had become a recurring theme in public agitation in the form of, for example, newsletters or public letters that are widely circulated in Muslim circles.

During an interfaith Bible-based debate held on 12 February 1998 at the Mwebechai mosque in the outskirts of Dar es Salaam, a confrontation occurred between the police and the gathered Muslims.[55] (The police were there to apprehend the leader of this gathering, Ustadh Magezi Shaʾbani Maranda, for what the authorities called inflammatory speeches and creation of religious tension.) The confrontation soon engulfed the passers-by and developed into widespread Muslim unrest for two days. Muslim protesters stoned government vehicles on the Morogoro road leading out of the city.[56] The protesters (who claimed that President Benjamin Mkapa's government favored Christians and was denying them freedom of assembly)[57] also marched on a CCM branch office and burned two government vehicles and set government flags afire. Paramilitary forces were brought in to back up the police. Some Muslims, including women, locked themselves inside the mosque for their own safety and came out only after the armed police had broken the front door and fired rounds of tear gas into the crowd in the mosque. In all, the police shot dead two people and arrested more than one hundred. The funerals for the dead (considered martyrs) drew huge crowds, the high turnout making a clear a political statement about Muslim rage at perceived government suppression. On 29 March 1998, Muslim women who claimed to have been tortured and humiliated while in police custody staged a peaceful sit-in in the Mwembechai mosque's compound. More Muslims arrived to show their support and to protest what they saw as oppression of Muslims.

Islamic assertiveness in Tanzania has been most evident in Zanzibar. Young people have increasingly and openly identified with an Islamic trend in this mainly Muslim society that has special status in the Tanzanian union. The Tanzanian government has worried about this upsurge in Islamic activism on the island. This led the government leaders (Nyerere and his successor President Ali Hassan Mwinyi) in the latter part of 1987 to make a number of speeches on national unity in which the secular nature of Tanzanian society was emphasized. This did not stop the unrest. Island resentment at the control exercised by the mainland over local affairs and the economic decline in Zanzibar erupted in May 1988 demonstrations in which two people died and eight were injured.[58] The demonstrations were sparked by remarks made by Sophia Kawawa (the wife of Rashid Kawawa, the then CCM national secretary general), the head of a CCM-affiliated association for Tanzanian women (UWT).

In the antigovernment demonstration, the groups participating included some Saudi-educated Zanzibaris who helped channel the religious and political discontent into an activist Islamist direction. Various Zanzibari organizations had questioned the control exercised by the mainland over affairs in the islands. These groups had sprung up in the Gulf countries, in Britain, and the Scandinavian countries. Because Zanzibar had joined the Organization of the Islamic Conference, even if only for a brief period, indicated President Mwinyi's willingness (unlike his predecessor) to acknowledge Zanzibaris' aspirations/desire to associate with Muslim/Middle Eastern countries (especially via the OIC) as a way of ameliorating their poor economic situation.

Islamic assertiveness in Zanzibar can be traced back to the activities of the Karume regime, which curtailed religious education/Arabic classes in schools and generally discouraged Zanzibaris from traveling outside the island.[59] With the death of Karume, his successor Aboud Jumbe attempted to cultivate a religious constituency for his own political ambitions. By establishing Bamita (the council of Tanzanian mosques) he sought to attract oil-rich Arab money to Zanzibar. During this period, some Zanzibaris got the opportunity to further their Islamic education in the Gulf region, and those who were studying in mainland Tanzania got access for the first time to Islamic literature easily available in Dar es Salaam through MSAUD (the Muslim Student Association of the University of Dar es Salaam). In Zanzibar itself, a number of religious scholars were active providing religious education to a small circle of students. Jumbe's efforts notwithstanding, he was in the end forced to resign as the vice-president of Tanzania due to his perceived failure to check separatist tendencies in Zanzibar. Yet during the leadership of his successor, Ali Hassan Mwinyi (another Zanzibari who later became president of Tanzania), Islamic activism was to come out in the open with full force.[60]

The abandonment of the statist approach to development in Tanzania in the mid-1980s allowed autonomous religious organizations to assert themselves (whereas in the ujamaa era, a concerted attempt had been made to co-opt them). Religious politics was therefore to enjoy something of a resurgence in the post-Nyerere era. As the state control over the institutions of civil society began to ease (especially in the transitional period to multiparty politics) Mwinyi came increasingly under criticism from Christian groups[61] for not checking what was seen to be a rising wave of activist/"militant" Islamism.[62] The subsequent preparations for the multiparty general elections, 29 October 1995, underscored serious divisions and splits within the ruling CCM as it sought to choose a successor to Mwinyi, whose term of office was nearing an end. In the first round of preliminary voting, a Muslim candidate, Jakaya Kikwete (the former finance minister), was thought to have won. Nevertheless, by the time the presidential race was over, Benjamin Mkapa (Nyerere's choice) emerged as the party's presidential candidate amid rancor and bitterness over the whole voting process.

Among the people who were deeply disappointed and decided to defect from the party to join the opposition was professor Kighoma ʿAli Malima, who was an activist Muslim.[63] As Mwinyi's minister of education, he had been targeted for criticism by Christian groups for insisting on Muslims being promoted in government positions and in institutions of higher learning. Reacting to this pressure, Mwinyi had been forced to remove him from this sensitive ministry and appoint him as the vice-president of the planning commission. After Malima defected from CCM, he was named as the presidential candidate for the National Party for Reconstruction. He had deliberately made it clear to Tanzanian Muslims that he was seeking their vote: he was hoping they would vote as a bloc for his party. It was reported during this period that some Friday sermons in mosques had been calling for "proper voting," while an Anglican bishop had apparently warned of the danger of the country being plunged into chaos should religion decide the next president. Malima's death a few weeks later, on a fund-raising visit to London, eliminated a Muslim challenger in the elections. The general elections were now to be fought between two leading Christian contenders, Benjamin Mkapa of the old ruling CCM party,[64] and the anticorruption champion Augustine Mrema, leader of the main opposition party, the National Convention for Construction and Reform (NCCR-Mageuzi).

CCM's victory and Benjamin Mkapa's assumption of power (succeeding ʿAli Mwinyi as the president of Tanzania) seemed to indicate the country's opting for a system of presidency that alternates between Muslim and Christian candidates.[65]

Notes

1. I am grateful to ʿAbdalla Noor, of Jinja, Uganda, for making available to me relevant printed material, including newspaper coverage (in Luganda, English, and Kiswahili) of recent events dealing with the Muslim communities of East Africa.

2. They seek societal reform at the same time as they aspire (at least if one goes by their rhetoric) to bring about reform at the state level.

3. Personal communication with al-Amin Mazru'i. See also the discussion in Bakari and Yahya 1995, 234–51.

4. See Pouwels 1981, 329–45.

5. Farsy produced many students, including the Tanzania-based Shaykh Said Musa—a prolific writer in his own right.

6. See Bakari and Yahya 1995, 168–93, 247.

7. Ibid., 248.

8. Part of Kenya's colonial legacy involves the inheritance of a Western civil code (English common law) side by side with Islamic law. In matters of personal status, for example, Muslims could turn to qadi courts.

9. Muslims are concentrated in the coast and northeastern provinces (with significant representation in the populous western province). One-half of the Asian population is Muslim.

10. See the discussion in Bakari and Yahya 1995.

11. Bakari and Yahya 1995, 243–44.

12. Geist 1981.

13. See the Kenya Muslim monthly the *Message* No. 62(1996).

14. *Daily Nation,* 2 May 1992.

15. See Oded 1996, 406–15.

16. The grounds or, rather, pretext for denying the IPK permission to register itself as a political party was that it was a religiously based organization; in fact (except for its name) its constitution was nonsectarian.

17. Ibid., 406–7, and Bakari and Yahya 1995, 256. See also O'Brien in Hansen and Twaddle 1995, 213–15. The riots broke out in Mombasa in May and September 1992, and in Lamu in September and August 1993.

18. Oded 1996, 406–15.

19. Bakari and Yahya 1995, 256.

20. Ibid., 247.

21. Ibid.

22. See Sperling 1997.

23. Ibid. Shaykh Balala returned to Kenya in 1997 (when he was again issued a Kenyan passport) although he did not play much of a role in the elections. I heard that he was detained on the actual day of elections to forestall any problems he might create for the government.

24. Mazrui 1971, 184.

25. Uganda's current president, Museveni, touches briefly on the subject of religion and politics in Uganda in his book *Sowing the Mustard Seed,* (London: Macmillan Publishers Ltd. 1997, 41–42), without, however, indicating the role his government has played in favoring one leadership candidate over another.

26. Yet the Obote II regime's record was even worse: he came back with old scores to settle with the Baganda and other ethnic groups opposed to his rule (and so the cycle of violence started by Idi Amin continued).

27. *Tabligh* refers to the process of conveying or extending the "call" to a life of faith.

28. See "Who Are the Tabliqs; What Do They Want?" *New Vision,* Kampala, Uganda, Nov. 27, 1996, with references to Kayunga 1993.

29. Ibid.

30. Ibid.

31. *New Vision,* 4 Sept. 1992.

32. Jamil Mukulu, a former Christian who embraced Islam, obtained his Islamic education (specializing in the Arabic language) in Saudi Arabia in the 1980s.

33. Shaykh Kakeeto is reported to have two degrees from Saudi Arabia. By other accounts, he received his education from Pemba, Tanzania. His emphasis is on daw'a.

34. See "Who Are the Tabliqs?"

35. Ibid. See also "Are Muslims Being Sidelined?" *New Vision,* 28 Aug. 1996, 22.

36. See "Mufti Confirms Militant Clique," *New Vision,* 3 Mar. 1995.

37. See *Mambo Leo,* Mar.–Apr. 1923.

38. See Iliffe 1979.

39. See Nimtz 1980.

40. Iliffe 1979, 551.

41. Bienen 1967; 64.

42. el-Alawy, *Tanganyika Standard,* 20 Aug. 1959.

43. Bienen 1967, 64.

44. Swantz 1965, 34.

45. *Tanganyika Standard* (12, 14, 15 Oct. 1963); and the *Reporter* 1964, as cited in Swantz 1965, 34.

46. Mazru'i and Tidy 1984, 307.

47. Westerlund 1980, 103–4.

48. Owing to the fact that they were strictly for Muslims, the seminaries came under criticism of Christians. These complaints soon attracted the attention of the CCM leadership. See my dissertation (1992, 229–54).

49. See *Islamochristiana,* 1990, 180–81.

50. Uwamdi, which publishes the newspaper *Mizani,* is headed by Shaykh Musa Hussein, who is from Ujiji. See Balda 1993b, 228–31.

51. See Lodhi and Westerlund 1997.

52. Personal communication with Mohamed 'Abdul-Ghani in Kingston, Canada.

53. The interfaith debates are seen as capable of disrupting public peace.

54. See *Crescent International,* 1–15 Jun. 1993, for more on the pork episode.

55. The meeting was organized by members of Khidmat Dawat al-Islamia, according to Dar es Salaam's regional commissioner.

56. For local Muslim coverage of events, see *AN-NUUR,* 20–26 Feb. 1998; for the official explanation of events, consult the semi-official *Daily News* (14 Feb.).

57. Recent Muslim agitation against the government (see the Muslim newsletter *AN-NUUR)* includes a thirteen-page documented memorandum by the secretary of the Committee for the Defence of the Rights of Muslims, Juma Isa Ponda. This document draws up a list of charges against Mwalimu Julius Nyerere and Christian church groups, depicting them as architects of Muslim marginalization in Tanzania.

58. See *Country Report* 4 (1987), 2 (1989), 4 and 3 (1989), 9 (1989).

59. Personal communication in the summer of 1997 with Khatibu Rajabu, a Zanzibari who is writing a book on Islam and political developments in Zanzibar.

60. Some Zanzibari seem to think that Nyerere had nominated Mwinyi as his successor probably partly to placate Zanzibaris and partly to placate the feelings of those who thought the country was controlled by a Christian elite.

61. On growing Christian "fundamentalism" in Tanzania, see Lodhi and Westerlund 1997, which discusses the view of local activist Christian groups that consider Islam as an archenemy, especially since the collapse of Communism.

62. Nyerere himself had been unhappy with what he saw as Mwinyi's failure to curb Islamic "nationalism," which threatened to divide the country.

63. See the discussion in *Islamochristiana* 16 (1990), 171–82.

64. Despite the pre-election defections and internal disputes within CCM, the party emerged as the winner in the Oct. 29, 1995 multiparty polls (though not without all the opposition candi-

dates denouncing widespread polling irregularities—activity confirmed by the Commonwealth group of observers).

65. Despite the changed leadership, Islamic activism continues in Tanzania. Elsewhere in Africa, political Islam is making itself felt in various ways.

Bibliography

ʿAbdulla, Ahmed. 1965. "The Ambivalence of African Muslim Education," *East African Journal* (Feb.): 7–11.

el-ʿAlawy, H. S. 1959. "AMNUT hits back at Critics," *Tanganyika Standard,* Aug. 20.

Bakari, Mohamed, and Saad S. Yahya, eds. 1995. *Islam in Kenya.* Proceedings of the National Seminar on Contemporary Islam in Kenya. Nairobi: Mewa.

Balda, J. L. 1993a. "Swahili Islam: Continuity and Revival," *Encounter* (Mar.): 193–94; (Apr.): 1–29.

——. 1993b. "The Role of Kiswahili in East African Islam." In *Muslim Identity and Social Change in Sub-Saharan Africa,* ed. Louis Brenner, 226–38. Bloomington: Indiana University Press.

Bienen, Henry. 1967. *Tanzania: Party Transformation and Economic Development.* Princeton: Princeton University Press.

Chande, Abdin. 1998. *Islam, Ulamaa, and Community Development in Tanzania: A Study of Islamic Trends in Tanzania, East Africa.* San Francisco: Austin & Lawrier.

Court, David. 1979. "The Education System as a Response to Inequality." In *Politics and Public Policy in Kenya and Tanzania,* ed. Joel D. Barkan and J. J. Okumu. New York.

Farsy, Abdallah Salih. 1989. *The Shafiʿi Ulama of East Africa (ca. 1830–1970): A Hagiographic Account.* Trans., ed., and annotated Randall L. Pouwels. Madison: University of Wisconsin African Studies Center.

Geist, Judith K. 1981. "Coastal Agrarian Underdevelopment and Regional Imbalance in Kenya." Ph.D. diss., University of California, Berkeley.

Iliffe, John. 1979. *A Modern History of Tanganyika.* Cambridge: Cambridge University Press.

Kasozi, A. B. K. 1986. *The Spread of Islam in Uganda.* Nairobi: Oxford University Press.

Kayunga, A. 1993. "Islamic Fundamentalism in Uganda: The Tabliq Youth Movement." In *Studies in Living Conditions, Popular Movements, and Constitutions in Uganda,* ed. Mahmood Mamdani and Joe Oloka-Onyango.

Kiwanuka, K. M. 1973. "The Politics of Islam in Bukoba District." B.A. thesis, University of Dar es Salaam.

Lodhi, Abdulaziz, and David Westerlund. 1997. "African Islam in Tanzania." In *Majoritens Islam,* rev. English ed. London: Curzon.

Martin, Bradford G. 1971. "Notes on Some Members of the Learned Classes of Zanzibar and East Africa in the Nineteenth Century," *African Historical Studies* 4:525–46.

Mazrui, Ali A. 1971. "Islam and the English Language." In *Language Use and Social Change,* ed. W. H. Whiteley. London: Oxford University Press.

Mazrui, Ali, and Michael Tidy. 1984. *Nationalism and New States of Africa.* London: Heinemann.

Nimtz, August. 1980. *Islam and Politics in East Africa: The Sufi Order in Tanzania.* Minneapolis: University of Minnesota Press.

O'Brien, Donald B. Cruise. 1995. "Coping with the Christians: The Muslim Predicament in Kenya." In *Religion and Politics in East Africa,* ed. H. B. Hansen and M. Twaddle. London: Currey.

Oded, Arya. 1974. *Islam in Uganda: Islamization through a Centralized State in Pre-Colonial Africa.* Jerusalem: Israel Universities Press.

———. 1996. "Islamic Extremism in Kenya: The Rise and Fall of Sheikh Khalid Balala," *Journal of Religion in Africa* 26:406–15.

Pouwels, Randall L. 1981. "Sh. al-Amin b. Ali Mazrui and Islamic Modernism in East Africa," *International Journal of Middle Eastern Studies* 13:329–45.

———. 1987. *Horn and Crescent: Cultural Change and Traditional Islam on the East African Coast (800–1900).* Cambridge: Cambridge University Press.

Sperling, David. 1997. "Islam and the Religious Dimension of Conflict in Kenya." Paper presented at the conference on "Conflicts in the Horn of Africa," Nairobi, Kenya, 23–25 May.

Swantz, Lloyd. 1965. "Church, Mission, and State Relations in Pre and Post Independence Tanzania (1955–1964)." Syracuse University, Maxwell Graduate School of Citizenship and Public Affairs, African Studies Program, occasional paper no. 19.

Twaddle, Michael. 1988. "The Emergence of Politico-Religious Groupings in Late Nineteenth-Century Buganda," *Journal of African History* 29:81–92.

Westerlund, David. 1980. *Ujamaa na Dini: A Study of Some Aspects of Society and Religion in Tanzania (1961–1977).* Stockholm: Almquist & Wiksell International.

———. 1982. *From Socialism to Islam? Notes on Islam as a Political Factor in Contemporary Africa.* Uppsala: Scandinavian Institute of African Studies.

Zein, Abdul Hamid M. el-. 1974. *The Sacred Meadows.* Evanston, Ill.: Northwestern University Press.

Part IV

General Themes

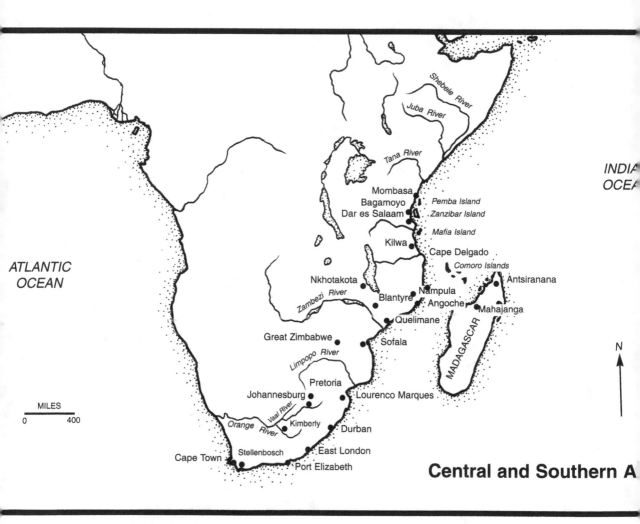

ATLANTIC
OCEAN

Shebele River

Juba River

Tana River

INDIA
OCEA

Mombasa
Bagamoyo
Dar es Salaam
Pemba Island
Zanzibar Island
Mafia Island
Kilwa
Cape Delgado
Comoro Islands
Nkhotakota
Nampula
Antsiranana
Zambezi River
Blantyre
Angoche
Mahajanga
Quelimane
Great Zimbabwe
Sofala
Limpopo River
MADAGASCAR
Pretoria
N
Johannesburg
Lourenco Marques
Vaal River
Orange River
Kimberly
Durban
Stellenbosch
East London
Cape Town
Port Elizabeth

MILES
0   400

Central and Southern A

CHAPTER 17

Islamic Law in Africa

Allan Christelow

he history of Islamic law in Africa is a vast and varied terrain, only roughly charted in now dated academic maps.[1] To venture through it, we need sturdy conceptual containers suitable for the many types of data to be collected. The most fundamental is that of Islamic law itself. The shari'a encompasses not only matters included in secular concepts of law, such as taxation, homicide, or inheritance, but also social and ritual comportment. What foods may one eat? What clothes may one wear? How and when should one pray? Wherever a variety of cultural traditions are in competition, as in sub-Saharan Africa, these are crucial questions.

Islamic law itself offers a variety of traditions. They serve as the basis for distinct ritual-legal communities within the wider community of Islam. There are the four classical *madhahib* (sing.: *madhhab*), the Hanafi, Maliki, Shafi'i, and Hanbali, and legal traditions associated with Shi'a and Ibadi Islam. Each tradition has developed a corpus of texts dealing with both general methods of legal reasoning and specific legal questions. In premodern settings, every region had its dominant tradition, but in some localities more than one tradition was present. An important question is how and why a particular tradition becomes established, and how it is adapted in day-to-day legal practice.

The evidence we have on legal practice, especially prior to the twentieth century, is usually anecdotal, and not always reliable. So one must proceed with caution, first in describing legal practice, then in locating points of change and analyzing the factors behind it. Changing patterns of production and trade, monetary circulation, migration, technology, military organization, education, health and climatic conditions, and political and religious rivalry can all contribute to affecting the course of legal change. In colonial and independent Africa, legal institutions of European origin, as well as customary ones, compete with Islamic law in responding to these changes.[2]

Islamic legal systems differ from traditional African ones in numerous ways, but they can be blended. Islamic law, in principle, is administered by literate specialists. But the ruler may assume a direct judicial role, in consultation with qualified legists, and the Islamic judge can be incorporated into a traditional system of officeholding. Islamic law places relatively greater emphasis on the rights and obligations of individuals, as opposed to kinship groups, in marriage, property relations, and obligations related to blood payments. It introduces a new concept of status and associated rights based on religion rather than membership in a territorial or kinship community. But especially in the field of real property rights, Islamic legists in practice have accommodated a wide array of different customary practices. Islamic law affords protection to property owners against arbitrary taxation and seizure, though sometimes it serves more as a discourse of protest than a systematically observed code. It also provides a system of commercial law that can foster long-distance trade with other Muslim communities. And Islamic law rejects the notion that harm may be caused through the exercise of occult powers.

In the analysis of judicial institutions and processes, it will be helpful to distinguish between three types that I will term informal, formal, and centralized. One can find a great many settings in the history of Islamic Africa where there is no organized state or where the state has but a limited role in judicial affairs. In such settings, people with questions on points of law might approach a local imam, a Quranic teacher, or a person with a pious reputation. This informal sector of the legal market still thrives in many parts of modern-day Islamic Africa, especially when it comes to matters of ritual and social comportment.

Formality comes with the establishment of distinct judicial institutions, governed by a clear set of rules, with judicial authority delegated by the ruler, or even assumed directly by him. Here we encounter the classic Muslim judge, the *qadi,* and the *mufti,* or official jurisconsult, men of suitable legal learning and moral reputation, but also men willing to trim their religious sails to accommodate the political winds. The establishment of such formal legal authority seldom proceeds without trouble. Rare is the qadi who has not been the subject of accusations of favoritism, corruption, or toadyism. Underlying such accusations one can usually find factional intrigue and high economic stakes. The office of qadi is that point where government authority most directly impinges on day-to-day affairs. Where the articulation of state and society are only partial, as in most of Islamic African history, this is bound to be a difficult position to manage.

Modern states have devised judicial systems that go beyond mere formality to centralization. They have introduced clearly defined hierarchies of appeal, and often codified law, in order to assure the uniform operation—and thus the predictability—of law.[3] Judges become part of nationwide bureaucratic systems, at least partially insulated from local political haggling, but, in the bargain, all the more subject to central control. In Africa, European colonial administrations began the adaptation of centralized systems in areas where they deemed it necessary. Independent African governments have continued the process.

Judicial centralization has affected Islamic law in Africa in a variety of ways. In some cases it has meant the relegation of Islamic law to a limited domain, particularly family law, while European codes are applied in criminal matters and the modern commercial sector, and the modern court system is grafted on to local custom when it comes to real property. But in some cases, it has also meant the centralization of Islamic legal systems, and, in the Sudan since the 1980s, the expansion of such a system to cover all domains of law and all categories of citizen. And in some cases, necessarily difficult to document, judicial centralization has led to deformalization of Islamic legal processes as litigants find the modern-sector courts too costly or too intimidating to deal with.

Finally, we need to be concerned with the roles of the spoken and written word, first, in the transmission, elaboration, and diffusion of legal traditions, and second, in keeping records. In the first area, we have a great wealth of written material, going back many centuries, including biographical literature, both learned and popular treatises, and collections of legal responses. The oral mode is more difficult to study, but many field researchers by now have documented poems, songs, sermons, and day-to-day polemics related to Islamic law. In recent decades, the electronic media, especially television and cassette tapes, have played a role.

While the Islamic tradition is a literate one, it is not exclusively literate. Much that is written is meant to be memorized and recited. This includes both the Quran and the classical compendia of the legal traditions. Grounded in veneration of the divine written word, Islamic law is skeptical of the human written word when it comes to establishing judicial facts, preferring the oral testimony of witnesses known for their integrity, or in some cases resorting to oaths. Modern states, whatever their religious leaning, have tended to privilege neither the divine word nor the human word but rather the officially registered word. Well before the European colonial onslaught, the Ottoman Empire made the *sijill*, the judicial register, a ubiquitous appurtenance of the qadi, at least in cities.[4] But in sub-Saharan Islamic Africa, the age of the register (with pages specially treated to resist hungry insects) would only come with colonial rule. This presents a problem for record-devouring historians.[5] Where written legal records do exist, some scholars, entranced with the erudition associated with the transmission and elaboration of legal traditions, are disappointed by the hurried, telegraphic style of records and the seemingly trivial, repetitive nature of most cases. But recent work in Middle East history has demonstrated the great potential of systematic work with the sijill.[6]

Having chosen our conceptual containers, we are ready to embark on a journey through regional and chronological blocks of African Islamic legal history.

The Establishment of Legal Traditions

The first centers of Islamic law in the West were Qayrawan, in the center of what is now Tunisia, and Cordoba, royal capital of al-Andalus, Muslim Spain. In both centers, the Maliki madhhab came to prevail, but only after long struggle. The reasons for its triumph range from the political leanings of these regions to patterns of travel to social affinities.

The formative period of Islamic legal institutions in the Maghrib and al-Andalus coincided with the first two centuries of the 'Abbasid Caliphate (750–950). The legists of the West felt little loyalty to the caliphs of far away Baghdad, who lent their support to the Hanafi rite. When westerners journeyed east for the pilgrimage or study, they usually went to Egypt and Madina. The latter was home to Malik Ibn Anas, and the center of his school. Thus while political sentiment worked against the Hanafi rite, travel patterns favored the Maliki.[7]

Reflecting the *sunna,* or tradition of Madina, Malik gave greater emphasis to kinship ties than to social status, a more important element in the cosmopolitan city of Kufa in Iraq, home of the Hanafi school.[8] This difference was relevant in such technical matters as rules on the suitability of marriage partners. Conceivably, the preference for the Maliki rite reflected the less cosmopolitan, more kinship centered character of the cities of the West as opposed to those of the 'Abbasid heartlands. This may also help explain the success of the Malikis in the bilad al-Sudan and upper Egypt.

The Maliki school gave authority to the views of prominent jurists *(ra'y),* and allowed for consideration of what was in the best interests of the community *(istislah).* Both these elements led to the elaboration of a highly refined Western Maliki legal tradition.[9] The flourishing of legal scholarship and the centrality of the judiciary was linked to the export westward of the 'Abbasid-era agricultural revolution, centered on intensive cultivation of new cash crops.[10] This both stimulated long-distance commerce and raised land values in and near cities. Jurisdiction over inheritance litigation and land transactions gave the office of qadi, and the study of Islamic law, considerable economic importance. Both the office and higher-level Islamic legal study tended to be dominated from generation to generation by wealthy urban families.

The emergent Maliki urban elite met challenges from several directions. In Cordoba, the dominant theme was conflict with royal authority.[11] The challenge in Qayrawan came from a combination of royal and rural popular sources. Berber-speaking hill people and pastoralists of the central Maghrib proved fertile ground for sectarian appeals, first from the Ibadi Kharijites. Their domain was limited to the central Maghrib, and eventually the Mzab oasis complex, with an offshoot on the island of Jarba off the coast of Tunisia.[12] Ibadi merchants were among the first Muslims to travel to the western Sudan. But, as we will see later with the Ibadis in Zanzibar, they seem to have been an insular community with no interest in proselytizing.

The second, more important challenge came with the Shi'ite Fatimids, who rallied to their cause the Kutama Berbers of what is now eastern Algeria. Fatimid jurists, led by al-Nu'man, provided a new role model of a judicial official actively engaged, through writing and preaching, in making Islamic teachings comprehensible to ordinary people.[13]. This example influenced what was to become the most widely diffused of all western Maliki writings, the *Risala* of Ibn Abi Zayd al-Qayrawani (b. 922–23), whose lifespan coincided closely with the period of Fatimid rule in Ifriqiya.[14] The *Risala* is a simple, clear, and easy-to-memorize synthesis of Islamic law, not an abstruse, specialized legal tract—qualities that assured its enduring value.

With the passage eastward of the Fatimids after 973, Maliki hegemony re-emerged, strengthened by the conflict. But the Malikis remained vulnerable on a key point. How was one to reconcile the universalistic aspirations of Islam with the parochialism of a local legal tradition? Al-Shafiʿi led the attack in the east, arguing that the key to restoring legal unity lay in rigorous study of the hadith, statements passed down orally from the Prophet Muhammad.[15] A young, idealistic Maghribi, such as the future Almohad *mahdi* Ibn Tumart, was bound to be struck by these arguments in favor of the primacy of Hadith and against the Maliki predilection for *raʾy*. These were an ideal intellectual weapon for an outsider from a mountain village to attack the entrenched power of the urban legists, while allying with reformers such as Ibn Rushd.[16]

But just as had been the case with the Fatimid challenge, the end result was not to break Maliki predominance, but to reinforce it. Having support among the skilled artisans, merchants, and religious scholars of the cities, the Maliki legists could be neither uprooted nor ignored, so Almohad rulers were obliged to seek their cooperation. Part of their strength lay in the commercial ties they had established with the western Sudan where, from the tenth century onward, they forged harmonious relations with local rulers, while making limited religious inroads.[17]

The next great classic of the Maliki tradition was the fourteenth-century *Mukhtasar* of the Cairene legist Khalil Ibn Ishaq. The author was thoroughly exposed to the rigorous, systematic legal reasoning of the Shafiʿis. And by the time he wrote it, the flourishing of long-distance trade had helped make the Maliki rite not just the parochial tradition of the Maghrib, but an ecumenical school reaching from the banks of the Niger to those of the upper Nile.[18] In Cairo, the great metropole of Islamic legal studies, one found endowed facilities to serve students from these far-flung regions and maintain some cohesion in the Maliki school.[19]

Along the Red Sea and Indian Ocean coasts, the establishment of the Shafiʿi rite follows a pattern roughly parallel to its Maliki counterpart in the west. This zone of Africa was linked to southern Arabia where, more successfully than in the Maghrib, state builders with their roots in desert and mountain tribespeople turned to sectarian versions of Islam (Zaydi Shiʿism in Yemen, Ibadism in Oman). But the orthodox Shafiʿi rite took root among townspeople.[20] It was they who built the Indian Ocean trading circuits, introducing Shafiʿi texts from Zanzibar to Indonesia. The Ibadis of Oman did establish political dominance along the East African coast, but religiously usually they kept to themselves.

The Elaboration and Adaptation of Legal Traditions

The period from the fourteenth through the nineteenth centuries is marked by stability and internal elaboration of Islamic legal traditions in the urban centers of the Arabic-speaking lands, and by vigorous efforts at adaptation in the Sudanic lands and in East Africa.

In the Maghrib by the fourteenth century, the emergence of sufi *tariqas* seems to have helped mediate the previously turbulent relations between urban centers and the countryside. The Maghrib also faced challenges in the form of the revival of Christian military power in Spain, and armed nomadic migratory movements from the east, known as the Hilalian invasions. The turbulent times brought many new legal questions, and an outpouring of legal response literature.[21] In a city such as Tunis, Islamic law not only governed social and economic life, but also shaped the physical structure of the city in every detail from the width of streets to the placement of windows.[22]

Starting in the sixteenth century, the sultanate of Morocco and the Ottoman provinces to the east take their now familiar form. But the boundaries of legal cultures did not coincide with those of polities. The eastern Maghrib—Tripolitania, Tunisia, and eastern Algeria—was more exposed to eastern Islamic influence than were Morocco and western Algeria. Ottoman policy in the cities was to reinforce their segmentation into distinct communities, each with its own formally recognized judicial authority.[23] One would assume that insofar as a foreign military governor intervened in judicial affairs, it was for reasons of strict political expediency *(siyasa),* rather than local custom or royal tradition.

In the Sudan belt and in East Africa, Muslims had to adapt their religion to settings not only where traditional religions still held sway, but where political and economic patterns were quite different from those in North Africa. South of the Sahara, only in Timbuktu can we find patterns closely resembling those to the north, with an autonomous class of Muslim scholars presiding over urban affairs.[24] This does not mean that Kano or Mombasa are less Islamic than Tunis or Cairo, only that their socioeconomic and political environments are different.

In Mediterranean North Africa, locally rooted traditions of authority disappeared in the course of long centuries of imperial rule from Rome or Constantinople/Istanbul. In the cities and their rural hinterlands, regimes of private property tenure held sway. Here the shari'a governs all property matters and is administered by a virtual corporation of Muslim scholars who, insofar as they do not challenge royal authority, conduct their business in autonomous fashion.[25]

South of the Sahara, locally rooted traditions of royal authority thrive.[26] Part of the Sudanic prince's power stems from his role as the ultimate arbiter of the disposition of all real property in his realm. Fully private property holding is often absent here.[27] A telling symptom of this is the absence (in the western Sudan, though not in Ethiopia or coastal East Africa) of *waqf,* or religious endowments, whose establishment is predicated upon the existence of private property.[28] As a source of funding for religious and legal education, the endowments underwrote the autonomy of the scholarly class.

In the western Sudan, Muslim traders originally lived outside the cities in a type of settlement that persists in parts of West Africa today as the *zango*. Where royal authority, and the great majority of people, remained tied to traditional religion, separate Muslim communities evolved their own identities, and an ideology of accommodation, the Suwarian tradition, named after al-Hajj Salim al-Suwari, a Muslim scholar of the fifteenth century or possibly earlier.[29] Such separate Muslim communities as the Juula and the Jakhanke followed Islamic law among themselves without directly attacking the traditional practices of their neighbors or rulers. In some respects, these groups resemble the Swahili of East Africa, or the religious lineages of North Africa, the marabouts, or *awlad sayyid,* who also saw themselves as bearers of true Islam, and expected less of ordinary tribesmen.[30] All of these might be termed religious enclave communities.

In West Africa, the barriers between these enclaves gradually eroded, culminating in a marked transformation toward the end of the fifteenth century. The embodiment of this transformation was an Islamic legist of North African origin, Muhammad al-Maghili. Unwilling to accept the political quietism of his fellow North African legists, he fled to Songhay and the Hausa states. He arrived at an opportune moment when such rulers as Askiya Muhammad of Songhay and Sarki Muhammad Rumfa of Kano were promoting the Islamization of their respective regimes. The growth of trade and concentration of political power were at the root of this change. Al-Maghili did not instigate this phenomenon but rather consecrated it.[31] The Islamization of traditional states in this period (c. 1500–c. 1700) extended through the Sudan belt to Bornu, Dar Fur, and Sinnar, producing remarkable syntheses of Islamic and traditional Sudanic institutions. These arrangements tended to be flexible, responding to changing economic and political circumstances.[32]

Two themes stand out in the Islamic legal discourse of these settings. The shari'a played a key role in arguing for or against the legitimacy of rulers. And it served to establish a region-wide status system, defining the qualities that separated Muslims from non-Muslims, a crucial matter since non-Muslims could be enslaved or made to pay heavy taxes.

Not long after al-Maghili's appearance in the west, there was a period of turbulence in the religious history of the east. In the Horn, Ahmad Gran led a *jihad* into the highlands of Ethiopia. But the jihadist forces crumbled with the death of their leader, leaving Islam as the religion of pastoralists in the arid lowlands, and of trading enclaves in the highlands. To the south, there are intriguing traces of an effort to win over to Islam the Mutapa in Zimbabwe in about 1560. But the military power of the Portuguese and the religious vitality of local tradition easily thwarted it. All that may have survived were a few possibly Islamic ritual practices among the Lembe people.[33] Except for the coast, East Africa remained a land of Muslim enclaves.

The late eighteenth and nineteenth centuries in the Western Sudan brought more intensified Islamization of states with a series of *jihads,* the most important of them that led by Shehu ʿUthman Dan Fodio in what was to become northern Nigeria.[34] The Sokoto jihadists did the most to advance Islamic law not by the sword but by the written and oral word, in both prose and verse, discussing the shariʿa in relation to situations and events familiar to their audience.[35] They also achieved this end through the promotion of commerce, a pattern Spaulding has argued for in Sinnar.[36] But, in the lands of the Sokoto caliphate, many old patterns continued. Just as the Habe *sarki,* the Fulani emir was the ultimate arbiter in matters of real property rights. Face veiled, surrounded by a bevy of royal titleholders, the new emir was still very much a Sudanic figure. While the emirs named *alkalai* to administer Islamic law, they maintained a large judicial role themselves. At least in this case, Sudanic royal authority and the shariʿa were by no means mutually exclusive. In many respects, they reinforced one another. The only surviving judicial records of the period take the form of correspondence between judges in different localities, usually inquiring as to the status of a particular person—Muslim or traditionalist, free or slave. This underscores the role of Islamic law in creating a uniform status system.[37]

The Colonial Era

Even before colonial conquest, Muslim legists in many parts of Africa dealt with questions stemming from growing European military and economic pressure. These most commonly involved the legality of trade with Europeans, and the debate was often framed in terms of whether such trade strengthened Europeans or weakened Muslims. In the Maghrib, the sale of horses and food were considered in relation to their potential military importance. The consumption of tobacco, often imported from European sources, involved questions of both economics and ritual purity.[38] In East Africa, the sale of elephant tusks to Europeans raised similar questions.[39]

Colonial conquest brought large-scale movements of population. In some cases, Muslims under European rule responded to arguments that Islamic law obliged them to undertake *hijra* (flight from infidel rule).[40] In South Africa, it was the Dutch East India Company that introduced the first Muslims, convicts and exiles from Southeast Asia.[41] Commercial development under colonial rule often facilitated the establishment of new Muslim merchant communities.

Both colonial regimes, such as the French in Algeria, and modernizing Muslim regimes, such as that of Muhammad ʿAli in the Sudan, and the Busaidi sultanate of Zanzibar, sought to centralize Muslim judicial systems. This reduced the degree of local political influence in judicial affairs, and it opened recruitment into judicial ranks to those who came from outside the traditional urban judicial elites.[42] The Mahdist regime in the Sudan can be understood as a reaction to Egyptian centralizing policies, but it introduced its own basis for centralization, eschewing the particularism of the madhahib to return to the pure roots of Islamic law, a policy not unlike that of the Almohads. Centralization made possible a more rigorous standardization in legal practice. In Egypt, starting in the 1920s, this led to domination of more conservative interpretations of Islamic law, particularly when it came to the rights of women.[43]

One aspect of the legal history of North Africa that has received scant attention is the abolition of slavery, carried out by the French in Algeria in 1848, and by Ahmad Bey in Tunisia.[44] Compared with sub-Saharan Africa, slaves were not a major portion of the work force, yet they were probably a substantial component in the households of the economic and political elite, and female slaves of Sudanic origin had a cultural role as practitioners of the *bori* or *zar* cults.[45] We have little knowledge of the legal status or economic and social roles of slaves following emancipation, or of subsequent history of cultural attitudes relating to race and slavery.[46] In some cities, such as Constantine, blacks virtually disappeared. More open cities with better economic opportunities, such as Tunis, seem to have attracted former slaves.[47] So may have certain oases, particularly Wargla.

In the 1890s and early 1900s, as French colonial power began to expand in West Africa, French jurists in North Africa promoted the export of the Algerian (and, by now, Tunisian) model of Franco-Muslim law to the south. They met with very limited success, influencing policy only in Mauritania and the "Four Communes" of Senegal.[48] This owed in part to the very different character of these lands, but also to a growing vogue in colonial circles to promote customary law as a barrier to the expansion of Islam.

The climax of French colonial enthusiasm for custom came with the Dahir Berbère in Morocco in 1930, which gave official sanction to Berber custom in mountain regions, while maintaining the jurisdiction of Islamic law in the cities and plains. By this time, however, Islamic law had become interwoven with the ideology of territorial nationalism, and the measure provoked a storm of protest.[49] Throughout Islamic Africa, as European-inspired principles of the territorial state took hold, the significance of Islamic law for creating a transterritorial status framework dwindled. Colonial powers attacked the framework by prohibiting the process, based on it, of producing slaves through raiding. Yet master-slave relations were often terminated within an Islamic framework that rendered former slaves into clients.[50] Antagonistic feelings, connected with the old status system endured in those areas where Islamic political formations had been involved in slave raiding (for example, northern and Middle Belt Nigeria).[51] Where instead early Muslim converts were often former slaves, victims of inter- or intra-ethnic warfare uprooted from tradition (southwestern Nigeria, South Africa), this pattern seems less applicable.[52]

British legal policy in Kenya roughly mirrored that of the French in Senegal. In the long-Islamized Kenya coastal strip, as in Dakar and Saint-Louis in Senegal, the Muslim courts received formal recognition. The interior of Kenya remained the preserve of African tradition and English law, with Islamic law recognized only informally. The Germans in Tanganyika followed more uniform policies, so that neither Islamic law nor the Swahili language were officially tied to coastal enclaves.

In both the Sudan and Nigeria, it fell to British colonial authorities to grapple with Islamic legal policy. The two settings were very different. In the riverine northern Sudan, the Egyptians had laid the foundations for judicial centralization.[53] The Egyptian intrusion and the Mahdist upheaval had undermined or destroyed traditional structures of local Muslim kingship, except perhaps in Dar Fur. In their absence, state-sponsored centralization could proceed unimpeded, with the importation of criminal codes from India, and the modernization of Islamic legal education.

In the 1920s, though the British considered favoring customary law, they opted to reinforce the Islamic court system, finding that the Muslim judges, with modern Islamic and Arabic education, were a convenient counterweight to both obstreperous European-educated "graduates" and cantankerous rural chiefs. During the 1920s and 1930s, the chief qadis of the Sudan issued a number of circulars on points of Islamic law to guide their subordinates that, in the context, were quite progressive.[54]

In the Horn of Africa, the Italians carried out a process of centralizing Muslim court systems in Somalia and Eritrea, while superimposing Italian courts at the higher level, along lines similar to French North Africa. In Ethiopia, given the association between Christianity and nationalism, the Italians found it opportune to make themselves seen as the benefactors of Islamic institutions. With the restoration of Haile Selassie after 1941, Islamic law took a more marginal role in Ethiopian schemes for judicial modernization.[55]

In the former lands of the Sokoto caliphate and the Bornu sultanate, the traditions of local Muslim kingship remained intact, and the British authorities of northern Nigeria did not directly challenge them. The traditional rulers retained their judicial roles with a minimum of British oversight, except on sensitive issues such as slavery and theft.[56] The local alkalai were appointed and supervised by traditional rulers. But the British did introduce the keeping of written records, by 1909 in the emir of Kano's judicial council, and gradually in other jurisdictions. In the 1930s, the British attempted to bring modern Islamic legal education from the Sudan. Nevertheless, traditional rulers managed to maintain an upper hand in judicial affairs through the 1950s.[57]

In southern Nigeria, the history of Islamic law was different. By the time the region came under British control in the early 1900s, there were a good many Muslims among the Yoruba, but there were also Christians, and many Yoruba stuck to their traditional religion. It was in this region that the commercial agricultural export economy first took root, and as the value of land rose, land remained within the framework of traditional law. Lagos was an enclave of British law, and Lagos barristers became advocates for extending the authority of the Nigeria supreme court into the interior.[58] This combination of the early development of European legal institutions in the region and the strength of Yoruba tradition left little scope for Islamic law. Thus, as in most of French West Africa, Islamic law among the Yoruba was administered on an informal basis by local *alfas*, who offered their advice to those who sought it and composed orally recited poems to edify those who did not. Hausa migrants in Yoruba cities had their own informal ethnic jurisdiction.[59]

The Yoruba case is an important example of the many situations in Africa where Islam took root as a religious practice but did not become associated with a state tradition in precolonial times. Colonial rule facilitated the spread of Islam as a religion, loosening the bonds of tradition and promoting trade. But it prevented the Islamization of political structures, and brought an alternative system of written law. As I have suggested, precolonial Islamization of the state did not obliterate traditional patterns, especially of rulership. It did, however, establish formal, state-sponsored Islamic legal structures. Such structures did not create strict religious conformity, but they did help establish what might be termed ritual consensus, recognizing perhaps some legitimate variation in orthodox practice, but marking other practices as beyond the pale.

The implications of different Islamic legal structures in Africa can be observed in the 1920s. By this time, rapid travel and communication tied the Islamic world together as never before. These factors combined with the conquest of the holy cities of Mecca and Madina by the puritanical Wahhabis to set off wide-ranging debates over ritual. Such questions as the permissibility of vocal prayer at funerals were not new ones, but they were pursued with unprecedented fervor. They tested a society's ability to maintain ritual consensus.

Two types of systems were able to weather these conflicts reasonably well. In Tunisia, where an old Islamic Mediterranean urban tradition persisted, modified little by French colonial rule, one could find the Shaykh al-Islam, Tahir Bin Ashur, in 1936, offering a learned commentary on all the conflicting responses of earlier generations of Muslim scholars to the question of funeral prayer, and concluding that no one should force their views on others. In Kano, the emir used his judicial powers to punish not particular views but their vociferous advocacy. *Shatima,* or verbal abuse liable to incite violence, was regularly and severely punished.

Two other types had greater difficulty establishing ritual consensus. Where Islamic legal matters were handled informally—through much of West Africa, most of East Africa, and all of the continent's center and south—disputes over how to pray (especially on Friday), how to mourn, or who should be imam, were difficult to resolve. Sometimes European courts or administrators had to settle the matter.[60] In Algeria, where a centralizing, ambivalently secularizing regime had dramatically altered traditional patterns, it was also difficult to establish ritual consensus. Funeral processions easily turned into brawls between sufi and Salafi.[61]

By the 1940s, as the prospect of an independent Nigerian nation with free and equal citizens began to loom as a reality, the British were forced to examine their Northern Region legal policy. The most sensitive issue turned out to be homicide law.[62] The reasons for this are complex. Most obviously, perhaps, a nation of free and equal citizens could not have a system of criminal law that discriminated among them on the basis of religion. But one must also understand the sensitivity of the issue in relation to the image of the northern traditional ruler. Jurisdiction over homicide cases was linked to their role as arbiter of life and death.[63] If this role were to be usurped by the Nigeria supreme court, at the instigation of a lawyer from

Lagos, the entire structure of traditional political authority was at risk. The matter was especially problematic in that the British colonial jurists had no credentials in Islamic law.

The West Africa Court of Appeal's overturning of a homicide verdict by the emir of Katsina in the Tsofo Guba case of 1948 marked the start of ten years of confusion, maneuvering, institutional tinkering, and hyperbolic rhetoric in Northern Region legal policy. At the end, the region's mercurial premier, Sir Ahmadu Bello, assented to the implementation of Northern Region penal and criminal codes based on the Sudanese model. British authorities offered soothing assurances that the new code was entirely consistent with Islamic law, for instance in punishing the consumption of alcohol. Not long thereafter, "Coca Cola Penal Code" entered the lexicon of the northern Nigerian bartender.

Islamic Law in Independent Nation-States

During the long gestation of modern nationalism in western Europe, legal unification and the centralization of judicial authority came to be cardinal principles. The new regimes in France after 1789 consecrated these principles by establishing a unified national law code and by eliminating legal distinctions based on ethnicity, religion, or social status. The only legal distinctions of consequence were between adults and minors, men and women, and citizens and noncitizens. A corollary to the principle that equality required homogeneity was the notion that separate legal status implied inequality, and possibly lack of patriotic commitment.[64]

Such propositions are potentially problematic in the development of legal systems in African nation-states. In countless African settings, legists and political thinkers have posed the question: Can national unity and the equality of citizens be achieved without concessions to legal pluralism? Or might one substitute a concept of legal harmonization for legal homogenization, allowing variations within a set of parameters? Further, are there certain universal legal norms that must be observed, requiring the reform if not elimination of traditional law? In those states with a history of formal or centralized Islamic legal institutions, there can be an additional question: Is not Islamic law a valid, even superior alternative to Western law? These are especially sensitive questions, for while people might "tune out" the dismal products of government-run media or government-appointed professors, the law is interactive in nature. Litigants must listen to a judge's verdict, and potential litigants may well respond in anger to a new legal policy.

The problems posed by Islamic law in independent African nations are by no means uniform, nor are their resolution. They can be illustrated by a discussion of four very different cases: Nigeria, the Sudan, Algeria, and Tanzania.

In Nigeria, the British authorities in the 1950s had devised a stopgap solution, composed of penal and criminal codes, and an intermediate-level appeals court, the Northern Region High Court in Kaduna, where a learned British justice might consult with Islamic legists. The regional formula survived for six years in independent

Nigeria. It came to include the establishment of a Northern Region Shariʿa Court of Appeal to supplement the high court in Kaduna, as well as the maintenance of the emirs' judicial roles. The military rulers who assumed power in 1966 took the secession of Biafra and the incessant political turbulence of the First Republic as proof of a need for stronger national institutions. Toward this end, they abolished the regional system, and with it the Northern Region Shariʿa Court of Appeal, and they terminated the judicial powers of the emirs. These measures had important consequences, some of them easy to detect, some of them not.

The most obvious are the arguments over establishing a national shariʿa court of appeal that nearly derailed the process of making a constitution for the Second Republic in 1978–79. This involved a good dose of political posturing, but also some substantial issues. Northerners, none more than veteran alkalai such as Abdulmalik Bappa Mahmud,[65] felt a very real resentment over supreme court justices with no background in Islamic law passing judgment in such matters. Southerners feared the establishment of Muslim courts in their region. Conservative northern politicians may have hoped to generate Yoruba Muslim support on this issue, but their hopes were misplaced. As David Laitin has shown, loyalty to the ancestral city takes precedence for the Yoruba over loyalty to religion. Within the north, young, modern-educated progressives such as Yusuf Bala Usman[66] argued that northern conservatives were merely using the shariʿa issue to bolster their feudal power. It was a Yoruba, General Obasanjo, who prodded the constituent assembly to end the shariʿa debate and get on with their business.

The impact of the termination of the emir's judicial powers is less easy to gauge. One problem is that people continued to take their cases to emirs or their subordinate officials for informal mediation. This alternative was far less costly than the government courts, and assured the application of familiar traditions discussed in a familiar language. But in instances where police power was involved, as in disciplining rabble-rousing preachers for abusive language, traditional rulers could no longer be effective. One such preacher, Muhammadu Marwa, known as Mallam Mai Tatsine, who had been disciplined by Kano's emir before 1966, was able to build a formidable following in the late 1970s, leading to a disastrous conflict in December 1980 in which federal troops had to be called in and some four thousand people were killed.[67] Efforts have been made to establish structures that might facilitate a ritual consensus among Nigerian Muslims, but the task is a formidable one.[68]

The Sudan shares many elements with Nigerian legal history, but in a different arrangement, and with a different result. While Islamic law in northern Nigeria, up to independence, was under the aegis of traditional rulers, in Sudan, the Islamic courts were linked to the central government, much as they were in Algeria. Though this facilitated legal modernization, it also set the stage for a tumultuous national debate over basic assumptions concerning how to interpret the shariʿa, particularly with regard to women and to non-Muslims. This culminated in Numayry's effort to impose Islamic law as national law in the mid-1980s.[69] and in his government's decision to execute the most prominent advocate of a liberal reading of Islamic law,

Mahmud Muhammad Taha.[70] The strength of the professional Islamic judiciary and the relative weakness of the European-trained legal elite and of exponents of customary law, as compared with Nigeria, was an important factor in these events.

Yet one must bear in mind that the Islamization of law in the Sudan has been initiated and sustained under military rule. In Sudan, as in Nigeria, military officers are concerned, on occasion obsessed, with homogeneity and uniformity, and with the primacy of the central state.[71] In Nigeria, this concern led Generals Gowon and Obasanjo to diminish the role of Islamic law. Sudan's generals made the opposite decision, that Islamic law should become the law in all matters for all categories of people. Hasan Turabi, long-time leader of the Muslim Brothers in the Sudan (but also a polished intellectual with a thorough Western education) constructed the ideological ramparts from which to defend these measures. One can just as easily paint Turabi as new-age jihadist, pursuing a centuries-old agenda of the Sudanic religious frontier, or as a modern nation builder, dedicated to building a national citizenry through assimilation. Perhaps he is a bit of both.

It can also be argued that the Sudan, more than other parts of Islamic Africa, finds itself caught between competing trends toward the globalization of legal cultures. Within the Islamic trend, there are two currents, one promoted by neighboring Saudi Arabia emphasizing integral application of Islamic law in such traditional domains as family and penal law. The other, associated more with Iran, stresses the Islamization of state institutions and economic policies.[72] The Western world, through the United Nations and various nongovernmental organizations such as Amnesty International, opposes discrimination based upon religion, ethnicity, or gender, and insists on humanitarian standards of punishment. Yet the representatives of both Islamic and Western legal culture in this case seldom if ever question the principle of judicial centralization, or speak of the need to adapt to local tradition.

The government of Algeria in the 1970s seemed a model of stability, a happy marriage between a secular political ideology and an Islamic national identity. But this image was to a large extent the product of the cautious silence of many Algerians. As they grew less cautious in the 1980s, the fissures in the Algerian system emerged. They centered on some rather old questions. One was whether Islamic law should be codified in a progressive reformist manner or a conservative one. The issue pitted the Westernized middle class of the cities against a combination of traditional conservatives, and, increasingly, Islamists. Many Algerians, perhaps most, preferred a policy of live-and-let-live when it came to arguments over ritual and social comportment. Insofar as it could, the regime pursued a policy of devolution on these questions, for instance leaving rules on alcohol to the local *wilaya*, or government, level. After much wrangling, a quite conservative family code was issued in 1984.[73] This neither pacified the Islamist constituency nor ended the rift within Algerian society.

In dealing with such problems, Algeria was hampered by two interacting factors. One was a legacy of French colonial rule that had bequeathed an official religious establishment under strong state control. The second factor was a phenomenon already noted in the 1930s—what we might call the globalization of Islamic ideology. Both revolutionary Iran and the conservative Gulf powers, each in their own way, promoted not just a personal return to Islam, but a collective, state-imposed one. The government-sponsored Islamic leadership of Algeria were cautious and pragmatic, and altogether lacking the charisma that could convince earnest young men, with bleak material prospects, tuned into global Islamic trends, to support a government widely perceived as corrupt. When the Islamic Salvation Front (FIS) was established in 1988, President Chadeli may have had in mind a strategy similar to General ʿUmar Hasan al-Bashir in the Sudan, with ʿAbbassi Madani playing the role of Hasan Turabi. But the Algerian military were too imbued with a sense of secular nationalism, and contempt for the simplistic formulas of some of the FIS preachers to allow this to happen. There was one other element. The Kabyles, with their own cultural identity, made up a substantial part of the electorate and had a major presence in the capital.[74]

The problem of Islamic law in African nation-building was not, however, intractable, as can be shown with the case of Tanzania. Before the creation of this state, the Arab elite on the island of Zanzibar had to rely on Islam as the basis of national integration. But in the early 1960s, the African majority of the island turned against their erstwhile masters, and Zanzibar joined mainland Tanganyika. Under Nyerere's leadership, Tanzania went on to elaborate a national system of family law. Through the national debates on this issue, a sense of pragmatism and compromise prevailed over doctrinaire insistence on national unity. The laws that emerged from this process offered options to reconcile both Christian and Islamic sensibilities.[75] One finds, in varying degrees, the same sort of tolerant pragmatism in the former French West Africa. How well this pragmatic spirit will survive the politicization of religion that has set in since the 1980s remains to be seen.[76]

One particular problem faced in most African countries with significant Muslim populations today is how to handle questions of ritual and social comportment that are outside the domain of the courts, or sometimes matters of family law in which national courts wish to refrain from making religious decisions. A typical government response, in cases ranging from Mali to South Africa, has been to set up national councils composed of Islamic leaders from around the country.[77] Frequently, the chief officers of such councils are given a judicial title—in Uganda, for instance, grand kadi (qadi).[78] These are perhaps not so much an effort to impose uniform answers as to prevent religious disputes from getting out of control. Judged by Western administrative or legal standards, these councils may seem an ineffectual oddity, aimed at promoting the political interests of national power holders, or the religious vanity of an external promoter. Their only real options are consensus or quiet disagreement. But one might argue that this is an old, and quite sensible, Islamic tradition.

A similar observation might be made regarding African qadis' courts. By the standards of well-heeled, Western-educated legal elites, these are usually a ramshackle affair. The furniture is minimal and timeworn. There is no air conditioning. But the atmosphere is one of quiet and dignity. The litigants do not prostrate themselves before the judge as they would before the emir. They do not cast anxious, bewildered looks at expensive lawyers or bewigged judges. For those with limited access to modern schooling and the modern economic sector, the qadi's court is financially and culturally accessible. In urban settings, where kinship networks have eroded, this court seems to be especially important to women. The rights afforded them by Islamic law—to maintenance payments following divorce, or to child support—are crucial to them.[79]

The qadis understandably feel a sense of pride in performing an essential role within their communities, and resentment at the power and prestige—and sometimes the arrogance—of secular judges and lawyers. But since its origins, the position of qadi has been a difficult and ambivalent one. The qadi, at least before rampant centralization, is both a servant of the community and an agent of the state. The degree to which the job is a difficult one, whether in ninth-century Qayrawan or twentieth-century Kano, might be seen as a measure of the gap between state and community.

Notes

1. Anderson 1955; Lewis 1980; Froelich 1965.
2. Roberts and Mann 1991.
3. Charnay 1970.
4. Sonbol 1996.
5. Christelow 1994a.
6. Sonbol 1996; Doumani 1995; Gerber 1994.
7. Turki 1971.
8. Coulson 1964.
9. Fiero 1992; Urvoy 1992.
10. Glick 1970.
11. Monès 1964.
12. Savage 1995; Platt 1985.
13. Dachraoui 1981.
14. Bercher 1953; Kenny 1992.
15. Coulson 1964.
16. Bel 1938.
17. Levtzion 1968.
18. Fadel 1996.
19. Walz 1978.
20. Messick 1993.
21. Berque 1978; Toledano 1978.
22. Hakim 1986.
23. Christelow 1985.
24. Saad 1983.

25. Munson; Green 1978; Combs-Shilling 1979.

26. Smith 1960, 1978; Levtzion 1968, 1973; Paden 1973.

27. O'Fahey and Abu Salim 1983.

28. Crummey forthcoming.

29. Wilks 1989; Sanneh 1989.

30. Gellner 1969; Stewart 1973.

31. Hunwick 1985; Starratt 1991; Barkindo 1987.

32. Spaulding 1977.

33. Mandivenga 1984; Parfitt 1999.

34. Robinson 1985; Last 1967.

35. Hiskett 1984; Boyd and Mack 1997.

36. Spaulding 1977, 1985a.

37. Tafawa Balewa 1989.

38. Cigar 1978; Saad 1983.

39. Cassanelli 1982.

40. Danziger 1976; Duffield 1981; Works 1976.

41. Shell 1993; see also chapter 15.

42. Christelow 1985; Pouwels 1987; Green 1978; McHugh 1994.

43. Sonbol 1996; Hill 1979.

44. Brown 1974.

45. Paques 1964.

46. Munson 1993.

47. Largueche 1991, Largueche 1996.

48. Christelow 1992.

49. Brown 1973.

50. Lovejoy and Hogendorn 1993; Sikainga 1996.

51. Kastfelt 1994; Burnham 1996.

52. Ryan 1978; Laitin 1986; Mohammed 1992; Shell 1993.

53. Daly 1987.

54. Fleuhr-Lobban 1987.

55. Trimingham 1964.

56. Christelow 1994a.

57. Naniya 1993.

58. Adewoye 1977; Luckham 1978.

59. Ryan 1978; Salamone 1996.

60. Launay 1977; Laitin 1986; Miles 1994.

61. Merad 1972; Christelow 1997.

62. Keay and Richardson 1966.

63. Rathbone 1993.

64. Brubaker 1992.

65. Mahmud 1986.

66. Usman 1979.

67. Christelow 1994b.

68. Umar 1993; Kukah 1993.

69. Kok 1991; O'Fahey 1995; Bleuchot 1991.

70. An-Na'im 1990; Khayati 1991.

71. Voll and Voll 1985; Warburg 1995.

72. Mallat 1993.

73. Mayer 1995; Vandevelde 1985; Bormans 1977.

74. Ruedy 1994.
75. Omari 1984.
76. Kettani 1985; Sanneh 1997; Mazrui 1993.
77. Brenner 1993; Naudè 1985;
78. Oded 1974; Kasozi 1985.
79. Brown 1993.

Bibliography

Adewoye, T. O. 1977. *The Judicial System of Southern Nigeria (1854–1954): Law in a Dependency.* London: Longman.

Anderson, J. N. D. 1955. *Islamic Law in Africa.* London: Cass.

An-Naʿim, Abdullahi Ahmed. 1990. *Toward an Islamic Reformation: Civil Liberties, Human Rights, and International Law.* Syracuse: Syracuse University Press.

Barkindo, Bawuro. 1987. "The Role of al-Maghili in the Reforms of Sarki Muhammad Rumfa," *Kano Studies,* n.s, no. 3:85–110.

Bel, Alfred. 1938. *La religion musulmane en Berberie: Esquisse d'histoire et de sociologie religieuses.* Paris.

Bercher, Léon, 1953. *La Risala de Ibn Abi Zayd al-Qayrawani.* Algiers: Bibliothèque Arabe-Française.

Berque, Jacques. 1978. *L'intérieur du Maghreb, XV–XIXe siècle.* Paris: Gallimard.

Bleuchot, Hervé. 1991. "Islam, droit pénal, et politique: Sur deux ouvrages de Sadiq al-Mahdi." In *Sudan: History, Identity, Ideology,* ed. H. Bleuchot. Reading: Ithaca Press.

Bobboyi, Hamidu. 1993. "Relations of the Bornu ʿUlama with the Sayfawa Rulers: The Role of the *Mahrams.*" *Sudanic Africa* 4:175–204.

Bormans, Maurice. 1977. *Statut personnel et famille au Maghreb de 1940 à nos jours.* Paris: Mouton.

Boyd, Jean, and Beverly Mack. 1997. *The Collected Works of Nana Asmau bint Usman Dan Fodio.* Bloomington: Indiana University Press.

Brenner, Louis, ed. 1993. *Muslim Identity and Social Change in Sub-Saharan Africa.* Bloomington: Indiana University Press.

Brown, Beverly B. 1993. "Islamic Law, Qadhi's Courts, and Women's Legal Status: The Case of Kenya," *Journal of the Institute of Muslim Minority Affairs* 14:94–101.

Brown, Kenneth. 1973. "The Impact of the *Dahir Berbère* in Salé." In *Arabs and Berbers,* ed. E. Gellner and C. Micaud. London: Duckworth.

Brown, Leon Carl. 1974. *The Tunisia of Ahmad Bey (1837–1855).* Princeton: Princeton University Press.

Brubaker, Rogers. 1992. *Citizenship and Nationhood in France and Germany.* Harvard University Press.

Brunschwig, Henri. 1965. "Justice Religieuse et Justice Laique dans la Tunisie des Deys et des Beys," *Studia Islamica* 23:27–70.

Burnham, Philip. 1996. *The Politics of Cultural Difference in Northern Cameroun*. Edinburgh: Edinburgh University Press.

Cassanelli, Lee. 1982. *The Shaping of Somali Society*. Philadelphia: University of Pennsylvania Press.

Charnay, Jean-Paul. 1965. *La vie musulmane en Algérie d'après la jurisprudence de la première moitié du vingtième siècle*. Paris.

———. 1970. "Dialectique entre droit musulman et juridisme industriel," *Studia Islamica* 32:77–87.

Chenoufi, Ali. 1977. *Un savant tunisien du XIXe siècle: Muhammad al-Sanusi, sa vie et son oeuvre*. Tunis: Publications de l'Université de Tunis.

Christelow, Allan. 1985. Muslim Law Courts and the French Colonial State in Algeria. Princeton: Princeton University Press.

———. 1992. "The Muslim Judge and Municipal Politics in Colonial Algeria and Senegal." In *Comparing Muslim Societies*, ed. Juan R. I. Cole. Ann Arbor: University of Michigan Press.

———. 1994a. *Thus Ruled Emir Abbas: Selected Cases from the Emir of Kano's Judicial Council*. East Lansing: Michigan State University Press.

———. 1994b. "Maitatsine," *Oxford Encyclopedia of Modern Islam*.

———. 1997. "In Search of One Word's Meaning: *Zaman* in Early Twentieth Century Kano," *History in Africa* 24:95–115.

Cigar, Norman. 1978. "Conflict and Community in an Urban Milieu: Fez under the 'Alawis (ca. 1666–1830)," *Maghreb Review* 3:3–13.

Clarke, Peter. 1982. *West Africa and Islam*. London: Arnold.

Combs-Schilling, Elaine. 1979. *Sacred Performances*. New York: Columbia University Press.

Coulson, Noel J. 1964. *A History of Islamic Law*. Edinburgh: Edinburgh University Press.

Crummey, Donald. Forthcoming. *Land and State in Sub-Saharan Africa*.

Dachraoui, Farhat. 1981. *Le califat Fatimide au Maghreb*. Tunis: Publications de l'Université de Tunis.

Daly, Martin. 1985. *Modernization in the Sudan: Essays in Honor of Richard Hill*. New York: L. Barber Press.

———. 1987. *Empire on the Nile: The Anglo-Egyptian Sudan (1898–1934)*. Cambridge: Cambridge University Press.

Danziger, Raphael. 1976. *Abd al-Qadir and the Algerians*. New York: Africana Press.

Demeersman, André. 1978. "La fonction de Cheikh al-Islam en Tunisie de la fin du 18e siècle au début du 20e siècle," *IBLA* 41:215–70.

Doumani, Beshara. 1995. *Rediscovering Palestine: Merchants and Peasants of Jabal Nablus (1700–1900)*. Berkeley: University of California Press.

Duffield, Mark. 1981. *Maiurno: Capitalism and Rural Life in Sudan*. London: Ithaca Press.

Fadel, Muhammed. 1996. "The Social Logic of *Taqlid* and the Rise of the Mukhtasar." *Islamic Law and Society* 3:2, 193–223.

Fiero, María Isabel. 1992. "Heresy in al-Andalus." In *The Legacy of Muslim Spain,* ed. Salma Khadra al-Jayyusi. Leiden: E. J. Brill.

Fluehr-Lobban, Carolyn. 1987. *Islamic Law and Society in the Sudan.* London: Cass.

Froelich, J-C. 1965. "Droit musulman et droit coutumier." In *Etudes du droit africain et du droit malagache,* ed. M. Alliot et al. Paris.

Geertz, Clifford. 1968. *Islam Observed: Religious Development in Morocco and Indonesia.* Chicago: University of Chicago Press.

Gellner, Ernest. 1969. *Saints of the Atlas.* London: Weidenfeld and Nicholson.

Gerber, Haim. 1994. *State, Society, and Law in Islam.* Albany: State University of New York Press.

Glick, Thomas F. 1970. *Irrigation and Society in Medieval Valencia.* Cambridge: Harvard University Press.

Goody, Jack. 1986. *The Logic of Writing and the Organization of Society.* Cambridge: Cambridge University Press.

Green, Arnold. 1978. *The Tunisian Ulama (1873–1915).* Leiden: E. J. Brill.

Hakim, Besim Salim. 1986. *Arab-Islamic Cities: Building and Planning Principles.* London: Kegan Paul.

Hill, Enid. 1979. *Mahkama: Studies in the Egyptian Legal System.* London: Ithaca Press.

Hiskett, Mervyn. 1984. *The Development of Islam in West Africa.* London: Longman.

Hourani, Albert. 1962. *Arabic Thought in the Liberal Age.* London: Oxford University Press.

Hunwick, John. 1985. *Sharia in Songhay: The Replies of al-Maghili to the Questions of Askia al-Hajj Muhammad.* London: The British Academy.

Kapteijns, Lidwein. 1985. "Islamic Rationales for the Changing Role of Women in the Western Sudan." In *Modernization in the Sudan,* ed. Martin Daly. New York: L. Barber Press.

Kasozi, Abdu B. K. 1985. "The Uganda Muslim Supreme Council: An Experiment in Muslim Administrative Centralization and Institutionalization," *Journal of the Institute of Muslim Minority Affairs* 6:34–52.

Kastfelt, Niels. 1994. *Religion and Politics in Nigeria: A Study in Middle Belt Christianity.* London: Tauris.

Keay, E. A., and S. S. Richardson. 1966. *The Native and Customary Courts of Nigeria.* London.

Kenny, Joseph. 1992. *The Risala: Treatise on Maliki Law.* Minna, Nigeria: Islamic Education Trust.

Kettani, Ali. 1985. "Muslims in Tanzania: A Rejoinder," *Journal of the Institute of Muslim Minority Affairs* 6:219–20.

Khayati, Mustapha. 1991. "Introduction à la pensée de Mahmud Muhammad Taha, réformiste et martyr." In *Sudan: History, Identity, Ideology,* ed. Hervé Bleuchot. Reading: Ithaca Press.

Kok, Peter Nyot. 1991. "Conflict over Laws in the Sudan: From Pluralism to Monolithicism." In *Sudan: History, Ideology, Identity,* ed. H. Bleuchot. Reading: Ithaca.

Kukah, Matthew Hasan. 1993. *Religion, Politics, and Power in Northern Nigeria.* Ibadan: Spectrum.

Laitin, David. 1986. *Hegemony and Culture: Politics and Religious Change among the Yoruba.* Chicago: University of Chicago Press.

Largueche, Abdelhamid. 1991. "La minorité noire de Tunis au XIXe siècle," *Annuaire de l'Afrique du Nord* 30:135–53.

Largueche, Dalenda. 1996. "Confined, Battered, and Repudiated Women in Tunis since the Eighteenth Century." In *Muslim Women, the Family and Divorce Laws in Islamic History,* ed. Amira El-Azhary Sonbol. Syracuse: Syracuse University Press.

Last, D. M. 1967. *The Sokoto Caliphate.* London: Longman.

Launay, Robert. 1977. "The Birth of a Ritual: The Politics of Innovation in Dyula Islam," *Savanna* 6:145–54.

Levtzion, Nehemia. 1968. *Muslims and Chiefs in West Africa.* London: Oxford University Press.

———. 1973. *Ancient Ghana and Mali.* New York: Africana.

Levtzion, Nehemia, and Humphrey Fisher, eds. 1977. *Rural and Urban Islam in West Africa.* Boulder, Colo.: Lynne Rienner.

Lewis, I. M. 1980. *Islam in Tropical Africa.* 2nd ed. Bloomington: Indiana University Press.

Lovejoy, Paul, and Jan Hogendorn. 1993. *Slow Death for Slavery: The Course of Abolition in Northern Nigeria (1897–1936).* Cambridge: Cambridge University Press.

Luckham, Robin. 1978. "Imperialism, Law, and Structural Dependence: The Ghana Legal Profession," *Development and Change* 9:201–48.

Maher, Vanessa. 1974. *Women and Property in Morocco.* Cambridge: Cambridge University Press.

Mahmud, Abdulmalik Bappa. 1986. *A Brief History of Sharia in the Defunct Northern Nigeria.* Kaduna.

Mallat, Chibli. 1993. *The Renewal of Islamic Law.* Cambridge: Cambridge University Press.

Mandivenga, Ephraim C. 1984. "Muslims of Zimbabwe: Origins, Composition and Current Strength," *Journal of the Institute of Muslim Minority Affairs* 5:393–99.

Mayer, Ann Elizabeth. ed. 1985. *Property, Social Structure, and Law in the Modern Middle East.* Albany: State University of New York Press.

———. 1995. "Reform of Personal Status Law in North Africa: A Problem of Islamic or Mediterranean Laws?" *Middle East Journal,* 49:432–46.

Mazrui, Alamin. 1993. "Ethnicity and Pluralism: The Politicization of Religion in Kenya," *Journal of the Institute of Muslim Minority Affairs* 14:191–201.

McHugh, Neil. 1994. *Holy Men of the Blue Nile: The Making of an Arab-Islamic Community in the Nilotic Sudan (1500–1850).* Evanston, Ill.: Northwestern University Press.

Merad, Ali. 1972. *Le réformisme musulmane en Algérie de 1925 à 1940.* Paris: Mouton.

Messick, Brinkley. 1993. *The Calligraphic State: Textual Domination and History in a Muslim Society.* Berkeley: University of California Press.

Miles, William F. S. 1994. *Hausaland Divided: Colonialism and Independence in Niger and Nigeria.* Ithaca: Cornell University Press.

Mohammed, Ahmed Rufai. 1992. "The Popular Phase of Islam in Ebiraland," *Islam et sociétés au sud du Sahara* 6:47–64.

Monès, H. 1964. "Le role des hommes de religion dans l'histoire de l'Espagne musulmane jusqu'à la fin du califat," *Studia Islamica,* 20:47–88.

Munson, Henry. 1993. *Religion and Power in Morocco.* New Haven: Yale University Press.

Naniya, Tijani Muhammad. 1993. "The Dilemma of the *'Ulama'* in a Colonial Society: The Case Study of Kano Emirate." *Journal of Islamic Studies* 4:151–60.

Naudè, J. A. 1985. "Islam in South Africa: A General Survey," *Journal of the Institute of Muslim Minority Affairs* 6:21–33.

Oded, Arye. 1974. *Islam in Uganda.* Jerusalem.

O'Fahey, R. S. 1995. "The Past in the Present? The Issue of *Sharia* in the Sudan." In *Religion and Politics in East Africa,* ed. Michael Twaddle and Holger Bengt Hansen. London: Currey, and Athens: Ohio University Press.

O'Fahey, R. S., and M. I. Abu Salim. 1983. *Land in Dar Fur: Charters and Related Documents from the Dar Fur Sultanate.* Cambridge: Cambridge University Press.

Omari, C. K. 1984. "Christian-Muslim Relations in Tanzania: The Socio-political Dimension," *Journal of the Institute of Muslim Minority Affairs* 5:373–90.

Paden, John. 1973. *Religion and Political Culture in Kano.* Berkeley: University of California Press.

———. 1986. *Ahmadu Bello: Sardauna of Sokoto.* London: Hodder and Stoughton.

Paques, Viviana. 1964. *L'arbre cosmique dans la pensée populaire et dans la vie quotidienne Nord Ouest Africaines.* Paris: Musée de l'Homme.

Parfitt, Tudor. 1999. *Journey to the Vanished City.* London: Phoenix.

Platt, Katie. 1985. "Island Puritanism." In *Islamic Dilemmas,* ed. Ernest Gellner. Berlin: Mouton.

Pouwels, Randall. 1987. *Horn and Crescent: Cultural Change and Traditional Islam on the East African Coast (800–1900).* Cambridge: Cambridge University Press.

Rathbone, Richard. 1993. *Murder and Politics in Colonial Ghana.* Cambridge: Cambridge University Press.

Repp, Richard. 1977. "The Altered Role and Nature of the Ulema." In *Studies in Eighteenth Century Islamic History,* ed. Thomas Naff and R. C. Owen. Carbondale: Southern Illinois University Press.

———. 1988. "Qanun and Sharia in the Ottoman Context." In *Islamic Law: Social and Historical Contexts,* ed. Aziz Al-Azmeh. London: Routledge.

Roberts, Richard, and Kristin Mann. 1991. *Law in Colonial Africa.* Portsmouth: Heinemann.

Robinson, David. 1985. *The Holy War of Umar Tal.* London: Oxford University Press.

Rosen, Lawrence. 1989. *The Anthropology of Justice: Law as Culture in an Islamic Society.* Cambridge: Cambridge University Press.

Ruedy, John. 1994. *Islamism and Secularism in North Africa.* New York: St. Martin's.

Ryan, Patrick. 1978. *Imale: Yoruba Participation in the Muslim Tradition.* Missoula, Mont.: Scholar's Press.

Saad, Elias. 1983. *Social History of Timbuktu: The Role of Muslim Scholars and Notables (1400–1900).* Cambridge: Cambridge University Press.

Salamone, Frank A. 1996. "The Waziri and the Thief: Hausa Islamic Law in a Yoruba City, a Case Study from Ibadan, Nigeria," *African Studies Review* 39:125–40.

Sanneh, Lamin. 1989. *The Jakhanke Muslim Clerics: A Religious and Historical Study of Islam in Senegambia.* Lanham, Md.: University Press of America.

———. 1997. *The Crown and the Turban: Muslims and African Pluralism.* Boulder, Colo.: Westview.

Savage, Elizabeth. 1995. *The Islamic Conquest of North Africa: A Gateway to Hell, a Gateway to Heaven.* Princeton: Darwin.

Savage, Elizabeth, ed. 1992. *Perspectives on the Human Commodity: The Trans-Saharan Slave Trade.* London: Cass.

Shell, Robert. 1993. "From Rites to Rebellion: Islamic Conversion, Urbanization, and Ethnic Identities in the Cape of Good Hope, 1797 to 1904," *Canadian Journal of History* 28:410–57.

Sikainga, Ahmad A. 1996. *Slaves into Workers.* Austin: University of Texas Press.

Smith, M. G. 1960. *Government in Zazzau.* London: Oxford University Press.

———. 1978. *The Affairs of Daura.* Berkeley: University of California Press.

Sodiq, Yushua. 1996. "An Analysis of Yoruba and Islamic Inheritance Laws," *Muslim World* 86:313–33.

Sonbol, Amira El-Azhary, ed. 1996. *Women, the Family, and Divorce Laws in Islamic History.* Syracuse: Syracuse University Press.

Soyinka, Wole. 1975. *Death and the King's Horsemen.* New York: Norton.

Spaulding, Jay. 1977. "The Evolution of the Islamic Judiciary in Sinnar," *International Journal of African Historical Studies* 10:408–26.

———. 1985a. *The Heroic Age in Sinnar.* East Lansing: Michigan State University Press.

———. 1985b. "The End of Nubian Kingship in Sudan (1720–1762)." In *Modernization in the Sudan,* ed. Martin Daly. London: Croom Helm.

Starratt, Priscilla. 1991. "Oral History in Muslim Africa: al-Maghili Legends in Kano." Ph.D. diss., University of Michigan.

Stewart, Charles. 1973. *Islam and Social Order in Mauretania.* London: Oxford University Press.

Tafawa Balewa, Abubakar. 1989. *Shaihu Umar.* New York: Weiner.

Toledano, Henry. 1978. *Judicial Practice and Family Law in Morocco: The Chapter on Marriage from Sijilmasi's al-Amal al-Mutlaq.* Boulder, Colo.: Westview.

Trimingam, J. S. 1964. *Islam in East Africa.* London: Oxford University Press.

Turki, A. M. 1971. "La vénération pour Malik et la physionomie du malikisme andalou," *Studia Islamica* 33: 41–65.

Umar, Muhammad Sani. 1993. "Changing Islamic Identity in Nigeria from the 1960s to the 1980s." In Brenner 1993.

Urvoy, Dominique. 1992. "The ʿUlamaʾ of al-Andalus (849–877)." In *The Legacy of Muslim Spain,* ed. Salma Khadra al-Jayyusi. Leiden: E. J. Brill.

Usman, Yusuf Bala. 1979. *For the Liberation of Nigeria.* London: New Beacon.

Vandevelde, Hélène. 1985. "Le code algérien de la famille," *Maghreb-Machrek* 107:52–64.

Vatin, Jean Claude. 1984. "Exotisme et rationnalité: à l'origine de l'enseignement du droit en Algérie (1879–1909)." In *Connaissances du Maghreb,* ed. Vatin et al. Paris: CNRS.

Voll, John, and Sarah Potts Voll. 1985. *The Sudan: Unity and Diversity in a Multicultural State.* Boulder, Colo.: Westview.

Walz, Terence. 1978. *Trade between Egypt and the Bilad al-Sudan.* Cairo: Institut français d'archéologie orientale du Caire.

Warburg, Gabriel. 1995. "Mahdism and Islamism in Sudan," *International Journal of Middle East Studies* 27:219–36.

Wilks, Ivor. 1989. *Wa and Wala: Islam and Polity in Northwestern Ghana.* Cambridge: Cambridge University Press.

Works, John. 1976. *Strangers in a Strange Land: Hausa Immigrants in Chad.* New York: Columbia University Press.

CHAPTER 18

Muslim Women in African History

Roberta Ann Dunbar

> *A discussion of women and Islam must be seen in the context of class, country, and above all, the Quran. It is more accurate to say what a particular country does not permit women to do than to say what Islam permits or forbids.*
> —Ira G. Zepp[1]

> *It has not been the case that woman-sympathetic discourses have been entirely lacking in the history of Islam after all, but that they have not been able to attain authority.*
> —Ayesha M. Imam[2]

As members of society, women reside in social and political contexts that propose images and expected roles. Historical factors of culture, colonial rule, and post-independent political and economic patterns constitute pervasive shaping themes of context. Government, the law, and ideology—arenas dominated by men—set its tone. But women interpret, negotiate, mediate, and act, as men do. Until recently, quite different traditions of scholarship have informed our understanding of these matters: historical literature has more often characterized Islam by describing the context, whereas the social sciences have focused more on practice. Men and women do not necessarily experience religion the same way.[3] Does this mean—as it has so often been portrayed—that women's experience is any less Islamic?

The following narrative emphasizes women's roles, experiences, and the way they have fashioned their identities as Muslims in different arenas of life. It looks upon women as actors, and explores examples of African Muslim women as adepts in spirit possession; as teachers and spiritual leaders; and as political actors and agents of change. The preceding chapters have described the history of Islam's spread throughout the subcontinent and the primary features of Muslim law in Africa—the various contexts in which women live. The themes of political economy, regionalism, and family law found in those chapters provide important background to the discussion below.

Adepts in Spirit Possession

Questions about why women practice spirit possession have fueled much scholarly debate.[4] Are women who engage in spirit possession exhibiting some kind of psychological catharsis made necessary by the stress of their relatively low status in hierarchical societies? Or do spirit possession and the social obligations practitioners impose represent strategies that women develop to create an arena to express their individual persona and negotiate more favorable rewards from their domestic situation? Do women find spirit possession useful as a buffer to patriarchal hegemony in the broader society? Women's views have been much less visible in the literature on African Muslim societies until scholars began the deconstruction of Muslim societies' social categories.[5] The attention of these scholars to women's conceptions of men, their world, and its relationship to women illumines the negotiated nature of gender and the moral order. These studies have enlarged our focus by going beyond the personal experience of possession and the motivations for it to considering how these cults offer possibilities—at least at the symbolic level—for the realignment of public values. Nowhere is this more clear than in discussions about spirit possession—most notably *bori* in West Africa and *zar* in northeastern Africa.

From the earliest instances of Islamic transformation of community in Hausaland, spatial separation of the sexes has defined a gendered world.[6] Today, several degrees of seclusion obtain depending on the form of marriage, and in the rural areas, wealth. For the most part, married Muslim women in Hausa-speaking areas live within female quarters of their husband's home, going out only with his permission and only for medical, ceremonial, and, in some instances, social visits to friends. The segregated world has its own dynamic, ranging from the busy and complex management of a royal household in Kano[7] to the autonomous economic world women generate with the help of children and servants from within their quarters.[8] Multiple marriages, and alternatives to second and succeeding marriages available in *karuwanci*,[9] offer opportunities for choice, including the practice of spirit possession, or bori. To married women, bori is an occasion for celebration, music, and dance, albeit within the confines of their own homes. The social support of other women and material gifts given by her husband to one possessed, overcome isolation and permit a woman to negotiate attention. But if bori is liberating of the spirit, it does not create equality of the sexes; in contexts where both male and female adepts practice, they operate in spheres divided by sex, with the male sphere being the more innovative and in control of the more important spirits.[10] Perhaps this, too, is an aspect of gender relationships that may expand and contract depending upon historical factors.

Although decried by authorities for its association with the spirits of the pre-

Islamic past, bori spirits acquire new names and identities reflective of the culture's historical experience, including Islam and colonialism. Mounting their adepts in ritualized performances, they fashion a complex symbolism that offers both explanation and commentary on contemporary life. In her recent work on bori, Susan O'Brien has argued that far from being marginal to Hausa society, bori spirits, adepts, and public ceremonies are and have been central to the fashioning of a dynamic equilibrium or tension in the society as a whole.[11] Coupled with the official positions sometimes held by women associated with bori and the economic exchanges involved, bori is revealed to have a large public role.

In countries of the Horn, especially Ethiopia, and Sudan, women's expression of the spirit life found outlets through spirit possession zar and the pious completion of orthodox religious duties. Much recent research has emphasized the dynamic quality of women's institutional life in the complex cultural society of Sudan.[12] Demarcated into a separate, gendered world by physical, social, and religious conventions, women have made of that separation an arena for spiritual expression and for the creation of networks that promote spiritual, psychological, and material support. Although disdained by orthodox leaders and reformists alike for counter-conventional behaviors, zar leaders and practitioners do not participate in its rituals in self-conscious opposition to religion. To a greater extent than in West Africa, membership in zar is ubiquitous, and as some have suggested, may fulfill for women a comparable function to that of the many sufi rituals. Writing of Sinnar, Susan Kenyon has said that "Zar and zikr fulfil similar needs, ritual, emotional, and social, and largely cater to mutually exclusive members. . . . They differ in methods, organization, and ritual, but not in doctrine or basic belief."[13] As if to remind themselves of their subordination in the midst of these gatherings of women, the leaders of both zar and of spirit healers speak through the predominantly male voices of their spirits.[14]

In East Africa in the 1870s, missionaries commented upon the material benefits women accrued through gifts necessary to appease the spirit that possessed them.[15] Today in Mombasa, the visitation of a spirit, or *pepo,* upon a person (usually a woman) leads her to find a female or male ritual specialist *(mganga)* who understands the spirit's demand and exorcises it. The sexually divided sphere of spirits seen in bori appears in some East African regions as well. On northern Mafia Island, two types of spirits have been described. The first is associated with land spirits and is the specialty of the Pokomo. The second is open to the Pokomo and others, but is primarily female in membership and bears an affinity with the zar cult of northeastern Africa. On Mafia, women see these as sea spirits that prevent them from having children.[16] It is tempting to view this association of sea spirits with sterility as an oblique reframing of women's experience under Omani rule and its legacy.

Scholars have called attention to similarities in the domain of emotional expressiveness between spirit possession and sufi ritual practices.[17] As Islam became more widely adopted by African populations, sufi brotherhoods and ceremonial practices associated with Muslim holy days attracted the participation of women. At the end of the twentieth century, one may point to this phenomenon and at least speculate that, in some Muslim societies, Islamic spiritualism may have begun to erode the utility of the spirit cults.

Muslim Women as Teachers and Spiritual Leaders

Although Islam counsels the value of formal education—an ideal often shared by prophets and Muslim reformers alike—it is also true that in countries of Africa south of the Sahara with substantial Muslim populations, the numbers of girls attending school is significantly lower than elsewhere. The reasons for such a situation are many, but lie largely in the Westernized nature of education, indigenous social roles that assign young girls significant domestic responsibilities, and fears that girls will be rendered unsuitable for marriage by experiences of school life.

Nevertheless, for centuries women have pursued education and roles as teachers within the realm of Quranic education. Because of the gender segregation of many Muslim African societies, the role of women as teachers is critical in the assessment and development of women's education in both the formal and the nonformal settings. This is particularly true where public schools have become battlegrounds for the expression of conflict between religion and secularism.

Through their poetry and homilies, women scholars have contributed significantly to the intellectual development of the Muslim world in Africa. Jean Boyd and Murray Last first highlighted the role of the daughters of 'Uthman dan Fodio in assimilating the vast numbers of non-Muslim women incorporated into the Sokoto empire. In particular, Nana Asma'u, well-known in her own right for her religious writings, founded the 'Yan Taru movement to extend Muslim education of women out into the rural areas.[18] While exceptional, she was not unique for her time: among other female shaykhs, Khadijia of the Ahl-al-Aqil group in Mauritania is said to have taught 'Abd al-Qadir, the leader of the Torodo revolution.[19]

Hajiya Iya Isiaku and Hajiya 'A'isha Mahmoud, interviewed in Kano in the 1980s, were educated by family members, especially their fathers and successive husbands. Their careers were typical in that they continued the tradition of private education tutoring their students at home. Another woman, Hajiya Maria Mai Tafsiri, the one who knows *tafsiri*, or exegesis, has bridged both the private and public worlds in her work: taught by her father, she had accomplished advanced religious studies by the time of her marriage at age thirteen. Her scholarly reputation was enhanced by the broadcast of her recitations on local television and radio in Kano. Hajiya Maria also runs an Islamiyya school for married women and children. The education of other scholars, such as Hajiya Yelwa Ina and Hajiya Rabi Wali, combined training at home, in formal Quranic schools, and in government girls schools. There is no apparent pattern to suggest why these women chose to become scholars. Most had begun their studies at a young age and continued them through several marriages; *tariqa* membership of both Qadiriyya and Tijaniyya as well as no tariqa affiliation were reported; all asserted the importance of encouragement and instruction received from fathers, mothers, and husbands; and Hajiya Rabi in particular was conscious of the tradition of Nana Asma'u's 'Yan Taru.[20]

The line between women's activities as educators and as spiritual leaders is rarely distinguished, in part because they often overlap. Thus Boyd and Last noted that an important function of the 'Yan Taru was to extend the *baraka* of Shehu 'Uthman dan Fodio and organize a cult around it.[21] In Nigeria, 'A'isha, a *muqaddama* and hadith expert, and Safiya 'Umar Falke, also a muqaddama, were well-known women mystics in Kano during the colonial period.[22] In contemporary Kano, women leaders in both the Tijaniyya and Qadiriyya tariqas teach women recruits the prayers and rituals associated with their tariqas. Hajiya Laraba Kabara, the highest-ranking Qadiriyya woman, attended Quranic school but did not complete advanced studies. Her several marriages ended in failure and she remained childless. Attracted to the tariqa by a family friend, Hajiya Laraba is not only a prominent personage in Kano celebrations of the birthday of Shaykh 'Abd al-Qadir, but she has also made the pilgrimage many times, and thus has contacts with the wider Muslim world. Hajiya Hassana Ahmad Sufi, followed her mother into a career that combines mysticism and teaching. Known both as a scholar and mystic, she was the first woman student in the School for Arabic Studies in Kano, and has made a career of teaching advanced Muslim studies in a formal school as well as in an Islamiyya school she built privately at her home.[23]

Women like Ahmad and the others described above are at the forefront of the expansion of women's education in Nigeria in formal adult-education schools. These schools teach both Islamic and Western subjects, but emphasize the cultural integrity of Islam. Like other features of Islamic revival, such as adopting the chador, Muslim women see their schools as one further step to ultimate decolonization and cultural assurance.[24]

In southern Nigeria, Muhammad Jum'at Imam (1896–1959/60), the founder of the Mahdiyyat movement in Ijebul-Ode in 1941, held as a principal element of his instruction that women be educated and that they should attend mosques together with men. Muslim women were attracted by his teaching that there was no Quranic basis for purdah, and because, according to the recollections of followers, "He was a very religious man and of good character . . . who directed people in the right way."[25]

As late as the 1960s, Senegalese women were observed performing rites associated with pre-Islamic, African religions.[26] But recent history has witnessed a larger role for women to play within the context of the Muslim brotherhoods. In Senegal, where seclusion has not been as widespread as in northern Nigeria, many of these activities require public as well as private endeavor. Writing of this phenomenon, Christian Coulon observed that "women participate in their own way in Islam, manipulating it and accommodating it to their needs. They are active Muslims, even if their practices are informal, hidden, parallel, or heterodox; hence it is wrong to relegate the female Muslim universe to this twilight zone where it only appears to belong because of our inability to study it."[27]

Although the Muslim hierarchy restricts women to the private sphere, their participation in the worship of saints and ceremonies that engage prayer, singing, and dancing is a visible manifestation in public of women's spiritual life. Coulon suggests that in Senegal, "the Islam of the brotherhoods and *marabouts* has become primarily the religion of the women . . . because by its rational and explanatory nature it is linked, more than either reformist or fundamentalist Islam, to the traditional values transmitted by women."[28] These practices may be encouraged by one further feature of the tariqas. Women relatives of the tariqa leaders have assumed some of the old roles women held during the pre-Islamic period of the Wolof and Serer states. As relatives of the caliphs, they share in the grace of the tariqas and are actively engaged in furthering their health.

Another way in which women's roles have increased are through the *dàira* (or *dahira*), originally Mouride associations that emerged in urban milieus during the 1950s, but now appear to be common among all brotherhoods and in rural areas as well. Mouride leaders initially discouraged the da'iras because their membership included both sexes. However, in time, the resources made available to the brotherhood through its fund-raising projects won over the leaders on economic strength alone. Women contribute significantly to the economic success of these activities, since in the rural areas they are accustomed to gendered associational activities that combine both social and economic functions.[29]

One example of the spread of such activities beyond the capital city is provided by Leonardo Villalón's richly documented study of tariqa membership in Fatick, Senegal, where the da'iras accommodate women through women's sections of the group or by having a *présidente de femmes* or a *responsible cellule féminine*.[30] Of further interest is that in Fatick there is an all-women's daaira that was not attached to a particular marabout or tariqa, and whose membership consisted of women with varying tariqa affiliations. In addition to regular meetings, the members organize a major festival once a year and raise monies to support their members' attendance at the annual celebrations held in the "capital city" of each of the tariqas—Tivaouane, Touba, and Ndiassane, for instance. A famous religious singer from Kaolack, el-Hajj Tidiane Mbodj, is contracted by them for the annual celebration of the daaira precisely because his religious songs acknowledge the importance of all of the famous marabouts in Senegal without favoring any one of the brotherhoods. While such ecumenical activity fails to further the fortunes of any one marabout, the popularity of this festival sustains the importance of tariqa affiliation in general.[31]

Important to any discussion of Muslim women in Senegal are the women leaders of the Mourides. In the 1960s, Sokna Muslimatou, the sister of the then-reigning caliph of the Mourides, Falilou MBacke, was acknowledged for her spiritual leadership and her disciples. In the 1990s, this role is played by Sokna Magat Diop of Thiès, the daughter of Abdoulaye Iyakhine, a disciple of Shaykh Ibra Fall and Amadu Bamba. Instructed by her father in the duties of leadership, she was appointed by him to be his successor as head of the subgroup he had founded. She was further entwined with the Mouride leadership through a series of marriages—beginning with her first to Shaykh Ibra Fall—to members of the caliph's or Amadu Bamba's family. Since 1943, she has exercised the normal powers and duties of the head of an important section of the Mourides, and is widely acknowledged by the caliph for both her piety and organizational skills. Her leadership style is distinctive from that of male spiritual leaders. She never goes to mosques or conducts public prayers: her son does so instead while acknowledging that he is her "arm." Nor does she conduct marriages or baptisms, although she arranges many of the former and appoints imams to officiate; she is virtually a recluse, going out only on special occasions. She spends her days in prayer before her father's mausoleum, in study of Amadu Bamba's *qasaid* and practice of the *khalwa*—a severe regimen of fasting that can last up to forty days. Her disciples believe her reclusive, severe lifestyle only enhances the power of her baraka and her holiness.

Sokna Magat Diop's model has led to the creation of a subsection of her order that is concerned with justifying equality of the sexes in religious life. One of her daughters, NDeye, is the main organizer of a da'ira that contains both women and men (although "for the sake of form" she has a male copresident). Coulon raises the question, "Could it be that mysticism, in erasing or modifying the difference between the sexes, points the way towards acceptance of female authority in Islam?"[32] Other scholarship stresses rather the interdependence of women and male members in a daaira for Mame Diarra Bousso, the mother of Amadu Bamba. Men sing the qasaid and help women with the transportation of goods to Mame Diarra Bousso's tomb. However through their monthly contributions, women are primarily responsible for the alms gifts to the family during the annual *magal*, or pilgrimage to the tomb.[33]

In Sudan, religious leadership and the dynamic interplay of sufi orders and the orthodox *'ulama* are located within the male realm, although women's participation in Islamist movements in recent years may change that. While women and children may belong to the sufi tariqa, they are excluded from religious activities except for occasional participation as dancers, ululators, or praise-singers on the edges of public performances.[34] Religious beliefs are elaborated in Sudan outside orthodox Islam through spirits. Kenyon writes: "On the whole, they distinguish several different categories of spiritual beings and would not agree with Trimingham (1949, 172 ff.) that all are basically subcategories of *jinn*. This spirit world is very real to most women and alongside their daily prayers is a range of other routine practices aimed at conciliating and propitiating the many spiritual entities which can upset the order of their world."[35]

Two of the spiritual specialists Kenyon studied use many of the same techniques—especially possession—in their counseling roles. However, one of them, Bitt al-Jamil, operates as a religious teacher, seer, and healer; the other, Soreya, was the leader of a *tombura zar* in Sinnar. Neither of these women was literate or had received any religious training. Bitt al-Jamil worked through a spirit medium, Bashir Fath al-Rahman, and did not use other spirits in her work. Bitt al-Jamil was acknowledged to be unique because of her grace and spiritual power, unprecedented for a woman anywhere else in Sudan. She fills a unique role as Muslim spiritual leader without portfolio through the advice she administered during her many sessions. She and Soreya, the zar leader, position themselves at the frontier between the orderly canons of formal religion that all aspire to fulfill, and the disorderly realm of the personal spirits. Their wisdom and the faith and material networks of their clients perpetuate a strongly gender-demarcated and segregated world. "This idea of sexual segregation as a social asset and a personal virtue is a positive and moral approach"[36] that expresses women's view of religion and society.

Turning to East Africa, in Somalia pastoral ideas of community, strongly patriarchal in the precolonial period, only deepened the dependence and oppression of women as the ideology of clan became the primary expression of identity in the colonial and postcolonial worlds.[37] However, along the Benadir coast, the expansion of Islam during the nineteenth century included among the ʿulamaʾ a woman who was both a religious scholar and a mystic. Dada Masiti (1804–24 June 1921), was born into the Al-Ahdal clan of the Asharaf in Brava. As a girl of six, she was kidnapped to Zanzibar. Rescued by family members ten years later, she returned home to devote herself to religious studies and mysticism. A prolific poet, she composed a eulogy, "Shaykhi Chifa Isiloowa," that is still performed. Copies of it are kept by families in Brava.

Dada Masiti is the only female saint in Somalia whose tomb is honored by an annual ziyara. A eulogy written for her by Sahikh Qasim conveys a poetic persona similar to, yet different from, her counterpart in West Africa, Nana Asmaʾu:

> *She is noble, she is chaste, she is pious,*
> *And the daughter of noble descendants.*[38]

In contemporary Brava, Quranic classes are taught mainly by women teachers.[39] Further research might show whether Dada Masiti's career provides an East African parallel to Nana Asmaʾu's ʾYan Taru.

Further south in East Africa, sufism, spirit possession, gender, and class generated a complex range of social and religious forces influencing women.[40] The sufi orders came to the Swahili coast in the 1870s, and from the outset their focus challenged "the absence of women and slaves at the core of Islamic life."[41] Both the Qadiriyya, more prevalent in Tanganyika, and the Habib Saleh in Lamu attracted people of low status, including women, and challenged the formal, hierarchical conceptions of the Omani and freeborn upper classes. Women members of the Qadiriyya participated in mosque activities (something the Ahmadiyya, another brotherhood found in Bagamoyo, did not allow). The Qadiriyyas even endorsed female leadership, as witnessed by the story of Sheikh Binti Mtumwa, who founded a branch of the order in Nyasaland that attracted women disciples over a twenty-year period.[42]

Like the possession cults, tariqa membership enabled women to establish an autonomous sphere of action and some self-determination. Thus, Islam in East Africa has stood for both authority and the state, on the one hand, and innovation and opposition, on the other. It is not surprising that, in the context of Swahili society in the twentieth century, women, former slaves, and other groups of low status have found ways of understanding the religion that makes possible both greater assimilation into the larger world of universal Islam and opposition to the more patriarchal hegemony of the elite.

❨ ❨ ❨

Historical documentation on Muslim women's roles as healers, scholars, and teachers, while still meager, has been enriched by recent scholarship that focuses on their particular accomplishments. Spirit possession, long viewed as elements of popular or marginal culture whether practiced by women or men, must now be viewed within a broader conceptualization of Islam that acknowledges it as an important spiritual expression by practicing Muslims. Regional variations occur in the openness of sufi orders to women. The incorporation of women is apparently more profound in West and East Africa than elsewhere. Although the issue merits more systematic comparative analysis, Muslim women in-fluence formal as well as non-formal education more than has often been recognized.

As women have played more visible roles in Islamist revivals, their educational policies become embroiled in larger political debates. This is the subject of the next section.

Associations: Women as Agents of Change

During the twentieth century, women's membership in religious associations increased due to the decline of older forms of women's organizational life.[43] A heightened awareness of Islamic identity became particularly acute when efforts to improve women's status were closely identified with outsiders. As economic deterioration threatened the autonomy of states from the mid-1970s on, opposition to the imposition of externally created institutions blended with rejuvenated expressions of cultural allegiance. It is in these situations that Islam as a powerful source of culture has often become the focal point of opposition to external domination.

Furthermore, fundamentalist Muslims often link stricter moral standards for women to cures for broader social and economic ills.[44] Therefore, efforts by nationals or outsiders to enlarge the scope of women's lives are met with opposition by a strong 'ulama' and those supporting the reformist tradition. As women seek to participate in the "democratization" process in Africa, tensions over the correct Islamic interpretation of women's political potential have expanded. Women embraced distinctive Muslim dress, including the veil, and began to form Muslim women's political organizations. Sudan, Nigeria, Senegal, Niger, Kenya, and Tanzania offer contrasting cases for study.

❨ ❨ ❨

A number of scholars have explored recently the relationship of gender to broader issues of identity politics in Africa and elsewhere in the Muslim world. Works like Moghadam's *Identity Politics and Women* (1994) and Hale's *Gender Politics in Sudan* (1996) formulate important theoretical questions about religion as an instrument of cultural politics and the consequences for women when it becomes the basis of political hegemony. Moreover, Hale's penetrating analysis of gender and cultural politics in the Sudan adds the important factors of political economy and class/gender competition to those crucial to the rise of Islamist hegemony in that country.

Some of Hale's key points merit development: The roots of Islamist transformation of gender and cultural identities in Sudan took hold in the 1950s and 1960s as curricular reforms and media images sought to "naturalize"[45] the curricula at all instructional levels. Extensive labor migration to the Gulf states by males in the 1970s and 1980s resulted initially in an expanding work arena for women. However, as women began to enter high-level professional and managerial positions, their presence provoked Islamists who reflected the interests of the urban middle class. President Numayri sought to obscure class differences and promoted political unity, bringing former Islamist opponents into his government, giving legitimacy to their concerns. Then, assuming the mantle of religious leader, Numayri, with the Islamists, launched debates in the 1980s about personal laws and appropriate kinds of education and work for women. After 1989, these debates began to produce lower enrollments of women in certain types of medical and technical training and the exclusion of women from high-ranking (and better-salaried) positions.

Women in the Sudan Communist Party's women's union supported education for Sudanese women, but they otherwise avoided confrontation on issues they considered "religious and private" vs. "secular and public." Islamists in Ikhwan and the National Islamic Front were more successful in meeting women's needs through development designed to strengthen Islamic society in the social welfare, economic, and commercial sectors. Even though many of them abhorred women's public engagement in politics, the Islamists were the only party to elect women (two) to the people's assembly. By their activism, creative recruitment, and powerful media, Islamists managed to shift the center and terms of public debates for even those who, in other respects, opposed them.[46]

The construction of Islamic womanhood in the context of class competition and interests means, in Hale's view, that there are distinct limits to the emancipatory aspects of Islamist programs. Control of women remains central to the male-dominated state. Hale concludes that greater revolutionary potential lies in indigenous aspects of ongoing women's culture: economic networks like the *sanduq* rotating credit and the *toumeen* consumer cooperatives; and the religious networks seen in zar.[47]

☾ ☾ ☾

In Nigeria, royal women held important titles and administrative responsibilities at the Bornouan and Habe courts. While it appears that such titles were lost with the reformist jihad, the role of royal women in the management of the palace, the education and integration of slave women, and the intellectual life of the Sokoto is well known. The biography of Nana Asma'u provides a dramatic instance of women's traditional hegemony of the domestic side of life taking on a public aspect and scale.[48]

During the colonial period, Muslim women in the north were excluded from public fora. The legacy of colonial constitutions that preserved powerful regional interests and the near-autonomy of the emirates further discouraged women's entrance into public life.

The political culture of northern Nigeria during the postcolonial period has been relatively consistent insofar as women's place is concerned. It features two camps. One, representing the legatees of the jihad, supported women's education, but not the vote: women did not have the franchise in northern Nigeria until 1976. Once the vote was granted, this side worried about the impact of alien feminist ideas on Muslim women and insisted that the legal reforms carried out in 1979 not include personal and family law. The other pole, represented by the teacher and political leader Aminu Kano, emphasized women's rights, political emancipation, and education. He embraced alternative interpretations of religious texts, but disassociated their reforms from Western ideas—and certainly from feminist ideas.[49]

Initially, women's wings of the political parties were consigned to managing ceremonial issues. They drew heavily upon *karuwai* (see note 9) because of the public nature of their activities. During the Second Republic (1979–83), women's wings worked to get out the women's vote, but the party, not the women's wing leaders, created their agendas. Military rulers have opened the way for greater participation of women in the assemblies, in administrative posts, and constitutional conventions.[50] More recently, women's organizations themselves have come to the fore to develop an agenda for women that the political parties had failed to accomplish.

The first Nigerian women's group was the National Council of Women's Societies, founded in the 1950s. After 1965, the Muslim Sisters Organization organized women school graduates around concerns for Muslim women.[51] Bolanle Awe chaired a national commission on women in the 1980s that sought to increase the numbers of women as voters and candidates for office. The commission was superseded by Women in Nigeria (WIN) in 1982 and the Federation of Muslim Women's Associations of Nigeria (FOMWAN) in 1985. These two groups have emerged as important voices for women's issues in the last decade. WIN's scope is national and its leaders have encouraged women across ethnic, religious, and class lines to join their efforts. FOMWAN, on the other hand, promotes Islam and interpretations of it designed to improve women's status. From the outset, FOMWAN shouldered the lead of both politicizing Muslim women and at the same time fashioning an agenda acceptable to those who wished to speak out as Muslim women on national issues. Their initial declaration in 1985 called for the establishment of shari'a courts, upheld Muslim women's rights in the workplace, and urged the rejection of the IMF loan then being considered.[52] Like Muslim women in other parts of the world, they have argued the need for more women scholars to be involved in the interpretation of the law and the hadith.[53]

The Muslim male political leadership has endorsed FOMWAN, but has also sought to mobilize them on the behalf of male leaders. Given the turmoil that continues to characterize Nigerian politics, it is not at all clear that women's issues will be at the center of either constitutional reform or political activism. The question remains: Why should women's groups not assert their rightful if unfamiliar role in resolving the problems of civil and political life? By bringing together women from all over the country, and by diligently emphasizing women's needs, they may increase their number to a point where Nigeria's sorry travail of politics can be transformed.

☾ ☾ ☾

If an Islamic framework made possible the entry of Muslim women into politics in Nigeria, the same has not been true in Senegal. The relatively large scope of women's religious activities and leadership in the brotherhoods does not carry over into the realm of political campaigns and officeholding, although this may be changing.

Such a history is not surprising, given French colonial policies and the secular nature of the state. Feminist groups, though composed of Muslim women, focus their objectives and strategies outside of and at times in opposition to the religious associations. On the other hand, the activities of the da'ira may include support for political candidates. Thus, women disciples of the Tidjani marabout Shaykh Tidjane Sy, who make up the Dahiratou Khaury waal baraka, collect money for A. Aram Diene, a member of the national assembly.[54] Granted the vote in 1956, women were not elected to the national assembly until 1973. By 1991, they constituted about 12 percent of assembly membership. In the 1990s, women entered the ministerial ranks at the national cabinet level and were elected to positions of leadership in urban councils and rural groups in increasing numbers. At the end of the decade, 15 percent of civil servants were women.[55]

A more problematic challenge for women in the Senegalese political arena has been the increasing prominence of the radical reformist tendency in Islam that advocates an orthodoxy hostile to public roles for women. Over the course of three decades beginning in the 1920s, young intellectuals who identified with radical reformism in the broader Muslim world formed the Muslim Fraternity and the Union Culturelle Musulmane. In the 1970s and 1980s, young men trained abroad in Muslim centers of higher education forged an educated, vocal, and increasingly visible class that supported academic research and newspapers through a variety of associations within the Federation of Islamic Associations of Senegal (FAIS).

The continued success of a shaky alliance between the brotherhoods and the government may determine the political future for women. So long as the brotherhoods remain important political actors, women's religious and political leadership will continue to thrive within them. The interesting question is: What happens when the two realms of women activists—those in the daʾiras and the feminists acting in the secular realm—meet?[56] Men in these associations favor a restricted role for women in politics.

Another example from the francophone countries merits attention: Niger. Until the early 1990s, women's organizations in Niger were either wings of political parties (before 1974) or the creation of the state. The leadership sprang from the educated political elite, and although members of it were Muslim, policies were framed within the context of secular reform. The Association of Nigerien Women (established in 1975) advocated legal reform from the outset. However, government proposals and drafts of family codes languished in the face of Muslim and chiefly opposition.

The opening up of the political climate in Niger following the national conference in 1991 fostered the explosion of political parties and associations, including women's associations. Among the several new women's groups is one representing women's concerns within a consciously Muslim framework. In 1995, this group called upon the government to promote the teaching of Islam in public schools.[57] Women have actively engaged in transforming their relationship to identity and politics in Niger. A mass rally in May 1991 achieved the selection of women in the planning process for the national conference. Even in a conservative Muslim stronghold like Maradi, women have negotiated redefinitions of social categories of respectability that have enabled political alliances to occur that in the past would have been impossible.[58]

(((

Muslim women in Kenya and Tanzania have participated in politics in recent years as members of the major political parties, but few such parties have had a Muslim mandate. Kenya's political culture has veered more toward the reconstruction of ethnicity than of religion in the core political debates.

In centuries past, East African Muslim women held important political posts and wielded significant social and economic power. Both oral traditions and early Portuguese accounts noted that, pre-1600, Swahili communities accorded high social status to some women. As queens and women of influence, they played important roles in public affairs in the coastal towns.[59]

After 1600, however, during the Portuguese and early Omani periods, less is known about women's activities. Intermarriage between men living in coastal towns and women of the adjacent hinterland, while perhaps not as frequent as it had been in earlier periods, undoubtedly continued. Following the abolition of slavery, former slaves joined the recent immigrants of Hadhramis, Asians, and Comorians as people with little vested interest in coastal social hierarchy. Former slave women with their children formed the nucleus of landless, female-headed households. Many remained in service to their former owners as a matter of both religious belief and a lack of economic alternatives. Slave owners sometimes gave plots of land to former slaves who remained with them, and these were passed down to their children. If, in the early twentieth century, they were driven by economic circumstances to the larger cities like Mombasa, they depended on prostitution, sewing, and food processing for their livelihoods.[60]

Women in Mombasa, whether freeborn, descendants of slaves, or descendants of Omani, had many experiences in common. This is shown in a study of the life histories of three Muslim women collected by Sarah Mirza and Margaret Strobel in the 1980s. Although differences in ethnicity and social place gave these women different social and material prospects, many features of their lives illuminate and typify women's situation. All three women married more than once; all three achieved a desired divorce by insisting that their husbands repudiate them; all experienced infertility (common on the coast) and/or suffered the ravages of high infant mortality rates; and all lived in households predominantly female in composition. The latter pattern, while not a majority one, was significant enough to be remarked upon by census takers throughout the twentieth century.[61]

Omani and Twelve Tribes women spent much of their lives in seclusion, although there were exceptions. The importance of male authority and guardianship sprang from both Muslim and indigenous African practices. But in reality, women, especially those confronting economic necessity, engaged in a variety of activities and careers at different stages of their lives. The associational life of Muslim women in the first half of the twentieth century was profoundly shaped by the urban experience. Dance associations—especially in the towns like Mombasa—were a major feature of women's activities and played an important role in women's cultural expression and social change. Groups recruiting their membership from specific social categories organized major festivals, weddings, and dance competitions. The intensity of the latter often led to violence and they were banned by the colonial government after a time. But through them, women established mutual aid (within the groups); they promoted change in dress and styles through their dances; they developed their organizational skills; and they expressed social criticism, both to reestablish norms and to rebel against the patriarchal practices of home and state.[62]

Following World War II, dance competitions began to decline, but in their stead, many of the women who had been involved in them became active in "modern associations" that sought to influence politics and social policy. The Muslim Women's Institute and Muslim Women's Cultural Association in Mombasa provoked debates about the role of women in Arab society and supported the expansion of Arab Girls' Schools.[63]

In Kenya, however, these organizations of the postwar period remained more socially than politically focused. Reflecting the increasing importance of their Muslim identity in the broader context of Kenyan politics, they failed to support legal reforms proposed in the areas of divorce and inheritance or liberalizing measures for women in the mosques.[64] In Tanzania in the 1950s, Muslim women of Dar es Salaam created the women's wing of the Tanganyikan African National Union (Tanu). Through networks built by their dance and cooperative associations, women like Bibi Titi Mohammed used their cultural and organizational skills literally to create nationalism for Tanu, first in Dar es Salaam, then beyond. The testimony of women activists' life histories shows they were motivated by nationalism and improvement of the condition of women and children, but they did not understand this agenda to be opposed to Islam. Bibi Titi and others were devout Muslims who often paid a high personal price for their political work.[65]

After independence, Tanzania's President Nyerere espoused full political rights and participation for women: he replaced Tanu's women's wing with Umoja Ya Wanawake Tanzania (UWT—the Tanzanian women's organization). Under the one-party state, women increased their numbers in the civil service and professions, but their voices diminished as a political force.[66] Muslim women continued to be active in political life and founded some of the most important nongovernmental organizations concerned with gender issues. But the secular framework still holds: in a 1993 overview of the status of Tanzanian women, neither religion nor religious organizations appear in the text.[67] The reasons for this may lie with the nature of our sources on Tanzanian women, but it also seems likely that historical factors outlined above are important in the relatively muted role religion has played in Tanzania's political culture: the secular political ideology of the state; the minority status of Muslims; the regionally specific historical and cultural traditions of Islamic orthodoxy and law; and patterns of matriliny and cognatic descent that have accorded women greater equality than is found among Muslim populations elsewhere in sub-Saharan Africa.

Islam nevertheless is a factor in the politics of Tanzania because of the dynamic relationship between the two parts of the union: Zanzibar and mainland Tanganyika. During times of strains between the two territories, religious overtones come into the debates. Dissatisfaction with Tanzania's place in the global economy and the frustration of its citizens with declining services and rising costs have nourished scapegoating of Zanzibaris, the vast majority of whom are Muslim, because of their economic power. Coupled with ethnic and religious reconstruction elsewhere in the Muslim world, and in Africa, in Algeria and Sudan, this has led to heightened attention to women's morality as the standard-bearers of culture and religion. Such attention often evolves into policies and attitudes that are restrictive of Muslim women's freedom of speech and action. The evolution of Tanzanian politics will influence the course of women's political roles, be they victims or shapers of the force of religion in public life.

☾ ☾ ☾

Risking oversimplification we have teased out some comparative observations about Muslim women in Africa south of the Sahara. The relationship between religion and other aspects of their lives is complex. It is shaped by contextual elements of ideology, social structure, and political economy on the one hand, and by women's strategies on the other.

Differences of demography, underlying social structures, the age of Islam, and colonial history account for regional differences in women's experience of Islam to a greater degree than particular features of Muslim ideology. That does not mean, however, that ideology lacks importance. This is particularly visible in the domain of law and the state. The 1990s were not the first time that articulation of Islamic and secular law has been a vehicle for debating state authority and cultural identity. Family law often lies at the frontier of such debates because it touches people close to home. The status of women more than that of men is linked to family law because of their centrality to the biological and cultural reproduction of the system.

The alliance between the state and Islam is dynamic and has consequences for women. Unmenaced, the alliance is tolerant. But if menaced from without or within, it will harden. As with other kinds of cultural politics, Islamists draw inspiration, at least in part, from competition of social classes. In Sudan and Senegal, Islamists are educated, relatively wealthy, urban elites who have developed ties with the larger Muslim world from having studied or worked there. Nigeria's Islamists, on the other hand, represent a powerful, highly capitalized business class allied to an old aristocracy. The common element among all three is that they are strongly urbanized. How these forces play themselves out in rural Africa is much less clear.

Muslim women select different strategies to negotiate space for self-expression in the face of patriarchal hegemony. Spirit possession is one option that may be attractive especially for those whose social position requires seclusion but whose temperament or opportunity does not draw them to mysticism or teaching. Mysticism is an option that appears to cut across social class lines and cultural region, although the postures of the mystics vary in their relationship to the broader community. Thus, we see contrasts between Nana Asma'u and the Hajjiyas of Kano (learned leaders, member of the establishment) and Sokna Magat Diop (illiterate, devout, but able to organize as those in dahira and some zar networks do); and then again between these and challengers of the status quo, as with the East Africans and the Yoruba.

Muslim women in the late twentieth century resided in an era of great promise and great danger: great danger in that authoritarianism, in the hands of agents of military or social class, but justified in the name of religion, will impose greater physical, material, and psychological hardships on women than on men; great promise in that through political groups, ceremonial organizations, and education campaigns, women are finding new, essentially democratic arenas for public engagement and influence in the broader society. Cloaking their work in religion and piety, they offer fresh opportunities to assert community in these times of political alienation and economic duress. While the processes of these developments require further study, these features characterize Islam *and* Muslim women. If the exercise of condensing such rich and varied experience into so few pages has any merit, it is to broaden our conceptualization of Islam as well as to embrace our understanding of the condition of Muslim women.

Notes

1. Zepp 1992, 172.
2. Imam 1994, 137.
3. Coulon 1988, 115; Kenyon 1991, 31–32.
4. Berger 1976; Echard 1989; Stoller 1989; Lewis 1980.
5. Constantinides 1985; Boddy 1989; Kenyon 1991; O'Brien 1993.
6. Nast 1996.
7. Mack 1988, 1991.
8. Schildkrout 1983; Coles 1991; Frishman 1991.
9. The status of divorced women, *karuwai* (sing. *karuwa*), who do not live under the authority of a male guardian. Piault 1971; Barkow 1971; Pittin 1983.
10. Echard 1989.
11. O'Brien 1993, chapter 2.
12. Boddy 1988, 1989, 1992; Kenyon 1991; Hale 1996; Fluehr-Lobban 1994.
13. Kenyon 1991, 42–43.
14. Ibid., chapters 5 and 6.
15. Strobel 1979, 78–90.
16. Caplan 1982, 36.
17. Constantin 1987; Kenyon 1991.
18. Boyd and Last 1985; Boyd 1989; Asma'u 1997.
19. Coulon 1988, 120.
20. Sule and Starratt 1991, 34–40.
21. Cited in Coulon 1988, 123.
22. Paden 1973, 100, cited in Sule and Starratt 1991, 41.
23. Sule and Starratt 1991, 42, 44.
24. Ibid., 47.
25. Clarke 1988, 163–64, 179–80.
26. Falade 1971; Callaway and Creevey 1994, 44.
27. Coulon 1988, 115.
28. Ibid., 117–18.
29. Callaway and Creevey 1994, 48–49.
30. Villalón 1995, 154, 161.
31. Ibid., 162.
32. Coulon 1988, 130–31.
33. Rosander 1997.
34. Hale 1996, 84; Kenyon 1991, 37–38.
35. Kenyon 1991, 39.
36. Ibid., 184–221, 236.
37. Kapteijns 1991; 1994.

38. Kassim 1995, 27.

39. Arab League Educational, Cultural, and Scientific Organization (ALESCO), cited in Kassim 1995, 27.

40. Constantin 1987.

41. Strobel 1979, 77.

42. Constantin 1987, 65; see also Coulon 1988, 120–21.

43. Villalón 1995, 162; Nimtz 1980, 304 cited in Coulon 1988, 124; Le Guennec-Coppens 1983, 61–62.

44. Coulon 1988, 117.

45. Hale 1996, 202.

46. Ibid., chapter 4.

47. Ibid., 233–48.

48. Boyd 1989; Asma'u 1997.

49. Callaway and Creevey 1994, 144, 146, 149, 153.

50. Ibid., 149–53.

51. For historical analyses of Muslim women's organizations in Nigeria, see Abdullah 1997; Yusuf 1991.

52. Yusuf 1991, 100.

53. Imam 1994; Callaway and Creevey 1994, 156.

54. Ibid., 166.

55. Ibid., 170–72.

56. Ibid., 174–76; Coulon 1983, 127–41.

57. Dunbar 1991; Dunbar and Djibo 1992; Villalon 1994 *Camel Express Télématique,* 18 July 1995; Reynolds 1997.

58. Cooper 1995; 1997, chapter 8.

59. Pouwels 1987, 28.

60. Ibid., 93–194; Romero 1988.

61. Mirza and Strobel 1989, 10–12.

62. Strobel 1979; Geiger 1997, chapters 2 and 3.

63. Strobel 1979; Mirza and Strobel 1989.

64. Strobel 1979.

65. Geiger 1997.

66. Geiger 1997, chapter 8.

67. Tanzania Gender Networking Programme (TGNP) 1993.

Bibliography

Abdullah, Hussaina. 1997. "Religious Revivalism, Human Rights amd the Struggle for Women's Rights in Nigeria." Paper presented at the conference Cultural Transformations in Africa, 11–13 March. Cape Town: Centre for African Studies, University of Cape Town/Emory Law School, Emory University.

Asma'u, Nana. 1997. *Collected Works of Nana Asma'u, daughter of Usman dan Fodio,* ed. Jean Boyd and Beverly Mack. African historical sources series, no. 9. East Lansing: Michigan State University Press.

Barkow, Jerome. 1971. "The Institution of Courtesanship in the Northern States of Nigeria," *Génève-Afrique* 10:1–16.

Berger, Iris. 1976. "Rebels or Status-Seekers? Women as Spirit Mediums in East Africa." In *Women in Africa,* ed. Nancy J. Hafkin and Edna G. Bay, 157–81. Stanford: Stanford University Press.

Boddy, Janice. 1988. "Spirits and Selves in Northern Sudan: The Cultural Therapeutics of Possession and Trance," *American Ethnologist* 15:4–27.

———. 1989. *Wombs and Alien Spirits: Women, Men, and the Zar Cult in Northern Sudan.* Madison: University of Wisconsin Press.

———.1992. "Bucking the Agnatic System: Status and Strategies in Rural Northern Sudan." In *In Her Prime: New Views of Middle-Aged Women,* ed. Virginia Kerns and Judith K. Brown, 140–53. Urbana: University of Illinois Press.

Boyd, Jean. 1989. *The Caliph's Sister: Nana Asma'u (1793–1865), Teacher, Poet, and Islamic Leader.* London: Cass.

Boyd, Jean, and D. M. Last. 1985. "The Role of Women as *agents religieux* in Sokoto," *Canadian Journal of African Studies* 19:283–300.

Callaway, Barbara, and Lucy Creevey. 1994. *The Heritage of Islam: Women, Religion, and Politics in West Africa.* Boulder, Colo.: Lynne Rienner.

Camel Express Télématique, 18 July 1995.

Caplan, Pat. 1982. "Gender, Ideology, and Modes of Production on the Coast of East Africa," *Paideuma* 28:29–43.

Clarke, Peter B. 1988. "Charismatic Authority and the Creation of a New Order: The Case of the Mahdiyyat Movement in South-Western Nigeria." In *Charisma and Brotherhood in African Islam,* ed. Donal B. Cruise O'Brien and Christian Coulon, 157–82. Oxford: Clarendon.

Coles, Catherine. 1991. "Hausa Women's Work in a Declining Urban Economy." In Coles and Mack 1991, 183–91.

Coles, Catherine, and Beverly Mack. 1991. *Hausa Women in the Twentieth Century.* Madison: University of Wisconsin Press.

Constantin, F. 1987. "Condition féminine et dynamique confrérique en Afrique orientale," *Islam et sociétés au sud du Sahara* 1:58–69.

Constantinides, Pamela. 1985. "Women Heal Women: Spirit Possession and Sexual Segregation in a Muslim Society." In *Social Science and Medicine* 21:685–92.

Cooper, Barbara M. 1995. "The Politics of Difference and Women's Associations in Niger: Of 'Prostitutes,' the Public, and Politics," *Signs* 20:851–82.

———. 1997. *Marriage in Maradi: Gender and Culture in a Hausa Society in Niger (1900–1989).* Portsmouth, N.H.: Heinemann; Oxford: Currey.

Coulon, Christian. 1983. *Les Musulmans et le Pouvoir en Afrique Noire.* Paris: Karthala.

———. 1988. "Women, Islam, and *Baraka*." In *Charisma and Brotherhood in African Islam,* ed. Donal Cruise O'Brien and Christian Coulon, 113–33. Oxford: Clarendon.

Dunbar, Roberta Ann. 1991. "Islamic Values, the State, and 'the Development of Women': The Case of Niger." In Coles and Mack 1991, 69–89.

Dunbar, Roberta Ann, and Hadiza Djibo. 1992. *Islam, Public Policy, and the Legal Status of Women in Niger.* Prepared for the Office of Women in Development, Bureau for Research and Development, Agency for International Development. March. Contract no. PDC-0100-Z-00–9044–00.

Echard, Nicole. 1989. *Bori: Génies d'un culte de possession hausa de l'Ader et du Kurfey (Niger)*. Paris: Institut d'Ethnologie.

Falade, Solange. 1971. "Women of Dakar and Surrounding Urban Area." In *Women of Tropical Africa*, ed. Denise Paulme, 213–29. Berkeley: University of California Press.

Fluehr-Lobban, Carolyn. 1994. *Islamic Society in Practice*. Gainesville: University Press of Florida.

Frishman, Alan. 1991. "Hausa Women in the Urban Economy of Kano." In Coles and Mack 1991, 192–203.

Geiger, Susan. 1997. *TANU Women. Gender, and Culture in the Making of Tanganyikan Nationalism (1955–1965)*. Portsmouth, N.H.: Heinemann.

Le Guennec-Coens, F. 1983. *Femmes voilées de Lamu (Kenya)*. Paris: Editions Recherches sur le Civilisations.

Hale, Sondra. 1996. *Gender Politics in Sudan: Islamism, Socialism, and the State*. Boulder, Colo.: Westview.

Imam, Ayesha M. 1994. "Politics, Islam, and Women in Kano, Northern Nigeria." In *Identity Politics and Women: Cultural Assertions and Feminisms in International Perspectives*, ed. Valentine M. Moghadam, 123–44. Boulder, Colo.: Westview.

Kapteijns, Lidwien. 1991. "Women and the Somali Pastoral Tradition: Corporate Kinship and Capitalist Transformation in Northern Somalia." Boston: Working Papers in African Studies, no. 153. African Studies Center, Boston University.

———. 1994. "Women and the Crisis of Communal Identity: The Cultural Construction of Gender in Somali History." In *The Somali Challenge: From Catastrophe to Renewal?* ed. Ahmed I. Samatur, 211–32. Boulder, Colo.: Lynne Rienner.

Kassim, Mohamed M. 1995. "Islam and Swahili Culture on the Banadir Coast," *Northeast African Studies* 2 (n.s.):21–37.

Kenyon, Susan M. 1991. *Five Women of Sennar: Culture and Change in Central Sudan*. Oxford: Clarendon.

Lewis, I. M., ed. 1980. *Islam in Tropical Africa*. 2nd ed. London: International African Institute, with Hutchinson University Library for Africa.

Mack, Beverly. 1988. "Hajiya Ma'Daki: A Royal Hausa Woman." In *Life Histories of African Women*, ed. Patricia W. Romero, 47–77. London: Ashfield.

———. 1991. "Wives in Kano." In Coles and Mack 1991, 109–29.

Mirza, Sarah, and Margaret Strobel, eds. and trans. 1989. *Three Swahili Women: Life Histories from Mombasa, Kenya*. Bloomington: Indiana University Press.

Moghadam, Valentine M., ed. 1994. *Identity Politics and Women: Cultural Reassertions and Feminisms in International Perspective*. Boulder, Colo.: Westview.

Nast, Heidi J. 1996. "Islam, Gender, and Slavery in West Africa Circa 1500: A Spatial Archaeology of the Kano Palace, Northern Nigeria," *Annals of the Association of American Geographers* 86:44–77.

Nimtz, August H. 1980. *Islam and Politics in East Africa: The Sufi Order in Tanzania*. Minneapolis: University of Minnesota Press.

O'Brien, Susan. 1993. "Spirit Possession as Historical Source: Gender, Islam, and Healing in Hausa *Bori*." M.A. thesis in history, University of Wisconsin-Madison.

Oppong, Christine, ed. 1983. *Female and Male in West Africa*, 107–26 and 291–302. London: Allen & Unwin.

Paden, John N. 1973. *Religion and Political Culture in Kano*. Berkeley: University of California Press.

Piault, Colette. 1971. *Contribution à l'étude de la vie quotidienne de la femme Mawri: Etudes Nigeriennes,* 10. Niamey: CNRS.

Pittin, Renee I. 1983. "Houses of Women: A Focus on Alternative Life-Styles in Katsina City." In Oppong 1983, 291–302.

Pouwels, Randall L. 1987. *Horn and Crescent: Cultural Change and Traditional Islam on the East African Coast (800–1900)*. Cambridge: Cambridge University Press.

Reynolds, Eileen M. 1997. "The Democratic Transition in Niger (1991–1996): Women Leaders' Theories and Organizational Strategies for the Empowerment of Women." M.A. thesis, Clark University.

Romero, Patricia W. 1988. "Mama Khadija: A Life History as Example of Family History." In *Life Histories of African Women,* ed. Patricia W. Romero, 140–58. London: Ashfield.

Rosander, Eva Evers. 1997. "Le *dahira* de Mam Diarra Bousso à Mbacké." In *Transforming Female Identities: Women's Organizational Forms in West Africa,* ed. Eva Evers Rosander, 160–74. Seminar proceedings no. 31. Uppsala: Nordiska Afrikainstitutet.

Schildkrout, Enid. 1983. "Dependance and Autonomy: The Economic Activities of Secluded Hausa Women in Kano." In Oppong 1983, 107–26.

Stoller, Paul. 1989. *A Fusion of the Worlds: An Ethnography of Possession among the Songhay of Niger.* Chicago: University of Chicago Press.

Strobel, Margaret. 1979. *Muslim Women in Mombasa (1890–1975)*. New Haven: Yale University Press.

Sule, Balaraba B. M., and Priscilla E. Starratt. 1991. "Islamic Leadership Positions for Women in Contemporary Kano Society." In Coles and Mack 1991, 29–49.

Tanzania Gender Networking Programme (TGNP). 1993. *Gender Profile of Tanzania.* Dar es Salaam.

Villalón, Leonardo A. 1994. "Debating Change and Democracy in Niger: Transition and the Fate of the Code de la Famille." Paper presented at the African Studies Association meeting, Toronto, Canada, 3-6 Nov.

———. 1995. *Islamic Society and State Power in Senegal: Disciples and Citizens in Fatick.* Cambridge: Cambridge University Press.

Yusuf, Bilkisu. 1991. "Hausa-Fulani Women: The State of the Struggle." In Coles and Mack 1991, 90–108.

Zepp, Ira G. 1992. *A Muslim Primer: Beginner's Guide to Islam.* Westminster, Md.: Wakefield.

CHAPTER 19

Islamic Education and Scholarship in Sub-Saharan Africa

Stefan Reichmuth

In many African states and societies, Islamic education and its various institutions have held for long and still continue to hold a significant place in both individual and public life. The influence of this education was by no means restricted to Muslims alone but extended to patterns of general culture well beyond their communities. To be sure, Islamic learning is first and foremost supposed to provide the believer with access to the Quran, the Word of God, and to specific rituals, ethical norms, and patterns of behavior that are derived from God's message and from the words and deeds of his prophet. But besides that, it also transmits much broader patterns of learning, which, beyond basic literacy, equally include a wide range of subjects: law, theology and mysticism, Arabic grammar, poetry and literature, Islamic history, and finally a good deal of arithmetic, astronomy-cum-astrology, and medicomagical therapeutics. This intricate complex of learning, which involves children as well as young and aged adults and has a history of more than a thousand years in sub-Saharan Africa, came to have important differential and mediating functions for African societies.

Differential and Mediating Functions of Islamic Learning

Islamic learning, even at the elementary level of Quranic education, creates and reinforces basic differences between Muslims and non-Muslims. In many African regions, it provided the earliest pattern of schooling, setting Muslim children apart from those of other people, and gradually changing the prevailing attitudes to childhood and education, as well as to time and dress. Graduation from Quranic school frequently came to be celebrated as an initiation ceremony firmly embedded in Muslim communal life. At the same time, Islamic learning served to distinguish status, honor, and prestige among Muslims themselves. After long-standing contacts with Muslim foreigners, local groups of professional Islamic scholars came into their own, in a process that recurred time and again in various social settings.

Apart from this, although Quranic education was in most cases provided for both boys and girls, higher Islamic learning frequently came to be a male domain. Even if female learning, especially within the scholar families themselves, was by no means negligible, the basic pattern in this field reinforced separation between the sexes. Male predominance in public life was to prevail for a long time among African Muslims.

Another important differential provided by Islamic learning is communal and regional. This can be studied in the growth and development of important political and commercial centers in sub-Saharan Africa. Islamic scholars and traders contributed in no small way to the emergence and stability of such centers. Quite often, they would have their own distinct quarters or settlements, centered around their local mosques. In other cases, they were able to transform whole towns into distinct religious centers of their own. The religious and educational reputation of such places sometimes far outlived their political and commercial bloom. With their scholarly elite and their Islamic patterns of public life, centers of this kind provided important models for the political and cultural development in different parts of Africa.[1]

The mediating and integrating functions of Islamic learning and education are equally varied. This education is, first of all, designed to shape the believer's attitude toward God, cosmos, and time, and to relate it to the different stages and experiences of his life. In this respect, teachers and scholars very often perform crucial functions as advisers, spiritual guides, and healers. The concepts of sainthood that became widespread among African Muslims were largely based on these mediating functions of the Islamic teacher and scholar. At the social level, Islamic learning and its institutions made up a framework for different kinds of relations among Muslims themselves. They often brought together people from different ethnic and linguistic communities, as well as from different age groups and social layers. Institutions of Islamic learning became part of the prevailing social structure, in urban as well as in rural and nomadic contexts. As they provided an important source for the development of common ethical and legal norms, they also made an impact on the mutual relations between different professional and political classes and on the legitimation of public authority. Apart from this, Islamic scholars and students, being a highly mobile and sometimes truly cosmopolitan group, provided important links to the outside world for the communities they were living with.

These mediating functions at the social level were by no means restricted to Muslims alone. In many regions where Islam was established, Islamic learning not only distinguished Muslims from their non-Muslims neighbors, but also came to provide important patterns of common culture for both groups. Traces of this long-standing communication can be found in language, folklore, and historical legends, in dress and common festivals, and also in a widely shared range of therapeutical and divinatory practices, partly derived from local, partly from Islamic patterns. Many societies developed their own arrangements and institutions for social and cultural interaction between Muslims and non-Muslims. Motifs and topics derived from the scholars' literary culture sometimes played a crucial role in this process of cultural bargaining and exchange. For non-Muslim communities and states, Islamic scholars with their extended connections to large-scale trading networks provided vital links to the outside world, and they were often given important court positions. This cooperation found public and ritual recognition even in pagan royal festivals; certain important functions sometimes came to be reserved for Islamic scholars and dignitaries.[2]

Both differential and mediating functions of Islamic learning can be found at work in periods of social unrest and political upheaval. In such crises, groups of Islamic scholars with their students sometimes figured as conservative and loyalist elements. Not infrequently, however, they stood at the center of opposition and political change. This can be observed with particular clarity for the large Islamic movements of the eighteenth and nineteenth century in West Africa. Such movements often started out as religious-reform and preaching movements before they became directly involved in political and military struggles. With confrontation growing, full-scale ideologies of difference between believers and unbelievers were elaborated for the justification of violent or military action. Islamic learning, now gradually becoming a mass phenomenon, was used for this, but it also served to stabilize the resulting social and political arrangements once a new order was established. Commercial expansion in the Nile Valley and in East Africa since the eighteenth century equally made Islamic learning increasingly important for the articulation of commercial interest and political aims of the Muslim communities.

Islamic learning and education came under new challenges in the colonial and postcolonial period. The colonial powers oscillated in their policies between suppression of Muslim resistance and cooperation with Muslim groups—even to the extent of creating Muslim army units for both conquest and control of their domains. This also affected the position of Islamic scholars and educational institutions. For the Muslims themselves, Islamic learning and its reform became of primary importance, especially since new types of school education were being introduced by colonial administrators and Christian missionaries. As the political and military leaders of the Muslims lost power, the Islamic scholars on the whole gained in communal influence and public reputation. In most Muslim regions, Islamic schools continued to be run as private institutions, with or without recognition by the government, thus creating a private school sector subsidized by local Muslim communities. This sector existed alongside the public school system that was taking shape. Muslims also became increasingly committed to Western forms of education. Tension between the two systems found expression in different legal and organizational ways. Some countries ignored the Islamic sector; others gave it some recognition and tried to integrate it into the public educational system. From the two systems, and shaped by the manifold tensions between them, a new class of younger Muslim scholars and intellectuals came up. Many of them had already studied in Islamic institutions in the Arab countries. Since the 1980s, this younger Muslim elite group of mixed educational background has often become a cultural and political factor of its own, apart from the older generation of Islamic scholars and Muslim leaders. The struggle of the Muslim commmunities to cope with the different strands of learning and education in their countries is still going on. In this struggle, Islamic learning, increasingly geared to Arabic-language skills and strongly influenced by international models, has remained both a distinctive element and a forum for mediating social and political reform.

Variations in the Development of Quranic Learning

It is not easy to establish the historical depth of the patterns of Quranic learning that have been described for sub-Saharan Africa since the nineteenth century. Arab travelers and geographers were only casually interested in this form of education, which for them was just a familiar part of Muslim religious and communal life, not worth any closer attention.

The earliest black African group to be exposed to Islamic learning might have been the Ijnaw, among the Ibadis of the Jabal Nafusa in the early ninth century, who even produced a prominent Ibadi scholar and governor of the region. This man still spoke the language of Kanem, which shows the close links of the Ibadis to the Lake Chad region.[3] North African patterns of Quranic education can perhaps also be assumed for the trading communities of Awdaghust, Ghana, and others—although we know virtually nothing about the traders' children staying there.[4] Al-Bakri's famous account of the conversion of the king of Malal[5] shows that learning some pieces of the Quran for use during prayer was part even of a rather rudimentary conversion procedure. According to the same author, a copy of the Quran—allegedly sent by the caliph—had already become part of the regalia of the king of Kawkaw, suggesting recognition of the sacrality of the Quran within the states and societies of the sub-Saharan zone.[6] The first truly learned rulers in that region, according to one tradition of mixed black African and Berber origin, were the Banu Tanamak of Tadmakka, as reported by Ibn Hawqal (d. 988).[7] Ancient Tadmakka (most probably to be identified with present-day Essuk) and the Niger region of Kawkaw and old Kukiya are also the sites where the earliest traces of Arabic writing in sub-Saharan Africa, graffitis and tombstones dating from 1014 onward, have been identified.[8] It seems significant that the Essuk area also shows a concentration of inscriptions in the old Berber Tifinagh script, suggesting a long-standing cultural interaction of Berber and Arab culture in that region.

A further stage in the spread of Quranic education is reflected by Ibn Battuta. After his visit to Old Mali (1352–53), he praises the inhabitants of its capital: "Another [good feature] is their assiduity in prayer and their persistence in performing it in congregation and beating their children to make them perform it. . . . Another is their eagerness to memorize the great Koran. They place fetters on their children if there appears on their part a failure to memorize it and they are not undone until they memorize it."[9] He observed this several times, even in the family of the qadi, whose children he saw fettered with chains on the day of the great festival. The sometimes rather severe discipline forced upon children, especially boys, in Quranic schools, typical also of more recent ages in West Africa, thus finds its earliest witness in Ibn Battuta. It seems to have developed along with the establishment of congregational prayer as a public institution of major importance.

A particularly close connection of Quranic learning with a royal court can be reconstructed for the kingdom of Kanem/Bornu.[10] The founder of the Saifawa dynasty, Hummay b. 'Abd al-Jalil (c. 1075–86), is already celebrated in a praise-song (of unknown date) as a studious warrior: "The friend of youth, whose writing slate is of kabwi wood—At night a warrior on a coal-black horse; but when day dawns he is to be seen with his Quran in his hand."[11] The descendants of his alleged teacher Muhammad Mani played a prominent role as leading imams and kingmakers in the legends of origin as well as in the religious and political setup of the Sefuwa kingdom. The court and the capital of the Sefuwa kings in Kanem and later in Bornu became famous for their Quranic learning and for the calligraphic script that was developed there. Dated Quranic manuscripts from Bornu, in some cases with interlinear translations and glosses in the local language, are extant already for the seventeenth century, when local scholarship had come fully into its own.[12] Apart from the court, a tradition of rural school settlements *(mallemti)* had developed in the kingdom. These settlements were run by teachers of various origins and often granted considerable autonomy. Several migrant groups of different ethnic origins were absorbed into the kingdom by giving them chartered privileges for such semi-autonomous scholar settlements with a recognized 'alim as leader. The refined didactic method—divided into five clearly distinguished stages—for the training of the Quranic students in the rural *Sangaya* ("cornstalk hut") schools, which makes Bornu famous even today, is probably unique in West Africa: it transmits the ability not only to recite but also to write the Quran from memory with all the peculiarities of the Quranic orthography. Bornu attracted many students from the neighboring regions. From the eighteenth century onward, migrant scholars from Bornu traveled widely and obtained offices as teachers and imams in Hausaland and even within the Muslim settlements in Yorubaland, Borgu, and further west.

The rural Quranic school settlement, with families of teachers and scholars surrounded by a large number of students of different ages who served them and helped them about the household and in the fields, was a feature of not only Bornu: camps of scholars and students sharing the itinerant ways of life of nomadic and seminomadic groups became a common phenomenon in the western Sahara and among the Tuareg.[13] Rural school settlements were also widespread among the Juula and Fulbe scholars in the western Sudan. The Jakhanke communities,[14] the Juula of Ghana and Togo,[15] and the Torodbe of the Futa Toro[16] provide typical examples. Sometimes their teaching activities involved a considerable mobility of both scholars and students. The rural traveling school was already noticed by a European observer in Senegambia in the early seventeenth century.[17] It became an important institution shaping urban-rural relations in western and central Sudan. Many of the Islamic movements of the eighteenth century in West Africa had their origins in such, nearly autonomous, rural scholar communities, which often became places of resort in times of economic and political crises.

Descriptions of Quranic schools and their educational aims and customs were recorded by Islamic teachers and scholars themselves in the late nineteenth century. Especially, the detailed account given for Hausaland by Imam Umaru of Salga (1858–1934) shows the extent to which Quranic education had become embedded into social and cultural life among the Hausa.[18] In Kano, the majority of the inhabitants sent their sons to a Quranic school when the boy knew how to count up to ten. The teacher, with full authority over the student given to him by the father, would at first have him learn the opening sura *(al-fatiha)* and the last suras of the Quran by heart. The pupil then began to learn how to read and spell the Arabic letters and vowel signs. From this, he would be taught to read and recite the whole Quran, starting from the last *hizb* (sixtieth) and moving to the first. Celebrations used to be held for the finishing of every ten *ahzab*. The graduation ceremony *(walima)* would terminate the instruction period. The student, turbaned and beautifully dressed, had to recite the first part of the Quran in front of his teacher and a large crowd of other scholars, schoolmates, and relatives. The occasion was marked by the slaughtering of a bull and lavish feasting. The teacher was rewarded by the father of the student with payment and new clothes. (Lavish graduation ceremonies had already been mentioned—and criticized—by the Tuareg scholar Muhammad al-Lamtuni [fl. 1493] in his letter to al-Suyuti.)[19] The student, king of the occasion, would after that be regarded as fully initiated into adult life. Training in some of the available crafts and professions often having gone along with his Quranic instruction, marriage would soon follow. Further instruction might also be given.

This pattern of Quranic education, still existing in northern Nigeria (cf. McIntyre 1983) and in much similar ways in other West African Muslim societies, also involves elementary instruction in the obligatory rituals and in the symbolic and protective use of the Quranic verses as prayers for all sorts of personal needs and public occasions. Each community would follow its own pattern in this.[20] Writing is also part of the advanced stages of Quranic instruction, followed up to a varying extent according to personal interest and commitment of the student. For the spelling procedure, names of the Arab letters in local languages are still widely used. These names seem to be firmly rooted in ethnoreligious consciousness: in the case of the Fulbe in Ilorin, they remain the last trace of the Fulfulde language, which has been otherwise largely replaced by Yoruba, even within Fulbe families.

Girls' attendance at Quranic schools equally varies according to ethnic and local custom. Among the Yoruba of Ilorin, it has been very considerable, even in the past, and the walima ceremony, celebrated on the day before the wedding, is an important event for the bride. In Nigeria, the entrance age of Quranic schooling, formerly highly variable, has undergone a remarkable reduction in recent decades. This was most probably related to the spread of primary-school education, which has left many Quranic schools with additional nursery-school functions.

The West African patterns of Quranic education and its communal significance fully compare with the Quranic school *(chuo)* of the Swahili coast, and also with the eastern Sudanese *khalwa*.[21] The major role played by female Quranic teachers in Brava (see chapter 18) deserves further study: it shows that, in East Africa, female contribution to Islamic instruction has been an important factor, even if for the most part taking place only in privacy. Shinqit, in the western Sahara, provides a similar example for elementary literary education being handled largely by women. In any case, Quranic education had by the nineteenth century largely become a basic element of social status for many Muslim communities throughout sub-Saharan Africa, part of their sphere of public knowledge, and it was often complemented with a rich oral culture of religious poetry and praise in local languages.[22]

International Links

At the end of the fourteenth century at the very latest, Islamic learning had been fairly developed in several parts of West Africa and the East African coast. This can be gleaned from the accounts given by Ibn Sa'id (d. 1286), Ibn Battuta (d. 1368), Ibn Khaldun (d. 1406), and others. A prominent faqih from Ghana, al-Shaykh 'Uthman, who visited Egypt in 1394, became Ibn Khaldun's authority for the history of Mali and its neighbors—perhaps the first substantial contribution of a West African scholar to Arab historiography.

Several local centers of learning had emerged. Tadmakka, mentioned above, named after Mecca and closely resembling the Holy City,[23] seems to have been one of the earliest. Walata, the Massufa trading center visited by Ibn Battuta, inhabited by "Muslims who observe the prayer and study *fiqh* and memorize the Quran," had apparently emerged not too long before, being mentioned for the first time by him and by his contemporary al-'Umari (d. 1349).[24]

Perhaps the most important center further south was Zagha, in the Massina, which is largely identified with Ja/Dia and holds a prominent place as the original center of the Soninke scholarly diaspora, traced back to the days of ancient Wagadu/Ghana.[25] Ibn Battuta described the people of Zagha as already old in Islam, pious and interested in learning. The alleged tomb of the foundation figure of Juula Islamic scholarship, al-Hajj Salim al-Suwari, is shown to this day in Ja/Dia (see chapter 4). Ja seems to be quite typical also in the discontinuity of its local historical and scholarly traditions. With the change of its fortunes under Malian and Songhay rule, it lost its central position and came under the control of non-Muslim warrior clans (the Jawara), but nevertheless remained a city of marabouts with a strong reputation for spiritual and magic powers. Its traditions of origin were now projected further backwards, right into the times of the Prophets. Current local legend has it that even Moses and the pharaoh sought the assistance of the people of Ja in their magical competition, and Muhammad himself saw Ja's light shining in the darkness when he ascended to heaven with Jibril.[26] Historical traditions about other early centers like Tadmakka and, especially, Kukiya on the Niger, the alleged center of Songhay paganism with its old Arabic tombstones, show comparable disconuities and transformations.[27]

The city of Timbuktu, already touched by Ibn Battuta in 1353, came to absorb many of the scholarly traditions of the surrounding lands and of different ethnic groups. It also inherited Ja's older status as an inviolable center of learning and commerce and became a largely autonomous City of Scholars under Malian and Songhay rule, governed by its own patriciate of scholar families (see also chapter 3). As Timbuktu's rise and slow decline are uniquely documented by local Arabic historiography, the city may serve as a model center of Islamic scholarship in sub-Saharan Africa, running through different stages of attraction and diffusion of population and of Islamic influences, building up and transmitting a religious and urban tradition of lasting qualities.[28] Around 1500, Timbuktu had also established firm links to Islamic scholarship in the Middle East and North Africa. A similar consolidation of higher Islamic learning can be followed in Kanem-Bornu, whose ruler had even established a madrasa in Cairo. In the case of this kingdom, the royal capital itself became the main center of Islamic scholarship, especially after the foundation of Birnin Gazargamo and the shift of power eastward to Bornu.

The strands of Islamic scholarship that developed in West Africa at first largely followed trends in North Africa, then increasingly those from Egypt and the Hijaz. From the seventeenth century onward, they even fed back upon these centers themselves. The initial Ibadi impact, well attested in the early Arabic sources, does not seem to have left substantial traces south of the Sahara, if not for the famous Saghanughu scholar clan, who might perhaps be identified with the Ibadi sect called Saghanaghu, mentioned by Ibn Battuta for a place called Zaghari in the vicinity of the Niger.[29] Shi'i and Fatimid influences are even less visible. A lasting heritage of the Almoravid period is the predominance of the Maliki school in West Africa, but also one of the most widely used books about the Prophet, al-Qadi ʿIyad (d. 1149), *Kitab al-shifa,* which holds a very prominent place in scholarly training as well as in public recitation.[30] A direct impact of the Almoravids on developments in ancient Ghana is attested (cf. Ibn Khaldun in Levtzion and Hopkins, *Corpus,* 333); it is also probable further east for Kawkaw[31] and perhaps even for the kings of Kanem-Bornu, whose ancestry was still traced to the Veiled People *(al-mulaththamun)* by Mamluk scholars in fifteenth-century Egypt.[32]

Traces of relations with the Almohads can also be identified, especially for Kanem-Bornu. The earliest known scholar and poet from that kingdom, Ibrahim b. Yaʿqub al-Kanimi (d. c. 1212), made a career as a grammarian and poet at the Almohad court in Marrakesh.[33] Kanem-Bornu also maintained close relations with the Almohad Hafsids in Tunis.[34] The most striking Almohad heritage in the south is Ibn Tumart's short creed *al-Murshida,* which is still widely used as an introductory *tawhid* text in Nigeria, even if its author is never mentioned;[35] it was translated into

Hausa by a contemporary of 'Uthman b. Fodio. Other traces of Almohad theological and didactical tradition are yet to be identified (see below).

In the course of the fifteenth and sixteenth centuries, the religious and scholarly relations of the West Africans with Egypt and the Hijaz apparently became much closer. Students and visitors from the Bilad at-Takrur are mentioned for several prominent Egyptian scholars and sufis of that period.[36] Scholars from the Middle East also tried to develop relations with West Africa, entering into correspondence with its rulers and scholars and sending their writings to them. Most influential among West African scholars was Jamal al-Din al-Suyuti (d. 1505), whose assistance and mediation was even sought by the kings of Bornu and Songhay for obtaining formal recognition as vicegerents of the 'Abbasid caliph in Cairo.[37]

Some scholars traveled from the Middle East to the Bilad at-Takrur. The Meccan Abu Bakr b. Qasim al-Khazraji (d. 1404) became famous for his successful prayers for rain among his hosts. Al-Maqrizi met him after his return to Mecca. A later example of such travels were those of the Andalusian emigrant Shams al-Din Muhammad b. Yusuf al-Andalusi, who, having been appointed *Qadi'l-qudat* of the Malikis in Damascus, was banned to upper Egypt. He went from there to Takrur, where he died in 1514.

Local Islamic scholarship was strongly influenced and sometimes even initiated by the diffusion of the *Mukhtasar* of Khalil b. Ishaq (d. 1365), which after 1500 become the most authoritative textbook of Maliki fiqh and was much commented upon in the western and central Sudan and also in the western Sahara. Two figures were crucial for the spread of this book: One was Mahmud b. 'Umar Aqit (1463–1548), qadi of Timbuktu, who went on pilgrimage and visited the scholars of Cairo in 1509–10;[38] he propagated the *Mukhtasar* in his teaching and produced the first known local commentary on it. The other was the famous North African scholar al-Maghili (d. c. 1504), who visited West Africa during this period; he, too, wrote about the *Mukhtasar.*

One of two Berber scholars who studied with al-Maghili and who are known for their notes and comments on the *Mukhtasar* was Mahmud b. 'Umar Aqit's fellow traveler to Egypt Muhammad at-Tazakhti (d. 1529). This scholar later settled in Katsina. Here the Egyptian connection comes in again. The first introduction of the *Mukhtasar Khalil* by a scholar from Egypt is also mentioned for Kano in the *Asl al-Wanghariyyin;* thereafter, the Egyptian influence upon Islamic learning gradually superseded that of the Maghrib. It can be observed that the fuqaha of West Africa and of the western Sahara always remained in touch with the development of Maliki scholarship in Egypt, as can be seen from the *Mukhtasar* commentaries that they studied and quoted in their own writings.[39]

By the seventeenth century, the scholars of Timbuktu had gained considerable authority for the whole Maliki school. They took full part in the tobacco controversy that for a long time was fiercely disputed in Islam.[40] They also were important in spreading another key text of Islamic scholarship in West Africa, the *Umm al-Barahin,* by the famous theologian and ascetic of Tilimsan, Muhammad b. Yusuf al-

Sanusi (d. 1490). This short creed, one of three theological treatises by al-Sanusi, apparently became well liked both for its rational outlook and for the promise it made, to the faithful reader, of unfailing orthodoxy and salvation. Al-Sanusi's call for a rational understanding of one's faith and his strong condemnation of any unreflected imitation *(taqlid)* in matters of belief closely resemble earlier positions of the Almohads, whose didactic approach he seems to share. He claims to have developed a new way to sum up all the points of belief necessary for being saved during a difficult time, deducing them from the *shahada;* this, according to him, encompasses all necessary knowledge.[41] *Umm al-barahin* was to become the most authoritative creed in many parts of West Africa, especially among the Fulbe scholars, who even translated it into Fulfulde and regarded its learning-by-heart to be a basic obligation for the believer. Similar importance was given to al-Sanusi's three treatises in the Qibla region of the western Sahara.

The Timbuktu scholars Ahmad b. Ahmad b. 'Umar Aqit (d. 1583) and his famous son Ahmad Baba (d. 1627) were among the earliest commentators on this creed.[42] A student of Ahmad Baba, Muhammad b. Ahmad Baghyu'u, versified the creed in 1611, and the resulting Rajaz poem was probably the first Arabic text written by a West African to be commented upon by a Middle Eastern author: 'Abd al-Ghani al-Nabulusi (d. 1731), the famous Syrian sufi, wrote a commentary on it—*al-Lataif al-unsiyya ala nazm al-'Aqida al-Sanusiyya.* He did this at the request of a scholar-friend from Timbuktu (also called Ahmad al-Timbukti) who taught at the Haram. The two men had become friends during al-Nabulusi's stay in Medina in 1694.[43] Reception and spread of both *Mukhtasar Khalil* and *Umm al-barahin* illustrate perhaps more than anything else the West African connections with Middle Eastern and North African Islamic scholarship.

☾ ☾ ☾

Developments in eastern Africa took a more diverse turn. What perhaps comes closest to the happenings in West Africa, except for the process of continous Arabization that marks that period in the Funj and Dar Fur kingdoms, was the rise of rural centers of learning, combining legal teaching with sufism; such a development is attested for the Nile region from the sixteenth century on.[44] Some direct scholarly contacts with central Sudan can be identified, and the connection with Egypt was even stronger. The works of Khalil and al-Sanusi came to inspire Islamic learning and Arabic writing in eastern Sudan after the sixteenth century.

Islamic learning in Ethiopia and northern Somalia grew from Mamluk times in close relation to the Hijaz and Yemen, with lesser links also to Egypt. The size of the large group of Jabartis, Habashis, and Zayla'is mentioned by the Egyptian biographer al-Sakhawi for the fifteenth century looks impressive; this topic deserves a fuller study. Several in the group were famous sufis; others were slaves, often eunuchs who, in some cases, carved out considerable careers—for example, as wardens *(khuddam)* of the Haram in Medina. Sometimes they became strongly committed to Islamic education and learning. Most remarkable in this respect are three pious women: Khadija al-Sahrawiyya (d. 1480) from the Zayla' hinterland; and Safiyya bint Yaqut al-Habashi (d. 1468) and Yahib Allah al-Habashiyya (d. 1477), both of Ethiopian slave origin. They became scholarly authorities and transmitted their *ijazat* to al-Sakhawi himself.[45]

After the Muslim sultanates of Yifat (from the end of the thirteenth century to the early fifteenth) and Adal (the fifteenth century to the early sixteenth) and the jihad movement of Imam Ahmad Gran (1529–43), the city of Harar, capital of Adal since 1520, remained as an important commercial and religious center in southern Ethiopia, famous for its saints and Islamic schools.[46] This religious character remained at the basis of public order when Harar became again an independent emirate (1647–1875). A local tradition of fiqh scholarship—with considerable rivalry between Hanafites and Shafi'ites—appears with Hamid b. Siddiq, a Harari author of the eighteenth century.[47] He defended the old legal tradition of the Madhahib against its neglect by the moderns, echoing controversies common elsewhere at this time.

The development of the Muslim groups at the Swahili coast after 1500 is marked by strong discontinuities caused by immigration from the hinterlands, by the Portuguese conquests, and by the struggles against their rule and their missionary activities. The struggles thoroughly transformed the coastal communities themselves. Political and cultural leadership went in many places to South Arabian migrants, especially to the Shurafa, from Hadramaut. The religious and cultural revival brought about by these migrants after 1600 is described in chapter 12. The most significant was the rise of a written coastal literature in ki Swahili, whose earliest surviving manuscripts date from the eighteenth century but whose beginnings reach back well beyond that. Translations from Arabic religious and didactic poems belong to the earliest texts committed to writing. The contribution of the Hadramis stands out: the author of the oldest known poem (a translation from Arabic, al-Busiri's *Hamziyya*) belonged to the branch of the famous Sharifian family, of the 'Aydarus, resident in Lamu.[48]

In addition to these translations of Arabic poetry in praise of the Prophet, a new genre of epic poems *(utendi)* was created in the early eighteenth century, the contents being drawn from the life of Muhammad and other prophets. The oldest, *Utendi wa Tambuka (1728)*, written by Bwana Mwengo Athmani, in Pate, tells the story of the Prophet's Tabuk campaign against the Byzantines.[49] The topic might reflect the historical experience of struggle against a Christian power; the genre itself marks a new stage in the adaptation of Islamic lore to the interests of a broader local public. Swahili *Mashairi* poetry was widely used throughout the eighteenth and nineteenth century as a medium of public controversy and even legal dispute.[50] The Arabic religious literature of that period was dominated by Shafi'i fiqh under direct influence from Arabia. It firmly belonged to that Indian Ocean corpus of South Arabian scholarship that also came to prevail in the Malayan archipelago.[51]

The Swahili case, with its parallels to the religious and literary development in Southeast Asia, seems to fit into more general cultural trends within the Islamic world. It is striking that even the religious literature in Hausa in West Africa also had its beginnings during the same period. Here, too, a religious epic poem about the Prophet's battle of Badr *(Waakar Yaakin Badar)* marks the earliest sample so far recorded (apparently it came down in oral form). The author is alleged to be a scholar from Katsina, Muhammad Dan Masanih (d. 1667), who is known to have written a number of Arabic texts. The seventeenth century also marks the beginning in Hausaland of a local Arabic poetry for social and moral admonition and critique *(wa'z)*, with authors like Abdullahi Suka (fl. mid-seventeenth century), who became a legendary figure as a preacher in Kano.[52] Although no further examples of Hausa religious poetry are attested until around 1800, Arabic and Hausa samples together suggest some widening of Islamic cultural and public life that prepared the way for the Islamic movements of the late eighteenth and early nineteenth centuries (chapter 3).

Islamic Learning's Relations with the Modern State

By the nineteenth century, Islam had gained in political and cultural weight in many parts of sub-Saharan Africa. Most significant were the Islamic revolutions in West Africa that brought several groups of religious scholars, mainly of Fulbe origin, to political power. Perhaps for the first time in West African history, these movements led to the merger of the warrior and scholar classes, which had been often allied but never before fused.

For the states that emerged from the jihad movements of the eighteenth and early nineteenth centuries, political authority was formally derived from Islamic concepts and norms, and Islamic scholars who had been the guardians of these norms had now largely come to power themselves. This changed the character of public life and the role of Islam in it. Sometimes the rulers took on Islamic titles, and even if they later founded their own dynasties, adopted older titles and court ceremonies, and delegated their religious functions, Islam had now gained a central place in the political fabric. Founding scholars like 'Uthman b. Fodio and others frequently came to be regarded as saints, focusing general loyalties and religious emotions even after their demise far beyond the political loyalty paid to their heirs.

Another heritage of the jihad movements can be seen in the huge mass of devotional, didactic, and legal literature in Arabic and in several local languages that was produced by the movements' leaders and followers and their descendants. If there had been a trend toward creating a religious public culture since the seventeenth and eighteenth century, this was far superseded in the poetic and literary explosion sparked by the jihad. Under the rule of the Almamis of Futa Jalon, a large corpus of religious and didactic poetry in Fulfulde was created. The Arabic writings of the Sokoto caliphate far outnumber the whole former literary production in the central Sudan. Many of the poems and didactic works of the caliphate leaders are still in use today. Arabic became widely used for diplomacy and correspondence. The tradition of Quranic scholarship in Bornu still retained its reputation after the consolidation of the rule of the Shehus, but on the whole the center of gravity for Islamic learning in the central Sudan had clearly shifted to the west.

Other highly significant developments were connected with the preaching activities of the jihad movements. Local languages were increasingly used for religious
and didactic purposes. The jihad leaders had already preached in several languages,
if necessary with translators, during their preaching campaigns, and translation remained an integral part of teaching activities within the cities and schools of the
Sokoto caliphate. *Wa'z* poems in Fulfulde and Hausa became a major tool for the
propagation of Islamic morals and doctrines and also for the treatment of other
public issues.[53] It was this impact of the jihad that largely created Hausa written literature, especially in the field of religious and moral poetry. The spread of the Tijaniyya brotherhood was later to add to this. Another important result was the
establishment of Islamic preaching as part of the public order. Public preaching,
mainly during Ramadan and often in combination with Quranic exegesis *(tafsir)*,
became a recognized practice, and the preachers even managed to secure their liberty of critique vis-à-vis the rulers. Preaching culture—as an expression of public
norms and values, but also of opposition—became especially strong in urban society, as in Kano and among the Yoruba in Ilorin and even further south, beyond the
frontiers of the caliphate.[54] This recognized tradition of public preaching, dating
back to the jihad, was to have far-reaching consequences for the cultural and political development in the colonial and postcolonial era.

The East African coast, too, witnessed a widening of Islamic learning and a
growing depth of local standards of literacy and scholarship under Omani rule. The
Swahili language was already becoming a lingua franca for many ethnic groups in
East Africa. The sultans of Zanzibar, especially Barghash (1870–88) tried to develop
an Islamic judiciary and a unified administration for both the islands and the parts
of the hinterland that had come under their rule. Demands for Islamic learning and
literacy in Arabic and Swahili increased. This was the time when the term *ustaarabu*
(to be Arab-like) became synonymous in Swahili with being cultured or civilized
(see chapter 12). A new generation of Islamic scholars of southern Arabian origin—
mainly from the Banadir coast and the Comoros—came to settle in Zanzibar, and
they made the island an attractive center of learning. Toward the end of the century,
local scholars of coastal origin began to play an increasing role, especially within the
sufi brotherhoods that were spreading throughout the sultanate. Islamic scholars
also engaged in disputes and controversies with the Christian missionaries. At the
same time, these men also contributed to the collection of Swahili poetry and to
linguistic studies and Bible translation projects that were being undertaken by Christian missionary scholars.[55] These activities, like those of West Africa's Imam 'Umaru
Salga mentioned earlier, highlight the crucial role played by Islamic scholars in the
development of African studies in Europe.

The colonial conquests in sub-Saharan Africa had ambiguous results for the development of Islamic learning in Africa. As the Muslim states were conquered and
incorporated into larger empires, the unchallenged patronage of Islamic scholars
and schools was ended. Colonial administrations and Christian missions collaborated in the establishment of European forms of education, with the missions coming to set up and run, to a large extent, the educational institutions in non-Muslim

areas. Although Muslim reservations about Western education—as it often came to be called—were less pronounced and enduring than often assumed,[56] there can be no doubt that the unequal educational development led to social imbalances between Muslim and non-Muslim regions and communities that continue to haunt some African states even today.[57] On the other hand, some recognition of the Muslims' cultural and religious interests had often to be given, for collaboration with them was sought both in the administration and the military forces. Forms of Islamic religious and legal training were therefore developed and supervised by colonial administrators, sometimes leading to the establishment of new kinds of institutions that came to have a communal dynamics of their own.[58] This implied some formal recognition of Islamic religious instruction and of Arabic. Even if the development of public education in the colonial and postcolonial states for the most part followed European patterns and was largely based on the European languages, a beginning had been made that would lead in several cases to the full establishment of Arabic and Islamic studies in the public education system at all levels up to university. This development depended very much on the numerical and political weight of the Muslims in any given country. Some Muslim groups were quite successful in setting up their own educational societies, and these established and ran Western schools for their children. They were of particular importance among the Muslims of Lagos and Yorubaland, where associations like the Young Ansar-Ud-Deen Society (founded in 1923) contributed to the rise of an influential Muslim middle class in several urban communities.

Despite the educational and cultural challenges, Islamic learning continued to develop; it even expanded into those regions and towns where Muslims came to settle anew in the colonial period. The colonial period saw a rise and diversification of the literary production in Arabic, often in connection with the development of the sufi brotherhoods, but also with the increasing travel activities of the Islamic scholars, both within and outside sub-Saharan Africa. A growing interest in the Arabic language and the expanding contacts with the centers of Islamic learning in the Arab world led to the introduction of new types of Arab schools in several African countries. This process, started mainly in the 1930s and 1940s, gained momentum in the 1960s after many of the former colonies gained independence.

From the 1970s onward, a dense network of Arabic schools emerged in many regions with a Muslim population. It continues to expand and has by now become a full educational sector of its own in many African countries.[59] Organized by local scholars and associations and funded to a large extent by communal effort, these schools are an impressive witness to local involvement in educational and communal development projects, at a time when state activities in this field have been running into deepening crises. Principals and graduates of these schools often struggled very hard to obtain some recognition by their governments. Some countries did recognize them and tried to bring them under government control. Issues of cultural and communal autonomy and diversity are frequently at stake here, especially in francophone Africa, where the Arabic orientation of these schools is frequently viewed by state authorities and administrative elites as a threat to the prevailing

French patterns of public education. The reformed Arabic schools developed in close contact with Arab models and institutions, being partly attached to them (for example, the al-Azhar Institute in Ilorin, Nigeria). But this new school sector clearly maintains its connections with the older local institutions of Islamic learning, which a review of the educational books used brings out clearly. The books show a distinct blend of local and Arab materials.

In contrast to the older Islamic schools, female attendance and participation in the Arabic schools is very high, often reaching more than half of the student population. Local production of Arabic and Islamic literature has also strongly increased due to these schools' efforts. Several translations of the Quran into African languages have been undertaken by leading educational figures. The new Arabic schools and the writings produced by their founders and graduates demonstrate again both the distinctive and mediating functions of Islamic learning in the African setting: they both contribute to a distinct socialization of the younger generation of Muslims and, at the same time, create a discourse with clearly modernizing tendencies.[60]

In recent decades, a new type of Islamic organization and educational institution has grown that brings graduates of both public schools and the Arabic school sector into common fields of action. Many of their founders and members studied in Arab countries, and the organizations themselves are often in close contact with international Islamic bodies. Their enterprises fall mainly into the daʿwa category, which includes educational, missionary, and, not infrequently, political activities. Their leaders are official Islamic dignitaries, university lecturers and graduates, and students. They are particularly active in the field of students' and women's organizations and in the development of Islamic media programs. Their political activities range from educational lobbying and the production of religious publications to interreligious dialogue and polemic and public participation in political demonstrations and controversies.[61] A central issue for many of them is the foundation of an Islamic university, something that has been discussed for a long time in several countries but that so far has been realized only in Mbale (Uganda) and Say (Niger) in cooperation with the Organisation of the Islamic Conference (OIC) (see chapter 16).

Several daʿwa organizations maintain strong links to Arab and Islamic countries (for example, to Saudi Arabia, Libya, Sudan, Iran, and Pakistan) and to international bodies like the Muslim World League, the Islamic Call Organisation, and ISESCO.[62] These connections, and their local constituencies, are not without influence on the Islamic issues they propagate—issues that sometimes cause serious challenges to the state and to other Muslims. The daʿwa organizations represent a new stage in the educational development of the Muslims, as they merge different educational experiences within and outside their countries into a new public presence of Islam. In their divergent and sometimes quite controversial outlook, they reflect the internal and external challenges faced by Muslim societies today. Islamic education and scholarship have remained crucial fields for the Muslims' response to these challenges.

Notes

1. See Eisenstadt, Abitbol, and Chazan 1988.
2. For Borgu, see Farias 1998.
3. Levtzion 1978, 643.
4. Abu Yazid, the North African Khariji leader born in Kawkaw around 883, had his Quranic instruction back home in Tawzar; cf. Ibn Khaldun 1968, 7, 26f.
5. Levtzion and Hopkins 1981, *Corpus of Early Arabic Sources for West African History* (hereafter, *Corpus*), 82.
6. *Corpus*, 87.
7. *Corpus*, 51.
8. Farias 1990.
9. *Corpus*, 296.
10. For Kanem/Bornu, see Bobboyi 1992, 1993.
11. Hodgkin 1975, 90.
12. Bivar 1960, 1968.
13. al-Shinqiti 1958, 517ff.; Norris 1975, 109–17.
14. Sanneh 1989.
15. Wilks 1968.
16. Willis 1978.
17. Jobson 1623, quoted in Sanneh 1989, 163.
18. Mischlich 1908, 20–31; Ferguson 1973, 116–19, 260–66.
19. Norris 1975, 45.
20. Sanneh 1989, chapters 7 and 8; Mommerstegh 1991; Reichmuth 1993a, 180ff.; 1998 101–13.
21. Velten 1898, 56–59; Pouwels 1987, 80–88; al-Bayli 1972.
22. Pouwels 1987, 85.
23. al-Bakri, *Corpus*, 85.
24. *Corpus*, 276; 284ff.
25. Saad 1983, 31; Salvaing 1983; Sakai 1990.
26. Sakai 1990, 219.
27. Farias 1990, 1993a, 1993b.
28. Reichmuth 1997, 230.
29. Wilks 1968, 173ff.; Saad 1983, 59. Saghanughu is an alternate spelling of the Saganogo in Chapter 4.
30. Reichmuth 1993a, 171.
31. Hunwick 1980; Forias 1990, 75ff.; Lange 1991.
32. Ibn Hajar 4:168f.; quoted in full by al-Sakhawi 5:126.
33. Bencherifa 1991; Hunwick 1995, 17f.
34. Cf. Ibn Khaldun, *Corpus*, 332.
35. Reichmuth 1998, 120.
36. Winter 1982, 223f.; Levtzion 1986.
37. Norris 1975, 412f.; Levtzion 1986, 200ff.; Hunwick 1990, 85–89.
38. Ahmad Baba 1989, 607f.; al-Sa'di 1981, ar.38/fr.63.
39. Bivar and Hiskett 1962, 130ff.; Osswald 1993, 19.
40. Batran 1995.
41. al-Sanusi. Introduction to his own commentary; cf. also Zouber 1977, 53, n. 3; Brenner 1985, 58ff.
42. Zouber 1977, 42, 103ff., 121f.

43. al-Nabulusi 1996, 366, 429; Brockelmann 1937–49, Suppd. II, 355.
44. Chapter 5; Ibn Dayf Allah 1974, 40–45; O'Fahey 1994, 13; Norris 1990, 2ff.;
45. al-Sakhawi 12, 30, 71, 133.
46. For Harar's early historical and hagiographical tradition, see Wagner 1978.
47. Brunschvig 1976.
48. Poem dated 1062/1652 according to Knappert 1979, 103f.
49. Knappert 1979, 11f.; Dammann 1993.
50. Dammann 1993, 15.
51. Pouwels 1987; Becker 1967, 87.
52. Hunwick 1995, 32f.; cf. Burdon 1908, 38, 93.
53. Boyd and Furniss 1996.
54. Reichmuth 1997, 1998.
55. O'Fahey 1994, 9ff.; Topan, 918.
56. See, for example, Tibenderana 1983.
57. Kiyimba 1990, 94ff.
58. E.g. the *School of Arabic Studies (SAS)* in Kano, Nigeria, Reichmuth 1993a, 188ff.

59. For Mali, see Kaba; Brenner 1986, 1993; for Nigeria, Reichmuth 1993a, 172–83; for southern Kenya since the 1970s, Sperling 1993.

60. For studies on particular Islamic reformists and educationists in Senegal, Loimeier 1994; for Kenya, Lacunza Balda 1991, Kagabo 1997; for a case study of Ilorin, Nigeria, Reichmuth 1998, chapter 4.

61. For the whole spectrum of organizations and their international links, see Otayek 1993; for educational and missionary da'wa in Nigeria, see Reichmuth 1993a, 195ff.; see Loimeier 1997, chapter 5, on the Izala movement; for radical da'wa in East Africa, see chapter 16 of this volume.

62. For a short overview, see Hunwick 1997.

Bibliography

Abdulaziz, M. H. 1996. "The Influence of the Qasida on the Development of Swahili Rhymed and Metred Verse." In Sperl and Shackle, 1996, 411–28.

Ahmad Baba al-Tinbukti. 1398/1989. *Nayl al-ibtihaj bi-tatriz al-dibaj,* ed. A. A. al-Harama. Tarabulus: Kulliyyat al-da'wa al-islamiyya.

Al-Hajj, M. A. 1968. "A Seventeenth Century Chronicle on the Origins and Missionary Activities of the Wangarawa," *Kano Studies* 1, no. 4:7–16.

Batran, A. A. 1995. Harb fatawa al-tadkhin bayn al-'ulama al-muslimin min shimal wa-gharb Ifriqiya fi al-'aqdayn al-awwal wa-al-thani min zuhur al-tibgh, in:Jami'at Muhammad al-khamis-Ma'had al-dirasat al-ifriqiyya, al-Rabat and Jami'at Sidi Muhammad b. 'Abd Allah, Kulliyyat al-Adab wa-l-'ulum al-insaniyya, Sayis-Fas, *Fas wa-Ifriqiya. al-'Alaqat al-iqtisadiyya wa-l-thaqafiyya wa-l-ruhiyya,* 183–233. Rabat and Sais-Fes.

al-Bayli, A. 1972. al-Ta'lim fi l-khalwa al-sudaniyya al-Kuttab, *Majallat al-dirasat al-sudaniyya (Bulletin of Sudanese Studies)* 3 no.2: 79–91.

Becker, C. H. 1967. "Materialien zur Kenntnis des Islam in Deutsch-Ostafrika." In C. H. Becker, *Islamstudien: Vom Werden und Wesen der islamischen Welt,* 2:63–115. Repr. Hildesheim: Olms Verlag.

Bencheneb, H. 1995. "Al-Sanusi." *Encyclopedia of Islam,* 8, 20–22.

Bencherifa, M. 1991. *Ibrahim al-Kanimi: unmudhaj mubakkar li-l-tawassul al-thaqafi bayn al-Maghrib wa-bilad al-Sudan.* Rabat: Publications de l'Institut des Etudes Africaines.

Bivar, A. D. H. 1960. "A Dated Kuran from Bornu," *Nigeria Magazine* 65 (Jun.): 199–205.

———. 1968. "The Arabic Calligraphy of West Africa," *African Language Review* 7:3–15.

Bivar, A. D. H., and M. Hiskett. 1962. "The Arabic Literature of Nigeria to 1804: A Provisional Account," *BSOAS* 25:104–48.

Bobboyi, H. 1992. "The Ulama of Borno: A Study of the Relations between Scholars and State under the Saifawa (1470–1808)." Ph.D. diss., Northwestern University.

———. 1993. "Relations of the Borno Ulama with the Sayfawa Rulers: The Role of the Mahrams," *Sudanic Africa* 4:175–204.

Boyd, J., and G. Furniss. 1996. "Mobilize the People: The Qasida in Fulfulde and Hausa as Purposive Literature." In Sperl and Shackle 1996, 1:429–49.

Brenner, L. 1985. "Un enseignement théologique en Fulfulde: Le kabbe." In L. Brenner, *Réflexions sur le savoir islamique an Afrique de l'ouest,* 55–77. Talence: Centre d'Etude d'Afrique Noire, Université de Bordeaux..

———. 1986. "Al-Hajj Saad Umar Touré and Islamic Educational Reform in Mali," *Bayreuth African Studies Series 5: Language and Education in Africa,* 5–23. Bayreuth.

———. 1993a. "La culture arabo-islamique au Mali." In *Le radicalisme islamique au sud du Sahara: Da'wa, arabisation et critique de l'Occident,* ed. R. Otayek, 161–95. Paris: Karthala.

Brenner, L. ed. 1993b. *Muslim Identity and Social Change in Sub-Saharan Africa,* 179–97 and 198–209. London: Hurst & Co.

Brockelmann, C. 1937–49. *Geschichte des arabischen Litteratur,* Vols. I–II, Suppl. I–III. Leiden: E. J. Brill.

Brunschvig, R. 1976. "L'Islam enseigné par Hamid b. Siddiq de Harar (XVIIIe siècle)." In R. Brunschvig, *Etudes d'Islamologie,* 1:329–38. Paris: Maissoneuve et Larose.

Burdon, J. A. 1909. *Northern Nigeria: Historical Notes on Certain Emirates and Tribes.* London: Waterlow and Sons.

Dammann, E. 1993. *Verzeichnis der Orientalischen Handschriften in Deutschland 24,1. Afrikanische Handschriften: 1, Handschriften in Swahili und anderen Sprachen Afrikas.* Stuttgart: Franz Steiner Verlag.

Eisenstadt, S. N., M. Abitbol, and N. Chazan, eds. 1988. *The Early State in African Perspective: Culture, Power, and Division of Labor.* Leiden: E. J. Brill.

The Encyclopedia of Islam. New Edition. 1954–. Leiden: E. J. Brill.

Farias, P. F. de Moraes. 1990. "The Oldest Extant Writing of West Africa: Medieval Epigraphs from Essuk, Saney, and Egef-n-Tawaqqast (Mali)." *Journal des africanistes* 60, no. 2:65–113.

———. 1993a. "Text as Landscape: Cultural Reappropriations of Medieval Inscriptions in the Seventeenth and Late Twentieth Centuries (Essuk, Mali)." In *Threefold Wisdom: Islam, the Arab World, and Africa: Papers in Honour of Ivan Hrbek,* ed. O. Hulec and M. Mendel, 53–71. Praha: Oriental Institute, Academy of Sciences of the Czech Republic.

————. 1993b. *Histoire Contre Mémoire. Epigraphie, Chroniques, Tradition orale et Lieux d'Oubli dans le Sahel Malien.* Rabat: Publications de l'Institut des Etudes Africaines.

————. 1998. "For a non-culturalist historiography of Beninois Borgu." In *Regards sur le Borgou: Pouvoir et altérité dans une region Ouest-Africaine,* ed. E. Boesen, C. Hardung and R. Kuba, 39–69. Paris and Montreal: L'Harmattan.

Ferguson, D. E. 1973. "Nineteenth-Century Hausaland. Being a Description by Imam Imoru of the Land, Economy, and Society of His People." Ph.D. diss., University of California, Los Angeles.

al-Ghazzi, N. 1979. *al-Kawakib al-saira bi-ayan al-mia al-ashira.* Ed. J. S. Jabbur, 2nd ed. Beirut: Das al-afaq al-jadida.

Hiskett, M. 1975. *A History of Hausa Islamic Verse.* London: School of Oriental and African Studies, University of London.

Hodgkin, T., ed., 1975. *Nigerian Perspectives.* 2nd ed. London: Oxford University Press.

Hunwick, J. O. 1980. "Gao and the Almoravids: A Hypothesis." In *West African Culture Dynamics,* ed. B. Swartz and R. Dumett, 251–75. The Hague: Mouton & Co.

————. 1990. "Askia al-Hajj and his Successors: The Account of al-Imam al-Takruri," *Sudanic Africa* 1:85–89.

————. 1997. "Sub-Saharan Africa and the Wider World of Islam: Historical and Comparative Perspectives." In *African Islam and Islam in Africa,* ed. D. Westerlund and E. E. Rosander, 28–54. London: Hurot & Co.

Hunwick, J. O., ed. 1995. *Arabic Literature of Africa:* vol. 2, *The Writings of Central Sudanic Africa.* Leiden: E. J. Brill.

Ibn Dayf Allah, M. N. 1974. *Kitab al-tabaqat fi khusus al-awliya wa-l-salihin wa-l-ulama wa-l-shu'ara fi l-Sudan.* Ed. Y. F. Hasan, al-Khartum. 2nd ed. Khartoum: Karthoum University Press.

Ibn Hajar. 1390/1970. *Inbah al-Ghumr.* 4. Hyderabad: Matba'at Majlis Da'irat el-Ma'arif al-'Uthmaniyya.

Ibn Khaldun. 1968. *Kitab al-ibar.* 7. Beirut: Das al-Kitab al Lubnani and Maktabat al-Madrasa.

Kagabo, J. 1997. "Ilm wa ta'lim: Savoir et enseignement islamiques en Afrique de l'Est." In *Madrasa: La transmission du savoir dans le monde Musulman,* ed. N. Grandin and M. Gaborieau, 267–76. Paris. Editions Arguments.

Kiyimba, A. 1990. "The Muslim Community in Uganda through One Hundred and Forty Years: The Trials and Tribulations of a Muslim Minority," *Journal of African Religion and Philosophy* 1, no. 2:92–120. Kampala.

Knappert, J. 1979. *Four Centuries of Swahili Verse.* London.

Lacunza Balda, J. 1993. "Tendances de la litterature islamique swahili." In *Les Swahili entre Afrique et Arabie,* ed. F. Le Guennec-Coppens and P. Caplan, 19–38. Paris: Karthala.

Lange, D. 1991. "Les rois de Gao-Sané et les Almoravides," *JAH* 32:251–75.

Levtzion, Nehemia. 1978. "The Sahara and the Sudan from the Arab Conquest of the Maghrib to the Rise of the Almoravids." In *The Cambridge History of Africa,* ed. J. D. Fage. 2:637–84. Cambridge: Cambridge University Press.

————. 1986. "Mamluk Egypt and Takrur (West Africa)." In *Studies in Islamic History and Civilization in Honour of David Ayalon,* ed. M. Sharon, 183–207. Leiden 1986; repr. Aldershot 1994.

Levtzion, N. and J. Hopkins. 1981. *Corpus of Early Arabic Sources for West African History.* Cambridge: Cambridge University Press.

Loimeier, R. 1994. "Cheikh Touré: Du reformisme a l'islamisme, un musulman senegalais dans le siècle," *Islam et Sociétés au Sud du Sahara* 8: 99–112.

————. 1997. *Islamic Reform and Political Change in Northern Nigeria.* Evanston: Northwestern University Press.

al-Maqrizi. 1995. *Durar al-ʿuqud al-farida fi tarajim al-aʿyan al-mufida,* ed. A. Dirwish and M. al-Misri. Damascus: Manshurat Wizarat al-Thaqafa.

McIntyre, J. 1983. "Context and Register in Quranic Education: Words and Their Meanings in the Register of Kano Malams." In *Sprache, Geschichte, und Kultur in Afrika: Vorträge, gehalten auf dem 3. Afrikanistentag,* ed. R. Voyen and U. Claudi, 37–59. Hamburg: Buske Verlag.

Mischlich, A. 1908. "Über Sitten und Gebräuche in Hausa." *Mitteilungen des Seminars für Orientalische Sprachen (MSOS),* 2, no. 11:3.

Mommerstegh, G. 1991. "L'éducation Coranique au Mali: Le pouvoir des mots sacrés." In *L'Enseignement Islamique au Mali,* ed. B. Sanankoua and L. Brenner, 45–61. Bamako: Editions Jamana.

al-Nabulusi, A. 1986. *al-Haqiqa wa-l-majaz fi l-rihla ila bilad al-Sham wa-Misr wa-l-Hijaz,* ed. A. A. Haridi. Cairo: al-Haiʾa al-Misriyya al-ʿamma li-l-kitab.

Norris, H. T. 1975. *The Tuaregs: Their Islamic Legacy and Its Diffusion in the Sahel.* Warminster: Aris and Phillips.

————. 1990. *Sufi Mystics of the Niger Desert: Sidi Mahmut and the Hermits of Air.* Oxford: Clarendon Press.

O'Fahey, R. S., ed. 1994. *Arabic Literature of Africa.* Vol. 1, *The Writings of Eastern Sudanic Africa to c. 1900.* Leiden: E. J. Brill.

O'Fahey, R. S. and Knut Vikør. 1996. "A Zanzibari Waqf of Books: The Library of the Mundhiri Family," *Islamic Africa* 7:5–23.

Osswald, R. 1993. *Schichtengesellschaft und islamisches Recht: Die Zawaya und Krieger der Westsahara im Spiegel von Rechtsgutachten des 16.–19. Jahrhunderts.* Wiesbaden: Harrassowitz.

Otayek, R., ed. 1993. *Le radicalisme islamique au sud du Sahara: Daʿwa, arabisation, et critique de l'Occident.* Paris: Karthala.

Pouwels, R. 1987. *Horn and Crescent: Cultural Change and Traditional Islam on the East African Coast (800–1900).* Cambridge: Cambridge University Press.

Reichmuth, S. 1993a. "Islamische Bildung und ihr Verhältnis zum staatlichen Bildungswesen." In *Muslime in Nigeria: Religion und Gesellschaft im politischen Wandel seit den 50er Jahren,* ed. J. M. Abun-Nasr, 165–99. Münster 1993. LIT Verlag.

————. 1993b. "Islamic Learning and Its Interaction with 'Western' Education in Ilorin, Nigeria." In Brenner 1993b, 179–97.

———. 1996. "Education and the Growth of Religious Associations among Yoruba Muslims—the Ansar-Ud-Deen Society of Nigeria," *Journal of Religion in Africa* 26, no. 4:365–405.

———. 1997. "A Regional Centre of Islamic Learning in Nigeria: Ilorin and Its Influence on Yoruba Islam." In *Madrasa: La transmission du savoir dans le monde Musulman,* ed. N. Grandin and M. Gaborieau, 229–45. Paris 1997. Editions Arguments.

———. 1998. *Islamische Bildung und soziale Integration in Ilorin (Nigeria) seit ca. 1800.* Münster: LIT Verlag.

Saad, E. 1983. *Social History of Timbuktu: The Role of Muslim Scholars and Notables (1400–1900).* Cambridge: Cambridge University Press.

al-Saʿdi, ʿA. 1981. *Taʾrikh al-Sudan.* Ed. and trans. O. Houdas. Paris (repr. of Paris ed. 1913–14): A. Maisonneuve.

Sakai, S. 1990. "Traditions orales Ja: Histoire et Idéologie dans une ancienne cité islamique." In *Boucle du Niger—approches multidisciplinaires,* ed. J. Kawada, 2:211–58. Tokyo: Institut de Recherches sur les Langues et cultures d'Aioe et Afrique.

al-Sakhawi. 1412/1992. *al-Daw al-lamiʿ li-ahl al-qarn al-tasiʿ.* Cairo: 1313/1896; repr. Beirut: 1412/1992 Dar al-Jil.

Salvaing, B. 1983. "A propos de Dia et de ses lettrés au XIXe siècle," *Annales de l'Université Abidjan* 1, no. 11: 119–35.

Sanneh, L. 1989. *The Jakhanke Muslim Clerics: A Religious and Historical Study of Islam in Senegambia.* Lanham: University Press of America.

al-Sanusi, Muhammad b. Yusuf. [1051/1641]. *Kitab Umm al-barahin fiʿ ilm al-tawhid.* Text with author's commentary. Collection of Oriental Manuscripts, Institute for History, Archeology, and Ethnography, Russian Academy of Sciences, Makhachkala/Daghestan, MS 1005 (Syrian copy dated 1051/1641).

al-Shinqiti, A. 1378/1958. *al-Wasit fi tarajim udabaʾ Shinqit,* Cairo: Muassasat al-Khanji.

Sow, A. I. 1966. *La femme, la vache, la foi: écrivains & poètes du Fouta Djalo.* Paris: Julliard.

Sperl, S., and C. Shackle, eds. 1996. *Qasida Poetry in Islamic Asia and Africa.* 1:411–28 and 429–49. Leiden: E. J. Brill.

Sperling, D. 1993. "Rural Madrasas of the Southern Kenya Coast (1971–92)." In Brenner 1993b, 198–209.

Tibenderana, P. K. 1983. "The Emirs and the Spread of Western Education in Northern Nigeria (1910–46)," *JAH* 24:517–34.

Topan, F. 1997. "Swahili," *Encyclopedia of Islam,* 9:917f.

Velten, C. 1898. "Sitten und Gebräuche der Suaheli," *MSOS* 1:9–85.

Wagner, E. 1978. *Legende und Geschichte: Der Fath Madinat Harar von Yahya Nasrallah.* Wiesbaden: Harrassowitz.

Wilks, I. 1968. "The Transmission of Islamic Learning in Western Sudan." In *Literacy in Traditional Societies,* ed. J. Goody. Cambridge: Cambridge University Press.

Willis, J. R. 1978. "The Torodbe Clerisy: A Social View," *JAH* 14:195–212.

Winter, M. 1982. *Society and Religion in Early Ottoman Egypt: Studies in the Writings of Abd al-Wahhab al-Shaʿrani.* New Brunswick: Transaction Books.

Wüstenfeld, F. 1881. *Geschichte der Fatimiden-Chalifen: Nach Arabischen Quellen.* Göttingen: Dieterich.

Yahaya, I. Y. 1988. *Hausa a Rubuce: Tarihin Rubuce Rubuce Cikin Hausa.* Zaria: Gaskiya Corporation.

Zouber, M. A. 1977. *Ahmad Baba de Tombouctou (1556–1627): Sa vie et son oeuvre.* Paris: Maissoneuve et Larose.

CHAPTER 20

Sufi Brotherhoods in Africa

Knut S. Vikør

A lthough it is evident that Islam in Africa is closely interwoven with sufism, there has been considerable disagreement over the result of this influence; has it been a political and radical force or a conservative and pious one? Partly, this stems from a lack of clarity over the term *sufi brotherhood* itself. This is a translation of the Arabic term *tariqa*, which covers a much broader range of meaning than those normally conveyed by the English terms *order* or *brotherhood*. To simplify matters, we may distinguish between two meanings of the word. On the one hand, a tariqa is a method, or Way, that a Muslim may follow to reach a personal religious experience.[1] On the other hand, *tariqa* is used for the organizational framework that may be set up to transmit and practice this method. Only the second of the two meanings fits with our concept of brotherhood, but this organization is a consequence of, not a prerequisite for, the sufi experience: We may, and do, have tariqa-Ways without tariqa-brotherhoods; but we cannot have tariqa-brotherhoods without tariqa-Ways.

These organizational frameworks, the orders or brotherhoods, may then acquire functions beyond those of practicing the sufi Way, which in particular circumstances may make the tariqa-brotherhoods into political or economic actors that thus become "visible" to the student of political and social history. But it should always be remembered that these are external, and, in essence, haphazard results of the tariqa's existence. They are never the result of the contents of the tariqa-Way or the religious experience around which the brotherhood was set up. For this reason, it is possible to look past the social and political epiphenomena that make the order seem one day militant and the next otherworldly, and focus instead on how they see themselves and the relations between them.

The central core of a Way is the *wird*, the prayer ritual that is specific for the Way and that is transmitted from teacher to student in a chain of transmission *(silsila)* from the founder, and beyond him to the Prophet or a Companion, down to the present day. With the wird is transmitted not only a mystical knowledge, but also an identity and, ultimately, an authority that constitute the tariqa as a spiritual entity.

The wird may form part of a ritual, or *dhikr,* that is performed regularly among a group of adherents of the Way. This dhikr is performed at regular, often weekly, gatherings. Together with the often massive gatherings on the date of birth *(mawlid)* or death *(hawliyya)* of the founder, it makes the Way externally visible. Once a group of followers has formed around a Way and its shaykh, it may be formally organized, with more advanced initiates *(muqaddams)* becoming teachers and midlevel leaders. This, then, is the Way as brotherhood, and its structure will normally grow in complexity if the shaykh develops a following beyond the local community and remote groups are formed. However, the shaykh may also remain a local figure, with no particular organization required.

The Arrival of Sufism in West Africa

The organization of a brotherhood is thus often a practical and pragmatic response to the growth of a particular shaykh's audience. However, it is also possible to see the solidification of a sufi identity and organization as part of a more general historical development. That is the case when we look at the early history of sufism in West Africa, which was closely linked to the Sahara and the history of the "scholarly lineages" there. These lineages were transmitters of knowledge from a Maghrib where sufism had played a dominant role since the thirteenth century,[2] but within a different social context from that of the Maghrib.

Such groups are a typical feature of the Sahara, cutting across ethnic and language barriers from the *zawaya* of Mauritania, through the Tuareg *inesleman,* and on to the Libyan *mrabit.*[3] These were groups that in various ways lost power to "warrior" or "noble" tribes or groups; developing a "spiritual" role could, for them, become a strategy to raise their standing in relation to the other tribes socially—and also economically, in that such a role easily went together with developing trading relations. It could also be transformed into political capital by giving them functions as mediators between conflicting "warrior" tribes. These groups eventually became the carriers of Islamic scholarship and sufi influence in the interface between North and West Africa. Early on, this would take a "magical" form—the provision of amulets, *gris-gris,* and other supernatural methods of controlling nature. The power would be vested in special people and became known as *baraka.*[4] It would be linked to the lineage, and the spiritual power of a historical ancestor thus diffused to his extended family. Clearly, the more powerful the ancestor's baraka, the higher the standing of the group. This would give the group a motivation to enhance the perception of the ancestor's baraka.

With the strengthening of the Islamic model of thought, the power to control nature was linked to a relationship with God. Baraka became *wilaya,* "friendship with God." Like baraka, wilaya was proved by the miraculous events attributed to the ancestor, but it was also a way to raise a lineage's spiritual status compared with that of rivals. Wilaya was also displayed by piety and godfearingness, which was linked to learning. A *wali* could thus establish his standing and that of his extended family, not only by his personal fame as a pious man but by his measurable activities in writing and of teaching.

Another way to establish this status was to link the wali to a category of saints and holy men inside or outside the Sahara through a silsila. This would increase the standing of the possessor of wilaya by linking him to a recognized network of saintly men from the Middle Eastern heartlands. For this to help the lineage in general, however, the adoption of the silsila had to be made retroactively. The lineage's status was focused on the ancestor's baraka and wilaya, and thus the ancestor or someone close to him must have been the one who had joined the silsila,[5] by meeting one of the famous shaykhs from outside and "taking" the line from him.

The development of the status of the lineage, from an isolated baraka to the international silsila, can thus be seen as a way to accumulate a spiritual or "symbolic capital"[5] that could translate into both economic and political capital, either in competition with the nonscholarly *(hasani, imajeghan, sa`di)* groups or independently from them. As in the economic field, it is competition with other actors that forces the spiral of accumulation—the need to add to the spiritual status already acquired.

The focus of the silsila was the status of the saints mentioned in it, more than the tariqa identity of the line itself. By linking a lineage and its ancestor to a particular silsila, the name of the tariqa would however also be attached to the ancestor, and the awareness of tariqa specificities seems to have grown slowly among Saharan scholars from the seventeenth century. Beyond the lineage itself, there was, however, never any structured following of the brotherhood type before the end of the eighteenth century. Although the history of individual sufi attachments in the Sahara was thus a slow process that probably started in the seventeenth century, we cannot talk of sufi brotherhoods there, nor anywhere south of the desert, much before 1800.

The Ways: An Overview

Since most silsilas go back to a common set of early authorities, the distinctions between them may sometimes be fluid. The chains form a series of "family trees" that branch out into ever finer distinctions as shaykhs modify the wird or develop separate subidentities. This could happen either earlier or later in the development of the line. A particular Way may thus be named from one of the early founders, such as `Abd al-Qadir al-Jilani (d. 1166) or Abu 'l-Hasan al-Shadhili (d. 1258), or by the name of one of the shaykhs who branched out. Thus it may be useful to group them by family. The most important families for Africa are the Qadiriyya, Khalwatiyya, and Shadhiliyya Ways.

The Qadiriyya

The first development of the Qadiriyya in Africa is linked to the Saharan scholarly and trading lineage of the Kunta. It is not clear when the Kunta scholars started to consider themselves as Qadiri. The internal traditions claim that the connection was made at the time of their ancestor Ahmad al-Bakkaʾi (d. 1514)[6]—a great source for inherited wilaya—with a line to the equally famous scholar al-Maghili. There is, however, no evidence that al-Maghili ever dispensed the Qadiriyya or any other wird. The realization of a Qadiri identity more probably developed in the course of the seventeenth and eighteenth centuries. It came to prominence only with the scholar and political leader Sidi al-Mukhtar al-Kunti (1729–1811).[7]

The Muhtariyya

Al-Mukhtar belonged to the Awlad al-Wafi branch living in the oasis-town of Wadan. Not being of the dominant family, he went away to Walata to study and acquired a reputation for scholarliness and piety; he also possessed an ability to settle disputes among rival lineages. With an established scholarly status, he returned to Wadan in 1793 and made a partly unsuccessful bid for leadership among his lineage group. Only after he withdrew and established his own center at al-Hilla did he gain acceptance as the major scholarly and political leader of the Wafi branch and the Kunta at large.

Al-Mukhtar was initiated into the Qadiriyya by ʿAli b. Najib b. Shuʿayb, who did not belong to the Kunta lineage. The core of the organization was his family and the Kunta lineage.[8] Only Kunta could aspire to the highest levels of the brotherhood—that of being initiated directly by the Mukhtar family—and only that family, the founder and his descendants, constituted the summit. Below these levels of leadership, the brotherhood drew in adherents at two levels: *tilmidh* and *murid*. Both words mean "student," but the level of attachment was quite different. A murid was an individual member who took active part in the rituals and could give the wird to others, second-level teachers who were not necessarily Kunta. The tilmidhs formed groups, made up of zawaya, hasani, Berbers, "blacks," or any other who had gained the protection of the Kunta by attaching themselves to al-Mukhtar. They could do this either by physically moving to a Kunta community or simply by recognizing al-Mukhtar as their leader.

This level of group attachment seems to have been an innovation of al-Mukhtar's (it was copied by other Saharan brotherhoods, both Mukhtaris, such as Shaykh Sidiya, and others such as the Fadiliyya). The organization, while built around al-Mukhtar's Kunta family, extended the lineage's authority by attaching tilmidh groups on a Qadiri basis—clearly a new development. It seems that the traditional wilaya authority was no longer sufficient; something new had to be added to it. The reasons for this can easily be found in the political situation of the Kunta of Wadan.[9]

Besides the difficulties al-Mukhtar had in asserting his authority among the Kunta, there were also external problems. At the beginning of the eighteenth century, the dominant tribe of the oasis was the zawaya group Idaw al-Hajj—allies of the Kunta. The Idaw al-Hajj being weakened by a war with a rival group, the Kunta had gained supremacy over the oasis. This led a group of the Idaw al-Hajj to move away and establish a new center under the leadership of Sidi Mahmud (d. 1786), a scholar widely acclaimed for his piety, learning, and charisma; even the Kunta had to recognize his position. Thus, at the time al-Mukhtar returned to Wadan, the Kunta were about to be embroiled in a conflict with a rival scholarly group, and new resources of legitimacy were needed. It is not difficult to see how this situation might have precipitated al-Mukhtar's introduction of a new type of spiritual authority beyond the wilaya, since that was something the rival group might match.

At al-Mukhtar's death, the Way was continued by his son Muhammad. Muhammad died in 1826. The most widely recognized shaykh of the brotherhood thereafter was Muhammad's student Shaykh Sidiya (d. 1856), of the Awlad Ibiri zawaya lineage, farther west in the Sahara, with a center in Boutilmit.[10] His career largely mirrored that of al-Mukhtar. Coming from a minor lineage, he established his position first as a mediator and later as a scholar and shaykh of the Mukhtariyya Qadiriyya. He had his own tilmidh-groups—so many they almost doubled the size of his "lineage"—and gained economic and political power in the southwestern Sahara. His intellectual influence reached even farther. Sidiya was followed by his grandson, Sidiya "Baba," who maintained the position well into the twentieth century. He died in 1924.

The Mukhtariyya's political role was most important in the Sahara. Outside that region, both the Kunta and Shaykh Sidiya preferred to function as mediators. An exception was al-Mukhtar's great-grandson Ahmad al-Bakka'i, who became an archenemy of the later Tijani, al-Hajj 'Umar (discussed below).

The Fadiliyya

Another Saharan Way that gained influence was the Fadiliyya.[11] They did this both peacefully—to the south, in Senegal—and militarily—to the north, in Morocco. This branch of the Qadiriyya takes its name from Muhammad Fadil Mamin (c. 1795–1868), of the Ahl Jih al-Mukhtar zawaya lineage. Its center was in the western part of Mauritania, the Hawd region. Muhammad Fadil seems, like Mukhtar, to have developed an autochthonous branch of the Qadiriyya. Coming from a minor scholarly family, he never left the Sahara but studied with various local teachers.[12]

The "tariqa identity" of the family seems indeed to have been inclusive, Muhammad Fadil's father Mamin is said to have dispensed both the Nasiriyya Shadhiliyya, the new Tijaniyya, and the Qadiriyya wirds. When Fadil came to be identified primarily with the Qadiriyya, it may have been through the influence of al-Mukhtar's example further east: the two Ways were never linked (and later became rivals),[13] but the Fadiliyya took many organizational features from the model of al-Mukhtar and Shaykh Sidiya—for example, the tilmidh adherence and collection of *hadaya* gifts.

Although the Fadiliyya reached a wide influence in the region during the founder's lifetime, it was the next generation that spread it farther afield. Fadil's nephew Muhammad w. Muhammad Fadil took it to the Adrar, to the east, and his son Saʿd Buh (d. 1917) established a strong center in the Gibla region to the west, close to the coast.[14] Saʿd Buh's influence spread south of the Senegal River, where it grew to dominate his branch, but—although his influence on West African sufism was far greater—Saʿd Buh sometimes came under the shadow of his brother Sidi al-Mustafa. This brother, more commonly known under the nickname Maʾ al-ʿAynayn (1831–1910),[15] went northward, where he established centers, first in Tinduf then in Smara, in the Saqiyat al-Hamraʾ region. Continuing his father's work of sufi scholarship—and being a much more prolific author—Maʾ al-ʿAynayn developed close contacts with the Moroccan sultan, who supported him economically and was in turn initiated into the Saharan brotherhood. Maʾ al-ʿAynayn became involved in Moroccan politics, and with the sultan started a military campaign against the French, first in Mauritania and later in Morocco. His political action led to a celebrated disagreement with his brother Saʿd Buh, who under quite different circumstances had accepted the French presence and issued a fatwa against an "unrealistic" and disruptive jihad against France.[16]

Al-Barnawi

These Saharan orders were not the only Qadiri influences in West Africa. Several communities in the central Bilad al-Sudan may have had connections with the Qadiriyya as early as the seventeenth century,—for example, that of ʿAbd Allah al-Barnawi al-Himyari, the Kalumbardo community, in Bornu.[17] This community was visited by the scholar Ahmad al-Yamani (d. 1701), who traversed the region on his way from the Nile Valley to Morocco, teaching the Kalumbardos and others. A local Qadiri silsila includes his name.

ʿUthman dan Fodio

Our knowledge about the Kalumbardo is scanty, but we know much more about another scholarly community that grew in Hausaland in the late 1700s—that of the Fulani teacher ʿUthman dan Fodio, the jihadist and founder of the Sokoto state (1754–1817).[18] ʿUthman collected a number of wirds from various Ways, but his main identification was with the Qadiriyya—not, however, through the Kunta line. He accepted the wird of the Mukhtariyya Qadiris only late in his life, in 1812.

It is not clear whether ʿUthman first received the Qadiri wird during his early years of learning with his family. His main silsila goes through the Saharan teacher Jibril b. ʿUmar, with whom he studied for about a year while in his early twenties. Jibril, who had visited Egypt and the Hijaz, gave ʿUthman initiations in both the Khalwati and Qadiri Ways.

The Qadiriyya gave ʿUthman the impetus for his political movement. When he was ready to start his reform activity in 1794, ʿAbd al-Qadir al-Jilani, the original founder the Way, appeared to him in a vision and authorized the movement. In celebration of the moment, ʿUthman wrote a poem in Fulfulde entitled *al-Qadiriyya*, and the community he founded in the town of Degel were known as the Kadirawa.[19] The Qadiriyya, while thus connected to the jihad, did not exist as a corporate group in Sokoto during its early years. It was only after the emergence of a competing, organized, tradition—that of the Tijaniyya order—from the second half of the century, that the Qadiriyya started to develop into a structured order in this region.

The Qadiriyya in the East

In the Sudan, several holy families attach themselves to a Qadiri lineage. This dates back to the first period of Islam in the Sudan.[20] The region's direct contact with Egypt and the Hijaz may indeed have resulted in early influences from sufi learning. If so, however, sufi thought remained linked to the established holy families as a "family heirloom" until the nineteenth century, and any sufi identity became part of the general history of the lineages and their relations to each other.

Sufism in Somalia also developed via scholarly groups establishing themselves among more powerful and rival tribes.[21] In the more fertile regions of southern Somalia, these groups seem to have taken the form of settled agricultural communities, living in the physical space between the nomadic tribes. Although they have been called "tariqa communities," their identification with particular tariqas was weak.[22] The genealogical attachments these scholarly groups claimed to the Arabs of the Hijaz seems to have been more important for them.

It is only in the nineteenth century that we see the arrival of a clear, named tariqa in this region. Some settlements with a Qadiri identity arose from the 1820s, but the order's main impetus is linked to Shaykh Uways b. Muhammad al-Barawi (1847–1909). Centered on his native town Brava, his branch, sometimes called the Uwaysiyya, spread throughout East Africa, reaching Mozambique and Madagascar.[23] Uways's family was already linked to the Qadiriyya, but he went to Baghdad to receive reinitiation there. Returning to Brava in 1881, his leadership helped in spreading the Way through a series of settled communities, in particular in the southern parts of Somalia, where it became dominant.

We know, however, that the region's more marked Qadiri identity was not only the result of Uways's personality: another branch of the order was set up by ʿAbd al-Rahman al-Zaylaʿi (d. 1882), in Kolonkol, in the Ogaden region, further north.[24]

Uways, for his part, traveled widely in East Africa, and was invited to Zanzibar by Sultan Barghash in 1884.[25] He made the city the second center for his branch and initiated a number of local followers. Sufi Ways were already present in Zanzibar, but they were mostly confined to the Arab inhabitants; thus in particular, the ʿAydarusiyya/ʿAlawiyya branches of the Qadiriyya[26] which were family Ways closed to outsiders. Uways's branch and other new brotherhoods of the 1880s changed this situation by being independent of family and ethnic identites, eventually opening up to the African majority.

The first of Uways's students were Somalis like himself, but when recruits like ʿAbd Allah Mjana Khayri and Mzee b. Fereji started spreading into the mainland, a powerful organization was soon formed. It spread from Tanganyika into eastern

Congo and Rwanda, with centers in Tabora, Ujiji, and Rufiji.[27] The Maji-Maji rebellion in 1905–7 had an interesting effect: while sufi brotherhoods played little or no role in the movement itself, they spread very quickly in its wake. It seems they were filling an ideological or spiritual need left open after the defeat of the rebellion.[28]

The Uwaysiyya was not the only Qadiri branch in Tanganyika; in fact, the branch formed by Shaykh Ramiyya in Bagamoyo in 1905 may have surpassed it and become the largest Qadiri branch in the region.[29] This was a purely "African"-based branch. Ramiyya (d. 1931), a former slave from the Congo, grew to prominence in Bagamoyo because of his scholarliness. He had already set up a school teaching Islamic sciences when he was initiated into the Qadiriyya by a traveler from the Middle East—independently of the Somali/Uwaysi line. Ramiyya quickly developed a hierarchical structure around his brotherhood; and his success in business was no doubt another factor in the success of the branch. Both he and his son and successor Muhammad were active in nationalist politics, which among Muslims in Tanganyika was closely linked to the sufi brotherhoods.

This development was in clear contrast to that of Kenya, to the north, where the "traditional" model of sufi Ways—closely linked to the Arab traders and closed to the African majority—prevailed. There was therefore little sufi development there outside the Somali borderlands. However, the invigorated Qadiriyya did spread southward, into Malawi and Mozambique.[30] The major agent in this seems not to have been travelers going from Tanzania southward, but young students coming up from Malawi seeking learning in Zanzibar and other learning centers, then being influenced by and initiated into the Qadiriyya or the Shadhiliyya there; in other words, a first generation of local Muslim scholars based in exoteric sciences sent out a second generation for *ijazas* from respected scholars abroad, and the students only then learned of and joined the new brotherhoods. Major names here were Thabit b. Muhammad Ngawnje (d. 1959), ʿAbd al-Qahir Kapalase, and Masʿud b. Muhammad Mtawla. There is also the well-known case of a woman shaykh, the former slave Mtumwa bt. ʿAli (d. 1958), who, living in Zanzibar in her youth, there took the Qadiriyya and carried it to the Nkhotakhota region of Malawi, where she became the dominant scholar. She initiated both men and women into the order.[31]

Except in Kenya, the sufi brotherhoods clearly played a major part in spreading Islam in East Africa. The majority of Muslims there adhere to one or another brotherhood, the Qadiriyya, overall, being the dominant one. The social basis for the orders in African society was varied: both the slave trader Rumaliza and the slave Ramiyya were shaykhs of the Qadiriyya order. The admission of former slaves into high office in the orders was undoubtedly important, both as a way to garner support, in particular among African communities on the coast, and as a way for these individuals to gain leadership of their communities; often, as in the case of Ramiyya, this would place them over their former masters. The social crisis and economic upheavals in the region after the onset of colonialism allowed the order of walis to provide a new framework for stability. This facilitated the opening of lines of contact and identity stretching beyond the political and social borders that events had made obsolete.[32]

The Muridiyya

Of the orders derived from the Qadiri silsila, the best-known is without doubt the Muridiyya of Senegal. This was founded around 1905 by Ahmad Bamba Mbacké (d. 1927), a Wolof teacher.[33] He came from a scholarly family at the court of the king, *damel*, of Kayor; his father also had relations with the Gambian resistance leader Ma Ba.

His sufi silsila went to the Mukhtariyya Qadiriyya through Shaykh Sidiya, as well as to the Fadiliyya. Having been initiated by Shaykh Sidiya Baba in person, he started to dispense the Qadiriyya from his center in the Baol region. The number of supporters he recruited caused alarm among the French colonial authorities, although Bamba neither then nor later ever showed any interest in politics. Still, the French exiled him, first to Gabon in 1895, then, on his return in 1902, to Mauritania, where he rejoined Shaykh Sidiya. His absence did not stop his support from growing; rather, the contrary occurred. While he was in Mauritania, Bamba also established his own wird, despite his continued good contact with Shaykh Sidiya and the Qadiriyya. Only in 1912 was Bamba allowed to return. He settled in Diourbel, in Baol, where he stayed until his death in 1927. The French moved his tomb to the town of Touba, which became and remains the center of the order.

After Bamba's death, a crisis of leadership occurred. Two of Bamba's brothers disputed with his son over who should become successor, *khalifa-général*. In the end, and with colonial patronage, the son, Mustafa Mbacké, prevailed; but the brothers retained wide support, and on their own deaths were each succeeded by a *khalifa*. The unity of the order was preserved, not least by celebrating the wilaya of the founder in the annual pilgrimage to his tomb in Touba, the "grand *magal*." On Mustafa's death in 1945, the succession was again in dispute among the family, but again unity was preserved. The Muridiyya today is one single order.

The ethos of labor and organization of the students into communities *(da'iras)*, in which they engage in agricultural or other labor for a fixed period of time, has become the hallmark of the order; it has also made the order an important economic actor in Senegal. The production of groundnuts was its preserve, but as this has declined, the order has moved into new areas of international trade. The students are sent to France, Italy, and the United States, where they are economically active but internally organized in traditional dara fashion.[34]

The Khalwatiyya

The second of the three major "families" that have marked the history of the Ways in Africa is the Khalwatiyya. It derives its name from the importance it lays on the brethren going into seclusion *(khalwa)* for contemplation and purification; this, it is said, should be done at least once in a lifetime, and preferably at regular intervals.[35]

As was the case with the slow arrival of the Qadiriyya tariqa in West Africa, the details of the Khalwatiyya's local beginnings are shrouded in mystery. This mystery is linked to Sidi Mahmud al-Baghdadi (d. c. 1550), who is said to have brought the Way in an Ottoman form[36] to Aïr in the Niger Sahara. It seems to be established that there was such a Way in Aïr in the late seventeenth century, although it may be prudent to hesitate on its identification with the presumed founder a century earlier. The Mahmudiyya seems to have survived in Aïr, or possibly among the closed sufi communities in Hausaland, down to the late eighteenth century, for 'Uthman dan Fodio lists it among his own Ways, but separate from the Khalwati Way that he took from his Aïr teacher, Jibril.[37] Thus, two different Khalwati Ways were being disseminated from the Aïr region at this time. None reached an organizational form, however, and the Mahmudiyya Way seems to have died out in ensuing decades, only to be revived in the twentieth century by a local *mallam,* Musa Abatul (d. 1959), who in fact claimed that the Khalwatiyya was native to Aïr.[38]

The Sammaniyya

Another branch of the Khalwatiyya, which had significant impacts on the Nilotic Sudan, was that of Muhammad b. al-Karim al-Samman, a student of the Egyptian Khalwati shaykh Mustafa al-Bakri.[39] The Sammaniyya was spread into the Sudan by Ahmad al-Tayyib b. al-Bashir (1742–1824). He was initiated into the Way on several visits to Mecca and traveled widely in the Sudan to form the basis for the new tariqa. This, then, was a clear manifestation of tariqa-Way as a more active principle than had prevailed in the Sudan earlier. It is not clear, however, to what degree an organization beyond that of a series of initiations existed at this time.[40] Yet its influence remained strong; the Sudanese Mahdi started his career as a shaykh of the Sammaniyya, and—notwithstanding the difference in content—the movement he built was clearly influenced by the tariqa model.[41]

The Tijaniyya

It is, however, another derivative—one with its own name—that is the most famous representative of the Khalwati Way in Africa: the order of Ahmad al-Tijani.[42] In fact, the history of sufi orders in West Africa is in many ways the history of the spread and diversification of the Tijaniyya order.

It may be incorrect to classify the Tijaniyya as a member of the Khalwati family, because the founder, Ahmad al-Tijani (d. 1815 in Fez) did not accept the prevailing silsila system. Instead, he claimed that the Way had been revealed to him in a vision from the Prophet, and that the silsila thus went directly from himself to the Prophet, making his previous Khalwati initiation void and wrong. He was in fact the "seal of *wilaya*," in the same way that the Prophet Muhammad was the seal of prophethood; for this reason, his Way was the ultimate one, and no other Way was acceptable. However, in practical terms it seems useful to distinguish between joining the order and taking the wird. Most members of sufi brotherhoods will have only one as "their order"—the one with which they identify—although the scholarly among them may acquire any number of wirds from other orders. In the case of the Tijani, if one joined the order and maintained this as one's primary affiliation, then, generally, it was necessary to leave all other wirds. But it appears to have been perfectly possible for members of other orders to add the Tijani wird to their previous wirds, and even for them to dispense it. Exclusivism thus went with the identity, not the spiritual wird itself.

The Hafiziyya

The first expansion of the Tijani Way to the south came in western Sahara, from where several shaykhs visited Fez and met with Ahmad al-Tijani. The most important of these was Muhammad al-Hafiz w. al-Mukhtar (1760–1830), of the Idaw ʿAli lineage, based in the Shinqit region.[43] He stayed with al-Tijani for several years and on his return to the Sahara started spreading the Way, in particular among his lineage. His Way was specified by not using a contemplative khalwa. Unlike the Mukhtari Way of the same area, it used a loud dhikr.

During the leadership of Hafiz's student Mawlud Fal (b. 1773/4), the Hafiziyya spread throughout Mauritania and the western Sahara, and students took it as far as Adamawa, south of Lake Chad, and into the Nilotic Sudan. Thus, while retaining its core in the Idaw ʿAli lineage, this Way was spread beyond its region, and by a leader not of that lineage.

Al-Hajj ʿUmar

The most important propagator of the Tijaniyya order was al-Hajj ʿUmar b. Saʿid Tall (1796–1864). Indeed, if any division should be made in the history of sufism in West Africa, it is before and after al-Hajj ʿUmar. He was of the same scholarly Fulani background as ʿUthman dan Fodio, but his activity was in the west, in Futa Toro in Senegal.

After primary studies with his family, he settled as an itinerant teacher in the Futa Jallon region to the south. Here he met a teacher of the Tijaniyya Way, a follower of Mawlud Fal called ʿAbd al-Karim al-Naqil.[44] ʿUmar went on the pilgrimage to Mecca in 1828–31 and was there reinitiated into the Way by a student of al-Tijani and the order's deputy in the Hijaz, Muhammad al-Ghali. He appointed ʿUmar khalifa, representative, for the order in West Africa. This was perhaps not a very high position, in that the order hardly existed there at the time. But it was of great importance to ʿUmar, who on his return built much of his authority on this appointment.

ʿUmar's reputation as a religious leader, formed during his stay in Mecca, was firmly established on his slow return journey. He stayed for eight years in Sokoto and developed a close relationship with dan Fodio's successor, Muhammad Bello, marrying his daughter. When ʿUmar continued westward in 1839, passing through the sister *jihadi* state of Masina, he left behind Tijani communities in both places.

'Umar's main fame came from the jihad he led from 1852 (see chapter 6). He was, however, also a leading scholar; in fact, he is considered the second most important shaykh of the tariqa after the founder Ahmad al-Tijani himself, and his major work on the order, the *Rimah hizb al-Rahim,* is generally printed together with the order's "source book," the *Jawahir al-ma'ani.* [45] Few if any Islamic thinkers of West Africa has had greater impact on the outside world.

Originally, his Tijanism was not directed against other tariqas, as can be seen from his relations with Sokoto. However, as his jihad developed, he came into increasing rivalry with other Ways in the area, in particular the Mukhtariyya Qadiriyya. Under Ahmad al-Bakka'i, that order took an increasingly active political role on the side of Masina, soon a rival of 'Umar's new state. That religious questions were subservient can be seen in Masina's support of the pagan Segu kingdom against 'Umar, but 'Umar still found it necessary to develop an ideological justification for his war with a fellow Islamic and strictly jihadist state. From this time, he made a clearer spiritual distinction between the two Ways, the expression "the Qadiriyya and the Tijaniyya are like iron and gold" became common among the 'Umarians.[46]

'Umar's supporters in his wars were his students, the community of Tijani *talibés.* Their composition changed somewhat during his movement. In the early, pre-jihad phase (1839–45), when he stayed in Jegunko in Futa Jallon, spiritual factors seem to have been dominant in recruiting, and these students later were the ones more reluctant to take up the sword.[47] It was also in this period that 'Umar did most of his writing. Later, from 1846, he recruited more widely among the Futa Toro youth, and while these, too, were committed Tijani brethren, they were more militant in outlook. As the jihad got under way, political and military affairs thus came to dominate both 'Umar and the community.

Yet the basis was still the Tijani community and identity. The talibés' relation to 'Umar was that of murid to shaykh; they came to him individually and in doing so broke all bonds with their earlier social identity, merging into a new *jama'a* community. 'Umar's authority came from his position as khalifa of the order, a title he used most of his life, even after he had established himself as a jihadi leader and head of a new state. In this way, 'Umar developed the tariqa-organization in two related ways: as a method of structuring adhesion to his movement and giving it identity, and as a way to establish and legitimize his authority over the movement and the state. The idea of a jihad was with him at least from his stay in Sokoto, and his organization, while apparently set up for scholarly purposes, was certainly easily transformable into a military force. It must therefore be assumed that, while 'Umar was without doubt a genuine mystic and renowned scholar, he also built his Tijani pattern of organizaton and personal authority consciously for the purpose of carrying out the jihad.

The Tijaniyya after 'Umar

After 'Umar's death in 1864, his son Ahmad took over leadership of the state and the order.[48] When his political venture was finally crushed by the French in 1893, it caused a crisis of leadership for the order. Whereas under 'Umar it had been centrally led through his authority as khalifa, it was later characterized by a fragmentation into many centers, and indeed internal fragmentation of these centers themselves. This did not, however, stop the spreading of the order.

Already during Ahmad's period as head of the 'Umarian state, rivalry had arisen with his brother Agibu. When Ahmad fled after the defeat, Agibu established himself in the town of Bandiagara (the location of 'Umar's grave) as head of the family and order, under the protection of the French. Several family members maintained their loyalty to Ahmad or other family members, however, and Agibu was not able to command total support of the 'Umarian family. A nephew, Alfa Hashim (d. 1931), went to the Hijaz and spread the 'Umarian Tijaniyya from there to Indonesia and elsewhere. In the twentieth century, Sayyidi Nuru Tall (d. 1980) of Dakar became one of the most prominent leaders of the 'Umarian Tijaniyya. He was appointed *grand marabout* of the AOF by the French, with whom he kept close relations.[49] Although Nuru's status in the Tijaniyya was undoubtedly high, Tijani leaders outside the family have developed branches independent of the 'Umarians, and with far greater mass support.

The Hamawiyya

The most controversial of these developed in the middle Niger region. This was the branch of Ahmad Hamahu'llah b. Muhammad, of Nioro in northwestern Mali.[50] Hamahu'llah had one foot in the Saharan tradition of sufism and one in Sahelian Tijaniyya; his father was of a zawaya background from Tichit, his mother a Fulani.[51] He received his authority directly from the Maghrib, being initiated into the Way by Muhammad b. 'Abd Allah al-Akhdar, a North African with contacts in the Tlemcen (minority) branch of the Maghribian Tijaniyya. When, shortly before his death in 1909 al-Akhdar met the young Hamahu'llah, he is said to have recognized him as the new khalifa of the brotherhood.

Hamahu'llah's reputation spread rapidly, and his branch had followers in most of French West Africa after only a decade of existence.[52] Hamahu'llah was often harassed by the French authorities because of his abstention from public and official gatherings, thus by implication ignoring the colonial authority. Although he appointed a number of muqaddams from 1914 onwards, he himself was always a reclusive figure, something that possibly strengthened the saintliness that his followers saw in him. For his rejection, he was—like Ahmad Bamba and other nonpolitical sufi leaders—sent into exile, first to Mauritania, then to Côte d'Ivoire; like Bamba, he came back strengthened by it. Hamahu'llah himself and his brotherhood did not themselves seek or play any political role, but a conflict with a rival group, the Tinwajyu, led to clashes for which the French blamed Hamahu'llah. He was thus finally exiled to France, where he died in 1943.

Hamahu'llah's relations with the Umarian Tijanis were also marked by rivalry, but his position as leader of the upper Niger Tijaniyya was strengthened when one of the most respected members of the Umarian family, Cerno Bokar,[53] joined Hamahu'llah. Thus, the Hamawi branch survived the French repression. After 1958, it grew rapidly under the leadership of Hamahu'llah's son Muhammad. The branch spread to Burkina, Côte d'Ivoire, and Central Africa.[54]

Tivawane

The Umarian family is also represented in Senegal. However, the development of the order in this country, where it has become clearly the most widespread tariqa, has mainly been through two other branches, neither of them related to Umar's family. One is the Sy branch. The founder of this was the Tukolor scholar al-Hajj Malik Sy (1855–1922), who was initiated into the Tijaniyya by his uncle, a student of al-Hajj Umar.[55] He settled in Tivawane just north of Dakar and started to draw followers in considerable numbers from the Wolof of the area.

After Malik Sy died, divisions started to appear as the leadership of the order came into dispute. The conflict arose primarily between two of al-Hajj Malik's son's, Abd al-Bakr (Abdabacar) who took over the leadership, and Abd al-Aziz, who challenged him. The followers divided their loyalties between the two. Although Abd al-Bakr was generally recognized as the khalifa until his death in 1957, supporters of Abd al-Aziz started to set up parallel structures of the order. After Abd al-Bakr's death, the pattern reemerged, now between Abd al-Aziz, who took over as khalifa after his brother, and Abd al-Bakr's son Cheikh Tidiane.

Cheikh Tidiane's son, the young Mustafa Sy, with his father's support, established an Islamic organization—Da'irat al-Mustarshidin wal-Mustarshidat—which, while not a sufi tariqa (having no wird), in many ways is a modernized organizational expression of the Abd-Bakrian wing of the Sy branch of the Tijaniyya.[56] In spite of these fissions and organizational differences, the branch and the family do recognize each other as belonging to the same spiritual structure; although they may have separate annual rallies, the khalifa will formally appear also at the rally organized by his rival and give it his approval.

The Niassiyya

The other major branch of the Tijaniyya in Senegal, the Niassene, or Niassiyya, is smaller, in Senegal, than the Sy branch, but, unlike the Sy, its influences extend far outside that country. Its major base is outside Senegal, and it is particularly strong in Nigeria, where it is clearly the dominant tariqa.[57]

The founder of the branch was Abd Allah (Aboulaye) Niasse (d. 1922), who took the Tijani wird from Ma Ba, the Gambian student of Umar and jihadist in his own right.[58] After the defeat of the jihad, Abd Allah left militancy and started to teach the Tijaniyya, establishing a center in Kaolack on the Saloum River. Having some success in gathering followers, he was succeeded by his son Muhammad. But it was another son, Ibrahim "Baya" Niasse (1902–75) who soon started to gather the greater following and can be considered the real founder of the Niassiyya branch from about 1930.

The Niasse family is interesting because, unlike the Sy, it does not spring from a tradition of political or religious leaders. They are, to the contrary, of caste (blacksmith) origin, which may have had effects on the nature of its support in Senegal and the fact that it is less dominant there than elsewhere. Also, Ibrahim Niasse, although he was of the same "main-line" Tijanis as the Sy, supported *qabd*, praying with hands folded across the chest—a statement of great import that challenged the dominant view of the Maliki *madhhab* and set his branch apart from all other Tijani branches in West Africa.[59]

The introduction of the Niassiyya branch into Nigeria dates back to Ibrahim Niasse's pilgrimage to Mecca in 1937. There he met 'Abd Allah Bayero, the emir of Kano, who accepted Niasse as his teacher and took the branch home to Kano, inviting Ibrahim to come there. There was already a Tijani presence in the city: a major branch of it was lead by the scholar Muhammad Salga. On the latter's death in 1938, however, the majority of the Salgawa followers accepted the Niassiyya, thus forming the basis for the brotherhood, which rapidly spread in Nigeria to outshine the older Qadiriyya.[60] One factor that helped the promotion of this branch was the rivalry between Sokoto, the center of the jihad and where the Qadiriyya held sway, and the larger urban and commercial center of Kano. The latter city became the center of the Tijaniyya in Nigeria, and the adoption of the Tijaniyya became a way of self-assertion for this region vis-à-vis the Sokoto Qadiris.

The branch of Ibrahim Niasse, itself born out of a family split, has not escaped the same fissionary tendency as its rivals. Ibrahim tried to break this by appointing a son-in-law, Alioune Cisse, as his successor; this has, however, led to a split between Ibrahim's descendants and those of Cisse.[61] In spite of this, the branch has grown, and the non-Senegalese sections recognize Kaolack as its spiritual center, sending students and delegations there.

The Shadhiliyya

The third of the major families of sufi Ways that spread in Saharan and sub-Saharan Africa is the Shadhiliyya, a family of orders that dominates Maghribi Islam. It spread into the Saharan regions, particularly through the Nasiriyya suborder that has its center at Tamagrut on the southern Moroccan desert side. However, it was eclipsed by the Qadiriyya (and the Tijaniyya of the Idaw 'Ali) in the desert regions, and while some West African shaykhs took the Shadhili wird, its organizational role remained marginal in West Africa.

In East Africa, however, the Shadhiliyya has become the major brotherhood, alongside the Qadiriyya. Like the latter, it arrived in the region around 1880. The main propagater was Muhammad Ma'ruf (1853–1905), from a Hadhrami family in the Comoro Islands.[62] He broke from the 'Alawiyya that dominated his community and was initiated into the Yashrutiyya, a branch of the Shadhiliyya, by his compatriot 'Abd Allah Darwish. Ma'ruf was apparently in conflict with the authorities: he traveled to Madagascar and later to Zanzibar to escape problems. In both places, he worked actively and with considerable success to recruit people to his Way, in particular in Zanzibar, where his order came to outshine the Qadiriyya. Like the latter, it spread to the mainland among the non-Arab as well as new converts to Islam. It also spread south to Malawi, but was constrained by the Qadiriyya, which already was in place. Nevertheless, some of the most prominent scholars there, like ʿAbd Allah b. Hajj Mkwanda (d. 1930), joined the Shadhiliyya. The two orders soon came into conflict over the issue of certain rituals, the Shadhilis condemning the Qadiri usages as non-shariʿa.[63]

The Sudan saw an early influence from Shadhili shaykhs, mostly through influence from Egypt. This can be noticed as early as the seventeenth century, but these were only affiliations by individual shaykhs to a scholarly and saintly tradition that was yet without any organizational existence.[64] Organization was to appear only in the eighteenth century, with a new set of orders that were all influenced by the Moroccan scholar Ahmad b. Idris (d. 1837).

Idrisi Orders: The Sanusiyya

Ibn Idris, who spent most of his career in Mecca and the Yemen, never visited sub-Saharan Africa, but several of his students made their careers there.[65] He is atypical in that not only was no structured brotherhood set up with his name, but he did not even establish a distinct Way, preferring the standard Shadhili wird. Yet several students spoke of the "teachings of Ibn Idris" in a manner not much different from that of a founder of a Way.

His most famous student was Muhammad b. ʿAli al-Sanusi (1787–1859).[66] Another Maghribi, he studied in Fez, Cairo, and Mecca, where he met Ibn Idris and became his student. He then returned west to Cyrenaica and established a brotherhood among the Bedouin there. He thus fell into the pattern of the Saharan scholarly family, except that he did not belong to the region; in that sense, he had no family or tribal background and particular interests to further. Instead, he established a tariqa-organization in a way not known before in the area. This continued the spiritual role of mediating common to the traditional mrabit tribes; but it also went beyond this: it integrated members of the various strong tribes into the order, provided religious services (teaching the young, registering marriages, taking care of the poor), and—and this was primary—ensured the peace in a more forceful manner. As his main weapon, al-Sanusi used his own charisma which was inherited by his successors.[67]

Like Ibn Idris, al-Sanusi made a point of collecting as many different wirds as possible. He listed more than fifty different tariqas in his published works, and was initiated into many others. However, his main adhesion was to the Shadhiliyya, through Ibn Idris, and it seems that he largely considered the aim of his brotherhood to be spreading Ibn Idris's teachings. The order had its basis in Cyrenaican Bedouin society, but was never restricted to this. It quickly spread to urban areas and to neighboring regions to the west and east, as well as to the Hijaz, where al-

Sanusi spent much of his life in scholarly pursuits. It also spread southward, first to Kufra in al-Sanusi's lifetime, then further into the Chad regions during the time of his son, Muhammad al-Mahdi. It largely followed the trade routes that grew in the Sanusi-guaranteed peace, and at its outer extremities in Niger and Wadai, the Sanusi order was primarily an organization for traders, local or from the north.[68] The order also set up lodges and organized non-Bedouin groups in the desert to the south, so it does not seem to have considered itself restricted to the Bedouin areas.

This extension was, however, halted. The French had, quite incorrectly, formed an image of the Sanusiyya as a militant, anti-French and anti-Christian sect of fanatics. When the advancing French forces encountered the Sanusi in Chad, they decided to strike first and attacked several lodges.[69] The Sanusi were initially saved by the French inability to follow them into the desert, but the ensuing struggle—fought by local (mostly non-Bedouin) tribes in the name of the Sanusiyya—started a transformation of the order that eventually, after the Italian invasion in 1911, made them a guerilla force in Libya.

South of the Sahara, the difference between the "original" Sanusi tariqa and the "transformed" military combatants can be seen in Niger, where a young Tuareg, Kaossan, raised a shortlived military rebellion against the French in 1916 in the name of the Sanusiyya and with the blessing of the leadership.[70] This revolt found no echo among the existing Sanusi lodges and notables in Zinder; they adapted to the colonial situation.

The Sanusiyya continued to exist in Niger for some time. Yet, with the center in Cyrenaica crushed during the war and the French repression of the lodges in Chad, even the purely pious elements of the order eventually became extinct.

The Khatmiyya

Another order set up by a student of Ibn Idris has, while nonmilitant and less spectacular, become a dominant force in Sudanese Islam. This is the Khatmiyya, established by Muhammad 'Uthman al-Mirghani (1793–1852).[71] Of Hijazi origin, he went to the Sudan to proselytize in 1815. He soon developed some independence from his master and, unlike al-Sanusi, set up a tariqa-like structure independent from Ibn Idris during the latter's lifetime. This came to be known as the Khatmiyya: like al-Tijani, al-Mirghani claimed to be a "seal" *(khatim)* of the sufis. Besides underlining his own elevated status this was not, however, linked to the kind of exclusiveness and rejection of tradition that we find in al-Tijani. Like Ibn Idris and al-Sanusi, the sufi doctrines of the Khatmiyya must mainly be considered a continuation of traditional sufism.

While the order spread widely during Muhammad 'Uthman's lifetime, its success was based on the work of his successors—in particular, his son Muhammad al-Hasan al-Mirghani. The leadership remained with the family, but was regionalized in district sections around a central lodge at al-Saniyya in eastern Sudan. However, as the family was not of Sudanese origin, it strengthened its local roots by initiating local religious leaders into the order. In this way, its externality to the region made it merge the family-based Mirghani leadership to a set of local structures. Its structure thus was different from the maraboutic model of the west, where most of the orders (and branches) were led by families originating in the region. This shared feature of the Khatmiyya and the Sanusiyya—externality—led both to create stronger organizations than was common in their areas.

The Khatmiyya came into conflict with the Mahdi movement that arose in Sudan around 1880. While the Mahdi may not have been as anti-sufi as often portrayed, he clearly saw the Khatmiyya as a potential force of opposition, and fought it. After the defeat of the Mahdists in 1899, however, the brotherhood grew considerably, and soon became the dominant force in Sudanese Islam—a force that after independence was transformed into political capital in the multiparty system. While there is still rivalry with the Mahdi supporters in the Ansar—now a parallel system of adherence to that of the Khatmiyya—the major current sufi challenger is probably the Tijaniyya Niassiyya, which has spread rapidly in the Sudan since 1950.[72]

The Rashidiyya

A third student of Ibn Idris, the Sudanese Ibrahim al-Rashid (1813–74), was the only one of the three discussed here who established his Way in his native land.[73] Younger than al-Sanusi and al-Mirghani, he was with Ibn Idris at his death. He appears initially to have followed al-Sanusi, so long as the latter conceived of himself primarily as an Ibn Idris organizer. But when the Sanusiyya started to develop its own identity in Cyrenaica, al-Rashid left and returned to the Sudan to form a tariqa of his own.[74]

The Rashidiyya—seen as a rival by the dominant Khatmiyya order—had the advantage that Ibrahim al-Rashid, coming from a local scholarly family, could draw on established loyalties. He seems also to have had the more or less tacit support of the Ibn Idris family, who had not yet, however, established any corporate presence. This may have helped push the Khatmiyya into a more marked independence from the Idrisi legacy.

While al-Rashid did follow the other Idrisi derivatives in establishing a formal structure by initiating local leaders, his order was not so well cemented as that of the Khatmiyya. Thus, on al-Rashid's death, it developed in different directions, each branch with a separate identity. Several of these branches spread outside the Sudan: the most famous is no doubt the Salihiyya of Somalia, best known because of the more or less tangential role it played in anticolonial organization.

The Salihiyya

The Salihiyya brotherhood was formed in the Sudan by al-Shaykh Muhammad Salih (d. 1919), a nephew of al-Rashid. He was the "official" heir of the master, but his tariqa became known under his own name.[75] Salih stayed for some time in Mecca, and there the Way spread to pilgrims, in particular to some from India and regions around the Indian Ocean. It gained a strong foothold in Somalia, where it was first spread among the Abyssinian population by a former slave, Muhammad Gulid (d. 1918).[76]

A separate attempt to spread the order in Ogaden was made by Muhammad 'Abd Allah Hasan (1864–1920), a leader who raised a jihad against the British and the Italians. Traveling to Mecca, he was initiated by Muhammad Salih, and on his return to Somalia he tried to gather support for the brotherhood in both Mogadishu and the interior. He had so much success that in 1895 he proclaimed himself overall khalifa of the order in Somalia. Exactly how far he actively sought leadership of the jihad that broke out four years later, and what role the order played in it, is unclear.

'Abd Allah Hasan was a scholar much as Dan Fodio and al-Hajj 'Umar. Like his rival Uways, he wrote poetry in Somali, and he helped to promote writing in the vernacular. On his arrival in Mogadishu, he is said to have preached reform of the local Islam, against the use of tobacco and qat, as well as the worshipping of graves. He thus came into a heated conflict with Uways, the Qadiri leader in the south (it was a Salihi supporter who killed Uways in 1909). However, it may be that this fiery image has, to say the least, been enhanced by projection into the past of a strict attitude that he held as leader of the jihad.

In any case, he did not receive the backing of the Salihiyya at large; he was repudiated by the leader of the order in Mecca.[77] Still, the jihad remained identified with the order until it ended with 'Abd Allah Hasan's death in 1920–21.

The Ahmadiyya-Dandarawiyya

Other branches of the Ibn Idris tradition also spread on the Horn and East Africa. Some identify the Bardera community of southern Somalia with the teachings of Ibn Idris. However, its establishment c. 1815 was probably too early for an Idrisi affiliation, or indeed for any specific tariqa affiliation at all.[78] Toward the end of the century, however, an Idrisi community was set up in Geledi. This used the name of Ahmadiyya, which refers to Ahmad b. Idris, but in East Africa is mostly identified with the Dandarawiyya branch.

This was yet another subbranch of the Rashidiyya, formed by an Egyptian student of Ibrahim al-Rashid, Muhammad b. Ahmad al-Dandarawi (1839–1910). It spread in Egypt, the Sudan, and along the East African coast from northern Somalia to Tanzania.[79] There were a number of Ahmadi-Dandarawi communities in Somalia, and from there it spread to Zanzibar and thence to the mainland coast at the beginning of the twentieth century.[80] However, the brotherhood in East Africa remained restricted to the Somali and Arab diaspora communities and thus did not share the success of the Qadiriyya and Shadhiliyya-Yashrutiyya.

The Isma'iliyya

Other Sudanese orders related to the Ibn Idris tradition have roots in the tradition of wilaya and of local teachers who spread learning without any particular tariqa. Some of these formed a following of their own in the nineteenth century— for example, Muhammad al-Majdhub and Isma'il al-Wali (d. 1863).[81] Isma'il was a student of Muhammad 'Uthman al-Mirghani, who established a regional tariqa on the traditional model of scholarship in Kordofan in western Sudan. Ethnic rivalry forced it to mark some distance from the Khatmiyya, which was more associated with the northern region.

After Isma'il's death, the brotherhood acquired a more structured organization, eventually spreading to the rest of the Sudan. A split occurred between Isma'il's two sons, the "traditionalist" Makki (d. 1906), who inherited the leadership, and the younger al-Azhari, who had studied in Egypt. The latter was unhappy with the traditionalist approach of his brother and moved to Omdurman, near Khartoum, gathering followers there.[82] During the Mahdiyya, the two brothers were on opposite sides: Makki was pro-Mahdi; al-Azhari was killed fighting against the Mahdi. The followers of the younger brother came to consider themselves a separate branch, the Azhariyya. On the whole, then, the Isma'iliyya represents a local compromise between the "traditional" and the "Idrisi" organizational model, although there was little difference in the spiritual teachings of Isma'il and of his Idrisi colleagues.

The Idrisiyya

Although Ibn Idris himself never established either a Way or a brotherhood, his descendants have not been so reticent.[83] A branch of the family settled in Zayniyya in Luxor in Egypt, and formed an Idrisiyya order there at the end of the nineteenth century. From there it spread into the Sudan and it has developed a strong base there. A much more reclusive and quietist order than the Khatmiyya, it has an elitist appearance and has refused any overt participation in public or political life. However, its spiritual status gives it a noticeable potential influence.

The Development of the Brotherhoods

The general direction of the dissemination of the Ways has on the whole been from north to south, although east-west movements have also been significant. West African sufism was heavily influenced from the Sahara; Sudanese sufis took their inspiration partly from Egypt, partly from the Hijaz; and southern Somalia was an important stagepost for the spread of Ways to East Africa. Only the dissemination of the Qadiriyya into the interior, west and north-westward from Zanzibar, breaks this north-south pattern in a major way.

Given this pattern, it is noticeable that the distribution of the individual orders is not necessarily reproduced north-south. The most evident example of this is the Shadhiliyya, which largely dominates Maghribi sufism with a number of expanding suborders, such as the Nasiriyya, Darqawiyya, Madaniyya, and so on. In West Africa, these are either quite absent or overshadowed by various branches of the Qadiriyya (which are present but less dominant in the central Maghrib) and, later, the Tijaniyya, which, while originally Maghribi and spreading through the Sahara, took its major vitality from a link in the Hijaz. The most active Shadhili orders in sub-Saharan Africa are those of the east: the Idrisi derived orders in the Sudan and Somalia, and the Darqawi derivation in East Africa.

The other striking feature is the importance of a few individuals in "setting the direction" of tariqa distribution: al-Mukhtar al-Kunti and Uways al-Barawi for the Qadiriyya; al-Hajj 'Umar for the Tijaniyya; Ibn Idris and, more locally, Shaykh Ma'ruf, for the Shadhiliyya and derivations. These men not only inspired those who joined their own branch, but even, it appears, independent organizers outside it: al-Mukhtar's most successful contemporary, Muhammad Fadil, was a fellow Qadiri; alongside the 'Umarians, Tijani branches outside the 'Umar-Muhammad Ghali sil-sila dominate West Africa; and the Uwaysian is only one out of several equally strong Qadiri branches in East Africa. But in each period and region, the tariqa family that made the leap of innovation still dominates.

This indicates that while interregional scholarly contacts and influence is es-sential in the spread of sufi ideas, the key to their development is local. They grow because they answer needs or can be used in a particular context. When a dominant innovator introduces a tariqa pattern in an area, not only his followers but those who seek a similar pattern of behavior in rivalry or independence will tend to stick closely to the model, and thus stay in the same tariqa family but with a different sil-sila. The spread and increased complexity of the sufi model is the result of conscious actions for a purpose.

This also emphasizes that Ways develop through competition. There are two tendencies here. On the one hand, there was an "inclusivist" and tolerant attitude, the founders collecting initiations from a variety of Ways and tariqa families; local Mauritanian shaykhs freely disseminated both the Qadiri, Nasiri, and the theoreti-cally exclusivist Tijani wird; and the Nigerian leader Nasiru Kabara led several brotherhoods at the same time. On the other hand, rivalry and competition be-tween brotherhoods on the ground could be real and on occasion lead to clashes, even deaths. Again, the key factor is the context, the particular circumstance, not differences in the spiritual contents of the Ways.

What It Means to Be a Sufi

One such context was the structurality of the Saharan scholarly lineages, as seen above, where the "accumulation" of sufi patterns were strategies to promote the po-sition of one's own lineage. In this case, the sufi pattern grew out from kinship and lineage, and while followers (murids) were attracted on an individual basis, adhe-sion was often also on a kinship and lineage basis (the tilmidhs).

As the Ways grew in new surroundings, however, new patterns of organization and of relationships between shaykh and murid emerged, different from a kinship basis. This relationship could have several elements. The most basic was the accep-tance of a certain shaykh, local or distant, as one's guide in return for spiritual or material benefits. This could be an individual choice, or have a collective element in that the shaykh in question was seen to "represent" a certain group or category to which the follower belonged. Another level of adhesion was for the follower to take part in the rituals of the brotherhood, on a regular basis (as dhikrs) or by attending the annual birth and death, mawlid and hawliyya, gatherings, either locally or for a larger region. They could also signal their choice in other ways, by how they performed prayer or funerary rituals and the like, when these were distinctive to a particular brotherhood.

Once the follower received special instruction and was given some of the secret knowledge of the wird, he became an initiate and, progressing up the path of knowledge and experience, could himself start to teach the lower ranks as a muqaddam. An important part of the process was often for the seeker to isolate himself physically for a time in a meditation khalwa. Each brotherhood and branch differed widely in how many levels of muqaddams and other midlevel leaders there would be, and in how strictly they were controlled from a center. Typically, the authority of the muqaddams and their freedom of action would be restricted during the founder's lifetime or while the brotherhood was geographically concentrated. After the expansion of the brotherhood, central control could either be established by regular gatherings of the local shaykhs, or by the shaykh regularly traveling to the various countries. The number of intermediary levels in the organization did not necessarily have any relation to the level of mystical stages that an initiate had to go through in his (or her) search.[84]

Fissiparous Tendencies

It follows from the history of sufi brotherhoods that there is always a balance between a cohesive force—the spiritual authority of the shaykh or saint—and a fissionary tendency; all Ways, after all, split away from other Ways, and this is also apparent in African brotherhoods. It is perhaps seen most clearly in the Senegalese orders, where there is a pattern: a founder of a branch establishes his fame through his own spiritual means by establishing a following; his legitimacy is based on this following, although his formal appointment into the position of teacher is ascribed to a distant family member or a leading shaykh outside the family. Unlike in the Sahara, this association of the family with a silsila is not carried beyond at most one or two steps up.

Once the branch is set up, however, legitimacy is inherited, not acquired, but it is invariably a matter of contention. This pattern appears in the ʿUmarian Tijaniyya itself, in the other Tijani branches of Senegal, and in the Muridiyya and other orders in the region, with some variations. It is however noticeable that all the Tijani branches maintain the Tijani identity as primary. Names used for subbranches, such as Niassiyya, Malikiyya, and Hamawiyya, appear to be subordinate to the Tijani identity. This is in marked contrast to, in particular, the Sudan, where branches seem very quickly to split off and establish their own identity as different from that of the mother Way; this is true not just for those set up by Ibn Idris's students, but, even more so, for the following generation of Rashidi and Khatmi derivations.

This corresponds to two contrasting ways in which the lines of authority go;

that is, two different ways of building the link between followers and the founder's family (besides the Saharan model, where the lineage structure is the focus of the brotherhood). The one in the early history of Sudanese orders we may call a "grafting" model, whereby a shaykh from outside travels to various regions and initiates local scholarly leaders and walis into his Way. Thus the order is "grafted" onto various local structures of wilaya, which are drawn into a new and wider network. The new structure is transethnic and interregional; the local element is inscribed into an existing and fairly stable structure of authority. Only by moving away physically and making a clean break can an aspiring local shaykh hope to establish himself independently (such as Isma'il al-Wali's son al-Azhari), and even then it will be with difficulty. Authority is assigned from above.

In what might be called the "maraboutic" model of the Senegalese orders, on the other hand, the shaykh is designated from below. The basis of the order is the free association of the commoner or lower-level student to his marabout/shaykh. The prestige of the latter is based on the number of adherents he can claim, which he can then bring to the brotherhood of his choice, and he is given a status accordingly. A discontented member of the leadership can thus easily gain the support of a number of midlevel shaykhs, and thereby their following, creating his own power basis.

Although there clearly are limits to how far the midlevel shaykh can manipulate this situation, this model does emphasize a certain freedom of movement. No doubt, the fissionary tendencies that we see in all Senegalese orders stem from their basis in this contractual maraboutic model of authority.

The Social Background

The brotherhoods thus vary as to what degree they are linked to social groups. Typically, the founders of Ways and branches come from families with a reputation for learning and scholarship, but the contrast between the Sy family's traditional links with the local rulers and the Kaolack family's background in a lower-ranking blacksmith caste is striking. The brotherhoods may also be differentiated socially by their recruitment: in Senegal, the Tijanis at least earlier had a reputation for attracting more urban and highly educated members than the Muridiyya. Or the differentiation may be ethnic, as, in East Africa, between the Arabic diaspora community, an Africanized Shirazi (Swahili) class, and urban and rural Africans.

The admission of women to the brotherhoods has been a very common matter of contention between them.[85] It is not exceptional to see women belonging to the saintly families playing important informal roles, both as scholars teaching the ritual and Islamic sciences and in the actual running of the brotherhood.[86] It is less common to see women having formal positions, as teachers and leaders of both men and women, but one case has already been mentioned: Mtumwa bt. 'Ali of Malawi. Another example is Sokhna Magat Diop, of Senegal, the daughter of one of Ahmad Bamba's muqaddams. She took formal leadership of her father's branch of the Muridiyya when he died in 1943.[87] She functions as "a marabout like the others," with full and recognized authority over the branch, although she normally stays out of the public eye, leaving speechmaking to her son. Interestingly, while her father was known as a nonconformist shaykh, called the "Mahdi of Thiès," she herself has brought the branch into a clearly traditional and moderate Muridi model.

A typical feature of many of the brotherhoods has been their development as settled communities. This started in the Saharan period, when both al-Mukthar and Shaykh Sidiya established communities for their tilmidh adherent lineages, although they themselves may not have lived in them. Later, these communities were of many different types, and in examining the nature of the brotherhoods, it helps to study what kinds of settled communities they formed.

The most common type of structure is the sufi lodge *(zawiya)*, which may simply be the house where the dhikr is performed and where the shaykh may stay. Sometimes, however, the zawiya can take on wider functions. The Sanusiyya made them into small oasis communities in which the shaykhs and students would live; poor families might come to cultivate gardens and be protected, and these places became stageposts for trading networks.

In some communities, agricultural aspects dominated. These became primarily farming establishments, for individuals or groups, originally around a local scholar or holy man, but later to be integrated into the universe of sufi Ways as brotherhood communities. This seems to be the case for the Somali jama'as. The Muridi groundnut-producing daras is a special case of such a farming community: the murids, instead of settling in the community on a permanent basis, served there for a certain period as part of their cycle of initiation into the brotherhood. In the twentieth century, newer types of organization have developed, of which the *da'iras* are a striking example, appearing to build on a "modern" organizational model inserted into the postcolonial civil society.

Piety and Scholarship

The organizations are thus set up to promote the brotherhoods' main goals of piety and mysticism. The most important fields for the sufi scholarship have been piety and *tawhid*, the unity of God. A survey of manuscripts in some major collections of West African Islamic manuscripts recently cataloged shows that works on piety and praise of the Prophet equal those of *fiqh* in number. Only a minority of titles deal with actual sufi themes, even in the libraries of sufi centers.[88]

This centrality of piety in their works, contrasted with the more "scholastic" sciences, shows the importance that the orders and their leaders placed on disseminating an ideal of behavior, rather than on engaging in competitive disputation with rival scholars. Thus, the various orders spread and taught the same books—in particular, such basic works as the *Umm al-Barahin* of Muhammad b. Yusuf al-Sanusi on theology and the *Risala* of Ibn Abi Zayd al-Qayrawani on Maliki law.

The didactic direction of the writings by the sufi scholars of Africa is also shown by the increased centrality of writing in the vernacular—in particular, poetry of piety and praise for the Prophet. Most of the authors wrote in Arabic, but many also used local languages. This clearly was of great importance in widening the basis for their teachings. This is a general phenomenon of modern African Islam, and is not limited to those who established sufi orders (although it is one of their important characteristics).

The above does not mean that the scholars were not aware of the debates in the world of sufi and general Islamic thought. They participated in them. We have mentioned the stature of al-Hajj 'Umar in the Tijaniyya generally, and the importance of his scholarly work; we could also venture the extensive, and polemical, writings of the founder of the Sanusiyya in *usul al-fiqh*.

A suggestion has been made that the new orders that grew up in the eighteenth and nineteenth century share certain polemical ideas that set them apart from the earlier tariqas; however, this has been challenged. Although, as has already been mentioned, the Khatmiyya and the Tijaniyya share the term "seal of *wilaya*," the term (which did not originate with either of them) appears in such different contexts that it cannot be seen as a common idea.

The concept that has been most clearly linked to the idea of "Neo-sufism" is that of the *tariqa Muhammadiyya,* which both the Tijani and Ibn Idris orders use.[89] It is, however, not a new concept, and it does not mean, as has been suggested, that the sufi changes his spiritual aim from experiencing a "unity with God" to the more prosaic "unity with the Prophet." The ultimate aim remains the same. The term is saying, in part, that the seeker must follow the model behavior of the Prophet as far as that seeker is able; it is an ideal of piety. But more specifically, the term refers to seeing the Prophet in the flesh, in a vision, awake—talking to him and touching him. The tariqa Muhammadiyya is a silsila of sufis in which each member of the chain has had this experience, which is evidently one of extremely high spiritual standing. For al-Tijani, it was not really a chain at all; he himself had taken it directly from the Prophet. For the Idrisis, however, this elevated chain, or Way, comprised three or four scholars—a silsila going back to the supernatural figure of al-Khidr and continuing to Ibn Idris and those of his students who claimed the same status (thus, al-Sanusi and al-Mirghani). However, for these latter Ways—although the Muhammadiyya was the most elevated Way they had taken, and was thus given pride of place in their denomination of themselves—it was far from their only one; it was always supported by other, non-Muhammadi silsilas. In more prosaic terms, what the tariqa Muhammadiyya means is that those who attach themselves to it claim a higher stature in the spiritual field than the fellow orders. This could of course be transformed into an active resource in times of rivalry and competition, but it did not in itself have a social or political implication.

The Brotherhoods and Social Change

This leads to the question of the brotherhoods, the tariqa-organizations, as agents for political change. It is clear from the survey above that the different orders, when classified by Way, do not split into a quietist/militant dichotomy. The militant 'Umarian jihad was very much based on the Tijani order, but when the jihad was over the order did not collapse; rather, it spread and forged new and deeper roots in society. In the Idrisi tradition, the Sanusi resistance stems from the same root as the "quietist" Khatmiyya and the withdrawn modern Idrisiyya. The brothers Sa'd Buh and Ma' al-'Aynayn took opposite paths in politics but spread the same Fadili Way from their father. Thus, the "militancy" of the orders does not stem from their teachings, nor do the "militants" create a sufism that requires political activity to survive.

The tariqa-Way is thus irrelevant for the political potential of the orders: it is the organizational aspects of the orders that make them into possible political actors. As we noticed, the organization is not historically an essential means of dissemination of the Way; it is, however, a natural way of formalizing the relationship of teacher to student. When it did not arise in early African sufism, it was because this relationship was already defined by the lineage, and any new form of authority outside the lineage model was both foreign and unnecessary. This changed, but when it did, there must have been a reason for it.

We may see several elements in the creation of tariqa-organization: First there is the formalizing of the relationship between student and teacher, a relationship that is one of absolute (spiritual) authority and obedience. Second there is the creation of a hierarchy in this relationship: the teacher leads the student through several stages of esoteric knowledge, the mastery of one being a requirement for the initiation into the next. There is no need for this esoteric hierarchy to be transformed into an organizational status system, but clearly the existence of such a multilayered hierarchy can be the basis for the development of multiple levels of organization. From this may follow a third element of organization—the centralization of esoteric knowledge, and from this emerges leadership.

An established brotherhood can also have organizational functions beyond the ranks of the initiates proper. Apart from helping with the mundane matters of life and the dissemination of learning of various kinds in a community, the shaykh, and through him his brotherhood, can become a focus of identity. The commoner who knows that his local shaykh ("marabout") is a member of the Tijaniyya order will consider himself "attached" to that order, while having no formal ties to it. He may therefore look to the shaykh, and beyond him to the brotherhood, for help when other avenues are closed or when he for other reasons considers the shaykh the one most likely to support him. In this way, the brotherhood can become a focus for regional, ethnic, or social identity.

The organization and the lines of identity it creates stem from the spiritual work of the order, and are not created for the purpose of political activity. However, these elements are extremely well suited for political organization. A sufi order as described here has a clear identity; it has the committed support of a population on the basis of an existing category (which may be ethnic or regional); and it has an internal organization that is independent (that is, not merely a reflection of family or other structures) wherein the higher ranks of the leadership can, in theory, command the complete support of the lower ranks. It is a potentially explosive combination. The sufi order, when fully organizational, thus contains the potential to become a political actor, but a transformation of the functions of the order is required for this to happen.

Of the cases above, we see the tariqa structure used for political purposes when the Mukhtariyya gained ascendancy over rival clans; we see it also in the Tijani jihad of al-Hajj ʿUmar, and in the history of the Sanusiyya and the Salihiyya from the Idrisi tradition. We do not, however, see much of it in the jihads of ʿUthman b. Fodio and dan of Sheku Ahmadu in Masina—both of them Qadiri sufis. Why with some and not with others? Part of the answer can be linked to differences in strength of the orders' organizational patterns. In Hausaland, ʿUthman's affiliation to the Qadiriyya was mainly as a Way, not to it as an organization. Although the Qadiriyya was used as a focus of identity, it did not hold sufficient power for him to build his jihad on it. However, that is not a complete answer, for Sidi al-Mukhtar was in much the same situation and he was able to add the Qadiri affiliation to the "spiritual resources" needed for the political transformation of his lineage. There was nothing in the sufi model to stop ʿUthman using it in a similar way for his new community. That that did not happen must be because the external context was different.

Sidi al-Mukhtar wanted to tilt the balance of power to his clan, so he added the resource of a stronger tariqa organization to the lineage's status as a line of walis. This was both sufficient and required. ʿUthman, on the other hand, did not stand in a similar situation of structural rivalry with parallel lineage-based groups. His goal was revolutionary, and references to the early *hijra* and community of the Prophet supplied the required identity and models of behavior. His decentralized model of disseminating "grants of jihad" by issuing flags was both flexible and sufficient for the spread of the movement. Thus, the tariqa model was one of spiritual importance for him, but not one relevant for the struggle. Furthermore, the Mukhtariyya, like the Sanusiyya but unlike Hausaland, developed in an stateless environment. In such a situation, a transformational pattern of organization, when needed, was more likely to be found in a "religious" source, sufism. The Sokoto jihad, on the other hand, was against an existing state structure and would thus seek the more clearly state-oriented hijra model.

Al-Hajj ʿUmar, like ʿUthman, worked in a region where state structures were well developed. However, in his case the ideology and legitimacy of these structures were too close to his own for him easily to take over the Sokoto model for jihad. He was a "second-generation jihadist"; there had been several jihad movements in the region before his, and the rival state of Masina had a strong jihad charisma. The social basis for his community was also less clear-cut than in ʿUthman's. Because of this, he needed a new element—something that could be a focus of identity, authority, and organization for him. He found all three in the Tijaniyya tariqa. This is not to say that ʿUmar was any less genuine in his sufi concern than ʿUthman; we have ample proof of his scholarliness. Yet both ʿUthman and ʿUmar seem to have been conscious militants who set out on the path of militant reform. It was the circumstances of their struggle that were different, and these led one to take a strong tariqa model and the other to not do so.

A third major case, that of the Sanusi resistance, was different from both the other two. The Sanusiyya created their organization not for political ends, but only to promote piety and learning in Bedouin society. One reason for their strong internal structure was probably that they lacked a local family or tribal basis, such as the other Saharan sufi orders had. Militancy was forced upon them later by outsiders—the French. However, when that situation occurred and the local people started to use the Sanusi identity as a focus for resistance—for lack of any other—the potion of organization and identity seems to have been very effective, at least in the Cyrenaican heartland, where they forced the Italian invaders into a stalemate for almost two decades.

Thus, the sufi orders are not themselves conscious agents for social and political change. Their aim is to promote the Way of spiritual growth. They do, however, represent a resource that can be used for social and political purposes in the strategic jockeying for positions in a segmented society, or as a focus for identity and organization in a transformational struggle for a new political order. The Ways, however, are not dependent on either of these purposes, and have survived the political changes, strengthened and more widely disseminated. They are currently under attack from a new quarter—from Islamic "reformists" who see them as *depassé,* as carriers of "African" traditions that they want to replace with Islamic ones. But there seems to be a capacity for the brotherhoods to accommodate this "reformist" tendency and create new structures more adapted to the modern society, such as the different Senegalese da'iras. It is likely that the current debates may lead to the internal development of the sufi brotherhoods, rather than to their demise.

Have the sufi brotherhoods "Africanized" an Arabic or "global" Islam? It has been suggested that these brotherhoods, by providing an outlet for local leadership, have promoted a self-assertion in the face of non-African dominance.[90] It would, however, rather seem that their function has been to internationalize the Islam of Africa, by bringing the existing local leaders into contact with networks that span the continents and in which geographic and ethnic background is of minor importance.

Certainly, the brotherhoods have helped spread Islam to new territories—in particular, in the last hundred years, in continental East Africa. But their main function seems to have been to deepen and intellectualize the Islam of peoples who already knew it, not only among the scholars but also, through spreading writing in the vernacular, by teaching the basics of Islam and emphasizing personal piety and exemplary behavior, to Muslims at large. In the end, this effect is probably of greater import than its external functions as a focus for political combat and jihad.

Notes

1. Anawati and Gardet 1986; Baldick 1989; Schimmel 1975.

2. Trimingham 1970, 157; 1971, 44–51.

3. Stewart 1976; McDougall 1986; Evans-Pritchard 1949; Peters 1990a; Hamani 1989; Bernus 1981.

4. In East Africa, the term *buruhan* was used; Trimingham 1964, 94.

5. Cf. Bourdieu 1977, 176–83.

6. Batran 1974, 42; Stewart 1973, 37; Hunwick 1985, 43–4, 1999.

7. Brenner 1988, 36–43; Batran 1979; Ould Cheikh 1991; McDougall 1986.

8. Stewart 1973, 112–15; Brenner 1988, 42.

9. Ould Cheikh 1991.

10. Stewart 1973.

11. McLaughlin 1997.

12. Ibid., 87–91.

13. Ibid., 84–87, 71; Stewart 1973, 166; Martin 1976, 126; Triaud 1996, 426.

14. McLaughlin 1997, 174–6, 189–96.

15. Ibid., 176–89; Martin 1976, 125–51; Harmon 1992.

16. Ould Abdallah 1997.

17. Lavers 1971, 1987.

18. Last 1967; Hiskett 1994; Brenner 1988; el-Masri 1963.

19. Last 1967, lix, 216; Hiskett 1994, 67.

20. Karrar 1992, 21–35.

21. Cassanelli 1982; Reese 1996; Lewis 1984.

22. Lewis 1984, 144.

23. Martin 1976, 152–76.

24. Ibid., 178; cf. also Cerulli 1957, 188.

25. Coulon 1987, 116.

26. Vikør 1996, 134; cf. also Lewis 1984, 138; Trimingham 1964, 102.

27. Nimtz 1980, 58–59.

28. Ibid., 66.

29. Ibid., 95–192.

30. Greenstein 1976–77.

31. Ibid.; Constantin 1987a, 86–88.

32. Constantin 1988.

33. O'Brien 1971, 1975; Behrman 1970; Seesemann 1993.

34. Ebin 1991; Schmidt di Friedberg 1994.

35. Triaud 1988.

36. Norris 1989, 130; 1990, 149.

37. Brenner 1988, 47.

38. Triaud 1983.

39. Karrar 1992, 43–48; Levtzion 1994.

40. Karrar 1992, 48.

41. See chapter 7.

42. Abun-Nasr 1965; Martin 1969; 1976, 68–98; Vikør 1996, 25–29.

43. Ould Abdallah 1996; McLaughlin 1997, 82–83; Stewart 1973, 30; Abun-Nasr 1965, 102–6.

44. Martin 1976, 69; Robinson 1985, 94.

45. Radtke 1995b; Hunwick 1992.

46. Trimingham 1959, 98.

47. Robinson 1985, 112–24, 136.

48. Brenner 1984, 21–27; Oloruntimehin 1972, 147–316.

49. Garcia 1997.

50. Soares 1997; Hamès 1985; Brenner 1984, 45–59; Hunwick and Soares 1996.

51. Hamès 1997, 337–60; Soares 1997, 114.

52. Soares 1997, 120.

53. Brenner 1984.

54. Savadogo 1986; Soares 1997, 150–61.

55. Marone 1970, 140–41; Villalón 1995, 67–68, 139–40; M'Bow 1995.

56. Villalón 1995, 239–42; Villalón and Kane 1995; Diop 1981.

57. Villalón 1995, 140–42; Grey 1988; Kane 1989; Paden 1973, 73–146; Hiskett 1980; Loimeier 1997.

58. Quinn 1972, 1979.

59. Vikør 1995, 223–26; cf. also Paden 1973, 109, 126, 179, 185–86.

60. Paden 1973, 197–202; Kane 1989; cf. also item on Nasiru Kabara, Hunwick 1996, 321–23.

61. Villalón 1995, 141.

62. ʿAlawi 1934; Martin 1976, 152-58.

63. Greenstein 1976–77, 21, 31.

64. Karrar 1992, 35–39.

65. O'Fahey 1990, 1994.

66. Vikør 1995.

67. Ibid., 132–61; Peters 1990b.

68. Cordell 1977; Ciammaichella 1987.

69. Triaud 1987, 1995.

70. Triaud 1995, 819–920; Salifou 1973.

71. Karrar 1992, 42–102.

72. Ibid., 120–24.

73. O'Fahey 1990, 154–62; Karrar 1992, 103–10; Sedgwick 1998, 74–92.

74. Vikør 1995, 165–70.

75. O'Fahey 1990, 163–65; Karrar 1992, 109–10.

76. Cerulli 1957, 189–90; Lewis 1984, 138–39.

77. Lewis 1984, 139.

78. Cassanelli 1982, 135–36.

79. O'Fahey 1990, 163–64; Cassanelli 1982, 213, 237; Cerulli 1957, 190; Reese 1996, 321–33; Sedgwick 1998, 104–79.

80. O'Fahey 1990, 166; Nimtz 1980, 61, 123–24, 130.

81. Karrar 1992, 39, 71; Radtke 1992a, 1995a; Ibrahim 1980; Hofheinz 1996.

82. Ibrahim 1980, 86–92.

83. O'Fahey 1990, 125–39, 171–79; Karrar 1992, 116–20.

84. See Trimingham 1971, 152–54.

85. Nimtz 1980, 80; O'Fahey 1990, 97; Vikør 1995, 57.

86. Cf. Vikør 1995, 27, 205.

87. Coulon and Reveyrand 1990.

88. Muhammad 1995–97; Kane 1997.

89. Radtke 1992b, 1996, 120–28; Vikør 1996, 80–81, 227.

90. O'Brien 1981.

Bibliography

Abun-Nasr, Jamil M. 1965. *The Tijaniyya: A Sufi Order in the Modern World.* London: Oxford University Press.

'Alawi, Ahmad b. 'Abd al-Rahman. 1934. *Manaqib al-Sayyid Muhammad b. Ahmad b. Abi Bakr al-Shadhili al-Yashruti.* Cairo: Mustafa al-Babi al-Halabi.

Anawati, G. C. and Louis Gardet. 1986. *Mystique musulmane: Aspects et tendances, expériences et techniques.* Paris: J. Vrin.

Baldick, Julian. 1989. *Mystical Islam: An Introduction to Sufism.* London: I. B. Tauris.

Batran, 'Abd al-Aziz. 1974. 'The Qadiriyya-Mukhtaryya brotherhood in West Africa: the concept of tasawwuf in the writings of Sidi al-Mukhtar al-Kunti (1729–1811)," *Transafrican Journal of History* 4:41–70.

————. 1979. "The Kunta, Sidi al-Mukhtar al-Kunti and the Office of *Shaykh al-Tariqa'l-Qadiriyya.*" In Willis 1979, 113–46.

Behrman, Lucy C. 1970. *Muslim Brotherhoods and Politics in Senegal.* Cambridge, Mass.: Harvard University Press.

Bernus, Edmond. 1981. *Touaregs Nigériens: Unité culturelle et diversité régionale d'un peuple pasteur.* Paris: Editions de l'Office de la Recherche Scientifique et Technique Outre-Mer.

Bourdieu, Pierre. 1977. *Outline of a Theory of Practice.* Cambridge: Cambridge University Press.

Brenner, Louis. 1984. *West African Sufi: The Religious Heritage and Spiritual Search of Cerno Bokar Saalif Taal.* London: C. Hurst & Co.

————. 1988. "Concepts of *Tariqa* in West Africa: The Case of the Qadiriyya." In O'Brien and Coulon 1988, 33–52.

Cassanelli, Lee V. 1982. *The Shaping of Somali Society: Reconstructing the History of a Pastoral People, 1600–1900.* Philadelphia: University of Pennsylvania Press.

Cerulli, Enrico. 1957. *Somalia. Scritti vari editi ed inediti, I: Storia della Somalia. L'islam in Somalia.* Rome: A cura dell'amministrazione fiduciaria italiana della Somalia.

Ciammaichella, Glauco. 1987. *Libyens et Français au Tchad (1897–1914): La confrérie senoussie et le commerce transsaharien.* Paris: Editions du CNRS.

Constantin, François. 1987a. "Le saint et le prince: Sur les fondements de la dynamique confrérique en Afrique orientale." In Constantin 1987b, 85–109.

————, ed. 1987b. *Les Voies de l'islam en Afrique orientale.* Paris: Karthala.

————. 1988. "Charisma and the Crisis of Power in East Africa." In O'Brian and Coulon 1988, 67–90.

Cordell, Dennis. 1977. "Eastern Libya, Wadai and the Sanusiya: A Tariqa and a Trade Route," *Journal of African History* 18:21–36.

Coulon, Christian. 1987. "Vers une sociologie des confréries en Afrique orientale." In Constantin 1987b, 111–33.

Coulon, Christian, and Odile Reveyrand. 1990. *L'islam au feminin: Sokhna Magat Diop, Cheikh de la confrérie mouride (Sénégal).* Bordeaux: Centre d'Etudes d'Afrique Noire.

Diop, Moumar Komba. 1981. "Fonctions et activités des dahira mourides urbains (Sénégal)," *Cahiers d'études africaines* 21:79–91.

Ebin, Vicki. 1991. "Mouride Traders and International Trade Networks." Paper presented at the "Islamic Identities in Africa" conference, London, Apr. 18–20.

Evans-Pritchard, E. E. 1949. *The Sanusi of Cyrenaica.* Oxford: Clarendon Press.

Garcia, Sylvianne. 1997. "Al-Hajj Seydou Nourou Tall, 'grand marabout' tijani: l'histoire d'une carrière (v: 1880–1980)." In Robinson and Triaud 1997, 247–75.

Greenstein, Robert. 1976–77. "*Shaykhs* and *Tariqa*s: The Early Muslim *'Ulama'* and *Tariqa* Development in Malawi, c. 1885–1949." History research seminar papers, University of Malawi.

Grey, Christopher. 1988. "The Rise of the Niassene Tijaniyya, 1875 to Present," *Islam et sociétés au sud du Sahara* 2:34–60.

Hamani, Djibo. 1989. *Au carrefour du Soudan et de la Berberie: Le sultanat touareg de l'Ayar.* Niamey: Institut de Recherches en Sciences Humaines.

Hamès, Constant. 1985. "Cheikh Hamallah, ou qu'est qu'une confrérie islamique (tarîqa)?" *Archives de sciences sociales des religions* 55:67–83.

———. 1997. "Le premier exil de Shaikh Hamallah et la mémoire hamalliste (Nioro-Mederdra, 1925)." In Robinson and Triaud 1997, 337–60.

Harmon, Stephen A. 1992. "Shaykh Ma' al-'Aynayn: Armed resistance and French policy in Northwest Africa, 1900–1910," *Jusur* 8:1–22.

Hiskett, Mervyn. 1980. "The 'Community of Grace' and its opponents, the 'Rejecters': A debate about theology and mysticism in Muslim West African with special reference to its Hausa Expression," *African Language Studies* 17:99–140.

———. 1994. *The Sword of Truth: The Life and Times of the Shehu Usuman dan Fodio.* 2nd edn. Evanston: Northwestern University Press.

Hofheinz, Albrecht. 1996. "Internalising Islam: Shaykh Muhammad Majdhub, Scriptural Islam and Local Context in Early Nineteenth-Century Sudan." Dr. philos diss., University of Bergen.

Hunwick, John O. 1985. *Shari'a in Songhay: The Replies of al-Maghili to the questions of Askia al-hajj Muhammad.* Oxford: Oxford University Press.

———. 1992. "An Introduction to the Tijani Path: Being an Annotated Translation of the Chapter Headings of the Kitab al-Rimah of al-Hajj 'Umar," *Islam et sociétés au sud du Sahara,* 6:17–32.

———. 1996. *Arabic Literature of Africa, II: The Writings of Central Sudanic Africa to c. 1900.* Leiden: E. J. Brill.

———. 1999. "Tasawwuf: In Africa South of the Maghrib during the 19th and 20th Centuries." In *Encyclopaedia of Islam:* New edition. 10:339–40.

Hunwick, John O., and Benjamin Soares. 1996. "Falkeiana IV: The Shaykh as the Locus of Divine Self-disclosure: A poem in praise of Shaykh Hamahu 'llah," *Sudanic Africa* 7:97–112.

Ibrahim, Mahmoud Abdalla. 1980. "The History of the Isma'iliyya Tariqa in the Sudan: 1792–1914." Ph.D. diss., University of London.

Kane, Ousmane. 1989. "La Confrérie 'Tijaniyya Ibrahimiyya' de Kano et ses liens avec la za-wiya mère de Kaolack". *Islam et sociétés au sud du Sahara* 3:27–40.

———. 1997. *al-Makhtutat al-mahfuza fi Maktabat al-shaykh Mur Mubay Sisi wa-maktabat al-hajj Malik Si wa-maktabat al-shaykh Ibrahim Niyas*. London: Furqan.

Karrar, Ali Salih. 1992. *The Sufi Brotherhoods in the Sudan*. London: Chr. Hurst & Evanston: Northwestern University Press.

Last, Murray. 1967. *The Sokoto Caliphate*. London : Longmans.

Lavers, John E. 1971. "Islam in the Bornu Caliphate," *Odu* 5:27–53.

———. 1987. "Two Sufi Communities in Seventeeth and Eighteenth Century Borno." Paper presented at the "Sufism in Africa" workshop, London, Sept. 17–18.

Levtzion, Nehemia. 1994. "Eighteenth Century Renewal and Reform in Islam: The Role of Sufi Turuq in West Africa." In *Islam in West Africa: Religion: Society and Politics to 1800,* [1–18]. Aldershot: Variorum.

Lewis, I. M. 1984. "Sufism in Somaliland: A Study in Tribal Islam." In *Islam in Tribal Societies: From the Atlas to the Indus,* ed. Akbar S. Ahmed and David M. Hart, 127–68. London: Routledge and Kegan Paul.

Loimeier, Roman. 1997. *Islamic Reform and Political Change in Northern Nigeria*. Evanston: Northwestern University Press.

McDougall, Ann. 1986. "The Economics of Islam in the Southern Sahara: The Rise of the Kunta Clan," *Asian and African Studies* 20:45–60.

McLaughlin, Glen Wade. 1997. "Sufi, Saint, Sharif: Muhammad Fadil Wuld Mamin: His Spiritual Legacy, and the Political Economy of the Sacred Nineteenth Century Mauritania." Ph.D. diss, Northwestern University.

Marone, Ibrahima. 1970. "Le Tidjanisme au Sénégal," *Bulletin d'IFAN* 32:136–215.

Martin, Bradford G. 1969. "Notes sur l'origine de la tariqa des Tiganiyya et sur les débuts d'al-Hagg 'Umar," *Revue des Etudes Islamiques* 2:267–90.

———. 1976. *Muslim Brotherhoods in Nineteenth-Century Africa*. Cambridge: Cambridge University Press.

el-Masri, F. H. 1963. "The life of Shehu Usuman dan Fodio before the Jihad," *Journal of the Historical Society of Nigeria,* 2:435–48.

M'Bow, Penda. 1995. "Querelles de succession au sein de la confrérie Tidjane de Tivaouane dans les années 50." Paper presented to seminar, University of Bergen.

Muhammad, Baba Yunus. 1995–97. *Fihris Makhtutat Dar al-watha'iq al-qawmiya al-Nayjiriya bi-Kaduna*. Ed. J.O. Hunwick, 2 vols, London: Furqan.

Nimtz, August H. 1980. *Islam and Politics in East Africa: The Sufi Order in Tanzania*. Minneapolis: University of Minnesota Press.

Norris, H.T. 1989. "'À la recherche de Sîdî Mahmûd al-Baghdâdî': The *Silsila* of the Mahmûdiyya Tarîqa in the 'Qudwa'," *Islam et sociétés au sud du Sahara* 3:128–58.

———. 1990. *Sufi Mystics of the Niger Desert: Sidi Mahmud and the Hermits of Air*. Oxford: Clarendon Press.

O'Brien, Donal B. Cruise. 1971. *The Mourides of Senegal: The Political and Economic Organization of an Islamic Brotherhood*. Oxford: Clarendon Press.

———. 1975. *Saints and Politicians: Essays in the Organisation of a Senegalese Peasant Society.* Cambridge: Cambridge University Press.

———. 1981. "La filière musulmane: Confréries soufies et politique en Afrique noire," *Politique Africaine* 1:7–30.

O'Brien, Donal B. Cruise, and Christian Coulon, eds. 1988. *Charisma and Brotherhood in African Islam.* Oxford: Clarendon Press.

O'Fahey, R.S. 1990. *Enigmatic Saint: Ahmad Ibn Idris and the Idrisi Tradition.* London: Chr. Hurst & Evanston: Northwestern University Press.

———. 1994. *Arabic Literature of Africa, I: The Writings of Eastern Sudanic Africa to c. 1900.* Leiden: E. J. Brill.

Oloruntimehin, B.O. 1972. *The Segu Tukolor Empire.* London: Longman.

Ould Abdallah, A. Dedoud. 1996. "La Hafiziyya dans la Tijaniyya ouest-africaine (1800–1864)." Paper presented at the "Tijaniya Traditions and Societies in West Africa in the 19th and 20th Centuries" conference, Urbana, Ill., Apr. 1–5.

———. 1997. "Guerre sainte ou sédition blâmable: un débat entre shaikh Sa'd Bu et son frère Ma al-Ainain." In Robinson and Triaud 1997, 119–53.

Ould Cheikh, Abdel Wedoud. 1991. 'Identité tribale et pouvoir islamique. Quelques remarques sur une épître de al-Shaikh Sîdi Muhammad al-Kuntî (m. 1826), *al-Risala al-Ghallawiyya'.* Paper presented at the "Islamic Identities in Africa" conference, London Apr. 18–20.

Paden, John N. 1973. *Religion and Political Culture in Kano.* Berkeley: University of California Press.

Peters, Emrys L. 1990a. *The Bedouin of Cyrenaica.* Cambridge: Cambridge University Press.

———. 1990b. "The Sanusi Order and the Bedouin." In Peters 1990a, 10–28.

Popovic, Alexandre, and Gilles Veinstein, eds. 1996. *Les voies d'Allah: Les ordres mystiques dans l'islam des origines à aujourd'hui.* Paris: Fayard.

Quinn, Charlotte A. 1972. *Mandingo kingdoms in the Senegambia: Traditionalism, Islam and European Expansion.* London: Longman.

———. 1979. "Maba Diahou and the Gambian Jihad, 1850–1890." In Willis 1979, 233–58.

Radtke, Bernd. 1992a. "Lehrer-Schüler-Enkel: Ahmad b. Idris, Muhammad 'Utman al-Mirgani, Isma'il al-Wali," *Oriens* 32:94–132.

———. 1992b. "Between Projection and Suppression: Some Considerations concerning the Study of Sufism." In *Shi'a Islam, Sects and Sufism,* ed. Frederick de Jong, 70–82. Utrecht: Houtsma Stichting.

———. 1995a. "Isma'il al-Wali: Ein sudanesischer Theosoph des 19. Jahrhunderts," *Der Islam* 72:148–55.

———. 1995b. "Studies on the Sources of the *Kitab Rimah Hizb al-Rahim* of al-hajj 'Umar," *Sudanic Africa* 6:73–113.

———. 1996. "*Ibriz*iana," *Sudanic Africa* 7:113–58.

Reese, Scott Steve. 1996. "Patricians of the Benadir: Islamic Learning, Commerce and Somali Urban Identity in the Nineteenth Century." Ph.D. diss., University of Pennsylvania.

Robinson, David. 1985. *The Holy War of Umar Tal: The Western Sudan in the Mid-Nineteenth Century.* Oxford: Clarendon Press.

Robinson, David, and Jean-Louis Triaud, eds. 1997. *Le temps des marabouts: Itinéraires et stratégies islamiques en Afrique occidentale française v. 1880–1960.* Paris: Karthala.

Salifou, André. 1973. *Kaoussan ou la révolte Sénoussiste.* Niamey: Centre Nigérien de Recherches en Sciences Humaines.

Savadogo, Boukary. 1986. "La Tidjaniyya hamawiyya au Moogo central," *Islam et sociétés au sud du Sahara* 10:7–23.

Schimmel, Annemarie. 1975. *Mystical Dimensions of Islam.* Chapel Hill: University of North Carolina Press.

Schmidt di Friedberg, Ottavia. 1994. *Islam, solidarietà e lavoro: I muridi senegalesi in Italia.* Torino: Edizioni della Fondazione Giovanni Agnelli.

Sedgwick, Mark J. R. 1998. "The Heirs of Ahmad Ibn Idris: The Spread and Normalization of a Sufi Order, 1799–1996." Dr. philos. diss., University of Bergen.

Seesemann, Rüdiger. 1993. *Ahmadu Bamba und die Entstehung der Muridiya: Analyse religiöser und historischer Hintergründe.* Berlin: Klaus Schwarz.

Soares, Benjamin F. 1997. "The Spiritual Economy of Nioro du Sahel: Islamic Discourses and Practices in a Malian Religious Center." Ph.D. diss., Northwestern University.

Stewart, Charles C. 1973. *Islam and Social Order in Mauritania.* Oxford: Clarendon Press.

———. 1976. "Southern Saharan Scholarship and the *Bilad al-Sudan*," *Journal of African History* 17:73–93.

Triaud, Jean-Louis. 1983. "Hommes de religion et confréries islamiques dans une société en crise, l'Aïr au XIXe et XX siècles: le cas de la Khalwatiyya," *Cahiers d'études africaines* 23:239–80.

———. 1987. *Tchad 1900–1902: Une guerre franco-libyenne oubliée? Une confrérie musulmane, la Sanûsiyya face à la France.* Paris: L'Harmattan.

———. 1988. "*Khalwa* and the Career of Sainthood: An Interpretative Essay." In O'Brian and Coulon 1988, 53–66.

———. 1995. *La légende noire de la Sanûsiyya: Une confrérie musulmane saharienne sous le regard français (1840–1930).* Paris: Editions de la Maison des sciences de l'homme.

——— 1996. "L'Afrique occidentale et centrale." In Popovic and G. Veinstein 1996, 417–27.

Trimingham, J. Spencer. 1959. *Islam in West Africa.* Oxford: Clarendon Press.

———. 1964. *Islam in East Africa.* Oxford: Clarendon Press.

———. 1970. *A History of Islam in West Africa.* London: Oxford University Press.

———. 1971. *The Sufi Orders in Islam.* London: Oxford University Press.

Vikør, Knut S. 1995. *Sufi and Scholar on the Desert Edge: Muhammad b. ʿAli al-Sanusi and His Brotherhood.* London: Chr. Hurst & Evanston: Northwestern University Press.

———. 1996. *Sources for Sanusi Studies.* Bergen: Centre for Middle Eastern Studies.

Villalón, Leonardo A. 1995. *Islamic Society and State Power in Senegal: Disciples and Citizens in Fatick.* Cambridge: Cambridge University Press.

Villalón, Leonardo A., and Ousmane Kane. 1995. "Entre confrérisme, réformisme et is-lamisme: Les Murstarshidin du Sénégal," *Islam et sociétés au sud du Sahara* 9:119-201.

Willis, John Ralph, ed. 1979. *Studies in West African Islamic History, I: The Cultivators of Islam.* London: Frank Cass.

CHAPTER 21

Prayer, Amulets, and Healing

David Owusu-Ansah

Prayers and amulets are two of the common means by which African societies
have addressed illness. Through such agencies, the spiritual causes of sickness
are appealed to, or confronted, to let go of afflictions. The theory of disease that
ascribes illness to spiritual sources reflects a philosophical duality in which the outer
signs of ailments are ascribed to hidden spiritual imbalance. The explanation of sickness as presented above is not a suggestion that these societies have no appreciation of
natural causation of illness. In fact, as Dennis Warren has explained in an essay on the
Bono of Ghana, or as in separate presentation by W. Z. Conco and Gloria Waite on
the Bantus of the southern tier of Africa,[1] natural causes are anticipated for "ordinary
and common human illness." Conco observed of the Bantu that "in the beginning of
disease no supernatural danger is felt [for sickness] and home remedies are given."
Thus, it is in relation to prolonged and dangerous conditions that thoughts of spiritual origination of illness have been expressed.[2]

The tradition by which sickness is attributed to spirit causation is widely accepted. From Steve Feierman's discussion of the social roots of health and healing in
modern Africa, to the collection of essays in *African Therapeutic Systems,* edited by
Z. A. Ademuwagun and others, the medical tradition in which the spiritual world is
believed to be source for the endangerment of mental and physical health is articulated.[3] To be sick, therefore, is to be in the hold of a spirit-causing agent and, hence,
it is the ultimate purpose of healing to restore normal health.

Conditions perceived to be abnormal are many and varied. The fear of a difficult
birth, the possibility of loss of wealth and property, the loss of children to childhood
diseases, barrenness, sudden deaths (especially of individuals in the prime of life),
and chronic sickness are but a short list of maladies that undermine the stability of
personal and community life. As in all societies, indigenous communities have developed ideological interpretations of disease causation and a list of agents believed

responsible for the ailments. In her general reference to the Bantu of East Central Africa, Waite classified the disease causing agents to include ancestral spirits, witch- craft, and violation of taboos that protect society from spiritual pollution. Among the Bantu, the High God is even thought of as a disease-causing agent. But while the Supreme Being featured prominently in Waite's list, among the Akan-speakers of West Africa it is the host of intermediary lesser gods, witches and family ancestors, that are often thought of as culprits. As to which of these agents might a sickness be attributed, ordinary persons can only speculate. It is for this reason that expert ser- vices are sought.

Religious personages are collectively identified by the public as possessing ex- pert diagnostic and healing capabilities. Louis Brenner's "esoteric paradigm" is an excellent summary of the epistemological foundation upon which religious knowl- edge is evaluated. Here, Brenner revisits the concept of duality in which he classi- fied knowledge as belonging to either a public or sacred domain.[4] In the profane environment, religious ideas and concepts take the form of myths, songs, and prayers that are often recited during public rituals.[5] For the sacred or esoteric cate- gory, expert knowledge is acquired only through formal training and long periods of apprenticeship and initiations—a process that is best represented in Brookman- Amissah's work.[6]

Using case interviews conducted with trainees at the Akonnedi Shrine in Ghana, Brookman-Amissah investigated the vocation of the call to the priesthood as it was understood in Ghanaian societies. Several of the interviewees were being trained to become attendants at family shrines, but it was also noted that many had become possessed by spirit sources with which they had no previous contacts—a condition that illustrates access to sacred knowledge as being a privilege bestowed by the spirit world. The critical value of the priesthood profession then is to serve both the spirit and the profane worlds—that is, to mediate between the visible and the invisible domains and to protect society from spirit pollution. It was on this im- portant priestly function that Brookman-Amissah focused.

Brookman-Amissah researched how trainees at the shrine were prepared to communicate with the spirit world. The priests were instructed to become highly disciplined so as to receive clear and accurate prognostications from the gods—the logic being that, the better disciplined and well trained the specialist was, the more reliable would be the diagnosis and treatments. It was not uncommon for persons seeking cures to travel from specialist to specialist in search of the most effective practitioners.[7] Waite says there was a time when all health concerns in the Eastern Bantu environment were brought before a single medicine person; over the cen- turies, however, as social concerns increased, specialization developed. Thus, in Bantu Africa, as in the western regions of sub-Saharan Africa, witch doctors, herbal- ists, and many categories of local priests emerged. These specialists established med- ical traditions that treated sickness and also rendered innocuous the effects of witchcraft and offensive magic.

To cure or prevent misfortune, practitioners suggested, for example, ritual baths prepared from herbal medicine. The burning of herbal incense was another common means of purification for the soul, or for warding off evil spirits. The offering of sacrifices to counter the effects of harmful spirits was a familiar function of the religious specialist. Often, amulets and charms were prescribed as protective or healing agents. Prayerful words and thoughts, which could be short and extemporaneous or formal and long, were essential to the healing process.

☾   ☾   ☾

Such means of warding off the effects of illness were employed by traditional healers. In fact, local practitioners were well established as healers prior to the arrival of Islam in Africa. Muslim holy men therefore competed against these persons. A classic example of such an encounter is evident in al-Bakri's report on the Islamization of the early Malinke kingdom of Malal in the western Sudan (an account of the episode appears in chapter 3). When all local remedies failed to redress the calamitous condition of drought, the ruler of Malal found it necessary to try out a prayerful solution offered by the visiting Muslim holy man. The dramatic effectiveness of the Muslim remedy over that performed by "sorcerers" led to the destruction of palace shrines and to the monarch's house accepting Islam as an alternate religious practice.

Competition between the systems was unavoidable in some circumstances. In several communities, however, the availability of both modes of redressing imbalances was seen by those who sought medicine as offering additional choices. This pluralistic/pragmatic approach was recorded often in the nineteenth-century history of the non-Muslim Asante of West Africa,[8] whose contacts with Islamic culture date back to the mid-eighteenth century. Several Muslim residents of the Asante capital of Kumase produced and distributed Islamic prayers and amulets as protective and curative devices.[9] In fact, Asantehene [King] Osei Tutu Kwame (ruled 1804–23) was said to have shown particular interest in Muslim amulets and prayers; several Muslims at the capital serviced the palace, as was recorded by many European agents who visited Kumase.[10] Both sacrifices and rituals performed by indigenous practitioners and amulets and prayers offered by Muslims were perceived to contribute to Asante national security. Arabic manuscripts collected from nineteenth-century Asante reveal that the Muslims of Kumase possessed esoteric sources from which they made charms thought able to cure leprosy, bed-wetting, smallpox, sexual impotency, and many other diseases common in the region.[11] The specific contents of the manuscripts will be discussed later.

Many seekers of medicine, including the Asante, worked from the premise that the best communication with the spirit world could be achieved through the services of practitioners who were disciplined and well trained; it therefore was considered best neither to depend solely on local practitioners nor to ignore them in favor of Muslim holy men; the object, rather, was to rely on medicine that was perceived to be efficacious. In the case of the Asante royal house, the search for the best medicine was conducted through the office of the Nsumankwaahene—a hereditary, protobureaucratic position occupied by the head priest of the Asantehene. It was an eclectic tradition: the head of the royal priesthood looked at the past records of accomplishment of both local and Muslim medicine. A dramatic display of magical powers by a religious personage—as that at Malal, or a similar, Asante, episode reported in the 1860s—confirmed belief in the efficacy of such an approach.[12]

Such eclectic practice was not limited to nineteenth-century Asante. Trimingham comments on how indigenous religions of East Africa rapidly became inadequate in the nineteenth and twentieth centuries.[13] New diseases demanded new skills. Hartwig identified a number of diseases that spread in the East African hinterlands as commercial contacts with the Swahili coast expanded. Along the long-distance trade routes, epidemics such as smallpox and cholera that had hitherto been common to Indian Ocean communities were introduced. Furthermore, diseases that had been confined to certain interior regions of East Africa were transmitted for the first time to other districts.[14] The frequent devastation caused by old and new diseases resulted in increased accusations being made about sorcery and witchcraft in some East African communities, and the situation lent itself to the eclectic approach. Muslim prayers and amulets were among the most commonly prescribed treatments.

Prayers, Amulets, and Controversy

In discussions about the history of medicine in Egypt and the Arab world, both natural and supernatural procedures are present. In the earlier decades of the eleventh century, for example, Ibn Sina empirically discussed such medical topics as gynecology, cardiac drugs, tuberculosis, and medical plants. In operations for cataract and in castrations of slaves intended as eunuchs, surgery was performed by Muslim specialists. In many rural communities of Africa, circumcision continues to be performed by Muslim specialists. In fact, as Humphrey Fisher observed in his "Islamic healing in Black Africa," there is considerable literature in Arabic manuscripts to demonstrate that Muslim specialists in Africa had knowledge on "vaccination or inoculation against smallpox, the treatment of guinea-worm, dealing with gun wounds, the medical care of horses, and diagnosis and treatment of hemorrhoids."[15] Such information on secular remedies notwithstanding, it is the efficacy of prayers and amulets that immediately comes to mind when the subject of Islamic healing is addressed.

Lewis (1968) and Horton (1974) argued that Islam was accepted in Africa because of the degree of similarity between the African and Islamic cosmologies: both worldviews, they pointed out, recognize the multiplicity of spirits. I have demonstrated elsewhere that this simple resemblance of cosmologies is not sufficient premise to interpret Islamic conversions in Africa.[16] But Lewis's and Horton's explanation for the Islamization of Africa finds a perfect application when it is adopted to explain interests in Muslim prayers and charms as medicine. Indeed, as expressed by Asantehene Osei Tutu Kwame to British consul Joseph Dupuis, the royal interest in Islamic prayers and amulets was based on the conviction that "those objects had come directly from the higher god." In the hierarchical structure of the Akan spirit world, medicine that came from the direct word of the Supreme Being was understood to be more powerful than local ones thought of as originating only from intermediary powers—the lesser gods.[17] In addition to the recognized powers of the "higher god," it has been observed that Muslim literacy was itself seen by the oral societies of Africa to be magical and, therefore, a potential source of healing.[18] The demand for Muslim prayers/amulets as curative and preventive devices, and belief in their efficacy, has thus not been restricted to African Islamic societies.

In this regard it is interesting to note that it has been demonstrated by medical research that a treatment in which both patient and doctor believe can work miracles.[19] Again, we return to the idea of hidden knowledge and detailed training. The holy men who produced prayers and amulets ascribed the efficacy of their medicine to sacred sources, and while aspects of this Muslim perception about the relationship between the sacred and the profane is a legacy from the pre-Islamic *jahiliyya* era, the historian Neil McHugh has pointed to sufficient evidence supporting the observation that Islamic mysticism and the spiritual interpretation of holistic medicine were reenforced in the rise of sufism.[20] Through asceticism, abstinence, meditation, and good works, sufis became closer to God; such proximity to the Supreme Being bestowed beneficent power *(baraka)* that brought blessing to devotees and even onto the communities in which the sufi resided. However, even though Muslim clerics or holy men may not be practicing sufis, it is important to note that they, like the ascetic sufis, have been perceived as having supernatural perception *(batin)*—specialized and hidden knowledge that is acquired from years of training. Similar to the conclusions arrived by Brookman-Amissah in his assessment of indigenous medical practices, Brenner identified the activities that bestowed *baraka* and *batin* on holy men as fundamentally essential to the efficacy of their prayers and amulets.[21]

The specialized and esoteric knowledge of the holy man *(ilm al-batin)*, is quite different from the *zahir* category (including the basic reading and writing of Arabic, the primary study of the Quran and the prophetic hadith), which is carried out in public. As specialized information, *batin* knowledge was protected. For example, Pouwels has observed that Swahili Muslims place so much value on the books from which they derive such materials that often those sources are inherited as patrimony in an artisan family. Since many of the scripts adopted for Muslim spiritual healing are esoteric, and therefore private, the availability of similar documents from early nineteenth-century Asante presents unique opportunities for analysis. And we do have more than nine hundred folios of Arabic manuscripts that were assembled on behalf of Asantehene Osei Tutu Kwame (ruled 1804–23) by Muslim functionaries serving the Kumase palace.

Historians agree that the corpus is part of an Asante military paraphernalia lost in an 1826 expedition against Danes, other Europeans, and their local coastal allies.

Detailed history of the Kumase manuscripts can be found elsewhere.[22] In this chapter, it is sufficient to mention that some of the documents were correspondence exchanged between writers of the manuscripts and their coreligionists in Kumase. Also included are instructions that were solely intended for the making of prayer and amulets to secure magical protection for soldiers on the battlefield, and others (mentioned in the preceding section) that give instructions on the use of amulets to treat smallpox, bed-wetting, sexual impotency, leprosy, headaches, and difficult childbirth. Samples from the corpus are presented below as examples of instructions that were to fill the content of amulets for healing. Because of the poor quality of the manuscripts, as well as the invariable hands in which they were written, literal translation was often impossible. In my paraphrased translation, however, the reader is made aware of the contents and purposes of the amulets.

(a) Instructed amulets to afford easy childbirth conditions:

    1. A special magical seal *(khatim)* was required;

    —write 3 times the prayer "O God! The God of Jibril, Mikha`il and the Prophet Musa and the Prophet Muhammad (Peace be upon them) and of Harun;"

    —write 3 times the incantation "cause it to come out from the mother's stomach 'Musaisa, Musaisa;"

    —it was instructed that the written statements be washed into a solution and given to the expecting mother to drink.[23]

    2. To protect a difficult pregnancy, the Quranic passages (Q. 2:55; 17:111, and 18:1) were to be combined with the ground-up root of a tree.

    —the medicine was to be drunk or inserted.[24]

(b) Instruction for the making of amulets that assured multiple health benefits—guaranteeing great strength, relieving headaches, and increasing favors with women. Described as the talisman of Prophet Muhammad's cousin Ali, the content instructed:

    • write the *du'a* (incantation) "God, He is not a father and He is not a son. There is no power without God. O! You who permits. You are the One. There is no god but Him. The living. You who created the skies and the earth. The infallible."

    —the above was to combined with a *khatim* and made into a talisman.

    —this same prayer, if written 6 times, washed into a solution and mixed with water for bathing, the user will never be harmed.[25]

(c) The series of instructions that guaranteed happy marriages included:

    1. To find a wife and secure marriage,

    —on Wednesday, write Surat al-Yusuf (Q.12). Wash the material that has been written into a solution.

    —on Thursday, before sunrise, wash the previously written material, sit on a stone and wash yourself with it.

    —after washing with it, continue sitting on the stone till sunrise.

    —the result will be prosperity during the year.

—this amulet is also useful in the recovery of lost slaves; and therefore in ensuring the permanency of marriages.

—to make the amulet, write the recommended passages on your right foot, rub some meat on the leg and give it to either the slave or wife to eat. By this process, the amulet is internalized and therefore made effective.[26]

d) Charms constructed to cure smallpox or protect against the spread of diseases counseled the following:

1. For curing *judari* (smallpox), the construction of a seal *khatim* was the sole content suggested;

—the seal was to be washed and solution used to cook food. When eaten, the afflicted would be cure if God willed it.[27]

2. Another *khatim* was instructed as protection against epidemic.

—the prescribed material was to be used for bathing.[28]

This small, but typical, sample of the manuscripts dealing with the making of amulets included, as will be noted, identifiable Quranic chapters and verses, the invocation of certain *asma`*, or names, and *khawatim,* or what are generally referred to as seals or magical squares. As is evident in the above paraphrased translations, it was also typical to instruct that amulet contents be rubbed into objects or be used for soaking, washing, or bathing. It was equally common to find amulets folded, suspended, inserted, or buried at specified locations.[29]

The application of prophetic hadith and Quranic verses as sources for spiritual protection *(ruqya)* is understood by Muslims. In fact, the whole Quran is sometimes seen as a protection for the believer—"We send down, of the Quran, that which is a remedy and mercy to the believer (Q. 17:44)." But here, too, as it was observed in traditional African cosmology, the relationship between the sacred and the profane is underscored. That is, even though the holy book identified itself as only a spiritual remedy to those who believe, it is perceived by Muslims to have the ability to heal physical ailments as well. It is not surprising to find these Quranic verses prescribed for healing. This obvious source notwithstanding, the practice was still a specialized profession. To be sure, Islamic medicine was a religious science that required knowledge in astrology and numerology (especially for the construction of khawatim). By its nature, therefore, the practice involved ritual performances and spiritual retreat *(khalwa).* Sometimes this required several days of fasting and contemplation.

The selection of Quranic verses for amulet making was not arbitrary. The ability to know which chapter or verse, or combination of passages, to use, at what time and for what purpose, required *batin* knowledge. Occasionally, as implied in Cod. Arab. CCCII., vol.2, fo. 49a, knowledge of medical plants was necessary. Examples of the mixing of medical herbs and Arabic texts for healing are reported in the respective writings of Ryan and Pouwels.[30] Thus, the Muslim holy man applied a multiplicity of spiritual sources in preparing amulets and prayers to treat not only physical but also psychological and spiritual ailments.

The efficacy of the prayers and amulets was not in doubt "because the result [was] foreordained by God."[31] The issue of greater theological debate, however, was about the appropriateness for Muslims to rely on these objects. In the *Muqaddima*, Ibn Khaldun called on Muslims to avoid reliance on practices that were characteristically magical. He argued that the use of charms, irrespective of the purpose for which they were applied, corrupted the believer because the created object, rather than God himself, became the focus of adoration. Further, he reasoned that since the Quran attests to limits in human knowledge, it was logical that the educated *batin* scholar could lack clear understanding of things spiritual; thus, makers and users of amulets could go astray. The fifteenth-century North African jurist al-Maghili saw amulet making as a heretical activity that was to be severely punished. His absolute opposition is evidenced in his counseling of Askia Muhammad of the western Sudanese empire of Songhay. The wrongfulness of the practice, Maghili argued, was in the manipulation of the Quran. Even worse was the application of astrology and divination to the art. It was, therefore, the responsibility of Muslim rulers, Askia Muhammad was advised, to put an end to all such practices. Practitioners who disobeyed the royal injunction were to be denied Muslim burial upon death.[32]

In contrast, other scholars looked upon the practice with some favor. Ibn Abi Zayd al-Qayrawani, a tenth-century Maliki jurist, expressed such a position in his *Risala*. To the extent that their medical value was proven, the celebrated fourteenth-century mufti of Tunis, Imam Ibn 'Arafa, was said to have favored the use of amulets. Ibn 'Arafa argued that both unbelievers and menstruating women could wear Quranic passages as talisman as long as the contents were protected from direct contact with their bodies.[33]

Despite controversy on the medical application of amulets, manuscripts from the nineteenth-century Asante and examples of talismans found elsewhere in Africa indicate that Muslim prayers and amulets were in widespread and great demand. Several sources useful to amulet makers are known to have circulated, among them the *Dala'il al-Khayrat* of the fifteenth-century Moroccan scholar Abu 'Abd Allah Muhammad al-Jazuli and treatises on folk medicine and magic by al-Suyuti. A discussion on the favorable conjunctures of the stars and how they influence the efficacy of amulets was explained in *al-Durr al-Manzu' wa Khulasat al-Sirr al-Maktum fi 'Ilm al-Talasam wa'l-Nujum*, which was completed about 1733 by Shaykh Muhammad al-Katsinawi al-Fulani. The *Shumus al-Anwar wa Kunuz al-Asrar al-Kubra* of Ibn al-Hajj al-Tilimsani al-Maghribi returns to a discussion of the exclusive production of prayers and amulets from certain *asma'* and Quranic passages.

Whether their healing objects were constructed from magical squares, Quranic passages, or astrological signs, the practitioners who made them believed in their efficacy, God Willing. The case of the Islamization of Malal was cited above to illustrate that conflict could have resulted from competition between indigenous practitioners and Muslim holy men. History, however, supplies ample evidence to support the view that there was pluralistic application of Islamic prayers and amulets.[34]

Notes

1. Warren 1979, 120–24; Conco 1979, 71–80; Waite 1992; Mbiti 1969.

2. Conco 1979, 74.

3. Feierman 1985, 75–147.

4. Brenner 1984 and forthcoming.

5. Gaba 1973.

6. Brookman-Amissah 1975.

7. Janzen 1978 remains among the best works on pluralism in African therapeutic practices. The flexibility of choice inherent in this pluralistic therapeutic practice also accounts for the African reactions to Western and Islamic cures.

8. Fisher 1973a discusses the issue of "mixing" Islamic practices with traditional African ones. For further discussion on religious eclecticism, see chapter 3 or Levtzion 1968.

9. For a Maliki discussion on Muslim residency among non-Muslim communities in West Africa, see chapter 4.

10. See Bowdich 1819, passim; Dupuis 1824, passim.

11. Levtzion 1965, 99–119.

12. See Owusu-Ansah 1996, 355–35, esp. 358.

13. Trimingham 1964, 120–25.

14. Hartwig 1975, 63–73; Hartwig and Patterson 1978.

15. See Gran 1979, 339–48; Shilosh 1968, 235–48; Fisher 1973b, 23–47. In endnotes 13 through 18, Fisher presents a detailed examination of the cases of inoculations and vaccinations that took place in Muslim societies in West Africa.

16. Owusu-Ansah 1987; Lewis 1968. See also Horton 1971.

17. Dupuis 1824, 161–63.

18. Goody 1968; Hunwick 1976.

19. Frank 1973; Quimby 1972.

20. McHugh 1994, chapter 3; Gran 1979, 343–45; in this volume, see chapter 20.

21. Brenner 1995; Pouwels 1987; McHugh 1994.

22. For the detailed story and analysis of the "Arabic Manuscripts from the Guinea Coast," classified at the Royal Library of Copenhagen as "Cod. Arab. cccii," see Levtzion 1965; see also Kea 1984; Wilks, Levtzion, and Haight 1986.

23. Cod. Arab. cccii, vol. 3, f. 57b.

24. Ibid., vol. 2, f. 49a.

25. Ibid., vol. 2, f. 218a.

26. Ibid., vol. 1, f. 32b.

27. Ibid., f. 20b.

28. Ibid., vol. 3., f. 56b–57a.

29. For further, see Hunter 1977; and Handloff 1982, 185–94.

30. See summary of the Arabic text in the translations identified in endnotes 23 and 24. Scholarly discussions on the subject are in Ryan 1978; and Pouwels 1987, 84–93.

31. Tritton 1972, 128–33. See also the works of Abu Muhammad Ibn Hazm (Hazm 1911/12).

32. Ibn Khaldun 1967, vol. 3, 150–59. For more references to the views of al-Maghili, see Hunwick 1985, 89, 89n, 91n.

33. Zayd 1945, 318; for commentary on the position of Imam ʿArafa, see Nafrawi 1464, 442.

34. Fisher 1973a. For further discussion on religious eclecticism, see chapter 3.

Bibliography

Abdalla, Ismail H. 1997. *Islam, Medicine, and Practitioners in Northern Nigeria.* Lewiston, N.Y.: Mellen.

Bowdich, Thomas. 1819. *Mission from Cape Coast Castle to Ashantee.* London: Cass.

Brenner, Louis. Forthcoming. "Esoteric Paradigm." In *Encyclopedia of African Religions and Philosophy*, ed., V. Y. Mudimbe. Amsterdam: Kluwer Academic Press.

————. 1984. "The 'Esoteric Sciences' in West African Islam." Paper presented at the conference "Changing Role of the ʿUlama." Evanston, Ill.

————. 1995. "Sufism in Africa." Paper presented at the African Studies Association conference, Orlando, Florida, Nov.

Brett, Michael. 1973. *Northern Africa: Islam and Modernization.* London: Cass.

Brookman-Amissah, J. 1975. *The Traditional Education of the Indigenous Priesthood in Ghana.* University of Cape Coast.

Conco, W. Z. 1979. "The African Bantu Traditional Practice of Medicine." In *African Therapeutic Systems,* ed. Z. A. Ademuwagun et al., 71–80. Waltham, Mass.: Crossroads.

Dupuis, Joseph. 1824. *Journal of a Residence in Ashantee.* London: Cass.

Feierman, Stephen. 1985. "Struggle for Control: The Social Roots of Health and Healing in Modern Africa," *African Studies Review* 28:75–147.

Fisher, Humphrey. 1973a. "Conversion Reconsidered: Some Historical Aspects of Religious Conversion in Black Africa," *Africa* 43:27–40.

————. 1973b. "Hassebu: Islamic Healing in Black Africa." In *Northern Africa: Islam and Modernization,* ed. M. Brett, 23–47. London.

Frank, Jerome D. 1973. *Persuasion and Healing: A Comparative Study of Psychotherapy.* Baltimore: Johns Hopkins University Press.

Gaba, C. R. 1973. *Scriptures of an African People: Ritual Utterances of the Anlo.* New York: NOK.

Goody, Jack, ed. 1968. *Literacy in Traditional Societies.* Cambridge: Cambridge University Press.

Gran, Peter. 1979. "Medical Pluralism in Arab and Egyptian History: An Overview of Class Structures and Philosophies of the Main Phases," *Social Science and Medicine* 13B:339–48.

Handloff, Robert. 1982. "Prayer, Amulets, and Charms: Health and Social Control," *African Studies Review* 25:185–94.

Hartwig, Gerald. 1975. "Economic Consequences of Long-Distance Trade in East Africa: The Disease Factor," *African Studies Review* 18:63–73.

Hartwig, Gerald, and K. David Patterson, eds. 1978. *Disease in African History: An Introductory Survey and Case Studies.* Durham, N.C.: Duke University Press.

Hazm, Abu Muhammad Ibn. 1911/12. *Kitab al-Fisal fi'l Milal.* 5 vols. Cairo: n.p.

Hodgson, Marshall G. S. 1974. *The Venture of Islam: Conscience and History in a World Civilization.* vol. 1. Chicago: University of Chicago Press.

Horton, Robin. 1971. "African Conversion," *Africa* 41:85–108.

Hunter, Thomas. 1977. "Development of Islamic Tradition of Learning among the Jahanke of West Africa." Ph.D. diss., University of Chicago.

Hunwick, John O. 1985. *Shari'a in Songhay: The Replies of al-Maghili to the Questions of Askia al-Hajj Muhammad.* London: Oxford University Press.

———. 1976. *Islam in Africa: Friend or Foe.* Accra: University of Ghana.

Ibn Khaldun. 1967. *The Muqaddimah: An Introduction to History.* Trans Franz Rosenthal, vol. 3. Princeton: Princeton University Press.

Janzen, John M. 1978. *The Quest for Therapy in Lower Zaire.* Berkeley: University of California Press.

Kea, Ray. 1984. "A Note on Muslim Visitors at Christianborg (Gold Coast) in the Early Nineteenth Century." Paper read at the Islam in Africa conference: "The Changing Role of the 'ulama.'" Evanston, Ill.

Kjekshus, Helge. 1965. *Ecology Control and Economic Development in East African History.* Berkeley: University of California Press.

Levtzion, Nehemia. 1965. "Arabic Manuscripts from Early Nineteenth Century Kumase," *Transactions of the Historical Society of Ghana* 8:99–119.

———. 1968. *Muslim Chiefs and Clerics in West Africa.* London: Oxford University Press.

Lewis, I. M., ed.. 1968. *Islam in Tropical Africa.* London: Oxford University Press.

Mbiti, John S. 1969. *African Religions and Philosophy.* New York: Praeger.

McHugh, Neil. 1994. *Holymen of the Blue Nile.* Evanston, Ill.: Northwestern University Press.

al-Nafrawi, Ahmed b. Ghunaym. 1464. *Al-Fawakih ad-Dawani Sharh 'ala Risalat ibn Abi Zayd al-Qayrawani.* Cairo: n.p.

Owusu-Ansah, David. 1987. "Islamization Reconsidered: An Examination of Asante Responses to Muslim Influence in the Nineteenth Century," *Asian and African Studies* 21:145–63.

———. 1991. *Islamic Talismanic Tradition in Nineteenth Century Asante.* Lewiston, N.Y.: Mellen.

———. 1996. "The Asante Nkramo Imamate: Conflicting Traditions." In *The Cloth of Many Colored Silks: Papers on History and Society, Ghanaian and Islamic, in Honor of Ivor Wilks,* ed. John Hunwick and Nancy Lawler, 355–65. Evanston, Ill.: Northwestern University Press.

Pouwels, Randall L. 1987. *Horn and Crescent: Cultural Change and Traditional Islam on the East African Coast (800–1900).* Cambridge: Cambridge University Press.

Quimby, Lucy. 1972. "The Psychology of Magic among the Dyula." Paper presented at the Manding studies conference at the School of Oriental and African Studies, London.

Ryan, Patrick. 1978. *Imale: Yoruba Participation in Muslim Tradition: A Study of Classical Piety.* Missoula, Mont.: Scholars.

Shilosh, Ailon. 1968. "The Interaction between the Middle Eastern and Western Systems of Medicine," *Social Science and Medicine* 2:235–48.

Trimingham, J. S. 1964. *Islam in East Africa.* Oxford: Clarendon Press.

Tritton, A. S. 1972. "The Healing Art and the Limits of Change in Nature According to Ibn Hazm," *Bulletin of the School of Oriental and African Studies* 35:128–33.

Waite, Gloria. 1992. *A History of Traditional Medicine and Health Care in Pre-colonial East-central Africa.* Lewiston, N.Y.: Mellen.

Warren, Dennis M. 1979. "Bono Traditional Healers." In *African Therapeutic Systems,* ed. Z. A. Ademuwagun et al. Waltham, Mass.: Crossroads.

Wilks, Ivor, Nehemia Levtzion, and Bruce Haight. 1986. *Chronicles from Gonja: A Tradition of West African Muslim Historiography.* Cambridge: Cambridge University Press.

Zayd, Ibn Abi. 1945. *Risala,* ed. and trans. L. Bercher. Alger: Cabonel.

CHAPTER 22

Islamic Art and Material Culture in Africa

René A. Bravmann

To look at the arts and material culture of Islamic Africa is to engage a particularly vital frontier, one marked by the blending of belief and the artistic imagination. Africa is a long-ignored portion of Islamic civilization, a religious culture that has helped shape much of Africa and its creativity. Islamicists, however, have rarely been inclined to consider Africa (except for the heavily Arabized northern fringe of the continent): it has always been regarded as too provincial, too far removed from the heartland of Islam with its sophisticated metropolitan centers, imperial courts, and famed seats of learning. Located at the extreme edge of this civilization and conditioned by apparently different historical and cultural forces, Africa's monuments and creativity, typically marginalized or ignored, remain an eternal other—they exist but go unnoticed and unattended.

That this continues to be the case can be seen in the spate of volumes and exhibition catalogs that have appeared since the mid-1970s, a period marked by a general resurgence of Western interest in things Islamic. Such works fail to reveal Africa's contributions. Museums have been anxious to exhibit their Islamic holdings, and yet only the *Heritage of Islam* (along with a modest companion installation organized by David Heathcote and devoted to the arts and material culture of the Hausa of northern Nigeria), a highly successful international exhibition seen by large audiences both in Europe and the United States, touched upon Africa's wider artistic role within the Islamic world.[1]

How, one must ask, has this come to pass? After all, Islam in Africa is nearly as old as the faith itself and has, over the past millennium and more, come to influence much of the continent north of the equatorial forest and east of the great Rift Valley. Even regions normally regarded by African Muslims themselves as *dar al-harb*, lands of unbelief, have often proved to be fertile soil for Muslims and their faith. For example, in this volume see the revealing chapter on South Africa (chapter 15); or see the many writings of Ivor Wilks and others based upon European and Arabic sources, that describe the vital links binding Muslims and non-Muslims in nineteenth-century Asante.[2] That Islam has had a decided influence upon formal developments in architecture, weaving traditions, sculpture, and the decorative arts is now patently obvious, for everywhere one sees a blending of the message and requirements of the faith with local beliefs, values, and sensibilities. The resultant mix—never fixed; always in a state of dynamic adjustment and flux—tells us that Africa and Islam have surely made something of each other that is quite extraordinary, if only we care to look.

If the process of Islamization on the continent has in fact been so resonant, if it has resulted in such noteworthy achievements, why have they not been included in a wider vision of the Islamic phenomenon? Why not consider the diversity of mind and sensibility encountered in Hausaland or the Swahili coast in surveys of the Islamic world? Why do Islamicists persist in locating the cultural center of gravity of this religious civilization the way they have, thereby excluding vast portions of Muslim Africa? Karin Adahl, an art historian of Islam, begins to address precisely such questions in a recent essay but falls prey to many of the attitudes of her predecessors. For Adahl, much of Africa has not been considered by her colleagues because there are neither the necessary number of monographs nor the "comprehensive documentation of artifacts" that might allow for a history of the arts and material culture.[3] She is, of course, correct on this point, for much remains to be done. Adahl then goes on to submit, with unusual academic candor, that the arts of Islamic Africa, except for those of the Maghreb and Egypt that fully conform to classic Islamic canons, have been ignored simply because they lack "a certain quality." This is apparently due to the fact that in much of Muslim Africa "there is no court art, no major production centres for ceramics, carpets or manuscripts."[4] For Adahl, Islamic art and architecture, the high monuments and art forms of this civilization—the products of sophisticated metropolitan workshops that flourished over a period of centuries "in the central Islamic world, i.e., from Spain to India, from Turkey to Egypt"—are qualitatively different from that found in Africa. The perfection of form for Adahl, achieved in the arts of "glass, metalwork, woodwork, ivory, textiles, carpets, book-making, and painting" by Muslim artists in the heartlands of Islam, is simply not to be found in Africa. There Muslim creativity has been of another order, a pale and distant reflection of high Islamic culture and the home of only "simple and mostly second rate items."[5]

Adahl's essay serves as the introduction to *Islamic Art and Culture in Sub-Saharan Africa,* a volume published in 1995, edited by Adahl and her colleague Berit Sahlstrom and based upon papers delivered at an international conference hosted by Uppsala in 1992.[6] The thrust of this gathering was to explore Africa's contribution to Islamic civilization; it included participants from the disciplines of archeology, cultural anthropology, art and architectural history, and aesthetics. Adahl was one of the conveners of the conference and a founding member of the Uppsala Research Group for African and Islamic art. A specialist in Islamic art, with particular expertise in the Khamsa of Nizami and the broader topic of orientalism, she has more recently developed an interest in the subject of African Islam based upon a residency in Libya and travels in West Africa.

Adahl's introductory essay is an attempt to define what is Islamic in the arts and material culture of Muslim Africa and how this relates to creativity in the wider Muslim world—a daunting task, especially for someone with a traditional grounding in the arts of Islam, and one who is a relative newcomer to the subject of Islam in Africa. The resulting work shows that Adahl, while sympathetic, is never quite sure how to define the arts of the continent, for she is never really able to shed her centrist notions of what constitutes Islamic art, never really able to escape her training and intellectual perspective. The creative tension between Islam and African societies and the very process of Islamization itself are not addressed, although a number of the contributions in the volume touch upon this vital theme. In the end, Adahl would have done well to hearken to the words of Clifford Geertz, who so brilliantly explored the development of the faith in Morocco and Indonesia in *Islam Observed* many years ago. Why, Geertz asks, are Morocco and Indonesia so different despite being influenced by a single creed? What is it about Islam and local cultures, about the blending of so called "Great" and "Little" traditions, that results in such contrasting Islamic civilizations? For Geertz the process of Islamization is crucial, as is true in this volume, and it must be examined in a sensitively balanced manner. His words resonate for anyone attempting to understand the nature and character of African Islam:

> In both societies [Moroccan and Indonesian], despite the radical differences in the actual historical course and ultimate (that is contemporary) outcome of their religious development, Islamization has been a two-sided process. On the one hand, it has consisted of an effort to adapt a universal, in theory standardized and essentially unchangeable, and unusually well-integrated system of ritual and belief to the realities of local, even individual, moral and metaphysical perception. On the other, it has consisted of a struggle to maintain, in the face of this adaptive flexibility, the identity of Islam not just as religion in general but as the particular directives communicated by God to mankind through the preemptory prophecies of Muhammad.[7]

If Adahl had heeded Geertz's words it might have helped to decenter her narrative and allowed her to pursue her goal of trying to define "what is Islamic" about the arts of Muslim Africa in a more satisfying manner.

If Islamicists continue to ignore Africa, it is also true, as John Picton noted in his illuminating contribution to the Uppsala conference, that Africanists interested in the arts and material culture of the continent often fail "to reveal the presence of Islam."[8] While Picton's chapter "Islam, Artifact and Identity in South-western Nigeria" is important in many respects here, I simply want to touch upon some of his thoughts regarding Yoruba identity and Islam. The Yoruba present us with a particularly poignant case of not revealing Islam, for this culture and its artistry have been the subject of intense scrutiny since the late-colonial period. The scholarly literature on the Yoruba is vast, surely the largest for any African society, and includes some of the most discerning studies we have from the continent. Yoruba have themselves contributed impressively to this bibliography, especially in the field of aesthetics, where fluency in the language and a sensitivity to the expressive modes and nuances of culture have been critical. Trailblazing examinations of the relationship of art to society and especially of the religious, social, and political dimensions of Yoruba creativity appear almost annually and continue to probe the subtle links between art, music, dance, oratory, and drama that mark this civilization.

What we know about Yoruba artists and their careers is impressive; in fact, at the time this chapter was being written, people in New York were viewing the exhibition "Master Hand: Individuality and Creativity among Yoruba Sculptors" at the Metropolitan Museum of Art—the result of nearly two generations of critical inquiry beginning with the work of Father Kevin Carroll and more recently undertaken by Abiodun, Drewal, and Pemberton.[9] This was not a typical exhibition of objects by anonymous African craftsmen but rather a close examination of the works and lives of thirty influential Yoruba artists, a curatorial feat that is simply not possible for any other African culture.

Picton challenges our very assumptions about what we have come to call Yoruba, and demonstrates just how crucial the Fulani jihads of the nineteenth century were in the fashioning of Yoruba identity and consciousness. Islam began rather modestly among the Yoruba in the 1840s, but its influence grew dramatically, especially in western and northern Yorubaland, so that by the end of the colonial period, nearly 50 percent of the population regarded themselves as believers. That Islam has become an important part of Yoruba life in this century should be self-evident, and yet, as Picton notes, the substantial literature on this culture and its artistry remains curiously silent on the subject.[10]

What we do learn emerges from almost parenthetical observations: that Lamidi Fakeye and Yesefu Ejigboye, two well-known Yoruba sculptors, are practicing Muslims; that Oyo leatherworking derives much of its inspiration and vigor from Muslim Nupe and Hausa models; that Ifa divination, so crucial to Yoruba religious and social life, shares many features with Muslim Yoruba divining techniques and practices. Such snippets of information are, of course, intriguing, but they do not begin to challenge seriously our old and outdated notions of a pristine and monolithic Yoruba society. We urgently need cultural studies that seriously consider the Islamic factor in Yorubaland, as was done over twenty years ago by the historian Gbadamosi in his important book *The Growth of Islam among the Yoruba, 1848–1908*.[11] To continue to ignore this crucial aspect of Yoruba history and identity will never allow us to measure the fullness of the culture's social and artistic imagination. I would like to submit, in accord with Picton's admonition, that we will never truly grasp what has taken place in Yorubaland, or engage the history in and of the arts over the last century and a half, until we begin to address the impact of Islam upon Yoruba society.

Although it is a rather glaring example, Yorubaland is simply one instance of our unwillingness to take into account the influence of Islam. It happens elsewhere, and because so many Africanists (art historians, anthropologists, and so on) continue to "fail to reveal" the Islamic presence, it skews and often distorts our very vision of African creativity. The western Sudan, specifically the area included within the modern-day Republic of Mali—a region long subject to the process of Islamization—presents us with a number of such cases of neglect. Dogon art and culture, for example, long hailed as exemplars of traditional Sudanic civilization and a people ever vigilant to the potential encroachment of Islam, cannot be fully understood or appreciated without considering the impact of Muslim mystical texts like the *Kabbe,* written early in this century by the Fulani cleric and scholar Cerno Bokar of Bandiagara and apparently utilized in Dogon rituals today.[12]

Songhay spirit possession *(ghimbala),* so prevalent throughout the inland Niger Delta of eastern Mali, can ultimately make sense only if we acknowledge how it was reshaped during the nineteenth century by the Muslim reformer Shaykh Amadu of Masina. Ghimbala today, according to Gibbal, is the result of extraordinary accommodations, a blending of Quranic and Songhay invocations, of ritual acts said to be prescribed by the Quran and sanctioned by the ancient spirits that have always inhabited this Songhay-dominated portion of the Niger River.[13] Possession ceremonies today still follow an ancient calendric cycle, but out of deference to Muslim sensibilities, especially those shaped by the fundamentalist strain of Islam that has emerged in recent years in Mali, they are no longer held during the month of Ramadan. Such fusion and blending of tradition and Islam is perhaps best expressed by one of Sarah Brett-Smith's Bamana informants, the sculptor-blacksmith Kojugu: "We cite the owners of the Qur'an (i.e. Muslims) and the owners of the Qur'an cite us. All these things are mixed up together (i.e. all the beliefs current in the Mande world, both Islamic and traditional are interdependent)."[14] In Brett-Smith's stellar volume *The Making of Bamana Sculpture,* one is never far removed from the presence of Islam; it is always there lurking in the shadows of this monumental study, but, as she asserts in her introduction, given the thrust of the work it is a dimension that will have to "be left to others to investigate."[15]

Having said this, let me temper these comments by noting that important contributions on the arts and material culture of Islam, the result of impressive fieldwork and penetrating analysis, have begun to appear in the last two decades. These contributions are indeed rich, as well as full of promise for future research.[16] They tell us that Trimingham's bleak evaluations of the impact of Islam on African creativity, found in his pioneering work from the late-colonial period, need to be seriously reexamined. For Trimingham, the process of Islamization was inimical to African artistry and material culture because it could and would not tolerate their intimate connection to traditional values and beliefs. Conversion to Islam, it was his contention, invariably resulted in the rooting out of animist symbols, and when these were displaced "there [was] no aesthetic need to be satisfied which might be diverted to other artistic concerns."[17] In addition, the strong aniconic stance of the faith was considered a certain death knell for African visual and symbolic systems.

☾   ☾   ☾

Although it is still too early to write a comprehensive history of the arts and material culture of African Islam, given the large gaps in our knowledge, what can be demonstrated at this time is that the faith has forged a special and enduring relationship with its followers and that the arts of this vast area of Africa belong fully within the Islamic orbit. They serve as a vital testament to the remarkable diversity of mind and sensibility found within Islamic civilization, and they are, for me, among its most unique and enduring expressions. Never merely passive recipients of Islam, African members of the community of believers (the *umma*) shaped the religion whenever and wherever necessary to fit local needs and circumstances. Making something of each other, a synthesis developed that has proven to be rich and enduring. For the purposes of this chapter, I want to focus upon certain themes that strike me as particularly apposite in any attempt to begin to comprehend the artistry and character of African Islam. The discerning reader will notice that many of these themes are precisely those identified by scholars when more broadly discussing the arts and monuments within Islamic civilization.

I want to begin with the Word—the ways in which Allah's message, as embodied in the Quran, enriches and lends meaning to life itself. A passion for the words of God is evident everywhere in Muslim Africa so that, as Geertz noted in his study of Moroccan Islam, "the most mundane subjects seem set in a sacred frame."[18] These sounds and phrases of Allah lend a special tonality to existence; they create for the believer a potent acoustic quality to God's omnipresence, and they ultimately lie at the very heart of Muslim artistry. As I have noted elsewhere:

> The faithful not only feel and hear Allah's presence about them, they can actually see and touch it, for African Muslims transform the words of God, this passion for His sound, into clear and immutable shapes. African aesthetic sensibility merges everywhere with the literary and graphic potential of Islam, bringing a particular stability and form to God's words. African Islam . . . calls upon the skills of its scribes and scholars, as well as the cunning of its artists, to make visible God's presence in this world.[19]

To paint or weave God's words is to create from the deepest of sources, to produce works whose coercive power and affective beauty are undeniable.

One encounters numerous examples of these transformations of the words of Allah, the language of the Quran, on the African continent. Here I will consider a few of them. The first is a woven mat of natural and dyed grasses, an especially fine

Fig. 1. Woven into this Swahili prayer mat (mswala) *from northern Tanzania are references to Allah and to Muhammad the Chosen Prophet "Muhammadi Muhutari Nabiya." Tanzania National Museum Collection.*

product of Muslim Swahili plaiting, that is located in the Tanzania National Museum collection (fig. 1). Most likely made within the last two generations, it is a splendid example of a much older tradition of prayer mats documented by the German ethnographer Franz Stuhlmann at the turn of the nineteenth century.[20] Woven in the village of Moa, near the important coastal town of Tanga in northern Tanzania, it exhibits all the love for geometric pattern generally found in Swahili prayer mats, known as *mswala*. What distinguishes this mswala, and several examples collected near Moa by Stuhlmann for the Hamburgischen Kolonialinstitut nearly a century ago, is that the rhythms of geometry are framed and banded by God's words. Somehow, the artist managed to weave into this "place of prayer" (the literal meaning of the word *mswala*) Swahili verse rendered in Arabic characters. The script occurs within five narrow bands that run virtually the full length of the mat and in another band just inside its border. These strips are separated by woven bands consisting of geometric patterns; all is then edge-sewn to produce the mat. The bands of script are punctuated at regular intervals by the stirring invocation "In the name of God," known as the *bismillah*, while Allah's praise-name *Karamallah*, or "God the beneficent," occurs at several points throughout. A single reference to Muhammad the chosen prophet is to be found in the very center of the mat. The verses themselves are difficult to decipher for, according to Seyed Muhammad Maulana, a colleague from Mombasa, Kenya, they appear to be executed in a very localized script. What one cannot fail to appreciate, however, is that the weaver from Moa, using the humblest of materials, literally wove his passion for God and the prophet into a "place of prayer."[21]

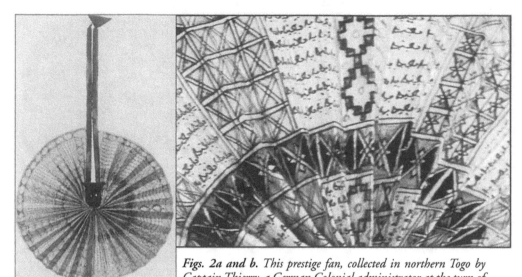

Figs. 2a and b. *This prestige fan, collected in northern Togo by Captain Thierry, a German Colonial administrator at the turn of the century, includes numerous references to one of Allah's 99 names, Ya Hafiz—"Oh Protector" or "Oh Guardian"—along its outer edge. Field Museum of Natural History. #104.941.*

Calligraphy is one of the great art forms of Islam, the visual equivalent to Quranic chanting, and some of the most dramatic examples of this tradition come from the African continent. An unusual piece in the collection of the Field Museum of Natural History in Chicago demonstrates that African Muslim artists are masters at presenting their passion for the word of God. A prestige fan, possibly of Hausa origin, is full of references to one of the ninety-nine excellent names of God, the *Asma al-Husna,* found in the Quran (fig. 2). Collected by Captain Thierry (a German colonial administrator stationed at the important trading town of Sansanne Mango in northern Togo) and acquired by the Field Museum in 1905, it is a calligraphic tour de force. Along the outer edge of the paper fan appears God's praise-name Ya Hafiz, meaning "Oh Protector," or "Oh Guardian," while the inner band includes the phrase "May God protect and preserve."[22] The fan, to be held by someone of high rank (it reminds me of a paper shield covered with calligraphic inscriptions held by the Asantehene Opoku Ware at his installation ceremony in Kumase in 1970) dramatically displays God's shielding presence.

☾ ☾ ☾

That God's sounds and words are indeed ubiquitous, that they are incapable of being confined and therefore may be heard and seen in the most remarkable places, is revealed in a striking Goboi masquerade costume located in the University of Pennsylvania Museum and collected in the Mende chiefdom of Bumpe in the

Fig. 3. (right) A Goboi masquerader photographed by William Hommel among the Mende of Kenema District, Sierra Leone in 1973. A collection of small wooden tablets with arabic inscriptions is visible in the hamper worn on the back of this Goboi.

Fig. 4. (below) Fifty-four miniature Quranic tablets with Arabic script are located in the hamper of a Goboi costume collected in the Mende Chiefdom of Bumpe sometime during the 1920s. University Museum, University of Pennsylvania.

1920s. Goboi masqueraders perform at virtually all functions of the Poro Society, the male secret organization so important to Mende culture. Goboi are entertainers of a high order and their striking costumes combine an abundance of raffia fiber, blue-and-white striped cotton cloth, cuts of red, black, and white homespun, mirrors, cowry shells, goatskin, and animal hair. In and of themselves, these are scintillating masked figures that cannot fail to please. But what ultimately fascinates the eye are the hampers, worn on the dancers' backs, which often contain bundles of miniature Quranic tablets with what appears to be Arabic script painted upon them. Such a Goboi was photographed in performance by William Hommel while in Mende country in 1973 (fig. 3). The hamper attached to the Goboi costume in the Pennsylvania museum collection is particularly well endowed with tablets—fifty-six to be exact—each of which has been painted with the dramatic proclamation Ya Allah (Oh God!) (fig. 4). This Goboi, from Mende country, an area of Sierra Leone still only lightly touched by Islam, reveals that even when traditional values and artistry remain vital, one can enter a world where Allah and African creativity meet and mingle.[23]

God's words are not only rendered visibly but they exist as well in a very different domain—that ineluctable environment of silence and secrecy within which amulets or talismans are conceived (see chapter 21). Quranic talismans have always been an important aspect of African Muslim life, a fact confirmed by nearly all visitors to the continent and by some of the extraordinary terra-cotta sculptures from the area of Jenne in Mali (dated from the eleventh to fourteenth centuries) that depict figures wearing leather-enclosed charms. The range of talismans created by Muslims in Africa is extraordinary: their shapes and the materials employed stagger the imagination; yet all amulets are alike in that they contain concealed truths. Whether written on paper and covered with carefully worked and dyed leather, or encased in copper or silver boxes, or held in a liquid suspension kept in a vial or carved bottle, like the Somali quluc, amulets are nearly always shielded from the public eye and kept within a culture's shadows. The owner of an amulet is the keeper of potent knowledge that is based upon carefully arranged and organized secrets, and thus is someone who possesses a particular treasure that cannot be known or shared by anyone else.

African Islamic charms, regardless of their outward form or intended purpose, appear to be composed of two parts—a written portion and a design or graphic element. Edmond Doutté, in his classic volume *Magie et Religion dans l'Afrique du Nord,* refers to these two elements as the *da'wa,* or spell, and the *jadwal,* or picture.[24] Some amulets include only a dawa; others have only a jadwal, with little or no writing; but many are glorious and creative works that combine the strengths of both elements. The da'wa may derive from a number of Islamic sources, including the Quran (surely the single most important reference), astrological treatises and divination manuals, or books on numerology; the jadwal may be based upon magical squares, images of the planets and their movements, or an impressive variety of geometric configurations. Famous makers of talismans devote years to perfecting their craft, for they must not only be well grounded in *zahir* (the study of the Quran, the commentaries upon the holy book, and exegesis), but they also need to pursue the study of *batin*, the inner and mystical aspects of the faith. Batin studies is a vast realm, one that cannot be fully encompassed by even the most dedicated individual, but those that persist are said to come to an understanding of not only the many forces at play in the world but of the hidden faces of God.

Since chapter 21 is almost wholly devoted to the topic of amulets, I want to confine my discussion to one example, a talisman that dramatically reveals what can happen in the continual interaction between Muslim and non-Muslim life in Africa. This particular amulet is found on the inner face of a mask, which in itself is a sculptural statement of inscrutable and mysterious forces, and therefore we are presented with an image that may be said to blend one secret with another. This Poro society mask (fig. 5), acquired in 1926 (and, like the Goboi costume, in the museum at the University of Pennsylvania), is attributed to the Toma of the Republic of Guinea. Poro masks, and there are many of them, are manifestations of the spiritual forces that guide this brotherhood and serve as guardians of its deepest secrets. This example combines a human face with the powerful beak of the hornbill; it thus instantly directs the mind to complex and barely understood notions of transformation. This could well have been the mask of a senior official of the Poro society, but we cannot be sure. What is certain, however, is that the face of the mask suggests powerful forces, and that inside the mask, on its inner surface, are drawn many squares that contain magical letters and numbers and a cryptic reference to chapter 3 of the Quran entitled "Palm Fiber." This short chapter is also known as the sura of Abu Lahab (the father of flame) and speaks of one of Muhammad's uncles, the only member of his own clan who opposed the prophet.[25] Sura III is an angry invective hurled specifically at Abu Lahab and his wife: it is also known as the cursing sura, and is generally voiced at moments of betrayal and treachery. This is fitting, for whatever else is expected of this Poro society mask, it surely must stand as an obdurate sentinel ever ready to defend this secret organization and its members against treason from within.

☾ ☾ ☾

A passion for the word of God and the ardent desire for talismans merges most dramatically in a specific period of African Islamic history, the nineteenth century jihads that occurred across the continent from Senegal to the Red Sea. The nineteenth century is filled with the names of Muslim leaders, religious reformers and militant nationalists who sought to purify and reinvigorate Islam and stem the tides of European encroachment. Among the former, surely the most famous was the Fulani social reformer and mystic 'Uthman dan Fodio, whose holy war against the Hausa states was permanently to change the political face and tenor of Islamic life in northern Nigeria. Of the militant resistors, the careers of al-Hajj 'Umar, the Mahdi, Muhammad Ahmad, and Muhammad 'Abdallah Hassan are remarkable for their

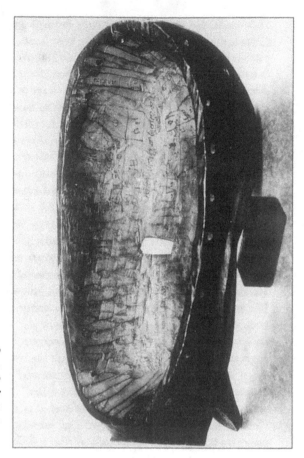

Fig. 5. *The inner surface of a Poro mask with powerful magical squares, letters, numbers, and a reference to chapter 3 of the Quran known as the Cursing Sura, or the Sura of Abu Lahab. University Museum, University of Pennsylvania. #Af 5373.*

unbending resistance to European force and their efforts to establish new political realms based upon Islamic principles. All of them fought against their oppressors and carried out a sacred religious obligation, by wielding the "sword of truth" and by waging battle "in the way of God."[26] To look at the swords, military banners, and other items associated with such campaigns allows us entry into the very nature of jihad, a duty sanctioned by the Quran and used by the Prophet himself in his attempt to spread the boundaries of nascent Islam. These objects are full of the very spirit and reality of holy war, for they include sacred words, cabalistic signs, and elaborate talismans that testify to the ever-present and guiding spirit of Allah.

One of the most protracted and bitter of the nineteenth-century jihads was the resistance movement, the Mahdiyya, waged between 1881 and 1895 by the Sudanese spiritual leader Muhammad Ahmad, the self-proclaimed Mahdi, or Messiah, against the combined might of British and Egyptian forces. The Mahdiyya had been active for nearly fifteen years when its leader died on 22 June 1895, nearly six months after the fall of Khartoum to the Mahdi's forces and the death of General Gordon. This crushing defeat had a profound effect upon Queen Victoria and the British Parliament and led to new and even more ferocious encounters between the British and the Mahdists. Khalipha ʿAbdullahi, the Mahdi's successor, bore the full fury of British revenge, and in decisive battles at Atbara and Omdurman, Anglo-Egyptian forces under Herbert Horatio Kitchener routed the khalipha's armies. By late 1899, the calipha himself was mortally wounded at the battle of Om-Dubraikat, shattering the final hopes of a Mahdist state and making the Anglo-Egyptian Sudan a colonial reality. In the full flush of victory, British troops returned home with a veritable cache of booty taken from their fallen victims. The sheer quantity of war trophies taken back to England was an impressive testament to the epic dimensions of the war waged against the Mahdists.

Among the spoils of war acquired by the British was a large, wooden slit drum, carved in the shape of a bullock, captured by Kitchener from the khalipha at the battle of Omdurma (fig. 6). The drum was presented to Queen Victoria by Kitchener, who was rewarded with a peerage for his role as commander at Omdurman and for ultimately crushing the Mahdist movement. The drum has been in the British Museum since 1937, a gift from King George V.[27] While such drums have long been associated with important traditional chiefs and leaders in the southern Sudan and adjacent portions of the Central African Republic, they are generally much smaller and devoid of surface decoration. The calipha's drum is not only monumental, perhaps testifying to his exalted status as the successor to the Mahdi, but it has been heightened sculpturally to fit within a militant Islamic context: "Mathematically precise floral patterns, a fretted crescent, meander (designs) and a single reference to a long-bladed scimitar are carved in broad bands across the flank

Fig. 6. Wooden slit drum captured from the Khalifa at the battle of Omdurman in the Anglo-Egyptian Sudan and presented to Queen Victoria by Lord Kitchener, commander at Omdurman. The Trustees of the British Museum, 1937. 11–8.1.

surfaces, their geometric regularity and precision reminiscent of ancient Islamic shapes expressing God's unity and presence."[28] Emblazoned with Muslim patterns, the booming sounds of this massively sculpted drum must have surely encouraged the khalipha's followers in battle.

That this jihad was waged with prayers, weapons, and a passionate belief in the holiness of their cause can be seen in the armor of faith that protected the Mahdi's soldiers confronting the might of the British Empire. A particularly fine sketch of the fervor and passion of holy war are the words written by Sir Charles Wilson, who described the courage of one of the Mahdi's commanders killed in the fierce battle near the wells of Abu Tlaih:

> I saw a fine old shaikh on horseback plant his banner in the center of the square, behind the camels. He was at once shot down falling on his banner. He turned out to be Musa, Amir of Daigham Arabs, from Kurdufan. I had noticed him in the advance, with his banner in one hand and a book of prayers in the other, and never saw anything finer. The old man never swerved to the right or left, and never ceased chanting his prayers until he had planted his banner in our square. If any man deserved a place in the Moslem paradise he did.[29]

Chanted prayers shielded the faithful, as did the many cotton banners and flags carried by mounted warriors that were filled with appliquéed exhortations regarding man's sacred military duty. One such flag, cited by Picton and Mack, contains the following message in Arabic: " Oh God, the Compassionate, the Merciful, the Living, the Eternal, the Almighty. There is no god but God and Muhammad is the Messenger of God. Muhammad al-Mahdi is the successor of the Messenger of God."[30] It is a message that would have elevated the spirits of the Mahdi's troops, a flag imbued with special amuletic properties and expressing the sacredness of holy war.

Of the many objects captured from the Mahdist troops, or taken in the wake of other jihadi movements, the vast majority demonstrate this desire for the presence of God. Soldiers and cavalrymen went to battle dressed in robes, quilted clothing, and protective headgear studded with amulets containing God's words. Chain mail, primarily of sixteenth- and seventeenth-century Mamluk Egyptian workmanship and used in the Fulani jihads in northern Nigeria, was often enhanced by micrographically engraved individual links with references to Allah and the Prophet. Swords, the supreme Muslim fighting weapon, were invariably inscribed with Allah's name and his blessings, while shorter, axe-like, branched weapons for close hand-to-hand combat (faintly echoing the longer and more elegant shapes of traditional throwing knives from the regions of Wadai and Dar Fur) had blades completely covered with etched Arabic script in a style known as Thuluth. On many of the battle axes, readable script is replaced by pure arabesques, calligraphic shapes that are neither Arabic consonants nor vowels, but even in such examples the intent is obvious and dramatic. The incessant quality of such unreadable etching reveals yet another level of communication, the ardent desire of the craftsman to capture the grace and flow of God's language thereby affording the weapon and its owner Allah's shielding presence and protection.

☾ ☾ ☾

A particularly rich arena for exploring the relationship of Islam to Africa and for examining the artistic results of this blending lies within the realm of Muslim festivals. Muslim holy days are impressive ritual events in which meaning is both created and released, and because they are often complex, unfolding over time, they have a rhythm and life of their own that can be contemplated and examined. To look even briefly at such festivals is to engage the remarkable diversity of mind and practice found within African Islam, to witness public demonstrations of communal belief and vivid enactments of religious sentiment. Festivals, by their very nature, enable the viewer to confront the full force of culture and artistry at work, to appreciate how they shape and focus the religious and expressive needs of believers. To look ever so briefly at Ramadan, the obligatory month of the fast, in two African communities—the Juula of Bobo-Dioulasso in Burkina Faso and the Gnawa of Marrakesh, Morocco—should demonstrate how this important religious obligation has been shaped by local values and sensibilities.[31]

For the Juula and Gnawa, the great fast of Ramadan is truly arduous, the daylight hours testing the believers resolve and devoted to reflection and self-examination. Fasting is crucial, indeed it is one of the five pillars of the faith, and its rigors are readily visible in both communities. Juula neighborhoods, normally distinguished by their intense commercial activity, are remarkably muted places during the daylight hours of Ramadan, while the Gnawa, nearly always a vital part of the J'Ma el Fnaa of Marrakesh, conspicuously absent themselves from the social heart of the city. Attendance at mosques increases dramatically and people spend much of their time reading large portions of the Quran and listening to the words of teachers and religious elders. Juula and Gnawa seek to observe the fast faithfully, for to follow God's directives during this month is said to be much more beneficial than at other times in the year.

The nights of Ramadan bring a release from the demands of the fast, and the Juula and Gnawa follow those words of the Quran that serve as a guide for nighttime behavior: "Eat and drink, until the white thread shows clearly to you from the black thread at dawn."[32] Entertainment and feasting are a very conspicuous feature of night life at Ramadan, but among the Juula and Gnawa, these nights, and especially those toward the end of the fast and the succeeding month, are highlighted by an unusual degree of creativity. In Bobo-Dioulasso, on any given evening, Juula children between the ages of six and fifteen perform dodo, a masquerade that includes stock animal and human characters and is wholly orchestrated and directed by the older children. Masks and costumes are created from pieces of tattered cloth, scraps of cardboard, discarded gourds, indeed whatever can be salvaged from the

Fig. 7. *Members of a dodo troupe in the final stages of preparation for their Ramadan performance. Photograph taken by the author in Bobo-Dioulasso, Burkina Faso in October 1972.*

world around them, and the results are a pure celebration of the artistry and ingenuity of childhood (fig. 7). A chorus of youthful voices, accompanied by drum rhythms rendered on old tin cans, sing songs appropriate to each of the masked characters. Children in Berrima and other Marrakshi neighborhoods where the Gnawa are concentrated also regale their elders with song and musical compositions, knowing full well that their efforts will be rewarded, for the nights of Ramadan call for people to demonstrate their generosity.

In each community, the eve of the twenty-seventh of Ramadan, known as the Lailat al-kadr, or the Night of Power, is especially important, for it was on this night that Allah first revealed the Quran to the Prophet Muhammad.[33] The unique character and magic of this night is explicitly stated in chapter 97 of the Quran, and both the Juula and Gnawa believe that evil spirits, or jinn, that have been bound by God's angels since the onset of Ramadan, are now even more fully secured, allowing the good angels and the spirit of God to descend into the world. Gnawa courtyards are carefully swept and washed, and special incense is burned in their corners to attract God's shielding presence. Gnawa homes require special protection at this time, for at the end of Ramadan the jinn will again be released to the world of the living, to their human hosts, and will need to be placated anew through nightlong possession ceremonies *(derdeba)*. Juula demonstrate their joy at Lailat al-Qadr with spectacular dances in which members from each of the Juula lineages perform. Unmarried girls, dressed in white waistcloths and covered with gold and silver jewelry, are led by a single dancer clad only in briefs and strands of colorful waist beads. Each of the leaders' bodies is covered with beautifully patterned designs painted with a mixture of rice flour and water, and each carries upon her head a set of stacked brass or imported enamel basins, from six to eight basins tall, that contain medicines and cowries and are tied in a string net. Drumming and dancing continue until just before dawn—an elegant display of that special Juula sensibility for parading their joy and closeness to God.

☾ ☾ ☾

Muslim Africa is also home to a fascinating tradition of popular prints devoted to religious subjects such as Muhammad's heroic battle at Badr, pilgrims on the hajj, a saint's tomb, and a generalized rendering of the Mosque of the Dome of the Rock. Printing houses in Egypt, Algeria, and Tunisia have spawned something of a minor industry, for these colorful prints are mass produced and affordable. They can be found for sale in markets and shops throughout much of West Africa and seen occupying an honored place on a sitting room wall in Muslim homes. Of all the subjects treated, surely the most popular is the one of al-Buraq, Muhammad's winged

Fig. 8. This print of al-Buraq was collected in Ghana in the late 1940s. Within the border surrounding the print is the first verse of sura 17 known as the Night Journey. In the rectangular box above the wings is the praise "al-Buraq, the Noble and Sympathetic Friend." Hearst Museum of Anthropology, Berkeley.

horse, which is said to have carried the Prophet on his mystical night journey *(isra)* from Mecca to Jerusalem and then on his nocturnal ascent *(mi'raj)* to the Dome of the Seven Heavens. A particularly fine example, most likely printed in Algeria, was collected in Ghana in the 1940s (fig. 8). The principal colors of this print are deep reds and plum, and they are particularly rich. The work is also more finely detailed than more recent examples and is more generously endowed with religious inscriptions: the first verse of sura 17, known as the Israelite, or the night journey, appears within the border of the print; references to Muhammad, Allah and al-Buraq are located in various medallions and around the saddle blanket; al-Buraq is extolled once again: "Praised be he who carried his servant (to) the distant mosque."[34]

Not only is the print of al-Buraq particularly popular in much of West Africa, but it also seems to have served as a visual catalyst for the many renditions of the winged steed currently being created by Muslim textile artists and scribes. Depictions of al-Buraq, often handled in a highly stylized manner, occur in numerous amulets from Sierra Leone, where they are elaborated with portions of Islamic verse. Left unfolded and placed above entryways, such charms are said to be particularly effective sentinels against evil forces, especially *tasalima*, or witches. Within the shimmering iridescence of Yoruba indigo tie-dyed cloths *(adire)*, a common theme is the crowned and winged al-Buraq with peacock tail-feathers, depicted as if on its mystical journey through a dark-blue night sky. The image of al-Buraq has even been absorbed into the contemporary world of advertising, for Nigerians can now sleep peacefully under "the blanket of your dreams," made of blended viscose by Mantex Manufacturing of Kano, and known commercially as Flying Horse Blankets.[35] The registered logo of this covering is a small image of al-Buraq in flight, although in this instance, the female-headed steed is openly smiling at the viewer; it may well suggest the sweetness of commercial success (fig. 9).

Images like those of al-Buraq are certainly fascinating, for they reveal the iconic potential tapped by Muslim artists in Africa. There is yet another face to Muslim creativity, however, that is much more common and visible—an artistry that conspicuously avoids representation in favor of a passionate pursuit of abstract shapes, a love of geometric patterns, sumptuous colors and exquisite textures. To look at such objects is to confront a world of humble items—cushions, robes, textiles, baskets, and jewelry—the things that we in the West classify as the "minor arts." In the hands of Muslim artists, however, these things are so consummately worked, so thoroughly ennobled, that they cannot fail to claim our attention.

A preference for beautifying the surface of objects with pure design has always marked the arts of Islam, has always been the dominant expressive mode of Muslim cultures, for religious dogma and theological opinion have consistently rejected the use of imagery as a valid avenue for the artistic imagination. That this orthodox authority could be ignored can be seen in artistry and monuments from much of the Islamic world, yet such proscriptions did have a decided effect for they fostered a particular outlook, a cast of mind and sensibility, that was to encourage the special delight for surface decoration and design that has come to exemplify the arts of Islam.

In any African Muslim community one quickly observes this particular aesthetic predilection. Humble objects—stools, ceramic containers, cushions, gowns, and hats—are all intensely personal items, but they are created and elaborated in such ways as to grace the lives of their owners. Surface patterns that initially appear to have been spontaneously created are in fact carefully planned and executed, sharing a level of refinement and formality found in the people themselves. Take for example a richly embroidered full-length man's gown *(riga)* from Kano, Nigeria, in the collection of the Metropolitan Museum of Art (fig. 10). This voluminous Hausa garment is made of white cotton enhanced with embroidered panels of natural silk, yet the embroidery is so subtle and intricate that to appreciate its beauty fully requires concentrated attention. The selection of a creamy silk for the embroidery of this white cloth suggests the desire for a subtle garment where modulation of texture and color is achieved through an eyelet-stitch technique that results in a denser surface and a slightly deeper cream tone. This type of *riga*, rather than the bolder and more colorful garments commonly found in local markets, is the kind of gown favored by Hausa men for important religious and social occasions.[36]

A particularly fine example of the combination of the sculptor's innate sensitivity to material with the organizing possibilities and patterns of geometry may be witnessed in a Dogon stool from the Republic of Mali (fig. 11). Among the Dogon, highly figured stools are invariably associated with men of substance, elders and

Fig. 9. *The registered logo for Flying Horse Blankets produced by Mantex Manufacturing in Kano, Nigeria with the image of a smiling al-Buraq in flight.*

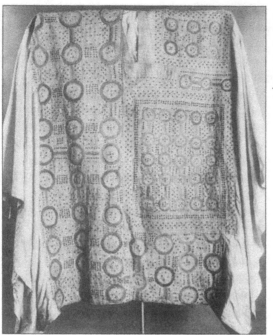

Fig. 10. A lavishly embroidered Hausa man's gown (riga). Eyelet stitching enhances the richness of the embroidery and dramatically reveals the chest panel containing a square of five circles across and five down. Metropolitan Museum of Art, #31979.206.279.

Fig. 11. This Dogon stool is influenced by the patterns and geometric precision of Islamic design. Its seat and the sides of the stool have been pierced and cut through to allow for the play of light upon the chevron, interlace and five square patterns. American Museum of Natural History. #90.2.3539.

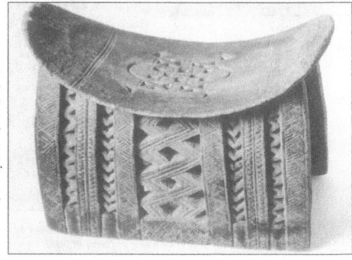

leaders known as *hogons*, who guide the life of village communities. Such stools have a round seat supported by generously sculpted caryatid figures that rest upon a circular base, and they are marvels of concentrated artistry. Regarded as objects of prestige, they are not sat upon but maintained as sculpted signs of authority, vested in living leaders by lineage ancestors from the past. This Dogon stool, however, is different in every conceivable way—its overall shape, its obvious evidence of use, and in the fact that it eschews the traditional Dogon love for intense sculptural figuration in favor of surface carving and embellishment that is both intricate and subtle. The example is wholly influenced by the patterns and geometric precision of Islam, for the seat itself and the sides of the stool have been generously pierced, allowing for the play of light upon the chevron, triangular, interlace and five-square patterns that dominate this graceful object. In this Dogon stool, the sculptor has reshaped form into delightfully complex Muslim patterns and configurations.

To spend time in an African Muslim community is to become acutely aware that one has entered a very distinct environment, one that is qualitatively different from a traditional or Christian setting. There are, of course, the obvious differences, certain sights and sounds that are immediately recognizable as Islamic: the mosque, the manner of dress, and the call to prayer that punctuate daily life. Another feature that impresses itself almost as quickly upon the visitor is the very private nature of family life, a factor that has inspired styles of Muslim domestic architecture found everywhere on the continent. Such architecture is remarkably consistent, especially in urban settings, as it is oriented not toward the outside world, but toward a set of interior spaces and courtyards within which life is conducted. Houses consist of solid and thick walls, and in Timbuktu and other towns along the Niger Bend, for example, one encounters single- and double-storied rectangular mud-brick homes with fortress-like walls that are buttressed at regular intervals. What impresses the viewer are these unrelenting slabs of mud brick that shut out the world and hide the life contained within them. Only an occasional wooden door, often embossed and studded with finely forged geometric iron shapes and knockers, announces the presence of a home. Such doors, and a few small openings at the second-story level filled with shuttered and grilled windows, are all that relieve the monotony of these mud walls and allow light and sound to penetrate.

Nothing illustrates the special character of Muslim domestic architecture quite as dramatically as Swahili towns on the east coast of Africa. These towns, born out of the interchange between coastal peoples with Muslim Arab, Persian, and, later in history, Indian or Malabar merchants, have a distinctive style, radiating a special character that is the result of a felicitous blending of Islam and African elements over the last ten centuries.[37] The Swahili were and are primarily townspeople, although never exclusively so, and it is only within the urban setting that one can truly appreciate the full flowering of Swahili civilization. The urban and urbane are in fact inseparable from the very definition of being Swahili, for as James de Vere Allen tells us, the Swahili themselves stress that culture can flourish only in towns, and is indeed the "prerogative of townsmen." To the Swahili, "culture is interpreted as a social patina, a way of life and knowledge of how to behave that can only be learned, indeed can only be practiced, by those living in towns."[38] The most visible expression of Swahili identity and culture is surely its stone houses, enhanced with coral-rag and stucco plasterwork and richly carved doors, created with a sense of style and a desire for privacy that is stunning.

Stone houses have been a feature of this coastal civilization since at least the thirteenth century, attesting to the prosperity enjoyed by various Swahili communities stretching from Mogadishu in Somalia to the southern coast of Tanzania. These homes, so utterly different from the wattle-and-daub mud houses of non-Swahili neighbors, dominate the townscapes of the coast and have always been an index of the heightened status enjoyed by their occupants. Grandly conceived, and constructed out of permanent materials, such houses (often two-storied) effectively wall off prosperous Swahili families from commoners and encourage a lifestyle imbued with a special urban elegance.[39] Public spaces and guest rooms are always located just inside the entrance of such homes, while more private spaces are situated beyond the generous courtyard and toward the back of the house. Special attention has always been paid to the rooms of the harem, insuring their seclusion from the courtyard, and creating a space for the women that is sumptuously decorated. Whole walls of the harem consist of elegantly carved and plastered niches that contain everything from imported glassware to exotic ceramics and brass items. Two-story houses enable the wealthiest Swahili families to accommodate housing for a suitable number of servants, while still ensuring the family a sufficient degree of privacy. In their grandeur and spaciousness Swahili stone houses have been not only perfectly designed for daily living but also to accommodate the most important of social events—births, marriages, and even the funerals of family members all within the confines of its shielding walls.

Having begun this excursion into the artistry and character of belief with a discussion of the importance of individual prayer and the believer's passion for the words of God, it seems only fitting to conclude with a look at Muslims praying together at the mosque, surely the most important religious institution and building within Islam. The word for mosque is *masjid*, and in Arabic it simply means "a place of prostration" before God. Thus a patch of ground covered by a mat, such as the marvelous Swahili mswala described earlier, fully qualifies as a masjid so long as the believer using it inclines himself before God with a pure heart. Indeed this mswala (the word literally means "a place of prayer") captures the very essence of the word as it appears in the Quran, for nowhere in this book of revelations does the word *masjid* specifically refer to a religious structure but simply to any place where God is worshipped. Anyone who has traveled among Muslims in Africa quickly realizes that a masjid may be the humblest of religious precincts. In rural Côte d'Ivoire, it was, and perhaps still is, not uncommon to find places of prayer whose perimeters were carefully marked with a group of stones or by inverted green bottles wedged into the ground. What was critical, as is the case with even the grandest mosques, was that each place of prayer be carefully aligned toward Mecca.

The root meaning of the word *masjid* immediately alerts us to other aspects of Muslim worship that need to be appreciated. Islam, among all the universalistic religions of the world, distinguishes itself by its structural and formal simplicity:

> There is no priesthood, no bewildering incantation, no solemn music, no curtained mysteries, no garments for sacred wear contrasted with those of the street and marketplace. All proceeds within a congregational unison in which the imam, or leader, does no more than occupy the space before the niche and set the time for the sequence of movements in which all participate.[40]

A Muslim service is remarkably direct, its flow utterly different from the intensely ceremonial liturgies found in most other great religious traditions. Prayer within Islam is essentially a solitary act, except for the Friday noon service, when Muslims congregate at the main mosque of their community, the *masjid al-jami,* or Friday mosque, to pray together and hear a sermon delivered by the imam or other notable. Although this is usually a short service, lasting less than an hour, what impresses the observer most forcibly is the sense of religious solidarity forged by the prayers, bowings, and homily. People are well dressed, most often in sparkling white clothing, and they form a chromatic community that sways, bends from side to side, and gracefully prostrates itself to the sounds of prayers and chanting. All the worshippers face the Mihrab niche, face east toward Mecca with a common purpose, a shared heart and mind, and this unity forged within the walls of the masjid al-jami is unforgettable.

Mosques in Africa, whether modest neighborhood buildings or impressive *masjid al-jami,* are all fundamentally places of prostration, religious spaces within which believers converse intimately with God. The mosque as a built environment is religious architecture that fully honors the ancient definition of the word *masjid,* a place dedicated to those who incline themselves before Allah. As such, a mosque does not require large processional spaces; it does not need to set aside room for a choir, or elevate portions of its interior for a hierarchy of religious officials. Its architectural requirements are remarkably minimal, a fact about the mosque that has been noted by Kenneth Cragg:

> It is essentially an essay in religious space: by definition it is a place for prostration. Hence the carpets (or more commonly in Africa, finely woven mats) and the unencumbered expanses of area, whether domed or pillared. The niche, or *mihrab*, is not a sanctuary. It is merely a mark of direction, a sign of the radius of the circle of which Mecca is the center. Calligraphy, or script, and color, are the only decoration. . . . The mosque, it might be said, is the architectural service and counterpart of a devotion consistent with Islam.[41]

Decorative elements are kept to a minimum: the *mihrab* may be elaborated with glazed tiling or intricate stucco patterns; glass or brass lamps illumine the niche and the wide, rather than deep, areas reserved for worship; columns may be topped by exquisitely carved capitals as is the case in the main prayer hall of the mosque at Qayrawan in Tunisia but this is rather exceptional. The *minbar* or pulpit, placed to the right of the *mihrab* and found in all Friday mosques, can be impressive examples of Islamic woodworking and marquetry (the ivory inlaid *minbar* built for the late-fifteenth-century Mamluk Sultan Qaitbay and now in the Victoria and Albert Museum in London is particularly splendid) but are typically little more than a raised platform of stone or mud-brick.[42] Mosque interiors are an exercise in artistic restraint and discretion for anything that might distract the worshippers attention and concentration is conspicuously avoided.

Mosques do nonetheless, physically dominate any African Muslim community, as they do everywhere in the Islamic world, and they are the most visible sign of the strength of commitment to the faith. While it is still premature to contemplate an in-depth history of African mosques, the antiquity of this architectural form and some of the broad stylistic developments associated with this building can be reconstructed from archaeological evidence and descriptive accounts by early Muslim and later European travelers. For East Africa (see chapter 12 for a discussion of the early Islamic presence on the Swahili coast), archeological investigations by Mark Horton at Shanga and Chittick at Kilwa strongly confirm that mosques were being erected at the very beginnings of Muslim settlement.[43]

In Shanga, the earliest evidence of a mosque, a simple tent-like structure, has been dated by Horton to the late eighth century. As the community grew in size and strength, this rudimentary mosque was reworked (indeed, twenty-five times, according to Horton) until finally abandoned in the early fifteenth century.[44] Building materials varied dramatically over time, from humble mud and mangrove beams to cut coral-and-lime plaster, suggesting not only a continual fluctuation in the fortunes of this early Swahili settlement but also how the members of Shanga constantly reinterpreted their most important religious structure. Horton's data from Shanga are critical, for they not only present us with a dynamic history of the shaping and reshaping of this particular community mosque, but suggest a basic developmental sequence that might well apply to mosques from much of the Swahili coast.

Mosques also appear to have been constructed in the oldest Muslim communities in West Africa—creations of North African merchants involved in the trans-Saharan trade. Recent archeological work in southern Mauritania, in what is presumed to have been the Muslim sector of the town of Kumbi Saleh, capital of the empire of Ghana, have unearthed the tenth-century foundations of a stone mosque. According to Devisse and Diallo, this early mosque was enlarged in the following century and enhanced by tile work, with distinctive Islamic decorative motifs and Arabic script.[45]

By the early fourteenth century, mosques built on a grand scale and in a dis-

Fig. 12. A typical Mande mosque constructed of mudbrick and, in this instance, surfaced with a thin concrete wash. Photograph taken by the author in the Wala community of Nakore in northwestern Ghana, November 1967.

tinctive Sudanese style (perhaps inspired by the Andalusian architect and poet al-Tuwayjin) were built within the empire of Mali at Gao, Timbuktu, and Jenne. This famous architect accompanied Mansa Musa on his trip home from the hajj in 1324 and is said to have worked extensively for the great ruler. According to Ibn Khaldun, al-Tuwayjin was apparently responsible for the construction of Mansa Musa's domed palace, a wonderful structure whose walls were decorated with arabesques in the most dazzling colors. His patron, delighted with the results, rewarded him with gold dust valued at twelve thousand mithkal for this work.[46]

Although we will probably never be able to attribute the so-called Sudanese style to a single architectural genius like al-Tuwayjin with any degree of certainty, what can be said with confidence is that this distinctive mosque type was surely the product of talented Manding builders residing within the medieval empire of Mali.[47]

Building with the humblest of materials, sun-dried mud bricks mixed with straw, these early Manding masons and their successors created some of the most remarkable sculptural and architectural examples of mosque architecture found anywhere in the Muslim world (fig.12). Constructed like fortresses, with battlemented walls and towers bristling with spikes, these mosques with gently sloping minarets have walls and buttresses pierced with projecting beams that serve as permanent scaffolding and help relieve their overall massiveness and horizontality. The interiors of such mosques present a different aspect, one of closeness and intimacy, for they are dominated by thick piers that support the roof, resulting in narrow aisles where congregants must place their prayer mats. Wherever the Muslim Manding settled, this mud-brick mosque architecture reappeared, a feature of their dispersion as distinctive as the language they speak. Mande mosques, like the other examples presented in this chapter, are vivid reminders that Islam and Africans have made something of each that is enduring—a testament to the artistry and character of belief.

Notes

1. See Heathcote 1977. This catalog includes a broad selection of Hausa artistry, ranging from leatherwork and gourd decoration to the arts of calligraphy and weaving. A modest catalog, it remains our basic source for the arts of this important culture.

2. See especially Wilks's monumental study of the Asante state (Wilks 1975). For the influence of Islam upon Asante regalia, see Bravmann and Silverman 1987.

3. Adahl 1995.

4. Ibid., 10.

5. Ibid., 17.

6. I want to thank Professors Karin Adahl and Berit Sahlstrom and the Research Group for African and Islamic art at Uppsala University for the opportunity to present my paper "Islamic Spirits and African Artistry in Trans-Saharan Perspective" to a discerning audience. This conference allowed me to share some preliminary thoughts on Sudanic aesthetic elements in Black Moroccan creativity and the artistic interface between North Africa, the Sahara, and Sudan.

7. Geertz 1971, 14–15.

8. Picton 1995.

9. Abiodun, Drewal, and Pemberton 1994.

10. Picton 1995, 87–89.

11. Gbadamosi 1978.

12. Brenner 1984. Brenner's biography of this Fulani cleric is a model study that thoroughly traces the spiritual path followed by Cerno Bokar.

13. Gibbal 1994, esp. chapter 8.

14. Brett-Smith 1994, 21.

15. Ibid., 20.

16. These include a number of eye-opening publications by Labelle Prussin on various aspects of African Islamic architecture and design, especially her 1986 volume. Mark's sensitive analysis of Muslim elements found in Cassamance masking and initiation ceremonies is discussed in Mark 1992. Our knowledge of Akan metalworking has been enlarged by Silverman's (1983) careful examination of North African metal basins and their impact upon the Akan. Lamp 1996 provides a thoughtful study of Baga cultural and artistic life in the face of Muslim reformist movements in contemporary Guinea.

17. Trimingham, 1959.

18. Geertz 1976, 1494.

19. Bravmann 1983, 19.

20. Stuhlmann 1910.

21. Bravmann 1983, 20.

22. Ibid., 25.

23. Ibid., 29.

24. Doutte 1908, 150–51.

25. Bravmann 1983, 44.

26. These phrases have been borrowed from Hiskett 1973, esp. chapter 6.

27. Information regarding the gifting of this drum to the British Museum was kindly supplied by Nigel Barley.

28. Bravmann 1995.

29. Samkange 1971, 410.

30. Picton and Mack 1979, 171.

31. The Gnawa of Marrakesh are descendants of Sudanese slaves and form a small but rather distinct community within Marrakesh. They are known as master healers of people struck by or possessed by the jinn, and their possession ceremonies *(derdeba)* are a marvelous blending of Sudanic expressive modes with elements derived from North African sufism.

32. Arberry 1955, sura 2, verse 183, p. 53.

33. Bravmann 1983, 68.

34. I want to acknowledge my debt to Diana de Treville for bringing this print of al-Buraq to my attention and for making available to me her translation (June 8, 1974) of its inscriptions.

35. I am indebted to John Lavers for the advertising label of this whimsical example of al-Buraq.

36. A fuller discussion of this handsome riga can be found in Bravmann 1983, chapter 6.

37. Middleton 1992 provides a superb study of this complex and sophisticated civilization.

38. Allen 1974, 134.

39. Middleton 1992, 63–68.

40. Cragg 1974, 56.

41. Ibid., 59.

42. Contadini 1995.

43. Horton 1996; Chittick 1974.

44. Horton 1996, chapters 9 and 10.

45. Devisse and Diallo 1993, 103 ff.

46. Ibn Khaldun, *Kitab al-'Ibar*, in Levtzion and Hopkins 1981, 335.

47. Prussin 1986, esp. chapter 6.

Bibliography

Abiodun, R., H. Drewel, and J. Pemberton. 1994. *The Yoruba Artist.* Washington, D.C.: Smithsonian Institution.

Adahl, K. 1995. "Islamic Art in Sub-Saharan Africa: Towards a Definition." In Adahl and Sahlstrom 1995.

Adahl, K., and B. Sahlstrom. 1995. *Islamic Art and Culture in Sub-Saharan Africa.* Uppsala: Acta Universitatsis.

Allen, J. de Vere. 1974. "Swahili Culture Reconsidered," *Azania* 9:105–38.

Arberry, A. J. 1955. *The Koran Interpreted.* New York: Macmillan.

Bravmann, R. A. 1983. *African Islam.* Washington, D.C.: Smithsonian Institution.

———. 1995. "Slit Drum." In Phillips 1995, 133.

Bravmann, R. A., and R. A. Silverman. 1987. "Painted Incantations: The Closeness of Allah and Kings in 19th-Century Asante." In *The Golden Stool: Center and Periphery*, ed. E. Schildkrout. New York: American Museum of Natural History.

Brenner, L. 1984. *West African Sufi*. Berkeley: Univerisity of California Press.

Brett-Smith, S. C. 1994. *The Making of Bamana Sculpture*. New York: Cambridge Univeristy Press.

Chittick, H. N. 1974. *Kilwa, an Islamic Trading City on the East African Coast*. Nairobi: British Institution in Eastern Africa.

Contadini, A. 1995. "Minbar for the Sultan Qa'itbay." In Phillips 1995, 595.

Cragg, K. 1974. *The House of Islam*. Belmont: Dickenson.

Devisse, J., ed. 1993. *Valles du Niger*. Paris: Editions de la Reunion des Musecs Nationaux.

Devisse, J., and B. Diallo. 1993. "Le Seuil de Wagadu." In *Vallées du Niger*, ed. J. Devisse. Paris.

Doutte, E. 1908. *Magie et Religion dans l'Afrique du Nord*. Algiers: A. Jourdan.

Gbadamosi, T. G. O. 1978. *The Growth of Islam among the Yoruba*. London: Longman.

Geertz, C. 1971. *Islam Observed*. Chicago: University of Chicago Press.

———. 1976. "Art as a Cultural System." In *Modern Language Notes*, 91:1474–99

Gibbal, J. M. 1994. *Genii of the River Niger*. Chicago: University of Chicago Press.

Heathcote, D. 1977. *The Arts of the Hausa*. London: Commonwealth Institute.

Horton, M. 1996. *Shanga, the Archaeology of a Muslim Trading Community on the Coast of East Africa*. London: Cambridge University Press.

Hiskett, M. 1973. *The Sword of Truth*. New York: Oxford University Press.

Josephy Jr., A. M., ed. 1971. *The Horizon History of Africa*. New York: American Heritage.

Lamp, F. 1996. *The Art of the Baga: A Drama of Cultural Reinvention*. New York: Museum for African Art.

Levtzion, Nehemia, and J. F. P. Hopkins, eds. 1981. *Corpus of Early Arabic Sources for West African History*. Trans. J. F. P. Hopkins. Cambridge: Cambridge University Press.

Mark, P. 1992. *The Wild Bull and the Sacred Forest*. Cambridge: Cambridge University Press.

Middleton, J. 1992. *The World of the Swahili*. New Haven: Yale University Press.

Phillips, T., ed. 1995. *Africa: The Art of a Continent*, 133 and 595. London: Royal Academy of Arts.

Picton, J. 1995. "Islam, Artifact, and Identity in South-western Nigeria." In *Islamic Art and Culture in Sub-Saharan Africa*, ed. K. Adahl and B. Sahlstrom. Uppsala.

Picton, J., and J. Mack. 1979. *African Textiles*. London: British Museums.

Prussin, L. 1986. *Hatumere: Islamic Design in West Africa*. Berkeley: University of California Press.

Samkange, S. 1971. "Wars of Resistance," In *The Horizon History of Africa*, ed. A. M. Josephy Jr.

Silverman, R. A. 1983. "Akan Kuduo: Form and Function." In Akan *Transformations: Problems in Ghanaian Art History*, ed. D. Ross and T. Garrard. Los Angeles: Museum of Cultural History.

Stuhlmann, F. 1910. *Handwerk und Industries in Ostafrika*. Hamburg: L. Friederichsen and Co.

Trimingham, J. S. 1959. *Islam in West Africa*. Oxford: Claredon Press.

Wilks, I. 1975. *Asante in the Nineteenth Century*. London: Cambridge University Press.

CHAPTER 23

Islamic Literature in Africa

Kenneth W. Harrow

What is "Islamic literature"? In this literary overview we seek to locate Muslim identities in actors whose awareness of themselves, as purveyors or critics of the faith, is reflected in their words as well as their acts. For the literary critic, this is reflected in the texts' participation in a discourse that identifies itself as Islamic.

Of necessity, the meaning of "Islam" here, or of a "Muslim discourse," is best seen in terms that are relative to the text as well as the culture. Islamic literature arose from the intersection between culture, discourse, text, and reader; that is, as relative to particular texts as well as to particular readers, and to the ways in which language has been used to construct related texts and ideas.

However the discourse on "Islam" is constructed, what any study of its literature in Africa demonstrates quite simply is the multivalent nature of what is meant when the term *Islam* is employed. Despite the common understanding of the term, it varies considerably with time, place, and text—sharing all the generic diversity of African culture, as well as particular idiosyncrasies of individual authors.

The history of Islamic writing in Africa might be conceived as that thought whose development was directly linked to Arab civilizations—that is, the Middle East and North Africa—as well as that which developed at a greater distance from the Islamic heartland and that therefore was more marked by syncretism or "foreign" incursions. The frequent privileging of the former rests upon a vision that might be termed Arabocentric, in which the "pure" tradition of Islam is seen to have unfolded within the core of Arab civilizations, in contrast to that of the "impure" ways of *al-mukhlit,* the "mixers" whose sub-Saharan traditions marked the processes of naturalization of Islam in Africa. In Africa, as elsewhere, the tension between the path of purity and that of mixing continues to inform the debates over the development of Islamic literature. However, on close inspection, one soon perceives that the processes deemed syncretic, the mixing deplored by the purists, have characterized the development of Islamic thought in general throughout history. The pejorative characterizations of Africanized forms of Islam might be deemed the result of prejudice.

Sub-Saharan Chronicles, Epics, and Oral Traditions

The ties between North African Islam and sub-Saharan Africa were multiple. The traders and religious leaders of the Maghrib carried Islam and Islamic thought across the desert into sub-Saharan Africa, especially from the eleventh century on. With the ascendancy of Musa as ruler of the Mande empire of Mali in the fourteenth century, Islam came to enjoy great prominence. The accounts dealing with the rise of Songhay in the fifteenth century and its powerful rulers—their reigns and great deeds, and their fall—are to be found in the major literary forms of the sixteenth and seventeenth centuries, including both oral epics and written chronicles.

Two of the principal sources of our knowledge about this period are the Arabic-language chronicles known as the *Ta'rikh el-Fettach*, or "The history of the researchers,"[1] and the *Ta'rikh es-Sudan*, or "The history of the blacks,"[2] written by Abderrahman es-Sa'di (1596–1655), a religious leader and political figure in the administration of Timbuktu. These two extensive works describe the Sudanic kingdoms from the point of view of the educated Muslim scribe. The written tradition of Arabic chroniclers and historians like Ibn Battuta is continued in the *Ta'rikh es-Sudan*, which is considered by historians to be the best account of the Songhay empire and the Moroccan protectorate that followed. However, the narratives of oral historians and praise-singers, known generally in West Africa as *griots*, also influenced the scribes, as we can see in the focus upon the genealogy of the Sonni dynasty and in the recounting of their origins and heroic accomplishments.

African epics such as *Sundiata, Askia Mohammed*,[3] and the *Ta'rikhs* were all marked by their deference to the supremacy of Islamic traditions. In addition to the written historical account of the rise and fall of the great Sudanic empire of Songhay that is provided in the *Ta'rikh es-Sudan*, there also exists an oral account of the dynasty of Askia Mohammed, *The Epic of Askia Mohammed*, that has survived for almost five hundred years. It celebrates the reign of the second great ruler of Songhay, Askia Mohammed, who supplanted the dynasty of his successor, Sonni 'Ali Ber (also known as Sonni 'Ali in the *Ta'rikh es-Sudan*).

It is often the case that when one ruler supplants another, the legitimizing account of the usurpation forms the basis of a dynastic epic. Such is the case here, where Askia Muhammad is portrayed as the legitimate and rightful ruler, despite his having to overcome his uncle, the king, as well as other cousins, to assume his role. Like Sundiata, he is oppressed at birth, and must prove his worth and establish his suzerainty by eliminating other pretenders. The epic echoes the historical facts in which Sonni 'Ali Ber died mysteriously on his return from a war. According to Thomas Hale, the transcriber of Nouhou Malio's 1981 recitation of the epic, Askia Muhammad then challenged Sonni 'Ali Ber's son to embrace Islam more fervently, and when the son refused, Askia Muhammad attacked and took over as ruler of the Songhay empire. Historical fact and epic account meet in the broad outlines of the events that followed: Askia Muhammad went on a pilgrimage to Mecca, and on his return undertook to expand his rule through a series of military expeditions that were justified in the name of the expansion of Islam.

Although Islam was not to be broadly accepted in the Sahel for many years, in oral and written texts Islam provided the principle of legitimizing rule on religious grounds, and of spreading the rule through jihad. Most of all, Muslim traditions and scholarship permitted the construction of epics and chronicles that elevated a dynasty to a regal stature. In *The Epic of Askia Mohammad*, one finds much evidence of traditional Soninke formulations and beliefs, as seen in the presence of sorcerers termed *sohanci*, in the powers of hunters, and especially in the social formulations that continued to define the world of the epical hero. The resulting epic is textured with layers of belief and discourse that reflect not only the original historical setting but the changes brought to the Songhay community in the years that followed.

☾ ☾ ☾

No African epic has received more attention than *Sundiata*.[4] Multiple versions of the epic have been recorded and transcribed, the two best-known being D. T. Niane's (1965) freer adaptation of Mamadou Kouyaté's version, and John Johnson's transcription of Fa-Digi Sosoko's recitation.[5] In all of the versions, the most striking episodes in the narration are grounded in a Malinke religious tradition that appears to be at a remove from Islamic beliefs. This is apparent in the role played by Sundiata's mother, Sogolon, the "buffalo woman" of Do. The tale of her conquest by two hunters is informed by magical events and practices that appertain to Malinke traditional beliefs. The Malinke dual hunting deity, Kondolon Ni Sané, whom Niane describes as guardians of the bush and forest, would seem to be the model for the two hunters who kill the totem buffalo whose spirit is transformed into Sogolon.

In terms of the epic's overall structure, Sundiata's relationship with his mother governs the first half of the narrative, and it is not until her death that he is able to begin his return from exile, leading to his conquests and ascension to greatness. However, even before Sundiata or Sogolon appear as characters in the epic, we are presented with a characteristic mixture of Islamic and non-Islamic Malinke elements. Thus, Kondolon Ni Sané (the dual hunting god) is mentioned first not in Sogolon's story but in the recitation of Sundiata's genealogy on his father's side. Although the male line is traced back to one of Muhammad's companions, Bilali, "faithful servant of the Prophet Muhammad," it is also one of those paternal ancestors, Mamadi Kané, who is called a "hunter king" and is "loved by Kondolon Ni Sané."[6] The descendants of Mamadi Kané are honored by the title of Simbon (hunter), and through that same paternal lineage Sundiata earns the honorific Son of the Lion. As grace, power, and stature are joined in the person of Sundiata, so, too, are brought together the Malinke and Islamic traditions that confer such qualities.

Niane explains that the word rendered as "grace" in the text is actually *baraka,* a term commonly employed in the Arab world to designate a divine blessing or the power that derives from it. Here it is baraka that assures the gifted Malinke hunter his success: "By the [baraka] of my master the great Simbon my arrows have hit her and now she lies not far from your walls."[7]

Sundiata is infused with a sense of mission—destiny, fate, determined by Allah—while all the major steps taken to accomplish that fate are marked by Malinke spiritualism. The principal opponent Sundiata is to overcome is an evil magician, Soumaoro, who can be conquered only by a greater spiritual force. That force can be unleashed by Sundiata only after his sister acquires the secret of Soumaoro's magic, and after Sundiata reacquires his own personal griot, Balla Fasséké. The destruction of Soumaoro's "fetishes" is not represented as the conquest of monotheistic Islam over polytheistic Sosso, but as the apotheosis of the Son of the Buffalo.[8] Although Mamoudou Kouyaté evokes Mansa Moussa, "beloved of God," in his final chapter, it is the eternity of Mali, not God, that is stressed, and the epic ends on the injunction to the listener not to seek to know the secrets to which only the initiated griots have rights—"secrets" belonging to Malinke tradition, not Islam.

Throughout the epic, Muslim beliefs are naturalized, as we can see every time Sundiata gives thanks to God. Equally natural are the sacrifices that he would have known to make as Son of the Buffalo. The blurring of the lines between Malinke tradition and Islam suggests the longevity of the syncretism.

South of the kingdoms of Mali and Songhay, there arose a series of cities in which Islam gradually began to take hold, especially from the fifteenth century. In northern Nigeria, the Hausa cities of Kano and Katsina became important centers of Islamic activity. The oral traditions of Hausaland have retained the memory of earlier reformist movements, as we can see in the development of *labarai* (oral tales). In a tale, recorded and analyzed by Priscilla Starratt (1996), a conventional struggle is recounted: a traditional *bori* priest is pitted against a Muslim holy man *(malam)* in a contest staged by the ruler. The ruler has placed a horse inside a house; he is the only person to know the house's contents. What, he asks, is in the house? The *bori* priest divines his answer: a horse. When the malam is asked the same question, he prays to Allah for guidance and is provided with a different answer: a white bull with horns. The ruler, expecting to find the horse still there, orders the walls of the house demolished. To the ruler's amazement, a white bull is found. Though the ruler waits years for the bull to change back to a horse, it remains a bull. Through this miracle, God insures the successful transplantation of the true faith to Katsina.

The confrontation between the Hausa bori priest and the Muslim malam establishes the tale's framework, providing a setting frequently found in many African oral traditions: magical contestation of power forms the central action. The first level of meaning to emerge from this dialectical contest involves God's greatness, to which the triumph of the malam attests. The magical transformation of the beast suggests a further hermeneutical level, one in which God's intervention entails greater issues of struggle, or jihad, and interpretation *(ijtihad)*. The subordination of the identities of the beasts to God's will and the demolition of the walls surrounding the miraculous transformation both suggest mystic meanings commensurate with the traditions of Islamic wisdom literature. Finally, the insertion of this timeless parable into the specific context of the labarai with the issue of the conversion of the Hausa at Katsina, and with the accommodation of the ruler to Islam in this important urban center of northern Nigeria where the major nineteenth century jihads took place, mark the tale's dialogical quality. The labarai, when considered as a Muslim text, may be viewed as containing both the message of the religious victory of Islam along with the intertextual elements of a pre-Islamic Hausa universe intertwined in the language, structure, and expression of the tale. The tale concludes on this note: "Islam entered our land. That's what I know."⁹ But along with this triumphant entry, the tale reminds us of the strength of the bori specialist (he was, after all, "correct" in his divination).

Interestingly, the version of the tale that we have was recited by someone who was himself a malam, Malam Sabo Lawan Kabara. In his account, the narrative both communicates and performs the actions that are translated into the triumph of Islam over traditional Hausa beliefs. At the beginning of the account, the storyteller makes mention of the "ruler from Katsina," whose name, we are told, Sabo Lawan Kabara cannot remember. The arrival of Islam in Katsina is rehearsed in the tale itself by the actions of the traders whose movements echo the advance of Islam: "These servants of God [the malamai] who kept coming to trade were bringing Islam, until Islam spread in the land." The receptiveness of Katsina to the faith was imaged in the desire of the unnamed ruler for the truth: "So this Ruler said he wanted to see what was the truth. Was Islam the truth? Or was it this Bori here that was being practiced?"¹⁰

The malam's defeat of the bori is allegorized by the actors themselves. Thus, as the malam gathers his followers to "exert themselves" in prayer to overcome the bori, he tells them, "If we don't do it with our effort, Islam will never be able to spread here." The narrator concludes his account of the malam's triumph on a wonderfully ambiguous note. Although the horse was transformed into a white bull, just as the bori's power was supplanted by that of the malam, the permanence of the triumph cannot be guaranteed by the malam-narrator himself: "The bull was put aside for many years as he [the ruler] was thinking that it would change back into a horse, until he grew tired of keeping it. I don't know, but I never heard about the day that it changed back into a horse." Although irony informs the malam's victory statement, that victory itself contains its own ambiguities: the ultimate spread of Islam depends upon convincing a "pagan" ruler; the figure that comes to represent the triumph of the faith, a white bull, is nevertheless a transformed version of an earlier figure. Many boris of Kano, in competition with the malams of Katsina, are themselves also Muslim. The tale eschews absolutist solutions all the while proclaiming, "Only Islam. Islam alone." Islam would then appear to be portrayed on the surface as a victorious conqueror from abroad, while the subtext suggests the transformation of an already existent religious discourse ("Don't revert to listening to the talk of the Bori").[11]

The oral tale can be read on two levels: that provided by the immediate circumstances of the actual performance and that of the original pattern of the story. As such, this bi-level narration can be read as a surface mythic historicization of the conquest and spread of Islam by the malams, as well as an unstated repetition of the victory of Katsina over Kano. This pattern is repeated in the tale's own history, as Starratt demonstrates:

> Despite the well worn oft repeated nature of the tale, it would appear that its ultimate Islamic motif comes from another legend of a mental duel between a Bori priest and a malam. The setting for this legend was, however, in Gobir where the Islamic reformer Shehu dan Fodio and a Bori priest contest to identify the true religion. Sarkin Gobir finds that God changed a female calf into a male calf. It would appear that the miracle of God changing an enclosed animal in a Bori priest versus malam contest has been moved from Gobir to Katsina.[12]

Thus we see the intersection of a preexistent discourse, an oral text, and its implied readers celebrating the triumph of the Islamic text.

East African Literature

The Swahili language was employed in the creation of a rich literary tradition, both oral and written. The earliest of the Swahili poets is a legendary poet-warrior-hero, Fumo Liyongo [*fumo* means king, or chief], whose origins lay in the state of Shanga, located on Pate Island. The oldest level of ruins at Shanga dates to the eighth century A.D. and the most recent to the fourteenth century. If Fumo Liyongo lived at the height of Shanga's power, it would have been in the tenth century, and the oral tradition that eventually gave birth to the epic or heroic poem *(utendi)* that celebrates his life would have dated to around that period. Scholars differ greatly on this dating; some set the epic at a later period.

The utendi is a long poem in Swahili consisting of four-line stanzas with end rhymes. It was originally intended to be sung or chanted with musical accompaniment in a public recital. According to ʿAbdulaziz, it was first recorded in the eighteenth century in the Pate region, and was based on Arabic models.[13] The form has survived and is today used for pedagogical or moral instruction as well as for recitation of classical, historical legends and epics. Arabic legends, Islamic beliefs, and traditional African hero stories all appear in the poems.

The *Utendi wa Liyongo* reflects the dual cultural heritage of the Swahili. At the beginning of the narrative, the sultan of Pate, Daudi Mringwari, fears that the handsome and fearless warrior Fumo Liyongo will usurp his throne. According to some versions, Daudi (Liyongo's cousin), rules by virtue of Islamic laws of succession, having been the son of the previous ruler, Mringwari I; however, Liyongo would have succeeded to the throne following the African tradition of matrilinear succession (descent through the female line). Other versions reverse the situation, claiming Liyongo's rightful place by virtue of Islamic patrilinear customs, and Daudi's rights according to traditional African matrilinear customs. In all cases, the two customs are in conflict, and would seem to represent an older African matrilinear system in conflict with the new Islamic patrilineage.

Sultan Daudi arranges a marriage between Liyongo and a Galla woman, hoping that Liyongo would leave Shanga, following matrilocal marriage customs of the day, and reside with his wife's people on the mainland. While Liyongo is away, the sultan plots with conspirators in Liyongo's new forest home to have him assassinated, but the plan is foiled by the hero. Liyongo is then tricked into returning to Pate for a dance-tourney, where he is captured and imprisoned. With his mother's help, Liyongo escapes, only to be betrayed by his own son and killed.

The figure of the warrior who meets his fate joins the Muslim emphasis on man's relationship with God and traditional African praise-singing that celebrates the man of strength. The two meet in Liyongo's own self-praise, sung in *The Song of Liyongo*:

> *I made my breast into a shield I unblock where there is a blockage,*
> *I do not fear thorns, nor sharp stings that might sting me.*
>
> *Dying for God and that ship that goes to meet Him,*
> *Do not fear the people of the world even if they hit you with ten thousand arrows.*

Like Sundiata, the Son of the Lion, Liongo also metaphorizes courage in the form of the fearless beast:

> *The lion roars with a thundrous roar;*
> *A tremendous roar, which kills pity in man.*
>
> *The best male lions carry shield and sword;*
> *fighting for their luck until their eyes shut.*
>
> *They take the bodies, feeding swords and rapiers,*
> *heroic lions piercing skin and flesh.*

Arabic influences seem distant from these lines, which conclude rather tamely with a coda that appears to be tacked on, as if submitting to a formal requirement to have an acceptable Muslim perspective:

> [The poet] will receive a reward [which] the generous God will pay him
> on the day of retribution when He will pay the wicked and the good.[14]

Death and the poet meet at the edges of transcendental self-overcoming: the lion consumes not only fear and human weakness, but the very instruments of mortality conceived and shaped by the human hand, "feeding swords and rapiers" with his breast. The familiar line concerning the day of retribution, read against the image of heroic lions, echoes the violence of teeth tearing into flesh, reducing the ethics to pitiful proportions when compared with the ravenous forces of the beast. The poetic figure of the hero is marked by strength, not goodness.

☾ ☾ ☾

During the eighteenth and nineteenth centuries, Swahili poets developed verse marked by Islamic exhortations and laments. One of the major Swahili poets, Sayyid Abdallah (d. 1810), presents us with a powerful homily on the inevitability of death, the transitoriness of wealth, and the dangers of damnation facing the human soul for those who disregard divine injunctions. His treatment of the inevitability of death suggests a less heroic stance than that of the lion. Rather, he advances a philosophic notion of acceptance for the inevitability of a force that governs nature as well as human life. The imagery he employs in the following lines of his *Inkishafi* delineates these aspects of death, while the poet's intimate relationship with the reader is suggested by the first-person point of view in which he addresses the reader:

> *Hear the meaning when I speak to you:*
> *life resembles a lamp-flame in the wind;*
> *it cannot be stopped when it goes out;*
> *one moment one sees it, then it has gone out.*
>
> *Or it resembles a roaring fire,*
> *in a clearing, in the bushes;*
> *there descends a cloudful of rain in the woods,*
> *and it is extinguished; you could not blow it into life again.*[15]

Other Swahili poets deal with the beauty of their beloved, the joys of loving, and sorrows over failed love. One finds common the belief among the Swahili Muslims that the preservation and propagation of Islamic doctrine, as in the form of homiletic verse, are "believed to give the mortals *thawab*—or Heavenly credit—that is expected to help them enter Paradise."[16]

Not surprisingly, the vibrant poetic traditions of Somali literature[17] bear resemblances to the Swahili. Islam and poetry meet in several ways in Somalia. The poet often shares in the power of the judicial council whose rulings are based upon customary law (the judgments of the "tree of customary law"). In contrast, the shaykh is the dispenser of the judgments of "the tree of truth"—that is, Islamic jurisprudence. Somali culture meets at their intersection; according to Abdirashid Ali Shermarke, "Somali culture [is] firmly based upon a dual structure: Islam and Somali poetry."[18] Until very recently, the poetry in question was entirely oral, and this had its impact upon Islamic practices in Somalia.

The oral tradition creates a reverence for the word, for recitation, and for the one who memorizes text: the passage through the gateway of faith is begun with the learning and recitation of the *shahada*—the credo—and culminates with the night of the recitation, in which the youthful initiate recites the entire Quran by heart. Additionally, reverence for the spoken word, when viewed from the Islamic context, is common to Somali as to Swahili beliefs: *thawab* is obtained by repetition of the holy verse. Conversely the power invested in the oral curse springs equally from the ability of the shaykh to evoke Allah's punishment for transgressors. Here poetry itself becomes, in the words of the Prophet addressed to the poet Hassan Ibn Tabit, "more potent than falling arrows in the darkness of dawn." A beautiful Somali version of this concept can be seen in the words of the poet Qamaan Bulxan (d. 1928): "O Cali, the Everlasting One has driven on the words of your poem/the rustling wind of the warm breeze has carried them."[19] It is no surprise that the poet's vaunting is hedged by the shaykh's accusations of irreverence, summed up in the Quranic warning, "Poets are followed by none save erring men" (26:227).

One of the great Somali poets of the nineteenth century, Mahammad Abdullah Hasan (d. 1921), celebrated in verse the defeat of the English forces led by Richard Corfield.[20] (This poem was central to one of Somali's major novels, *Close Sesame* [1983], by Nuruddin Farah.) Hasan extols traditional Muslim values, here set in the context of resistance to colonial invasions—similar to the exhortations in the religious writings of Muslim religious leaders in West Africa of the late-nineteenth and early twentieth centuries. Religious values lend legitimacy to the expression of powerful anticolonial sentiments:

> *You have died, Corfield, and are no longer in this world*
> *A merciless journey was your portion.*
> *When, Hell-destined, you set out for the Other World*
> *Those who have gone to Heaven will question you, if God is willing;*
> *When you see the companions of the faithful and the jewels of Heaven,*
> *Answer them how God tried you.*
> *Say to them: "From that day to this the Dervishes never ceased their assaults upon us.*
> *The British were broken, the noise of battle engulfed us;*
> *With fervour and faith the Dervishes attacked us."*[21]

The personal voice of the poet is heard in the poet's direct address to Corfield, in the biting tone that builds a powerful rhetoric of self-righteousness. Most striking is the oral dimension in which an implied/commanded performance is invoked in the words the poet places into the mouth of the defeated British officer. The repetition of the line, "With fervour and faith the Dervishes attacked us," crosses the borders of character and narrator, as if the officer's voice were obliged to echo a truth beyond its power to control.

(((

Women have also developed an oral tradition in Somali culture. Working with Mariam Omar Ali, Lidwien Kapteijns (1996) recorded a series of Somali *sittaat,* or women's praise-songs, for the "mothers of the believers," the early women of Islam. Recordings made at sessions of recitations of the sittaat in Djibouti revealed a tradition of community gatherings of the women in which Amina, the Prophet's mother, his foster-mother, Hagar, Mary, and the Prophet's wives and daughters were praised, extolled, and supplicated. "Oh God, you, Fatima, best of women, aren't you residing in the light and won't you quickly take us there?"[22] The pattern inscribed into the praise-singing is recognizably one of an oral tradition more closely aligned to the Somali than to that of the written Arabic text; this can be noted in its techniques of intensification, emphasis and stress through repetition, parallel structure, and powerful, short, declamatory lines. And at the same time, its lexicon is purely Islamic, beginning with the conventional blessing "Peace be upon you," and the imagery of Eve as a gift and a light:

> Peace be upon you, Grandmother Eve
> Peace be upon you, she is [Adam's] rib
> Peace be upon you, she is his wife
> Peace be upon you, a gift to him
> Peace be upon you, his light
> Peace be upon you, God loved her
> Peace be upon you, God was good to her
> Peace be upon you, God elevated her
> Peace be upon you, God was good to her
> Peace be upon you, and gave her to Adam.[23]

Originally serving as the basis for Somali feminist sensibility as well as spirituality, the sittaat sessions now face an uncertain future due to the pressures of more culturally "pure" approaches derived from the Islamic heartland.

Contemporary Literature: Critics and Defenders of Islam

In contemporary Islamic literature, much of which is written in European languages, Islam may be presented in a positive or negative light. When the work casts Islam in a positive, light, as an ethical faith, often the action takes the form of a jihad with twin meanings—struggle against external evil, and against evil impulses and weaknesses within. The latter conflict is commonly represented in a novel or short story in which the struggle within is intended to lead to self-overcoming. In narratives cast in the form of a quest, mythic projections of this theme are seen in the tales and epics that depict man or woman in a state of weakness or ignorance, overcoming obstacles to greater self-fulfillment. Islamic virtue is then a matter of inner strength, the key to self-transformation and to self-realization. On a quieter note, it is associated with those models of deportment or self-control whose character had been formed by this struggle.

On the other hand, when Islam is depicted in a negative light, the inner struggle is absent, and corruption takes an external form: hypocritical behavior, contradictions between word and deed, and typically base motivations of power and greed betray the absence of any inner strength or outward opposition to evil. Jihad is absent. With this emphasis on morality, and, implicitly, on obedience to higher moral principle, if not to higher authority, corrupt or hypocritical Muslim authorities are presented as archvillains, often standing accused of harboring a spirit of fatalism, projecting a message of inertia and passivity. A number of Sembène Ousmane's films and novels have set the tone for francophone "iconoclasts," those most critical of Islam.

☾ ☾ ☾

Shaykh Hamidou Kane's *L'Aventure ambiguë,*[24] set in northern Senegal during the late-colonial period, offers a classic example of the positive depiction of Islam. Like many other Islamic texts, the novel reflects structures of power through its discourses, continuing traditions that date back to pre-Islamic times and that were maintained by generations of griots, "Masters of the Word." Similar to the basic conflict that has animated Somali poetry, the struggle between shaykh and poet for authority over the spoken word, Kane's "ambiguous adventure" can best be viewed in terms of a triangular struggle among secular and sacred authorities for control over representations of the word. At one corner of the triangle are the forces of secular modernism, represented by the French, and more particularly by the administrator Paul Lacroix, for whom civilization is associated with progress, and who finds incredible the Muslim notion of the end of the world. At a second corner is to be found traditional African worldly authority, occupying a position identified by Coulon as that of the prince.[25] Here it is the rulers of the Diallobe clan, and especially the Grande Royale, who occupies this place. Lastly, there are the *marabouts,* as Coulon calls the leaders of the various sufi brotherhoods—religious leaders who also mobilized mass opposition to oppressive power. At the extreme end of maraboutic, spiritual opposition to secular power is to be found Le Maître, the spiritual guide to other-worldly comprehension and faith. His outward appearance, like his stern pedagogical practices, belies an esoteric asceticism grounded in the mystic apprehension of God's nature. For the family of Samba Diallo, secular power matters only so as to better enable the believer to practice his faith: "We are among the last men in the world to possess God as He veritably is in his oneness."[26] The Maître's thoughts convey the opposition between spiritual and secular power: "The Maître profoundly believed that the worship of God was incompatible with any exaltation of man. Now, at heart all forms of nobility were pagan. Nobility is the exaltation of man; faith is above all humility."[27]

For the mystic, the Divine is approached through the Word, as it is expressed in the evening prayer, the liminal moment when awareness of death is at its greatest and when one's smallness before the immensity of what sufis refer to as Reality or the Truth—attributes of God—are most sensibly felt. In contrast to the Europeans' alphabet, to the printed word associated with the conquering colonialists' earthly power, is to be found "la Parole," the creative, generative matrix whose force is manifested in the baraka of the Maître. The Word is the sword of the Maître with which he conquers not only earthly opponents but death itself: "He has the Word which is made of nothing, but which lasts and lasts."[28] More intriguingly, for the Maître, "la Parole" is the architecture of the world, and even the world itself. By extension, "paradise was built with the Words he recited, with the same brilliant lights . . . the same power."[29] Lastly, the image of word/world creativity is given striking form as an act of weaving, an image duplicated by the Dogon in their traditions: "The Word weaves that which exists."[30] Often mistaken as a purely existential period novel, Kane's masterpiece cannot be understood except as an expression of sufi mystical values.

☾ ☾ ☾

The focus on the holy man—saint or marabout—provides the center for much literature tinged with mysticism. The individual mystic appears most prominently in the Sudanese Tayeb Salih's *Wedding of Zein* (1968); the marabout, or master, features in Kane's *L'Aventure ambiguë* (1961). In the Guinean Camara Laye's *Le Regard du roi* (1954), the classic text of the sufi way, it is the *murshid,* the guide or spiritual teacher, who figures prominently, while the notions of *tariqa* and *dhikr* (see earlier chapters) inform the novel. All three novels portray Islam in a positive light.

On the surface, one might think that Laye chose an unlikely subject with which to convey sufi values in *Le Regard du roi,* a modern allegory whose setting vaguely corresponds to Laye's native Guinea. The protagonist, Clarence, is a somewhat arrogant white man who finds himself in reduced circumstances somewhere in Africa. He is skeptical, but inquisitive about what he encounters. Although he does not understand much of what he sees, he is an ideal figure for the initiate or pilgrim who starts on the religious journey from the lowest of levels.

One can find elements of Kafka that mark the incoherence of Clarence's initial state—his sense of being lost; and one can identify the setting, however as clearly that of a Sahelian landscape not unlike the Guinea uplands, with the march south into the forest. Yet these features tend to remain peripheral to the central religious imagery and meaning of the novel. Laye's upbringing in Kouroussa, Guinea, would have exposed him to many of the spiritual elements that found their way into this novel: various Islamic brotherhoods, including the Tijaniyya, had existed in the region for a long period of time.

In general, Islamic devotion is expressed through the submission of one's will to that of God. The adoration and prostration of a crowd before the figure of the king at the beginning of *Le Regard du roi* is only the outward manifestation of the Muslim belief: when a beggar informs Clarence that "one is not allowed to breathe"[31] as the king makes his salutation, he is expressing the absoluteness of its nature. Clarence is unaccustomed to such absoluteness.

For the mystic, white is black and black is white: the world of appearance is deceptive, ultimately unreal, in comparison with spiritual reality. The beggar whom Clarence encounters wears ragged clothes and has uncouth ways. Yet he can show

Clarence the way to the path he is seeking, answers his questions, and acts as his guide. He is Clarence's first spiritual teacher, and from the start he takes it upon himself to explain the significance of what is happening. It is the beggar who tells Clarence he is not allowed to breathe when the king makes his salutation, and that the gold worn by the king is "one of the signs of love . . . the purest kind of love."[32]

Clarence's thoughts are set in motion by the beggar's words and he accepts the beggar's offer to represent him before the king. Soon the beggar tempers and corrects Clarence's inexperience and impatience as he explains, "There are always certain obstacles."[33] Although Clarence can see the king at a distance, he knows that "never before had he been so far from his goal as he was now."[34] Unable to cross the barriers between himself and the king, Clarence accepts the beggar's advice to seek the king in the south, presumably where he will be traveling, and to allow the beggar to act as his guide. The journey thus begins with the basic sufi elements: a way, or *tariqa,* a guide, or *murshid,* and a goal of perfection to be won at the end in union with the divine.

Clarence passes through various stages, as is to be expected in such a journey; stages of ignorance, of life sunk in fleshly pleasures, and other states ultimately constitutive not only of the human condition, but of the obstacles between the human and the divine. The greatest of these obstacles ultimately proves itself to be legalism itself, the tendency established within Islam, as within all human societies, to ground notions of self-fulfillment in moral conduct—what are termed "rights" in the novel. Clarence has to learn that it is divine favor, not human rights, that will bring him closer to his goal. In the end it is not justice but love that brings Clarence to enlightenment. According to Trimingham, sufism developed mystical techniques that would "enable the seeker to arrive at *ma'rifa*"—the direct perception of God.[35]

When one considers the stages through which Clarence passes, the succession of guides he encounters, beginning with the beggar; when one considers the imagery, including whirling dancers who evoke the figure of dervishes, details of acts of devotion, or dhikr, such as salaaming, the prominence of Muslim imagery like a crescent-shaped ax forged in devotion to the king, the negative attitude toward merit and the importance of love, and finally the entire metaphor of the journey along a path, a way that resembles the sufi Way of Purification,[36] it becomes evident that the principal features of the allegory are grounded in sufi Islam.

☾ ☾ ☾

In his collection *Les Contes d'Amadou Koumba* (1947), Birago Diop has also given memorable features to these Islamic mysteries, drawing upon mostly Wolof traditions in Senegal. We can see mystic elements in many stories, such as "L'Héritage" and "La Biche et les deux chasseurs" (1947). In "La Biche," a marabout's spittle is ingested by a deer when it chews some grass, and thus the deer acquires the knowledge and the power of the marabout's word. The marabout, whose Wolof title is serigne, can infuse his spittle with his baraka because "good or bad words dissolve in the saliva, like honey in water, so that it retains a certain measure of their power."[37] In this story, Diop succeeds in appropriating and synthesizing Islamic and Wolof elements. The *serigne* is portrayed as returning from his pilgrimage to Mecca, the spiritual source of his power. However great the merit of that power, it subsists alongside another, the ancestral, which Diop is careful to present as even more venerable and puissant. Diop's images of ancestral presence—in the wind that blows, in the water that flows, as his poetry would have it—is here evoked in terms of its antiquity: "M'bile's knowledge, though great, was of too recent date; and if she knew that the earth was old, very old, and that the trees were old, very old, and that grass had existed since time immemorial, she did not know that the pact concluded between the ancestors of N'Dioumane [the hunter] and the earth, the trees and the grass was as old as the race of huntsmen."[38] From the power of the Word, to the marabout's spittle, to the ancestors' pact, Diop traces the declension of the forms of power through which African forms of Islam are joined to traditional patterns of belief.

In a thousand ways of representing the paradoxes, the illusions, the mysteries, the ambivalences of life, African writers have constructed a distinctively African Islamic edifice with their words—by stringing the pearls of their verses, as the Swahili conceit would have it. Swahili and Somali textual traditions, like their Songhay, Hausa, and Wolof counterparts, and often like those developed in Europhonic texts as well, converge at the one central point of the Islamic discourse—the special powers of the poetic, spoken, recited, chanted, evocatory word. Its esoteric properties rest upon exoteric form, allowing for the interplay between outward and inner meanings. Unlike the printed sign, whose primary quality is its interchangeableness, its capacity to be translated and telegraphed, the baraka, or power/blessing of the word, is inseparable from the status of the agents who articulate it: poets, shaykhs, marabouts, murshids, *fuqaha* (legal scholars)—as Mamadou Dia (1980) has said, these voices that can be traced from the distant past to the present have elaborated an anthology, a discursive tapestry, with "so many dazzling manifestations of a creative spirit and of a philosophical subtlety that owes its flourishing to Islam."[39]

Mysticism versus Scripturalism

The imagery that Mamadou Dia employs in extolling the tapestry of Islamic texts in Africa is well suited to reflect the spiritualism of African Islam. However, it fits less well the austere, formalistic features of the Islamic legalism, sometimes termed scripturalism.

Geertz identifies *sayyid* and *zawiya* complexes as forms of maraboutism, and indeed they are particular kinds of sufism found in Morocco, though with variants located elsewhere in sub-Saharan Africa. They provide contrasting models for the dominant trends of Islamic practice that Geertz named "scripturalist," and that are marked by an exoteric, legalist approach to religion. We can understand the sufi's view of scripturalism by considering the figure of the grandfather in Tayeb Salih's "A Handful of Dates":

> I loved to give rein to my imagination and picture to myself a tribe of giants
> living behind that wood, a people tall and thin with white beards and sharp
> noses, like my grandfather. . . . [A]s for his beard, it was soft and luxuriant
> and as white as cotton-wool—never in my life have I seen anything of a
> purer whiteness or greater beauty. My grandfather must also have been ex-
> tremely tall, for I never saw anyone in the whole area address him without
> having to look up at him.[40]

Purity, height, and respect can all serve as metaphors for moral stature.

In this story, the grandfather is placed in opposition to Masood, an imprudent neighbor who loses his property to the grandfather. Masood is blessed with a beautiful singing voice, a gurgling laugh, and by the ability to love—but according to the grandfather, he is "indolent." The austerity of the grandfather, so impressive to the child, is shown to be hard-hearted and unforgiving. The grandfather loves the methodological process of achieving religious stature: the memorization of the words of the Quran, the obligations that are met in prayer, the cleanliness in ablutions. This is the outward show of scripturalism, that form of Islam that Geertz sets in opposition to maraboutism.

In many works, mysticism and legalism, baraka and scripture, marabout and faqih, are often at odds with each other. In his collection *The Wedding of Zein and Other Stories* (1968), Salih gives sympathetic and spontaneous portrayals of sufi mystical values, especially as seen in the simple villager Zein, in contrast to the legalism characteristic of the ruling religious authorities. Zein, the village fool, comes to be engaged to the village belle, Nima. How does this "miracle" come about? The differing versions—some emphasize the influence of a dream, others the stubbornness of Nima in deciding to make a sacrifice—reflect the differences within the community.

Two central characters in the story, the imam and the saintly Haneen, embody opposing principles. The imam is represented negatively: gloomy, serious, unfrivolous, continually evoking the fear of death, he tells the assemblage of believers about their moral obligations, but inspires only uneasiness or vague sentiments of guilt or self-righteousness in them. In Martin Lings's terms,[41] he stands for exoteric, legalistic, formalistic Islam, and is limited in his understanding of things to their outer level of meaning. (By way of contrast, note Lings's evocative line suggesting the mystic's hermeneutic credo: "Every verse of the Koran has 'an outside and an inside'"[29].) For the Imam, Haneen's truth does not exist: "Haneen . . . represented the mystical side of the spiritual world, a side he did not recognize."[42] The imam has had ten years of university training and is the only one in the village to concern himself with the politics of the outside world. For Salih, he is a prisoner of the world of forms, trapped by the most insidious of lures, moral righteousness grounded in literal interpretations of texts—the limitation of the exoteric. As such, his insistence on one pure, correct Truth blinds him to the productive textuality of the mystic's contradictory perspectives, summed up by Lings as a double consciousness: "The full-grown Sufi is thus conscious of being, like other men, a prisoner of a world of forms, but unlike them he is also conscious of being free, with a freedom which immeasurably outweighs his imprisonment. He may therefore be said to have two centres of consciousness, one human and one Divine, and he may speak now from one and now from another, which accounts for certain apparent contradictions."[43]

In contrast to the imam, Haneen is the image of the sufi saint. His word is wholly oral: as with the common people, God's blessing is always on his lips, an expression whose mechanical expression is transformed by his life into genuine spiritual power. Unlike the imam, he is not attached to material things: for six months of the year he wanders with only his prayer rug and pitcher (page 44); he eats at the home of the poor people, has no visible wealth or position of importance, no discernible family ties. The villagers venerate him, in his life and in his death. In his relationship to Zein, he functions as the sufi guide. Haneen represents an idealized form of the Sudanese mystic. But in a larger sense, he highlights the two approaches to the text, to the word, that inform much of African Islamic writing: written versus oral; literal, moral, learned, exoteric readings versus popular, hidden, esoteric approaches.

Taken negatively, scripturalism provides a focus upon hypocrisy or failed ethical behavior, and as such it is represented in a wide range of critical writings: Sembène Ousmane's criticism of Islam (at this level) in works like *Vehi Ciosane* and *Xala* is obviously a criticism of the unethical deployment of religious authority; the censuring of Islam as seen in Yambo Ouologuem's *Devoir de Violence* and Ayi Kwei Armah's *Two Thousand Seasons* is also best understood in this way.[44] Other depictions of Muslim models of righteousness are numerous. The majority of Muslim characters in much recent African fiction—as in Wole Soyinka's *The Swamp Dwellers, The Interpreters, A Season of Anomy,* the more recent works of Nigerian writers, such as Ibrahim Tahir's *The Last Imam,* Zaynab Alkali's *The Virtuous Woman,* as well as popular Hausa fiction—testify to a growing desire of writers to focus entirely upon comportment as defined according to a Muslim ethos.[45]

☾ ☾ ☾

A key text that problematizes the social codes of Islam in contemporary Senegalese society is Mariama Bâ's *Une si longue lettre* (1980). Mariama Bâ's novel is one of the first francophone African novels to be written by a woman. It takes the unusual form of an epistolary novel—one not commonly seen after the eighteenth century. By taking this approach, Bâ is able to provide the reader with a certain closeness to the protagonist, Ramatoulaye, almost as if we were sharing in her diary.

The novel begins with a letter written by Ramatoulaye to her close friend Aissatou. The letter recounts the events surrounding the death of Ramatoulaye's husband, Modou. Ramatoulaye records the moment when she received the news of his death, her reactions, and especially the details of her actions and thoughts during the period of mourning. The account provides us with a portrait of the Muslim practices of dealing with death, and more particularly the Senegalese Wolof version of those practices.

The invocation of Quranic verses as the instrument of Allah's compassion for the widow is given in moving terms, although the first-person point of view has the strange effect here of creating a distance between the narrator and the scene: "Comforting words from the Koran fill the air; divine words, divine exhortations to virtue, warnings against evil, exaltation of humility, of faith. Shivers run through me. My tears flow and my voice joins weakly in the fervent 'Amen' which inspires the crowd's ardour at the end of each verse."[46] The conventionality of the sentiment is marked by the sets of rhetorical oppositions—virtue/evil, comforting words/warnings.

Unsurprisingly, she soon is questioning tradition. As the relatives and friends paying condolences make financial contributions, she reflects, "A disturbing display of inner feeling that cannot be evaluated now measured in francs! And again I think how many of the dead would have survived if, before organizing these festive funeral ceremonies, the relative or friend had bought the life-saving prescription or paid for hospitalization."[47] The disturbing thought, couched here as an abstract reflection, grows as her questioning of the ceremonial pattern is laid out:

> Alas, it's the same story of the eighth and fortieth days, when those who have "learned" belatedly make up for lost time. Light attire showing off slim waistlines, prominent backsides, the new brassiere or the one bought at the second-hand market, chewing sticks wedged between teeth, white or flowered shawls, heavy smell of incense and of *gongo,* loud voices, strident laughter. And yet we are told in the Koran that on the third day the dead body swells and fills its tomb; we are told that on the eighth it bursts; and we are also told that on the fortieth day it is stripped. What then is the significance of these joyous, institutionalized festivities that accompany our prayers for God's mercy? Who has come out of self-interest? Who has come to quench his own thirst? Who has come for the sake of mercy? Who has come that he may remember?[48]

Ramatoulaye sets the scene for us to judge the social standards of contemporary Muslim society in Dakar, and in the process she elaborates a Muslim code of righteousness that she holds up as the model for her own comportment. "I hope to carry out my duties fully. My heart concurs with the demands of religion. Reared since childhood on their strict precepts, I expect not to fail."[49]

Given this rigorous introduction to the character, and to Muslim practice, it comes as something of a surprise when we learn that Ramatoulaye's husband had totally abandoned the religious standard upheld by his wife, and that that standard served not only to comfort her, but as an instrument to condemn him:

> The *mirasse* commanded by the Koran requires that a dead person be stripped of his most intimate secrets; thus is exposed to others what was carefully concealed. These exposures crudely explain a man's life. With con-

sternation, I measure the extent of Modou's betrayal. His abandonment of his first family (myself and my children) was the outcome of the choice of a new life. [Modou took a second, young wife.] He rejected us. He mapped out his future without taking our existence into account.[50]

It is after this point that we learn that Modou had secretly married one of his daughter's best friends, after which he abandoned his old family and ignored all responsibilities to them.

The Ramatoulaye who takes this stern position toward her wayward husband is not the image of the traditional, submissive Muslim wife. We learn that Modou and Ramatoulaye, in their youth, had considered themselves part of a new generation of "évolués"—that is, modern, emancipated Africans. They had adopted European education and mores as their own, all the while joining in the struggle for independence when the time came. Strikingly, it is Ramatoulaye who depicts her education as an "emancipation." In describing herself and her female schoolmates from different parts of West Africa, she writes, "We were true sisters, destined for the same mission of emancipation."[51] The language she employs in elaborating on that "emancipation" is decidedly colonialist: "To lift us out of the bog of tradition, superstition and custom, to make us appreciate a multitude of civilizations without renouncing our own, to raise our vision of the world, cultivate our personalities, strengthen our qualities, to make up for our inadequacies, to develop universal moral values in us: these were the aims of our admirable headmistress."[52] Ramatoulaye's celebration of this education, so much in contrast with the conflicted accounts of Shaykh Hamadou Kane in his *L'Aventure ambiguë*, strongly echo the themes of negritude, especially as propounded by Léopold Senghor. They demarcate the path of what she terms the "New Africa" that lies ahead "for the promotion of the black woman."[53] But at the same time, she recognizes that that path "has not been at all fortuitous," just as her marriage to the New African Modou declined into a sad account of betrayal and rejection.

The period of mourning comes to an end. *Une si longue letter*, having begun with the portrait of the Muslim wife forced to deal with abandonment and death, reliant upon her faith and its practices to see her through, now shifts: Ramatoulaye finds herself forced to deal more and more with her children's problems rather than her own, and increasingly she turns to traditional Wolof practice—to her griot and her fortunetelling. She also turns to her "emancipated" friend Aissatou, who is able to afford her the necessary financial assistance to achieve a degree of freedom on her own. In short, as she passes from the portrayal of herself as daughter and wife to mother, Islamic practices and beliefs fade into the background; considerations of identity—national identity and female identity—come to the fore. Islam is thus contextualized as a facet of the identity for the modern Senegalese woman, not as the governing principle by which her life is to be lived and her values determined. Islam's moral imperatives enable her to lay to rest her old life. But in her final thoughts recorded in the novel, it plays no role in her elaboration of her hopes for the future.

Purism versus Syncretism

Here we shift the focus of our reading from mysticism versus scripturalism to purism versus syncretism. This will enable us better to note the tensions and divisions that arose as a consequence of the processes by which various African societies appropriated and modified Islamic practices and beliefs.

An example of the intermingling of Islamic and traditional Soninke beliefs can be seen in the *Ta'rikh es-Sudan*'s description of the battle for Gao, where Askia Mohamed's descendants relied on three protective spirits, incarnated in a snake, a hen, and an ox, "thanks to whom the city maintains its invulnerability."[54] When Askia Mohamed was endangered in battle with the Bargantche, however, he sought salvation by addressing a prayer to Allah: "Oh my God, I implore you in memory of that day when I stood next to the head of your messenger in his mausoleum."[55] What emerges is a syncretic portrait of two systems of belief.

Similarly, a close study of Fulani oral literature and of the sufi orders (especially the Tijaniyya) of the region of Mali, brings us to Hampâté Bâ's project to remain faithful to both the Islamic and the Fulani traditions. For Bâ (1972), the meeting of the two was not confrontational but harmonious, mutually stimulating because of the capacity of the Fulani base to grow and incorporate Muslim values. Affirming that strong compatibilities may be shown to exist between Islam and the tenets of traditional African religions, Bâ concludes that "Islam took hold and grew in sub-Saharan Africa upon the foundations of traditional religion."[56] Bâ himself illustrated this in his masterly epic poem *Kaïdara,* a quest tale of Fulani initiation.

In the African francophonic novel, a type of "dual consciousness" emerges characteristic of al-Mukhlit writing. We can see this in Kamara Laye's semi-autobiographical novel *L'Enfant noir,* in which the culture's "magico-religious syncretism" recurs repeatedly in ritual and practice.[57] The central episodes of the novel revolve around the Malinke practices of initiation, including the night of Konden Diara and the actual initiation itself, along with evocations of Allah and recognition of the observance of Ramadan. When Laye prepares to leave his home for the coast, the celebration is depicted as involving a mixed company of those associated with Muslim ties and others with traditional Malinke practices: "On the eve of my departure all the marabouts and witchdoctors [*feticheurs*], friends and notables, and indeed anyone else who cared to cross our threshold attended a magnificent feast in our concession."[58] To insure her son's protection, Laye's mother consults the wisest marabouts while his father makes sacrifices to the ancestors. His mother obtains an elixir from Kankan, prepared by the marabout from water used to wash a slate on which appropriate Quranic verses have been written. This is a familiar example of "popular" Islam, although careful attention to the characters' speech, as well as to the calendar, offers more striking examples, particularly ones relating to views of illness and death.

At times, an expression such as "thanks be to God" can evoke a familiar Muslim sensibility. The confrontation with death, so carefully constructed and circumscribed in traditional non-Islamic Africa—in the case of this novel, in Malinke terms—reveals basic beliefs: the novel's youthful protagonist experiences fear before the spirit of his departed companion Check; for the more mature narrator of the novel, a conventional Muslim sensibility guides his thoughts as he asserts that the soul of Check was preceding them on the path of God: "Quand je songe aujourd'hui à ces jours lointains, je ne sais plus très bien ce qui m'effrayait tant, mais c'est sans doute que je ne pense plus à la mort comme j'y pensais alors: je pense plus simplement. Je songe à ces jours, et très simplement je pense que Check nous a précédés sur le chemin de Dieu, et que nous prenons tous un jour ce chemin."[59] The patterns of this passage, so typical of the novel, are decidedly oral, with their repetitions and simple syntax. The naturalization of the doctrine of destiny suggests the ease with which Islam came to be accepted within a Malinke universe.

In a number of novels, the conflict between traditional beliefs and Islamic ones has revealed skeptical attitudes toward traditional ways increasingly regarded as retrograde. In *Les Soleils des indépendances* (1968), Ahmadou Kourouma of Côte d'Ivoire depicts a Malinke universe in which the forces of traditional religious as well as Muslim authority are intertwined, both equally impotent in the face of the corrupt and powerful state. Kourouma is the master ironist: in the fallen world of postindependence Togobala (generally the region of Côte d'Ivoire), both Islam and Malinke traditions are portrayed as desiccated, impotent. Nevertheless, they are what frame the world and inform reality for the believers. As Fama, the novel's protagonist, leaves the city to return to his ancestral homeland, he reflects upon the nature of the Malinke: "Malinke are full of duplicity because deep down inside they are blacker than their skin, while the words they speak are whiter than their teeth. Are they fetish-worshipers or Muslims? A Muslim heeds the Koran, a fetish-worshiper follows the Koma; but in Togobala, everyone publicly proclaims himself a devout Muslim, but everyone privately fears the fetish. Neither lizard nor swallow!"[60] For Kourouma, social identity is constructed like a mask; that is why he employs irony to demystify both Muslims and "fetish-worshipers." The narrator does not stand, as does the European missionary, outside and above the narration: his laughter is directed toward the sources of his own painful awareness, an awareness that is informed by the sense of an identity that is marked by fragmentation. For the purist, this incompleteness is a sign of the failure to free oneself from Jahiliyya, pre-Islamic darkness. For Kourouma, there is no earlier golden age of the Prophet and his companions by which the allegory of life can measure a standard of perfection.

☾ ☾ ☾

For Ahmed Sheikh Bangura, the central conflict in the Nigerian Ibrahim Tahir's *The Last Imam* (1984) involves "the social crises that result from the conflict between puritanical concerns with orthodoxy and accommodationism."[61] In this rich and complex novel set in northern Nigeria, the figure who strives to bring a pure form of Islam into the lives of the people of Bauchi is a brilliant and unbending imam. His purism leads him into conflict with his father, the preceding imam who had less difficulty accommodating traditional custom, the political authorities, Islamic creed, and the community. His own desires for a woman named Aisha, whom he takes as a concubine after having married four wives, and his struggle for his son's loyalty, all complicate the initial conflict between orthodox Islam and what the imam calls "Hausa heathen custom." At one point in the novel, the inhabitants hear a supernatural hyena moan, a moan that had always served as an evil omen. The novel's narration does not identify the moan for the reader as being a true or false omen, but the imam reads it in strictly scripturalist fashion: "To show Moses his power, Allah had turned the Mount Sinai into dust, to protect him he had parted the sea and to save Joseph he had sent down a ram from the sky . . . the miracles of the past had nothing to do with superstitions. Certainly not with the moan of a hyena."[62]

We read the imam as a man who is a believer, an uncompromising absolutist—but not a hypocrite, and not an evil figure. Unlike the religious charlatans of much of the earlier West African literature by authors like Sembène Ousmane, Ahmadou Kourouma, Aminata Sow Fall, or even Wole Soyinka, this imam is generally portrayed as admirable, but tragic. He refuses to see where his rigidity condemns him and leads to his failure. Between syncretism of any form and the pure truth of his faith, there is no accommodation. As he puts it when contesting his father's request that he make a public display of taking his wife's chastity, "So you want me to disobey the laws of my faith just to satisfy a common Hausa heathen custom?" (page 22). The narrator remarks, following the imam's question, "It was more of an accusation than it was a question."

The novel does not itself share in the imam's accusations. Like Kourouma's "neither lizard nor swallow," the people of Bauchi are mostly just human, open to past ways while embracing the new order and its hegemony. The reasonableness of the emir when he speaks to the imam, whom he both respects and attempts to save, sets off the rigor of the purist's unaccommodating faith:

> Learned men, books, the Word of God—forget about them now and talk to me as a man. That is why I called you here and not to a meeting of the Elders with the Vizir and all the rest. And I speak to you now as a man, a friend and a brother. That is how I think of you, for if you would only remember, your father taught me and educated me as his own son. And when my father, the late Emir died, I relied on him for advice. His counsel was always good, prudent and wise and we never did anything, even if it did not touch upon the spiritual health of the land, without asking him. These things I have not forgotten.[63]

But when the imam replies, it is clear that he cannot bend to the appeal of reasonableness: "My lord, I find it impossible to speak simply as a man. My duty to you, to the people of this land and above all to the kingdom of Allah and His Word forbid that I should" (page 196). The use of such terms as "idols" and "fetish priests" harks back to the reformist movements that swept across northern Nigeria and West Africa, and is effectively captured in the words employed by Askia Muhammad in his report to Al-Maghili on the conquest of the Dogon:

> Then I released everyone who claimed that he was a free Muslim and a large number of them went off. Then after that I asked about the circumstances of some of them, and about their country and behold they pronounced the *shahada:* "There is no God save God. Muhammad is the messenger of God." But in spite of that they believe that there are beings who can bring them benefit or do them harm other than God, Mighty and Exalted is He. They have idols and they say: "The fox has said so and so, and thus it will be so and so. . . ." So I admonished them to give up all that and they refused to do so without the use of force.[64]

Askia Muhammad's lapidary conclusion must be set over against the humanism of the emir in *The Last Imam,* whose attempt to speak to the imam as a "man, a friend, a brother" evokes the contemporary reader's sympathies far more than Askia Mohammed's casual reference to conversion by the sword.

☾ ☾ ☾

A final example of a postmodern version of cultural cross-fertilizing syncretism might be seen in Nuruddin Farah's *Maps,*[65] wherein Farah informs dreams and memories, mixed fantasies, and collected world visions with Islamic figures like the winged white horse, al-Buraq, that bore Muhammad aloft, and pre-Islamic Somali images of the deity like the crow. In his works, the personal, the fantastic, and the transcendental all intersect. Farah brings us to the limit where the devotional and the postmodern word, richly textured with the mix of traditions and languages, serves to express multiplicity and ambiguity, plurality and uncertainty.

This quality of recent Europhonic African literature must be read against the thoughts expressed by the Senegalese poet Moussa Ka, who sums up the positive acceptance of the role of Islamic values within the context of African-language literature:

> Wolof, Arabic, and all other languages are equally valuable:
> All poetry is fine, that aims at praising the Prophet.[66]

Notes

1. Kaʿti 1913.
2. al-Saʿdi 1900; Gérard 1981; Hale 1990.
3. Niane 1965; Hale 1996. The version of *The Epic of Askia Mohamed* under consideration was recited by the griot, or praise-singer, Nouhou Malio, and was recorded and transcribed in 1980–81. It is included in Thomas Hale's *Scribe, Griot, and Novelist* 1990. For a collection of twenty-five African oral epics, see Johnson, Hale, and Belcher's 1997 *Oral Epics from Africa*.
4. Niane 1965; Johnson and Sosoko 1986.
5. Although Niane 1965 is a freer adaptation, we are focusing upon it because of its widespread usage. In fact, the Johnson version demonstrates similar qualities showing both Islamic and traditional Malinke influences.
6. Niane 1965, 2, 3.
7. Ibid., 3.
8. Ibid., 70.
9. Starratt 1996, 164.
10. Ibid., 163.
11. All quotes are from Starrat 1996, 164.
12. Ibid., 165.
13. Pouwels 1992, 270; Abdulaziz 1979, 55. The earliest written Islamic literature in KiSwahili dates to the seventeenth century, with Arabic writing predating it (Knappert 1979). The earliest poem is Aidarusi's *Hamziyya,* which dates to 1652 (Knappert 1979).
14. Knappert 1979, 94.
15. Ibid., 165.
16. Shariff 1991, 42.
17. Samatar 1982; Ahmed 1991.
18. All quotes from Ahmed 1991, 79.
19. Quotes from Ahmed 1991, 85.
20. Andrzejewski and Lewis, 1964.
21. Ibid., 72.
22. Kapteijns 1996, 129.
23. Ibid., 127.
24. Kane 1961.
25. Coulon 1981.
26. Kane 1961, 9.
27. Ibid., 33. My trans.
28. Ibid., 75. My trans.
29. Ibid., 53. My trans.
30. Ibid., 131. My trans.
31. Laye 1954/1971, 35.
32. Ibid., 33–34.
33. Ibid., 37.
34. Ibid., 36.
35. Trimingham 1971, 145.
36. Ibid., 151.
37. Diop 1947, 34.
38. Ibid., 36.
39. Dia 1980, 36.
40. Quotations from Salih 1978, 23.

41. Lings 1977.

42. Salih 1978, 94.

43. Lings 1977, 14.

44. Sembène Ousmane 1965, 1973; Ouologuem 1968; Armah 1973.

45. Soyinka 1958, 1965, 1973; Tahir 1984; Alkali 1987.

46. Bâ 1980, 5.

47. Ibid., 6.

48. Ibid., 8.

49. Ibid.

50. Ibid., 9.

51. Ibid., 15.

52. Ibid., 16.

53. Ibid.

54. Hale 1991, 137.

55. Ibid., 136.

56. Bâ 1972, 138.

57. Laye 1953. The term is Lemuel Johnson's, used in an essay on al-Mukhlit writing entitled "Crescent and Consciousness" (in Harrow 1991), in which he focuses on Camara Laye and Cheikh Hamidou Kane.

58. Ibid., 136.

59. Ibid., 180. "When I remember now those distant days, I no longer know exactly what frightened me so, but it is certain that I no longer think about death as I thought then; I think more simply. I remember those days, and quite simply I think that Check preceded us on the path to God, and that we all take that path one day" (my translation).

60. Kourouma 1968, 72.

61. Bangura 1996, 182.

62. Tahir 1984, 207.

63. Kourouma 1968, 196.

64. Hunwick 1985, 77.

65. Farah 1986.

66. Cited in Gérard 1981, 73.

Bibliography

Abdulaziz, M. 1979. *Muyaka: Nineteenth Century Swahili Popular Poetry.* Nairobi: n.p.

Ahmed, Ali Jimale. 1991. "Of Poets and Sheikhs." In Harrow 1991.

al-Maghili, Mohammad b. Abd al-Karim. 1932. *The Obligations of the Princes.* Trans. T. H. Baldwin. Beirut: n.p.

al-Saʿdi, Abd Al-Rahman. 1900. *Taʾrikh es-Sudan.* Trans. O. Houdas. Paris: Leroux.

Alkali, Zaynab. 1987. *The Virtuous Woman.* Ikeja, Nigeria: Longman Nigeria.

Andrzejewski, B. W., and I. M. Lewis. 1964. *Somali Poetry.* Oxford: Clarendon.

Armah, Ayi Kweh. 1973. *Two Thousand Seasons.* Nairobi: East Africa Publishing.

Bâ, Hampaté. 1972. *Aspects de la civilisation africaine.* Paris: Présence africaine.

———. 1968. *Kaïdara*. Paris: Julliard.

Bâ, Mariama. 1980. *Une si longue lettre*. Dakar: Les Nouvelles éditions africaines (in English as *So Long a Letter*, trans. Modupé Bodé-Thomas. London: Heinemann, 1981).

Bangura, Ahmed Sheikh. 1996. "The Quest for Orthodoxy in Ibrahim Tahir's *The Last Imam*." In Harrow 1996.

Cambridge History of Arabic Literature, The. 1983, 1990, 1992. Vols. 1–4. Cambridge: Cambridge University Press.

Chouikh, Mohamed. 1988. *La Citadelle*. Algeria. Independent Film.

Coulon, Christian. 1981. *Le Marabout et le prince*. Paris: Pedone.

Dia, Mamadou. 1980. *Islam and civilisations négroafricains*. Dakar: Nouvelles éditions africaines.

Diop, Birago. 1947. *Les contes d'Amadou Koumba*. Paris: Présence africaine (in English as *Tales of Amadou Koumba*, trans. Dorothy Blair. Burnt Mill, Harlow: Longman, 1985).

Farah, Nuruddin. 1983. *Close Sesame*. London: Allison & Busby.

———. 1986. *Maps*. London: Pan.

Geertz, Clifford. 1968. *Islam Observed*. Chicago: University of Chicago Press.

Gérard, Albert. 1981. *African Language Literatures*. Washington, D.C.: Three Continents.

Hale, Thomas. 1990. *Scribe, Griot, and Novelist*. Gainesville: University of Florida Press.

———. 1991. "Can a Single Foot Follow Two Paths?" In Harrow 1991.

———. 1996. *The Epic of Askia Mohammed*. Bloomington: Indiana University Press.

Harrow, Kenneth W., ed. 1991. *Faces of Islam in African Literature*. Portsmouth N.H.: Heinemann.

———. 1996. *The Marabout and the Muse*. Portsmouth, N.H.: Heinemann.

Hiskett, Mervyn. 1973. *The Sword of Truth: The Life and Times of Shehu Usman dan Fodio*. London: School of Oriental and African Studies.

———. 1975. *A History of Hausa Islamic Verse*. London: School of Oriental and African Studies.

Hunwick, John O. 1985. *Sharia in Songhay: The Replies of Al-Maghili to the Questions of Askia al-Hajj Mohammed*. New York: Oxford University Press.

Ibn Battuta. 1975. *Ibn Battuta in Black Africa*. Trans. Said Hamdun and Noel King. London: Rex Collins.

Johnson, John William, and Fa-Digi Sosoko. 1986. *The Epic of Son-Jara: A West African Tradition*. Bloomington: Indiana University Press.

Johnson, John William, Thomas A. Hale, and Stephen Belcher. 1997. *Oral Epics from Africa*. Bloomington: Indiana University Press.

Johnson, Lemuel. 1991. "Crescent and Consciousness: Islamic Orthodoxies and the West African Novel." In Harrow 1991.

Kane, Cheikh Hamidou. 1961. *L'Aventure ambiguë*. Paris: Julliard (in English as *Ambiguous Adventure*, trans. Katherine Woods. New York: Collier, 1963).

Kapteijns, Lidwien, with Miriam Omar Ali. 1996. "*Sittaat:* Somali Women's Songs for the 'Mother of the Believers.'" In Harrow 1996.

Ka'ti, Mahmoud. 1913. *Tar'ikh al-Fattash.* Trans. O. Houdas and M. Delafosse. Paris: Leroux.

Knappert, Jan. 1979. *Four Centuries of Swahili Verse.* London: Heinemann.

Kourouma, Ahmadou. 1968. *Soleils des indépendances.* Montreal: Presses de l'Université de Montréal.

Laye, Camara. 1953. *L'Enfant noir.* Paris: Plon.

———. 1954. *Le Regard du roi.* Paris: Plon (in English as *The Radiance of the King,* trans. James Kirkup. New York: Collier, 1971).

Lings, Martin. 1977. *What Is Sufism?* Berkeley: University of California Press.

Niane, Djibril Tamsir. 1965. *Sundiata.* Harlow, U.K.: Longmans.

Ouologuem, Yambo. 1968. *Devoir de Violence.* Paris: Seuil.

Pouwels, Randall L. 1992. "Swahili Literature and History in the Post-Structuralist Era," *The International Journal of African Historical Studies* 25.2 (1992): 261–283.

Salih, Tayeb. 1969. *Season of Migration to the North.* Trans. Denys Johnson-Davies. London: Heinemann.

———. 1978. *The Wedding of Zein and Other Stories* [1968]. Trans. Denys Johnson-Davies. London: Heinemann.

Samatar, Said S. 1982. *Oral Poetry and Somali Nationalism.* London: Cambridge University Press.

Sembène Ousmane. 1973. *Vehi Ciosane.* Paris: Présence africaine.

———. 1965. *Xala.* Paris: Présence africaine.

Shariff, Ibrahim Noor. 1991. "Islam and Secularity in Swahili Literature: An Overview." In Harrow 1991.

Soyinka, Wole. 1973. *A Season of Anomy.* London: Rex Collins.

———. 1965. *The Interpreters.* London: Deutsch.

———. 1963. *The Swamp Dwellers* [1958]. In *Three Plays.* Ibadan: Mbari.

Starratt, Priscilla. 1996. "Islamic Influences on Oral Traditions in Hausa Literature." In Harrow 1996.

Tahir, Ibrahim. 1984. *The Last Imam.* Boston: Routledge & Kegan Paul.

Trimingham, J. Spencer. 1971. *The Sufi Orders in Islam.* London; Oxford University Press.

CHAPTER 24

Music and Islam in Sub-Saharan Africa

Eric Charry

From Senegal in the west to Indonesia in the east, music flourishes in, and is an essential part of, Muslim societies, achieving remarkable degrees of technical and aesthetic sophistication, widespread patronage, and striking diversity. The breadth of the range of music in the (for the most part) predominantly Muslim African countries surveyed here is daunting; each country has its own local and national cultures, parts of which are often shared with neighboring countries. As Islam took root throughout Africa it influenced and was influenced by local cultures in a variety of ways, sometimes stifling, sometimes stimulating musical expression. One of the goals of this chapter is finding common ground to discuss the various ways that Islam has impacted music in Africa south of the Sahara. Another goal is to bring together and survey diverse relevant writings on Islam and music in sub-Saharan Africa. Due to the fragmented nature of the sources and the vast music cultures concerned, this is more of a tentative beginning than a grand synthesis.[1]

The Nature of Islamic and Arab Influence

A fundamental task in the study of the relationship between Islam and music in Africa is, insofar as is possible, isolating for discussion Islamic doctrine and its local interpretations, the Arabian and broader Arab cultures that gave birth to and nourished Islam, and the African cultures into which Islam was brought.

Islam has affected African musics both socially and musically. By suppressing some forms of musical expression, such as certain kinds of drumming and dancing, sparking others, such as those associated with certain Muslim festivals, and lending status to certain musicians attached to local Muslim rulers, the introduction of Islam has impacted the kinds of music available to African societies, their uses of music, and the roles of musicians. By providing new technical musical materials, such as that embodied in solo recitation of the Quran, and enhancing some genres with new lyric content, such as the use of quotations from the Quran, Islam has impacted on the raw materials of musical performance.

The Arab culture that engendered Islam has traveled throughout much of Africa and affected music making, but it took root in much less uniform ways than that of Islamic doctrine. Some musical traits embodied in both Quranic recitation and Arab music, like monophony (single voice or unison singing) and a high degree of melodic ornamentation, permeate whole music cultures, perhaps due to similarities with local practices. But other aspects were more selectively accepted or rejected: the abstract nature of pieces of music; combining instrumental pieces into concert suites; technical terminology; and the use of certain musical instruments. Arab influences may have spread across Africa from Egypt well before the advent of Islam. The likely possibility that some influences may have initially spread from sub-Saharan Africa to Egypt via the slave trade and migration is still awaiting serious sustained scholarly inquiry.

Placed within the larger context of music in the world of Islam, Africa has two faces.[2] North Africa is allied with other broad musical traditions of the core Muslim world, such as Arab and Turkish, that share certain core characteristics of music making deeply rooted in the recitation of the Quran and embodied in a tonal universe known as *maqam:* monophony; improvisation; segmented or modular melodic structure; and melodic intricacy. Outside this core world is a second geographic area where these traditions and the maqam phenomenon are further removed from local practices, including Central Asia and North India. Sub-Saharan Africa, along with island and peninsular Southeast Asia, form a third Muslim area furthest removed from the influence of musical traditions in the core Muslim world.

Local African cultures that received Islam accepted musical elements in a variety of ways. Some of the contributing factors included geographic proximity and conformity of local traditions to the Arabian heartland, the duration of the Islamization process, and the intensity of the encounter of local traditions with Islam. In North Africa, whole Arab instrumental ensembles and their repertories took root and developed regional dialects. In coastal East Africa, a similar kind of process occurred wherein imported Arab instruments formed the core of ensembles that eventually established their own repertories based in local Swahili culture that came to be a mainstay of national identities. West African societies were much less apt to accept major parts of Arab music culture, most likely due to the geographic and cultural divide.

One of the least investigated areas of African music is the process by which Islam has impacted local traditions. The entries in the bibliography below represent a drop in the bucket of the totality of writing on African music. To be sure, many other studies of African music address issues of Islamic influence peripherally, but in general, fundamental questions of how and why an African music culture would and could adapt foreign elements have been addressed piecemeal throughout the continent, with reference to single musical traditions. These writings point to several major areas of impact, which can serve as a basis for a broader view:

- the use in local musics of quotations from the Quran and other Islamic sources;

- new genres of music associated with Muslim religious occasions, spiritual leaders, or Muslim musicians;

- alteration, suppression, and even eradication of some traditional forms of music;

- the establishment of separate classes of musicians;

- the introduction of new musical instruments;

- and new sound materials (styles of vocal and melody production, and tuning systems).

Islamic Religious Doctrine

Artistic expression associated with the recitation of the Quran contains fundamental characteristics of musical practice in the core Muslim world. In addition to the core genres of Quranic recitation and the call to prayer *(adhan)*, Muslim religious expression encompasses other genres such as chants of the *dhikr* (the sufi remembrance ceremony), songs called *madih* eulogizing the Prophet and his family,[3] and other chants associated with *mawlid* festivities (celebrating the birth of Muhammad). These genres form a shared body of works throughout the Muslim world, albeit with regional styles. The recitation of the Quran in particular carries Islamic sound ideals in their most essential form, and, as Lois Ibsen al Faruqi has noted, "There seems to be little doubt that the chanting of the Holy Book, the Quran, is the most important single agent of the musical dissemination process. It is the Quranic chant which is the clearest embodiment of the salient features of the music of the Muslims."[4]

Recitation of the Quran

The Quran exists in both written and oral traditions, but prayer, consisting of the profession of the faith *(shahada)* and recitations from the Quran, is meant to be heard rather than read.[5] The language of the Quran (the work that is the ultimate religious authority in Islam—the revelations communicated orally from Allah, God, to the prophet Muhammad via the intermediary angel Jibril) is classical Arabic, and everywhere in the Muslim world it is transmitted orally in Arabic in a style of delivery rooted in the Arab world. Being of divine origin, recitation of the Quran is one of the unifying forces in the Muslim world, carrying Arab aesthetics of melody wherever it goes.

A minimal education in Islam consists of memorizing parts of the Quran, and the vast majority of African Muslims have at least a passing acquaintance with this practice. *Tajwid,* the system of proper articulation and duration of syllables, and the sectioning off of words from each other that regulates the recitation of the Quran, is believed to reflect the way it was originally heard by Muhammad. Learning the Quran means learning to recite it according to the rules of tajwid, a duty of devout Muslims everywhere.

Although Quranic recitation carries core Muslim aesthetics of music making, it is considered distinct from musical performance on the basis of its text, which is of divine origin, and its intent. Herein lies a problem with Western terminology: while Quranic recitation fits a Western definition of music, most Muslims would not consider it music. Rather, the florid artistic rendering in public performance of the verses of the Quran are considered "recitation," not "singing" or "music." Even so, musical features of Quranic recitation have influenced music making in African Muslim countries.

In Egypt, two different styles of Quranic recitation are related to two different performance contexts. One, *murattal* style, is appropriate for personal private renditions or group prayer, and is aimed toward the clear syllabic presentation of the text, close to the speech end of a continuum; the other, *mujawwad* style, is for public performance, firmly rooted in maqam, the Arab melodic system, and is intended to produce an emotional effect on listeners through a more artistic melodic rendition full of ornamentation and melismas. To promote spontaneity of expression and avoid imposing a fixed melody on the Quranic text, mujawwad style is performed only publicly; practice is done on non-Quranic texts. Cassettes of this style are common in African marketplaces.[6]

Egyptian reciters of the Quran are particularly prized abroad; the government receives requests and sends reciters to all countries of the Islamic world. Al-Azhar University in Cairo maintains institutes that train professional Quran reciters and has played an important role in disseminating Egyptian styles of recitation throughout the Muslim world.[7] For centuries, Egyptian-educated scholars and reciters have taught south of the Sahara, and Africans have gone to Egypt and other West Asian countries to study, insuring an essential unity of Quranic recitation in Muslim Africa, although regional differences would most likely be found.[8]

The religious duties of every Muslim prescribed in the Quran, known as the five pillars of Islam (*shahada, salat, zakat, Ramadan,* and *hajj*), mark the major occasions for recitation of sacred texts as well as celebrations (except for *zakat,* or almsgiving). Salat, prayer done five times daily, is the major bond that ties together the sonic world of Islam. The *adhan,* performed by a *mu'adhdhin* (cantor), announces to the community each of the five daily prayer times. Prayer consists of recitations from the Quran, which begin with a verse known as *isti'adhah* (see figure 1). Directly following this is the *basmalah,* a one-line invocation that precedes each *sura* (chapter) of the Quran.[9] Then follows the first of the 115 *suwar* (chapters) in the Quran, known as *al-fatihah* (the opening), consisting of seven verses. While salat can be performed in the privacy of the home, the Muslim community comes together for the Friday midday prayer at the mosque, which can be preceded by an extended public recitation from the Quran. Shahada, the profession of the faith, is heard as part of the adhan.

The adhan, isti'adhah, basmalah, al-fatihah, and shahada (figure 1) are the most widely heard verses in the Muslim world, and their delivery constantly infuses Muslim communities with Islamic aesthetics of oral expression. They are primarily heard from the mouths of imams (prayer leaders), mua'dhdhins, and professional reciters across Africa, but musicians may also use them in performance, such as the griots (hereditary professional oral historians and musicians) of western Africa, who for the most part are educated and devout Muslims.

Figure 1. THE MOST COMMONLY HEARD VERSES IN ISLAM

Adhan (call to prayer)

Allah-u Akbar (4 times)
  Allah is most great

Ashhadu an la ilah-a illa 'llah (2 times)
  I testify that there is no God besides Allah

Ashhadu anna Muhammedan rasul Allah (2 times)
  I testify that Muhammad is the apostle of Allah

Hayya'ala 'l-salat (2 times)
  Come to prayer

Hayya'ala 'l-falah (2 times)
  Come to salvation

Allah-u Akbar (2 times)
  Allah is most great

La ilah-a illa 'llah
  There is no God besides Allah

Isti'adhah

'a'uudhu bi llaahi mina sh-shaytaani r-rajiim
  I take refuge in God from the power of evil.

Basmalah

bi smi llaahi r-rahmaani r-rahiim
  In the name of God, the Merciful and Compassionate.

Al-Fatihah (The Opening)

Al ham du li llaah rab bi l 'aa la miin
  Praise be to Allah, Lord of the Worlds

Al rah maan al ra hiim
  The beneficent, the Merciful

Maa li ki yaw mid diin,
   Owner of the Day of Judgment

Iy yaa ka na'budu wa iy yaa ka nas ta 'iin
   Thee (alone) we worship; Thee (alone) we ask for help.

Ah di naa l si raa ta l mu sta qiim
   Show us the straight path

Si raa ta la dhii na an 'am ta 'a lay him
   The path of those whom Thou hast favored

Ghay til magh duu bi 'a lay him wa laad da liin
   Not (the path) of those who earn Thine anger nor of those who go astray.

Shahada (profession of the faith)

Ashadu an la ilah-a illa 'llah
   I testify that there is no God besides Allah

Ashadu anna Muhammedan rasul Allah
   I testify that Muhammad is the apostle of God

Pop singers also infuse their music with verses from the Quran. For example, Baaba Maal, a singer from the Tokolor (a Fulbe branch) homeland in northern Senegal, begins his piece "Joulowo"[10] by singing the invocation preceding any recitation from the Quran (the isti'adhah) followed by the first line of al-fatihah, after which he switches to his native Pulaar, praising God:

audu bi llahi mina s-saytani r-rajim
   (I take refuge in God from the power of evil)

Al ham du li llah rab bi l a la min
   (Praise be to Allah, Lord of the Worlds)

Allah.

Mory Kante, Guinea's most commercially successful singer, in the course of his piece "Inch Allah"[11] sings three verses from the adhan and then the first verse of the al-fatihah. Then he continues on in his native Maninka tongue with greetings and praises to his patrons:

Allah-u Akbar, Allah-u Akbar
   (Allah is most great, Allah is most great)

[Ashhadu an] la ilah-a illa 'llah
   ([I testify that] there is no God besides Allah)

[Ashhadu anna] Muhammadan rasul Allah
   ([I testify that] Muhammad is the apostle of Allah)

Al ham du li llah rab bi l a la min
(Praise be to Allah, Lord of the Worlds).

This bringing in of verses from the Quran to popular music is widespread in West Africa, but in well-circumscribed contexts. Usually the subject matter of the song will dictate the appropriateness of mixing devotional and nondevotional texts. Baaba Maal's piece referred to above is a call for his fellow citizens to take up prayer. As the most aggressive disseminators of Islam in West Africa, Fulbe singers such as Maal might be expected to draw on the Quran. Pieces dedicated to important Fulbe leaders—such as "Taara" (He has gone), a widely performed piece dedicated to the nineteenth-century jihad leader al-Hajj ʿUmar Tal—routinely draw Islamic verses into performance. For example, in the course of a performance of "Taara,"[12] noted Mandinka singer Tata Bambo Kouyate, a female griot from Mali, suddenly interjects the verse "la ilah-a illa Allaha" (There is no God besides Allah) in the midst of Mandinka praises of al-Hajj ʿUmar Tal. Although the words are among the most fundamental in all Islam, her singing style is Maninka, as is the musical accompaniment, which consists of a single acoustic guitar. Mory Kante's piece "Inch Allah" represents perhaps the border of acceptability. *Akwaba Beach,* the album on which "Inch Allah" appears, was the best-selling African record of its time, with its hit "Yeke Yeke" making strong appearances as a single on European pop record charts and in dance clubs. Kante's Muslim sensibility allows pieces like "Inch Allah" and "Yeke Yeke" to stand side by side on a single album. Each piece has its place within his repertory.[13]

In stark contrast to popular singers integrating Islamic verses into their music, musical instruments have been used to accompany commentary on the Quran. Malian composer and musician Sorry Bamba questioned the venerable Malian writer Amadou Hampate Ba about this apparently uncommon practice.

> **Bamba:** Papa, I listened with pleasure to the commentaries in the Fula language on the Quran you did on Radio Mali. It was the first time that I heard the Quran accompanied by the ngoni [a lute] and I wondered what caused you to do that?

> **Ba:** It is to reach as many people as possible. I know that the people love the sound of Bazoumana Cissoko's ngoni. Through his music, the audience will listen better to the message that I make on the Quran.[14]

In Ba's interpretation of Islam, the combination of righteous intent (to draw listeners to the Quran) and an appropriate vehicle (an elderly respected musician playing the *ngoni,* a classical instrument in the sense that it typically accompanies deep oral history), justified the use of a musical instrument next to the Quran.

Most musicians in Muslim societies who perform for Muslim patrons have had at least a minimal Islamic education, with many gaining fluency in Arabic. Being schooled in or exposed to proper recitation of the Quran has had a greater impact on singing in North Africa than it has further south, perhaps because sub-Saharan styles of singing are further removed from Quranic recitation styles. In one Senegalese town, it is typical for a mu'adhdhin to come from the griot class,[15] but it is not clear how widespread this practice may be. Neither really is the extent of the influence of Quranic recitation styles on the griots of western Africa very clear. Until further research is carried out, it will have to suffice to generalize that a western African sahel and savannah praise singing style differs from neighboring non-Muslim singing styles (usually from the south), in part due to the influence of Muslim recitation or singing styles. On the other hand, the impact that early training in Quranic recitation had on shaping the vocal style of the great Egyptian singer Umm Kulthum is widely acknowledged and appreciated.[16] Growing up in a core Muslim culture where Quranic recitation and other singing styles are similar, the mutual influences would be much more direct than elsewhere.

Muslim Festivals and Occasions for Music

The main occasions for the florid mujawwad-style recitations of the Quran include: immediately preceding the Friday afternoon communal prayer in the mosque; every night during the month of Ramadan; and radio broadcasts. But there are also numerous other kinds of music making associated with Muslim celebrations.[17] Two such occasions are associated with Ramadan, the month of fasting from sunup to sundown: *laylat al-qadr* (the night of majesty), on the twenty-seventh night of Ramadan, commemorating the first revelation of the Quran to Muhammad; and *'id al-fitr* (the lesser feast), marking the end of Ramadan. The greatest celebration in the Islamic calendar in many parts of Africa is *'id al-adha* (the feast of the sacrifice), also known as *'id al-kabir* (the greater feast) or Tabaski in many African countries, commemorating the sacrifice of a lamb by Abraham, marking the end of the hajj that takes place several months after Ramadan. 'Id al-fitr and 'id al-kabir are major events for musicians and singers attached to the Hausa Kano court in Nigeria, for Dagbamba drummers in Ghana, and for many others. The spectacular music making at the fourteenth-century court of Mali described by Ibn Battuuta took place on these two feast days, as well as at the Friday communal prayers.[18]

During the month of Ramadan, music may also play an important part in daily activities. In Nigeria, for example, Yoruba and Hausa singers and musicians go house to house waking up Muslims for breakfast before daybreak; this also occurs among the Dagbamba in northern Ghana.[19] Yoruba call this vocal genre *were*,[20] which may have been transformed into another genre called *apala,* which uses a Yoruba *dundun* (drum) ensemble. Apala eventually began to be played on other occasions and gradually became entertainment music.[21]

Sakara, a genre of Yoruba Muslim-based entertainment music consisting of a vocalist accompanied by a frame drum *(sakara),* a gourd struck with rings on the fingers *(igba)*, and a plucked lute *(molo)*, later replaced by a fiddle *(goje)*, bears some of the vocal traits of Quranic recitation. Sakara was popular in the mid-twentieth century and was played at various Islamic festivals, weddings, and naming ceremonies. It was eventually eclipsed by apala as a favorite Yoruba Muslim popular music. By the 1970s, a genre known as *fuji* emerged, featuring the dundun and other talking drums as well as frequent use of quotations from the Quran,[22] similar to the example of Baaba Maal above. Another Yoruba and Hausa Muslim genre known as *waka* was performed at marriages and to welcome home Muslims from the hajj.[23] The use of drums, including drummers who would accompany notable Muslims to and from the prayer grounds on the major festivals,[24] may seem unusual, given the close association of drums with African deities and power societies that could compete directly with Islam. But among Yoruba, at least, those drums associated with non-Islamic religious traditions are not used in Muslim contexts. The dundun ensemble, on the other hand, is used in both Muslim and non-Muslim ceremonies, and dundun specialists are predominantly Muslim.[25]

Mawlid (or *maulidi*), the birthday of Muhammad, on the twelfth day of the month Rabii Awwal, is another important occasion for singing, instrument playing, and dancing. The telling of the story of Muhammad's birth may also be performed at other times of the year. In Lamu, Kenya (Lamu is the name of the major town as well as the island and archipelago on which it is situated), an important center of Swahili culture, maulidi is cause for a week-long festival. In the mosques of Lamu, a frame drum *(tari)*, flute *(nai)*, and small drum *(kigoma)* are used in religious celebrations like maulidi. A sharp distinction is made wherein these instruments are used exclusively in religious contexts; instruments used for other kinds of dancing are not used on religious occasions. The Damba festival of the Dagbamba of northern Ghana centers around mawlid, and represents not just the peaceful coexistence of Islam and local drumming traditions, but a real African affinity for synthesis.[26] On the birthday of the Prophet, *luna* (talking drum) playing accompanies recitations from the Quran while the luna drummers *(lunsi)* escort Muslim clerics to the chief's compound where the birth is formally announced. The drummers are an important part of activities throughout the subsequent week leading up to the ritual naming ceremony devoted to the Prophet, and they even echo with their drums the words of the Muslim leader when he announces that the newborn's name is Muhammad. After the naming ceremony, the "strongly Muslim emphasis in the event shifts—Damba becomes devoted to the land, chieftaincy, social networks, and Dagbamba values."[27] The *Mi'raj*, the Prophet's ascension, the night of 26/27 Rajab, is occasionally celebrated in a similar way to mawlid in various parts of Africa.

Sufi dhikr ceremonies are not usually attached to a festival or single specific occasion but they often take place on Thursday afternoons or on specially designated occasions. The ceremonies can take a variety of forms that can include recitations, singing, and dancing. *Dhikr* can refer to verses or formulas said during the daily prayers, to private meditative rhythmic breathing and chanting of formulas, and to a communal ceremony, called *hadra,* wherein musical instruments are played along with singing and dancing.[28] A concert of instrumental and vocal music, called *sama,* is also related to dhikr ceremonies. Pilgrimages to the tombs of important sufi leaders, such as the Grand Maggal of the Mouride sufi order in Senegal, or those of the North African Gnawa, may also be occasions for song and dance.[29]

Perhaps furthest removed from core Islamic practice everywhere, occupying the fringes of Islamic religious activity, are the ceremonies of the Gnawa, professional musicians and healers of sub-Saharan origin brought to North Africa centuries ago in the slave trade. Their ceremonies, called *derdeba* (in Morocco and Algeria) and *stambali* (in Tunisia) differ from the sufi hadra in that *jinns,* supernatural beings, are introduced and they are aimed at healing individuals.[30] In Essaouria, an important Gnawa center in Morocco, Gnawa ceremonies gradually resume after Ramadan (during which time they are not held), culminating during the month of Chabane (immediately preceding Ramadan) with ceremonies every night except Friday. Gnawa can also be found entertaining the public at Jamaa al-Fna, the famed plaza in Marrakesh. Since the 1970s, Gnawa traditions have been secularized and popularized for a broader public by groups such as Nass el Ghiwane from Morocco. Other kinds of spirit possession ceremonies *(zaar* and *tambura)* aimed at curing individuals and with minimal Muslim components also take place in Sudan.[31]

While the Islamic holy month of Ramadan has spawned what can be considered Muslim musical genres, it has also acted to attenuate others. For example, Ramadan is a month of unemployment for professional *jembe* drummers in western Africa. One of their main sources of income is playing for weddings, which are halted during this month. During id al-adha, however, jembe drumming and *bala* (xylophone) playing are quite common as part of the general festivities. The ancient Sosso bala, the instrument believed to date back to the time of the Maninka hero Sunjata (thirteenth century) is usually taken out and played in Niagassola, Guinea, and jembe drummers tour the village, playing compound to compound.

Islamic Views on Music

The role of music in Islam has long been a topic of debate among Muslims. The Quran has nothing explicit to say about the use of music: different verses have been cited as being implicitly for or against it. The hadith, authoritative collections of sayings from the prophet Muhammad and anecdotes about his life, have been cited in the debate, but widely varying conclusions have been drawn from the same passages. In short, outside of a few core tenets, Islamic doctrine, ultimately stemming from the Quran and the hadith, is not so much a singular canon but rather a body of divergent interpretations at different times and places.

Arguments concerning the role of music center around the term *sama,* which refers to listening to chanting and singing of religious texts. Sama' can be contrasted with *tarab* (delight, pleasure) and *ghina* (singing), both of which have more secular connotations having to do with the reception or the performance, respectively, of music, and neither of which would be used to refer to Quranic recitation or other kinds of religious expression. Arguments against sama stress that it is associated with worldly pleasures that diverts one from a religious life. "One might speculate as well that it is not so much the un-Islamic associations of music (luxury and vice) that call up objection as it is music's compelling power, which makes it a rival with Islam for human souls."[32] This concept of competing for human souls is a powerful reason why Muslims have acted to suppress certain power societies associated with drumming and masked dancers, such as *komo* in Guinea and Mali. Arguments for sama stress that through it, primarily chanting and singing, one can come closer to God.[33]

While widespread sufism encouraged a healthy atmosphere for music, several Islamic reform movements would try to reshape local practice. One such case was the holy war led by Fulani scholar 'Uthman dan Fodio against perceived Hausa backsliding in the early nineteenth century, leading to the establishment of the Fulani Sokoto empire covering parts of Niger, Nigeria, and Cameroon. Writings by 'Uthman dan Fodio and others around this time, conveniently discussed, excerpted, and translated by Veit Erlmann (1986), shed light not only on Hausa musical practice, but also on local Muslim attitudes toward local musics. String and wind instruments were scorned or condemned, at least in part because of the contexts in which they were played. Certain kinds of drumming were allowed, notably that for military purposes. The Sokoto reforms, however, were to have limited long-term impact on Hausa music culture.[34]

Muslim dogma concerning representational art, to quote a chapter of the same name by René Bravmann, has had varying degrees of impact on African mask traditions, and consequently on the accompanying drumming and dancing.[35] A fundamental objection to representational art is that the act of fashioning or creating it by human beings is an attempt at usurping the powers of Allah, the Creator. Therefore, "the highest term of praise which in the Christian world can be bestowed upon the artist, in calling him a creator, in the Muslim world serves to emphasize the most damning evidence of his guilt."[36] This concept leads not only to the suppression of certain kinds of art, but also to the development of other kinds of more abstract art.

> Therefore, although the Quran does not give any specifications, injunctions or prohibitions about the arts in general or about music in particular, the ideas carried in that revelation, and in the minds of the peoples who received it and were moved by it, made certain types of artistic expression more suitable than other.

> First of all, since no being in nature could properly represent God, tawhid [the oneness and utter "other-ness" of God] caused the Muslims to emphasize abstract content in their arts.[37]

In North Africa, the idea of abstract content in the arts can be seen in the instrumental and vocal suites named after the musical materials out of which they are made (maqam). A similar practice occurs among the griots of Mauritania, who name pieces after the melodic modes in which they are set. But just south in Mali, and throughout sub-Saharan Africa, this is rare. Pieces are typically named after important individuals (in the griot tradition), or after events celebrating groups of individuals (as in drumming pieces for initiations or certain classes of people).

Sufism

Islamic mysticism, known as sufism, not only allows music, but puts it to great use.[38] Sufism in its broadest sense can embrace "those tendencies in Islam which aim at direct communion between God and man."[39] Many Ways (turuq, sing. tariqa) of accomplishing this have developed in sufism, and by the thirteenth century turuq took on the more institutionalized aspect of an order with a founder who passed down the tradition through a chain (silsila) of disciples, who would receive the wird (access), "the substance of the tariqa defined in one or more prayers or cycles of prayers."[40] The earliest tariqa, and the most widespread in sub-Saharan Africa, stems from ʿAbd al-Qadir, the twelfth-century founder of the Qadiriyya order based in Baghdad. In addition to the Qadiriyya order, the Tijaniyya order, founded in the eighteenth century by Ahmad al-Tijani in Morocco, is found throughout West Africa due to the nineteenth-century jihads of its Fulbe adherents, especially al-Hajj ʿUmar Tal (see chapter 20).

According to sufi thought, the value of samaʿ, listening to religious music, is determined by the righteousness of the listener. As a means to explore the spiritual world, it is admissible; as entertainment or diversion, it is not. Sufis cite sura 33, verses 41–42 of the Quran as the inspiration for their dhikr ceremony, which can include singing, dancing, and even musical instruments: "O ye who believe! Remember Allah with much remembrance. And glorify Him early and late." This citation for the use of music in praise of God brings to mind psalm 150 of the Old Testament, which is similarly taken as inspiration by African American Pentecostal church members.

Whereas recitation of the Quran conforms closely to norms established in the Arab world, sufi dhikrs tend to be shaded more by local musical practice. In general, the further away the genre is from Quran recitation, the more it will reflect local culture. Even so, dhikrs appear to retain certain general characteristics. The most extensive reporting on the musical aspects of a dhikr come from Sudan, where Artur Simon has carefully documented the various components of the ceremony.[41]

The unique nature of Senegalese sufism has led to its pervasive influence on popular singers such as Youssou Ndour and Baaba Maal.[42] Sufism is very strong in Senegal, with almost all of the Muslim population belonging to either the Tijaniyya (the majority), Mouride, or Qadiriyya orders. Sufi leaders have taken on such an aura of sainthood that they often have replaced Allah or Muhammad as the subjects of praise-songs and poetry, contributing to a distinctly Senegalese brand of Sufism. The griot praise-singing tradition may have been adapted by non-griots (who would not normally take up public singing) to praise the religious elite, rather than the political and social elite. Shaykh Amadu Bamba Mbacke, the founder of the Mouride offshoot of the Qadiriyya order in the late-nineteenth century, is venerated the most and has been the object of countless praise-songs and recordings. A distinction has been made by Fiona McLaughlin between popular Islamic music, such as the poems and songs connected with various sufi ceremonies, usually sung in Arabic, and Islamic popular music, such as songs in praise of sufi leaders commercially recorded by popular singers, usually in local languages such as Wolof or Pulaar.[43]

North African Gnawa approach the outer boundaries of sufism. Gnawa claim descent from Bilal (or Sidi Bilali), the black African slave freed by Muhammad who then became his mu'adhdhin. But there is neither a biological nor initiatory chain linking Bilal (who was a eunuch) to any specific Gnawa families. Gnawa were brought to North Africa as slaves from south of the Sahara, most notably of Bambara (a catch-all term referring to any number of Malian peoples) or Hausa descent. The situation of the Gnawa has been compared to that of Africans in the Americas who forged new religions and musics by combining the belief systems of the lands from where they came with those of their new homes.[44] The link of Gnawa to Bilal may be indicative of their pre-slave status in Mali, where widespread oral traditions indicate that Bilal was the ancestor of the royal Keita lineage. A similar kind of descent, but from Surakata, a companion to Muhammad, has been claimed by Maninka, Wolof, and Soninke griots, perhaps as a move to enhance their prestige in Muslim society.[45]

Gnawa musical instruments bear closer relationships to those used south of the Sahara than those in North Africa or the core Muslim world. The *guimbri* (sometimes called *sintir*), a large plucked lute with a rectangular, box-like body, bears many marks of the Bamana ngoni played in Mali (which has a rounded body). The *shaqshaqa* (Arabic: *qarqabat*) are large metal castanets that resemble those used by Hausa women.[46] The large, double-headed drum called *ganga* (Arabic: *tabl*) played with one curved and one straight stick is similar to drums played throughout the Sahel, particularly the Hausa ganga from Nigeria.

The Arab Culture of Islam

The Arab culture that gave rise to Islam in the seventh century spawned one of the great classical music traditions of the world. Beginning in the ninth century, Arabic treatises dealing with all aspects of music theory began to appear, with Baghdad emerging as the major center. While the florid mujawwad style of recitation of the Quran took root wherever the seeds of Islam were planted, other realms of Arab music had mixed success in the Muslim world.

Arab musical instruments and their associated repertories took hold in North Africa. To a lesser extent Arab instruments were also adopted, but much later, in parts of coastal East Africa. The further removed areas of West Africa, however, did not accept these elements so readily, perhaps because they did not have ready access to the instruments nor a community of Arab patrons. Comparisons of the Arab-based musical traditions in North Africa, East Africa, and Mauritania illustrate the varied ways in which Arab traditions have mixed with local African cultures, relatively independent of Islamic doctrine.

Early in the ninth century, a renowned Baghdad musician named Ziryab fled to Andalusia (southern Spain), where he founded a conservatory of music. Music was patronized at the Andalusian courts, and beginning in the twelfth century, when Hispano-Arabs began fleeing the centers of Seville, Cordoba, Valencia, and Granada to the Maghrib, the musicians among them reestablished their Andalusian traditions in Tunis (Tunisia), Tlemcem and Constantine (Algeria), and Fez (Morocco). These traditions of ultimate Arab origin still survive, and the genre of music played, which consists of suites of instrumental and vocal pieces, is called Maluf (in Tunisia and Libya) or Nubah (in Morocco and Algeria).[47]

Certain Arab or West Asian instruments, such as the 'ud and rebab, spread north from Spain into Europe, eventually becoming transformed into the guitar and violin, respectively. The early spread of instruments from Muslim lands south into sub-Saharan Africa is a sensitive topic fraught with generalizations often based on scant evidence. There are clear cases of foreign imports, and there are also cases in which lack of evidence makes it hazardous to speculate on the direction of the flow of influences.[48]

Several instruments associated with sufi activities have clearly been imported south of the Sahara, where they have largely retained their Muslim associations. The tabala (a drum), primarily found outside mosques, is used to announce many events associated with the Islamic calendar. In Senegal, adherents of the Qadiriyya sufi order use a set of tabala, most likely inspired by their sabar drumming traditions, in their religious ceremonies.[49] The bendir (a frame drum) is also an Arab (or West Asian) import used in Hausa Qadiriyya dhikr ceremonies.[50]

Instruments like the plucked lutes (for example, the Maninka koni, Fulbe hoddu, Wolof xalam, Hausa gurumi) and bowed lutes (for example, the Dagbamba gondze, and Hausa goge) that are played throughout the West African sahel and savanna present more difficult problems of attribution. They are primarily played by Muslim peoples, but their origins are unclear. The similarity of ancient Egyptian plucked lutes to those of West Africa is uncanny, pointing perhaps to a diffusion process dating back almost four thousand years.[51] It has been assumed that fiddles were imported from either North Africa or Egypt, but substantial historical information has been lacking.[52]

Equally puzzling are the origins of other instruments that are widespread in the Sahel regions of Senegal, Mali, Niger, Ghana, and Nigeria. Hourglass-shaped squeeze drums (tama, luna, dundun), large double-headed bass drums (dundun, gun-gon, ganga), and the more geographically limited long trumpets (kakaki) associated with Hausa and Fulani royalty all have close associations with Muslim peoples, but their origins have yet to be adequately explored. These might be considered Muslim instruments not because they are used in Islamic contexts, but because they are primarily played by Muslim peoples.

The musical genre known as *taarab*, from the Arabic "to be moved or agitated," presents a fascinating example of a mixture of East African, Egyptian, and Indian Ocean elements, relatively free of religious associations.[53] Primarily played at weddings, taarab is the predominant popular music along the Swahili coast (northern Mozambique to southern Somalia), with important centers in Zanzibar (the island that spawned the genre), Dar es Salaam and Tanga (Tanzania), and Mombasa and Lamu (Kenya). It is even appreciated further afield in parts of neighboring countries such as Democratic Republic of the Congo (Zaire) and Burundi. In contrast to the strength of Islam and weakness of Arab culture in much West African music, taarab music exemplifies Arab influence without the accompanying Islamic doctrine.

The origins of taarab are often dated to the 1870s, when the third Omani sultan to rule from Zanzibar sent one of his musicians to study in Egypt, thereby opening up his court to Arab music. By the turn of the century, the Zanzibari court was home to an Egyptian Arab music rooted in the *takht* ensemble that was flourishing in Egypt. The male takht (male musicians performing for a male audience) initially predominated at the Zanzibar court: a solo singer accompanied by a male chorus; *'ud* (lute); *qanun* (dulcimer); *nay* (flute); violin; and *riqq* (a tambourine). In 1905, Akhwani Safaa was founded, the first of what would be many independent "musical clubs" not attached to the court. Based on the male takht tradition, Akhwani Safaa sang in Arabic for an Arab elite and became established as the Arab concert music end of a taarab continuum that would soon extend to local traditions.

The other end of the taarab continuum was established by the greatest taarab singer of all time, Siti Bint Saad in the 1920s. Singing about life in Zanzibar in her native KiSwahili language rather than about love in Arabic, she was accompanied by an ensemble leaning toward the more percussive female takht ensembles of Egypt; an early photograph shows her playing the *tar* (a tambourine), along with three men playing an ud, a riqq, and a violin (held in an Indian-style position).[54] Siti Bint Saad, widely considered the mother of taarab, made hundreds of records for HMV, Columbia, and Odeon in the late 1920s and early 1930s. Due to her influence, taarab began to open up to women and the local African rather than Arab population. As part of this process, the music drew on the local *ngoma* traditions of drumming and dancing. Rather than functioning as a concert music as the takht ensemble music did in Egypt, taarab ensembles with female singers would play for women's clubs at weddings, where guests would encircle the musicians and dance, bringing the tradition more in line with African drumming traditions. After the revolution in Zanzibar in 1964, the Arab presence in taarab was further de-emphasized with an increased presence of women, of the KiSwahili language, and of Western popular musical influences.

Less tangible evidence of Arab influence, because it has brewed over the course of centuries, if not millennia, can be found in the musics of southern desert groups such as the Moors and Tuaregs. In contrast with their southern neighbors, Moorish and Tuareg women play string instruments, a rarity further south, as well as percussion instruments. The playing position of the Moorish *ardin,* a harp with a calabash resonator, resembles that of ancient Egyptian harps. Several other morphological features of the instruments point to the east. Moorish music resembles Arab music in several ways: suites of instrumental and vocal pieces make up a concert performance; the technical terminology for melody creation is much more extensive than that found further south; and the rhythmic materials associated with their drums is closer to Arab music (see the discography: Mauritania).

Varieties of vocal music related to certain poetic forms of pre-Islamic Arabian society are also in use throughout the Muslim world, most notably the *qasidah* used in sufi ceremonies.[55]

The Impact on Local Traditions

In addition to bringing in a relatively bounded musical system intact (Quranic recitation) as well as various musical instruments, the adoption of Islam has impacted on the development as well as decline of certain genres of the local music cultures. The most notorious example of the latter concerns drumming and dancing, particularly that associated with local religious power and initiation societies. Drumming was opposed on several grounds: that it was associated with representational masks that conflicted with Islamic prohibitions on such kinds of art; that the masks represented spirits or deities in direct conflict with Islamic doctrine; and that it was associated with dancing related to the realm of worldly pleasures. Wherever masks are found, there are also drums that accompany their outing. But the relationship between local Muslim doctrine and practice is by no means straightforward, and there could be considerable disjunctures. As Bravmann (1974) and more recently Peter Mark (1992) have shown, Muslim and pre-Muslim practices (such as mask traditions) can coexist and complement each other: "This give and take between Muslim and traditional cultures, each conditioning the other, has governed—has indeed characterized—the entire history of the religion in West Africa."[56] One song from upper Guinea sung by women in the course of circumcision celebrations demonstrates local recognition of this mutual conditioning. The song honors Alpha Kabine, a Muslim leader who lifted earlier restrictions on music and dance in circumcisions celebrations.

> *Our dances and songs*
> *In honor of our children*
> *Will not at all kill*
> *Our faith in Islam.*
> *May you forever remain serene,*
> *Oh, Alpha Kabiné the great*
> *Our authentic ancestor!*
> *We devote the time*

> *For our cherished Islamic rites*
> *But without sacrificing our songs*
> *And dances for our cherished children.*[57]

With respect to masked dancing and its accompanying drumming that is wide-spread in Africa, the actual form of a mask may be as important a consideration in its survival as is the blasphemous spirit to which it is oriented. The presence of a face on a wooden mask, thereby conflicting with Muslim prohibitions on representation, might contribute to its demise at the hands of Muslim reformers.[58] Masking traditions such as the Senegambian Mandinka *kankuran* made of long strips of tree bark with no discernible face, usually accompanied by the Mandinka three-drum *tantango* (also called *seruba*) ensemble, have not only survived in Muslim villages and societies, but are widely accepted facts of life. On the other hand, wooden *komo* (or *koma*) masks and their related drumming and dancing in Mali and Guinea are becoming extinct. Writing in the early 1970s, Gilbert Rouget noted that in eastern Guinea,

> Twenty five years ago, traditional religion was still very much alive at Karala. In the Fifties, Islam zealots managed to get the "fetishes" burnt. The mysteries of the koma, the secret society of the masks, corner-stone of the religion, were exposed to the eyes of women and the non-initiated.
>
> Since then, koma rites have not been carried out in this village, now completely Moslem.[59]

To be sure, the jembe drums that accompanied the komo masks are still quite active, but in a more secularized context.

Masking, drumming, and dancing traditions of the Baga people of coastal Guinea may have suffered due to Muslim fanaticism.[60] Throughout the twentieth century, the gradual encroachment of Islam led to a decline of Baga ritual. In the mid 1950s, Muslim zealots invaded Bagaland and targeted sacred masks. Associated drumming traditions were devalued, only to be renewed in a more public context of national ballet troupes established after independence. Lester Monts has documented a less traumatic but similarly transforming fifteen-year period in a Liberian village, where Islam and its proponents gradually displaced local secret power societies and their related musics with more acceptable versions.[61]

Certain genres of local music cultures have expanded due to the advance of Islam rather than declined. Repertories of griots of western Africa, largely made up of pieces dedicated to heroic individuals within their societies, have broadened to include prominent Muslims into the fold. A significant portion of the pieces narrated and sung by Senegambian Mandinka *jelis* (griots) are dedicated to Fulbe Muslim leaders and clerics such as Alfa Yaya, Hama Ba (Maba Diakhou), and the aforementioned al-Hajj ʿUmar Tal.[62] These are the pieces that tend to draw quotations from the Quran, prayers, and other bits of Islamic wisdom in performance. Muslim leaders often had praise-singers in their entourage, and at times encouraged a healthy atmosphere for certain kinds of music. In Kankan, Guinea, a thriving devout Muslim community that featured the renowned Cheikh Muhammad Cherif (known as Le grand Cherif), a great Islamic mystic who attracted followers from all over West Africa, provided a supportive atmosphere for Maninka jelis who in turn composed pieces appropriately honoring their Muslim patrons.[63]

☾ ☾ ☾

The status of musicians within a society is often linked with the pervasiveness of Islam in that society. Musicians in African Muslim societies may be stigmatized by a perceived association with a variety of activities that could be construed as counter to an orthodox Muslim way of life, such as song and dance, the intermingling of the sexes, the drinking of alcohol, and, more seriously, playing for power or spirit associations that would come into direct conflict with the fundamental tenet of Islam that there is but one God. Due to this stigma, professional musicians among the devout Fulani of northern Cameroon, for instance, are primarily non-Fulani.[64] Griots and other musicians attached to Muslim rulers may also enjoy certain degrees of prestige and privilege.

It is often difficult to separate out the factors of Islam and professionalism in determining reasons for a low social status of musicians in African Muslim societies. Praise-singers earning wealth at the expense of patrons fearful of losing their reputations if they are not forthcoming with appropriate remuneration exemplify one aspect of professionalism that contributes to a dim view of musicians in some societies. But recently, outside observers have begun to appreciate the give and take that goes on in the negotiation of various kinds of power in African societies. Maninka jelis, for instance, may be willing to accept and even propagate a stereotyped image of lower social status to make their patrons bigger, enhancing their own spiritual powers in the process.[65]

Among the Hausa of Nigeria, musicians and praise-singers as a whole have been reported as having a low social status, but within their class there is a hierarchy determined in part by the Muslim milieu.[66] Court musicians, who are devout Muslims, enjoy the prestige of accompanying the processions of the Hausa and Fulani royalty and aristocracy during certain Muslim festivals; they also have access to the emir's palace. Musicians in the Hausa *bori* cult, on the other hand, do not enjoy such prestige, in part because of their association with a non-Islamic spirit world. Hausa musical instruments also have degrees of prestige attached to them. The most prestigious is the kakaki, a long metal trumpet to be played only for chiefs. Next in line is the *kotso,* an hourglass drum played with the hand, which can be played not only for chiefs but also for a variety of aristocracy and important persons outside the royal court.[67] Other instruments, such as the *garaya* (a lute), played for the bori cult, have little prestige attached to them.

❨ ❨ ❨

To conclude: Islamic and Arab aesthetics of artistic expression have been inter-preted and articulated in different ways across Africa. Sorting out the various strains of interpretation and articulation is no easy task. For example, East Coast taarab, North African classical, and Egyptian singers might all share certain musical traits, as do griot singers from Mauritania such as Dimi Mint Abba, who represented her country at the Umm Kulthum festival in Tunis in the mid 1970s. But in Dimi Mint Abba's music there is also an intangible element that comes from the south. Just across the Mauritanian border, in Mali, female Maninka jelis such as Ami Koita and Tata Bamba Kouyate sing in a style removed from their northern neighbors, but they, too, have an intangible element that distinguishes them from some of their closest neighbors. Just adjacent to the Maninka heartland in southern Mali, singers from the Wasulu region such as Oumou Sangare are even farther removed from the Arab singing styles to the north.

To be sure, one can identify characteristics such as ornamentation, vibrato, melismas, vocal nasality, tonal organization, polyrhythm, polyphony, instrumenta-tion, song texts, and the role of music and musicians in a society that can be (and have been) cited to distinguish one style from another. The role of Islam in the ebb and flow that goes into the crystallization of a music culture is a fledgling field of in-quiry in African music studies, certainly compared with the other disciplines repre-sented in this book. As this area of inquiry matures, it should have much to say about the African genius for adaptation, not only within Africa, but wherever an African presence has been felt in the world. And it also should have much to say about the adaptability of Islam to local environments.

Notes

1. I have benefited from three earlier general surveys of music and Islam in Africa: Anderson 1971; Duvelle 1972; and Simon 1983. For brief regional overviews of music in Africa that take Islam into account, see Cooke 1998 and Wendt 1998. For more extended regional coverage, see Kubik 1982, 1989; also see the individual country entries in the forthcoming revised edition of the *New Grove Dictionary of Music and Musicians*. I thank Virginia Danielson for insightful comments on earlier drafts of this chapter.

2. The following concepts of core characteristics, Muslim music culture areas, and degrees of influence are drawn from al Faruqi 1983–84, and al Faruqi and al Faruqi 1986 (summarized here and in the next paragraph).

3. Touma 1996, 159–62.

4. al Faruqi 1981b, 12.

5. Essential sources for music and religious expression in the core Muslim world include Danielson 1995, Farmer 1957, al Faruqi and al Faruqi 1986, Nelson 1985, Shiloah 1995, and Touma 1996, all of which contain further bibliographic references.

6. An example of murattal style led by Alhaji Bai Konte from the Gambia can be heard on Pevar 1978-disc ("Ramadan, evening prayer in the Konte compound"); an example of mujawwad style by Muhammad Manobala from Liberia is on Monts 1998-disc.

7. Nelson 1985, 138–39.

8. For example, Lester Monts indicates that Muhammad Manobala (see note 6 above) studied in West Asia. Also see L. Kaba's (1974, 73ff.) discussion of West Africans studying at Al-Azhar.

9. Nelson 1985, 19.

10. Maal 1991-disc.

11. Kante 1987-disc.

12. Kidel 1991-vid.

13. For another example of Muslim influence in Guinean music, see Kaba and Charry forthcoming.

14. Bamba and Prevost 1996, 150. My translation from the French.

15. McLaughlin 1997, 564–65.

16. Danielson 1997.

17. See Trimingham 1980, 65–67, for a brief overview of festivals in the Islamic calendar.

18. Chernoff 1985, 110; Besmer 1974; Levtzion and Hopkins 1981, 292–93, 416.

19. Chernoff 1979, 131.

20. Adegbite 1989, 36, 38–40.

21. Euba 1971, 178.

22. Waterman 1998; 1990, 36–39.

23. Euba 1971, 177–78; Mack 1986; Ames and King 1971, 135.

24. Euba 1971, 176–78.

25. Omibiyi-Obidike 1979, 46–47.

26. Kinney 1970; Locke 1990.

27. Locke 1990, 20.

28. Trimingham 1971, 201–7.

29. McLaughlin 1997, 565–66; Paques 1991, 60–66. The distinctions between dhikr, hadra, and sama' may vary over time and place, but in general hadra (invoking the presence of the Prophet) is a communal dhikr (remembrance) involving chanting, often leading to very excited states of religious ecstasy or trance, and sama' (audition) is more of a spiritual concert leading to calmer religious states. For more, see Rouget 1985, 262–79.

30. Lievre 1987, 42–43.

31. Lapassade 1976, 203; Grame 1970; Simon 1998, 554–55.

32. Nelson 1985, 189.

33. Robson 1938 provides a good introduction to sources in debates about the role of music in Islam, with translations of two well-known tracts that take opposite sides. For more on sama' and the role of music in Islam, see Rouget 1985, 255, 314; Shiloah 1995, 31ff.; and the listing of sources in al Faruqi and al Faruqi 1986, 449–55.

34. Erlmann 1986, 10–20, 31. See L. Kaba 1974 for a discussion of the Wahhabiyya Islamic reform movement in French West Africa in the mid-twentieth century.

35. Bravmann 1974, 15–27.

36. Thomas W. Arnold, quoted in Bravmann 1974, 16.

37. al Faruqi 1981b, 13.

38. Shiloah 1995, 40–41; Touma 1996, 162.

39. Trimingham 1971, 1.

40. Ibid., 214.

41. Simon 1974, 1980a-disc, 1989, 1998.

42. McLaughlin 1997.

43. Ibid., 565. This tradition has spread beyond the borders of Senegal. Baba Djan Kaba 1992-disc from Guinea has recorded a piece in praise of Shaykh Amadu Bamba (titled "Touba Famake") and on the same disc praised the religious leaders of Kankan, Guinea (in the piece "Kankan").

44. Lapassade 1976, 1982.

45. Conrad 1985; Zemp 1966.

46. Ames and King 1971, 10.

47. For more information on the Arab-Andalusian ensembles, see Chelbi 1985, Davis 1996, 1997a, 1997b, Schuyler 1978, Shiloah 1995, and Wendt 1998.

48. Blench 1984 provides a good overview of possible foreign imports into sub-Saharan Africa. Also see Hause 1948, Djedje 1980, Erlmann 1983b, the distribution maps in al Faruqi and al Faruqi 1986, and Charry 1996.

49. Boubacar Diagne 1992-disc; Soule and Millot 1993-vid.

50. Ames and King 1971, 13.

51. Charry 1996.

52. Djedje 1980, 1992.

53. Information on taarab is drawn from Graebner 1991, 1993, Fargion 1993, and the excellent series of CDs on the Globestyle label (see listings for Kenya and Tanzania in the discography).

54. Graebner 1994, 349.

55. Danielson 1997; al Faruqi 1981a, 260–61; McLaughlin 1997, 566, 575–77; Simon 1974, 1980a-disc; Touma 1996, 96.

56. Bravmann 1974, 29.

57. M. Kaba 1995, 108. This is my English translation of Kaba's French translation of the original Maninka. See ibid. for other songs related to Islam and local Maninka practices.

58. Mark 1992, 143.

59. Rouget 1972-disc.

60. Lamp 1996, 223ff.

61. Monts 1998.

62. Knight 1973, 1983.

63. Kaba and Charry forthcoming.

64. Arnott 1980; Erlmann 1983a, 192–93.

65. Hoffman 1995, 45.

66. Ames 1973; Besmer 1998.

67. Besmer 1998; Ames n.d.-disc.

Bibliography

General Islam and Music

Danielson, Virginia. 1995. "Devotional Music." In *Oxford Encyclopedia of the Modern Islamic World,* ed. John L. Esposito, 1:364–68. New York: Oxford University Press.

Farmer, Henry G. 1957. "The Music of Islam." In *New Oxford History of Music,* ed. Egon Wellesz, vol. 1: *Ancient and Oriental Music.* London: Oxford University Press, 421–77.

al Faruqi, Lois Ibsen. 1981a. *An Annotated Glossary of Arabic Musical Terms.* Westport, Conn.: Greenwood.

———. 1981b. "Round Table on Islamic Influences." In International Musicological Society: *Report of the Twelfth Congress* (Berkeley, 1977), ed. Daniel Heartz and Bonnie Wade, 11–13. Kassel/Philadelphia: Barenreiter/American Musicological Society.

———. 1983–84. "Factors of Continuity in the Musical Cultures of the Muslim World," *Progress Reports in Ethnomusicology* 1 (2):1–18. Baltimore County: Department of Music, University of Maryland.

———. 1985. "Music, Musicians and Muslim Law," *Asian Music* 17 (1):3–36.

al Faruqi, Isma'il R. and Lois Lamya al Faruqi. 1986. *The Cultural Atlas of Islam*. New York: Macmillan.

Nelson, Kristina. 1985. *The Art of Reciting the Qur'an*. Austin: University of Texas Press.

Robson, James. 1938. *Tracts on Listening to Music, being Dhamm al-malahi by Ibn abi l-Dunya and Bawariq al-ilma, by Majd al-Din al-Tusi al-Ghazali*. London: Royal Asiatic Society.

Rouget, Gilbert. 1985. *Music and Trance: A Theory of the Relations between Music and Possession*. Chicago: University of Chicago Press.

Shiloah, Amnon. 1995. *Music in the World of Islam: A Socio-Cultural Study*. Detroit: Wayne State University Press.

Touma, Habib. 1996. *The Music of the Arabs*. New exp. ed. Portland, Oreg.: Amadeus.

General African and Regional

Anderson, Lois Ann. 1971. "The Interrelation of African and Arab Musics: Some Preliminary Considerations." In *Essays on Music and History in Africa*, ed. Klaus Wachsmann, 143–69. Evanston: Northwestern University Press.

Arnott, D. W. 1980. "Fulani Music." In *The New Grove Dictionary of Music and Musicians*, ed. Stanley Sadie, 7:23–25. London: Macmillan.

Blench, Roger. 1984. "The Morphology and Distribution of Sub-Saharan Musical Instruments of North African, Middle Eastern, and Asian, Origin," *Musica Asiatica* 4:155–91.

Bravmann, René A. 1974. *Islam and Tribal Art in West Africa*. Cambridge: Cambridge University Press.

Charry, Eric. 1996. "West African Lutes: An Historical Overview," *Galpin Society Journal* 49:3–37.

———. 2000. *Mande Music: Traditional and Modern Music of the Maninka and Mandinka of Western Africa*. Chicago: University of Chicago Press.

Conrad, David. 1985. "Islam in the Oral Traditions of Mali: Bilali and Surakata," *Journal of African History* 26 (1):33–49.

Cooke, Peter. 1998. "East Africa: An Introduction." In *The Garland Encyclopedia of African Music*, ed. Ruth Stone, 598–609. New York: Garland.

DjeDje, Jacqueline Cogdell. 1980. *Distribution of the One String Fiddle in West Africa*. Monograph Series in Ethnomusicology, no. 2. Los Angeles: Program in Ethnomusicology, Dept. of Music, University of California.

———. 1992. "Music and History: An Analysis of Hausa and Dagomba Fiddle Traditions." In *African Musicology: Current Trends 2*, ed. Jacqueline Cogdell DjeDje, 151–79. Los Angeles: African Studies Center, University of California.

Duvelle, Charles. 1972. "Oriental Music in Black Africa." In *African Music: Meeting in Yaounde, Cameroon* (Feb. 23–27, 1970), UNSECO, 95–117. Paris: La Revue Musicale.

Graebner, Werner. 1991. "Tarabu—Populäre Musik am Indischen Ozean." In *Populäre Musik in Afrika,* ed. Veit Erlmann, 181–200. Berlin: Museum für Völkerkunde.

———. 1994. "Swahili Musical Party: Islamic Taarab Music of East Africa." In *World Music: The Rough Guide,* ed. Simon Broughton et al., 349–55. London: Rough Guides.

Hause, H. E. 1948. "Terms for Musical Instruments in the Sudanic Languages," *Journal of the American Oriental Society,* supplement, 7:1–70.

Kaba, Lansiné. 1974. *The Wahhabiyya: Islamic Reform and Politics in French West Africa.* Evanston, Ill.: Northwestern University Press.

Kaba, Mamadi. 1995. *Anthologie de chants mandingues (Côte d'Ivoire, Guinée, Mali).* Paris: L'Harmattan.

Kubik, Gerhard. 1982. *Musikgeschichte in Bildern 1 (10): Ostafrika.* Leipzig: VEB Deutscher Verlag für Musik Leipzig.

———. 1989. *Musikgeschichte in Bildern 1 (11): Westafrika.* Leipzig: VEB Deutscher Verlag für Musik Leipzig.

———. 1998. "Intra-African Streams of Influence." In *The Garland Encyclopedia of African Music,* ed. Ruth Stone, 293–326. New York: Garland.

Levtzion, Nehemia, and J. F. P. Hopkins, eds. 1981. *Corpus of Early Arabic Sources for West African History.* Trans. J. F. P. Hopkins. Cambridge: Cambridge University Press.

Lievre, Viviane. 1987. *Danses du Maghreb d'une rive à l'autre.* Paris: Karthala.

Simon, Artur. 1983. "Islam und Musik in Afrika." In *Musik in Afrika,* ed. Artur Simon, 297–309. Berlin: Museum für Völkerkunde, 297–309.

Trimingham, J. Spencer. 1971. *The Sufi Orders in Islam.* Oxford: Oxford University Press.

———. 1980. *The Influence of Islam upon Africa.* 2nd ed. London: Longman.

Wegner, Ulrich. 1984. *Afrikanische Saiteninstrumente.* Berlin: Museum für Völkerkunde.

Wendt, Caroline Card. 1998. "North Africa: An Introduction." In *The Garland Encyclopedia of African Music,* ed. Ruth Stone, 532–48. New York: Garland.

Zemp, Hugo. 1966. "La Legende des griots Malinke," *Cahiers d'Etudes Africaines* 24:611–42.

Cameroon

Erlmann, Veit. 1983a. "Marginal Men, Strangers, and Wayfarers: Professional Musicians and Change among the Fulani of Diamare (North Cameroon)," *Ethnomusicology* 27 (2):187–225.

———. 1983b. "Notes on Musical Instruments among the Fulani of Diamare (North Cameroon)," *African Music* 6 (3):16–41.

Egypt

Castelo-Branco, Salwa el-Shawan. 1980. "The Socio-Political Context of al-musika al-ʿarabiyyah in Cairo, Egypt: Policies, Patronage, Institutions, and Musical Change (1927–77)," *Asian Music* 12 (1):86–128.

Danielson, Virginia. 1997. *The Voice of Egypt: Umm Kulthum, Arabic Song, and Egyptian Society in the Twentieth Century.* Chicago: University of Chicago Press.

Racy, Ali Jihad. 1988. "Sound and Society: The *Takht* Music of Early-Twentieth Century Cairo," *Selected Reports in Ethnomusicology* 7:139–70.

The Gambia

Knight, Roderic. 1973. "Mandinka Jaliya: Professional Music of The Gambia." 2 vols. Ph.D. diss., University of California, Los Angeles.

———. 1983. "Manding/Fula Relations as Reflected in the Manding Song Repertoire," *African Music* 6 (2):37–47.

Ghana

Chernoff, John Miller. 1979. *African Rhythm and African Sensibility: Aesthetics and Social Action in African Musical Idioms.* Chicago: University of Chicago Press.

———. 1985. "The Drums of Dagbon." In *Repercussions: A Celebration of African-American Music,* ed. Geoffrey Haydon and Dennis Marks, 101–27. London: Century.

Kinney, Sylvia. 1970. "Drummers in Dagbon: The Role of the Drummer in the Damba Festival," *Ethnomusicology* 14 (2):258–65.

Locke, David, featuring Abubakari Lunna. 1990. *Drum Damba: Talking Drum Lessons.* Crown Point, Ind.: White Cliffs Media.

Guinea

Kaba, Lansiné, and Eric Charry. Forthcoming. "Mamaya: Renewal and Tradition in the Manninka Music of Kankan, Guinea (1935–45)." In *The African Diaspora: A Musical Perspective,* ed. Ingrid Monson. New York: Garland.

Lamp, Frederick. 1996. *Art of the Baga: A Drama of Cultural Reinvention.* New York: Museum for African Art/Prestel Verlag.

Kenya

Boyd, Alan. 1981. "Music in Islam: Lamu, Kenya, a Case Study." In *Discourse in Ethnomusicology 2: A Tribute to Alan P. Merriam,* ed. Caroline Card et al., 82–98. Bloomington: Ethnomusicology Publications Group, Indiana University.

Kingei, Geoffrey. 1992. "Language, Culture, and Communication: The Role of Swahili Taarab Songs in Kenya (1963–1990)." Ph.D. diss., Howard University.

Ntarangwi, Mwenda G. 1998. "Taarab Texts, Gender, and Islam in an Urban East African Context: Social Transformations among the WaSwahili of Mombasa, Kenya." Ph.D. diss., University of Illinois, Urbana-Champaign.

Liberia

Monts, Lester. 1998. "Islam in Liberia." In *The Garland Encyclopedia of African Music,* ed. Ruth Stone, 327–49. New York: Garland.

Mali

Bamba, Sorry, with Liliane Prevost. 1996. *De la Tradition à la World Music.* Paris: L'Harmattan.

Hoffman, Barbara. 1995. "Power, Structure, and Mande *Jeliw,*" In *Status and Identity in West Africa: Nyamakalaw of Mande,* ed. David Conrad and Barbara Frank, 36–45. Bloomington: Indiana University Press.

Mauritania

Guignard, M. 1973. *Musique, honneur, et plaisir au Sahara: Etude psychologique et musicologique de la société Maure.* Paris: Geuthner.

Nikiprowetzky, Tolia. 1960–69. *Trois aspects de la musique africaine: Mauritanie, Senegal, Niger.* Paris: Office de Cooperation Radiophonique.

Norris, H. T. 1968. *Shinqiti Folk Literature and Song.* London: Oxford University Press.

Morocco

Grame, Theodore C. 1970. "Music in the Jmaa al-Fna of Marrakesh," *Musical Quarterly* 56 (1):74–87.

Lapassade, Georges. 1976. "Les gnaoua d'Essaouira," *L'Homme et la société* 39/40:191–215.

———. 1982. *Gens de l'ombre, transes et possessions.* Paris: Meridiens/Anthropos.

Paques, Viviana. 1991. *La Religion des esclaves: Recherches sur la confrérie marocaine des Gnawa.* Bergamo: Moretti & Vitali.

Schuyler, Philip. 1978. "Moroccan Andalusian Music," *World of Music* 20 (1):33–46.

———. 1979. "A Repertory of Ideas: The Music of the Rwais, Berber Professional Musicians from Southwestern Morocco." Ph.D. diss., University of Washington.

———. 1981. "Music and Meaning among the Gnawa Religious Brotherhood of Morocco," *World of Music* 23 (1):3–12.

Nigeria

Adegbite, Ademola. 1989. "The Influence of Islam on Yoruba Music," *Orita* 21 (1):32–43.

Ames, David W. 1973. "Igbo and Hausa Musicians: A Comparative Examination," *Ethnomusicology* 17 (2):250–78.

Ames, David W., and Anthony V. King. 1971. *Glossary of Hausa Music and Its Social Contexts.* Evanston: Northwestern University Press.

Bender, Wolfgang. 1973. *Waka-Sakara-Apala-Fuji: Islamisch beeinfluste Musik der Yoruba in Nigeria und Benin.* Universität Bayreuth.

Besmer, Fremont. 1971. "Hausa Court Music in Kano, Nigeria." Ph.D. diss., Teachers College, Columbia University.

———. 1974. *Kí'dàn Dárán Sállà: Music for the Eve of the Muslim Festivals of 'id Al-Fitr and 'id Al-Kabiir in Kano, Nigeria.* Bloomington: African Studies Program, Indiana University.

———. 1998. "Hausa Performance." In *The Garland Encyclopedia of African Music,* ed. Ruth Stone, 515–29. New York: Garland.

Erlmann, Veit. 1986. *Music and the Islamic Reform in the Early Sokoto Empire: Sources, Ideology, Effects.* Stuttgart: Franz Steiner.

Euba, Akin. 1971. "Islamic Musical Culture among the Yoruba: A Preliminary Survey." In *Essays on Music and History in Africa,* ed. Klaus Wachsmann, 171–81. Evanston: Northwestern University Press.

Mack, Beverly. 1986. "Songs from Silence: Hausa Women's Poetry." In *Ngambika: Studies of Women in African Literature,* ed. Carole Boyce Davies and Anne Adams Graves, 181–90. Trenton, N.J.: Africa World.

Omibiyi-Obidike, Mosunmola Ayinke. 1979. "Islam Influence on Yoruba Music," *African Notes* 8 (2):37–54.

Waterman, Christopher. 1990. *Jùjú: A Social History and Ethnography of an African Popular Music.* Chicago: University of Chicago Press.

———. 1998. "Yoruba Popular Music." In *The Garland Encyclopedia of African Music,* ed. Ruth Stone, 471–87. New York: Garland.

Senegal

Cruise O'Brien, Donal B. 1971. *The Mourides of Senegal: The Political and Economic Organization of an Islamic Brotherhood.* London: Oxford University Press.

McLaughlin, Fiona. 1997. "Islam and Popular Music in Senegal: The Emergence of a 'New Tradition,'" *Africa* 67 (4):560–81.

Mark, Peter. 1992. *The Wild Bull and the Sacred Forest: Form, Meaning, and Change in Senegambian Initiation Masks.* Cambridge: Cambridge University Press.

Sudan

Simon, Artur. 1974. "Islamische und afrikanische Elemente in der Musik de Nordsudan am Beispiel de Dikr," *Hamburger Jahrbuch zur Musikwissenschaft* 1:249–78.

———. 1981. "Round Table on Islamic Influences." In *International Musicological Society: Report of the Twelfth Congress* (Berkeley 1977), ed. Daniel Heartz and Bonnie Wade, 13–18. Kassel/Philadelphia: Barenreiter/American Musicological Society.

———. 1989. "Musical Traditions, Islam, and Cultural Identity in Sudan." In *Perspectives on African Music,* ed. Wolfgang Bender, 25–41. Bayreuth: Breitinger.

———. 1998. "Music in Sudan." In *The Garland Encyclopedia of African Music,* ed. Ruth Stone, 549–73. New York: Garland.

Tanzania

Askew, Kelly. 1997. "Performing the Nation: Swahili Musical Performance and the Production of Tanzanian National Culture." Ph.D. diss., Harvard University.

Fair, Laura. Forthcoming. "'You Men Should Stop Oppressing and Stealing from the Poor': Negotiating Community, Identity, and Power through Taarab Music." In *Pastimes and Politics: Gender, Culture, and Identity in Zanzibar (1890–1945)*. Ed. Laura Fair. Athens: Ohio University Press.

Fargion, Janet Topp. 1993. "The Role of Women in Taarab in Zanzibar: An Historical Examination of a Process of 'Africanisation'," *World of Music* 35 (2):109–25.

Farhan, Idi. 1992. "Introduction of Taarab to Zanzibar in the Nineteenth Century," *International Conference on the History and Culture of Zanzibar* (Dec. 14–16, 1992; Zanzibar); proceedings, vol. 1.

Graebner, Werner. 1993. Book review of "Jukwaa la Taarab—Zanzibar" by Issa Mgana, *World of Music* 35 (1):102–7.

Tunisia

Chelbi, M. 1985. *Musique et societe en Tunisie*. Tunis: Salammbo.

Davis, Ruth Frances. 1996. "Arab-Andalusian Music in Tunisia," *Early Music* 24 (3):423–37.

———. 1997a. "Cultural Policy and the Tunisian Ma'lúf: Redefining a Tradition," *Ethnomusicology* 41 (1):1–21.

———. 1997b. "Traditional Arab Music Ensembles in Tunis: Modernizing Al-Turath in the Shadow of Egypt," *Asian Music* 28 (2):73–108.

Selected Discography

General

Jenkins, Jean. 1994. *Music in the World of Islam*. 3 vols. Topic, TCSD 901 to 903 (originally issued in 1974 as 6 vols. on Tangent).

Chad

Brandily, Monique. n.d. *An Anthology of African Music*, UNESCO collection, vol. 9: *Chad, Music of Kanem*. Barenreiter Musicaphon, BM30L2309.

Egypt

Kulthum Umm. n.d. *Om Kalsoum: Al Atlal*. Sono Cairo, 101.

The Gambia

Pevar, Mark D. 1978. *Music from The Gambia*, vol. 1. Folkways, FE 4521.

Guinea

Kaba, Baba Djan. 1992. *Kankan*. Sonodisc, CD 5510.

Kante, Mory. 1987. *Akwaba Beach*. Barclay/Polydor, 833 119–2.

Rouget, Gilbert. 1972. *Musique d'Afrique Occidentale*. Recorded 1952. Vogue, LDM 30116. Reissued 1999 on *Guinée: Musique des Malinké*. Le Chant du Monde, CNR 2741112.

Kenya

Boyd, Alan. 1992. *Music of the Waswahili of Lamu, Kenya.* 3 vols. Smithsonian Folkways, 04093 to 04095 (originally issued 1976–1985).

Maulidi & Musical Party. 1990. *Mombasa Wedding Special.* GlobeStyle, CDORBD 058.

Various. 1994. *Songs the Swahili Sing.* Original Music, OMCD 024 (originally issued 1983).

Liberia

Monts, Lester, producer. 1998. "Vai Call to Prayer, performed by Muhammad Manobala," on CD accompanying *The Garland Encyclopedia of African Music,* ed. Ruth Stone. New York: Garland.

Mali

Koita, Ami. 1993. *Songs of Praise.* Stern's Africa, STCD 1039.

Kouyate, Tata Bambo. 1985. *Jatigui.* Globestyle, CD ORB 042.

Sangare, Oumou. 1991. *Moussolou.* World Circuit, WCD 021.

Mauritania

Chighaly, Aicha Mint. 1997. *Griote de Mauritanie.* Inedit, W 260078.

Duvelle, Charles. 1996. *Musique Maure.* Ocora, ORC 28.

Eide, Khalifa Ould, and Dimi Mint Abba. 1990. *Moorish Music from Mauritania.* World Circuit, WCD 019.

Morocco

Gnaoua d'Essaouira. 1993. *Maroc: Haadra des Gnaoua d'Essaouira.* OCORA, C560006.

Nass el Ghiwane. 1992. *Le Meilleur de Nass el Ghiwane: Maroc, Chants d'espoir.* Blue Silver, 071–2.

Schuyler, Philip D. 1970. *Musical Anthology of the Orient,* UNESCO collection, vol. 27, *Morocco 1: The Music of Islam and Sufism in Morocco.* Barenreiter Musicaphon, BM30SL2027.

———. 1972. *Music of Morocco: The Pan-Islamic Tradition.* Lyrichord, LLST 7240.

———. 1978. *The Rwais: Moroccan Berber Musicians from the High Atlas.* Lyrichord, LLST 7316.

Niger

Nikiprowetzky, Tolia. 1990. *Anthologie de la musique du Niger.* OCORA, C 559056.

Nigeria

Ames, David. n.d. *An Anthology of African Music,* UNESCO collection, vols. 6 and 7, *Nigeria-Hausa Music 1 and 2.* Barenreiter Musicaphon, BM 30L 2306 and 2307.

Yoruba Music. 1992. *Yoruba Street Percussion.* Original Music, OMCD 016.

Senegal

Ames, David. 1955. *Wolof Music of Senegal and The Gambia.* Folkways, P462.

Diagne, Boubacar. 1992. *Tabala Wolof: Sufi Drumming of Senegal.* Village Pulse, VPU-1002.

Maal, Baaba. 1991. *Baayo.* Mango, 162539907–2.

Kala, Musa Dieng. 1996. *Shakawtu: The Faith.* Shanachie, 64072.

Sudan

Simon, Artur. 1980a. *Dikr und madih: Islamische Gesänge und Zeremonien/Islamic Songs and Ceremonies. Sudan.* Museum für Völkerkunde Berlin, Museum Collection, MC10.

———. 1980b. *Musik der Nubier/Nordsudan; Music of the Nubians/Northern Sudan.* Museum für Völkerkunde Berlin, Museum Collection, MC 9.

Tanzania

Black Star & Lucky Star Musical Clubs. 1989. *Nyota.* Gobestyle, CDORB 044.

Music of Zanzibar. 1988–89. *Taarab 1: Abdullah Mussa Ahmed & Seif Salim Saleh: Ganoon, Ud, and Violin; Taarab 2: Ikhwani Safaa Musical Club; Taarab 3: Ghazzy Musical Club, El Arry; Taarab 4: Culture Music Club.* GlobeStyle CDORB 032; 033; 040; 041.

Selected Videography

Genini, Izza. 1994. *Morocco, Body and Soul.* New York: First Run/Icarus Films.

Haydon, Geoffrey, and Dennis Marks. 1984. *Repercussions 5: Drums of Dagbon.* Chicago Home Video.

Kidel, Mark, producer and director. 1991. *Bamako Beat: Music from Mali.* BBC, London.

Soule, Beatrice, and Eric Millot, directors. 1993. *Djabote: Doudou N'Diaye Rose.* Montpelier, Vt.: Multicultural Media.

Glossary

adhan—Call to prayer.

ʿalim (pl. ʿulamaʾ)—A scholar.

baraka—Blessing, spiritual grace.

bori—Spirit possession among the Hausa.

daʾira or dahira—In Senegal, religious associations of the Muridiyya brotherhood.

dar al-harb—"The land(s) of war," part of the world not governed by Muslims and the *shariʿa* (q.v.).

dar al-Islam—"The land(s) of Islam," referring to the part of the world governed by Muslims and the *shariʿa* (q.v.).

dara or daara—Community, used in particular in Senegal of the agricultural communities of the Muridiyya brotherhood, in contract with the mostly urban *daʾiras* of the same country.

dhikr—"Remembering" God, reciting the names of God; a religious service practiced by all mystical brotherhoods.

faqih (pl. fuqahaʾ)—An ʿalim who is learned in *fiqh* (q.v.).

fatwa—A legal pronouncement handed down by a Muslim jurisconsult.

fiqh—The science of religious law (shariʿa, q.v.).

hadith—Prophetic tradition; an account of what the Prophet said or did; second in authority to the Quran.

hajj—The pilgrimage to Mecca; one of the five pillars of Islam.

hajji—A pilgrim, or a sobriquet of one who completed the *hajj*.

hijra—The emigration of the Prophet Muhammad from Mecca to Medina; emigration from land(s) of unbelief *(kufr)*.

ijaza—Authorization given by a mentor to transmit knowledge, or to teach a specfic text.

jamaʿa—Community, often used of agricultural settlements.

jeli—Maninka hereditary profession, oral historian–musician. Also known as griot.

jihad (fi sabil Allah)—"Struggle for God's sake"; mostly used for religiously sanctioned war. In West Africa, common name for a series of Fulani-based revolutions from Senegal to Cameroon in the nineteenth century.

Glossary

jizya—The poll-tax levied on non-Muslims by Muslim authorities.

khalifa (pl. khulafaʿ)—"Representative"; the Arabic word for "caliph," it also means a regional leader or head of a breakaway branch within a sufi brotherhood (higher than *muqaddam* and *shayh*, qq.v.)

khalwa—A retreat, often for forty days.

khutba—The sermon given during the Friday prayers by a mosque official, the *khatib*.

madhhab—"Rite" or "school of law"; one of the four major divisions of Sunni Islam, which differ in some points of law and performance of the ritual prayers.

madrasa—A college, where the Islamic sciences are taught.

mahdi—"The rightly guided one"; the restorer of religion and justice, who will rule before the end of the world.

mallam—Hausa, from Arabic *muʿallam* (teacher): Islamic scholar *(ʿalim)*.

marabout—Saint and charismatic religious personality, derived from *murabit*, a warrior-monk who inhabited a *ribat* (q.v.). Equivalent of *shaykh* (q.v.); sufi leader.

mawlid—Celebration of the birthday of the Prophet, a saint, or a sufi *shaykh* (q.v.).

mganga—Swahili term for a ritual specialist and/or healer.

muʾadhdhin—The one who does the *adhan* (call to prayer).

mudir—A specialized Swahili term applied to mid-level officials of the Zanzibar Sultanate.

mufti—A jurisconsult who gives *fatwa* (q.v.).

muqaddam—Leader of a sufi brotherhood.

murid—Student, follower of a sufi brotherhood. Alt.: *tilmidh* (pl. *talamidh*).

mwalimu or **walimu**—A Swahili term for a religious teacher of any kind.

mwanavyuoni or **wanazuoni**—A more specialized Swahili term for a religious scholar (*ʿalim*, q.v.).

nazir—Supervisor.

pepo—Swahili term for a spirit that "visits" one possessed.

qadi—A Muslim judge, a scholar who is employed by an Islamic regime to render judgments in a court based on the *shariʿa* (q.v.).

qasida (pl. qasaʾid)—A verse form often associated in Africa with eulogies of important religious leaders.

ribat—Originally, a fortified convent on the frontiers of Islam; one of the terms (like *zawiya*, q.v.) denoting the residence of mystics.

samaʾ—A concert of spiritual or devotional music.

sanduq—In Sudan, rotating credit associations.

shahada—Islam confession of faith, which states that "There is no god but God, and Muhammad is His messenger."

shariʿa—The religious law of Islam.

sharif (pl. shurafaʾ)—This refers to a putative descendant of the Prophet Muhammad, or of his near family.

shaykh—An honorific term applied informally to a highly esteemed (male) personage. A patriarch or a religious scholar, or head of a sufi lodge (*zawiya,* q.v.).

sufi—A Muslim mystic, who often belongs to one of the mystical brotherhoods.

sunna—A normative custom of the Prophet or of the early Muslim community, as set forth in the *hadith* (q.v.).

tafsir—Exegesis of the Quran.

tariqa (pl. turuq)—A mystical path or "Way" to an experience of God by the *sufi* (q.v.); often organized as a brotherhood.

ʿulamaʾ—Scholars (sing. *ʿalim*).

wali (pl. awliyaʾ)—A holy person, a saint.

wilaya or **walaya**—"Friendship with God," the status of saint (*wali,* q.v.).

wird (pl. awrad)—Prayer ritual that is distinctive for and identity marker of a sufi Way (*tariqa,* q.v.).

zakat—The alms tax obligatory for all Muslims.

zar—Literally, "the red wind"; in countries of northern Africa and the Middle East, the term extends to associations of men and/or women who practice healing rituals that may include spirit possessions and counsel clients as healers.

zawiya (pl. zawaya)—The residence of mystics, like *ribat* (q.v.); also, clerical tribes of the Sahara.

Contributors

Edward A. Alpers is Professor of African History at UCLA. His research and writing focus on the political economy of international trade in eastern Africa through the nineteenth century. He has published *Ivory and Slaves in East Central Africa* (1974) and *Walter Rodney: Revolutionary and Scholar* (1982), as well as a wide range of book chapters and articles. Alpers continues to write about the history of Islam in northern Mozambique, and he is past president of the African Studies Association (1994).

René A. Bravmann is Professor of Art at the University of Washington in Seattle. Considered to be one of the leading authorities worldwide in his field of African art history, he has published a number of important works in the history of African Islamic art. Among these are *Islam and Tribal Art in West Africa* (1974) and *African Islam* (1983).

Abdin Chande is Assistant Professor of Islamic and African Studies at St. Mary's College of Maryland. His contribution to this volume is part of his ongoing research on Islam in East Africa. He has published several articles on this subject and is author of *Islam, Ulamaa and Community Development in Tanga, Tanzania.*

Eric Charry is an Associate Professor in the Music Department at Wesleyan University. He has published numerous articles on various aspects of music in West Africa, and his book, *Mande Music,* is forthcoming from the University of Chicago Press.

Allan Christelow is Professor and Chair of the History Department at Idaho State University. His specialties include the history of Islamic legal institutions in Africa, and Islamic intellectual life and religious movements in the nineteenth and twentieth centuries, particularly in Algeria. He is the author of *Muslim Law Courts and the French Colonial State in Algeria* (1985) and *Thus Ruled Emir Abbas: Selected Cases from the Emir of Kano's Judicial Council* (1994).

Roberta Ann Dunbar is Associate Professor of African Studies in the Department of African and Afro-American Studies at the University of North Carolina, Chapel Hill. Her field of specialization is nineteenth- and twentieth-century social history of Africa, with particular emphasis in gender, law, and Islam. She is the author of articles and book chapters on women in Niger, most notably "Islamic Values, the

States, and 'Development of Women': the Case of Niger" in *Hausa Women in the Twentieth Century* (ed. C. M. Coles and B. B. Mack) and "Rhetoric of Inclusion—Acts of Exclusion: Political Transition and Women's Prospects in Niger" to appear in *Democratic Transitions in Africa* (ed. C. Newbury and P. Robinson).

Kenneth W. Harrow is Professor of English at Michigan State University. A highly regarded specialist in African literature, he has written articles dealing with sufism and feminist issues in African literature and cinema. Harrow is the author of *Thresholds of Change in African Literature* (1994), and he has edited *Faces of Islam in African Literature* (1991) and *The Marabout and the Muse* (1996).

Lansiné Kaba is Professor of African and African-American Studies and Dean of the Honors College at the University of Illinois at Chicago, and president of the African Studies Association, 1999–2000. He has published numerous articles on African history and politics. His book *The Wahhabiyya, Islamic Reform and Politics in French West Africa* (1974) received the Herskovits Award from the ASA. His new book, *Cheikh Mohhammad Chérif de Kankan et son temps, 1870–1955,* is in press.

Lidwien Kapteijns is Professor of History and Chairwoman of Women's Studies at Wellesley College, where she teaches courses in African and Middle Eastern History. She has published several books about the precolonial and early colonial history of the Sudan, and is now working on a history of Somalia. Her new book, *Women's Voices in a Man's World: Women and the Pastoral Tradition in Northern Somali Oral Literature, c. 1880-1980* is in press.

Nehemia Levtzion is Bamberger and Fuld Professor of the History of the Muslim Peoples at the Hebrew University of Jerusalem. He is the author of *Muslims and Chiefs in West Africa* (1968), *Ancient Ghana and Mali* (1973 and 1980), and *Islam in West Africa: Religion, Society, and Politics to 1800* (1994). He produced, with J. F. P. Hopkins, the *Corpus of Early Arabic Sources for West African History.* He was Dean of Humanities at the Hebrew University (1977–81), President of the Open University of Israel (1987–92), and since 1997 he has been the Chairman of the Council for Higher Education's Planning and Budgeting Committee.

William F. S. Miles is Professor of Political Science at Northeastern University in Boston. As a Fulbright research scholar in 1983, he was affiliated with Bayero University in Kano, Nigeria. Miles is the author of *Elections in Nigeria: A Grassroots Perspective* (1988) and *Hausaland Divided: Colonialism and Independence in Nigeria and Niger* (1994).

David Owusu-Ansah is Professor of History at James Madison University. In addition to several scholarly articles and chapters on Islam, Islamic politics, and religious conversion in Africa, he is the author of *Islamic Talismanic Tradition in Nineteenth-Century Asante* (1991), and with D. M. McFarland he has co-authored the *Historical Dictionary of Ghana* (1995).

Michael Pearson is Professor of History at the University of New South Wales in Sydney, Australia. His research interests include the early modern history of India and East Africa, and the Indian Ocean. He has published widely on these subjects, and among his most notable titles are *India and the Indian Ocean, 1500–1800* (1987 and 1999); *Pilgrimage to Mecca: The Indian Experience* (1996); and *Port Cities and Intruders: The Swahili Coast, India, and Portugal in the Early Modern Era* (1998).

Randall L. Pouwels is Professor of African History at the University of Central Arkansas in Conway, Arkansas. Besides African Islamic history, his research interests include African historiography, and orality and literacy in African societies. Pouwels has made several important contributions in his fields of interest, including *Horn and Crescent: Cultural Change and Traditional Islam on the East African Coast, 800–1900* (1987) and an annotated translation of A. S. Farsy's *The Shafi'i Ulama of East Africa, 1820–1970: A Hagiographic Account* (1989). He is the founder and serving president of the African Islamic Studies Association.

Stefan Reichmuth is Professor of Islamic Studies at Ruhr-Universität in Bochum, Germany. He has conducted research on Arabic dialects and oral traditions in the eastern Sudan, on Islamic learning and education in Nigeria, and on Islam among the Yoruba. Among his most noteworthy publications are "A Regional Centre of Islamic Learning in Nigeria: Ilorin and Its Influence on Yoruba Islam" (1997); and "The Interplay of Local Developments and Transnational Relations in the Islamic World: Perceptions and Perspectives"(1998).

David Robinson is University Distinguished Professor of History and African Studies at Michigan State University. He has worked primarily on the recent history of francophone and Islamic West Africa, and has published *The Holy War of Umar Tal* (1985); (with J. Hanson) *After the Jihad: The Reign of Ahmad al-Kabir in the Western Sudan* (1991); and (with J.-L. Triaud) *Le Temps des Marabouts* (1997). He has served as a past editor of the *Journal of African History* (1990–94), and currently is the vice president of the West African Research Association.

Robert C.-H. Shell is Senior Lecturer in the History department and is the Director of the Population Research Unit at Rhodes University in East London, South Africa. His research interests include comparative slavery, Islamic history, urbanization, and historical demography. In addition to several important articles, Shell's most notable publication has been *Children of Bondage: A Social History of Slavery at the Cape of Good Hope, 1652–1838* (1994).

Jay Spaulding is a Professor in the Department of History at Keane College of New Jersey in Union, New Jersey. A specialist in the history of northeastern Africa, Spaulding has published numerous substantial scholarly works, including (with R. S. O'Fahey) *Kingdoms of the Sudan* (1974); *The Heroic Age in Sinnar* (1985); and *An Islamic Alliance: Ali Dinar and the Sanusiyya (1906–1916)* (1994).

David Sperling is a Senior Lecturer in the Department of History at the University of Nairobi, Kenya. His main interests lie in the history of Islam in East Africa during the nineteenth and twentieth centuries, particularly the adoption and growth of Islam in rural African communities. His writings include chapters in, among others, *Muslim Identity and Social Change in Sub-Saharan Africa* (ed. L. Brenner) and *Revealing Prophets: Prophecy in Eastern African History* (ed. D. Anderson and D. Johnson).

Jean-Louis Triaud is a historian of African Islamic history and a Professor at the Université de Provence in Aix-en-Provence, France. He is the editor of the annual *Islam et Sociétés au Sud du Sahara*. His recent publications include *La légende noire de la Sanusiyya. Une confrérie musulmane saharienne sous le regard français* (1995); (with Ousmane Kane) *Islam et islamismes au sud du Sahara* (1998); and (with J.-P. Chrétien) *Histoire d'Afrique. Les enjeux de mémoire* (1999).

Knut S. Vikør is the Director of the Centre for Middle Eastern and Islamic Studies at the University of Bergen, Norway. He has written on the economic and political history of the central Sahara, sufi orders in nineteenth-century North Africa, and Islamic law. His publications include *Sufi and Scholar on the Desert Edge: Muhammad b. Ali al-Sanusi and His Brotherhood* (1995); *Sources for Sanusi Studies* (1996); *The Oasis of Salt: The History of Kawar, a Saharan Centre of Salt Production* (1999). He is the editor of the annual *Sudanic Africa: A Journal of Historical Sources.*

John Obert Voll is Professor of Islamic History at Georgetown University in Washington, D.C., where he holds a joint appointment in the History Department and in the Center for Muslim-Christian Understanding. He is past president of the Middle East Studies Association. He has written or edited books and articles on modern Sudanese history and modern movements of Islamic revival. Among his most noteworthy books are (with J. L. Esposito) *Islam and Democracy* (1996) and *Islam, Continuity, and Change in the Modern World* (1982 and 1994).

Peter von Sivers is Associate Professor of Classical Middle Eastern History at the University of Utah. He has served as a past editor of the *International Journal of Middle Eastern Studies* and as a past chair of the Near and Middle Eastern Committee of the Social Science Research Council. A highly regarded authority in his field, von Sivers is the author of articles, chapters, and books on Middle Eastern and North African history in the classical period and the nineteenth century. Currently, he is completing a world history textbook for Longman Publishers.

Ivor Wilks was on the faculty of the University of Ghana from 1953 to 1966. Presently, he is the Herskovits Professor Emeritus of African Studies, Northwestern University, and holds an Honorary Professorship at the University of Wales, Lampeter. He is the author of numerous scholarly publications on West African history. His books include the Herskovits Award–winning *Asante in the Nineteenth Century: The Structure and Evolution of a Political Order* (1975); *Wa and Wala: Islam and Polity in Northwestern Ghana* (1989); *Forests of Gold: Essays on the Akan and the Kingdom of Asante* (1993); and (with N. Levtzion and B. Haight) *Chronicles from Gonja: A West African Tradition of Muslim Historiography* (1986).

Index